for ~~Lucy~~
and _her_ imagination

Christmas, 1979

The Madwoman in the Attic

The Madwoman in the Attic

THE WOMAN WRITER AND THE NINETEENTH-CENTURY LITERARY IMAGINATION

SANDRA M. GILBERT
and SUSAN GUBAR

NEW HAVEN AND LONDON
YALE UNIVERSITY PRESS
1979

Designed by Sally Harris and set in Monophoto Baskerville type. Printed in the United States of America by Halliday Lithograph, West Hanover, Mass.

Published in Great Britain, Europe, Africa, and Asia (except Japan) by Yale University Press, Ltd., London. Distributed in Australia and New Zealand by Book & Film Services, Artarmon, N.S.W., Australia; and in Japan by Harper & Row, Publishers, Tokyo Office.

Library of Congress Cataloging in Publication Data

Gilbert, Sandra M
   The madwoman in the attic.

   Includes bibliographical references and index.
   1. English literature—Women authors—History and criticism. 2. English literature—19th century—History and criticism. 3. Dickinson, Emily, 1830–1886. 4. Milton, John, 1608–1674—Influence. 5. Fall of man in literature. 6. Women in literature. 7. Women authors—Biography. I. Gubar, Susan, joint author. II. Title.
PR115.G5   820′.9′9287   78–20792
ISBN 0-300-02286-7

Acknowledgment is made to the following for permission to reprint portions of this book, originally published in slightly different form:

Feminist Studies, for "The Genesis of Hunger, according to *Shirley*" (by Susan Gubar) and "Horror's Twin: Mary Shelley's Monstrous Eve" (by Sandra Gilbert).
Novel, for "Sane Jane and the Critics" (by Susan Gubar) and "A Revisionary Company" (by Sandra Gilbert and Susan Gubar).
PMLA, for "Patriarchal Poetry and Women Readers: Reflections on Milton's Bogey" (by Sandra Gilbert).
Signs, for "Plain Jane's Progress" (by Sandra Gilbert) and "The Female Monster in Augustan Satire" (by Susan Gubar).
The Cornell Review, for portions of "Liber Scriptus: The Metaphor of Literary Paternity" (by Sandra Gilbert).
Indiana University Press, for portions of "Introduction: Gender, Creativity, and the Woman Poet" (by Sandra Gilbert and Susan Gubar), in Gilbert and Gubar, ed., *Shakespeare's Sisters: Feminist Essays on Women Poets* (Indiana University Press, 1979).

Acknowledgment is made for permission to quote from the following:

Thomas H. Johnson, ed. *The Poems of Emily Dickinson.* Cambridge, Mass.: The Belknap Press of Harvard University Press. Copyright 1951, 1955 by the President and Fellows of Harvard College. By permission of the publishers and the Trustees of Amherst College.
Thomas H. Johnson, ed. *The Complete Poems of Emily Dickinson.* Boston, Mass.: Little, Brown and Company. Copyright 1914, 1935, 1942 by Martha Dickinson Bianchi. Copyright 1929, © 1957, 1963 by Mary L. Hampson. By permission of the publishers.
Ruth Stone. *Cheap.* Copyright © 1975 by Ruth Stone. By permission of Harcourt Brace Jovanovich, Inc.

This book is as much for Edward, Elliot, and Roger, as it is for Kathy, Molly, Sandra, Simone, Susan, and Susanna.

The strife of thought, accusing and excusing, began afresh, and gathered fierceness. The soul of Lilith lay naked to the torture of pure interpenetrating inward light. She began to moan, and sigh deep sighs, then murmur as if holding colloquy with a dividual self: her queendom was no longer whole; it was divided against itself. . . . At length she began what seemed a tale about herself, in a language so strange, and in forms so shadowy, that I could but here and there understand a little.

—George MacDonald, *Lilith*

It was not at first clear to me exactly what I was, except that I was someone who was being made to do certain things by someone else who was really the same person as myself—I have always called her Lilith. And yet the acts were mine, not Lilith's.

—Laura Riding, "Eve's Side of It"

Contents

Preface   xi

Part I. Toward a Feminist Poetics

1. The Queen's Looking Glass: Female Creativity, Male
   Images of Women, and the Metaphor of Literary
   Paternity   3
2. Infection in the Sentence: The Woman Writer and the
   Anxiety of Authorship   45
3. The Parables of the Cave   93

Part II. Inside the House of Fiction: Jane Austen's Tenants of Possibility

4. Shut Up in Prose: Gender and Genre in Austen's
   Juvenilia   107
5. Jane Austen's Cover Story (and Its Secret Agents)   146

Part III. How Are We Fal'n?: Milton's Daughters

6. Milton's Bogey: Patriarchal Poetry and Women
   Readers   187
7. Horror's Twin: Mary Shelley's Monstrous Eve   213
8. Looking Oppositely: Emily Brontë's Bible of Hell   248

Part IV. The Spectral Selves of Charlotte Brontë

9. A Secret, Inward Wound: *The Professor*'s Pupil   311
10. A Dialogue of Self and Soul: Plain Jane's Progress   336
11. The Genesis of Hunger, According to *Shirley*   372
12. The Buried Life of Lucy Snowe   399

Part V. Captivity and Consciousness in George Eliot's Fiction

13. Made Keen by Loss: George Eliot's Veiled Vision   443
14. George Eliot as the Angel of Destruction   478

Part VI. Strength in Agony: Nineteenth-Century Poetry by Women

15. The Aesthetics of Renunciation   539
16. A Woman—White: Emily Dickinson's Yarn of Pearl   581

Notes   651

Index   699

Preface

This book began with a course in literature by women that we taught together at Indiana University in the fall of 1973. Reading the writing of women from Jane Austen and Charlotte Brontë to Emily Dickinson, Virginia Woolf, and Sylvia Plath, we were surprised by the coherence of theme and imagery that we encountered in the works of writers who were often geographically, historically, and psychologically distant from each other. Indeed, even when we studied women's achievements in radically different genres, we found what began to seem a distinctively female literary tradition, a tradition that had been approached and appreciated by many women readers and writers but which no one had yet defined in its entirety. Images of enclosure and escape, fantasies in which maddened doubles functioned as asocial surrogates for docile selves, metaphors of physical discomfort manifested in frozen landscapes and fiery interiors—such patterns recurred throughout this tradition, along with obsessive depictions of diseases like anorexia, agoraphobia, and claustrophobia.

Seeking to understand the anxieties out of which this tradition must have grown, we undertook a close study of the literature produced by women in the nineteenth century, for that seemed to us to be the first era in which female authorship was no longer in some sense anomalous. As we explored this literature, however, we found ourselves over and over again confronting two separate but related matters: first, the social position in which nineteenth-century women writers found themselves and, second, the reading that they themselves did. Both in life and in art, we saw, the artists we studied were literally and figuratively confined. Enclosed in the architecture of an overwhelmingly male-dominated society, these literary women were also, inevitably, trapped in the specifically literary constructs of what Gertrude Stein was to call "patriarchal poetry." For not only did a nineteenth-century woman writer have to inhabit ancestral mansions (or cottages) owned and built by men, she was also constricted and restricted by the Palaces of Art and Houses of Fiction male writers authored. We decided, therefore, that the striking coherence we noticed in literature by women could be explained by a common, female impulse to struggle free from social and literary confinement through strategic redefinitions of self, art, and society.

As our title's allusion to *Jane Eyre* suggests, we began our own definition of these redefinitions with close readings of Charlotte Brontë, who seemed to us to provide a paradigm of many distinctively female anxieties and abilities. Thus, although we have attempted to maintain a very roughly chronological ordering of authors through-out the book, this often under-appreciated nineteenth-century novelist really does occupy a central position in our study: through detailed analyses of her novels, we hope to show new ways in which all nineteenth-century works by women can be interpreted. As our table of contents indicates, however, we eventually felt that we had to branch out from Brontë, if only to understand her more fully. For in the process of researching our book we realized that, like many other feminists, we were trying to recover not only a major (and neglected) female literature but a whole (neglected) female history.

In this connection, the work of social historians like Gerda Lerner, Alice Rossi, Ann Douglas, and Martha Vicinus not only helped us but helped remind us just how much of women's history has been lost or misunderstood. Even more useful for our project, however, were the recent demonstrations by Ellen Moers and Elaine Showalter that nineteenth-century literary women *did* have both a literature and a culture of their own—that, in other words, by the nineteenth century there was a rich and clearly defined female literary sub-culture, a community in which women consciously read and related to each other's works. Because both Moers and Showalter have so skillfully traced the overall history of this community, we have been able here to focus closely on a number of nineteenth-century texts we consider crucial to that history; and in a future volume we plan similar readings of key twentieth-century texts. For us, such touch-stones have provided models for understanding the dynamics of female literary response to male literary assertion and coercion.

That literary texts are coercive (or at least compellingly persuasive) has been one of our major observations, for just as women have been repeatedly defined by male authors, they seem in reaction to have found it necessary to act out male metaphors in their own texts, as if trying to understand their implications. Our literary methodology has therefore been based on the Bloomian premise that literary history consists of strong action and inevitable reaction. Moreover, like such phenomenological critics as Gaston Bachelard, Simone de Beauvoir, and J. Hillis Miller, we have sought to describe both the experience that generates metaphor and the metaphor that creates experience.

Reading metaphors in this experiential way, we have inevitably ended up reading our own lives as well as the texts we study, so that the process of writing this book has been as transformative for us as the process of "attempting the pen" was for so many of the women we discuss. And much of the exhilaration of writing has come from working together. Like most collaborators, we have divided our responsibilities: Sandra Gilbert drafted the section on "Milton's daughters," the essays on *The Professor* and *Jane Eyre*, and the chapters on the "Aesthetics of Renunciation" and on Emily Dickinson; Susan Gubar drafted the section on Jane Austen, the essays on *Shirley* and *Villette*, and the two chapters about George Eliot; and each of us has drafted portions of the introductory exploration of a feminist poetics. We have continually exchanged and discussed our drafts, however, so that we feel our book represents not just a dialogue but a consensus. Redefining what has so far been male-defined literary history in the same way that women writers have revised "patriarchal poetics," we have found that the process of collaboration has given us the essential support we needed to complete such an ambitious project.

Besides our own friendship, however, we were fortunate enough to have much additional help from colleagues, friends, students, husbands, and children. Useful suggestions were offered by many, including Frederic Amory, Wendy Barker, Elyse Blankley, Timothy Bovey, Moneera Doss, Robert Griffin, Dolores Gros Louis, Anne Hedin, Robert Hopkins, Kenneth Johnston, Cynthia Kinnard, U. C. Knoepflmacher, Wendy Kolmar, Richard Levin, Barbara Clarke Mossberg, Celeste Wright, and, especially, Donald Gray, whose detailed comments were often crucial. We are grateful to many others as well. The encouragement of Harold Bloom, Tillie Olsen, Robert Scholes, Catharine Stimpson, and Ruth Stone aided us in significant ways, and we are particularly grateful to Kenneth R. R. Gros Louis, whose interest in this project has enabled us to teach together several times at Indiana and whose good will has continually heartened us. In this connection, we want especially to thank our home institutions, Indiana University and the University of California at Davis, which also encouraged us by generously providing travel money, research grants, and summer fellowships when no other funding agencies would.

We must thank, too, the people connected with Yale University Press who helped make this book possible. In particular, Garrett Stewart, chosen as outside advisor by the Press, was an ideal reader, whose enthusiasm and perceptiveness were important to our work; Ellen Graham was a perfect editor, whose exemplary patience helped guide this project to completion; and Lynn Walterick was a superb and sympathetic copyeditor, whose skillful questions invariably helped us find better answers. Without Edith Lavis's dedication in preparing the manuscript, however, their efforts would have been in vain, so we must thank her as well, while we must also thank Mrs. Virginia French for devoted childcare without which even the act of composition would have been impossible, Gretchen Paulig for invaluable help in indexing, and both Eileen Frye and Alison Hilton for very useful suggestions about illustrations. As this book goes to press we want to note, too, that Hopewell Selby occupies a special place in our thoughts. Finally, we want most of all to acknowledge what has been profoundly important to both of us: the revisionary advice and consent of our husbands, Elliot Gilbert and Edward Gubar, and our children, Roger, Kathy, and Susanna Gilbert, and Molly and Simone Gubar, all of whom, together, have given us lives that are a joy to read.

I
Toward a Feminist Poetics

Illustration on the preceding page: *Astarte Syriaca*, by Dante Gabriel Rossetti. Courtesy of the City of Manchester Art Galleries.

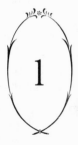

The Queen's Looking Glass: Female Creativity, Male Images of Women, and the Metaphor of Literary Paternity

And the lady of the house was seen only as she appeared in each room, according to the nature of the lord of the room. None saw the whole of her, none but herself. For the light which she was was both her mirror and her body. None could tell the whole of her, none but herself.

—Laura Riding

Alas! A woman that attempts the pen
Such an intruder on the rights of men,
Such a presumptuous Creature is esteem'd
The fault can by no vertue be redeem'd.
    —Anne Finch, Countess of Winchilsea

As to all that nonsense Henry and Larry talked about, the necessity of "I am God" in order to create (I suppose they mean "I am God, I am not a woman"). . . . this "I am God," which makes creation an act of solitude and pride, this image of God alone making sky, earth, sea, it is this image which has confused woman.

—Anaïs Nin

Is a pen a metaphorical penis? Gerard Manley Hopkins seems to have thought so. In a letter to his friend R. W. Dixon in 1886 he confided a crucial feature of his theory of poetry. The artist's "most essential quality," he declared, is "masterly execution, which is a kind of male gift, and especially marks off men from women, the begetting of one's thought on paper, on verse, or whatever the matter is." In addition, he noted that "on better consideration it strikes me that the mastery I speak of is not so much in the mind as a puberty in the life of that quality. The male quality is the creative gift."[1]

3

Male sexuality, in other words, is not just analogically but actually the essence of literary power. The poet's pen is in some sense (even more than figuratively) a penis.

Eccentric and obscure though he was, Hopkins was articulating a concept central to that Victorian culture of which he was in this case a representative male citizen. But of course the patriarchal notion that the writer "fathers" his text just as God fathered the world is and has been all-pervasive in Western literary civilization, so much so that, as Edward Said has shown, the metaphor is built into the very word, *author*, with which writer, deity, and *pater familias* are identified. Said's miniature meditation on the word *authority* is worth quoting in full because it summarizes so much that is relevant here:

> *Authority* suggests to me a constellation of linked meanings: not only, as the OED tells us, "a power to enforce obedience," or "a derived or delegated power," or "a power to influence action," or "a power to inspire belief," or "a person whose opinion is accepted"; not only those, but a connection as well with *author*—that is, a person who originates or gives existence to something, a begetter, beginner, father, or ancestor, a person also who sets forth written statements. There is still another cluster of meanings: *author* is tied to the past participle *auctus* of the verb *augere*; therefore *auctor*, according to Eric Partridge, is literally an increaser and thus a founder. *Auctoritas* is production, invention, cause, in addition to meaning a right of possession. Finally, it means continuance, or a causing to continue. Taken together these meanings are all grounded in the following notions: (1) that of the power of an individual to initiate, institute, establish—in short, to begin; (2) that this power and its product are an increase over what had been there previously; (3) that the individual wielding this power controls its issue and what is derived therefrom; (4) that authority maintains the continuity of its course.[2]

In conclusion, Said, who is discussing "The Novel as Beginning Intention," remarks that "All four of these [last] abstractions can be used to describe the way in which narrative fiction asserts itself psychologically and aesthetically through the technical efforts of the novelist." But they can also, of course, be used to describe both the author and the authority of any literary text, a point Hopkins's sexual/aesthetic theory seems to have been designed to elaborate. Indeed, Said himself later observes that a convention of most literary texts is "that the unity or integrity of the text is maintained by a series of genealogical connections: author—text, beginning-middle-end, text—meaning, reader—interpretation, and so on. *Underneath all these is the imagery of succession, of paternity, or hierarchy*" (italics ours).[3]

There is a sense in which the very notion of paternity is itself, as Stephen Dedalus puts it in *Ulysses*, a "legal fiction,"[4] a story requiring imagination if not faith. A man cannot verify his fatherhood by either sense or reason, after all; that his child is *his* is in a sense a tale he tells himself to explain the infant's existence. Obviously, the anxiety implicit in such storytelling urgently needs not only the reassurances of male superiority that patriarchal misogyny implies, but also such compensatory fictions of the Word as those embodied in the genealogical imagery Said describes. Thus it is possible to trace the history of this compensatory, sometimes frankly stated and sometimes submerged imagery that elaborates upon what Stephen Dedalus calls the "mystical estate" of paternity[5] through the works of many literary theoreticians besides Hopkins and Said. Defining poetry as a mirror held up to nature, the mimetic aesthetic that begins with Aristotle and descends through Sidney, Shakespeare, and Johnson implies that the poet, like a lesser God, has made or engendered an alternative, mirror-universe in which he actually seems to enclose or trap shadows of reality. Similarly, Coleridge's Romantic concept of the human "imagination or esemplastic power" is of a virile, generative force which echoes "the eternal act of creation in the infinite I AM," while Ruskin's phallic-sounding "Penetrative Imagination" is a "possession-taking faculty" and a "piercing . . . mind's tongue" that seizes, cuts down, and gets at the root of experience in order "to throw up what new shoots it will."[6] In all these aesthetics the poet, like God the Father, is a paternalistic ruler of the fictive world he has created. Shelley called him a "legislator." Keats noted, speaking of writers, that "the antients [*sic*] were Emperors of vast Provinces" though "each of the moderns" is merely an "Elector of Hanover."[7]

In medieval philosophy, the network of connections among sexual, literary, and theological metaphors is equally complex: God the

Father both engenders the cosmos and, as Ernst Robert Curtius notes, writes the Book of Nature: both tropes describe a single act of creation.[8] In addition, the Heavenly Author's ultimate eschatological power is made manifest when, as the *Liber Scriptus* of the traditional requiem mass indicates, He writes the Book of Judgment. More recently, male artists like the Earl of Rochester in the seventeenth century and Auguste Renoir in the nineteenth, have frankly defined aesthetics based on male sexual delight. "I . . . never Rhym'd, but for my Pintle's [penis's] sake," declares Rochester's witty Timon,[9] and (according to the painter Bridget Riley) Renoir "is supposed to have said that he painted his paintings with his prick."[10] Clearly, both these artists believe, with Norman O. Brown, that "the penis is the head of the body," and they might both agree, too, with John Irwin's suggestion that the relationship "of the masculine self with the feminine-masculine work is also an autoerotic act . . . a kind of creative onanism in which through the use of the phallic pen on the 'pure space' of the virgin page . . . the self is continually spent and wasted. . . . "[11] No doubt it is for all these reasons, moreover, that poets have traditionally used a vocabulary derived from the patriarchal "family romance" to describe their relations with each other. As Harold Bloom has pointed out, "from the sons of Homer to the sons of Ben Jonson, poetic influence [has] been described as a filial relationship," a relationship of "*sonship*." The fierce struggle at the heart of literary history, says Bloom, is a "battle between strong equals, father and son as mighty opposites, Laius and Oedipus at the crossroads."[12]

Though many of these writers use the metaphor of literary paternity in different ways and for different purposes, all seem overwhelmingly to agree that a literary text is not only speech quite literally embodied, but also power mysteriously made manifest, made flesh. In patriarchal Western culture, therefore, the text's author is a father, a progenitor, a procreator, an aesthetic patriarch whose pen is an instrument of generative power like his penis. More, his pen's power, like his penis's power, is not just the ability to generate life but the power to create a posterity to which he lays claim, as, in Said's paraphrase of Partridge, "an increaser and thus a founder." In this respect, the pen is truly mightier than its phallic counterpart the sword, and in patriarchy more resonantly sexual. Not only does the writer respond to his muse's quasi-sexual excitation with an out-pouring of the aesthetic energy Hopkins called "the fine delight that fathers thought"—a delight poured seminally from pen to page—but as the author of an enduring text the writer engages the attention of the future in exactly the same way that a king (or father) "owns" the homage of the present. No sword-wielding general could rule so long or possess so vast a kingdom.

Finally, that such a notion of "ownership" or possession is embedded in the metaphor of paternity leads to yet another implication of this complex metaphor. For if the author/father is owner of his text and of his reader's attention, he is also, of course, owner/possessor of the subjects of his text, that is to say of those figures, scenes, and events—those brain children—he has both incarnated in black and white and "bound" in cloth or leather. Thus, because he is an *author*, a "man of letters" is simultaneously, like his divine counterpart, a father, a master or ruler, and an owner: the spiritual type of a patriarch, as we understand that term in Western society.

Where does such an implicitly or explicitly patriarchal theory of literature leave literary women? If the pen is a metaphorical penis, with what organ can females generate texts? The question may seem frivolous, but as our epigraph from Anaïs Nin indicates, both the patriarchal etiology that defines a solitary Father God as the only creator of all things, and the male metaphors of literary creation that depend upon such an etiology, have long "confused" literary women, readers and writers alike. For what if such a proudly masculine cosmic Author is the sole legitimate model for all earthly authors? Or worse, what if the male generative power is not just the only legitimate power but the only power there is? That literary theoreticians from Aristotle to Hopkins seemed to believe this was so no doubt prevented many women from ever "attempting the pen"—to use Anne Finch's phrase—and caused enormous anxiety in generations of those women who were "presumptuous" enough to dare such an attempt. Jane Austen's Anne Elliot understates the case when she decorously observes, toward the end of *Persuasion*, that "men have had every advantage of us in telling their story. Education has been theirs in so much higher a degree; the pen has been in their

hands" (II, chap. 11).[13] For, as Anne Finch's complaint suggests,
the pen has been defined as not just accidentally but essentially a
male "tool," and therefore not only inappropriate but actually alien
to women. Lacking Austen's demure irony, Finch's passionate
protest goes almost as far toward the center of the metaphor of literary paternity as Hopkins's letter to Canon Dixon. Not only is "a
woman that attempts the pen" an intrusive and "presumptuous
Creature," she is absolutely unredeemable: no virtue can outweigh
the "fault" of her presumption because she has grotesquely crossed
boundaries dictated by Nature:

> They tell us, we mistake our sex and way;
> Good breeding, fassion, dancing, dressing, play
> Are the accomplishments we shou'd desire;
> To write, or read, or think, or to enquire
> Wou'd cloud our beauty, and exaust our time,
> And interrupt the conquests of our prime;
> Whilst the dull mannage, of a servile house
> Is held by some, our outmost art and use.[14]

Because they are by definition male activities, this passage implies,
writing, reading, and thinking are not only alien but also inimical
to "female" characteristics. One hundred years later, in a famous
letter to Charlotte Brontë, Robert Southey rephrased the same notion:
"Literature is not the business of a woman's life, and it cannot be."[15]
It cannot be, the metaphor of literary paternity implies, because it
is physiologically as well as sociologically impossible. If male sexuality
is integrally associated with the assertive presence of literary power,
female sexuality is associated with the absence of such power, with
the idea—expressed by the nineteenth-century thinker Otto Weininger—that "woman has no share in ontological reality." As we
shall see, a further implication of the paternity/creativity metaphor
is the notion (implicit both in Weininger and in Southey's letter)
that women exist only to be acted on by men, both as literary and
as sensual objects. Again one of Anne Finch's poems explores the
assumptions submerged in so many literary theories. Addressing three
male poets, she exclaims:

> Happy you three! happy the Race of Men!
> Born to inform or to correct the Pen
> To proffitts pleasures freedom and command

> Whilst we beside you but as Cyphers stand
> T' increase your Numbers and to swell th' account
> Of your delights which from our charms amount
> And sadly are by this distinction taught
> That since the Fall (by our seducement wrought)
> Our is the greater losse as ours the greater fault.[16]

Since Eve's daughters have fallen so much lower than Adam's sons, this passage says, *all* females are "Cyphers"—nullities, vacancies— existing merely and punningly to increase male "Numbers" (either poems or persons) by pleasuring either men's bodies or their minds, their penises or their pens.

In that case, however, devoid of what Richard Chase once called "the masculine *élan*," and implicitly rejecting even the slavish consolations of her "femininity," a literary woman is doubly a "Cypher," for she is really a "eunuch," to use the striking figure Germaine Greer applied to all women in patriarchal society. Thus Anthony Burgess recently declared that Jane Austen's novels fail because her writing "lacks a strong male thrust," and William Gass lamented that literary women "lack that blood congested genital drive which energizes every great style."[17] The assumptions that underlie their statements were articulated more than a century ago by the nineteenth-century editor-critic Rufus Griswold. Introducing an anthology entitled *The Female Poets of America*, Griswold outlined a theory of literary sex roles which builds upon, and clarifies, these grim implications of the metaphor of literary paternity.

> It is less easy to be assured of the genuineness of literary ability in women than in men. The moral nature of women, in its finest and richest development, partakes of some of the qualities of genius; it assumes, at least, the similitude of that which in men is the characteristic or accompaniment of the highest grade of mental inspiration. We are in danger, therefore, of mistaking for the efflorescent energy of creative intelligence, that which is only the exuberance of personal "feelings unemployed." . . . The most exquisite susceptibility of the spirit, and the capacity to mirror in dazzling variety the effects which circumstances or surrounding minds work upon it, may be accompanied by *no power to originate, nor even, in any proper sense, to reproduce.* [Italics ours][18]

Since Griswold has actually compiled a collection of poems by women, he plainly does not believe that all women lack reproductive or generative literary power all the time. His gender-definitions imply, however, that when such creative energy appears in a woman it may be anomalous, freakish, because as a "male" characteristic it is essentially "unfeminine."

The converse of these explicit and implicit definitions of "femininity" may also be true for those who develop literary theories based upon the "mystical estate" of fatherhood: if a woman lacks generative literary power, then a man who loses or abuses such power becomes like a eunuch—or like a woman. When the imprisoned Marquis de Sade was denied "any use of pencil, ink, pen, and paper," declares Roland Barthes, he was figuratively emasculated, for "the scriptural sperm" could flow no longer, and "without exercise, without a pen, Sade [become] *bloated*, [became] a eunuch." Similarly, when Hopkins wanted to explain to R. W. Dixon the aesthetic consequences of a *lack* of male mastery, he seized upon an explanation which developed the implicit parallel between women and eunuchs, declaring that "if the life" is not "conveyed into the work and . . . displayed there . . . the product is one of those *hens' eggs* that are good to eat and look just like live ones but never hatch" (italics ours).[19] And when, late in his life, he tried to define his own sense of sterility, his thickening writer's block, he described himself (in the sonnet "The Fine Delight That Fathers Thought") both as a eunuch and *as a woman*, specifically a woman deserted by male power: "the widow of an insight lost," surviving in a diminished "winter world" that entirely lacks "the roll, the rise, the carol, the creation" of male generative power, whose "strong / Spur" is phallically "live and lancing like the blow pipe flame." And once again some lines from one of Anne Finch's plaintive protests against male literary hegemony seem to support Hopkins's image of the powerless and sterile woman artist. Remarking in the conclusion of her "Introduction" to her *Poems* that women are "to be dull / Expected and dessigned" she does not repudiate such expectations, but on the contrary admonishes herself, with bitter irony, to *be* dull:

> Be caution'd then my Muse, and still retir'd;
> Nor be dispis'd, aiming to be admir'd;

> Conscious of wants, still with contracted wing,
> To some few friends, and to thy sorrows sing;
> For groves of Lawrell, thou wert never meant;
> Be dark enough thy shades, and be thou there content.[20]

Cut off from generative energy, in a dark and wintry world, Finch seems to be defining herself here not only as a "Cypher" but as "the widow of an insight lost."

Finch's despairing (if ironic) acceptance of male expectations and designs summarizes in a single episode the coercive power not only of cultural constraints but of the literary texts which incarnate them. For it is as much from literature as from "life" that literate women learn they are "to be dull / Expected and dessigned." As Leo Bersani puts it, written "language doesn't merely describe identity but actually produces moral and perhaps even physical identity. . . . We have to allow for a kind of dissolution or at least elasticity of being induced by an immersion in literature."[21] A century and a half earlier, Jane Austen had Anne Elliot's interlocutor, Captain Harville, make a related point in *Persuasion*. Arguing women's inconstancy over Anne's heated objections, he notes that "all histories are against you—all stories, prose, and verse. . . . I could bring you fifty quotations in a moment on my side the argument, and I do not think I ever opened a book in my life which had not something to say upon woman's inconstancy" (II, chap. 11). To this Anne responds, as we have seen, that the pen has been in male hands. In the context of Harville's speech, her remark implies that women have not only been excluded from authorship but in addition they have been subjust to (and subjects of) male authority. With Chaucer's astute Wife of Bath, therefore, Anne might demand, "Who peynted the leoun, tel me who?" And, like the Wife's, her own answer to her own rhetorical question would emphasize our culture's historical confusion of literary authorship with patriarchal authority:

> By God, if wommen hadde writen stories,
> As clerkes han withinne hir oratories,
> They wolde han writen of men more wikednesse
> Than all the mark of Adam may redresse.

In other words, what Bersani, Austen, and Chaucer all imply is that, precisely because a writer "fathers" his text, his literary creations (as we pointed out earlier) are his possession, his property. Having defined them in language and thus generated them, he owns them, controls them, and encloses them on the printed page. Describing his earliest sense of vocation as a writer, Jean-Paul Sartre recalled in *Les Mots* his childhood belief that "to write was to engrave new beings upon [the infinite Tables of the Word] or . . . to catch living things in the trap of phrases." [22] Naive as such a notion may seem on the face of it, it is not "wholly an illusion, for it is his [Sartre's] truth," as one commentator observes[23]—and indeed it is every writer's "truth," a truth which has traditionally led male authors to assume patriarchal rights of ownership over the female "characters" they engrave upon "the infinite Tables of the Word."

Male authors have also, of course, generated male characters over whom they would seem to have had similar rights of ownership. But further implicit in the metaphor of literary paternity is the idea that each man, arriving at what Hopkins called the "puberty" of his creative gift, has the ability, even perhaps the obligation, to talk back to other men by generating alternative fictions of his own. Lacking the pen/penis which would enable them similarly to refute one fiction by another, women in patriarchal societies have historically been reduced to *mere* properties, to characters and images imprisoned in male texts because generated solely, as Anne Elliot and Anne Finch observe, by male expectations and designs.

Like the metaphor of literary paternity itself, this corollary notion that the chief creature man has generated is woman has a long and complex history. From Eve, Minerva, Sophia, and Galatea onward, after all, patriarchal mythology defines women as created by, from, and for men, the children of male brains, ribs, and ingenuity. For Blake the eternal female was at her best an Emanation of the male creative principle. For Shelley she was an epi-psyche, a soul out of the poet's soul, whose inception paralleled on a spiritual plane the solider births of Eve and Minerva. Throughout the history of Western culture, moreover, male-engendered female figures as superficially disparate as Milton's Sin, Swift's Chloe, and Yeats's Crazy Jane have incarnated men's ambivalence not only toward female sexuality but toward their own (male) physicality. At the same time, male texts, continually elaborating the metaphor of literary paternity, have continually proclaimed that, in Honoré de Balzac's ambiguous words, "woman's virtue is man's greatest invention."[24] A characteristically condensed and oracular comment by Norman O. Brown perfectly summarizes the assumptions on which all such texts are based:

> Poetry, the creative act, the act of life, the archetypal sexual act. Sexuality is poetry. The lady is our creation, or Pygmalion's statue. The lady is the poem; [Petrarch's] Laura is, really, poetry.[25]

No doubt this complex of metaphors and etiologies simply reflects not just the fiercely patriarchal structure of Western society but also the underpinning of misogyny upon which that severe patriarchy has stood. The roots of "authority" tell us, after all, that if woman is man's property then he must have authored her, just as surely as they tell us that if he authored her she must be his property. As a creation "penned" by man, moreover, woman has been "penned up" or "penned in." As a sort of "sentence" man has spoken, she has herself been "sentenced": fated, jailed, for he has both "indited" her and "indicted" her. As a thought he has "framed," she has been both "framed" (enclosed) in his texts, glyphs, graphics, and "framed up" (found guilty, found wanting) in his cosmologies. For as Humpty Dumpty tells Alice in *Through the Looking Glass*, the "master" of words, utterances, phrases, literary properties, "can manage the whole lot of them!"[26] The etymology and etiology of masculine authority are, it seems, almost necessarily identical. However, for women who felt themselves to be more than, in every sense, the properties of literary texts, the problem posed by such authority was neither metaphysical nor philological, but (as the pain expressed by Anne Finch and Anne Elliot indicates) psychological. Since both patriarchy and its texts subordinate and imprison women, before women can even attempt that pen which is so rigorously kept from them they must escape just those male texts which, defining them as "Cyphers," deny them the autonomy to formulate alternatives to the authority that has imprisoned them and kept them from attempting the pen.

The vicious circularity of this problem helps explain the curious passivity with which Finch responded (or pretended to respond) to male expectations and designs, and it helps explain, too, the centuries-long silence of so many women who must have had talents comparable to Finch's. A final paradox of the metaphor of literary paternity is the fact that in the same way an author both generates and imprisons his fictive creatures, he silences them by depriving them of autonomy (that is, of the power of independent speech) even as he gives them life. He silences them and, as Keats's "Ode on a Grecian Urn" suggests, he stills them, or—embedding them in the marble of his art—kills them. As Albert Gelpi neatly puts it, "the artist kills experience into art, for temporal experience can only escape death by dying into the 'immortality' of artistic form. The fixity of 'life' in art and the fluidity of 'life' in nature are incompatible." [27] The pen, therefore, is not only mightier than the sword, it is also *like* the sword in its power—its need, even—to kill. And this last attribute of the pen once again seems to be associatively linked with its metaphorical maleness. Simone de Beauvoir has commented that the human male's "transcendence" of nature is symbolized by his ability to hunt and kill, just as the human female's identification with nature, her role as a symbol of immanence, is expressed by her central involvement in that life-giving but involuntary birth process which perpetuates the species. Thus, superiority—or authority—"has been accorded in humanity not to the sex that brings forth but to that which kills." [28] In D. H. Lawrence's words, "the Lords of Life are the Masters of Death"—and therefore, patriarchal poetics implies, they are the masters of art. [29]

Commentators on female subordination from Freud and Horney to de Beauvoir, Wolfgang Lederer, and most recently, Dorothy Dinnerstein, have of course explored other aspects of the relationship between the sexes that also lead men to want figuratively to "kill" women. What Horney called male "dread" of the female is a phenomenon to which Lederer has devoted a long and scholarly book. [30] Elaborating on de Beauvoir's assertion that as mother of life "woman's first lie, her first treason [seems to be] that of life itself—life which, though clothed in the most attractive forms, is always infested by the ferments of age and death," Lederer remarks upon woman's own tendency to "kill" *herself* into art in order "to appeal to man":

> From the Paleolithic on, we have evidence that woman, through careful coiffure, through adornment and makeup, tried to stress

the eternal type rather than the mortal self. Such makeup, in Africa or Japan, may reach the, to us, somewhat estranging degree of a lifeless mask—and yet that is precisely the purpose of it: where nothing is lifelike, nothing speaks of death.[31]

For yet another reason, then, it is no wonder that women have historically hesitated to attempt the pen. Authored by a male God and by a godlike male, killed into a "perfect" image of herself, the woman writer's self-contemplation may be said to have begun with a searching glance into the mirror of the male-inscribed literary text. There she would see at first only those eternal lineaments fixed on her like a mask to conceal her dreadful and bloody link to nature. But looking long enough, looking hard enough, she would see—like the speaker of Mary Elizabeth Coleridge's "The Other Side of the Mirror"—an enraged prisoner: herself. The poem describing this vision is central to the feminist poetics we are trying to construct:

> I sat before my glass one day,
>   And conjured up a vision bare,
> Unlike the aspects glad and gay,
>   That erst were found reflected there—
> The vision of a woman, wild
>   With more than womanly despair.
>
> Her hair stood back on either side
>   A face bereft of loveliness.
> It had no envy now to hide
>   What once no man on earth could guess.
> It formed the thorny aureole
>   Of hard unsanctified distress.
>
> Her lips were open—not a sound
>   Came through the parted lines of red.
> Whate'er it was, the hideous wound
>   In silence and in secret bled.
> No sigh relieved her speechless woe,
>   She had no voice to speak her dread.
>
> And in her lurid eyes there shone
>   The dying flame of life's desire,
> Made mad because its hope was gone,

> And kindled at the leaping fire
> Of jealousy, and fierce revenge,
>   And strength that could not change nor tire.
>
> Shade of a shadow in the glass,
>   O set the crystal surface free!
> Pass—as the fairer visions pass—
>   Nor ever more return, to be
> The ghost of a distracted hour,
> That heard me whisper, 'I am she!'[32]

What this poem suggests is that, although the woman who is the prisoner of the mirror/text's images has "no voice to speak her dread," although "no sigh" interrupts "her speechless woe," she has an invincible sense of her own autonomy, her own interiority; she has a sense, to paraphrase Chaucer's Wife of Bath, of the authority of her own experience.[33] The power of metaphor, says Mary Elizabeth Coleridge's poem, can only extend so far. Finally, no human creature can be completely silenced by a text or by an image. Just as stories notoriously have a habit of "getting away" from their authors, human beings since Eden have had a habit of defying authority, both divine and literary.[34]

Once more the debate in which Austen's Anne Elliot and her Captain Harville engage is relevant here, for it is surely no accident that the question these two characters are discussing is woman's "inconstancy"—her refusal, that is, to be fixed or "killed" by an author/owner, her stubborn insistence on her own way. That male authors berate her for this refusal even while they themselves generate female characters who (as we shall see) perversely display "monstrous" autonomy is one of the ironies of literary art. From a female perspective, however, such "inconstancy" can only be encouraging, for—implying duplicity—it suggests that women themselves have the power to create themselves as characters, even perhaps the power to reach toward the woman trapped on the other side of the mirror/text and help her to climb out.

Before the woman writer can journey through the looking glass toward literary autonomy, however, she must come to terms with the images on the surface of the glass, with, that is, those mythic masks male artists have fastened over her human face both to lessen their dread of her "inconstancy" and—by identifying her with the "eternal types" they have themselves invented—to possess her more thoroughly. Specifically, as we will try to show here, a woman writer must examine, assimilate, and transcend the extreme images of "angel" and "monster" which male authors have generated for her. Before we women can write, declared Virginia Woolf, we must "kill" the "angel in the house."[35] In other words, women must kill the aesthetic ideal through which they themselves have been "killed" into art. And similarly, all women writers must kill the angel's necessary opposite and double, the "monster" in the house, whose Medusa-face also kills female creativity. For us as feminist critics, however, the Woolfian act of "killing" both angels and monsters must here begin with an understanding of the nature and origin of these images. At this point in our construction of a feminist poetics, then, we really must dissect in order to murder. And we must particularly do this in order to understand literature by women because, as we shall show, the images of "angel" and "monster" have been so ubiquitous throughout literature by men that they have also pervaded women's writing to such an extent that few women have definitively "killed" either figure. Rather, the female imagination has perceived itself, as it were, through a glass darkly: until quite recently the woman writer has had (if only unconsciously) to define herself as a mysterious creature who resides behind the angel or monster or angel/monster image that lives on what Mary Elizabeth Coleridge called "the crystal surface."

For all literary artists, of course, self-definition necessarily precedes self-assertion: the creative "I AM" cannot be uttered if the "I" knows not what it is. But for the female artist the essential process of self-definition is complicated by all those patriarchal definitions that intervene between herself and herself. From Anne Finch's Ardelia, who struggles to escape the male designs in which she feels herself enmeshed, to Sylvia Plath's "Lady Lazarus," who tells "Herr Doktor . . . Herr Enemy" that "I am your opus, / I am your valuable,"[36] the woman writer acknowledges with pain, confusion, and anger that what she sees in the mirror is usually a male construct, the "pure gold baby" of male brains, a glittering and wholly artificial child. With Christina Rossetti, moreover, she realizes that the male artist often "feeds" upon his female subject's face "not as she is but as she fills his dreams."[37] Finally, as "A Woman's Poem" of 1859 simply puts it, the woman writer insists that "You [men] make the worlds wherein you move. . . . Our world (alas you make that too!)" —and in its narrow confines, "shut in four blank walls . . . we act our parts."[38]

Though the highly stylized women's roles to which this last poem alludes are all ultimately variations upon the roles of angel and monster, they seem on the surface quite varied, because so many masks, reflecting such an elaborate typology, have been invented for women. A crucial passage from Elizabeth Barrett Browning's *Aurora Leigh* suggests both the mystifying deathliness and the mysterious variety female artists perceive in male imagery of women. Contemplating a portrait of her mother which, significantly, was made after its subject was dead (so that it is a kind of death mask, an image of a woman metaphorically killed into art) the young Aurora broods on the work's iconography. Noting that her mother's chambermaid had insisted upon having her dead mistress painted in "the red stiff silk" of her court dress rather than in an "English-fashioned shroud," she remarks that the effect of this unlikely costume was "very strange." As the child stared at the painting, her mother's "swan-like supernatural white life" seemed to mingle with "whatever I last read, or heard, or dreamed," and thus in its charismatic beauty, her mother's image became

> by turns
> Ghost, fiend, and angel, fairy, witch, and sprite;
> A dauntless Muse who eyes a dreadful Fate;
> A loving Psyche who loses sight of Love;
> A still Medusa with mild milky brows,
> All curdled and all clothed upon with snakes
> Whose slime falls fast as sweat will; or anon
> Our Lady of the Passion, stabbed with swords
> Where the Babe sucked; or Lamia in her first
> Moonlighted pallor, ere she shrunk and blinked,
> And shuddering wriggled down to the unclean;
> Or my own mother, leaving her last smile

In her last kiss upon the baby-mouth
My father pushed down on the bed for that;
Or my dead mother, without smile or kiss,
Buried at Florence.[39]

The female forms Aurora sees in her dead mother's picture are extreme, melodramatic, gothic—"Ghost, fiend, and angel, fairy, witch, and sprite"—specifically, as she tells us, because her reading merges with her seeing. What this implies, however, is not only that she herself is fated to inhabit male-defined masks and costumes, as her mother did, but that male-defined masks and costumes inevitably inhabit *her*, altering her vision. Aurora's self-development as a poet is the central concern of Barrett Browning's *Bildungsroman* in verse, but if she is to be a poet she must deconstruct the dead self that is a male "opus" and discover a living, "inconstant" self. She must, in other words, replace the "copy" with the "individuality," as Barrett Browning once said she thought she herself had done in her mature art.[40] Significantly, however, the "copy" selves depicted in Aurora's mother's portrait ultimately represent, once again, the moral extremes of angel ("angel," "fairy," and perhaps "sprite") and monster ("ghost," "witch," "fiend").

In her brilliant and influential analysis of the question "Is Female to Male as Nature Is to Culture?" the anthropologist Sherry Ortner notes that in every society "the psychic mode associated with women seems to stand at both the bottom and the top of the scale of human modes of relating." Attempting to account for this "symbolic ambiguity," Ortner explains "both the subversive feminine symbols (witches, evil eye, menstrual pollution, castrating mothers) and the feminine symbols of transcendence (mother goddesses, merciful dispensers of salvation, female symbols of justice)" by pointing out that women "can appear from certain points of view to stand both under and over (but really simply outside of) the sphere of culture's hegemony."[41] That is, precisely because a woman is denied the autonomy—the subjectivity—that the pen represents, she is not only excluded from culture (whose emblem might well be the pen) but she also becomes herself an embodiment of just those extremes of mysterious and intransigent Otherness which culture confronts with worship or fear, love or loathing. As "Ghost, fiend, and angel, fairy, witch, and sprite," she mediates between the male artist and the Unknown, simultaneously teaching him purity and instructing him in degradation. But what of her own artistic growth? Because that growth has for so long been radically qualified by the angel- and monster-imagery the literary woman sees in the looking glass of the male-authored text, some understanding of such imagery is an essential preliminary to any study of literature by women. As Joan Didion recently noted, "writing is an aggression" precisely because it is "an imposition . . . an invasion of someone else's most private space."[42] Like Leo Bersani's observation that an "elasticity of being [is] induced by an immersion in literature," her remark has special significance in this connection. A thorough study of those male constructs which have invaded the "most private space" of countless literate women would require hundreds of pages—indeed, a number of excellent books have been devoted to the subject[43]—but we will attempt here a brief review of the fundamental extremes of angel and monster, in order to demonstrate the severity of the male text's "imposition" upon women.

The ideal woman that male authors dream of generating is always an angel, as Norman O. Brown's comment about Laura/poetry suggested. At the same time, from Virginia Woolf's point of view, the "angel in the house" is the most pernicious image male authors have ever imposed upon literary women. Where and how did this ambiguous image originate, particularly the trivialized Victorian angel in the house that so disturbed Woolf? In the Middle Ages, of course, mankind's great teacher of purity was the Virgin Mary, a mother goddess who perfectly fitted the female role Ortner defines as "merciful dispenser of salvation." For the more secular nineteenth century, however, the eternal type of female purity was represented not by a madonna in heaven but by an angel in the house. Nevertheless, there is a clear line of literary descent from divine Virgin to domestic angel, passing through (among many others) Dante, Milton, and Goethe.

Like most Renaissance neo-Platonists, Dante claimed to know God and His Virgin handmaid by knowing the Virgin's virgin attendant,

Beatrice. Similarly, Milton, despite his undeniable misogyny (which we shall examine later), speaks of having been granted a vision of "my late espoused saint," who

> Came vested all in white, pure as her mind.
>   Her face was veiled, yet to my fancied sight,
> Love sweetness goodness, in her person shined
>   So clear, as in no face with more delight.

In death, in other words, Milton's human wife has taken on both the celestial brightness of Mary and (since she has been "washed from spot of childbed taint") the virginal purity of Beatrice. In fact, if she could be resurrected in the flesh she might now be an angel in the house, interpreting heaven's luminous mysteries to her wondering husband.

The famous vision of the "Eternal Feminine" (*Das Ewig-Weibliche*) with which Goethe's *Faust* concludes presents women from penitent prostitutes to angelic virgins in just this role of interpreters or intermediaries between the divine Father and his human sons. The German of *Faust's* "Chorus Mysticus" is extraordinarily difficult to translate in verse, but Hans Eichner's English paraphrase easily suggests the ways in which Goethe's image of female intercessors seems almost to be a revision of Milton's "late espoused saint": "All that is transitory is merely symbolical; here (that is to say, in the scene before you) the inaccessible is (symbolically) portrayed and the inexpressible is (symbolically) made manifest. The eternal feminine (i.e. the eternal principle symbolized by woman) draws us to higher spheres." Meditating on the exact nature of this eternal feminine, moreover, Eichner comments that for Goethe the "ideal of contemplative purity" is always feminine while "the ideal of significant action is masculine."[44] Once again, therefore, it is just because women are defined as wholly passive, completely void of generative power (like "Cyphers") that they become numinous to male artists. For in the metaphysical emptiness their "purity" signifies they are, of course, *self-less*, with all the moral and psychological implications that word suggests.

Elaborating further on Goethe's eternal feminine, Eichner gives an example of the culmination of Goethe's "chain of representatives of the 'noblest femininity'": Makarie, in the late novel *Wilhelm Meister's Travels*. His description of her usefully summarizes the philosophical background of the angel in the house:

> She ... leads a life of almost pure contemplation.... in considerable isolation on a country estate ... a life without external events—a life whose story cannot be told as there is no story. Her existence is not useless. On the contrary ... she shines like a beacon in a dark world, like a motionless lighthouse by which others, the travellers whose lives do have a story, can set their course. When those involved in feeling and action turn to her in their need, they are never dismissed without advice and consolation. She is an ideal, a model of selflessness and of purity of heart.[45]

She has no story of her own but gives "advice and consolation" to others, listens, smiles, sympathizes: such characteristics show that Makarie is not only the descendent of Western culture's cloistered virgins but also the direct ancestress of Coventry Patmore's angel in the house, the eponymous heroine of what may have been the middle nineteenth century's most popular book of poems.

Dedicated to "the memory of her by whom and for whom I became a poet," Patmore's *The Angel in the House* is a verse-sequence which hymns the praises and narrates the courtship and marriage of Honoria, one of the three daughters of a country Dean, a girl whose unselfish grace, gentleness, simplicity, and nobility reveal that she is not only a pattern Victorian lady but almost literally an angel on earth. Certainly her spirituality interprets the divine for her poet-husband, so that

> No happier post than this I ask,
>   To live her laureate all my life.
> On wings of love uplifted free,
>   And by her gentleness made great,
> I'll teach how noble man should be
>   To match with such a lovely mate.[46]

Honoria's essential virtue, in other words, is that her virtue makes her *man* "great." In and of herself, she is neither great nor extraordinary. Indeed, Patmore adduces many details to stress the almost pathetic ordinariness of her life: she picks violets, loses her gloves, feeds her birds, waters her rose plot, and journeys to London on a train with her father the Dean, carrying in her lap a volume of Petrarch borrowed from her lover but entirely ignorant that the book is, as he tells us, "worth its weight in gold." In short, like Goethe's Makarie, Honoria has no story except a sort of anti-story of selfless innocence based on the notion that "Man must be pleased; but him to please / Is woman's pleasure."[47]

Significantly, when the young poet-lover first visits the Deanery where his Honoria awaits him like Sleeping Beauty or Snow White, one of her sisters asks him if, since leaving Cambridge, he has "outgrown" Kant and Goethe. But if his paean of praise to the *Ewig-Weibliche* in rural England suggests that he has not, at any rate, outgrown the latter of these, that is because for Victorian men of letters Goethe represented not collegiate immaturity but moral maturity. After all, the climactic words of *Sartor Resartus*, that most influential masterpiece of Victorian sagacity, were "Close thy *Byron;* open thy *Goethe*,"[48] and though Carlyle was not specifically thinking of what came to be called "the woman question," his canonization of Goethe meant, among other things, a new emphasis on the eternal feminine, the angel woman Patmore describes in his verses, Aurora Leigh perceives in her mother's picture, and Virginia Woolf shudders to remember.

Of course, from the eighteenth century on, conduct books for ladies had proliferated, enjoining young girls to submissiveness, modesty, self-lessness; reminding all women that they should be angelic. There is a long and crowded road from *The Booke of Curtesye* (1477) to the columns of "Dear Abby," but social historians have fully explored its part in the creation of those "eternal feminine" virtues of modesty, gracefulness, purity, delicacy, civility, compliancy, reticence, chastity, affability, politeness—all of which are modes of mannerliness that contributed to Honoria's angelic innocence. Ladies were assured by the writers of such conduct books that "There are Rules for all our Actions, even down to Sleeping with a good Grace," and they were told that this good Grace was a woman's duty to her husband because "if Woman owes her Being to the Comfort and Profit of man, 'tis highly reasonable that she should be careful and diligent to content and please him."[49]

The arts of pleasing men, in other words, are not only angelic
characteristics; in more worldly terms, they are the proper acts of a
lady. "What shall I do to gratify myself or to be admired?" is not
the question a lady asks on arising, declared Mrs. Sarah Ellis, Victorian England's foremost preceptress of female morals and manners,
in 1844. No, because she is "the least engaged of any member of the
household," a woman of right feeling should devote herself to the
good of others.[50] And she should do this silently, without calling
attention to her exertions because "all that would tend to draw away
her thoughts from others and fix them on herself, ought to be avoided
as an evil to her."[51] Similarly, John Ruskin affirmed in 1865 that
the woman's "power is not for rule, not for battle, and her intellect
is not for invention or creation, but for sweet orderings" of domesticity.[52] Plainly, both writers meant that, enshrined within her home,
a Victorian angel-woman should become her husband's holy refuge
from the blood and sweat that inevitably accompanies a "life of
significant action," as well as, in her "contemplative purity," a living
memento of the otherness of the divine.

At times, however, in the severity of her selflessness, as well as in
the extremity of her alienation from ordinary fleshly life, this nineteenth-century angel-woman becomes not just a memento of otherness
but actually a *memento mori* or, as Alexander Welsh has noted, an
"Angel of Death." Discussing Dickens's heroines in particular and
what he calls Victorian "angelology" in general, Welsh analyzes
the ways in which a spiritualized heroine like Florence Dombey
"assists in the translation of the dying to a future state," not only
by officiating at the sickbed but also by maternally welcoming the
sufferer "from the other side of death."[53] But if the angel-woman in
some curious way simultaneously inhabits both this world and the
next, then there is a sense in which, besides ministering to the dying,
she is herself already dead. Welsh muses on "the apparent revers-
ibility of the heroine's role, whereby the acts of dying and of saving
someone from death seem confused," and he points out that Dickens
actually describes Florence Dombey as having the unearthly serenity
of one who is dead.[54] A spiritual messenger, an interpreter of mysteries
to wondering and devoted men, the *Ewig-Weibliche* angel becomes,
finally, a messenger of the mystical otherness of death.

As Ann Douglas has recently shown, the nineteenth-century cult of such death-angels as Harriet Beecher Stowe's little Eva or Dickens's little Nell resulted in a veritable "domestication of death," producing both a conventionalized iconography and a stylized hagiography of dying women and children.[55] Like Dickens's dead-alive Florence Dombey, for instance, Louisa May Alcott's dying Beth March is a household saint, and the deathbed at which she surrenders herself to heaven is the ultimate shrine of the angel-woman's mysteries. At the same time, moreover, the aesthetic cult of ladylike fragility and delicate beauty—no doubt associated with the moral cult of the angel-woman—obliged "genteel" women to "kill" themselves (as Lederer observed) into art objects: slim, pale, passive beings whose "charms" eerily recalled the snowy, porcelain immobility of the dead. Tight-lacing, fasting, vinegar-drinking, and similar cosmetic or dietary excesses were all parts of a physical regimen that helped women either to feign morbid weakness or actually to "decline" into real illness. Beth March's beautiful ladylike sister Amy is thus, in her artful way, as pale and frail as her consumptive sibling, and together these two heroines constitute complementary halves of the emblematic "beautiful woman" whose *death*, thought Edgar Allan Poe, "is unquestionably the most poetical topic in the world."[56]

Whether she becomes an *objet d'art* or a saint, however, it is the surrender of her self—of her personal comfort, her personal desires, or both—that is the beautiful angel-woman's key act, while it is precisely this sacrifice which dooms her both to death and to heaven. For to be selfless is not only to be noble, it is to be dead. A life that has no story, like the life of Goethe's Makarie, is really a life of death, a death-in-life. The ideal of "contemplative purity" evokes, finally, both heaven and the grave. To return to Aurora Leigh's catalogue, then—her vision of "Ghost, fiend, and angel, fairy, witch, and sprite" in her mother's portrait—there is a sense in which as a celestial "angel" Aurora's mother is also a somewhat sinister "ghost," because she wears the face of the spiritualized Victorian woman who, having died to her own desires, her own self, her own life, leads a posthumous existence in her own lifetime.

As Douglas reminds us too, though, the Victorian domestication of death represents not just an acquiescence in death by the selfless, but also a secret striving for power by the powerless. "The tombstone," she notes, "is the sacred emblem in the cult of the overlooked."[57]

Exorcised from public life, denied the pleasures (though not the pains) of sensual existence, the Victorian angel in the house was allowed to hold sway over at least one realm beyond her own household: the kingdom of the dead. But if, as nurse and comforter, spirit-guide and mystical messenger, a woman ruled the dying and the dead, might not even her admirers sometimes fear that, besides dying or easing death, she could *bring* death? As Welsh puts it, "the power of an angel to save implies, even while it denies, the power of death." Speaking of angelic Agnes Wickfield (in *David Copperfield*), he adds a sinister but witty question: "Who, in the language of detective fiction, was the last person to see Dora Copperfield alive?"[58]

Neither Welsh nor Dickens does more than hint at the angel-woman's pernicious potential. But in this context a word to the wise is enough, for such a hint helps explain the fluid metamorphoses that the figure of Aurora's mother undergoes. Her images of "Ghost, fiend, and angel, fairy, witch and sprite," we begin to see, are inextricably linked, one to another, each to its opposite. Certainly, imprisoned in the coffinlike shape of a death angel, a woman might long demonically for escape. In addition, if as death angel the woman suggests a providentially selfless mother, delivering the male soul from one realm to another, the same woman's maternal power implies, too, the fearful bondage of mortality into which every mother delivers her children. Finally, the fact that the angel woman manipulates her domestic/mystical sphere in order to ensure the well-being of those entrusted to her care reveals that she *can* manipulate; she can scheme; she can plot—stories as well as strategies.

The Victorian angel's scheming, her mortal fleshliness, and her repressed (but therefore all the more frightening) capacity for explosive rage are often subtly acknowledged, even in the most glowing texts of male "angelographers." Patmore's Honoria, for instance, proves to be considerably more duplicitous than at first she seemed. "To the sweet folly of the dove," her poet-lover admits, "She joins the cunning of the snake." To be sure, the speaker shows that her wiliness is exercised in a "good" cause: "to rivet and exalt his love." Nevertheless,

> Her mode of candour is deceit;
> And what she thinks from what she'll say

(Although I'll never call her cheat)
Lies far as Scotland from Cathay.[59]

Clearly, the poet is here acknowledging his beloved's potential for what Austen's Captain Harville called "inconstancy"—that is, her stubborn autonomy and unknowable subjectivity, meaning the ineradicable selfishness that underlies even her angelic renunciation of self.

Similarly, exploring analogous tensions between flesh and spirit in yet another version of the angel-woman, Dante Gabriel Rossetti places his "Blessed Damozel" behind "golden barriers" in heaven, but then observes that she is still humanly embodied. The bars she leans on are oddly warm; her voice, her hair, her tears are weirdly real and sensual, perhaps to emphasize the impossibility of complete spirituality for any woman. This "damozel's" life-in-death, at any rate, is still in some sense physical and therefore (paradoxically) emblematic of mortality. But though Rossetti wrote "The Blessed Damozel" in 1846, sixteen years before the suicide of his wife and model Elizabeth Siddal, the secret anxieties such imagery expressed came to the surface long after Lizzie's death. In 1869, to retrieve a poetry manuscript he had sentimentally buried with this beloved woman whose face "fill[ed] his dreams"—buried as if woman and artwork were necessarily inseparable—Rossetti had Lizzie's coffin exhumed, and literary London buzzed with rumors that her hair had "continued to grow after her death, to grow so long, so beautiful, so luxuriantly as to fill the coffin with its gold!"[60] As if symbolizing the indomitable earthliness that no woman, however angelic, could entirely renounce, Lizzie Siddal Rossetti's hair leaps like a metaphor for monstrous female sexual energies from the literal and figurative coffins in which her artist-husband enclosed her. To Rossetti, its assertive radiance made the dead Lizzie seem both terrifyingly physical and fiercely supernatural. "'Mid change the changeless night environeth, / Lies all that golden hair undimmed in death," he wrote.[61]

If we define a woman like Rossetti's dead wife as indomitably earthly yet somehow supernatural, we are defining her as a witch or monster, a magical creature of the lower world who is a kind of antithetical mirror image of an angel. As such, she still stands, in Sherry Ortner's words, "both under and over (but really simply outside of) the sphere of culture's hegemony." But now, as a representative of otherness, she incarnates the damning otherness of the flesh rather than the inspiring otherness of the spirit, expressing what—to use Anne Finch's words—men consider her own "presumptuous" desires rather than the angelic humility and "dullness" for which she was designed. Indeed, if we return to the literary definitions of "authority" with which we began this discussion, we will see that the monster-woman, threatening to replace her angelic sister, embodies intransigent female autonomy and thus represents both the author's power to allay "his" anxieties by calling their source bad names (witch, bitch, fiend, monster) and, simultaneously, the mysterious power of the character who refuses to stay in her textually ordained "place" and thus generates a story that "gets away" from its author.

Because, as Dorothy Dinnerstein has proposed, male anxieties about female autonomy probably go as deep as everyone's mother-dominated infancy, patriarchal texts have traditionally suggested that every angelically selfless Snow White must be hunted, if not haunted, by a wickedly assertive Stepmother: for every glowing portrait of submissive women enshrined in domesticity, there exists an equally important negative image that embodies the sacrilegious fiendishness of what William Blake called the "Female Will." Thus, while male writers traditionally praise the simplicity of the dove, they invariably castigate the cunning of the serpent—at least when that cunning is exercised in her own behalf. Similarly, assertiveness, aggressiveness—all characteristics of a male life of "significant action"—are "monstrous" in women precisely because "unfeminine" and therefore unsuited to a gentle life of "contemplative purity." Musing on "The Daughter of Eve," Patmore's poet-speaker remarks, significantly, that

> The woman's gentle mood o'erstept
>   Withers my love, that lightly scans
> The rest, and does in her accept
>   All her own faults, but none of man's.[62]

Luckily, his Honoria has no such vicious defects; her serpentine cunning, as we noted earlier, is concentrated entirely on pleasing her lover. But repeatedly, throughout most male literature, a sweet heroine inside the house (like Honoria) is opposed to a vicious bitch outside.

Behind Thackeray's angelically submissive Amelia Sedley, for instance—an Honoria whose career is traced in gloomier detail than that of Patmore's angel—lurks *Vanity Fair*'s stubbornly autonomous Becky Sharp, an independent "charmer" whom the novelist at one point actually describes as a monstrous and snaky sorceress:

> In describing this siren, singing and smiling, coaxing and cajoling, the author, with modest pride, asks his readers all around, has he once forgotten the laws of politeness, and showed the monster's hideous tail above water? No! Those who like may peep down under waves that are pretty transparent, and see it writhing and twirling, diabolically hideous and slimy, flapping amongst bones, or curling around corpses; but above the water line, I ask, has not everything been proper, agreeable, and decorous. . . . [63]

As this extraordinary passage suggests, the monster may not only be concealed *behind* the angel, she may actually turn out to reside *within* (or in the lower half of) the angel. Thus, Thackeray implies, every angel in the house—"proper, agreeable, and decorous," "coaxing and cajoling" hapless men—is really, perhaps, a monster, "diabolically hideous and slimy."

"A woman in the shape of a monster," Adrienne Rich observes in "Planetarium," "a monster in the shape of a woman / the skies are full of them." [64] Because the skies *are* full of them, even if we focus only on those female monsters who are directly related to Thackeray's serpentine siren, we will find that such monsters have long inhabited male texts. Emblems of filthy materiality, committed only to their own private ends, these women are accidents of nature, deformities meant to repel, but in their very freakishness they possess unhealthy energies, powerful and dangerous arts. Moreover, to the extent that they incarnate male dread of women and, specifically, male scorn of female creativity, such characters have drastically affected the self-images of women writers, negatively reinforcing those messages of submissiveness conveyed by their angelic sisters.

The first book of Spenser's *The Faerie Queene* introduces a female monster who serves as a prototype of the entire line. *Errour* is half woman, half serpent, "Most lothsom, filthie, foule, and full of vile disdaine" (1.1.126). She breeds in a dark den where her young suck on her poisonous dugs or creep back into her mouth at the sight of hated light, and in battle against the noble Red-crosse Knight, she spews out a flood of books and papers, frogs and toads. Symbolizing the dangerous effect of misdirected and undigested learning, her filthiness adumbrates that of two other powerful females in book 1, Duessa and Lucifera. But because these other women can create false appearances to hide their vile natures, they are even more dangerous.

Like Errour, Duessa is deformed below the waist, as if to foreshadow *Lear*'s "But to the girdle do the Gods inherit, Beneath is all the fiend's." When, like all witches, she must do penance at the time of the new moon by bathing with herbs traditionally used by such other witches as Scylla, Circe, and Medea, her "neather parts" are revealed as "misshapen, monstruous."[65] But significantly, Duessa deceives and ensnares men by assuming the shape of Una, the beautiful and angelic heroine who represents Christianity, charity, docility. Similarly, Lucifera lives in what seems to be a lovely mansion, a cunningly constructed House of Pride whose weak foundation and ruinous rear quarters are carefully concealed. Both women use their arts of deception to entrap and destroy men, and the secret, shameful ugliness of both is closely associated with their hidden genitals—that is, with their femaleness.

Descending from Patristic misogynists like Tertullian and St. Augustine through Renaissance and Restoration literature—through Sidney's Cecropia, Shakespeare's Lady Macbeth and his Goneril and Regan, Milton's Sin (and even, as we shall see, his Eve)—the female monster populates the works of the satirists of the eighteenth century, a company of male artists whose virulent visions must have been particularly alarming to feminine readers in an age when women had just begun to "attempt the pen." These authors attacked literary women on two fronts. First, and most obviously, through the construction of cartoon figures like Sheridan's Mrs. Malaprop and

Fielding's Mrs. Slipslop, and Smollett's Tabitha Bramble, they implied that language itself was almost literally alien to the female tongue. In the mouths of women, vocabulary loses meaning, sentences dissolve, literary messages are distorted or destroyed. At the same time, more subtly but perhaps for that reason even more significantly, such authors devised elaborate anti-romances to show that the female "angel" was really a female "fiend," the ladylike paragon really an unladylike monster. Thus while the "Bluestocking" Anne Finch would find herself directly caricatured (as she was by Pope and Gay) as a character afflicted with the "poetical Itch" like Phoebe Clinket in *Three Hours After Marriage*,[66] she might well feel herself to be indirectly but even more profoundly attacked by Johnson's famous observation that a woman preacher was like a dog standing on its hind legs, or by the suggestion—embedded in works by Swift, Pope, Gay, and others—that *all* women were inexorably and inescapably monstrous, in the flesh as well as in the spirit. Finally, in a comment like Horace Walpole's remark that Mary Wollstonecraft was "a hyena in petticoats," the two kinds of misogynistic attacks definitively merged.[67]

It is significant, then, that Jonathan Swift's disgust with the monstrous females who populate so many of his verses seems to have been caused specifically by the inexorable failure of female art. Like disgusted Gulliver, who returns to England only to prefer the stable to the parlor, his horses to his wife, Swift projects his horror of time, his dread of physicality, on to another stinking creature—the degenerate woman. Probably the most famous instance of this projection occurs in his so-called dirty poems. In these works, we peer behind the facade of the angel woman to discover that, say, the idealized "Caelia, Caelia, Caelia, shits!" We discover that the seemingly unblemished Chloe must "either void or burst," and that the female "inner space" of the "Queen of Love" is like a foul chamber pot.[68] Though some critics have suggested that the misogyny implied by Swift's characterizations of these women is merely ironic, what emerges from his most furious poems in this vein is a horror of female flesh and a revulsion at the inability—the powerlessness—of female arts to redeem or to transform the flesh. Thus for Swift female sexuality is consistently equated with degeneration, disease, and death, while female arts are trivial attempts to forestall an inevitable end.

Significantly, as if defining the tradition of duplicity in which even Patmore's uxorious speaker placed his heroine, Swift devotes many poems to an examination of the role deception plays in the creation of a saving but inadequate fiction of femininity. In "A Beautiful Young Nymph," a battered prostitute removes her wig, her crystal eye, her teeth, and her padding at bedtime, so that the next morning she must employ all her "Arts" to reconstruct her "scatter'd Parts."[69] Such as they are, however, her arts only contribute to her own suffering or that of others, and the same thing is true of Diana in "The Progress of Beauty," who awakes as a mingled mass of dirt and sweat, with cracked lips, foul teeth, and gummy eyes, to spend four hours artfully reconstructing herself. Because she is inexorably rotting away, however, Swift declares that eventually all forms will fail, for "Art no longer can prevayl / When the Materialls all are gone."[70] The strategies of Chloe, Caelia, Corinna, and Diana—artists manqué all—have no success, Swift shows, except in temporarily staving off dissolution, for like Pope's "Sex of Queens," Swift's females are composed of what Pope called "Matter too soft," and their arts are thus always inadequate.[71]

No wonder, then, that the Augustan satirist attacks the female scribbler so virulently, reinforcing Anne Finch's doleful sense that for a woman to attempt the pen is monstrous and "presumptuous," for she is "to be dull / Expected and dessigned." At least in part reflecting male artists' anxieties about the adequacy of their *own* arts, female writers are maligned as failures in eighteenth-century satire precisely because they cannot transcend their female bodily limitations: they cannot *conceive* of themselves in any but reproductive terms. Poor Phoebe Clinket, for instance, is both a caricature of Finch herself and a prototype of the female dunce who proves that literary creativity in women is merely the result of sexual frustration. Lovingly nurturing the unworthy "issue" of her muse because it attests to the "Fertility and Readiness" of her imagination, Phoebe is as sensual and indiscriminate in her poetic strainings as Lady Townley is in her insatiable erotic longings.[72] Like mothers of illegitimate or misshapen offspring, female writers are not producing what they ought, the satirists declare, so that a loose lady novelist is, appropriately enough, the first prize in *The Dunciad*'s urinary contest, while a chamberpot is awarded to the runner-up.

For the most part, eighteenth-century satirists limited their depiction of the female monster to low mimetic equivalents like Phoebe Clinket or Swift's corroding coquettes. But there were several important avatars of the monster woman who retained the allegorical anatomy of their more fantastic precursors. In *The Battle of the Books*, for instance, Swift's "Goddess Criticism" clearly symbolizes the demise of wit and learning. Devouring numberless volumes in a den as dark as Errour's, she is surrounded by relatives like Ignorance, Pride, Opinion, Noise, Impudence, and Pedantry, and she herself is as allegorically deformed as any of Spenser's females.

> The Goddess herself had claws like a Cat; her Head, and Ears, and Voice, resembled those of an Ass; Her Teeth fallen out before; Her Eyes turned inward, as if she lookt only upon Herself; Her diet was the overflowing of her own Gall: Her Spleen was so large, as to stand prominent like a Dug of the first Rate, nor wanted Excrescencies in forms of Teats, at which a Crew of ugly Monsters were greedily sucking; and what is wonderful to conceive, the bulk of Spleen increased faster than the Sucking could diminish it.[73]

Like Spenser's Errour and Milton's Sin, Criticism is linked by her processes of eternal breeding, eating, spewing, feeding, and redevouring to biological cycles all three poets view as destructive to transcendent, intellectual life. More, since all the creations of each monstrous mother are her excretions, and since all her excretions are both her food and her weaponry, each mother forms with her brood a self-enclosed system, cannibalistic and solipsistic: the creativity of the world made flesh is annihilating. At the same time, Swift's spleen-producing and splenetic Goddess cannot be far removed from the Goddess of Spleen in Pope's *The Rape of the Lock*, and—because she is a mother Goddess—she also has much in common with the Goddess of Dullness who appears in Pope's *Dunciad*. The parent of "Vapours and Female Wit," the "*Hysteric* or *Poetic* fit," the Queen of Spleen rules over all women between the ages of fifteen and fifty, and thus, as a sort of patroness of the female sexual cycle, she is associated with the same anti-creation that characterizes Errour, Sin, and Criticism.[74] Similarly, the Goddess of Dullness, a nursing mother worshipped by a society of dunces, symbolizes the failure of

culture, the failure of art, and the death of the satirist. The huge
daughter of Chaos and Night, she rocks the laureate in her ample lap
while handing out rewards and intoxicating drinks to her dull sons.
A Queen of Ooze, whose inertia comments on idealized Queens of
Love, she nods and all of Nature falls asleep, its light destroyed by
the stupor that spreads throughout the land in the milk of her
"kindness."[75]

In all these incarnations—from Errour to Dullness, from Goneril
and Regan to Chloe and Caelia—the female monster is a striking
illustration of Simone de Beauvoir's thesis that woman has been
made to represent all of man's ambivalent feelings about his own
inability to control his own physical existence, his own birth and
death. As the Other, woman comes to represent the contingency of
life, life that is made to be destroyed. "It is the horror of his own
carnal contingence," de Beauvoir notes, "which [man] projects
upon [woman]."[76] In addition, as Karen Horney and Dorothy
Dinnerstein have shown, male dread of women, and specifically the
infantile dread of maternal autonomy, has historically objectified
itself in vilification of women, while male ambivalence about female
"charms" underlies the traditional images of such terrible sorceress-
goddesses as the Sphinx, Medusa, Circe, Kali, Delilah, and Salome,
all of whom possess duplicitous arts that allow them both to seduce
and to steal male generative energy.[77]

The sexual nausea associated with all these monster women helps
explain why so many real women have for so long expressed loathing
of (or at least anxiety about) their own, inexorably female bodies.
The "killing" of oneself into an art object—the pruning and preening,
the mirror madness, and concern with odors and aging, with hair
which is invariably too curly or too lank, with bodies too thin or
too thick—all this testifies to the efforts women have expended not
just trying to be angels but trying *not* to become female monsters.
More significantly for our purposes, however, the female freak is
and has been a powerfully coercive and monitory image for women
secretly desiring to attempt the pen, an image that helped enforce
the injunctions to silence implicit also in the concept of the *Ewig-
Weibliche*. If becoming an *author* meant mistaking one's "sex and way,"
if it meant becoming an "unsexed" or perversely sexed female, then
it meant becoming a monster or freak, a vile Errour, a grotesque

Lady Macbeth, a disgusting goddess of Dullness, or (to name a few later witches) a murderous Lamia, a sinister Geraldine. Perhaps, then, the "presumptuous" effort should not be made at all. Certainly the story of Lilith, one more monster woman—indeed, according to Hebrew mythology, both the first woman *and* the first monster— specifically connects poetic presumption with madness, freakishness, monstrosity.

Created not from Adam's rib but, like him, from the dust, Lilith was Adam's first wife, according to apocryphal Jewish lore. Because she considered herself his equal, she objected to lying beneath him, so that when he tried to force her submission, she became enraged and, speaking the Ineffable Name, flew away to the edge of the Red Sea to reside with demons. Threatened by God's angelic emissaries, told that she must return or daily lose a hundred of her demon children to death, Lilith preferred punishment to patriarchal marriage, and she took her revenge against both God and Adam by injuring babies— especially male babies, who were traditionally thought to be more vulnerable to her attacks. What her history suggests is that in patri- archal culture, female speech and female "presumption"—that is, angry revolt against male domination—are inextricably linked and inevitably daemonic. Excluded from the human community, even from the semidivine communal chronicles of the Bible, the figure of Lilith represents the price women have been told they must pay for attempting to define themselves. And it is a terrible price: cursed both because she is a character who "got away" and because she dared to usurp the essentially literary authority implied by the act of naming, Lilith is locked into a vengeance (child-killing) which can only bring her more suffering (the killing of her own children). And even the nature of her one-woman revolution emphasizes her helplessness and her isolation, for her protest takes the form of a refusal and a departure, a flight of escape rather than an active rebellion like, say, Satan's. As a paradigm of both the "witch" and the "fiend" of Aurora Leigh's "Ghost, fiend, and angel, fairy, witch and sprite," Lilith reveals, then, just how difficult it is for women even to attempt the pen. And from George MacDonald, the Victorian fantasist who portrayed her in his astonishing *Lilith* as a paradigm of the self-tormenting assertive woman, to Laura Riding, who depicted her in "Eve's Side of It" as an archetypal woman Creator, the problem Lilith represents has been associated with the problems of female authorship and female authority.[78] Even if they had not studied her legend, literary women like Anne Finch, bemoaning the double bind in which the mutually dependent images of angel and monster had left them, must have gotten the message Lilith incarnates: a life of feminine submission, of "contemplative purity," is a life of silence, a life that has no pen and no story, while a life of female rebellion, of "significant action," is a life that must be silenced, a life whose monstrous pen tells a terrible story. Either way, the images on the surface of the looking glass, into which the female artist peers in search of her *self*, warn her that she is or must be a "Cypher," framed and framed up, indited and indicted.

As the legend of Lilith shows, and as psychoanalysts from Freud and Jung onward have observed, myths and fairy tales often both state and enforce culture's sentences with greater accuracy than more sophisticated literary texts. If Lilith's story summarizes the genesis of the female monster in a single useful parable, the Grimm tale of "Little Snow White" dramatizes the essential but equivocal relationship between the angel-woman and the monster-woman, a relationship that is also implicit in Aurora Leigh's bewildered speculations about her dead mother. "Little Snow White," which Walt Disney entitled "Snow White and the Seven Dwarves," should really be called Snow White and Her Wicked Stepmother, for the central action of the tale—indeed, its only real action—arises from the relationship between these two women: the one fair, young, pale, the other just as fair, but older, fiercer; the one a daughter, the other a mother; the one sweet, ignorant, passive, the other both artful and active; the one a sort of angel, the other an undeniable witch.

Significantly, the conflict between these two women is fought out largely in the transparent enclosures into which, like all the other images of women we have been discussing here, both have been locked: a magic looking glass, an enchanted and enchanting glass coffin. Here, wielding as weapons the tools patriarchy suggests that women use to kill themselves into art, the two women literally try to kill each other with art. Shadow fights shadow, image destroys image in the crystal prison, as if the "fiend" of Aurora's mother's portrait should plot to destroy the "angel" who is another one of her selves.

The story begins in midwinter, with a Queen sitting and sewing, framed by a window. As in so many fairy tales, she pricks her finger, bleeds, and is thereby assumed into the cycle of sexuality William Blake called the realm of "generation," giving birth "soon after" to a daughter "as white as snow, as red as blood, and as black as the wood of the window frame."[79] All the motifs introduced in this prefatory first paragraph—sewing, snow, blood, enclosure—are associated with key themes in female lives (hence in female writing), and they are thus themes we shall be studying throughout this book. But for our purposes here the tale's opening *is* merely prefatory. The real story begins when the Queen, having become a mother, metamorphoses also into a witch—that is, into a wicked "step" mother: " . . . when the child was born, the Queen died," and "After a year had passed the King took to himself another wife."

When we first encounter this "new" wife, she is framed in a magic looking glass, just as her predecessor—that is, her earlier self—had been framed in a window. To be caught and trapped in a mirror rather than a window, however, is to be driven inward, obsessively studying self-images as if seeking a viable self. The first Queen seems still to have had prospects; not yet fallen into sexuality, she looked outward, if only upon the snow. The second Queen is doomed to the inward search that psychoanalysts like Bruno Bettelheim censoriously define as "narcissism,"[80] but which (as Mary Elizabeth Coleridge's "The Other Side of the Mirror" suggested) is necessitated by a state from which all outward prospects have been removed.

That outward prospects *have* been removed—or lost or dissolved away—is suggested not only by the Queen's mirror obsession but by the absence of the King from the story as it is related in the Grimm version. The Queen's husband and Snow White's father (for whose attentions, according to Bettelheim, the two women are battling in a feminized Oedipal struggle) never actually appears in this story at all, a fact that emphasizes the almost stifling intensity with which the tale concentrates on the conflict in the mirror between mother and daughter, woman and woman, self and self. At the same time, though, there is clearly at least one way in which the King *is* present.

His, surely, is the voice of the looking glass, the patriarchal voice of judgment that rules the Queen's—and every woman's—self-evaluation. He it is who decides, first, that his consort is "the fairest of all," and then, as she becomes maddened, rebellious, witchlike, that she must be replaced by his angelically innocent and dutiful daughter, a girl who is therefore defined as "more beautiful still" than the Queen. To the extent, then, that the King, and only the King, constituted the first Queen's prospects, he need no longer appear in the story because, having assimilated the meaning of her own sexuality (and having, thus, become the second Queen) the woman has internalized the King's rules: his voice resides now in her own mirror, her own mind.

But if Snow White is "really" the daughter of the second as well as of the first Queen (i.e., if the two Queens are identical), why does the Queen hate her so much? The traditional explanation—that the mother is as threatened by her daughter's "budding sexuality" as the daughter is by the mother's "possession" of the father—is helpful but does not seem entirely adequate, considering the depth and ferocity of the Queen's rage. It is true, of course, that in the patriarchal Kingdom of the text these women inhabit the Queen's life can be literally imperiled by her daughter's beauty, and true (as we shall see throughout this study) that, given the female vulnerability such perils imply, female bonding is extraordinarily difficult in patriarchy: women almost inevitably turn against women because the voice of the looking glass sets them against each other. But, beyond all this, it seems as if there is a sense in which the intense desperation with which the Queen enacts her rituals of self-absorption causes (or is caused by) her hatred of Snow White. Innocent, passive, and self-lessly free of the mirror madness that consumes the Queen, Snow White represents the ideal of renunciation that the Queen has already renounced at the beginning of the story. Thus Snow White is destined to replace the Queen *because* the Queen hates her, rather than vice versa. The Queen's hatred of Snow White, in other words, exists before the looking glass has provided an obvious reason for hatred.

For the Queen, as we come to see more clearly in the course of the story, is a plotter, a plot-maker, a schemer, a witch, an artist, an impersonator, a woman of almost infinite creative energy, witty, wily, and self-absorbed as all artists traditionally are. On the other hand, in her absolute chastity, her frozen innocence, her sweet nullity, Snow White represents precisely the ideal of "contemplative purity" we have already discussed, an ideal that could quite literally kill the Queen. An angel in the house of myth, Snow White is not only a child but (as female angels always are) childlike, docile, submissive, the heroine of a life that *has no story*. But the Queen, adult and demonic, plainly wants a life of "significant action," by definition an "unfeminine" life of stories and story-telling. And therefore, to the extent that Snow White, as her daughter, is a part of herself, she wants to kill the Snow White *in herself*, the angel who would keep deeds and dramas out of her own house.

The first death plot the Queen invents is a naively straightforward murder story: she commands one of her huntsmen to kill Snow White. But, as Bruno Bettelheim has shown, the huntsman is really a surrogate for the King, a parental—or, more specifically, patriarchal—figure "who dominates, controls, and subdues wild ferocious beasts" and who thus "represents the subjugation of the animal, asocial, violent tendencies in man."[81] In a sense, then, the Queen has foolishly asked her patriarchal master to act for her in doing the subversive deed she wants to do in part to retain power over him and in part to steal his power from him. Obviously, he will not do this. As patriarchy's angelic daughter, Snow White is, after all, *his* child, and he must save her, not kill her. Hence he kills a wild boar in her stead, and brings its lung and liver to the Queen as proof that he has murdered the child. Thinking that she is devouring her ice-pure enemy, therefore, the Queen consumes, instead, the wild boar's organs; that is, symbolically speaking, she devours her own beastly rage, and becomes (of course) even more enraged.

When she learns that her first plot has failed, then, the Queen's story-telling becomes angrier as well as more inventive, more sophisticated, more subversive. Significantly, each of the three "tales" she tells—that is, each of the three plots she invents—depends on a poisonous or parodic use of a distinctively female device as a murder weapon, and in each case she reinforces the sardonic commentary on "femininity" that such weaponry makes by impersonating a "wise" woman, a "good" mother, or, as Ellen Moers would put it, an "educating heroine."[82] As a "kind" old pedlar woman, she offers to lace Snow White "properly" for once—then suffocates her with a very Victorian set of tight laces. As another wise old expert in female beauty, she promises to comb Snow White's hair "properly," then assaults her with a poisonous comb. Finally, as a wholesome farmer's wife, she gives Snow White a "very poisonous apple," which she has made in "a quite secret, lonely room, where no one ever came." The girl finally falls, killed, so it seems, by the female arts of cosmetology and cookery. Paradoxically, however, even though the Queen has been using such feminine wiles as the sirens' comb and Eve's apple subversively, to destroy angelic Snow White so that she (the Queen) can assert and aggrandize herself, these arts have had on her daughter an opposite effect from those she intended. Strengthening the chaste maiden in her passivity, they have made her into precisely the eternally beautiful, inanimate *objet d'art* patriarchal aesthetics want a girl to be. From the point of view of the mad, self-assertive Queen, conventional female arts *kill*. But from the point of view of the docile and selfless princess, such arts, even while they kill, confer the only measure of power available to a woman in a patriarchal culture.

Certainly when the kindly huntsman-father saved her life by abandoning her in the forest at the edge of his kingdom, Snow White discovered her own powerlessness. Though she had been allowed to live because she was a "good" girl, she had to find her own devious way of resisting the onslaughts of the maddened Queen, both inside and outside her self. In this connection, the seven dwarves probably represent her own dwarfed powers, her stunted selfhood, for, as Bettelheim points out, they can do little to help save the girl from the Queen. At the same time, however, her life with them is an important part of her education in submissive femininity, for in serving them she learns essential lessons of service, of selflessness, of domesticity. Finally, that at this point Snow White is a housekeeping angel in a *tiny* house conveys the story's attitude toward "woman's world and woman's work": the realm of domesticity is a miniaturized kingdom in which the best of women is not only like a dwarf but like a dwarf's servant.

Does the irony and bitterness consequent upon such a perception lead to Snow White's few small acts of disobedience? Or would Snow White ultimately have rebelled anyway, precisely because she *is* the Queen's true daughter? The story does not, of course, answer such questions, but it does seem to imply them, since its turning point comes from Snow White's significant willingness to be tempted by the Queen's "gifts," despite the dwarves' admonitions. Indeed, the only hint of self-interest that Snow White displays throughout the whole story comes in her "narcissistic" desire for the stay-laces, the comb, and the apple that the disguised murderess offers. As Bettelheim remarks, this "suggests how close the stepmother's temptations are to Snow White's inner desires."[83] Indeed, it suggests that, as we have already noted, the Queen and Snow White are in some sense one: while the Queen struggles to free herself from the passive Snow White in herself, Snow White must struggle to repress the assertive Queen in herself. That both women eat from the same deadly apple in the third temptation episode merely clarifies and dramatizes this point. The Queen's lonely art has enabled her to contrive a two-faced fruit—one white and one red "cheek"—that represents her ambiguous relationship to this angelic girl who is both her daughter and her enemy, her self and her opposite. Her intention is that the girl will die of the apple's poisoned red half—red with her sexual energy, her assertive desire for deeds of blood and triumph—while she herself will be unharmed by the passivity of the white half.

But though at first this seems to have happened, the apple's effect is, finally, of course, quite different. After the Queen's artfulness has killed Snow White into art, the girl becomes if anything even more dangerous to her "step" mother's autonomy than she was before, because even more opposed to it in both mind and body. For, dead and self-less in her glass coffin, she is an object, to be displayed and desired, patriarchy's marble "opus," the decorative and decorous Galatea with whom every ruler would like to grace his parlor. Thus, when the Prince first sees Snow White in her coffin, he begs the dwarves to give "it" to him as a gift, "for I cannot live without seeing Snow White. I will honor and prize her as my dearest possession". An "it," a possession, Snow White has become an idealized image of herself, a woman in a portrait like Aurora Leigh's mother, and as such she has definitively proven herself to be patriarchy's ideal woman, the perfect candidate for Queen. At this point, therefore, she regurgitates the poison apple (whose madness had stuck in her throat) and rises from her coffin. The fairest in the land, she will marry the most powerful in the land; bidden to their wedding, the egotistically assertive, plotting Queen will become a former Queen, dancing herself to death in red-hot iron shoes.

What does the future hold for Snow White, however? When her Prince becomes a King and she becomes a Queen, what will her life be like? Trained to domesticity by her dwarf instructors, will she sit in the window, gazing out on the wild forest of her past, and sigh, and sew, and prick her finger, and conceive a child white as snow, red as blood, black as ebony wood? Surely, fairest of them all, Snow White has exchanged one glass coffin for another, delivered from the prison where the Queen put her only to be imprisoned in the looking glass from which the King's voice speaks daily. There is, after all, no female model for her in this tale except the "good" (dead) mother and her living avatar the "bad" mother. And if Snow White escaped her first glass coffin by her goodness, her passivity and docility, her only escape from her second glass coffin, the imprisoning mirror, must evidently be through "badness," through plots and stories, duplicitous schemes, wild dreams, fierce fictions, mad impersonations. The cycle of her fate seems inexorable. Renouncing "contemplative purity," she must now embark on that life of "significant action" which, for a woman, is defined as a witch's life because it is so monstrous, so unnatural. Grotesque as Errour, Duessa, Lucifera, she will practice false arts in her secret, lonely room. Suicidal as Lilith and Medea, she will become a murderess bent on the self-slaughter implicit in her murderous attempts against the life of her own child. Finally, in fiery shoes that parody the costumes of femininity as surely as the comb and stays she herself contrived, she will do a silent terrible death-dance out of the story, the looking glass, the transparent coffin of her own image. Her only deed, this death will imply, can be a deed of death, her only action the pernicious action of self-destruction.

In this connection, it seems especially significant that the Queen's dance of death is a silent one. In "The Juniper Tree," a version of "Little Snow White" in which a *boy's* mother tries to kill him (for different reasons, of course) the dead boy is transformed not into a silent art object but into a furious golden bird who sings a song of vengeance against his murderess and finally crushes her to death with a millstone.[84] The male child's progress toward adulthood is a growth toward both self-assertion and self-articulation, "The Juniper Tree" implies, a development of the *powers* of speech. But the girl child must learn the arts of silence either as herself a silent image invented and defined by the magic looking glass of the male-authored text, or as a silent dancer of her own woes, a dancer who enacts rather than articulates. From the abused Procne to the reclusive Lady of Shallott, therefore, women have been told that their art, like the witch's dance in "Little Snow White," is an art of silence. Procne must record her sufferings with what Geoffrey Hartman calls "the voice of the shuttle" because when she was raped her tongue was cut out.[85] The Lady of Shallott must weave her story because she is imprisoned in a tower as adamantine as any glass coffin, doomed to escape only through the self-annihilating madness of romantic love (just as the Queen is doomed to escape only through the self-annihilating madness of her death dance), and her last work of art is her own dead body floating downstream in a boat. And even when such maddened or grotesque female artists make sounds, they are for the most part, say patriarchal theorists, absurd or grotesque or pitiful. Procne's sister Philomel, for instance, speaks with an unintelligible bird's voice (unlike the voice of the hero of "The Juniper Tree"). And when Gerard Manley Hopkins, with whom we began this meditation on pens and penises and kings and queens, wrote of her in an epigram "On a Poetess," he wrote as follows:

> Miss M. 's a nightingale. 'Tis well
> Your simile I keep.
> It is the way with Philomel
> To sing while others sleep.[86]

Even Matthew Arnold's more sympathetically conceived Philomel speaks "a wild, unquenched, deep-sunken, old-world pain" that arises from the stirrings of a "bewildered brain."[87]

Yet, as Mary Elizabeth Coleridge's yearning toward that sane and serious self concealed on the other side of the mirror suggested —and as Anne Finch's complaint and Anne Elliot's protest told us too—women writers, longing to attempt the pen, have longed to escape from the many-faceted glass coffins of the patriarchal texts whose properties male authors insisted that they are. Reaching a hand to the stern, self-determining self behind the looking-glass portrait of her mother, reaching past those grotesque and obstructive images of "Ghost, fiend, and angel, fairy, witch, and sprite," Aurora Leigh, like all the women artists whose careers we will trace in this book, tries to excavate the real self buried beneath the "copy" selves. Similarly, Mary Elizabeth Coleridge, staring into a mirror where her own mouth appears as a "hideous wound" bleeding "in silence and in secret," strives for a "voice to speak her dread."

In their attempts at the escape that the female pen offers from the prison of the male text, women like Aurora Leigh and Mary Elizabeth Coleridge begin, as we shall see, by alternately defining themselves as angel-women or as monster-women. Like Snow White and the wicked Queen, their earliest impulses, as we shall also see, are ambivalent. Either they are inclined to immobilize themselves with suffocating tight-laces in the glass coffins of patriarchy, or they are tempted to destroy themselves by doing fiery and suicidal tarantellas out of the looking glass. Yet, despite the obstacles presented by those twin images of angel and monster, despite the fears of sterility and the anxieties of authorship from which women have suffered, generations of texts *have* been possible for female writers. By the end of the eighteenth century—and here is the most important phenomenon we will see throughout this volume—women were not only writing, they were conceiving fictional worlds in which patriarchal images and conventions were severely, radically revised. And as self-conceiving women from Anne Finch and Anne Elliot to Emily Brontë and Emily Dickinson rose from the glass coffin of the male-authored text, as they exploded out of the Queen's looking glass, the old silent dance of death became a dance of triumph, a dance into speech, a dance of authority.

2 Infection in the Sentence: The Woman Writer and the Anxiety of Authorship

> The man who does not know sick women does not know women.
> —S. Weir Mitchell

> I try to describe this long limitation, hoping that with such power as is now mine, and such use of language as is within that power, this will convince any one who cares about it that this "living" of mine had been done under a heavy handicap. . . .
> —Charlotte Perkins Gilman

> A Word dropped careless on a Page
> May stimulate an eye
> When folded in perpetual seam
> The Wrinkled Maker lie
>
> Infection in the sentence breeds
> We may inhale Despair
> At distances of Centuries
> From the Malaria—
> —Emily Dickinson

> I stand in the ring
> in the dead city
> and tie on the red shoes
> . . . .
> They are not mine,
> they are my mother's,
> her mother's before,
> handed down like an heirloom
> but hidden like shameful letters.
> —Anne Sexton

What does it mean to be a woman writer in a culture whose fundamental definitions of literary authority are, as we have seen, both overtly and covertly patriarchal? If the vexed and vexing polarities of angel and monster, sweet dumb Snow White and fierce mad Queen, are major images literary tradition offers women, how does such imagery influence the ways in which women attempt the pen? If the Queen's looking glass speaks with the King's voice, how do its perpetual kingly admonitions affect the Queen's own voice? Since his is the chief voice she hears, does the Queen try to sound like the King, imitating his tone, his inflections, his phrasing, his point of view? Or does she "talk back" to him in her own vocabulary, her own timbre, insisting on her own viewpoint? We believe these are basic questions feminist literary criticism—both theoretical and practical—must answer, and consequently they are questions to which we shall turn again and again, not only in this chapter but in all our readings of nineteenth-century literature by women.

That writers assimilate and then consciously or unconsciously affirm or deny the achievements of their predecessors is, of course, a central fact of literary history, a fact whose aesthetic and metaphysical implications have been discussed in detail by theorists as diverse as T. S. Eliot, M. H. Abrams, Erich Auerbach, and Frank Kermode.[1] More recently, some literary theorists have begun to explore what we might call the psychology of literary history—the tensions and anxieties, hostilities and inadequacies writers feel when they confront not only the achievements of their predecessors but the traditions of genre, style, and metaphor that they inherit from such "forefathers." Increasingly, these critics study the ways in which, as J. Hillis Miller has put it, a literary text "is inhabited . . . by a long chain of parasitical presences, echoes, allusions, guests, ghosts of previous texts."[2]

As Miller himself also notes, the first and foremost student of such literary psychohistory has been Harold Bloom. Applying Freudian structures to literary genealogies, Bloom has postulated that the dynamics of literary history arise from the artist's "anxiety of influence," his fear that he is not his own creator and that the works of his predecessors, existing before and beyond him, assume essential priority over his own writings. In fact, as we pointed out in our discussion of the metaphor of literary paternity, Bloom's paradigm of the sequential historical relationship between literary artists is the relationship of father and son, specifically that relationship as it was defined by Freud. Thus Bloom explains that a "strong poet" must engage in heroic warfare with his "precursor," for, involved as he is in a literary Oedipal struggle, a man can only become a poet by somehow invalidating his poetic father.[3]

Bloom's model of literary history is intensely (even exclusively) male, and necessarily patriarchal. For this reason it has seemed, and no doubt will continue to seem, offensively sexist to some feminist critics. Not only, after all, does Bloom describe literary history as the crucial warfare of fathers and sons, he sees Milton's fiercely masculine fallen Satan as *the* type of the poet in our culture, and he metaphorically defines the poetic process as a sexual encounter between a male poet and his female muse. Where, then, does the female poet fit in? Does she want to annihilate a "forefather" or a "foremother"? What if she can find no models, no precursors? Does she have a muse, and what is its sex? Such questions are inevitable in any female consideration of Bloomian poetics. And yet, from a feminist perspective, their inevitability may be just the point; it may, that is, call our attention not to what is wrong about Bloom's conceptualization of the dynamics of Western literary history, but to what is right (or at least suggestive) about his theory.

For Western literary history *is* overwhelmingly male—or, more accurately, patriarchal—and Bloom analyzes and explains this fact, while other theorists have ignored it, precisely, one supposes, because they assumed literature had to be male. Like Freud, whose psychoanalytic postulates permeate Bloom's literary psychoanalyses of the "anxiety of influence," Bloom has defined processes of interaction that his predecessors did not bother to consider because, among other reasons, they were themselves so caught up in such processes. Like Freud, too, Bloom has insisted on bringing to consciousness assumptions readers and writers do not ordinarily examine. In doing so, he has clarified the implications of the psychosexual and sociosexual con-texts by which every literary text is surrounded, and thus the meanings of the "guests" and "ghosts" which inhabit texts themselves. Speaking of Freud, the feminist theorist Juliet Mitchell has remarked that "psychoanalysis is not a recommendation *for* a patriarchal society, but an analysis of one."[4] The same sort of statement could be made about Bloom's model of literary history, which is not a recommendation for but an analysis of the patriarchal poetics (and attendant anxieties) which underlie our culture's chief literary movements.

For our purposes here, however, Bloom's historical construct is useful not only because it helps identify and define the patriarchal psychosexual context in which so much Western literature was authored, but also because it can help us distinguish the anxieties and achievements of female writers from those of male writers. If we return to the question we asked earlier—where does a woman writer "fit in" to the overwhelmingly and essentially male literary history Bloom describes?—we find we have to answer that a woman writer does *not* "fit in." At first glance, indeed, she seems to be anomalous, indefinable, alienated, a freakish outsider. Just as in Freud's theories of male and female psychosexual development there is no symmetry between a boy's growth and a girl's (with, say, the male "Oedipus complex" balanced by a female "Electra complex") so Bloom's male-oriented theory of the "anxiety of influence" cannot be simply reversed or inverted in order to account for the situation of the woman writer.

Certainly if we acquiesce in the patriarchal Bloomian model, we can be sure that the female poet does not experience the "anxiety of influence" in the same way that her male counterpart would, for the simple reason that she must confront precursors who are almost exclusively male, and therefore significantly different from her. Not only do these precursors incarnate patriarchal authority (as our discussion of the metaphor of literary paternity argued), they attempt to enclose her in definitions of her person and her potential which, by reducing her to extreme stereotypes (angel, monster) drastically conflict with her own sense of her self—that is, of her subjectivity, her autonomy, her creativity. On the one hand, therefore, the woman writer's male precursors symbolize authority; on the other hand, despite their authority, they fail to define the ways in which she experiences her own identity as a writer. More, the masculine authority with which they construct their literary personae, as well as the fierce power struggles in which they engage in their efforts of self-creation, seem to the woman writer directly to contradict the terms of her own gender definition. Thus the "anxiety of influence" that a male poet experiences is felt by a female poet as an even more primary "anxiety of authorship"—a radical fear that she cannot create, that because she can never become a "precursor" the act of writing will isolate or destroy her.

This anxiety is, of course, exacerbated by her fear that not only can she not fight a male precursor on "his" terms and win, she cannot "beget" art upon the (female) body of the muse. As Juliet Mitchell notes, in a concise summary of the implications Freud's theory of psychosexual development has for women, both a boy and a girl, "as they learn to speak and live within society, want to take the father's [in Bloom's terminology the precursor's] place, and *only the boy will one day be allowed to do so.* Furthermore both sexes are born into the desire of the mother, and as, through cultural heritage, what the mother desires is the phallus-turned-baby, *both* children desire to be the phallus for the mother. Again, *only the boy can fully recognize himself in his mother's desire.* Thus *both* sexes repudiate the implications of femininity," but the girl learns (in relation to her father) "that her subjugation to the law of the father entails her becoming the representative of 'nature' and 'sexuality,' a chaos of spontaneous, intuitive creativity."[5]

Unlike her male counterpart, then, the female artist must first struggle against the effects of a socialization which makes conflict with the will of her (male) precursors seem inexpressibly absurd, futile, or even—as in the case of the Queen in "Little Snow White"— self-annihilating. And just as the male artist's struggle against his precursor takes the form of what Bloom calls revisionary swerves, flights, misreadings, so the female writer's battle for self-creation involves her in a revisionary process. Her battle, however, is not against her (male) precursor's reading of the world but against his reading of *her.* In order to define herself as an author she must redefine the terms of her socialization. Her revisionary struggle, therefore, often becomes a struggle for what Adrienne Rich has called "Re-vision—the act of looking back, of seeing with fresh eyes, of entering an old text from a new critical direction ... an act of survival."[6] Frequently, moreover, she can begin such a struggle only by actively seeking a *female* precursor who, far from representing a threatening force to be denied or killed, proves by example that a revolt against patriarchal literary authority is possible.

For this reason, as well as for the sound psychoanalytic reasons

Mitchell and others give, it would be foolish to lock the woman artist into an Electra pattern matching the Oedipal structure Bloom proposes for male writers. The woman writer—and we shall see women doing this over and over again—searches for a female model not because she wants dutifully to comply with male definitions of her "femininity" but because she must legitimize her own rebellious endeavors. At the same time, like most women in patriarchal society, the woman writer does experience her gender as a painful obstacle, or even a debilitating inadequacy; like most patriarchally conditioned women, in other words, she is victimized by what Mitchell calls "the inferiorized and 'alternative' (second sex) psychology of women under patriarchy."[7] Thus the loneliness of the female artist, her feelings of alienation from male predecessors coupled with her need for sisterly precursors and successors, her urgent sense of her need for a female audience together with her fear of the antagonism of male readers, her culturally conditioned timidity about self-dramatization, her dread of the patriarchal authority of art, her anxiety about the impropriety of female invention—all these phenomena of "inferiorization" mark the woman writer's struggle for artistic self-definition and differentiate her efforts at self-creation from those of her male counterpart.

As we shall see, such sociosexual differentiation means that, as Elaine Showalter has suggested, women writers participate in a quite different literary subculture from that inhabited by male writers, a subculture which has its own distinctive literary traditions, even— though it defines itself *in relation to* the "main," male-dominated, literary culture—a distinctive history.[8] At best, the separateness of this female subculture has been exhilarating for women. In recent years, for instance, while male writers seem increasingly to have felt exhausted by the need for revisionism which Bloom's theory of the "anxiety of influence" accurately describes, women writers have seen themselves as pioneers in a creativity so intense that their male counterparts have probably not experienced its analog since the Renaissance, or at least since the Romantic era. The son of many fathers, today's male writer feels hopelessly belated; the daughter of too few mothers, today's female writer feels that she is helping to create a viable tradition which is at last definitively emerging.

There is a darker side of this female literary subculture, however, especially when women's struggles for literary self-creation are seen in the psychosexual context described by Bloom's Freudian theories of patrilineal literary inheritance. As we noted above, for an "anxiety of influence" the woman writer substitutes what we have called an "anxiety of authorship," an anxiety built from complex and often only barely conscious fears of that authority which seems to the female artist to be by definition inappropriate to her sex. Because it is based on the woman's socially determined sense of her own biology, this anxiety of authorship is quite distinct from the anxiety about creativity that could be traced in such male writers as Hawthorne or Dostoevsky. Indeed, to the extent that it forms one of the unique bonds that link women in what we might call the secret sisterhood of their literary subculture, such anxiety in itself constitutes a crucial mark of that subculture.

In comparison to the "male" tradition of strong, father-son combat, however, this female anxiety of authorship is profoundly debilitating. Handed down not from one woman to another but from the stern literary "fathers" of patriarchy to all their "inferiorized" female descendants, it is in many ways the germ of a dis-ease or, at any rate, a disaffection, a disturbance, a distrust, that spreads like a stain throughout the style and structure of much literature by women, especially—as we shall see in this study—throughout literature by women before the twentieth century. For if contemporary women do now attempt the pen with energy and authority, they are able to do so only because their eighteenth- and nineteenth-century foremothers struggled in isolation that felt like illness, alienation that felt like madness, obscurity that felt like paralysis to overcome the anxiety of authorship that was endemic to their literary subculture. Thus, while the recent feminist emphasis on positive role models has undoubtedly helped many women, it should not keep us from realizing the terrible odds against which a creative female subculture was established. Far from reinforcing socially oppressive sexual stereotyping, only a full consideration of such problems can reveal the extraordinary strength of women's literary accomplishments in the eighteenth and nineteenth centuries.

Emily Dickinson's acute observations about "infection in the sentence," quoted in our epigraphs, resonate in a number of different ways, then, for women writers, given the literary woman's special concept of her place in literary psychohistory. To begin with, the words seem to indicate Dickinson's keen consciousness that, in the purest Bloomian or Millerian sense, pernicious "guests" and "ghosts" inhabit all literary texts. For any reader, but especially for a reader who is also a writer, every text can become a "sentence" or weapon in a kind of metaphorical germ warfare. Beyond this, however, the fact that "infection in the sentence *breeds*" suggests Dickinson's recognition that literary texts are coercive, imprisoning, fever-inducing; that, since literature usurps a reader's interiority, it is an invasion of privacy. Moreover, given Dickinson's own gender definition, the sexual ambiguity of her poem's "Wrinkled Maker" is significant. For while, on the one hand, "we" (meaning especially women writers) "may inhale Despair" from all those patriarchal texts which seek to deny female autonomy and authority, on the other hand "we" (meaning especially women writers) "may inhale Despair" from all those "foremothers" who have both overtly and covertly conveyed their traditional authorship anxiety to their bewildered female descendants. Finally, such traditional, metaphorically matrilineal anxiety ensures that even the maker of a text, when she is a woman, may feel imprisoned within texts—folded and "wrinkled" by their pages and thus trapped in their "perpetual seam[s]" which perpetually tell her how she *seems*.

Although contemporary women writers are relatively free of the infection of this "Despair" Dickinson defines (at least in comparison to their nineteenth-century precursors), an anecdote recently related by the American poet and essayist Annie Gottlieb summarizes our point about the ways in which, for all women, "Infection in the sentence breeds":

> When I began to enjoy my powers as a writer, I dreamt that my mother had me sterilized! (Even in dreams we still blame our mothers for the punitive choices our culture forces on us.) I went after the mother-figure in my dream, brandishing a large knife; on its blade was writing. I cried, "Do you know what you are doing? You are destroying my femaleness, my *female power*, which is important to me *because of you*!"[9]

Seeking motherly precursors, says Gottlieb, as if echoing Dickinson, the woman writer may find only infection, debilitation. Yet still she must seek, not seek to subvert, her *"female power,* which is important" to her because of her lost literary matrilineage. In this connection, Dickinson's own words about mothers are revealing, for she alternately claimed that "I never had a mother," that "I always ran Home to Awe as a child. . . . He was an awful Mother but I liked him better than none," and that "a mother [was] a miracle." [10] Yet, as we shall see, her own anxiety of authorship was a "Despair" inhaled not only from the infections suffered by her own ailing physical mother, and her many tormented literary mothers, but from the literary fathers who spoke to her—even "lied" to her—sometimes near at hand, sometimes "at distances of Centuries," from the censorious looking glasses of literary texts.

It is debilitating to be *any* woman in a society where women are warned that if they do not behave like angels they must be monsters. Recently, in fact, social scientists and social historians like Jessie Bernard, Phyllis Chesler, Naomi Weisstein, and Pauline Bart have begun to study the ways in which patriarchal socialization literally makes women sick, both physically and mentally. [11] Hysteria, the disease with which Freud so famously began his investigations into the dynamic connections between *psyche* and *soma,* is by definition a "female disease," not so much because it takes its name from the Greek word for womb, *hyster* (the organ which was in the nineteenth century supposed to "cause" this emotional disturbance), but because hysteria did occur mainly among women in turn-of-the-century Vienna, and because throughout the nineteenth century this mental illness, like many other nervous disorders, was thought to be caused by the female reproductive system, as if to elaborate upon Aristotle's notion that femaleness was in and of itself a deformity. [12] And, indeed, such diseases of maladjustment to the physical and social environment as anorexia and agoraphobia did and do strike a disproportionate number of women. Sufferers from anorexia—loss of appetite, self-starvation—are primarily adolescent girls. Sufferers from agoraphobia—fear of open or "public" places—are usually female, most frequently middle-aged housewives, as are sufferers from crippling rheumatoid arthritis. [13]

Such diseases are caused by patriarchal socialization in several ways. Most obviously, of course, any young girl, but especially a lively or imaginative one, is likely to experience her education in docility, submissiveness, self-lessness as in some sense sickening. To be trained in renunciation is almost necessarily to be trained to ill health, since the human animal', first and strongest urge is to his/her *own* survival, pleasure, assertion. In addition, each of the "subjects" in which a young girl is educated may be sickening in a specific way. Learning to become a beautiful object, the girl learns anxiety about—perhaps even loathing of—her own flesh. Peering obsessively into the real as well as metaphoric looking glasses that surround her, she desires literally to "reduce" her own body. In the nineteenth century, as we noted earlier, this desire to be beautiful and "frail" led to tight-lacing and vinegar-drinking. In our own era it has spawned in-numerable diets and "controlled" fasts, as well as the extraordinary phenomenon of teenage anorexia.[14] Similarly, it seems inevitable that women reared for, and conditioned to, lives of privacy, reticence, domesticity, might develop pathological fears of public places and unconfined spaces. Like the comb, stay-laces, and apple which the Queen in "Little Snow White" uses as weapons against her hated stepdaughter, such afflictions as anorexia and agoraphobia simply carry patriarchal definitions of "femininity" to absurd extremes, and thus function as essential or at least inescapable parodies of social prescriptions.

In the nineteenth century, however, the complex of social prescrip-tions these diseases parody did not merely urge women to act in ways which would cause them to become ill; nineteenth-century culture seems to have actually admonished women to *be* ill. In other words, the "female diseases" from which Victorian women suffered were not always byproducts of their training in femininity; they were the goals of such training. As Barbara Ehrenreich and Deirdre English have shown, throughout much of the nineteenth century "Upper- and upper-middle-class women were [defined as] 'sick' [frail, ill]; working-class women were [defined as] 'sickening' [infectious, dis-eased]." Speaking of the "lady," they go on to point out that "Society agreed that she was frail and sickly," and consequently a "cult of female invalidism" developed in England and America. For the products of such a cult, it was, as Dr. Mary Putnam Jacobi wrote in 1895, "considered natural and almost laudable to break down under all conceivable varieties of strain—a winter dissipation, a houseful of servants, a quarrel with a female friend, not to speak of more legitimate reasons.... Constantly considering their nerves, urged to consider them by well-intentioned but short-sighted advisors, [women] pretty soon become nothing but a bundle of nerves." [15]

Given this socially conditioned epidemic of female illness, it is not surprising to find that the angel in the house of literature frequently suffered not just from fear and trembling but from literal and figurative sicknesses unto death. Although her hyperactive stepmother dances herself into the grave, after all, beautiful Snow White has just barely recovered from a catatonic trance in her glass coffin. And if we return to Goethe's Makarie, the "good" woman of *Wilhelm Meister's Travels* whom Hans Eichner has described as incarnating her author's ideal of "contemplative purity," we find that this "model of selflessness and of purity of heart ... this embodiment of *das Ewig-Weibliche*, suffers from migraine headaches." [16] Implying ruthless self-suppression, does the "eternal feminine" necessarily imply illness? If so, we may have found yet another meaning for Dickinson's assertion that "Infection in the sentence breeds." The despair we "inhale" even "at distances of centuries" may be the despair of a life like Makarie's, a life that *"has no story."*

At the same time, however, the despair of the monster-woman is also real, undeniable, and infectious. The Queen's mad tarantella is plainly unhealthy and metaphorically the result of too much storytelling. As the Romantic poets feared, too much imagination may be dangerous to anyone, male or female, but for women in particular patriarchal culture has always assumed mental exercises would have dire consequences. In 1645 John Winthrop, the governor of the Massachusetts Bay Colony, noted in his journal that Anne Hopkins "has fallen into a sad infirmity, the loss of her understanding and reason, which had been growing upon her divers years, by occasion of her giving herself wholly to reading and writing, and had written many books," adding that "if she had attended her household affairs, and such things as belong to women ... she had kept her wits." [17] And as Wendy Martin has noted in the nineteenth century this fear of the intellectual woman became so intense that the phenomenon ... was recorded in medical annals. A thinking woman was considered such a breach of nature that a Harvard doctor reported during his autopsy on a Radcliffe graduate he discovered that her uterus had shrivelled to the size of a pea.[18]

If, then, as Anne Sexton suggests (in a poem parts of which we have also used here as an epigraph), the red shoes passed furtively down from woman to woman are the shoes of art, the Queen's dancing shoes, it is as sickening to be a Queen who wears them as it is to be an angelic Makarie who repudiates them. Several passages in Sexton's verse express what we have defined as "anxiety of authorship" in the form of a feverish dread of the suicidal tarantella of female creativity:

> All those girls
> who wore red shoes,
> each boarded a train that would not stop.
> . . . .
> They tore off their ears like safety pins.
> Their arms fell off them and became hats.
> Their heads rolled off and sang down the street.
> And their feet—oh God, their feet in the market place—
> ... the feet went on.
> The feet could not stop.
> . . . .
> They could not listen.
> They could not stop.
> What they did was the death dance.
>
> What they did would do them in.

Certainly infection breeds in these sentences, and despair: female art, Sexton suggests, has a "hidden" but crucial tradition of uncontrollable madness. Perhaps it was her semi-conscious perception of this tradition that gave Sexton herself "a secret fear" of being "a reincarnation" of Edna Millay, whose reputation seemed based on romance. In a letter to DeWitt Snodgrass she confessed that she had "a fear of writing as a woman writes," adding, "I wish I were a man

—I would rather write the way a man writes."[19] After all, dancing the death dance, "all those girls / who wore the red shoes" dismantle their own bodies, like anorexics renouncing the guilty weight of their female flesh. But if their arms, ears, and heads fall off, perhaps their wombs, too, will "shrivel" to "the size of a pea"?

In this connection, a passage from Margaret Atwood's *Lady Oracle* acts almost as a gloss on the conflict between creativity and "femininity" which Sexton's violent imagery embodies (or dis-embodies). Significantly, the protagonist of Atwood's novel is a writer of the sort of fiction that has recently been called "female gothic," and even more significantly she too projects her anxieties of authorship into the fairy-tale metaphor of the red shoes. Stepping in glass, she sees blood on her feet, and suddenly feels that she has discovered

> The real red shoes, the feet punished for dancing. You could dance, or you could have the love of a good man. But you were afraid to dance, because you had this unnatural fear that if you danced they'd cut your feet off so you wouldn't be able to dance. . . . Finally you overcame your fear and danced, and they cut your feet off. The good man went away too, because you wanted to dance.[20]

Whether she is a passive angel or an active monster, in other words, the woman writer feels herself to be literally or figuratively crippled by the debilitating alternatives her culture offers her, and the crippling effects of her conditioning sometimes seem to "breed" like sentences of death in the bloody shoes she inherits from her literary foremothers.

Surrounded as she is by images of disease, traditions of disease, and invitations both to disease and to dis-ease, it is no wonder that the woman writer has held many mirrors up to the discomforts of her own nature. As we shall see, the notion that "Infection in the sentence breeds" has been so central a truth for literary women that the great artistic achievements of nineteenth-century novelists and poets from Austen and Shelley to Dickinson and Barrett Browning are often both literally and figuratively concerned with disease, as if to emphasize the effort with which health and wholeness were won from the infectious "vapors" of despair and fragmentation. Rejecting the poisoned apples her culture offers her, the woman writer often becomes in some sense anorexic, resolutely closing her mouth on silence (since—in the words of Jane Austen's Henry Tilney—"a woman's only power is the power of refusal"[21]), even while she complains of starvation. Thus both Charlotte and Emily Brontë depict the travails of starved or starving anorexic heroines, while Emily Dickinson declares in one breath that she "had been hungry, all the Years," and in another opts for "Sumptuous Destitution." Similarly, Christina Rossetti represents her own anxiety of authorship in the split between one heroine who longs to "suck and suck" on goblin fruit and another who locks her lips fiercely together in a gesture of silent and passionate renunciation. In addition, many of these literary women become in one way or another agoraphobic. Trained to reticence, they fear the vertiginous openness of the literary marketplace and rationalize with Emily Dickinson that "Publication—is the Auction / Of the Mind of Man" or, worse, punningly confess that "Creation seemed a mighty Crack—/ To make me visible."[22]

As we shall also see, other diseases and dis-eases accompany the two classic symptoms of anorexia and agoraphobia. Claustrophobia, for instance, agoraphobia's parallel and complementary opposite, is a disturbance we shall encounter again and again in women's writing throughout the nineteenth century. Eye "troubles," moreover, seem to abound in the lives and works of literary women, with Dickinson matter-of-factly noting that her eye got "put out," George Eliot describing patriarchal Rome as "a disease of the retina," Jane Eyre and Aurora Leigh marrying blind men, Charlotte Brontë deliberately writing with her eyes closed, and Mary Elizabeth Coleridge writing about "Blindness" that came because "Absolute and bright, / The Sun's rays smote me till they masked the Sun."[23] Finally, aphasia and amnesia—two illnesses which symbolically represent (and parody) the sort of intellectual incapacity patriarchal culture has traditionally required of women—appear and reappear in women's writings in frankly stated or disguised forms. "Foolish" women characters in Jane Austen's novels (Miss Bates in *Emma*, for instance) express Malapropish confusion about language, while Mary Shelley's monster has to learn language from scratch and Emily Dickinson herself childishly questions the meanings of the most basic English words: "Will there really be a 'Morning'? / Is there such a thing as 'Day'?"[24] At the same time, many women writers manage to imply that the reason for such ignorance of language—as well as the reason for their deep sense of alienation and inescapable feeling of anomie—is that they have *forgotten* something. Deprived of the power that even their pens don't seem to confer, these women resemble Doris Lessing's heroines, who have to fight their internalization of patriarchal strictures for even a faint trace memory of what they might have become.

"Where are the songs I used to know, / Where are the notes I used to sing?" writes Christina Rossetti in "The Key-Note," a poem whose title indicates its significance for her. "I have forgotten everything / I used to know so long ago."[25] As if to make the same point, Charlotte Brontë's Lucy Snowe conveniently "forgets" her own history and even, so it seems, the Christian name of one of the central characters in her story, while Brontë's orphaned Jane Eyre seems to have lost (or symbolically "forgotten") her family heritage. Similarly, too, Emily Brontë's Heathcliff "forgets" or is made to forget who and what he was; Mary Shelley's monster is "born" without either a memory or a family history; and Elizabeth Barrett Browning's Aurora Leigh is early separated from—and thus induced to "forget"—her "mother land" of Italy. As this last example suggests, however, what all these characters and their authors really fear they have forgotten is precisely that aspect of their lives which has been kept from them by patriarchal poetics: their matrilineal heritage of literary strength, their "female power" which, as Annie Gottlieb wrote, is important to them *because of* (not in spite of) their mothers. In order, then, not only to understand the ways in which "Infection in the sentence breeds" for women but also to learn how women have won through disease to artistic health we must begin by redefining Bloom's seminal definitions of the revisionary "anxiety of influence." In doing so, we will have to trace the difficult paths by which nineteenth-century women overcame their "anxiety of authorship," repudiated debilitating patriarchal prescriptions, and recovered or remembered the lost foremothers who could help them find their distinctive female power.

To begin with, those women who were among the first of their sex to attempt the pen were evidently infected or sickened by just the feelings of self-doubt, inadequacy, and inferiority that their education in "femininity" almost seems to have been designed to induce. The necessary converse of the metaphor of literary paternity, as we noted in our discussion of that phenomenon, was a belief in female literary sterility, a belief that caused literary women like Anne Finch to consider with deep anxiety the possibility that they might be "Cyphers," powerless intellectual eunuchs. In addition, such women were profoundly affected by the sort of assumptions that underly an assertion like Rufus Griswold's statement that in reading women's writing "We are in danger ... of mistaking for the efflorescent energy of creative intelligence, that which is only the exuberance of personal 'feelings unemployed.'"[26] Even if it was not absurd for a woman to try to write, this remark implies, perhaps it was somehow sick or what we would today call "neurotic." "We live at home, quiet, confined, and our feelings prey upon us," says Austen's Anne Elliot to Captain Harville, not long before they embark upon the debate about the male pen and its depiction of female "inconstancy" which we discussed earlier. She speaks in what Austen describes as "a low, feeling voice," and her remarks as well as her manner suggest both her own and her author's acquiescence in the notion that women may be more vulnerable than men to the dangers and diseases of "feelings unemployed."[27]

It is not surprising, then, that one of Finch's best and most passionate poems is an ambitious Pindaric ode entitled "The Spleen." Here, in what might almost be a response to Pope's characterization of the Queen of Spleen in *The Rape of the Lock*, Finch confesses and explores her own anxiety about the "vaporous" illness whose force, she feared, ruled her life and art. Her self-examination is particularly interesting not only because of its rigorous honesty, but because that honesty compels her to reveal just how severely she herself has been influenced by the kinds of misogynistic strictures about women's "feelings unemployed" that Pope had embedded in *his* poem. Thus Pope insists that the "wayward Queen" of Spleen rules "the sex to fifty from fifteen"—rules women, that is, throughout their "prime" of female sexuality—and is therefore the "parent" of both hysteria and (female) poetry, and Finch seems at least in part to agree, for she notes that "In the Imperious *Wife* thou Vapours art." That is, insubordinate women are merely, as Pope himself would have thought, neurotic women. "Lordly *Man* [is] born to Imperial Sway," says Finch, but he is defeated by splenetic woman; he "Compounds for Peace . . . And *Woman*, arm'd with *Spleen*, do's servilely Obey." At the same time, however, Finch admits that she feels the most pernicious effects of Spleen within herself, and specifically within herself *as an artist*, and she complains of these effects quite movingly, without the self-censure that would seem to have followed from her earlier vision of female insubordination. Addressing Spleen, she writes that

> O'er me alas! thou dost too much prevail:
> I feel thy Force, whilst I against thee rail;
> I feel my Verse decay, and my crampt Numbers fail.
> Thro' thy black Jaundice I all Objects see,
>   As Dark, and Terrible as Thee,
> My Lines decry'd, and my Employment thought
> An useless Folly, or presumptuous Fault.[28]

Is it crazy, neurotic, splenetic, to want to be a writer? In "The Spleen" Finch admits that she fears it is, suggesting, therefore, that Pope's portrayal of her as the foolish and neurotic Phoebe Clinket had—not surprisingly—driven her into a Cave of Spleen in her own mind.

When seventeenth- and eighteenth-century women writers—and even some nineteenth-century literary women—did not confess that they thought it might actually be mad of them to want to attempt the pen, they did usually indicate that they felt in some sense apologetic about such a "presumptuous" pastime. As we saw earlier, Finch herself admonished her muse to be cautious "and still retir'd," adding that the most she could hope to do as a writer was "still with contracted wing, / To some few friends, and to thy sorrows sing." Though her self-effacing admonition is riddled with irony, it is also serious and practical. As Elaine Showalter has shown, until the end of the nineteenth century the woman writer really was supposed to take second place to her literary brothers and fathers.[29] If she refused to be modest, self-deprecating, subservient, refused to present her artistic productions as mere trifles designed to divert and distract readers in moments of idleness, she could expect to be ignored or (sometimes scurrilously) attacked. Anne Killigrew, who ambitiously implored the "Queen of Verse" to warm her soul with "poetic fire," was rewarded for her overreaching with charges of plagiarism. "I writ, and the judicious praised my pen: / Could any doubt ensuing glory then?" she notes, recounting as part of the story of her humiliation expectations that would be reasonable enough in a male artist. But instead "What ought t'have brought me honour, brought me shame."[30] Her American contemporary, Anne Bradstreet, echoes the frustration and annoyance expressed here in a discussion of the reception she could expect *her* published poems to receive:

> I am obnoxious to each carping tongue
> Who says my hand a needle better fits,
> A poet's pen all scorn I should thus wrong,
> For such despite they cast on female wits:
> If what I do prove well, it won't advance,
> They'll say it's stol'n, or else it was by chance.[31]

There is such a weary and worldly accuracy in this analysis that plainly, especially in the context of Killigrew's experience, no sensible woman writer could overlook the warning implied: be modest or else! Be dark enough thy shades, and be thou there content!

Accordingly, Bradstreet herself, eschewing Apollo's manly "bays," asks only for a "thyme or parsley wreath," suavely assuring her male readers that "This mean and unrefined ore of mine / Will make your glist'ring gold but more to shine." And though once again, as with Finch's self-admonitions, bitter irony permeates this modesty, the very pose of modesty necessarily has its ill effects, both on the poet's self-definition and on her art. Just as Finch feels her "Crampt Numbers" crippled by the gloomy disease of female Spleen, Bradstreet confesses that she has a "foolish, broken, blemished Muse" whose defects cannot be mended, since "nature made it so irreparable." After all, she adds—as if to cement the connection between femaleness and madness, or at least mental deformity—"a weak or wounded brain admits no cure." Similarly, Margaret Cavendish, the Duchess of Newcastle, whose literary activities actually inspired her contemporaries to call her "Mad Madge," seems to have tried to transcend her own "madness" by deploying the kind of modest, "sensible," and self-deprecatory misogyny that characterizes Bradstreet's *apologia pro vita sua.* "It cannot be expected," Cavendish avers, that "I should write so wisely or wittily as men, being of the effeminate sex, whose brains nature has mixed with the coldest and softest elements." Men and women, she goes on to declare, "may be compared to the blackbirds, where the hen can never sing with so strong and loud a voice, nor so clear and perfect notes as the cock; her breast is not made with that strength to strain so high."[32] But finally the contradictions between her attitude toward her gender and her sense of her own vocation seem really to have made her in some sense "mad." It may have been in a fleeting moment of despair and self-confrontation that she wrote, "Women live like Bats or Owls, labour like Beasts, and die like Worms." But eventually, as Virginia Woolf puts it, "the people crowded round her coach when she issued out," for "the crazy Duchess became a bogey to frighten clever girls with."[33]

As Woolf's comments imply, women who did *not* apologize for their literary efforts were defined as mad and monstrous: freakish because "unsexed" or freakish because sexually "fallen." If Cavendish's extraordinary intellectual ambitions made her seem like an aberration of nature, and Finch's writing caused her to be defined as a fool, an absolutely immodest, unapologetic rebel like Aphra Behn—the first really "professional" literary woman in England—was and is always considered a somewhat "shady lady," no doubt promiscuous, probably self-indulgent, and certainly "indecent." "What has poor woman done, that she must be / Debarred from sense and sacred poetry?" Behn frankly asked, and she seems just as frankly to have lived the life of a Restoration rake.[34] In consequence, like some real-life Duessa, she was gradually but inexorably excluded (even exorcized) not only from the canon of serious literature but from the parlors and libraries of respectability.

By the beginning of the bourgeois nineteenth century, however, both money and "morality" had become so important that no serious writer could afford either psychologically or economically to risk Behn's kind of "shadiness." Thus we find Jane Austen decorously protesting in 1816 that she is constitutionally unable to join "manly, spirited Sketches" to the "little bit (two Inches wide) of Ivory," on which, figuratively speaking, she claimed to inscribe her novels, and Charlotte Brontë assuring Robert Southey in 1837 that "I have

endeavored . . . to observe all the duties a woman ought to fulfil."
Confessing with shame that "I don't always succeed, for sometimes
when I'm teaching or sewing, I would rather be reading or writing,"
she dutifully adds that "I try to deny myself; and my father's approbation amply reward[s] me for the privation."[35] Similarly, in
1862 we discover Emily Dickinson telling Thomas Wentworth
Higginson that publication is as "foreign to my thought, as Fir-
mament to Fin," implying that she is *generically* unsuited to such
self-advertisement,[36] while in 1869 we see Louisa May Alcott's Jo
March learning to write moral homilies for children instead of
ambitious gothic thrillers. Clearly there is conscious or semiconscious
irony in all these choices of the apparently miniature over the
assuredly major, of the domestic over the dramatic, of the private
over the public, of obscurity over glory. But just as clearly the very
need to make such choices emphasizes the sickening anxiety of
authorship inherent in the situation of almost every woman writer
in England and America until quite recently.

What the lives and lines and choices of all these women tell us,
in short, is that the literary woman has always faced equally degrading options when she had to define her public presence in the
world. If she did not suppress her work entirely or publish it pseud-
onymously or anonymously, she could modestly confess her female
"limitations" and concentrate on the "lesser" subjects reserved for
ladies as becoming to their inferior powers. If the latter alternative
seemed an admission of failure, she could rebel, accepting the ostracism that must have seemed inevitable. Thus, as Virginia Woolf
observed, the woman writer seemed locked into a disconcerting
double bind: she had to choose between admitting she was "only a
woman" or protesting that she was "as good as a man."[37] Inevitably,
as we shall see, the literature produced by women confronted with
such anxiety-inducing choices has been strongly marked not only
by an obsessive interest in these limited options but also by obsessive
imagery of confinement that reveals the ways in which female artists
feel trapped and sickened both by suffocating alternatives and by
the culture that created them. Goethe's fictional Makarie was not,
after all, the only angelic woman to suffer from terrible headaches.
George Eliot (like Virginia Woolf) had them too, and perhaps we
can begin to understand why.

To consider the afflictions of George Eliot, however, is to bring to mind another strategy the insubordinate woman writer eventually developed for dealing with her socially prescribed subordination. Where women like Finch and Bradstreet apologized for their supposed inadequacies while women like Behn and Cavendish flaunted their freakishness, the most rebellious of their nineteenth-century descendants attempted to solve the literary problem of being female by presenting themselves as *male*. In effect, such writers protested not that they were "as good as" men but that, as writers, they *were* men. George Sand and (following her) George Eliot most famously used a kind of male-impersonation to gain male acceptance of their intellectual seriousness. But the three Brontë sisters, too, concealed their troublesome femaleness behind the masks of Currer, Ellis, and Acton Bell, names which Charlotte Brontë disingenuously insisted they had chosen for their androgynous neutrality but which most of their earliest readers assumed were male. For all these women, the cloak of maleness was obviously a practical-seeming refuge from those claustrophobic double binds of "femininity" which had given so much pain to writers like Bradstreet, Finch, and Cavendish.

Disguised as a man, after all, a woman writer could move vigorously away from the "lesser subjects" and "lesser lives" which had constrained her foremothers. Like the nineteenth-century French painter Rosa Bonheur, who wore male clothes so she could visit slaughterhouses and racecourses to study the animals she depicted, the "male-identified" woman writer felt that, dressed in the male "costume" of her pseudonym, she could walk more freely about the provinces of literature that were ordinarily forbidden to ladies. With Bonheur, therefore, she could boast that "My trousers have been my great protectors. . . . Many times I have congratulated myself for having dared to break with traditions which would have forced me to abstain from certain kinds of work, due to the obligation to drag my skirts everywhere."[38]

Yet though the metaphorical trousers of women like Sand and Eliot and the Brontës enabled them to maneuver for position in an overwhelmingly male literary tradition, such costumes also proved to be as problematical if not as debilitating as any of the more modest and ladylike garments writers like Finch and Bradstreet might be said to have adopted. For a woman artist is, after all, a woman—that is her "problem"—and if she denies her own gender she inevitably confronts an identity crisis as severe as the anxiety of authorship she is trying to surmount. There is a hint of such a crisis in Bonheur's discussion of her trousers. "I had no alternative but to realize that the garments of my own sex were a total nuisance," she explains. "But the costume I am wearing is my working outfit, nothing else. [And] if you are the slightest bit put off, I am completely prepared to put on a skirt, especially since all I have to do is to open a closet to find a whole assortment of feminine outfits."[39] Literal or figurative male impersonation seems to bring with it a nervous compulsion toward "feminine protest," along with a resurgence of the same fear of freakishness or monstrosity that necessitated male mimicry in the first place. As most literary women would have remembered, after all, it is Lady Macbeth—one of Shakespeare's most unsavory heroines —who asks the gods to "unsex" her in the cause of ambition.

Inalterably female in a culture where creativity is defined purely in male terms, almost every woman writer must have experienced the kinds of gender-conflicts that Aphra Behn expressed when she spoke of "my masculine part, the poet in me."[40] But for the nineteenth-century woman who tried to transcend her own anxiety of authorship and achieve patriarchal authority through metaphorical transvestism or male impersonation, even more radical psychic confusion must have been inevitable. Elizabeth Barrett Browning's two striking sonnets on George Sand define and analyze the problem such a woman faced. In the first of these pieces ("To George Sand, A Desire") Barrett Browning describes the French writer, whom she passionately admired, as a self-created freak, a "large-brained woman and large-hearted man / Self-called George Sand," and she declares her hope that "to woman's claim / And man's" Sand might join an "angel's grace," the redeeming strength "of a pure genius sanctified from blame." The implication is that, since Sand has crossed into forbidden and anomalous sociosexual territory, she desperately needs "purification"—sexual, spiritual, and social. On the other hand, in the second sonnet ("To George Sand, A Recognition") Barrett Browning insists that no matter what Sand does she is still inalterably female, and thus inexorably agonized.

> True genius, but true woman, dost deny
> The woman's nature with a manly scorn,
> And break away the gauds and armlets worn
> By weaker women in captivity?
> Ah, vain denial! that revolted cry
> Is sobbed in by a woman's voice forlorn.
> Thy woman's hair, my sister, all unshorn,
> Floats back dishevelled strength in agony,
> Disproving thy man's name. . . . [41]

In fact, Barrett Browning declares, only in death will Sand be able to transcend the constrictions of her gender. Then *God* will "unsex" her "on the heavenly shore." But until then, she must acquiesce in her inescapable femaleness, manifested by her "woman-heart's" terrible beating "in a poet fire."

Barrett Browning's imagery is drastic, melodramatic, even grotesque, but there are strong reasons for the intensity with which she characterizes Sand's representative identity crisis. As her own passionate involvement suggests, the problem Barrett Browning is really confronting in the Sand sonnets goes beyond the contradictions between vocation and gender that induced such anxiety in all these women, to include what we might call contradictions of genre and gender. Most Western literary genres are, after all, essentially male—devised by male authors to tell male stories about the world.

In its original form, for instance, the novel traditionally traces what patriarchal society has always thought of as a masculine pattern: the rise of a middle-class hero past dramatically depicted social and economic obstacles to a higher and more suitable position in the world. (Significantly, indeed, when a heroine rises—as in *Pamela*—she usually does so through the offices of a hero.) Similarly, our great paradigmatic tragedies, from *Oedipus* to *Faust*, tend to focus on a male "overreacher" whose virile will to dominate or rebel (or both) makes him simultaneously noble and vulnerable. From the rake-rogue to his modern counterpart the traveling salesman, moreover, our comic heroes are quintessentially male in their escapades and conquests, while from the epic to the historical novel, the detective story to the "western," European and American narrative literature has concentrated much of its attention on male characters who occupy powerful public roles from which women have almost always been excluded.

Verse genres have been even more thoroughly male than fictional ones. The sonnet, beginning with Petrarch's celebrations of "his" Laura, took shape as a poem in praise of the poet's mistress (who, we saw in Norman O. Brown's comment, can never herself be a poet because she "is" *poetry*). The "Great Ode" encourages the poet to define himself as a priestlike bard. The satiric epistle is usually written when a writer's manly rage transforms "his" pen into a figurative sword. And the pastoral elegy—beginning with Moscus's "Lament for Bion"—traditionally expresses a poet's grief over the death of a brother-poet, through whose untimely loss he faces and resolves the cosmic questions of death and rebirth.

It is true, of course, that even beyond what we might call the *Pamela* plot, some stories have been imagined for women, by male poets as well as male novelists. As we have seen, however, most of these stories tend to perpetuate extreme and debilitating images of women as angels or monsters. Thus the genres associated with such plot paradigms present just as many difficulties to the woman writer as those works of literature which focus primarily on men. If she identifies with a snow-white heroine, the glass coffin of romance "feels" like a deathbed to the female novelist, as Mary Shelley trenchantly shows in *Frankenstein*, while the grim exorcism from society of such a female "overreacher" as "Snow White's" Queen has always been a source of anxiety to literary women rather than the inspiration for a tale of tragic grandeur. It is Macbeth, after all, who is noble; Lady Macbeth is a monster. Similarly, Oedipus is a heroic figure while Medea is merely a witch, and Lear's madness is gloriously universal while Ophelia's is just pathetic. Yet to the extent that the structure of tragedy reflects the structure of patriarchy—to the extent, that is, that tragedy must be about the "fall" of a character who is "high"— the genre of tragedy, rather than simply *employing* such stories, itself necessitates them.[42]

To be sure, there is no real reason why a woman writer cannot tell traditional kinds of stories, even if they are about male heroes and even if they inevitably fit into male-devised generic structures. As Joyce Carol Oates has observed, critics often "fail to see how the creative artist shares to varying degrees the personalities of all his characters, even those whom he appears to detest—perhaps, at times, it is these characters he is really closest to."[43] It is significant, however, that this statement was made by a woman, for the remark suggests the extent to which a female artist in particular is keenly aware that she must inevitably project herself into a number of uncongenial characters and situations. It suggests, too, the degree of anxiety a literary woman may feel about such a splitting or distribution of her identity, as well as the self-dislike she may experience in feeling that she is "really closest to" those characters she "appears to detest." Perhaps this dis-ease, which we might almost call "schizophrenia of authorship," is one to which a woman writer is especially susceptible because she herself secretly realizes that her employment of (and participation in) patriarchal plots and genres inevitably involves her in duplicity or bad faith.

If a female novelist uses the *Pamela* plot, for instance, she is exploiting a story that implies women cannot and should not do what she is herself accomplishing in writing her book. Ambitious to rise by her own literary exertions, she is implicitly admonishing her female readers that they can hope to rise only through male intervention. At the same time, as Joanna Russ has pointed out, if a woman writer "abandon[s] female protagonists altogether and stick[s] to male myths with male protagonists . . . she falsifies herself and much of her own experience."[44] For though writers (as Oates implies) do use masks and disguises in most of their work, though what Keats called "the poetical Character" in some sense has "no self" because it *is* so many selves,[45] the continual use of male models inevitably involves the female artist in a dangerous form of psychological self-denial that goes far beyond the metaphysical self-lessness Keats was contemplating. As Barrett Browning's Sand sonnets suggest, such self-denial may precipitate severe identity crises because the male impersonator begins to see herself as freakish—not wholesomely androgynous but unhealthily hermaphroditic. In addition, such self-denial may become even more than self-destructive when the female author finds herself creating works of fiction that subordinate other women by perpetuating a morality that sanctifies or vilifies all women into submission. When Harriet Beecher Stowe, in "My Wife and I," assumes the persona of an avuncular patriarch educating females in their domestic duties, we resent the duplicity and compromise involved, as well as Stowe's betrayal of her own sex.[46] Similarly, when in *Little Women* Louisa May Alcott "teaches" Jo March to renounce gothic thrillers, we cannot help feeling that it is hypocritical of her to continue writing such tales herself. And inevitably, of course, such duplicity, compromise, and hypocrisy take their greatest toll on the artist who practices them: if a writer cannot be accurate and consistent in her art, how can her work be true to its own ideas?

Finally, even when male mimicry does not entail moral or aesthetic compromises of the kind we have been discussing, the use of male devised plots, genres, and conventions may involve a female writer in uncomfortable contradictions and tensions. When Elizabeth Barrett Browning writes "An Essay on Mind," a long meditative-philosophic poem of a kind previously composed mainly by men (with Pope's "Essay on Man" a representative work in the genre), she catalogues all the world's "great" poets, and all are male; the women she describes are muses. When in the same work, moreover, she describes the joys of intellectual discovery she herself must have felt as a girl, she writes about a schoolboy and *his* exultant response to the classics. Significantly, the "Essay on Mind" is specifically the poem Barrett Browning was discussing when she noted that her early writing was done by a "copy" self. Yet even as a mature poet she included only one woman in "A Vision of Poets"—Sappho—and remarked of her, as she did of George Sand, that the contradictions between her vocation and her gender were so dangerous that they might lead to complete self-destruction.[47]

Similarly, as we shall see, Charlotte Brontë disguised herself as a man in order to narrate her first novel, *The Professor*, and devoted a good deal of space in the book to "objective" analyses of the flaws and failings of young women her own age, as if trying to distance herself as much as possible from the female sex. The result, as with Barrett Browning's "Essay on Mind," is a "copy" work which exemplifies the aesthetic tensions and moral contradictions that threaten the woman writer who tries to transcend her own female anxiety of authorship by pretending she is male. Speaking of the Brontës' desire "to throw the color of masculinity into their writing," their great admirer Mrs. Gaskell once remarked that, despite the spiritual sincerity of the sisters, at times "this desire to appear male" made their work "technically false," even "[made] their writing squint."[48]

That Gaskell used a metaphor of physical discomfort—"squinting"—is significant, for the phenomenon of male mimicry is itself a sign of female dis-ease, a sign that infection, or at least headaches, "in the sentence" breed.

Yet the attempted cure is as problematical as the disease, a point we shall consider in greater detail in our discussions both of *The Professor* and of George Eliot. For as the literary difficulties of male-impersonations show, the female genius who denies her femaleness engages in what Barrett Browning herself called a "vain denial." Her "revolted cry / Is sobbed in by a woman's voice forlorn," and her "woman's hair" reveals her "dishevelled strength in agony," all too often disproving, contradicting, and subverting whatever practical advantages she gets from her "man's name." At the same time, however, the woman who squarely confronts both her own femaleness and the patriarchal nature of the plots and poetics available to her as an artist may feel herself struck dumb by what seem to be irreconcileable contradictions of genre and gender. An entry in Margaret Fuller's journal beautifully summarizes this problem:

> For all the tides of life that flow within me, I am dumb and ineffectual, when it comes to casting my thought into a form. No old one suits me. If I could invent one, it seems to me the pleasure of creation would make it possible for me to write. . . . I love best to be a woman; but womanhood is at present too straitly-bounded to give me scope. At hours, I live truly as a woman; at others, I should stifle; as, on the other hand, I should palsy, when I play the artist.[49]

Dis-eased and infected by the sentences of patriarchy, yet unable to deny the urgency of that "poet-fire" she felt within herself, what strategies did the woman writer develop for overcoming her anxiety of authorship? How did she dance out of the looking glass of the male text into a tradition that enabled her to create her own authority? Denied the economic, social, and psychological status ordinarily essential to creativity; denied the right, skill, and education to tell their own stories with confidence, women who did not retreat into angelic silence seem at first to have had very limited options. On the one hand, they could accept the "parsley wreath" of self-denial, writing in "lesser" genres—children's books, letters, diaries—or limiting their readership to "mere" women like themselves and producing what George Eliot called "Silly Novels by Lady Novelists."[50] On the other hand, they could become males *manqués*, mimics who disguised their identities and, denying themselves, produced most frequently a literature of bad faith and inauthenticity. Given such weak solutions to what appears to have been an overwhelming problem, how could there be a great tradition of literature by women? Yet, as we shall show, there is just such a tradition, a tradition especially encompassing the works of nineteenth-century women writers who found viable ways of circumventing the problematic strategies we have just outlined.

Inappropriate as male-devised genres must always have seemed, some women have always managed to work seriously in them. Indeed, when we examine the great works written by nineteenth-century women poets and novelists, we soon notice two striking facts. First, an extraordinary number of literary women either eschewed or grew beyond both female "modesty" and male mimicry. From Austen to Dickinson, these female artists all dealt with central female experiences from a specifically female perspective. But this distinctively feminine aspect of their art has been generally ignored by critics because the most successful women writers often seem to have channeled their female concerns into secret or at least obscure corners. In effect, such women have created submerged meanings, meanings hidden within or behind the more accessible, "public" content of their works, so that their literature could be read and appreciated even when its vital concern with female dispossession and disease was ignored. Second, the writing of these women often seems "odd" in relation to the predominantly male literary history defined by the standards of what we have called patriarchal poetics. Neither Augustans nor Romantics, neither Victorian sages nor Pre-Raphaelite sensualists, many of the most distinguished late eighteenth-century and nineteenth-century English and American women writers do not seem to "fit" into any of those categories to which our literary historians have accustomed us. Indeed, to many critics and scholars, some of these literary women look like isolated eccentrics.

We may legitimately wonder, however, if the second striking fact about nineteenth-century literature by women may not in some sense be a function of the first. Could the "oddity" of this work be associated with women's secret but insistent struggle to transcend their anxiety of authorship? Could the "isolation" and apparent "eccentricity" of these women really represent their common female struggle to solve the problem of what Anne Finch called the literary woman's "fall," as well as their common female search for an aesthetic that would yield a healthy space in an overwhelmingly male "Palace of Art"? Certainly when we consider the "oddity" of women's writing in relation to its submerged content, it begins to seem that when women did not turn into male mimics or accept the "parsley wreath" they may have attempted to transcend their anxiety of authorship by *revising* male genres, using them to record their own dreams and their own stories *in disguise*. Such writers, therefore, both participated in and—to use one of Harold Bloom's key terms—"swerved" from the central sequences of male literary history, enacting a uniquely female process of revision and redefinition that necessarily caused them to seem "odd." At the same time, while they achieved essential authority by telling their own stories, these writers allayed their distinctively female anxieties of authorship by following Emily Dickinson's famous (and characteristically female) advice to "Tell all the Truth but tell it slant—."[51] In short, like the twentieth-century American poet H. D., who declared her aesthetic strategy by entitling one of her novels *Palimpsest*, women from Jane Austen and Mary Shelley to Emily Brontë and Emily Dickinson produced literary works that are in some sense palimpsestic, works whose surface designs conceal or obscure deeper, less accessible (and less socially acceptable) levels of meaning. Thus these authors managed the difficult task of achieving true female literary authority by simultaneously conforming to and subverting patriarchal literary standards.

Of course, as the allegorical figure of Duessa suggests, men have always accused women of the duplicity that is essential to the literary strategies we are describing here. In part, at least, such accusations are well founded, both in life and in art. As in the white-black relationship, the dominant group in the male-female relationship rightly fears and suspects that the docility of the subordinate caste masks rebellious passions. Moreover, just as blacks did in the master-slave relationships of the American South, women in patriarchy have traditionally cultivated accents of acquiescence in order to gain freedom to live their lives on their own terms, if only in the privacy of their own thoughts. Interestingly, indeed, several feminist critics have recently used Frantz Fanon's model of colonialism to describe the relationship between male (parent) culture and female (colonized) literature.[52] But with only one language at their disposal, women writers in England and America had to be even more adept at doubletalk than their colonized counterparts. We shall see, therefore, that in publicly presenting acceptable facades for private and dangerous visions women writers have long used a wide range of tactics to obscure but not obliterate their most subversive impulses. Along with the twentieth-century American painter Judy Chicago, any one of these artists might have noted that "formal issues" were often "something that my content had to be hidden behind in order for my work to be taken seriously." And with Judy Chicago, too, any one of these women might have confessed that "Because of this duplicity, there always appeared to be something 'not quite right' about my pieces according to the prevailing aesthetic."[53]

To be sure, male writers also "swerve" from their predecessors, and they too produce literary texts whose revolutionary messages are concealed behind stylized facades. The most original male writers, moreover, sometimes seem "not quite right" to those readers we have recently come to call "establishment" critics. As Bloom's theory of the anxiety of influence implies, however, and as our analysis of the metaphor of literary paternity also suggests, there are powerful paradigms of male intellectual struggle which enable the male writer to explain his rebelliousness, his "swerving," and his "originality" both to himself and to the world, no matter how many readers think him "not quite right." In a sense, therefore, he conceals his revolutionary energies only so that he may more powerfully reveal them, and swerves or rebels so that he may triumph by founding a new order, since his struggle against his precursor is a "battle of strong equals."

For the woman writer, however, concealment is not a military gesture but a strategy born of fear and dis-ease. Similarly, a literary "swerve" is not a motion by which the writer prepares for a victorious accession to power but a necessary evasion. Locked into structures created by and for men, eighteenth- and nineteenth-century women writers did not so much rebel against the prevailing aesthetic as feel guilty about their inability to conform to it. With little sense of a viable female culture, such women were plainly much troubled by the fact that they needed to communicate truths which other (i.e. male) writers apparently never felt or expressed. Conditioned to doubt their own authority anyway, women writers who wanted to describe what, in Dickinson's phrase, is "not brayed of tongue"[54] would find it easier to doubt themselves than the censorious voices of society. The evasions and concealments of their art are therefore far more elaborate than those of most male writers. For, given the patriarchal biases of nineteenth-century literary culture, the literary woman did have something crucial to hide.

Because so many of the lost or concealed truths of female culture have recently been retrieved by feminist scholars, women readers in particular have lately become aware that nineteenth-century literary women felt they had things to hide. Many feminist critics, therefore, have begun to write about these phenomena of evasion and concealment in women's writing. In *The Female Imagination*, for instance, Patricia Meyer Spacks repeatedly describes the ways in which women's novels are marked by "subterranean challenges" to truths that the writers of such works appear on the surface to accept. Similarly, Carolyn Heilbrun and Catharine Stimpson discuss "the presence of absence" in literature by women, the "hollows, centers, caverns within the work—places where activity that one might expect is missing. . . or deceptively coded." Perhaps most trenchantly, Elaine Showalter has recently pointed out that feminist criticism, with its emphasis on the woman writer's inevitable consciousness of her own gender, has allowed us to "see meaning in what has previously been empty space. The orthodox plot recedes, and another plot, hitherto submerged in the anonymity of the background, stands out in bold relief like a thumbprint."[55]

But what is this other plot? Is there any *one* other plot? What is the secret message of literature by women, if there is a single secret message? What, in other words, have women got to hide? Most obviously, of course, if we return to the angelic figure of Makarie— that ideal of "contemplative purity" who no doubt had headaches precisely because her author inflicted upon her a life that seemed to have "no story"—what literary women have hidden or disguised is what each writer knows is in some sense her own story. Because, as Simone de Beauvoir puts it, women "still dream through the dreams of men," internalizing the strictures that the Queen's looking glass utters in its kingly voice, the message or story that has been hidden is "merely," in Carolyn Kizer's bitter words, "the private lives of one half of humanity." [56] More specifically, however, the one plot that seems to be concealed in most of the nineteenth-century literature by women which will concern us here is in some sense a story of the woman writer's quest for her own story; it is the story, in other words, of the woman's quest for self-definition. Like the speaker of Mary Elizabeth Coleridge's "The Other Side of a Mirror," the literary woman frequently finds herself staring with horror at a fearful image of herself that has been mysteriously inscribed on the surface of the glass, and she tries to guess the truth that cannot be uttered by the wounded and bleeding mouth, the truth behind the "leaping fire / Of jealousy and fierce revenge," the truth "of hard unsanctified distress." Uneasily aware that, like Sylvia Plath, she is "inhabited by a cry," she secretly seeks to unify herself by coming to terms with her own fragmentation. Yet even though, with Mary Elizabeth Coleridge, she strives to "set the crystal surface" of the mirror free from frightful images, she continually feels, as May Sarton puts it, that she has been "broken in two / By sheer definition." [57] The story "no man may guess," therefore, is the story of her attempt to make herself whole by healing her own infections and diseases.

To heal herself, however, the woman writer must exorcise the sentences which bred her infection in the first place; she must overtly or covertly free herself of the despair she inhaled from some "Wrinkled Maker," and she can only do this by revising the Maker's texts. Or, to put the matter in terms of a different metaphor, to "set the crystal surface free" a literary woman must shatter the mirror that has so long reflected what every woman was supposed to be. For these reasons, then, women writers in England and America, throughout the nineteenth century and on into the twentieth, have been especially concerned with assaulting and revising, deconstructing and reconstructing those images of women inherited from male literature, especially, as we noted in our discussion of the Queen's looking glass, the paradigmatic polarities of angel and monster. Examining and attacking such images, however, literary women have inevitably had consciously or unconsciously to reject the values and assumptions of the society that created these fearsome paradigms. Thus, even when they do not overtly criticize patriarchal institutions or conventions (and most of the nineteenth-century women we shall be studying do *not* overtly do so), these writers almost obsessively create characters who enact their own, covert authorial anger. With Charlotte Brontë, they may feel that there are "evils" of which it is advisable "not too often to think." With George Eliot, they may declare that the "woman question" seems "to overhang abysses, of which even pros-titution is not the worst."[58] But over and over again they project what seems to be the energy of their own despair into passionate, even melodramatic characters who act out the subversive impulses every woman inevitably feels when she contemplates the "deep-rooted" evils of patriarchy.

It is significant, then, that when the speaker of "The Other Side of a Mirror" looks into her glass the woman that she sees is a mad-woman, "wild / With more than womanly despair," the monster that she fears she really is rather than the angel she has pretended to be. What the heroine of George Eliot's verse-drama *Armgart* calls "basely feigned content, the placid mask / Of woman's misery" *is* merely a mask, and Mary Elizabeth Coleridge, like so many of her contem-poraries, records the emergence from behind the mask of a figure whose rage "once no man on earth could guess."[59] Repudiating "basely feigned content," this figure arises like a bad dream, bloody, envious, enraged, as if the very process of writing had itself liberated a madwoman, a crazy and angry woman, from a silence in which neither she nor her author can continue to acquiesce. Thus although Coleridge's mirrored madwoman is an emblem of "speechless woe" because she has "no voice to speak her dread," the poet ultimately speaks *for* her when she whispers "I am she!" More, she speaks for her in writing the poem that narrates her emergence from behind the placid mask, "the aspects glad and gay, / That erst were found reflected there."

As we explore nineteenth-century literature, we will find that this madwoman emerges over and over again from the mirrors women writers hold up both to their own natures and to their own visions of nature. Even the most apparently conservative and decorous women writers obsessively create fiercely independent characters who seek to destroy all the patriarchal structures which both their authors and their authors' submissive heroines seem to accept as inevitable. Of course, by projecting their rebellious impulses not into their heroines but into mad or monstrous women (who are suitably punished in the course of the novel or poem), female authors dramatize their own self-division, their desire both to accept the strictures of patriarchal society and to reject them. What this means, however, is that the madwoman in literature by women is not merely, as she might be in male literature, an antagonist or foil to the heroine. Rather, she is usually in some sense the *author's* double, an image of her own anxiety and rage. Indeed, much of the poetry and fiction written by women conjures up this mad creature so that female authors can come to terms with their own uniquely female feelings of fragmentation, their own keen sense of the discrepancies between what they are and what they are supposed to be.

We shall see, then, that the mad double is as crucial to the aggressively sane novels of Jane Austen and George Eliot as she is in the more obviously rebellious stories told by Charlotte and Emily Brontë. Both gothic and anti-gothic writers represent themselves as split like Emily Dickinson between the elected nun and the damned witch, or like Mary Shelley between the noble, censorious scientist and his enraged, childish monster. In fact, so important is this female schizophrenia of authorship that, as we hope to show, it links these nineteenth-century writers with such twentieth-century descendants as Virginia Woolf (who projects herself into both ladylike Mrs. Dalloway and crazed Septimus Warren Smith), Doris Lessing (who divides herself between sane Martha Hesse and mad Lynda Coldridge), and Sylvia Plath (who sees herself as both a plaster saint and a dangerous "old yellow" monster).

To be sure, in the works of all these artists—both nineteenth- and twentieth-century—the mad character is sometimes created only to be destroyed: Septimus Warren Smith and Bertha Mason Rochester are both good examples of such characters, as is Victor Frankenstein's monster. Yet even when a figure of rage seems to function only as a monitory image, her (or his) fury must be acknowledged not only by the angelic protagonist to whom s/he is opposed, but, significantly, *by the reader as well*. With his usual perceptiveness, Geoffrey Chaucer anticipated the dynamics of this situation in the *Canterbury Tales*.

When he gave the Wife of Bath a tale of her own, he portrayed her
projecting her subversive vision of patriarchal institutions into the
story of a furious hag who demands supreme power over her own life
and that of her husband: only when she gains his complete acceptance
of her authority does this witch transform herself into a modest and
docile beauty. Five centuries later, the threat of the hag, the monster,
the witch, the madwoman, still lurks behind the compliant paragon
of women's stories.

To mention witches, however, is to be reminded once again of
the traditional (patriarchally defined) association between creative
women and monsters. In projecting their anger and dis-ease into
dreadful figures, creating dark doubles for themselves and their
heroines, women writers are both identifying with and revising the
self-definitions patriarchal culture has imposed on them. All the
nineteenth- and twentieth-century literary women who evoke the
female monster in their novels and poems alter her meaning by virtue
of their own identification with her. For it is usually because she is
in some sense imbued with interiority that the witch-monster-mad-
woman becomes so crucial an avatar of the writer's own self. From a
male point of view, women who reject the submissive silences of
domesticity have been seen as terrible objects—Gorgons, Sirens,
Scyllas, serpent-Lamias, Mothers of Death or Goddesses of Night.
But from a female point of view the monster woman is simply a
woman who seeks the power of self-articulation, and therefore, like
Mary Shelley giving the first-person story of a monster who seemed
to his creator to be merely a "filthy mass that moves and talks," she
presents this figure for the first time from the inside out. Such a
radical misreading of patriarchal poetics frees the woman artist to
imply her criticism of the literary conventions she has inherited even
as it allows her to express her ambiguous relationship to a culture that
has not only defined her gender but shaped her mind. In a sense, as
a famous poem by Muriel Rukeyser implies, all these women ultimately embrace the role of that most mythic of female monsters, the
Sphinx, whose indecipherable message is the key to existence, because
they know that the secret wisdom so long hidden from men is precisely
their point of view.[60]

There is a sense, then, in which the female literary tradition we
have been defining participates on all levels in the same duality or

duplicity that necessitates the generation of such doubles as monster characters who shadow angelic authors and mad anti-heroines who complicate the lives of sane heroines. Parody, for instance, is another one of the key strategies through which this female duplicity reveals itself. As we have noted, nineteenth-century women writers frequently both use and misuse (or subvert) a common male tradition or genre. Consequently, we shall see over and over again that a "complex vibration" occurs between stylized generic gestures and unexpected deviations from such obvious gestures, a vibration that undercuts and ridicules the genre being employed. Some of the best-known recent poetry by women openly uses such parody in the cause of feminism: traditional figures of patriarchal mythology like Circe, Leda, Cassandra, Medusa, Helen, and Persephone have all lately been reinvented in the images of their female creators, and each poem devoted to one of these figures is a reading that reinvents her original story.[61] But though nineteenth-century women did not employ this kind of parody so openly and angrily, they too deployed it to give contextual force to their revisionary attempts at self-definition. Jane Austen's novels of sense and sensibility, for instance, suggest a revolt against both those standards of female excellence. Similarly, Charlotte Brontë's critical revision of *Pilgrim's Progress* questions the patriarchal ideal of female submissiveness by sub-stituting a questing Everywoman for Bunyan's questing Christian. In addition, as we shall show in detail in later chapters, Mary Shelley, Emily Brontë, and George Eliot covertly reappraise and repudiate the misogyny implicit in Milton's mythology by misreading and revising Milton's story of woman's fall. Parodic, duplicitous, extra-ordinarily sophisticated, all this female writing is both revisionary and revolutionary, even when it is produced by writers we usually think of as models of angelic resignation.

To summarize this point, it is helpful to examine a work by the woman who seems to be the most modest and gentle of the three Brontë sisters. Anne Brontë's *The Tenant of Wildfell Hall* (1848) is generally considered conservative in its espousal of Christian values, but it tells what is in fact a story of woman's liberation. Specifically, it describes a woman's escape from the prisonhouse of a bad marriage, and her subsequent attempts to achieve independence by establishing herself in a career as an artist. Since Helen Graham, the novel's protagonist, must remain incognito in order to elude her husband, she signs with false initials the landscapes she produces when she becomes a professional artist, and she titles the works in such a way as to hide her whereabouts. In short, she uses her art both to express and to camouflage herself. But this functionally ambiguous aesthetic is not merely a result of her flight from home and husband. For even earlier in the novel, when we encounter Helen before her marriage, her use of art is duplicitous. Her painting and drawing seem at first simply to be genteel social accomplishments, but when she shows one of her paintings to her future husband, he discovers a pencil sketch of his own face on the back of the canvas. Helen has been using the reverse side of her paintings to express her secret desires, and although she has remembered to rub out all the other sketches, this one remains, eventually calling his attention to the dim traces on the backs of all the others.

In the figure of Helen Graham, Anne Brontë has given us a wonderfully useful paradigm of the female artist. Whether Helen covertly uses a supposedly modest young lady's "accomplishments" for unladylike self-expression or publicly flaunts her professionalism and independence, she must in some sense deny or conceal her own art, or at least deny the self-assertion implicit in her art. In other words, there is an essential ambiguity involved in her career as an artist. When, as a girl, she draws on the backs of her paintings, she must make the paintings themselves work as public masks to hide her private dreams, and only behind such masks does she feel free to choose her own subjects. Thus she produces a public art which she herself rejects as inadequate but which she secretly uses to discover a new aesthetic space for herself. In addition, she subverts her genteelly "feminine" works with personal representations which endure only in tracings, since her guilt about the impropriety of self-expression has caused her to efface her private drawings just as it has led her to efface herself.

It is significant, moreover, that the sketch on the other side of Helen's canvas depicts the face of the Byronically brooding, sensual Arthur Huntingdon, the man she finally decides to marry. Fatally attracted by the energy and freedom that she desires as an escape from the constraints of her own life, Helen pays for her initial attraction by watching her husband metamorphose from a fallen angel into a fiend, as he relentlessly and self-destructively pursues a diabolical career of gaming, whoring, and drinking. In this respect, too, Helen is prototypical, since we shall see that women artists are repeatedly attracted to the Satanic/Byronic hero even while they try to resist the sexual submission exacted by this oppressive younger son who seems, at first, so like a brother or a double. From Jane Austen, who almost obsessively rejected this figure, to Mary Shelley, the Brontës, and George Eliot, all of whom identified with his fierce presumption, women writers develop a subversive tradition that has a unique relationship to the Romantic ethos of revolt.

What distinguishes Helen Graham (and all the women authors who resemble her) from male Romantics, however, is precisely her anxiety about her own artistry, together with the duplicity that anxiety necessitates. Even when she becomes a professional artist, Helen continues to fear the social implications of her vocation. Associating female creativity with freedom from male domination, and dreading the misogynistic censure of her community, she produces art that at least partly hides her experience of her actual place in the world. Because her audience potentially includes the man from whom she is trying to escape, she must balance her need to paint her own condition against her need to circumvent detection. Her strained relationship to her art is thus determined almost entirely by her gender, so that from both her anxieties and her strategies for overcoming them we can extrapolate a number of the crucial ways in which women's art has been radically qualified by their femaleness.

As we shall see, Anne Brontë's sister Charlotte depicts similar anxieties and similar strategies for overcoming anxiety in the careers of all the female artists who appear in her novels. From timid Frances Henri to demure Jane Eyre, from mysterious Lucia to flamboyant Vashti, Brontë's women artists withdraw behind their art even while they assert themselves through it, as if deliberately adopting Helen Graham's duplicitous techniques of self-expression. For the great women writers of the past two centuries are linked by the ingenuity with which all, while no one was really looking, danced out of the debilitating looking glass of the male text into the health of female authority. Tracing subversive pictures behind socially acceptable facades, they managed to appear to dissociate themselves from their own revolutionary impulses even while passionately enacting such impulses. Articulating the "private lives of one half of humanity," their fiction and poetry both records and transcends the struggle of what Marge Piercy has called "Unlearning to not speak." [62]

We must not forget, however, that to hide behind the facade of art, even for so crucial a process as "Unlearning to not speak," is still to be hidden, to be confined: to be secret is to be secreted. In a poignant and perceptive poem to Emily Dickinson, Adrienne Rich has noted that in her "half-cracked way" Dickinson chose "silence for entertainment, / chose to have it out at last / on [her] own premises."[63] This is what Jane Austen, too, chose to do when she ironically defined her work-space as two inches of ivory, what Emily Brontë chose to do when she hid her poems in kitchen cabinets (and perhaps destroyed her Gondal stories), what Christina Rossetti chose when she elected an art that glorified the religious constrictions of the "convent threshold." Rich's crucial pun on the word *premises* returns us, therefore, to the confinement of these women, a confinement that was inescapable for them even at their moments of greatest triumph, a confinement that was implicit in their secretness. This confinement was both literal and figurative. Literally, women like Dickinson, Brontë, and Rossetti were imprisoned in their homes, their father's houses; indeed, almost all nineteenth-century women were in some sense imprisoned in men's houses. Figuratively, such women were, as we have seen, locked into male texts, texts from which they could escape only through ingenuity and indirection. It is not surprising, then, that spatial imagery of enclosure and escape, elaborated with what frequently becomes obsessive intensity, characterizes much of their writing.

In fact, anxieties about space sometimes seem to dominate the literature of both nineteenth-century women and their twentieth-century descendants. In the genre Ellen Moers has recently called "female Gothic,"[64] for instance, heroines who characteristically inhabit mysteriously intricate or uncomfortably stifling houses are often seen as captured, fettered, trapped, even buried alive. But other kinds of works by women—novels of manners, domestic tales, lyric poems—also show the same concern with spatial constrictions. From Ann Radcliffe's melodramatic dungeons to Jane Austen's mirrored parlors, from Charlotte Brontë's haunted garrets to Emily Brontë's coffin-shaped beds, imagery of enclosure reflects the woman writer's own discomfort, her sense of powerlessness, her fear that she inhabits alien and incomprehensible places. Indeed, it reflects her growing suspicion that what the nineteenth century called "woman's place" is itself irrational and strange. Moreover, from Emily Dickinson's haunted chambers to H. D.'s tightly shut sea-shells and Sylvia Plath's grave-caves, imagery of entrapment expresses the woman writer's sense that she has been dispossessed precisely because she is so thoroughly possessed—and possessed in every sense of the word.

The opening stanzas of Charlotte Perkins Gilman's punningly titled "In Duty Bound" show how inevitable it was for a female artist to translate into spatial terms her despair at the spiritual constrictions of what Gilman ironically called "home comfort."

> In duty bound, a life hemmed in,
>   Whichever way the spirit turns to look;
> No chance of breaking out, except by sin;
>   Not even room to shirk—
>   Simply to live, and work.
>
> An obligation preimposed, unsought,
>   Yet binding with the force of natural law;
> The pressure of antagonistic thought;
>   Aching within, each hour,
>   A sense of wasting power.
>
> A house with roof so darkly low
>   The heavy rafters shut the sunlight out;
> One cannot stand erect without a blow;
>   Until the soul inside
>   Cries for a grave—more wide.[65]

Literally confined to the house, figuratively confined to a single "place," enclosed in parlors and encased in texts, imprisoned in kitchens and enshrined in stanzas, women artists naturally found themselves describing dark interiors and confusing their sense that they were house-bound with their rebellion against being duty bound. The same connections Gilman's poem made in the nineteenth century had after all been made by Anne Finch in the eighteenth, when she complained that women who wanted to write poetry were scornfully told that "the dull mannage of a servile house" was their "outmost art and use." Inevitably, then, since they were trapped in so many ways in the architecture—both the houses and the institutions—of patriarchy, women expressed their anxiety of authorship by comparing their "presumptuous" literary ambitions with the domestic accomplishments that had been prescribed for them. Inevitably, too, they expressed their claustrophobic rage by enacting rebellious escapes.

Dramatizations of imprisonment and escape are so all-pervasive in nineteenth-century literature by women that we believe they represent a uniquely female tradition in this period. Interestingly, though works in this tradition generally begin by using houses as primary symbols of female imprisonment, they also use much of the other paraphernalia of "woman's place" to enact their central symbolic drama of enclosure and escape. Ladylike veils and costumes, mirrors, paintings, statues, locked cabinets, drawers, trunks, strongboxes, and other domestic furnishing appear and reappear in female novels and poems throughout the nineteenth century and on into the twentieth to signify the woman writer's sense that, as Emily Dickinson put it, her "life" has been "shaven and fitted to a frame," a confinement she can only tolerate by believing that "the soul has moments of escape / When bursting all the doors / She dances like a bomb abroad."[66] Significantly, too, the explosive violence of these "moments of escape" that women writers continually imagine for themselves returns us to the phenomenon of the mad double so many of these women have projected into their works. For it is, after all, through the violence of the double that the female author enacts her own raging desire to escape male houses and male texts, while at the same time it is through the double's violence that this anxious author articulates for herself the costly destructiveness of anger repressed until it can no longer be contained.

As we shall see, therefore, infection continually breeds in the sentences of women whose writing obsessively enacts this drama of enclosure and escape. Specifically, what we have called the distinctively female diseases of anorexia and agoraphobia are closely associated with this dramatic/thematic pattern. Defining themselves as prisoners of their own gender, for instance, women frequently create characters who attempt to escape, if only into nothingness, through the suicidal self-starvation of anorexia. Similarly, in a metaphorical elaboration of bulimia, the disease of overeating which is anorexia's complement and mirror-image (as Marlene Boskind-Lodahl has recently shown),[67] women writers often envision an "outbreak" that transforms their characters into huge and powerful monsters. More obviously, agoraphobia and its complementary opposite, claustrophobia, are by definition associated with the spatial imagery through which these poets and novelists express their feelings of social confinement and their yearning for spiritual escape. The paradigmatic female story, therefore—the story such angels in the house of literature as Goethe's Makarie and Patmore's Honoria were in effect "forbidden" to tell—is frequently an arrangement of the elements most readers will readily remember from Charlotte Brontë's *Jane Eyre.* Examining the psychosocial implications of a "haunted" ancestral mansion, such a tale explores the tension between parlor and attic, the psychic split between the lady who submits to male dicta and the lunatic who rebels. But in examining these matters the paradigmatic female story inevitably considers also the equally uncomfortable spatial options of expulsion into the cold outside or suffocation in the hot indoors, and in addition it often embodies an obsessive anxiety both about starvation to the point of disappearance and about monstrous inhabitation.

Many nineteenth-century male writers also, of course, used imagery of enclosure and escape to make deeply felt points about the relationship of the individual and society. Dickens and Poe, for instance, on opposite sides of the Atlantic, wrote of prisons, cages, tombs, and cellars in similar ways and for similar reasons. Still, the male writer is so much more comfortable with his literary role that he can usually elaborate upon his visionary theme more consciously and objectively than the female writer can. The distinction between male and female images of imprisonment is—and always has been— a distinction between, on the one hand, that which is both metaphysical and metaphorical, and on the other hand, that which is social and actual. Sleeping in his coffin, the seventeenth-century poet John Donne was piously rehearsing the constraints of the grave in advance, but the nineteenth-century poet Emily Dickinson, in purdah in her white dress, was anxiously living those constraints in the present.

Imagining himself buried alive in tombs and cellars, Edgar Allan Poe was letting his mind poetically wander into the deepest recesses of his own psyche, but Dickinson, reporting that "I do not cross my Father's ground to any house in town," was recording a real, self-willed, self-burial. Similarly, when Byron's Prisoner of Chillon notes that "my very chains and I grew friends," the poet himself is making an epistemological point about the nature of the human mind, as well as a political point about the tyranny of the state. But when Rose Yorke in *Shirley* describes Caroline Helstone as living the life of a toad enclosed in a block of marble, Charlotte Brontë is speaking through her about her own deprived and constricted life, and its real conditions.[68]

Thus, though most male metaphors of imprisonment have obvious implications in common (and many can be traced back to traditional images used by, say, Shakespeare and Plato), such metaphors may have very different aesthetic functions and philosophical messages in different male literary works. Wordsworth's prison-house in the "Intimations" ode serves a purpose quite unlike that served by the jails in Dickens's novels. Coleridge's twice-five miles of visionary greenery ought not to be confused with Keats's vale of soul-making, and the escape of Tennyson's Art from her Palace should not be identified with the resurrection of Poe's Ligeia. Women authors, however, reflect the literal reality of their own confinement in the constraints they depict, and so all at least begin with the same unconscious or conscious purpose in employing such spatial imagery. Recording their own distinctively female experience, they are secretly working through and within the conventions of literary texts to define their own lives.

While some male authors also use such imagery for implicitly or explicitly confessional projects, women seem forced to live more intimately with the metaphors they have created to solve the "problem" of their fall. At least one critic does deal not only with such images but with their psychological meaning as they accrue around houses. Noting in *The Poetics of Space* that "the house image would appear to have become the topography of our inmost being," Gaston Bachelard shows the ways in which houses, nests, shells, and wardrobes are in us as much as we are in them.[69] What is significant from our point of view, however, is the extraordinary discrepancy between the almost consistently "felicitous space" he discusses and the negative space we have found. Clearly, for Bachelard the protective asylum of the house is closely associated with its maternal features, and to this extent he is following the work done on dream symbolism by Freud and on female inner space by Erikson. It seems clear too, however, that such symbolism must inevitably have very different implications for male critics and for female authors.

Women themselves have often, of course, been described or imagined as houses. Most recently Erik Erikson advanced his controversial theory of female "inner space" in an effort to account for little girls' interest in domestic enclosures. But in medieval times, as if to anticipate Erikson, statues of the Madonna were made to open up and reveal the holy family hidden in the Virgin's inner space. The female womb has certainly, always and everywhere, been a child's first and most satisfying house, a source of food and dark security, and therefore a mythic paradise imaged over and over again in sacred caves, secret shrines, consecrated huts. Yet for many a woman writer these ancient associations of house and self seem mainly to have strengthened the anxiety about enclosure which she projected into her art. Disturbed by the real physiological prospect of enclosing an unknown part of herself that is somehow also not herself, the female artist may, like Mary Shelley, conflate anxieties about maternity with anxieties about literary creativity. Alternatively, troubled by the anatomical "emptiness" of spinsterhood, she may, like Emily Dickinson, fear the inhabitations of nothingness and death, the transformation of womb into tomb. Moreover, conditioned to believe that as a house she is herself owned (and ought to be inhabited) by a man, she may once again but for yet another reason see herself as inescapably an object. In other words, even if she does not experience her womb as a kind of tomb or perceive her child's occupation of her house/body as depersonalizing, she may recognize that in an essential way she has been defined simply by her purely biological usefulness to her species.

To become literally a house, after all, is to be denied the hope of that spiritual transcendence of the body which, as Simone de Beauvoir has argued, is what makes humanity distinctively human. Thus, to be confined in childbirth (and significantly "confinement" was the key nineteenth-century term for what we would now, just as significantly, call "delivery") is in a way just as problematical as to be confined in a house or prison. Indeed, it might well seem to the literary woman that, just as ontogeny may be said to recapitulate phylogeny, the confinement of pregnancy replicates the confinement of society. For even if she is only metaphorically denied transcendence, the woman writer who perceives the implications of the house/body equation must unconsciously realize that such a trope does not just "place" her in a glass coffin, it transforms her into a version of the glass coffin herself. There is a sense, therefore, in which, confined in such a network of metaphors, what Adrienne Rich has called a "thinking woman" might inevitably feel that now she has been imprisoned within her own alien and loathsome body.[70] Once again, in other words, she has become not only a prisoner but a monster.

As if to comment on the unity of all these points—on, that is, the anxiety-inducing connections between what women writers tend to see as their parallel confinements in texts, houses, and maternal female bodies—Charlotte Perkins Gilman brought them all together in 1890 in a striking story of female confinement and escape, a paradigmatic tale which (like *Jane Eyre*) seems to tell *the* story that all literary women would tell if they could speak their "speechless woe." "The Yellow Wallpaper," which Gilman herself called "a description of a case of nervous breakdown," recounts in the first person the experiences of a woman who is evidently suffering from a severe postpartum psychosis.[71] Her husband, a censorious and paternalistic physician, is treating her according to methods by which S. Weir Mitchell, a famous "nerve specialist," treated Gilman herself for a similar problem. He has confined her to a large garret room in an "ancestral hall" he has rented, and he has forbidden her to touch pen to paper until she is well again, for he feels, says the narrator, "that with my imaginative power and habit of story-making, a nervous weakness like mine is sure to lead to all manner of excited fancies, and that I ought to use my will and good sense to check the tendency" (15–16).

The cure, of course, is worse than the disease, for the sick woman's mental condition deteriorates rapidly. "I think sometimes that if I were only well enough to write a little it would relieve the press of ideas and rest me," she remarks, but literally confined in a room she thinks is a one-time nursery because it has "rings and things" in the walls, she is literally locked away from creativity. The "rings and things," although reminiscent of children's gymnastic equipment, are really the paraphernalia of confinement, like the gate at the head of the stairs, instruments that definitively indicate her imprisonment. Even more tormenting, however, is the room's wallpaper: a sulphurous yellow paper, torn off in spots, and patterned with "lame uncertain curves" that "plunge off at outrageous angles" and "destroy themselves in unheard of contradictions." Ancient, smoldering, "unclean" as the oppressive structures of the society in which she finds herself, this paper surrounds the narrator like an inexplicable text, censorious and overwhelming as her physician husband, haunting as the "hereditary estate" in which she is trying to survive. Inevitably she studies its suicidal implications—and inevitably, because of her "imaginative power and habit of story-making," she revises it, projecting her own passion for escape into its otherwise incomprehensible hieroglyphics. "This wall-paper," she decides, at a key point in her story,

> has a kind of sub-pattern in a different shade, a particularly irritating one, for you can only see it in certain lights, and not clearly then.
>
> But in the places where it isn't faded and where the sun is just so—I can see a strange, provoking, formless sort of figure, that seems to skulk about behind that silly and conspicuous front design. [18]

As time passes, this figure concealed behind what corresponds (in terms of what we have been discussing) to the facade of the patriarchal text becomes clearer and clearer. By moonlight the pattern of the wallpaper "becomes bars! The outside pattern I mean, and the woman behind it is as plain as can be." And eventually, as the narrator sinks more deeply into what the world calls madness, the terrifying implications of both the paper and the figure imprisoned behind the paper begin to permeate—that is, to *haunt*—the rented ancestral mansion in which she and her husband are immured. The "yellow smell" of the paper "creeps all over the house," drenching every room in its subtle aroma of decay. And the woman creeps too— through the house, in the house, and out of the house, in the garden and "on that long road under the trees." Sometimes, indeed, the narrator confesses, "I think there are a great many women" both behind the paper and creeping in the garden,

> and sometimes only one, and she crawls around fast, and her crawling shakes [the paper] all over. . . . And she is all the time trying to climb through. But nobody could climb through that pattern—it strangles so; I think that is why it has so many heads. [30]

Eventually it becomes obvious to both reader and narrator that the figure creeping through and behind the wallpaper is both the narrator and the narrator's double. By the end of the story, moreover, the narrator has enabled this double to escape from her textual/architectural confinement: "I pulled and she shook, I shook and she pulled, and before morning we had peeled off yards of that paper." Is the message of the tale's conclusion mere madness? Certainly the righteous Doctor John—whose name links him to the anti-hero of Charlotte Brontë's *Villette*—has been temporarily defeated, or at least momentarily stunned. "Now why should that man have fainted?" the narrator ironically asks as she creeps around her attic. But John's unmasculine swoon of surprise is the least of the triumphs Gilman imagines for her madwoman. More significant are the madwoman's own imaginings and creations, mirages of health and freedom with which her author endows her like a fairy godmother showering gold on a sleeping heroine. The woman from behind the wallpaper creeps away, for instance, creeps fast and far on the long road, in broad daylight. "I have watched her sometimes away off in the open country," says the narrator, "creeping as fast as a cloud shadow in a high wind."

Indistinct and yet rapid, barely perceptible but inexorable, the progress of that cloud shadow is not unlike the progress of nineteenth-century literary women out of the texts defined by patriarchal poetics into the open spaces of their own authority. That such an escape from the numb world behind the patterned walls of the text was a flight from dis-ease into health was quite clear to Gilman herself. When "The Yellow Wallpaper" was published she sent it to Weir Mitchell, whose strictures had kept her from attempting the pen during her own breakdown, thereby aggravating her illness, and she was delighted to learn, years later, that "he had changed his treatment of

nervous prostration since reading" her story. "If that is a fact," she
declared, "I have not lived in vain." [72] Because she was a rebellious
feminist besides being a medical iconoclast, we can be sure that
Gilman did not think of this triumph of hers in narrowly therapeutic
terms. Because she knew, with Emily Dickinson, that "Infection in
the sentence breeds," she knew that the cure for female despair must
be spiritual as well as physical, aesthetic as well as social. What "The
Yellow Wallpaper" shows she knew, too, is that even when a supposedly "mad" woman has been sentenced to imprisonment in the
"infected" house of her own body, she may discover that, as Sylvia
Plath was to put it seventy years later, she has "a self to recover,
a queen." [73]

3 The Parables of the Cave

"Next then," I said, "take the following parable of education and ignorance as a picture of the condition of our nature. Imagine mankind as dwelling in an underground cave . . . "

—Plato

Where are the songs I used to know,
　Where are the notes I used to sing?
I have forgotten everything
　I used to know so long ago.
　　—Christina Rossetti

. . . there came upon me an overshadowing bright Cloud, and in the midst of it the figure of a Woman, most richly adorned with transparent Gold, her Hair hanging down, and her Face as the terrible Crystal for brightness [and] immediately this Voice came, saying, Behold I am God's Eternal Virgin-Wisdom . . . I am to unseal the Treasures of God's deep Wisdom unto thee, and will be as Rebecca was unto Jacob, a true Natural Mother; for out of my Womb thou shalt be brought forth after the manner of a Spirit, Conceived and Born again.

—Jane Lead

Although Plato does not seem to have thought much about this point, a cave is—as Freud pointed out—a female place, a womb-shaped enclosure, a house of earth, secret and often sacred.[1] To this shrine the initiate comes to hear the voices of darkness, the wisdom of inwardness. In this prison the slave is immured, the virgin sacrificed, the priestess abandoned. "We have put her living in the tomb!" Poe's paradigmatic exclamation of horror, with its shadow of solips-

93

ism, summarizes the Victorian shudder of disgust at the thought of
cavern confrontations and the evils they might reveal—the suffocation, the "black bat airs," the vampirism, the chaos of what
Victor Frankenstein calls "filthy creation." But despite its melodrama, Poe's remark summarizes too (even if unintentionally) the
plight of the woman in patriarchal culture, the woman whose cave-
shaped anatomy is her destiny. Not just, like Plato's cave-dweller,
a prisoner of Nature, this woman is a prisoner of her own nature,
a prisoner in the "grave cave" of immanence which she transforms
into a vaporous Cave of Spleen.[2]

In this regard, an anecdote of Simone de Beauvoir's forms a sort
of counter-parable to Plato's:

> I recall seeing in a primitive village of Tunisia a subterranean
> cavern in which four women were squatting: the old one-eyed
> and toothless wife, her face horribly devastated, was cooking
> dough on a small brazier in the midst of an acrid smoke; two
> wives somewhat younger, but almost as disfigured, were lulling
> children in their arms—one was giving suck; seated before a
> loom, a young idol magnificently decked out in silk, gold, and
> silver was knotting threads of wool. As I left this gloomy cave—
> kingdom of immanence, womb, and tomb—in the corridor
> leading upward toward the light of day I passed the male,
> dressed in white, well groomed, smiling, sunny. He was returning
> from the marketplace, where he had discussed world affairs
> with other men; he would pass some hours in this retreat of his
> at the heart of the vast universe to which he belonged, from
> which he was not separated. For the withered old women, for
> the young wife doomed to the same rapid decay, there was no
> universe other than the smoky cave, whence they emerged
> only at night, silent and veiled.[3]

Destroyed by traditional female activities—cooking, nursing, nee-
dling, knotting—which ought to have given them life as they themselves give life to men, the women of this underground harem are
obviously buried in (and by) patriarchal definitions of their sexuality.
Here is immanence with no hope of transcendence, nature seduced
and betrayed by culture, enclosure without any possibility of escape.
Or so it would seem.

Yet the womb-shaped cave is also the place of female power, the *umbilicus mundi,* one of the great antechambers of the mysteries of transformation. As herself a kind of cave, every woman might seem to have the cave's metaphorical power of annihilation, the power— as de Beauvoir puts it elsewhere—of "night in the entrails of the earth," for "in many a legend," she notes, "we see the hero lost forever as he falls back into the maternal shadows—cave, abyss, hell."[4] At the same time, as herself a fated inhabitant of that earth-cave of immanence in which de Beauvoir's Tunisian women were trapped, every woman might seem to have metaphorical access to the dark knowledge buried in caves. Summarizing the characteristics of those female "great weavers" who determine destiny—Norns, Fates, priestesses of Demeter, prophetesses of Gaea—Helen Diner points out that "all knowledge of Fate comes from the female depths; none of the surface powers knows it. Whoever wants to know about Fate must go down to the woman," meaning the Great Mother, the Weaver Woman who weaves "the world tapestry out of genesis and demise" in her cave of power. Yet individual women are imprisoned in, not empowered by, such caves, like Blake's symbolic worms, "Weaving to Dreams the Sexual strife/And weeping over the Web of life."[5] How, therefore, does any woman—but especially a literary woman, who thinks in images—reconcile the cave's negative meta-phoric potential with its positive mythic possibilities? Immobilized and half-blinded in Plato's cave, how does such a woman distinguish what she is from what she sees, her real creative essence from the unreal cutpaper shadows the cavern-master claims as reality?

In a fictionalized "Author's Introduction" to *The Last Man* (1826) Mary Shelley tells another story about a cave, a story which implicitly answers these questions and which, therefore, constitutes yet a third parable of the cave. In 1818, she begins, she and "a friend" visited what was said to be "the gloomy cavern of the Cumaean Sibyl." Entering a mysterious, almost inaccessible chamber, they found "piles of leaves, fragments of bark, and a white filmy substance resembling the inner part of the green hood which shelters the grain of the unripe Indian corn." At first, Shelley confesses, she and her male companion (Percy Shelley) were baffled by this discovery, but "At length, my friend . . . exclaimed 'This *is* the Sibyl's cave; these are sibylline leaves!' " Her account continues as follows.

On examination, we found that all the leaves, bark, and other substances were traced with written characters. What appeared to us more astonishing, was that these writings were expressed in various languages: some unknown to my companion . . . some . . . in modern dialects. . . . We could make out little by the dim light, but they seemed to contain prophecies, detailed relations of events but lately passed; names . . . and often exclamations of exultation or woe . . . were traced on their thin scant pages. . . . We made a hasty selection of such of the leaves, whose writing one, at least of us could understand, and then . . . bade adieu to the dim hypaethric cavern. . . . Since that period . . . I have been employed in deciphering these sacred remains. . . . I present the public with my latest discoveries in the slight Sibylline pages. Scattered and unconnected as they were, I have been obliged to . . . model the work into a consistent form. But the main substance rests on the divine intuitions which the Cumaean damsel obtained from heaven.[6]

Every feature of this cave journey is significant, especially for the feminist critic who seeks to understand the meaning not just of male but also of female parables of the cave.

To begin with, the sad fact that not Mary Shelley but her male companion is able to recognize the Sibyl's cave and readily to decipher some of the difficult languages in which the sibylline leaves are written suggests the woman writer's own anxieties about her equivocal position in a patriarchal literary culture which often seems to her to enact strange rituals and speak in unknown tongues. The woman may *be* the cave, but—so Mary Shelley's hesitant response suggests—it is the man who knows the cave, who analyzes its meaning, who (like Plato) authors its primary parables, and who even interprets its language, as Gerard Manley Hopkins, that apostle of aesthetic virility, was to do more than half a century after the publication of *The Last Man,* in his sonnet "Spelt from Sibyl's Leaves."

Yet the cave is a female space and it belonged to a female hierophant, the lost Sibyl, the prophetess who inscribed her "divine intuitions" on tender leaves and fragments of delicate bark. For Mary Shelley, therefore, it is intimately connected with both her own artistic authority and her own power of self-creation. A male poet or instructor may guide her to this place, but, as she herself realizes, she and she alone can effectively reconstruct the scattered truth of the Sibyl's leaves. Literally the daughter of a dead and dishonored mother—the powerful feminist Mary Wollstonecraft—Mary Shelley portrays herself in this parable as figuratively the daughter of the vanished Sybil, the primordial prophetess who mythically conceived all women artists.

That the Sibyl's leaves are now scattered, fragmented, barely comprehensible is thus the central problem Shelley faces in her own art. Earlier in her introduction, she notes that finding the cave was a preliminary problem. She and her companion were misled and misdirected by native guides, she tells us; left alone in one chamber while the guides went for new torches, they "lost" their way in the darkness; ascending in the "wrong" direction, they accidentally stumbled upon the true cave. But the difficulty of this initial discovery merely foreshadows the difficulty of the crucial task of reconstruction, as Shelley shows. For just as the path to the Sibyl's cave has been forgotten, the coherent truth of her leaves has been shattered and scattered, the body of her art dismembered, and, like Anne Finch, she has become a sort of "Cypher," powerless and enigmatic. But while the way to the cave can be "remembered" by accident, the whole meaning of the sibylline leaves can only be re-membered through painstaking labor: translation, transcription, and stitchery, re-vision and re-creation.

The specifically sexual texture of these sibylline documents, these scattered leaves and leavings, adds to their profound importance for women. Working on leaves, bark, and "a white filmy substance," the Sibyl literally wrote, and wrote *upon*, the Book of Nature. She had, in other words, a goddess's power of maternal creativity, the sexual/artistic strength that is the female equivalent of the male potential for literary paternity. In her "dim hypaethric cavern"—a dim sea-cave that was nevertheless *open* to the sky—she received her "divine intuitions" through "an aperture" in the "arched dome-like roof" which "let in the light of heaven." On her "raised seat of stone, about the size of a Grecian couch," she *conceived* her art, inscribing it on leaves and bark from the green world outside. And so fierce are her verses, so truthful her "poetic rhapsodies," that even in deciphering them Shelley exclaims that she feels herself "taken ... out of a world, which has averted its once benignant face from me, to one glowing with imagination and power." For in recovering and reconstructing the Sibyl's scattered artistic/sexual energy, Shelley comes to recognize that she is discovering and creating—literally *de-ciphering*—her own creative power. "Sometimes I have thought," she modestly confesses, "that, obscure and chaotic as they are, [these translations from the Sibyl's leaves] owe their present form to me, their decipherer. As if we should give to another artist, the painted fragments which form the mosaic copy of Raphael's Transfiguration in St. Peter's; he would put them together in a form, whose mode would be fashioned by his own peculiar mind and talent."[7]

Given all these implications and overtones, it seems to us that the submerged message of Shelley's parable of the cave forms in itself a fourth parable in the series we have been discussing. This last parable is the story of the woman artist who enters the cavern of her own mind and finds there the scattered leaves not only of her own power but of the tradition which might have generated that power. The body of her precursor's art, and thus the body of her own art, lies in pieces around her, dismembered, dis-remembered, disintegrated. How can she remember it and become a member of it, join it and rejoin it, integrate it and in doing so achieve her own integrity, her own selfhood? Surrounded by the ruins of her own tradition, the leavings and unleavings of her spiritual mother's art, she feels—as we noted earlier—like someone suffering from amnesia. Not only did she fail to recognize—that is, to remember—the cavern itself, she no longer knows its languages, its messages, its forms. With Christina Rossetti, she wonders once again "Where are the songs I used to know,/Where are the notes I used to sing?" Bewildered by the incoherence of the fragments she confronts, she cannot help deciding that "I have forgotten everything/I used to know so long ago."

But it is possible, as Mary Shelley's introduction tells us, for the woman poet to reconstruct the shattered tradition that is her matrilineal heritage. Her trip into the cavern of her own mind, despite (or perhaps because of) its falls in darkness, its stumblings, its anxious wanderings, begins the process of re-membering. Even her dialogue with the Romantic poet who guides her (in Mary Shelley's version of the parable) proves useful, for, as Northrop Frye has argued, a

revolutionary "mother-goddess myth" which allows power and dignity to women—a myth which is anti-hierarchical, a myth which would
liberate the energy of all living creatures—"gained ground" in the
Romantic period.[8] Finally, the sibylline messages themselves speak
to her, and in speaking to her they both enable her to speak for
herself and empower her to speak for the Sibyl. Going "down to the
woman" of Fate whom Helen Diner describes, the woman writer
recovers herself as a woman of art. Thus, where the traditional male
hero makes his "night sea journey" to the center of the earth, the
bottom of the mere, the belly of the whale, to slay or be slain by the
dragons of darkness, the female artist makes her journey into what
Adrienne Rich has called "the cratered night of female memory" to
revitalize the darkness, to retrieve what has been lost, to regenerate,
reconceive, and give birth.[9]

What she gives birth to is in a sense her own mother goddess and
her own mother land. In this parable of the cave it is not the male
god Osiris who has been torn apart but his sister, Isis, who has been
dismembered and destroyed. Similarly, it is not the male poet
Orpheus whose catastrophe we are confronting but his lost bride,
Eurydice, whom we find abandoned in the labyrinthine caverns of
Hades. Or to put the point another way, this parable suggests that
(as the poet H. D. knew) the traditional figure of Isis in search of
Osiris is really a figure of Isis in search of herself, and the betrayed
Eurydice is really (like Virginia Woolf's "Judith Shakespeare") the
woman poet who never arose from the prison of her "grave cave."
Reconstructing Isis and Eurydice, then, the woman artist redefines
and recovers the lost Atlantis of her literary heritage, the sunken
continent whose wholeness once encompassed and explained all
those figures on the horizon who now seem "odd," fragmentary,
incomplete—the novelists historians call "singular anomalies," the
poets critics call "poetesses," the revolutionary artists patriarchal
poets see as "unsexed," monstrous, grotesque. Remembered by the
community of which they are and were members, such figures gain
their full authority, and their visions begin to seem like conceptions
as powerful as the Sibyl's were. Emily Brontë's passionate A. G. A.,
Jane Lead's Sophia, H. D.'s *bona dea* all have a place in this risen
Atlantis which is their mother country, and Jane Eyre's friendship
for Diana and Mary Rivers, Aurora Leigh's love of her Italian

mother land together with her dream of a new Jerusalem, Emily
Dickinson's "mystic green" where women "live aloud," and George
Eliot's concept of sisterhood—all these visions and re-visions help
define the utopian boundaries of the resurrected continent.

That women have translated their yearnings for motherly or
sisterly precursors into visions of such a land is as clear as it is certain
that this metaphoric land, like the Sibyl's leaves and the woman
writer's power, has been shattered and scattered. Emily Dickinson,
a woman artist whose own carefully sewn together "packets" of
poetry were—ironically enough—to be fragmented by male editors
and female heirs, projected her yearning for this lost female home
into the figure of a caged (and female) leopard. Her visionary nostalgia demonstrates that at times the memory of this Atlantis could
be as painful for women writers as amnesia about it often was.
"Civilization—spurns—the Leopard!" she noted, commenting that
"Deserts—never rebuked her Satin— . . . [for] This was the Leopard's
nature—Signor— / Need—a keeper—frown?" and adding, poi-
gnantly, that we should

> Pity—the Pard—that left her Asia—
> Memories—of Palm—
> Cannot be stifled—with Narcotic—
> Nor suppressed—with Balm—[10]

Similarly, though she was ostensibly using the symbolism of traditional religion, Christina Rossetti described her pained yearning for
a lost, visionary continent like Dickinson's "Asia" in a poem whose
title—"Mother Country"—openly acknowledges the real subject:

> Oh what is that country
>   And where can it be
> Not mine own country,
>   But dearer far to me?
>
> Yet mine own country,
>   If I one day may see
> Its spices and cedars,
>   Its gold and ivory.
>
> As I lie dreaming
>   It rises, that land;

> There rises before me
>   Its green golden strand,
> With the bowing cedars
>   And the shining sand;
> It sparkles and flashes
>   Like a shaken brand.[11]

The ambiguities with which Rossetti describes her own relationship to this land ("Not mine own . . . But dearer far") reflect the uncertainty of the self-definition upon which her vision depends. Is a woman's *mother* country her "own"? Has Mary Shelley a "right" to the Sibyl's leaves? Through what structure of definitions and qualifications can the female artist claim her matrilineal heritage, her birthright of that power which, as Annie Gottlieb's dream asserted, is important to her *because of* her mother? Despite these implicit questions, Rossetti admits that "As I lie dreaming / It rises that land"—rises, significantly, glittering and flashing "like a shaken brand," rises from "the cratered night of female memory," setting fire to the darkness, dispersing the shadows of the cavern, destroying the archaic structures which enclosed it in silence and gloom.

There is a sense in which, for us, this book is a dream of the rising of Christina Rossetti's "mother country." And there is a sense in which it is an attempt at reconstructing the Sibyl's leaves, leaves which haunt us with the possibility that if we can piece together their fragments the parts will form a whole that tells the story of the career of a single woman artist, a "mother of us all," as Gertrude Stein would put it, a woman whom patriarchal poetics dismembered and whom we have tried to remember. Detached from herself, silenced, subdued, this woman artist tried in the beginning, as we shall see, to write like an angel in the house of fiction: with Jane Austen and Maria Edgeworth, she concealed her own truth behind a decorous and ladylike facade, scattering her real wishes to the winds or translating them into incomprehensible hieroglyphics. But as time passed and her cave-prison became more constricted, more claustrophobic, she "fell" into the gothic/Satanic mode and, with the Brontës and Mary Shelley, she planned mad or monstrous escapes, then dizzily withdrew—with George Eliot and Emily Dickinson—from those open spaces where the scorching presence of the

patriarchal sun, whom Dickinson called "the man of noon," emphasized her vulnerability. Since "Creation seemed a mighty Crack" to
make her "visible," she took refuge again in the safety of the "dim
hypaethric cavern" where she could be alone with herself, with a
truth that was hers even in its fragmentation.[12]

Yet through all these stages of her history this mythic woman artist
dreamed, like her sibylline ancestress, of a visionary future, a utopian
land in which she could be whole and energetic. As tense with
longing as the giant "korl woman," a metal sculpture the man named
Wolfe carves from flesh-colored pig "refuse" in Rebecca Harding
Davis's *Life in the Iron Mills*, she turned with a "wild, eager face,"
with "the mad, half-despairing gesture of drowning," toward her
half-conscious imagination of that future. Eventually she was to
realize, with Adrienne Rich, that she was "reading the Parable of
the Cave / while living in the cave"; with Sylvia Plath she was to
decide that "I am a miner" surrounded by "tears / The earthen
womb / Exudes from its dead boredom"; and like Plath she was to
hang her cave "with roses," transfiguring it—as the Sibyl did—with
artful foliage.[13] But her vision of self-creation was consistently the
same vision of connection and resurrection. Like the rebirth of the
drowned Atlantans in Ursula Le Guin's utopian "The New Atlantis,"
this vision often began with an awakening in darkness, a dim awareness of "the whispering thunder from below," and a sense that even
if "we could not answer, we knew because we heard, because we
felt, because we wept, we knew that we were; and we remembered
other voices."[14] Like Mary Shelley's piecing together of the Sybil's
leaves, the vision often entailed a subversive transfiguration of those
female arts to which de Beauvoir's cave-dwelling seamstresses were
condemned into the powerful arts of the underground Weaver
Woman, who uses her magical loom to weave a distinctively female
"Tapestr[y] of Paradise."[15] And the fact that the cave is and was
a place where such visions were possible is itself a sign of the power
of the cave and a crucial message of the parable of the cave, a message
to remind us that the cave is not just the place from which the past
is retrieved but the place where the future is conceived, the "earthen
womb"—or, as in Willa Cather's *My Antonia*, the "fruit cave"—from
which the new land rises.[16]

Elizabeth Barrett Browning expressed this final point for the later nineteenth century, as if to carry Mary Shelley's allegorical narrative one step further. Describing a utopian island paradise in which all creatures are "glad and safe. . . . No guns nor springes in my dream," she populated this peaceful land with visionary poets who have withdrawn to a life in dim sea caves—"I repair / To live within the caves: / And near me two or three may dwell, / Whom dreams fantastic please as well," she wrote, and then described her paradise more specifically:

> Long winding caverns, glittering far
>   Into a crystal distance!
> Through clefts of which, shall many a star
>   Shine clear without resistance!
> And carry down its rays the smell
> Of flowers above invisible.[17]

Here, she declared, her poets—implicitly female or at least matriarchal rather than patriarchal, worshipers of the Romantic mother goddess Frye describes—would create their own literary tradition through a re-vision of the high themes their famous "masculinist" counterparts had celebrated.

> . . . often, by the joy without
>   And in us overcome,
> We, through our musing, shall let float
>   Such poems—sitting dumb—
> As Pindar might have writ if he
> Had tended sheep in Arcady;
> Or Aeschylus—the pleasant fields
>   He died in, longer knowing;
> Or Homer, had men's sins and shields
>   Been lost in Meles flowing;
> Or poet Plato, had the undim
> Unsetting Godlight broke on him.

Poet Plato revised by a shining woman of noon, a magical woman like Jane Lead's "Eternal Virgin-Wisdom," with "her Face as the terrible Crystal for brightness!" In a sense that re-vision is the major subject of our book, just as it was the theme of Barrett Browning's earnest, female prayer:

> Choose me the cave most worthy choice,
>   To make a place for prayer,
> And I will choose a praying voice
>   To pour our spirits there.

And the answer to Barrett Browning's prayer might have been given by the sibylline voice of Jane Lead's Virgin-Wisdom, or Sophia, the true goddess of the cave: "for out of my Womb thou shalt be brought forth after the manner of a Spirit, Conceived and Born again."

II
Inside the House of Fiction: Jane Austen's Tenants of Possibility

Illustration on the preceding page: *John Gubbins Newton and His Sister*, attributed to John Zephaniah Bell (previously Jacques Laurent Agasse). From the Collection of Mr. and Mrs. Paul Mellon, Upperville, Virginia.

Shut Up in Prose:
Gender and Genre in Austen's
Juvenilia

Not a few of Jane Austen's personal acquaintances might have echoed
Sir Samuel Egerton Brydges, who noticed that "she was fair and
handsome, slight and elegant, but with cheeks a little too full," while
"never suspect[ing] she was an authoress."[1] For this novelist whose
personal obscurity was more complete than that of any other famous
writer was always quick to insist either on complete anonymity or on
the propriety of her limited craft, her delight in delineating just "3
or 4 Families in a Country Village."[2] With her self-deprecatory remarks about her inability to join "strong manly, spirited sketches,
full of Variety and Glow" with her "little bit (two Inches wide) of

107

Ivory,"[3] Jane Austen perpetuated the belief among her friends that her art was just an accomplishment "by a lady," if anything "rather too light and bright and sparkling."[4] In this respect she resembled one of her favorite contemporaries, Mary Brunton, who would rather have "glid[ed] through the world unknown" than been "suspected of literary airs—to be shunned, as literary women are, by the more pretending of their own sex, and abhorred, as literary women are, by the more pretending of the other!—my dear, I would sooner exhibit as a ropedancer."[5]

Yet, decorous though they might first seem, Austen's self-effacing anonymity and her modest description of her miniaturist art also imply a criticism, even a rejection, of the world at large. For, as Gaston Bachelard explains, the miniature "allows us to be world conscious at slight risk."[6] While the creators of satirically conceived diminutive landscapes seem to see everything as small because they are themselves so grand, Austen's analogy for her art—her "little bit (two Inches wide) of Ivory"—suggests a fragility that reminds us of the risk and instability outside the fictional space. Besides seeing her art metaphorically, as her critics would too, in relation to female arts severely devalued until quite recently[7] (for painting on ivory was traditionally a "ladylike" occupation), Austen attempted through self-imposed novelistic limitations to define a secure place, even as she seemed to admit the impossibility of actually inhabiting such a small space with any degree of comfort. And always, for Austen, it is women—because they are too vulnerable in the world at large—who must acquiesce in their own confinement, no matter how stifling it may be.

But it is precisely to the limits of her art that Austen's most vocal critics have always responded, with both praise and blame. The tone is set by the curiously backhanded compliments of Sir Walter Scott, who compares her novels to "cornfields and cottages and meadows," as opposed to "highly adorned grounds" or "the rugged sublimities of a mountain landscape." The pleasure of such fiction is, he explains, such that "the youthful wanderer may return from his promenade to the ordinary business of life, without any chance of having his head turned by the recollection of the scene through which he has been wandering."[8] In other words, the novels are so unassuming that they can be easily forgotten. Mundane (like cornfields) and small (like cottages) and tame (like meadows), they wear the "common-place face" Charlotte Brontë found in *Pride and Prejudice*, a novel Brontë scornfully describes as "a carefully fenced, highly cultivated garden, with neat borders and delicate flowers; but no glance of a bright, vivid physiognomy, no open country, no fresh air, no blue hill, no bonny beck."[9]

Spatial images of boundary and enclosure seem to proliferate when-ever we find writers coming to terms with Jane Austen, as if they were displaying their own anxieties about what she represents. Edward Fitzgerald's comment—"She is capital as far as she goes: but she never goes out of the Parlour"—is a classic in this respect, as is Elizabeth Barrett Browning's breezy characterization of the novels as "perfect as far as they go—that's certain. Only they don't go far, I think."[10] It is hardly surprising that Emerson is "at a loss to understand why people hold Miss Austen's novels at so high a rate," horrified as he is by what he considers the trivializing domes-ticity and diminution of her fiction:

> ... vulgar in tone, sterile in artistic invention, imprisoned in the wretched conventions of English society, without genius, wit, or knowledge of the world. Never was life so pinched and narrow. The one problem in the mind of the writer in both the stories I have read, *Persuasion*, and *Pride and Prejudice*, is marriage-ableness. All that interests in any character introduced is still this one, Has he or (she) the money to marry with, and conditions, conforming? 'Tis "the nympholepsy of a fond despair," say, rather, of an English boarding-house. Suicide is more respect-able.[11]

But the conventionally masculine judgment of Austen's triviality is probably best illustrated by Mark Twain, who cannot even bring himself to spell her name correctly in a letter to Howells, her staunch-est American defender: Poe's "prose," he notes, "is unreadable—like Jane Austin's," adding that there is one difference: "I could read his prose on salary, but not Jane's. Jane is entirely impossible. It seems a great pity that they allowed her to die a natural death."[12] Certainly D. H. Lawrence expresses similar hostility for the lady writer in his attack on Austen as "this old maid" who "typifies 'personality' instead of character, the sharp knowing in apartness instead of knowing in togetherness, and she is, to my feeling, thoroughly unpleasant, English in the bad, mean, snobbish sense of the word."[13]

Repeatedly, in other words, Austen was placed in the double bind she would so convincingly dramatize in her novels, for when not rejected as artificial and convention-bound, she was condemned as natural and therefore a writer almost in spite of herself. Imagining her as "the brown thrush who tells his story from the garden bough," Henry James describes Austen's "light felicity," her "extraordinary grace," as a sign of "her unconsciousness":

> ...as if...she sometimes, over her work basket, her tapestry flowers, in the spare, cool drawing-room of other days, fell a-musing, lapsed too metaphorically, as one may say, into wool gathering, and her dropped stitches, of these pardonable, of these precious moments, were afterwards picked up as little touches of human truth, little glimpses of steady vision, little master-strokes of imagination.[14]

A stereotypical "lady" author, Austen is here diminished into a small personage whose domestic productions result in artistic creation not through the exacting craft by which the male author weaves the intricate figures in his own carpets, but through fortuitous forgetfulness on the part of the lady (who drops her stitches unthinkingly) and through the presumably male critical establishment that picks them up afterwards to view them as charming miniatures of imaginative activity. The entire passage radiates James's anxiety at his own indebtedness to this "little" female precursor who, to his embarrassment, taught him so much of his presumably masterful art. Indeed, in a story that examines Austen's curious effect on men and her usefulness in male culture, Rudyard Kipling has one of his more pugnacious characters insist that Jane Austen "did leave lawful issue in the shape o' one son; an' 'is name was 'Enery James."[15]

In "The Janeites" Kipling presents several veterans from World War I listening to a shell-shocked ex-Garrison Artillery man, Humberstall, recount his experiences on the Somme Front, where he had unexpectedly discovered a secret unit of Austen fans who call themselves the Society of the Janeites. Despite the seeming discrepancy between Austen's decorously "feminine" parlor and the violent,

"masculine" war, the officers analyze the significance of their re-
stricting ranks and roles much as Austen analyzes the meaning of
her characters' limiting social positions. Not only does Humberstall
discover that Austen's characters are "only just like people you'd
run across any day," he also knows that "They're all on the make,
in a quiet way, in Jane." He is not surprised, therefore, when the
whole company is blown to pieces by one man's addlepated adherence
to a code: as his naming of the guns after Austen's "heavies" demonstrates, the ego that creates all the problems for her characters is the
same ego that shoots Kipling's guns. Paradoxically, moreover, the
firings of "General Tilney" and "The Lady Catherine de Bugg" also
seem to point our attention to the explosive anger behind the decorous
surfaces of Austen's novels, although the men in the trenches find in
the Austen guns the symbol of what they think they are fighting for.

Using Austen the same way American servicemen might have
exploited pin-up girls, the Society of Janeites transforms their heroine
into a nostalgic symbol of order, culture, England, in an apocalyptic
world where all the old gods have failed or disappeared. But Austen
is adapted when adopted for use by masculine society, and she
functions to perpetuate the male bonding and violence she would
herself have deplored. Clearly Kipling is involved in ridiculing the
formation of religious sects or cults, specifically the historical Janeites
who sanctified Austen into the apotheosis of propriety and elegance,
of what Ann Douglas has called in a somewhat different context
the "feminization" of culture. But Kipling implies that so-called
feminization is a male-dominated process inflicted upon women. And
in this respect he illustrates how Austen has herself become a victim
of the fictionalizing process we will see her acknowledging as women's
basic problem in her own fiction.

Not only a parody of what male culture has made of the cult of
Jane, however, "The Janeites" is also a tribute to Austen, who
justifies her deification as the patron saint of the officers by furnishing
Humberstall with what turns out to be a password that literally saves
his life by getting him a place on a hospital train. By pronouncing
the name "Miss Bates," Humberstall miraculously survives circumstances as inauspicious as those endured by Miss Bates herself, a
spinster in *Emma* whose physical, economic, and social confinement
is only mitigated by her good humor. Certainly Humberstall's special

fondness for *Persuasion*—which celebrates Captain Harville's "ingenious contrivances and nice arrangements . . . to turn the actual space to the best possible account"[16]—is not unrelated to his appreciation of Austen herself: "There's no one to touch Jane when you're in a tight place." From Austen, then, Humberstall and his companions have gained not only an analysis of social conventions that helps make sense of their own constricted lives, but also an example of how to inhabit a small space with grace and intelligence.

It is eminently appropriate that the Army Janeites try to survive by making the best of a bad situation, accepting their tight place and digging in behind the camouflage-screens they have constructed around their trenches. While their position is finally given away, their attitude is worthy of the writer who concerns herself almost exclusively with characters inhabiting the common sitting room. Critical disparagement of the triviality of this place is related to values that find war or business somehow qualitatively more "real" or "significant" than, for example, the politics of the family.[17] But critics who patronize or castigate Austen for her acceptance of limits and boundaries are overlooking a subversive strain in even her earliest stories: Austen's courageous "grace under pressure" is not only a refuge from a dangerous reality, it is also a comment on it, as W. H. Auden implied:

> You could not shock her more than she shocks me;
>   Beside her Joyce seems innocent as grass.
> It makes me most uncomfortable to see
>   An English spinster of the middle class
>   Describe the amorous effects of "brass,"
> Reveal so frankly and with such sobriety
> The economic basis of society.[18]

Although she has become a symbol of culture, it *is* shocking how persistently Austen demonstrates her discomfort with her cultural inheritance, specifically her dissatisfaction with the tight place assigned women in patriarchy and her analysis of the economics of sexual exploitation. At the same time, however, she knows from the beginning of her career that there is no other place for her but a tight one, and her parodic strategy is itself a testimony to her struggle with inadequate but inescapable structures. If, like Scott and Brontë,

Emerson and James, we continue to see her world as narrow or
trivial, perhaps we can learn from Humberstall that "there's no one
to touch Jane when you're in a tight place." Since this tight place
is both literary and social, we will begin with the parodic juvenilia
and then consider "the amorous effects of 'brass'" in *Northanger Abbey*
to trace how and why Austen is centrally concerned with the impossibility of women escaping the conventions and categories that, in
every sense, belittle them.

Jane Austen has always been famous for fireside scenes in which
several characters comfortably and quietly discuss options so seemingly trivial that it is astonishing when they are transformed into important ethical dilemmas. There is always a feeling, too, that we owe
to her narrator's art the significance with which such scenes are
invested: she seemed to know about the burdens of banality and the
resulting pressure to subject even the smallest gestures to close analysis.
A family in *Love and Freindship* (1790) sit by the fireplace in their "cot"
when they hear a knock on the door:

> My Father started—"What noise is that," (said he.) "It
> sounds like a loud rapping at the door"—(replied my Mother.)
> "it does indeed." (cried I.) "I am of your opinion; (said my
> Father) it certainly does appear to proceed from some uncommon
> violence exerted against our unoffending door." "Yes (exclaimed
> I) I cannot help thinking it must be somebody who knocks for
> admittance."
>
> "That is another point (replied he;) We must not pretend to
> determine on what motive the person may knock—tho' that
> someone *does* rap at the door, I am partly convinced." [19]

Clearly this discursive speculation on the knocking at the door ridicules the propensity of sentimental novelists to record even the most
exasperatingly trivial events, but it simultaneously demonstrates the
common female ennui at having to maintain polite conversation
while waiting for a prince to come. In other words, such juvenilia is
important not only because in this early work Austen ridicules the
false literary conventions that debase expression, thereby dangerously
falsifying expectations, especially for female readers, but also because

she reveals here her awareness that such conventions have inalterably shaped women's lives. For Jane Austen's parody of extravagant literary conventions turns on the culture that makes women continually vulnerable to such fantasies.

Laura of *Love and Freindship* is understandably frustrated by the banal confinement of the fireside scene: "Alas," she laments, "how am I to avoid those evils I shall never be exposed to?" Because she is allowed to pursue those evils with indecorous abandon, *Love and Freindship* is a good place to begin to understand attitudes more fully dramatized there than elsewhere in Austen's fiction. With a singular lack of the "infallible discretion"[20] for which it would later become famous, Austen's adolescent fiction includes a larger "slice of life" than we might at first expect: thievery and drunkenness, matricide and patricide, adultery and madness are common subjects. Moreover, the parodic melodrama of this fiction unfolds through hectic geographical maneuverings, particularly through female escapes and escapades quite unlike those that appear in the mature novels.

Laura, for instance, elopes with a stranger upon whom, she immediately decides, the happiness or misery of her future life depends. From her humble cottage in the vale of Uske, she travels to visit Edward's aunt in Middlesex, but she must leave immediately after Edward boasts to his father of his pride in provoking that parent's displeasure by marrying without his consent. Running off in Edward's father's carriage, the happy couple meet up with Sophia and Augustus at "M," but they are forced to remove themselves quickly when Augustus is arrested for having "gracefully purloined" his father's money. Alone in the world, after taking turns fainting on the sofa, the two girls set out for London but end up in Scotland, where they successfully encourage a young female relative to elope to Gretna Green. Thrown out in punishment for this bad advice, Laura and Sophia meet up with their dying husbands, naturally in a phaeton crash. Sophia is fittingly taken off by a galloping consumption, while Laura proceeds by a stagecoach in which she is reunited with her husband's long-lost family who have been traveling back and forth from Sterling to Edinburgh for reasons that are far too complicated and ridiculous to relate here.

Of course her contrivance of such a zany picaresque does not contradict Austen's later insistence on the limits of her artistic province, since the point of her parody is precisely to illustrate the dangerous delusiveness of fiction which seriously presents heroines like Laura (and stories like *Love and Freindship*) as models of reality. While ridiculing ludicrous literary conventions, Austen also implies that romantic stories create absurd misconceptions. Such novelistic clichés as love at first sight, the primacy of passion over all other emotions and/ or duties, the chivalric exploits of the hero, the vulnerable sensitivity of the heroine, the lovers' proclaimed indifference to financial considerations, and the cruel crudity of parents are all shown to be at best improbable; at worst they are shown to provide manipulative roles and hypocritical jargon which mask materialistic and libidinal egoism.

Living lives regulated by the rules provided by popular fiction, these characters prove only how very bankrupt that fiction is. For while Laura and Sophia proclaim their delicate feelings, tender sentiments, and refined sensibilities, they are in fact having a delightful time gratifying their desires at the expense of everyone else's. Austen's critique of the ethical effects of such literature is matched by her insistence on its basic falsity: adventure, intrigue, crime, passion, and death arrive with such intensity, in such abundance, and with such rapidity that they lose all reality. Surely they are just the hectic daydreams of an imagination infected by too many Emmelines and Emilias.[21] The extensive itinerary of a heroine like Laura is the most dramatic clue that her story is mere wish-fulfillment, one especially attractive to women who live at home confined to the domestic sphere, as do such heroines of Austen's nonparodic juvenilia as Emma Watson of *The Watsons* and Catharine of the early fiction "Catharine."

Significantly, however, Emma Watson and Catharine are both avid readers of romance, just as Austen herself was clearly one of those young women whose imagination had, in fact, been inalterably affected by all the escapist literature provided them, then as now. Not the least of the curious effects of *Love and Freindship* results from the contradiction between the narrator's insistent ridicule of her heroines and their liveliness, their general willingness to get on with it and catch the next coach. Laura and Sophia are really quite attractive in their exuberant assertiveness, their exploration and exploitation of the world, their curiously honest expression of their needs, their rebellious rejection of their fathers' advice, their demands for autonomy, their sense of the significance and drama of their lives and adventures, their gullible delight in playing out the plots they have admired. The girls' rebellion against familial restraints seems to have so fascinated Austen that she reiterates it almost obsessively in *Love and Freindship*, and again in a hilarious letter when she takes on the persona of an anonymous female correspondent who cheerfully explains, "I murdered my Father at a very early period of my Life, I have since murdered my Mother, and I am now going to murder my Sister."[22] The matricides and patricides make such characters seem much more exuberantly alive than their sensible, slow-witted, dying parents. It is this covert counterpoint that makes suspicious the overt "moral" of *Love and Freindship*, suggesting that though Austen appears to be operating in a repressive tradition, many of her generic moral signals are merely convenient camouflage.

At first glance, Sophia and Laura seem related to a common type in eighteenth-century literature. Like Biddy Tipkins of Steele's *The Tender Husband*, Coleman's *Polly Honeycombe*, and Lydia Languish of Sheridan's *The Rivals*, for instance, these girls are filled with outlandish fancies derived from their readings in the circulating library. Illustrating the dangers of feminine lawlessness and the necessity of female submission, female quixotes of eighteenth-century fiction typically exemplify the evils of romantic fiction and female assertion. The abundance of such heroines in her juvenilia would seem to place Austen in precisely the tradition Ellen Moers has recently explored, that of the educating heroine who preaches the necessity of dutiful restraint to female readers, cautioning them especially against the snares of romance. But Austen did not admire the prototypical Madame de Genlis; she was "disgusted" with her brand of didacticism[23] and with the evangelic fervor of novelists who considered themselves primarily moralists.[24]

Far from modeling herself on conservative conduct writers like Hannah Moore or Dr. Gregory or Mrs. Chapone,[25] Austen repeatedly demonstrates her alienation from the aggressively patriarchal tradition that constitutes her Augustan inheritance, as well as her agreement with Mary Wollstonecraft that these authors helped "render women more artificial, weak characters, than they would otherwise have been."[26] A writer who could parody *An Essay on Man* to read

"*Ride where you may*, Be Candid where you can" [italics ours] is not about to vindicate the ways of God to man.[27] Nor is she about to justify the ways of Pope to women. One suspects that Austen, like Marianne Dashwood, appreciates Pope no more than is proper.[28] Even Dr. Johnson, whom she obviously does value, has his oracular rhetorical style parodied, first in the empty abstractions and antitheses that abound in the juvenilia,[29] and later in the mouth of *Pride and Prejudice's* Mary Bennet, a girl who prides herself on pompous platitudes. Finally, Austen attacks *The Spectator* repeatedly, at least in part for its condescension toward female readers. The Regency, as well as her own private perspective as a woman, inalterably separates Austen from the Augustan context in which she is so frequently placed. Like her most mature heroine, Anne Elliot of *Persuasion*, she sometimes advised young readers to reflect on the wisdom of essayists who sought to "rouse and fortify the mind by the highest precepts, and the strongest examples of moral and religious endurance," but she too is "eloquent on a point in which her own conduct would ill bear examination" (*P*, I, chap. 11).

If Austen rejects the romantic traditions of her culture in a parody like *Love and Freindship*, she does so not by way of the attack on feminine flightiness so common in conduct literature, or, at least, she uses this motif to mask a somewhat different point. *Love and Freindship* is the first hint of the depth of her alienation from her culture, especially as that culture defined and circumscribed women. Far from being the usual appeal for female sobriety and submission to domestic restraints so common in anti-romantic eighteenth-century literature, *Love and Freindship* attacks a society that trivializes female assertion by channeling it into the most ridiculous and unproductive forms of behavior. With nothing to do in the world, Sophia and Laura become addicts of feeling. Like all the other heroines of Austen's parodic juvenilia, they make an identity out of passivity, as if foreshadowing the bored girls described by Simone de Beauvoir, who "give themselves up to gloomy and romantic daydreams":

> Neglected, "misunderstood," they seek consolation in narcissistic fancies: they view themselves as romantic heroines of fiction, with self-admiration and self-pity. Quite naturally they become coquettish and stagy, these defects becoming more conspicuous

at puberty. Their malaise shows itself in impatience, tantrums, tears; they enjoy crying—a taste that many women retain in later years—largely because they like to play the part of victims. . . . Little girls sometimes watch themselves cry in a mirror, to double the pleasure.[30]

Sophia and Laura do make a cult of passivity, fainting and languishing dramatically on sofas, defining their virtues and beauty in terms of their physical weakness and their susceptibility to overwhelming passions.

In this way, and more overtly by constantly scrutinizing their own physical perfections, they dramatize de Beauvoir's point that women, in typical victim fashion, become narcissistic out of their fear of facing reality. And because they pride themselves not only on their frailty but also on those very "accomplishments" that insure it, their narcissism is inextricably linked to masochism, for they have been successfully socialized into believing that their subordinate status in society is precisely the fulfillment they crave. Austen is very clear on the reasons for their obsessive fancies: Sophia and Laura are the victims of what Karen Horney has recently identified as the "overvaluation of love" and in this respect, according to Austen, they typify their sex.[31] Encouraged to know and care only about the love of men, Laura and Sophia are compulsive and indiscriminate in satisfying their insatiable need for being loved, while they are themselves incapable of authentic feeling. They would and do go to any lengths to "catch" men, but they must feign ignorance, modesty, and indifference to amatory passion. Austen shows how popular romantic fiction contributes to the traditional notion that women have no other legitimate aim but to love men and how this assumption is at the root of "female" narcissism, masochism, and deceit. She could hardly have set out to create a more heretical challenge to societal definitions of the feminine.

Furthermore, *Love and Freindship* displays Austen's concern with the rhetorical effect of fiction, not in terms of the moral issues raised by Dr. Johnson in his influential essay "On Fiction," but in terms of the psychological destruction such extravagant role models and illusory plots can wreak. De Beauvoir writes of "stagy" girls who "view themselves as romantic heroines of fiction"; and at least one of the reasons Laura and Sophia seem so grotesque is that they are living out predetermined plots: as readers who have accepted, even embraced, their status as characters, they epitomize the ways in which women have been tempted to forfeit interiority and the freedom of self-definition for literary roles. For if, as we might infer from Kipling, Austen herself was destined to become a sanctified symbol, her characters are no less circumscribed by fictional stereotypes and plots that seem to transform them into manic puppets. Like Anne Elliot, who explains that she will "not allow books to prove anything" because "men have had every advantage of us in telling their own story," Austen retains her suspicions about the effect of literary images of both sexes, and she repeatedly resorts to parodic strategies to discredit such images, deconstructing, for example, Richardson's influential ideas of heroism and heroinism.

Refusing to appreciate such angelic paragons as Clarissa or Pamela, Austen criticizes the morally pernicious equation of female virtue with passivity, or masculinity with aggression. From *Lady Susan* to *Sanditon*, she rejects stories in which women simply defend their virtue against male sexual advances. Most of her heroines resemble Charlotte Heywood, who picks up a copy of *Camilla* only to put it down again because "She had not *Camilla's* Youth, & had no intention of having her Distress." [32] Similarly, Austen criticizes the Richardsonian rake by implying that sentimental fiction legitimizes the role of the seducer-rapist, thereby encouraging men to act out their most predatory impulses. Sir Edward of *Sanditon* is only the last of the false suitors who models himself on Lovelace, his life's primary objective being seduction. For Austen, the libertine is a relative of the Byronic hero, and she is quite sure that his dangerous attractions are best defused through ridicule: "I have read the *Corsair*, mended my petticoat, & have nothing else to do," she writes in a letter that probably best illustrates the technique.[33] Because she realizes that writers like Richardson and Byron have truthfully represented the power struggle between the sexes, however, she does seek a way of telling their story without perpetuating it. In each of her novels, a seduced-and-abandoned plot is embedded in the form of an interpolated tale told to the heroine as a monitory image of her own more problematic story.

For all her ladylike discretion, then, Austen is rigorous in her revolt against the conventions she inherited. But she expresses her dissent under the cover of parodic strategies that had been legitimized by the most conservative writers of her time and that therefore were then (and remain now) radically ambiguous. Informing her recurrent use of parody is her belief that the inherited literary structures which are not directly degrading to her sex are patently irrelevant. Therefore, when she begins *Sense and Sensibility* with a retelling of *King Lear*, her reversals imply that male traditions need to be evaluated and reinterpreted from a female perspective: instead of the evil daughter castrating the old king by whittling away at his retinue of knights ("what need one?"), Austen represents the male heir and his wife persuading themselves to cheat their already unjustly deprived sisters of a rightful share of the patrimony ("Altogether, they will have five hundred a-year amongst them, and what on earth can four women want for more than that?" [*SS*, I, chap. 2]). When Maria Bertram echoes the caged bird of Sterne's *A Sentimental Journey*, complaining that the locked gates of her future husband's grounds are too confining—"I cannot get out, as the starling said"[34]—she reflects on the dangers of the romantic celebration of personal liberty and self-expression for women who will be severely punished if they insist on getting out.

Whether here, or in her parodies of Fanny Burney and Sir Samuel Egerton Brydges in *Pride and Prejudice*, Austen dramatizes how damaging it has been for women to inhabit a culture created by and for men, confirming perhaps more than any of her sisterly successors the truth of Mary Ellmann's contention that

> for women writers, as for Negro, what others have said bears down on whatever they can say themselves. Both are like people looking for their own bodies under razed buildings, having to clear away debris. In their every effort to formulate a new point of view, one feels the refutation of previous points of view—a weight which must impede spontaneity.[35]

Austen demystifies the literature she has read neither because she believes it misrepresents reality, as Mary Lascelles argues, nor out of obsessive fear of emotional contact, as Marvin Mudrick claims, nor because she is writing Tory propaganda against the Jacobins, as Marilyn Butler speculates,[36] but because she seeks to illustrate

how such fictions are the alien creations of writers who contribute
to the enfeebling of women.

But though Ellmann's image is generally helpful for an understanding of the female artist, in Austen's case it is a simplification.
Austen's culture is not a destroyed rubble around her corpse. On
the contrary, it is a healthy and powerful architec ure which she
must learn to inhabit. Far from looking under razed buildings or
(even more radically) razing buildings herself, Austen admits the
limits and discomforts of the paternal roof, but learns to live beneath
it. As we have seen, however, she begins by laughing at its construction, pointing out exactly how much of that construction actually
depends on the subjugation of women. If she wishes to be an architect
herself, however, she needs to make use of the only available building
materials—the language and genres, conventions and stereotypes
at her disposal. She does not reject these, she reinvents them. For
one thing, she has herself admired and enjoyed the literature of
such sister novelists as Maria Edgeworth, Mrs. Radcliffe, Charlotte
Lennox, Mary Brunton, and Fanny Burney. For another, as we
have seen, regardless of how damaging they have been, the conventions of romantic fiction have been internalized by the women of
her culture and so they do describe the psychology of growing up
female. Finally, these are the only available stories she has. Austen
makes a virtue of her own confinement, as her heroines will do also.
By exploiting the very conventions she exposes as inadequate, she
demonstrates the power of patriarchy as well as the ambivalence
and confinement of the female writer. She also discovers an effective
subterfuge for a severe critique of her culture. For even as she
dramatizes her own alienation from a society she cannot evade or
transcend, she subverts the conventions of popular fiction to describe
the lonely vulnerability of girls whose lives, if more mundane, are
just as thwarted as those they read about so obsessively. For all their
hilarious exaggeration, then, the incidents and characters of the
juvenilia reappear in the later novels, where they portray the
bewilderment of heroines whose guides are as inadequate as the
author's in her search for a way of telling their story.

Just as Laura languishes in the Vale of Uske at the beginning of
Love and Freindship, for example, the later heroines are confined to
homes noteworthy for their suffocating atmosphere. The heroine

of "Catharine" is limited to the company of an aunt who fears that
all contact with society will engage the girl's heart imprudently.
Living in her aunt's inexorably ordered house, Catharine has nothing
to do but retreat to a romantically constructed bower, a place of
adolescent illusions. Boredom is also a major affliction for Catherine
Morland and Charlotte Heywood, who are involved in the drudgery
of educating younger siblings in secluded areas offering few potential
friends, as it is for the seemingly more privileged Emma, who suffers
from intellectual loneliness, as well as the blazing fires, closed windows, and locked doors of her father's house. The Dashwood sisters
move into a cottage with parlors too small for parties, and Fanny
Price only manages to remove herself from her suffocatingly cramped
home in Portsmouth to the little white attic which all the other
occupants of Mansfield Park have outgrown. When the parental
house is not downright uncomfortable because of its inadequate
space, it is still a place with no privacy. Thus the only person able
to retreat from the relentlessly trivial bustle at the Bennets is the
father, who has his own library. Furthermore, as Nina Auerbach
has shown, all the girls inhabit houses that are never endowed with
the physical concreteness and comfort that specificity supplies.[37]
The absence of details suggests how empty and unreal such family
life feels, and a character like Anne Elliot, for example, faces the
sterile elegance of her father's estate confined and confused by one
of the few details the reader is provided, the mirrors in her father's
private dressing room.

One reason why the adventures of the later heroines seem to supply
such small relief to girls "doomed to waste [their] Days of Youth
and Beauty in a humble Cottage in the Vale" is that most, like
Laura, can only wait for an unpredictable and unreliable knock
on the door. What characterizes the excursions of all these heroines
is their total dependency on the whim of wealthier family or friends.
None has the power to produce her own itinerary and none knows
until the very last moment whether or not she will be taken on a
trip upon which her happiness often depends. All the heroines of
Austen's fiction very much want to experience the wider world
outside their parents' province; each, though, must wait until lucky
enough to be asked to accompany a chaperone who frequently
only mars the pleasure of the adventure. Although in her earliest

writing Austen ridicules the rapidity and improbability of coincidence in second-rate fiction, not a few of her own plots save the heroines from stagnation by means of the overtly literary device of an introduction to an older person who is so pleased with the heroine that "at parting she declares her sole *ambition* was to have her accompany them the next morning to Bath, whither they were going for some weeks." [38]

It is probably for this reason that, from the juvenilia to the post-humously published fragments, there is a recurrent interest in the horse and carriage. It is not surprising in the juvenilia to find a young woman marrying a man she loathes because he has promised her a new chaise, with a silver border and a saddle horse, in return for her not expecting to go to any public place for three years. [39] Indeed, not a few of the heroines recall the plight of two characters in the juvenilia who go on a walking tour through Wales with only one pony, ridden by their mother: not only do their sketches suffer, being "not such exact resemblances as might be wished, from their being taken as [they] ran along," so do their feet as they find themselves hopping home from Hereford. [40] Still, they are delighted with their excursion, and their passion for travel reminds us of the runaways who abound in Austen's novels, young women whose imaginations are tainted by romantic notions which fuel their excessive materialism or sexuality, and who would do anything with anyone in order to escape their families: Eliza Brandon, Julia and Maria Bertram, Lydia Bennet, Lucy Steele, and Georgianna Darcy are all "prepared for matrimony by an hatred of home, restraint, and tranquillity" (*MP*, II, chap. 3). Provided with only the naive clichés of sentimental literature, they insist on acting out those very plots Austen would—but therefore cannot—exorcise from her own fiction.

But hopping home from Hereford also recalls Marianne Dashwood who, like Fanny Price, is vitally concerned with her want of a horse: this pleasure and exercise is not at these girls' disposal primarily because of its expense and impropriety. Emma Woodhouse is subjected to the unwelcome proposals of Mr. Elton because she cannot avoid a ride in his carriage, and Jane Bennet becomes seriously ill at a time when her parents' horses cannot be spared. Similarly, Catherine Morland and Mrs. Parker are both victimized by male escorts whose recklessness hazards their health, if not their lives. It is no small testimony of her regard for their reciprocal partnership that Anne Elliot sees the lively and mutually self-regulating style of the Crofts' driving of their one-horse chaise as a good representation of their marriage. Coaches, barouche-landaus, and curricles are the crucial factors that will determine who goes where with whom on the expeditions to places like Northanger, Pemberly, Donwell Abbey, Southerton, and Lyme.

Every trivial social occasion, each of the many visits and calls endured if not enjoyed by the heroines, reminds us that women are dependent on fathers or brothers for even this most limited form of movement, when they are not indebted to wealthy widows who censure and criticize officiously.[41] Not possessing or controlling the means of transportation, each heroine is defined as different from the poorest men of her neighborhood, all of whom can convey themselves wherever they want or need to go. Indeed, what distinguishes the heroines from their brothers is invariably their lack of liberty: while Austen describes how younger brothers are as financially circumscribed as their sisters, for instance in their choosing of a mate, she always insists that the caste of gender takes precedence over the dictates of class; as poor a dependent as William Price is far more mobile than both his indigent sisters and his wealthy female cousins. For Austen, the domestic confinement of women is not a metaphor so much as a literal fact of life, enforced by all those elaborate rules of etiquette governing even the trivial morning calls that affect the females of each of the novels. The fact that "he is to purvey, and she to smile"[42] is what must have enraged and repelled readers like Brontë and Barrett Browning. As Anne Elliot explains, "We live at home, quiet, confined and our feelings prey upon us" (*P*, II, chap. 11).

According to popular moralists of Austen's day, what would be needed for a satisfied life in such uncongenial circumstances would be "inner resources." Yet these are what most of the young women in her novels lack, precisely because of the inadequate upbringing with which they have been provided by absent or ineffectual mothers. In fact, though Austen's juvenilia often ridicules fiction that portrays the heroine as an orphan or foundling or neglected stepdaughter, the mature novelist does not herself supply her female protagonists with very different family situations. In *A Vindication of the Rights of*

Woman Mary Wollstonecraft explained that "woman . . . a slave in every situation to prejudice, seldom exerts enlightened maternal affection; for she either neglects her children, or spoils them by improper indulgences." [43] Austen would agree, although she focuses specifically on mothers who fail in their nurturing of daughters. Emma Woodhouse, Emma Watson, Catharine, and Anne Elliot are literally motherless, as are such minor characters as Clara Brereton, Jane Fairfax, the Steele sisters, Miss Tilney, Georgianna Darcy, the Miss Bingleys, Mary Crawford, and Harriet Smith. But those girls who have living mothers are nonetheless neglected or overindulged by the absence of enlightened maternal affection.

Fanny Price "might scruple to make use of the words, but she must and did feel that her mother was a partial, ill-judging parent, a dawdle, a slattern, who neither taught nor restrained her children, whose house was the scene of mismanagement and discomfort . . . who had no talent, no conversation, no affection toward herself" (*MP*, III, chap. 8). Mrs. Price, however, is not much different from Mrs. Dashwood and Mrs. Bennet, who are as immature and silly as their youngest daughters, and who are therefore unable to guide young women into maturity. Women like Lady Bertram, Mrs. Musgrove, and Mrs. Bates are a burden on their children because their ignorance, indolence, and folly, resulting as they do in neglect, seem no better than the smothering love of those women whose officiousness spoils by improper indulgence. Fanny Dashwood and Lady Middleton of *Sense and Sensibility*, for example, are cruelly indifferent to the needs of all but their children, who are therefore transformed by such inauspicious attention into noisy, bothersome monsters. Lady Catherine de Bourgh proves conclusively that authoritative management of a daughter's life cannot be identified with nurturing love: coldly administering all aspects of her daughter's growth, overbearing Lady Catherine produces a girl who "was pale and sickly; her features, though not plain, were insignificant; and she spoke very little, except in a low voice." [44]

Because they are literally or figuratively motherless, the daughters in Austen's fiction are easily persuaded that they must look to men for security. Although their mothers' example proves how debilitating marriage can be, they seek husbands in order to escape from home. What feminists have recently called matrophobia—fear of becoming one's mother[45]—supplies one more motive to flee the parental house, as does the financial necessity of competing for male protection which their mothers really cannot supply. The parodic portrait in "Jack and Alice" of the competition between drunken Alice Johnson and the accomplished tailor's daughter, Lucy, for the incomparable Charles Adams (who was "so dazzling a Beauty that none but Eagles could look him in the Face") is thus not so different from the rivalry Emma Woodhouse feels toward Harriet Smith or Jane Fairfax over Mr. Knightley. And it is hardly surprising when in the juvenilia Austen pushes this fierce female rivalry to its fitting conclusion, describing how poor Lucy falls a victim to the envy of a female companion "who jealous of her superiour charms took her by poison from an admiring World at the age of seventeen."[46]

Austen ridicules the easy violence that embellishes melodrama even as she explores hostility between young women who feel they have no alternative but to compete on the marriage market. Like Charlotte Lucas, many an Austen heroine, "without thinking highly either of men or of matrimony," considers marriage "the only honourable provision for well-educated young women of small fortune, their pleasantest preservation from want" (*PP*, I, chap. 22). And so, at the beginning of *The Watsons*, one sister has to warn another about a third that, "There is nothing she would not do to get married. . . . Do not trust her with any secrets of your own, take warning by me, do not trust her." Because such females would rather marry a man they dislike than teach school or enter the governess "slave-trade,"[47] they fight ferociously for the few eligible men who do seem attractive. The rivalries between Miss Bingley and Miss Bennet, between Miss Dashwood and Miss Steele, between Julia and Maria Bertram for Henry Crawford, between the Musgrove sisters for Captain Wentworth are only the most obvious examples of fierce female competition where female anger is deflected from powerful male to powerless female targets.

Throughout the juvenilia, most hilariously in "Frederic and Elfrida," Austen ridicules the idea, promulgated by romantic fiction, that the only events worth recording are marriage proposals, marriage ceremonies, engagements made or broken, preparations for dances where lovers are expected, amatory disappointments, and elopements.

But her own fiction is essentially limited to just such topics. The implication is clear: marriage is crucial because it is the only accessible form of self-definition for girls in her society. Indeed, Austen's silence on all other subjects becomes itself a kind of statement, for the absences in her fiction prove how deficient are the lives of girls and women, even as they testify to her own deprivation as a woman writer. Yet Austen actually uses her self-proclaimed and celebrated acceptance of the limits of her art to mask a subversive critique of the forms of self-expression available to her both as an artist and as a woman, for her ridicule of inane literary structures helps her articulate her alienation from equally inadequate societal strictures.

Austen was indisputably fascinated by double-talk, by conversations that imply the opposite of what they intend, narrative statements that can only confuse, and descriptions that are linguistically sound, but indecipherable or tautological. We can see her concern for such matters in "Jack and Alice," where dictatorial Lady Williams is adamant in giving her friend unintelligible advice about a proposed trip to Bath:

> "What say you to accompanying these Ladies: I shall be miserable without you—t'will be a most pleasant tour to you—I hope you'll go; if you do I am sure t'will be the Death of me— pray be persuaded."[48]

Almost as if she were taking on the persona of Mrs. Slipslop or Mrs. Malaprop (that wonderful "queen of the dictionary") or Tabitha Bramble, Austen engages here in the same kind of playful nonsense that occurs in the narrator's introduction to the story of "Frederic and Elfrida" ("The Uncle of Elfrida was the Father of Frederic; in other words, they were first cousins by the Father's side") or in "Lesley Castle" ("We are handsome, my dear Charlotte, very handsome and the greatest of our Perfections is, that, we are entirely insensible of them ourselves"). Characteristically, in Austen's juvenilia one girl explains, "if a book is well written, I always find it too short," and discovers that her friend agrees: "So do I, only I get tired of it before it is finished."[49] What is so wonderful about these sentences is the "ladylike" way in which they quietly subvert the conventions of language, while managing to sound perfectly accept-able, even grammatically elegant and decorous.

With its insistent evocation of two generic frameworks, the *Bildungsroman* and the burlesque, *Northanger Abbey* (1818) supplies one reason for Austen's fascination with coding, concealing, or just plain not saying what she means, because this apparently amusing and inoffensive novel finally expresses an indictment of patriarchy that could hardly be considered proper or even permissible in Austen's day. Indeed, when this early work was published post-humously—because its author could not find a publisher who would print it during her lifetime—it was the harsh portrayal of the patriarch that most disturbed reviewers.[50] Since we have already seen that Austen tends to enact her own ambivalent relationship to her literary predecessors as she describes her heroines' vulnerability in masculine society, it is hardly surprising to find that she describes Catherine Morland's initiation into the fashionable life of Bath, balls, and marriage settlements by trying to come to terms with the complex and ambiguous relationship between women and the novel.

Northanger Abbey begins with a sentence that resonates as the novel progresses: "No one who had ever seen Catherine Morland in her infancy, would have supposed her born to be an heroine." And certainly what we see of the young Catherine is her unromantic physical exuberance and health. We are told, moreover, that she was "fond of all boys' plays, and greatly preferred cricket not merely to dolls, but to the more heroic enjoyments of infancy, nursing a dormouse, feeding a canary-bird, or watering a rose-bush" (I, chap. 1). Inattentive to books, uninterested in music or drawing, she was "noisy and wild, hated confinement and cleanliness, and loved nothing so well in the world as rolling down the green slope at the back of the house" (I, chap. 1). But at fifteen Catherine began to curl her hair and read, and "from fifteen to seventeen she was in training for a heroine" (I, chap. 1). Indeed her actual "training for a heroine" is documented in the rest of the novel, although, as we shall see, it is hard to imagine a more uncongenial or unnatural course of instruction for her or for any other spirited girl.

Puzzled, confused, anxious to please, and above else innocent and curious, Catherine wonders as she wanders up and down the two traditional settings for female initiation, the dance hall at Bath and the passageways of a gothic abbey. But Austen keeps on reminding us that Catherine is typical because she is *not* born to be a heroine: burdened with parents who were "not in the least addicted to locking up ... daughters", Catherine could "not write sonnets" and had "no notion of drawing" (I, chap. 1). There is "not one lord" in her neighborhood—"not even a baronet" (I, chap. 2)— and on her journey to Bath, "neither robbers nor tempests befriend" her (I, chap. 2). When she enters the Upper Rooms in Bath, "not one" gentleman starts with wonder on beholding her, "no whisper of eager inquiry ran round the room, nor was she once called a divinity by anybody" (I, chap. 2). Her room at the Abbey is "by no means unreasonably large, and contained neither tapestry nor velvets" (II, chap. 6). Austen dramatizes all the ways in which Catherine is unable to live up to the rather unbelievable accomplishments of Charlotte Smith's and Mrs. Radcliffe's popular paragons. Heroines, it seems, are not born like people, but manufactured like monsters, and also like monsters they seem fated to self-destruct. Thus *Northanger Abbey* describes exactly how a girl in search of her life story finds herself entrapped in a series of monstrous fictions which deprive her of primacy.

To begin with, we see this fictionalizing process most clearly in the first section at Bath. Sitting in the crowded, noisy Upper Rooms, awaiting a suitable partner, Catherine is uncomfortably situated between Mrs. Thorpe, who talks only of her children, and Mrs. Allen, who is a monomaniac on the subject of gowns, hats, muslins, and ribbons. Fit representatives not only of fashionable life but also of the state of female maturity in an aristocratic and patriarchal society, they are a constant source of irritation to Catherine, who is happy to be liberated from their ridiculous refrains by Isabella and John Thorpe. Yet if Mrs. Allen and Mrs. Thorpe are grotesque, the young Thorpes are equally absurd, for in them we see what it means to be a fashionable young lady or gentleman. Isabella is a heroine with a vengeance: flirting and feigning, she is a sister of the earlier Sophia and Laura who runs after men with a single-minded determination not even barely disguised by her protestations of sisterly affection for Catherine. Contorted "with smiles of most exquisite misery, and the laughing eye of utter despondency" (I, chap. 9), Isabella is continually acting out a script that makes her ridiculous. At the same time, her brother, as trapped in the stereotypes of masculinity as she is in femininity, continually contradicts himself, even while he constantly boasts about his skill as a hunter, his great gig, his incomparable drinking capacity, and the boldness of his riding. Not only, then, do the Thorpes represent a nightmarish version of what it means to see oneself as a hero or heroine, they also make Catherine's life miserable by preying on her gullibility and vulnerability.

What both the Thorpes do is lie *to* her and *about* her until she is entrapped in a series of coercive fictions of their making. Catherine becomes the pawn in Isabella's plot, specifically the self-consciously dramatic romance with James Morland in which Catherine is supposed to play the role of sisterly intimate to a swooning, blushing Isabella: Isabella continually gives Catherine clues that she ought to be soliciting her friend's confessions of love or eliciting her anxieties about separating from her lover, clues which Catherine never follows because she never quite catches their meaning. Similarly, John Thorpe constructs a series of fictions in which Catherine is first the object of his own amorous designs and then a wealthy heiress whom General Tilney can further fictionalize. Catherine becomes extremely uncomfortable as he manipulates all these stories about her, and only her ignorance serves to save her from the humiliating realization that her invitation to Northanger depends on General Tilney's illusive image of her.

When Henry Tilney points out to Catherine that "man has the advantage of choice, woman only the power of refusal" (I, chap. 10), he echoes a truth articulated (in a far more tragic circumstance) by Clarissa, who would give up choice if she could but preserve "the liberty of *refusal*, which belongs to my Sex."[51] But in Austen's parodic text, Henry makes a point that is as much about fiction as it is about marriage and dancing, his purported subjects: Catherine is as confined by the clichéd stories of the other characters as Austen is by her need to reject inherited stories of what it means to be a heroine. Unlike her author, however, Catherine "cannot speak well enough to be unintelligible" (II, chap. 1), so she lapses into silence when the Thorpes' version of reality contradicts her own, for instance when Isabella seats herself near a door that commands a good view of everybody entering because "it is so out of the way" (II, chap. 3), or when, in spite of John Thorpe's warnings about the violence of his horses, his carriage proceeds at a safe speed. Repeatedly, she does not understand "how to reconcile two such very different accounts of the same thing" (I, chap. 9). Enmeshed in the Thorpes' misinterpretations, Catherine can only feebly deflect Isabella's assertion that her rejection of John Thorpe represents the cooling of her first feelings: "You are describing what never happened" (II, chap. 3). While Catherine only sporadically and confusedly glimpses the discrepancies between Isabella's stated hatred of men and her continual coquetry, or John Thorpe's assertion that he saw the Tilneys driving up the Lansdown Road and her own discovery of them walking down the street, Austen is clearly quite conscious of the lies which John and his sister use to falsify Catherine's sense of reality, just as she is aware of the source of these lies in the popular fiction of her day.

Yet, despite her distaste for the falsity of fictional conventions, Austen insists quite early in the novel that she will not reject the practitioners of her own art: "I will not adopt that ungenerous and impolitic custom so common with novel-writers, of degrading by their contemptuous censure the very performances, to the number of which they are themselves adding" (I, chap. 5). In an extraordinary attack on critics of the novel, Austen makes it quite clear that she realizes male anthologists of Goldsmith, Milton, Pope, Prior, Addison, Steele, and Sterne are customarily praised ahead of the female creators of works like *Cecelia*, *Camilla*, or *Belinda*, although the work of such men is neither original nor literary. Indeed, as if to substantiate her feeling that prejudice against the novel is widespread, she shows how even an addicted reader of romances (who has been forced, like so many girls, to substitute novel reading for a formal education) needs to express disdain for the genre. In the important expedition to Beechen Cliff, we find Catherine claiming to despise the form. Novels, she says, are "not clever enough" for Henry Tilney because "gentlemen read better books" (I, chap. 14). But her censure is really, of course, a form of self-deprecation.

The novel is a status-deprived genre, Austen implies, because it is closely associated with a status-deprived gender. Catherine considers novels an inferior kind of literature precisely because they had already become the province of women writers and of a rapidly expanding female audience. Again and again we see the kind of miseducation novels confer on Catherine, teaching her to talk in inflated and stilted clichés, training her to expect impossibly villainous or virtuous behavior from people whose motives are more complex than she suspects, blinding her to the mundane selfishness of her contemporaries. Yet Austen declares that novel writers have been an "injured body," and she explicitly sets out to defend this species of composition that has been so unfairly decried out of "pride, ignorance, or fashion" (I, chap. 5).

Her passionate defense of the novel is not as out of place as it might first seem, for if *Northanger Abbey* is a parody of novelistic clichés, it also resembles the rest of the juvenilia in its tendency to rely on these very conventions for its own shape. Austen is writing a romance as conventional in its ways as those she criticizes: Catherine Morland's most endearing quality is her inexperience, and her adventures result from the Allens' gratuitous decision to take her as a companion on their trip to Bath, where she is actually introduced to Henry Tilney by the Master of Ceremonies, and where a lucky mistake causes his father to invite her to visit, appropriately enough, his gothic mansion. Like so many of Pamela's daughters, Catherine marries the man of her dreams and is thereby elevated to his rank. In other words, she succeeds in doing what Isabella is so mercilessly punished for wanting to do, making a good match. Finally, in true heroine style, Catherine rejects the false suitor for the true one[52] and is rescued for felicity by an ending no less aggressively engineered than that of most sentimental novels.

As if justifying both her spirited defense of sister novelists and the romantic shape of her heroine's story, Austen has Catherine admit a fierce animosity for the sober pages of history. Catherine tells Henry Tilney and his sister that history "tells [her] nothing that does not either vex or weary [her]. The quarrels of popes and kings, with wars or pestilences, in every page; *the men all so good for nothing, and hardly any women at all*—it is very tiresome" [italics ours] (I, chap. 14). She is severely criticized for this view; but she is, after all, correct, for the knowledge conferred by historians does seem irrelevant to the private lives of most women. Furthermore, Austen had already explored this fact in her only attempt at history, a

parody of Goldsmith's *History of England*, written in her youth and
signed as the work of "a partial, prejudiced, and ignorant Historian."[53] What is conveyed in this early joke is precisely Catherine's
sense of the irrationality, cruelty, and irrelevance of history, as well
as the partisan spleen of most so-called objective historians. Until
she can place herself, and two friends, in the company of Mary
Queen of Scots, historical events seem as absurdly distant from
Austen's common concerns as they do to Charlotte Brontë in *Shirley*,
George Eliot in *Middlemarch*, or Virginia Woolf in *The Years*, writers
who self-consciously display the ways in which history and historical
narration only indirectly affect women because they deal with
public events never experienced at first hand in the privatized lives
of women.

Even quite late in Austen's career, when she was approached to
write a history of the august House of Cobourg, she refused to take
historical "reality" seriously, declaring that she could no more write
a historical romance than an epic poem, "and if it were indispensable
for me to keep it up and never relax into laughing at myself or other
people, I am sure I should be hung before I had finished the first
chapter."[54] While in this letter she could defend her "pictures of
domestic life in country villages" with a sure sense of her own
province as a writer, Austen's sympathy and identification with
Catherine Morland's ignorance is evident elsewhere in her protesta-
tion that certain topics are entirely unknown to her. She cannot
portray a clergyman sketched by a correspondent because

> Such a man's conversation must at times be on subjects of
> science and philosophy, of which I know nothing; or at least
> be occasionally abundant in quotations and allusions which a
> woman who, like me, knows only her own mother tongue, and
> has read very little in that, would be totally without the power of
> giving. A classical education, or at any rate a very extensive
> acquaintance with English literature, ancient and modern,
> appears to me quite indispensible for the person who would do
> justice to your clergyman; and I think I may boast myself to
> be, with all possible vanity, the most unlearned and uninformed
> female who ever dared to be an authoress.[55]

Like Fanny Burney, who refused Dr. Johnson's offer of Latin lessons because she could not "devote so much time to acquire something I shall always dread to have known,"[56] Austen seems to have felt the need to maintain a degree of ladylike ignorance.

Yet not only does Austen write about women's miseducation, not only does she feel herself to be a victim of it; in *Northanger Abbey* she angrily attacks their culturally conditioned ignorance, for she is clearly infuriated that "A woman especially, if she have the misfortune of knowing anything, should conceal it as well as she can" (I, chap. 14). Though "imbecility in females is a great enhancement of their personal charms," Austen sarcastically admits that some men are "too reasonable and too well informed themselves to desire any thing more in woman than ignorance" (I, chap. 14). When at Beechen Cliff Henry Tilney moves from the subject of the natural landscape to a discussion of politics, the narrator, like Catherine, keeps still. Etiquette, it seems, would forbid such discussions (for character and author alike), even if ignorance did not make them impossible. At the same time, however, both Catherine and Austen realize that history and politics, which have been completely beyond the reach of women's experience, are far from sanctified by such a divorce. "What in the midst of that mighty drama [of history] are girls and their blind visions?" Austen might have asked, as George Eliot would in *Daniel Deronda*. And she might have answered similarly that in these "delicate vessels is borne onward through the ages the treasures of human affection."[57] Ignoring the political and economic activity of men throughout history, Austen implies that history may very well be a uniform drama of masculine posturing that is no less a fiction (and a potentially pernicious one) than gothic romance. She suggests, too, that this fiction of history is finally a matter of indifference to women, who never participate in it and who are almost completely absent from its pages. Austen thus anticipates a question Virginia Woolf would angrily pose in *Three Guineas*: "what does 'patriotism' mean to [the educated man's sister]? Has she the same reasons for being proud of England, for loving England, for defending England?"[58] For, like Woolf, Austen asserts that women see male-dominated history from the disillusioned and disaffected perspective of the outsider.

At the same time, the issue of women's reasons for "being proud of England, for loving England, for defending England" is crucial to the revision of gothic fiction we find in *Northanger Abbey*. Rather than rejecting the gothic conventions she burlesques, Austen is very clearly criticizing female gothic in order to reinvest it with authority. As A. Walton Litz has demonstrated, Austen disapproves of Mrs. Radcliffe's exotic locales because such settings imply a discrepancy between the heroine's danger and the reader's security.[59] Austen's heroine is defined as a reader, and in her narrative she blunders on more significant, if less melodramatic, truths, as potentially destructive as any in Mrs. Radcliffe's fiction. Catherine discovers in the old-fashioned black cabinet something just as awful as a lost manuscript detailing a nun's story. Could Austen be pointing at the real threat to women's happiness when she describes her heroine finding *a laundry list*? Moreover, while Catherine reveals her own naive delusions when she expects to find Mrs. Tilney shut up and receiving from her husband's pitiless hands "a nightly supply of coarse food" (II, chap. 8), she does discover that "in suspecting General Tilney of either murdering or shutting up his wife, she had scarcely sinned against his character, or magnified his cruelty" (II, chap. 15).

Using the conventions of gothic even as she transforms them into a subversive critique of patriarchy, Austen shows her heroine penetrating to the secret of the Abbey, the hidden truth of the ancestral mansion, to learn the complete and arbitrary power of the owner of the house, the father, the General. In a book not unfittingly pronounced *North/Anger*, Austen rewrites the gothic not because she disagrees with her sister novelists about the confinement of women, but because she believes women have been imprisoned more effectively by miseducation than by walls and more by financial dependency, which is the authentic ancestral curse, than by any verbal oath or warning. Austen's gothic novel is set in England because— even while it ridicules and repudiates patriarchal politics (or perhaps *because* it does so)—it is, as Robert Hopkins has shown, the most political of Jane Austen's novels. Hopkins's analysis of the political allusions in *Northanger Abbey* reveals not only the mercenary General's "callous lack of concern for the commonweal," but also his role "as an inquisitor surveying possibly seditious pamphlets." This means that Henry Tilney's eulogy of an England where gothic atrocities can presumably never occur because "every man is surrounded by a neighborhood of voluntary spies" (II, chap. 9) refers ironically to

the political paranoia and repression of the General, whose role as a
modern inquisitor reflects Austen's sense of "the nightmarish political
world of the 1790s and very early 1800s." [60] The writers of romance,
Austen implies, were not so much wrong as simplistic in their
descriptions of female vulnerability. In spite of her professed or
actual ignorance, then, Austen brilliantly relocates the villain of the
exotic, faraway gothic locale here, now, in England.

It is significant, then, that General Tilney drives Catherine from
his house without sufficient funds, without an escort for the seventy-
mile journey, because she has no fortune of her own. Ellen Moers
may exaggerate in her claim that "money and its making were
characteristically female rather than male subjects in English fiction," [61] but Austen does characteristically explore the specific ways
in which patriarchal control of women depends on women being
denied the right to earn or even inherit their own money. From
Sense and Sensibility, where a male heir deprives his sisters of their
home, to *Pride and Prejudice*, where the male entail threatens the
Bennet girls with marriages of convenience, from *Emma*, where Jane
Fairfax must become a governess if she cannot engage herself to a
wealthy husband, to *Persuasion*, where the widowed Mrs. Smith
struggles ineffectually against poverty, Austen reminds her readers
that the laws and customs of England may, as Henry Tilney glow-
ingly announces, insure against wife-murder (II, chap. 10), but
they do not offer much more than this minimal security for a wife
not beloved, or a woman not a wife: as Austen explains in a letter
to her favorite niece, "single women have a dreadful propensity for
being poor." [62] Thus, in all her novels Austen examines the female
powerlessness that underlies monetary pressure to marry, the injustice
of inheritance laws, the ignorance of women denied formal education,
the psychological vulnerability of the heiress or widow, the exploited
dependency of the spinster, the boredom of the lady provided with
no vocation. And the powerlessness implicit in all these situations is
also a part of the secret behind the graceful and even elegant surfaces
of English society that Catherine manages to penetrate. Like Austen's
other heroines, she comes to realize that most women resemble her
friend Eleanor Tilney, who is only "a nominal mistress of [the
house]"; her "real power is nothing" (II, chap. 13).

Catherine's realization that the family, as represented by the

Tilneys, is a bankrupt and coercive institution matches the discoveries of many of Austen's other heroines. Specifically, her realization that General Tilney controls the household despite his lack of
honor and feeling matches Elizabeth Bennet's recognition that her
father's withdrawal into his library is destructive and selfish, or
Emma Woodhouse's recognition that her valetudinarian father has
strengthened her egotism out of *his* selfish need for her undivided
attention. More than the discoveries of the others, though, Catherine's
realization of General Tilney's greed and coercion resembles Fanny
Price's recognition that the head of the Bertram family is not only
fallible and inflexible in his judgment but mercenary in his motives.
In a sense, then, all of Austen's later heroines resemble Catherine
Morland in their discovery of the failure of the father, the emptiness
of the patriarchal hierarchy, and, as Mary Burgan has shown, the
inadequacy of the family as the basic psychological and economic
unit of society.[63]

Significantly, all these fathers who control the finances of the
house are in their various ways incapable of sustaining their children.
Mr. Woodhouse quite literally tries to starve his family and guests,
while Sir Walter Elliot is too cheap to provide dinners for his daughters, and Sir Thomas Bertram is so concerned with the elegance of
his repast that his children only seek to escape his well-stocked table.
As an exacting gourmet, General Tilney looks upon a "tolerably
large eating-room as one of the necessities of life" (II, chap. 6), but
his own appetite is not a little alarming, and the meals over which
he presides are invariably a testimony to his childrens' and his
guest's deprivation. Continually oppressed at the General's table
with his incessant attentions, "perverse as it seemed, [Catherine]
doubted whether she might not have felt less, had she been less
attended to" [II, chap. 5]. What continues to mystify her about the
General is "why he should say one thing so positively, and mean
another all the while" (II, chap. 11). In fact, Austen redefines the
gothic in yet another way in *Northanger Abbey* by showing that
Catherine Morland is trapped, not inside the General's Abbey, but
inside his fiction, a tale in which she figures as an heiress and thus
a suitable bride for his second son. Moreover, though it may be less
obvious, Catherine is also trapped by the interpretations of the
General's children.

Even before Beechen Cliff Elinor Tilney is "not at home" to Catherine, who then sees her leaving the house with her father (I, chap. 12). And on Beechen Cliff, Catherine finds that her own language is not understood. While all the critics seem to side with Henry Tilney's "corrections" of her "mistakes," it is clear from Catherine's defense of herself that her language quite accurately reflects her own perspective. She uses the word *torment*, for example, in place of *instruct* because she knows what Henry Tilney has never experienced:

> "You think me foolish to call instruction a torment, but if you had been as much used as myself to hear poor little children first learning their letters and then learning to spell, if you had ever seen how stupid they can be for a whole morning together, and how tired my poor mother is at the end of it, as I am in the habit of seeing almost every day of my life at home, you would allow that to *torment* and to *instruct* might sometimes be used as synonymous words." [I, chap. 14]

Immediately following this linguistic debate, Catherine watches the Tilneys' "viewing the country with the eyes of persons accustomed to drawing," and hears them talking "in phrases which conveyed scarcely any idea to her" (I, chap. 14). She is convinced moreover that "the little which she could understand ... appeared to contradict the very few notions she had entertained on the matter before." Surely instruction which causes her to doubt the evidence of her own eyes and understanding *is* a kind of torment. And she is further victimized by the process of depersonalization begun in Bath when she wholeheartedly adopts Henry's view and even entertains the belief "that Henry Tilney could never be wrong" (I, chap. 14).

While the Tilneys are certainly neither as hypocritical nor as coercive as the Thorpes, they do contribute to Catherine's confused anxiety over the validity of her own interpretations. Whenever Henry talks with her, he mockingly treats her like a "heroine," thereby surrounding her with clichéd language and clichéd plots. When they meet at a dance in Bath, he claims to worry about the poor figure he will make in her journal, and while his ridicule is no doubt meant for the sentimental novels in which every girl covers reams of paper with the most mundane details of her less than heroic life, such ridicule gratuitously misinterprets (and confuses) Catherine. At Northanger, when she confides to Henry that his sister has taught her how to love a hyacinth, he responds with approbation: "a taste for flowers is always desirable in your sex, as a means of getting you out of doors, and tempting you to more frequent exercise than you would otherwise take!" This, although we know that Catherine has always been happy outdoors; she is left quietly to protest that "Mamma says I am never within" (II, chap. 7). Furthermore, as Katrin Ristkok Burlin has noticed, it is Henry who provides Catherine with the plot that really threatens to overwhelm her in the Abbey.[64] While General Tilney resembles the fathers of Austen's mature fiction in his attempts to watch and control his children as an author would "his" characters—witness the narcissistic Sir Walter and the witty Mr. Bennet—it is Henry Tilney who teaches Catherine at Beechen Cliff to view nature aesthetically, and it is he, as his father's son, who authors the gothic story that entraps Catherine in the sliding panels, ancient tapestries, gloomy passageways, funereal beds, and haunted halls of Northanger.

Of course, though Austen's portrait of the artist as a young man stresses the dangers of literary manipulation, Henry's miniature gothic *is* clearly a burlesque, and no one except the gullible Catherine would ever be taken in for a minute. Indeed, many critics are uncomfortable with this aspect of the novel, finding that it splits here into two parts. But the two sections are not differentiated so much by the realism of the Bath section and the burlesque of the Abbey scenes as by a crucial shift in Catherine, who seems at the Abbey finally to fall into literacy, to be confined in prose. The girl who originally preferred cricket, baseball, and horseback riding to books becomes fascinated with Henry Tilney's plot because it is the culminating step in her training to become a heroine, which has progressed from her early perusal of Gray and Pope to her shutting herself up in Bath with Isabella to read novels and her purchasing a new writing desk which she takes with her in the chaise to Northanger. Indeed, what seems to attract Catherine to Henry Tilney is his lively literariness, for he is very closely associated with books. He has read "hundreds and hundreds" of novels (I, chap. 14), all of which furnish him with misogynistic stereotypes for her. This man whose room at Northanger is littered with books, guns, and great-coats is a specialist in "young ladies' ways."

"Everybody allows that the talent of writing agreeable letters is peculiarly female," Henry explains, and that female style is faultless except for "a general deficiency in subject, a total inattention to stops, and a very frequent ignorance of grammar" (I, chap. 3). Proving himself a man, he says, "no less by the generosity of my soul, than the clearness of my head" (I, chap. 14), Henry has "no patience with such of my sex as disdain to let themselves sometimes down to the comprehension of yours." He feels, moreover, that "perhaps the abilities of women are neither sound nor acute—neither vigorous nor keen. Perhaps they want observation, discernment, judgment, fire, genius and wit" (I, chap. 14). For all his charming vivacity, then, Henry Tilney's misogyny is closely identified with his literary authority so that, when his tale of Northanger sounds "just like a book" to Catherine (II, chap. 5), she is bound to be shut up inside this "horrid" novel by finally acquiescing to her status as a character.

Yet Catherine is one of the first examples we have of a character who gets away from her author, since her imagination runs away with the plot and role Henry has supplied her. Significantly, the story that Catherine enacts involves her in a series of terrifying, gothic adventures. Shaking and sweating through a succession of sleepless nights, she becomes obsessed with broken handles on chests that suggest "premature violence" to her, and "strange ciphers" that promise to disclose "hidden secrets" (II, chap. 6). Searching for clues to some impending evil or doom, she finds herself terrified when a cabinet will not open, only to discover in the morning that she had locked it herself; and, worse, she becomes convinced of Mrs. Tilney's confinement and finds herself weeping before the monument to the dead woman's memory. The monument notwithstanding, however, she is unconvinced of Mrs. Tilney's decease because she knows that a waxen figure might have been introduced and substituted in the family vault. Indeed, when she does not find a lost manuscript to document the General's iniquity, Catherine is only further assured that this villain has too much wit to leave clues that would lead to his detection.

Most simply, of course, this section of *Northanger Abbey* testifies to

the delusions created when girls internalize the ridiculous expectations and standards of gothic fiction. But the anxiety Catherine
experiences just at the point when she has truly come like a heroine
to the home of the man of her dreams seems also to express feelings
of confusion that are more than understandable if we remember
how constantly she has been beset with alien visions of herself and
with incomprehensible and contradictory standards for behavior.
Since heroines are not born but made, the making of a heroine
seems to imply an unnatural acquiescence in all these incomprehensible fictions: indeed, Austen seems to be implying that the girl
who becomes a heroine will become ill, if not mad. Here is the
natural consequence of a young lady's sentimental education in
preening, reading, shopping, and dreaming. Already, in Bath, caught
between the contradictory claims of friends and relatives, Catherine
meditates "by turns, on broken promises and broken arches, phaetons
and false hangings, Tilneys and trap-doors" (I, chap. 11), as if she
inhabits Pope's mad Cave of Spleen. Later, however, wandering
through the Abbey at night, Catherine could be said to be searching
finally for her own true story, seeking to unearth the past fate of a
lost female who will somehow unlock the secret of her own future.
Aspiring to become the next Mrs. Tilney, Catherine is understandably obsessed with the figure of the last Mrs. Tilney, and if we take
her fantasy seriously, in spite of the heavy parodic tone here, we can
see why, for Mrs. Tilney is an image of herself. Feeling confined and
constrained in the General's house, but not understanding why,
Catherine projects her own feelings of victimization into her imaginings of the General's wife, whose mild countenance is fitted to a
frame in death, as presumably in life, and whose painting finds no
more favor in the Abbey than her person did. Like Mary Elizabeth
Coleridge in "The Other Side of a Mirror," Catherine confronts the
image of this imprisoned, silenced woman only to realize "I am she!"
Significantly, this story of the female prisoner is Catherine's *only*
independent fiction, and it is a story that she must immediately
renounce as a "voluntary, self-created delusion" (II, chap. 10)
which can earn only her self-hatred.

If General Tilney is a monster of manipulation, then, Catherine
Morland, as George Levine has shown, is also "an incipient monster,"
not very different from the monsters that haunt Austen's contem-

porary, Mary Shelley.[65] But Catherine's monstrosity is not just, as Levine claims, the result of social climbing at odds with the limits imposed by the social and moral order; it is also the result of her search for a story of her own. Imaginative and sensitive, Catherine genuinely believes that she can become the heroine of her own life story, that she can author herself, and thereby define and control reality. But, like Mary Shelley's monster, she must finally come to terms with herself as a creature of someone else's making, a character trapped inside an uncongenial plot. In fact, like Mary Shelley's monster, Catherine cannot make sense of the signs of her culture, and her frustration is at least partially reflected in her fiction of the starving, suffering Mrs. Tilney. That she sees herself liberating this female prisoner is thus only part of her delusion, because Catherine is destined to fall not just from what Ellen Moers calls "heroinism" but even from authorship and authority: she is fated to be taught the indelicacy of her own attempt at fiction-making. Searching to understand the literary problems that persistently tease her, seeking to find the hidden origin of her own discomfort, we shall see that Catherine is motivated by a curiosity that links her not only to Mary Shelley's monster, but also to such rebellious, dissatisfied inquirers as Catherine Earnshaw, Jane Eyre, and Dorothea Brooke.

Mystified first by the Thorpes, then by the Tilneys, Catherine Morland is understandably filled with a sense of her own otherness, and the story of the imprisoned wife fully reveals both her anger and her self-pity. But her gravest loss of power comes when she is fully "awakened" and "the visions of romance were over" (II, chap. 10). Forced to renounce her story-telling, Catherine matures when "the anxieties of common life began soon to succeed to the alarms of romance" (II, chap. 10). First, her double, Isabella, who has been "all for ambition" (II, chap. 10), must be completely punished and revealed in all her monstrous aspiration. Henry Tilney is joking when he exclaims that Catherine must feel "that in losing Isabella, you lose half yourself" (II, chap. 10); but he is at least partially correct, since Isabella represents the distillation of Catherine's ambition to author herself as a heroine. For this reason, the conversations about Isabella's want of fortune and the difficulty this places in the way of her marrying Captain Tilney raise Catherine's alarms about herself because, as Catherine admits, "she was as insignificant, and perhaps as portionless, as Isabella" (II, chap. 11).

Isabella's last verbal attempt to revise reality is extremely unsuccessful; its inconsistencies and artificialities strike even Catherine as false. "Ashamed of Isabella, and ashamed of having ever loved her" (II, chap. 12), Catherine therefore begins to awaken to the anxieties of common life, and her own fall follows close upon Isabella's. Driven from the General's house, she now experiences agitations "mournfully superior in reality and substance" to her earlier imaginings (II, chap. 13). Catherine had been convinced by Henry of the "absurdity of her curiosity and her fears," but now she discovers that he erred not only in his sense of Isabella's story ("you little thought of its ending so" [II, chap. 10]), but also in his sense of hers. Not the least of Catherine's agitations must involve the realization that she has submitted to Henry's estimate that her fears of the General were "only" imaginary, when all along she had been right.

This is why *Northanger Abbey* is, finally, a gothic story as frightening as any told by Mrs. Radcliffe, for the evil it describes is the horror described by writers as dissimilar as Charlotte Perkins Gilman, Phyllis Chesler, and Sylvia Plath, the terror and self-loathing that results when a woman is made to disregard her personal sense of danger, to accept as real what contradicts her perception of her own situation. More dramatic, if not more debilitating, examples can be cited to illustrate Catherine's confusion when she realizes she has replaced her own interiority or authenticity with Henry's inadequate judgments. For the process of being brainwashed that almost fatally confuses Catherine has always painfully humiliated women subjected to a maddening process that Florence Rush, in an allusion to the famous Ingrid Bergman movie about a woman so driven insane, has recently called "gaslighting."[66]

While "a heroine returning, at the close of her career, to her native village, in all the triumph of recovered reputation" would be "a delight" for writer and reader alike, Austen admits, "I bring my heroine to her home in solitude and disgrace" (II, chap. 14). Catherine has nothing else to do but "to be silent and alone" (II, chap. 14). Having relinquished her attempt to gain a story or even a point of view, she composes a letter to Elinor that will not pain her if Henry should chance to read it. Like so many heroines, from Snow White to Kate Brown, who stands waiting for the kettle to boil at the beginning of *Summer Before the Dark*, Catherine is left with nothing to do but wait:

> She could neither sit still, nor employ herself for ten minutes together, walking round the garden and orchard again and again, as if nothing but motion was voluntary; and it seemed as if she could even walk about the house rather than remain fixed for any time in the parlour. [II, chap. 15]

Her mother gives her a book of moral essays entitled *The Mirror*, which is what must now supplant the romances, for it tells stories appropriate to her "silence and sadness" (II, chap. 15). From this glass coffin she is rescued by the prince whose "affection originated in nothing better than gratitude" for her partiality toward him (II, chap. 15).

   In spite of Henry's faults and the inevitable coercion of his authority over her, his parsonage will of course be a more pleasant dwelling than either the General's Abbey or the parental cot. Within its well-proportioned rooms, the girl who so enjoyed rolling down green slopes can at least gain a glimpse through the windows of luxuriant green meadows; in other words, Catherine's future home holds out the promise that women can find comfortable spaces to inhabit in their society. Austen even removes Elinor Tilney from "the evils of such a home as Northanger" (II, chap. 16), if only by marrying her to the gentleman whose servant left behind the laundry list. Yet the happy ending is the result of neither woman's education since, Austen implies, each continues to find the secret of the Abbey perplexing. We shall see that in this respect Catherine's fate foreshadows that of the later heroines, most of whom are also "saved" when they relinquish their subjectivity through the manipulations of a narrator who calls attention to her own exertions and thereby makes us wonder whether the lives of women not so benevolently protected would have turned out quite so well.

   At the same time, even if the marriage of the past Mrs. Tilney makes us wonder about the future Mrs. Tilney's prospects for happiness, Austen has successfully balanced her own artistic commitment to an inherited literary structure that idealizes feminine submission against her rebellious imaginative sympathies. With a heavy reliance on characters who are readers, all of Austen's early parodies point us, then, to the important subject of female imagination in her mature novels. But it is in *Northanger Abbey* that this novelist most forcefully indicates her consciousness of what Harold Bloom might call her "belatedness," a belatedness inextricably related to her definition of herself as female and therefore secondary. Just as Catherine Morland remains a reader, Austen presents herself as a "mere" interpreter and critic of prior fictions, and thereby quite modestly demonstrates her willingness to inhabit a house of fiction not of her own making.

5 Jane Austen's Cover Story (and Its Secret Agents)

I am like the needy knife-grinder—I have no story to tell.
—Maria Edgeworth

I dwell in Possibility—
A fairer House than Prose—
More numerous of Windows—
Superior—for Doors—
—Emily Dickinson

... the modes of fainting should be all as different as possible and
may be made very diverting.
—*The Girls' Book of Diversions* (ca. 1840)

From Sappho to myself, consider the fate of women.
How unwomanly to discuss it!
—Carolyn Kizer

Jane Austen was not alone in experiencing the tensions inherent in being a "lady" writer, a fact that she herself seemed to stress when, in *Northanger Abbey*, she gently admonished literary women like Maria Edgeworth for being embarrassed about their status as novelists. Interestingly, Austen came close to analyzing a central problem for Edgeworth, who constantly judged and depreciated her own "feminine" fiction in terms of her father's commitment to pedagogically sound moral instruction. Indeed, as our first epigraph is meant to suggest, Maria Edgeworth's persistent belief that she had no story of her own reflects Catherine Morland's initiation into her fallen female state as a person without a history, without a name of her own, without a story of significance which she could herself

146

author. Yet, because Edgeworth's image of herself as a needy knife-grinder suggests a potential for cutting remarks not dissimilar from what Virginia Woolf called Austen's delight in slicing her characters' heads off,[1] and because her reaction against General Tilney—"quite outrageously out of drawing and out of nature"[2]—reflects Austen's own discretion about male power in her later books, Maria Edgeworth's career is worth considering as a preface to the achievement of Austen's maturity.

Although she was possibly one of the most popular and influential novelists of her time, Maria Edgeworth's personal reticence and modesty matched Austen's, causing Byron, among others, to observe, "One would never have guessed she could write *her name*; whereas her father talked, *not* as if he could write nothing else, but as if nothing else was worth writing."[3] Even to her most recent biographer, the name Edgeworth still means Richard Lovell Edgeworth, the father whose overbearing egotism amused or annoyed many of the people he met. And while Marilyn Butler explains that Richard Edgeworth must not be viewed as an unscrupulous Svengali operating on an unsuspecting child,[4] she does not seem to realize that his daughter's voluntary devotion could also inhibit and circumscribe her talent, creating perhaps an even more complex problem for the emerging author than outright coercion would have spawned. The portrait of Richard Edgeworth as a scientific inventor and Enlightenment theorist who practiced his pedagogy at home for the greater intellectual development of his family must be balanced against his Rousseauistic experiment with his first son (whose erratic and uncontrollable spirits convinced him that Rousseau was wrong) and his fathering twenty-two children by four wives, more than one of whom was an object of his profound indifference.

As the third of twenty-two and the daughter of the wife most completely neglected, Maria Edgeworth seems to have used her writing to gain the attention and approval of her father. From the beginning of her career, by their common consent, he became the impresario and narrator of her life. He first set her to work on censorious Madame de Genlis's *Adèle et Théodore*, the work that would have launched her career, if his friend Thomas Day had not congratulated him when Maria's translation was cancelled by the publishers. While Maria wrote her *Letters for Literary Ladies* (1795) as a response to the ensuing correspondence between Day and Richard Lovell Edgeworth about the issue of female authorship, it can hardly be viewed as an act of literary assertion.

For, far from defending female authority, this manuscript, which she described as "disfigured by all manner of crooked marks of papa's critical indignation, besides various abusive marginal notes,"[5] actually contains an attack on female flightiness and self-dramatization (in "Letters of Julia and Caroline") and a satiric essay implying that feminine arguments for even the most minor sorts of self-determination are manipulative, hypocritical, self-congratulatory, and irrational ("Essay on the Noble Science of Self-Justification"). She does include an exchange of letters between a misogynist (presumably modelled on Day) who argues that "female prodigies . . . are scarcely less offensive to my taste than monsters" and a defender of female learning (presumably her father) who claims that

> considering that the pen was to women a new instrument, I think they have made at least as good a use of it as learned men did of the needle some centuries ago, when they set themselves to determine how many spirits could stand upon its point, and were ready to tear one another to pieces in the discussion of this sublime question.[6]

But this "defense," which argues that women are no sillier than medieval theologians, is hardly a compliment, coming—as it does—from an enlightened philosopher, nor is the subsequent proposition that education is necessary to make women better wives and mothers, two roles Maria Edgeworth herself never undertook. Written for an audience composed of Days and Edgeworths, *Letters for Literary Ladies* helps us understand why Maria Edgeworth could not become an author without turning herself into a literary lady, a creature of her father's imagination who was understandably anxious for and about her father's control.

"Where should I be without my father? I should sink into that nothing from which he has raised me,"[7] Maria Edgeworth worried in an eerie adumbration of the fears expressed by George Eliot and a host of other dutiful daughter-writers. Because Richard Lovell Edgeworth "pointed out" to her that "to be a mere writer of pretty stories and novellettes would be unworthy of his partner, pupil &

daughter,"[8] Maria soon stopped writing the books which her early talent seemed to make so successful—not before, however, she wrote one novel without either his aid or his knowledge. Not only was *Castle Rackrent* (1800) one of her earliest and most popular productions, it contains a subversive critique of patriarchy surprisingly similar to what we found in *Northanger Abbey*.

As narrated by the trusty servant Thady Quirk, this history of an Irish ancestral mansion is told in terms of the succession of its owners, Irish aristocrats best characterized by their indolence, improvidence, and love for litigation, alcohol, and women. Sir Tallyhoos, Sir Patrick, Sir Murtagh, Sir Kit, and Sir Condy are praised and served by their loyal retainer, who nevertheless reveals their irresponsible abuse of their position in Irish society. *Castle Rackrent* also includes a particularly interesting episode about an imprisoned wife that further links it to the secret we discovered in the overlooked passageways of Northanger. All of the Rackrent landlords marry for money, but one of them, Sir Kit, brings back to Ireland a Jewish heiress as his wife. While Thady ostensibly bemoans what "this heretic Blackamore"[9] will bring down on the head of the estate, he actually describes the pathetic ignorance and vulnerability of the wealthy foreigner, who is completely at the mercy of her cruelly capricious husband. Her helplessness is dramatized, characteristically, in an argument over the food for their table, since Sir Kit insists on irritating her with the presence of sausages, bacon, and pork at every meal. Refusing to feed on forbidden, foreign foods, as so many later heroines will, she responds by shutting herself up in her room, a dangerous solution since Sir Kit then locks her up. "We none of us ever saw or heard her speak for seven years after that" (29), Thady calmly explains.

As if aware of the potential impact of this episode, the author affixes a long explanatory footnote attesting to the historical accuracy of what "can scarcely be thought credible" by citing "the celebrated Lady Cathcart's conjugal imprisonment," a case that might also have reminded Maria Edgeworth of the story of George I's wife, who was shut up in Hanover when he left to ascend to the English throne, and who escaped only through her death thirty-two years later.[10] Sir Kit is shown to follow the example of Lady Cathcart's husband when he drinks Lady Rackrent's good health with his table companions, sending a servant on a sham errand to ask if "there was anything at table he might send her," and accepting the sham answer returned by his servant that "she did not wish for anything, but drank the company's health" (30–31). Starving inside the ancestral mansion, the literally imprisoned wife is also figuratively imprisoned within her husband's fictions. Meanwhile, Thady loyally proclaims that Sir Kit was never cured of the gaming tricks that mortgaged his estate, but that this "was the only fault he had, God bless him!" (32).

When, after her husband's death, Lady Rackrent recovers, fires the cook, and departs the country, Thady decides that "it was a shame for her, being his wife, not to show more duty," specifically not to have saved him from financial ruin. But clearly the lady's escape is a triumph that goes far in explaining why *Castle Rackrent* was scribbled fast, in secret, almost the only work of fiction Maria Edgeworth wrote without her father's help. Indeed she insisted that the story spontaneously came to her when she heard an old steward's voice, and that she simply recorded it. We will see other instances of such "trance" writing, especially with regard to the Brontës, but here it clearly helps explain why *Castle Rackrent* remained *her* book, why she steadily resisted her father's encouragement to add "corrections" to it.[11]

Certainly, when viewed as a woman's creation, *Castle Rackrent* must be considered a critique of patriarchy, for the male aristocratic line is criticized because it exploits Ireland, that traditional old sow, leaving a peasantry starved and dispossessed. Rackrent means destructive rental, and *Castle Rackrent* is a protest against exploitative landlords. Furthermore, Thady Quirk enacts the typically powerless role of housekeeper with the same ambivalence that characterizes women like Elinor Tilney in *Northanger Abbey* and Nelly Dean in *Wuthering Heights*, both of whom identify with the male owner and enforce his will, although they see it as arbitrary and coercive. Yet, like Maria Edgeworth, the needy knifegrinder, even while Thady pretends to be of use by telling not his own story but his providers', his words are damaging, for he reveals the depravity of the very masters he seems to praise so loyally. And this steward who appears to serve his lords with such docility actually benefits from their decline, sets into motion the machinery that finishes them off, and even contributes to the demise of their last representative. Whether consciously or unconsciously,[12] this "faithful family retainer" manages to get the big house. Exploiting the dissembling tactics of the powerless, Thady is an effective antagonist, and, at the end of the story, although he claims to despise him, it is his own son who has inherited the power of the Rackrent family.

Pursuing her career in her father's sitting room and writing primarily to please him, Maria Edgeworth managed in this early fiction to evade her father's control by dramatizing the retaliatory revenge of the seemingly dutiful and the apparently weak. But in spite of its success and the good reception accorded her romance *Belinda*, she turned away from her own "pretty stories and novellettes" as "unworthy" of her father's "partner, pupil & daughter," deciding to pursue instead her father's projects, for example his *Professional Education*, a study of vocational education for boys. Devoted until his death to writing Irish tales and children's stories which serve as a gloss on his political and educational theories, Maria Edgeworth went as far as she could in seeing herself and presenting herself as her father's secretary: "I have only repeated the same opinions [Edgeworth's] in other forms," she explained; "A certain quantity of bullion was given to me and I coined it into as many pieces as I thought would be convenient for popular use."[13] Admitting frequently that her "acting and most kind literary partner" made all the final decisions, she explained that "it was to please my father I first exerted myself to write, to please him I continued." But if "the first stone was thrown the first motion given by him," she understandably believed that "when there is no similar moving power the beauteous circles vanish and the water stagnates."[14]

Although she was clearly troubled that without her author she would cease to exist or create, Maria Edgeworth solved the problem of what we have been calling "the anxiety of female authorship" by writing as if she were her father's pen. Like so many of her successors—Mrs. Gaskell, Geraldine Jewsbury, George Eliot, Olive Schreiner—she was plagued by headaches that might have reflected the strain of this solution. She was also convinced that her father's skill in cutting, his criticism, and invention alone allowed her to write by relieving her from the vacillation and anxiety to which she was so much subject.[15] In this respect Maria Edgeworth resembles

Dorothea Brooke of *Middlemarch*, for "if she had written a book she must have done it as Saint Theresa did, under the command of an authority that constrained her conscience" (chap. 10). Certainly we sense the strain in her biography, for example in the incident at Richard Lovell Edgeworth's deathbed: the day before he died, Marilyn Butler explains, Richard Edgeworth dictated to his daughter a letter for his publisher explaining that she would add 200 pages to his 480-page memoir within a month after his death. In the margin his secretary wrote what she apparently could not find the courage to say: "I never promised."[16] Like Dorothea Casaubon, who finally never promises to complete Casaubon's book and instead writes silently a message on his notes explaining why she cannot, Maria Edgeworth must have struggled with the conflict between her desire to fulfill her father's wishes by living out his plots and her need to assert her own talents. Unlike Dorothea, however, she finally wrote her father's book in spite of the pain doing so must have entailed.

Literally writing her father's book, however, was doing little more than what she did throughout her career when she wrote stories illustrating his theories and portraying the wise benevolence of male authority figures. At least one critic believes that she did manage to balance her father's standards with her personal allegiances. But even if she did covertly express her dissent from her father's values— by sustaining a dialogue in her fiction between moral surface and symbolic resistence[17]—what this rather schizophrenic solution earned her on the domestic front was her father's patronizing inscription on her writing desk:

> On this humble desk were written all the numerous works of my daughter, Maria Edgeworth, in the common sitting-room of my family. In these works which were chiefly written to please me, she has never attacked the personal character of any human being or interfered with the opinions of any sect or party, religious or political; . . . she improved and amused her own mind, and gratified her heart, which I do believe is better than her head.[18]

Even as *Castle Rackrent* displays the same critique of patriarchy we traced in *Northanger Abbey*, then, Mr. Edgeworth's condescending praise of *his* daughter's desk in *his* sitting room reminds us that

Austen also worked in such a decorous space. Likewise, just as Richard Lovell Edgeworth perceives this space as a sign of Maria's ladylike submission to his domestic control, Virginia Woolf suggests that such a writing place can serve as an emblem of the confinement of the "lady" novelist:

> If a woman wrote, she would have to write in the common sitting-room . . . . She was always interrupted. . . . Jane Austen wrote like that to the end of her days. "How she was able to effect all this," her nephew writes in his Memoir, "is surprising, for she had no separate study to repair to, and most of the work must have been done in the general sitting-room subject to all kinds of casual interruptions. She was careful that her occupation should not be suspected by servants or visitors or any persons beyond her own family party." Jane Austen hid her manuscripts or covered them with a piece of blotting-paper. . . . [She] was glad that a hinge creaked, so that she might hide her manuscript before any one came in.[19]

Despite the odd contradiction we sense between Woolf's repeated assertions elsewhere in *A Room of One's Own* that Austen was unimpeded by her sex and her clear-sighted recognition in this passage of the limits placed on Austen because of it, the image of the lady writing in the common sitting room is especially useful in helping us understand both Austen's confinement and the fictional strategies she developed for coping with it. We have already seen that even in the juvenilia (which many critics consider her most conservative work) there are clues that Austen is hiding a distinctly unladylike outlook behind the "cover" or "blotter" of parody. But the blotting paper poised in anticipation of a forewarning creak can serve as an emblem of a far more organic camouflage existing within the mature novels, even as it calls to our attention the anxiety that authorship entailed for Austen.

We can see Austen struggling after *Northanger Abbey* to combine her implicitly rebellious vision with an explicitly decorous form as she follows Miss Edgeworth's example and writes in order to make herself useful, justifying her presumptuous attempts at the pen by inspiring other women with respect for the moral and social responsibilities of their domestic duties, and thereby allowing her surviving

relatives to make the same claims as Mr. Edgeworth. Yet the repressive implications of the story she tells—a story, invariably, of the
need for women to renounce their claims to stories of their own—
paradoxically allow her to escape the imprisonment she defines and
defends as her heroines' fate so that, like Emily Dickinson, Austen
herself can finally be said to "dwell in Possibility—/ A fairer House
than Prose—" (J. 657).

Austen's propriety is most apparent in the overt lesson she sets out
to teach in all of her mature novels. Aware that male superiority is
far more than a fiction, she always defers to the economic, social,
and political power of men as she dramatizes how and why female
survival depends on gaining male approval and protection. All the
heroines who reject inadequate fathers are engaged in a search for
better, more sensitive men who are, nevertheless, still the representatives of authority. As in *Northanger Abbey*, the happy ending of an
Austen novel occurs when the girl becomes a daughter to her husband, an older and wiser man who has been her teacher and her
advisor, whose house can provide her with shelter and sustenance
and at least derived status, reflected glory. Whether it be parsonage
or ancestral mansion, the man's house is where the heroine can
retreat from both her parents' inadequacies and the perils of the
outside world: like Henry Tilney's Woodston, Delaford, Pemberley,
Donwell, and Thornton Lacy are spacious, beautiful places almost
always supplied with the loveliest fruit trees and the prettiest prospects. Whereas becoming a man means proving or testing oneself
or earning a vocation, becoming a woman means relinquishing
achievement and accommodating oneself to men and the spaces
they provide.

Dramatizing the necessity of female submission for female survival,
Austen's story is especially flattering to male readers because it
describes the taming not just of any woman but specifically of a
rebellious, imaginative girl who is amorously mastered by a sensible
man. No less than the blotter literally held over the manuscript on
her writing desk, Austen's cover story of the necessity for silence and
submission reinforces women's subordinate position in patriarchal
culture. Interestingly, what common law called "coverture" at this

time actually defined the married woman's status as suspended or "covered": "the very being or legal existence of the woman is suspended during the marriage," wrote Sir William Blackstone, "or at least is incorporated and consolidated into that of the husband: under whose wing, protection and cover, she performs everything."[20] The happiest ending envisioned by Austen, at least until her very last novel, accepts the necessity of protection and cover for heroines who wish to perform anything at all.

At the same time, however, we shall see that Austen herself "performs everything" under this cover story. As Virginia Woolf noted, for all her "infallible discretion," Austen always stimulates her readers "to supply what is not there."[21] A story as sexist as that of the taming of the shrew, for example, provides her with a "blotter" or socially acceptable cover for expressing her own self-division. Undoubtedly a useful acknowledgment of her own ladylike submission and her acquiescence to masculine values, this plot also allows Austen to consider her own anxiety about female assertion and expression, to dramatize her doubts about the possibility of being both a woman and a writer. She describes both her own dilemma and, by extension, that of all women who experience themselves as divided, caught in the contradiction between their status as human beings and their vocation as females.

The impropriety of female creativity first emerges as a problem in *Lady Susan*, where Austen seems divided between her delight in the vitality of a talented libertine lady and her simultaneous rejection of the sexuality and selfishness of her heroine's plots. In this first version of the taming of the shrew, Austen exposes the wicked wilfulness of Lady Susan, who gets her own way because of her "artful" (Letters 4, 13, and 17), "bewitching powers" (Letter 4), powers intimately related to her "clever" and "happy command of language" (Letter 8). Using "deep arts," Lady Susan always has a "design" (Letter 4) or "artifice" that testifies to her great "talent" (Letters 16 and 36) as a "Mistress of Deceit" (Letter 23) who knows how to play a number of parts quite convincingly. She is the first of a series of heroines, of varying degrees of attractiveness, whose lively wit and energetic imagination make them both fascinating and frightening to their creator.

Several critics have explored how Lady Susan's London ways are contrasted to her daughter's love of the country, how the mother's talkative liveliness and sexuality are balanced against the daughter's silence and chastity, how art is opposed to nature.[22] But, if Lady Susan is energetic in her pursuit of pleasure, her daughter is quite vapid and weak; indeed, she seems far more socialized into passivity than a fit representative of nature would be. Actually she is only necessary to emphasize Lady Susan's unattractiveness—her cruelty to her daughter—which can best be viewed as Austen's reflex to suppress her interest in such wilful sorts of women. For the relationship between Lady Susan and Frederica is not unlike that between the crafty Queen and her angelic step daughter, Snow White: Lady Susan seems almost obsessed with hatred of her daughter, who represents an extension of her own self, a projection of her own inescapable femininity which she tries to destroy or transcend even at the risk of the social ostracism she must inevitably incur at the end of the novel. These two, mother and daughter, reappear transformed in the mature novels into sisters, sometimes because Austen wishes to consider how they embody available options that are in some ways equally attractive yet mutually exclusive, sometimes because she seeks to illustrate how these two divided aspects of the self can be integrated.

In *Sense and Sensibility* (1811), as most readers of the novel have noted, Marianne Dashwood's sensibility links her to the Romantic imagination. Repeatedly described as fanciful, imaginative, emotionally responsive, and receptive to the natural beauty of trees and the aesthetic beauties of Cowper, Marianne is extremely sensitive to language, repelled by clichés, and impatient with the polite lies of civility. Although quite different from Lady Susan, she too allows her lively affections to involve her in an improper amorous involvement, and her indiscreet behavior is contrasted with that of her sister Elinor, who is silent, reserved, and eminently proper. If the imagination is linked with Machiavellian evil in *Lady Susan*, it is closely associated with self-destruction in *Sense and Sensibility*: when Elinor and Marianne have to confront the same painful situation— betrayal by the men they deemed future husbands—Elinor's stoical self-restraint is the strength born of her good sense while Marianne's indulgence in sensibility almost causes her own death, the unfettered play of her imagination seeming to result in a terrible fever that represents how imaginative women are infected and sickened by their dreams.

Marianne's youthful enthusiasm is very attractive, and the reader, like Colonel Brandon, is tempted to find "something so amiable in the prejudices of a young mind, that one is sorry to see them give way to the reception of more general opinions" (I, chap. 11). But give way they apparently must and evidently do. Eagerness of fancy is a passion like any other, perhaps more imprudent because it is not recognized as such. As delightful as it might first seem, moreover, it is always shown to be a sign of immaturity, of a refusal to submit. Finally this is unbecoming and unproductive in women, who must exert their inner resources for pliancy, elasticity of spirit, and accommodation. *Sense and Sensibility* is an especially painful novel to read because Austen herself seems caught between her attraction to Marianne's sincerity and spontaneity, while at the same identifying with the civil falsehoods and the reserved, polite silences of Elinor, whose art is fittingly portrayed as the painting of screens.

Pride and Prejudice (1813) continues to associate the perils of the imagination with the pitfalls of selfhood, sexuality, and assertion. Elizabeth Bennet is her father's favorite daughter because she has inherited his wit. She is talkative, satirical, quick at interpreting appearances and articulating her judgments, and so she too is contrasted to a sensible silent sister, Jane, who is quiet, unwilling to express her needs or desires, supportive of all and critical of none. While moral Jane remains an invalid, captive at the Bingleys, her satirical sister Elizabeth walks two miles along muddy roads to help nurse her. While Jane visits the Gardners only to remain inside their house waiting hopelessly for the visitors she wishes to receive, Elizabeth travels to the Collins' establishment where she visits Lady Catherine. While Jane remains at home, lovesick but uncomplaining, Elizabeth accompanies the Gardeners on a walking tour of Derbyshire. Jane's docility, gentleness, and benevolence are remarkable, for she suffers silently throughout the entire plot, until she is finally set free by her Prince Charming. In these respects, she adumbrates Jane Fairfax of Austen's *Emma* (1816), another Jane who is totally passive and quiet, despite the fact that she is repeatedly humiliated by her lover. Indeed, although Jane Fairfax is eventually driven to a gesture of revolt—the pathetic decision to endure the "slave-trade" of becoming a governess rather than wait for Frank Churchill to become her husband—she is a paragon of submissive politeness and patience throughout her ordeal, so much so that, "wrapped up in a cloak of politeness," she was to Emma and even to Mr. Knightley "disgustingly . . . suspiciously, reserved" (II, chap. 2).

Just as Jane Bennet forecasts the role and character of Jane Fairfax, Elizabeth Bennet shares much with Emma who, perhaps more than all the others, demonstrates Austen's ambivalence about her imaginative powers, since she created in Emma a heroine whom she suspected no one but herself would like.[23] A player of word games, a painter of portraits and a spinner of tales, Emma is clearly an avatar of Austen the artist. And more than all the other playful, lively girls, Emma reminds us that the witty woman is responding to her own confining situation with words that become her weapon, a defense against banality, a way of at least *seeming* to control her life. Like Austen, Emma has at her disposal worn-out, hackneyed stories of romance that she is smart enough to resist in her own life. If Emma is an artist who manipulates people as if they were characters in her own stories, Austen emphasizes not only the immorality of this activity, but its cause or motivation: except for placating her father, Emma has nothing to do. Given her intelligence and imagination, her impatient attempts to transform a mundane reality are completely understandable.

Emma and her friends believe her capable of answering questions which puzzle less quick and assured girls, an ability shown to be necessary in a world of professions and falsehoods, puzzles, charades, and riddles. But word games deceive especially those players who think they have discovered the hidden meanings, and Emma misinterprets every riddle. Most of the letters in the novel contain "nothing but truth, though there might be some truths not told" (II, chap. 2). Because readiness to talk frequently masks reticence to communicate, the vast majority of conversations involve characters who not only remain unaffected by dialogue, but barely hear each other talking: Isabella, Miss Bates and Mr. Woodhouse, Mrs. Elton and Mr. Weston are participating in simultaneous soliloquies. The civil falsehoods that keep society running make each character a riddle to the others, a polite puzzle. With professions of openness Frank Churchill has been keeping a secret that threatens to embarrass and pain both Emma and Jane Fairfax. Emma discovers the ambiguous nature of discourse that mystifies, withholds, coerces, and lies as much as it reveals.

Yet Austen could not punish her more thoroughly than she does, and in this respect too Emma resembles the other imaginative girls. For all these heroines are mortified, humiliated, even bullied into sense. Austen's heavy attack on Emma, for instance, depends on the abject failure of the girl's wit. The very brilliant and assertive playfulness that initially marks her as a heroine is finally criticized on the grounds that it is self-deluding. Unable to imagine her visions into reality, she finds that she has all along been manipulated as a character in someone else's fiction. Through Emma, Austen is confronting the inadequacy of fiction and the pain of the "imaginist" who encounters the relentless recalcitrance of the world in which she lives, but she is also exposing the vulnerable delusions that Emma shares with Catherine Morland before the latter learns that she has no story to tell. Not only does the female artist fail, then, her efforts are condemned as tyrannical and coercive. Emma feels great self-loathing when she discovers how blind she has been: she is "ashamed of every sensation but the one revealed to her—her affection for Mr. Knightley—Every other part of her mind was disgusting" (III, chap. 2).

Although Emma is the center of Austen's fiction, what she has to learn is her commonality with Jane Fairfax, her vulnerability as a female. Like the antithetical sisters we have discussed, Jane Fairfax and Emma are doubles. Since they are the most accomplished girls in Highbury, exactly the same age, suitable companions, the fact that they are not friends is in itself quite significant. Emma even believes at times that her dislike for Jane is caused by her seeing in Jane "the really accomplished young woman which she wanted to be thought herself" (II, chap. 2). In fact, she has to succumb to Jane's fate, to *become* her double through the realization that she too has been manipulated as a pawn in Frank Churchill's game. The seriousness of Emma's assertive playfulness is made clear when she behaves rudely, making uncivil remarks at Box Hill, when she talks indiscreetly, unwittingly encouraging the advances of Mr. Elton, and when she allows her imagination to indulge in rather lewd suppositions about the possible sexual intrigues of Jane Fairfax and a married man. In other words, Emma's imagination has led her to the sin of being unladylike, and her complete mortification is a prelude to submission as she becomes a friend of Jane Fairfax, at one with her too in her realization of her own powerlessness. In this respect, Mr. Elton's recitation of a well-known riddle seems ominous:

> My first doth affliction denote,
>> Which my second is destin'd to feel
> And my whole is the best antidote
>> That affliction to soften and heal.—   [I, chap. 9]

For if the answer is woe/man, then in the process of growing up female Emma must be initiated into a secondary role of service and silence.

Similarly, in *Northanger Abbey* Catherine Morland experiences "the liberty which her imagination had dared to take" as a folly which makes her feel that "She hated herself more than she could express" (II, chap. 10) so that she too is reduced to "silence and sadness" (II, chap. 15). Although Marianne Dashwood's sister had admitted that "thirty-five and seventeen had better not have anything to do with matrimony together" (I, chap. 8), Marianne allows herself at the end to be given away to Colonel Brandon as a "reward" (III, chap. 14) for his virtuous constancy. At nineteen she finds herself "submitting to new attachments, entering on new duties" (III, chap. 14). "With such a confederacy against her," the narrator asks, "what else could she do?" Even Elizabeth Bennet, who had "prided" herself on her "discernment," finds that she had never known even herself (II, chap. 13). When "her anger was turned against herself" (II, chap. 14), Elizabeth realizes that "she had been blind, partial, prejudiced, absurd" (II, chap. 13). Significantly, "she was humbled, she was grieved; she repented, though *she hardly knew of what*" (III, chap. 8; italics ours).

All of these girls learn the necessity of curbing their tongues: Marianne is silent when she learns submission and even when "a thousand inquiries sprung up from her heart . . . she dared not urge one" (III, chap. 10). When she finds that "For herself she was humbled; but she was proud of him" (III, chap. 10), Elizabeth Bennet displays her maturity by her modest reticence: not only does she refrain from telling both her parents about her feelings for Mr.

Darcy, she never tells Jane about Mrs. Gardiner's letter or about her lover's role in persuading Mr. Bingley not to propose. Whereas before she had scorned Mr. Collins's imputation that ladies never say what they mean, at the end of *Pride and Prejudice* Elizabeth refuses to answer Lady Catherine and lies to her mother about the motives for that lady's visit. Furthermore, Elizabeth checks herself with Mr. Darcy, remembering "that he had yet to learn to be laughed at, and it was rather too early to begin" (III, chap. 16).

Emma also refrains from communicating with both Mrs. Elton and Jane Fairfax when she learns to behave discreetly. She manages to keep Harriet's secret even when Mr. Knightley proposes to her. "What did she say?" the narrator coyly asks. "Just what she ought, of course. A lady always does" (III, chap. 13). And at this point the novelist indicates her own ladylike discretion as she too refrains from detailing the personal scene explicitly. The polite talk of ladies, as Robin Lakoff has shown, is devised "to prevent the expression of strong statements,"[24] but such politeness commits both author and heroine alike to their resolve "of being humble and discreet and repressing imagination" (I, chap. 17). The novelist who has been fascinated with double-talk from the very beginning of her writing career sees the silences, evasions, and lies of women as an inescapable sign of their requisite sense of doubleness.

Austen's self-division—her fascination with the imagination and her anxiety that it is unfeminine—is part of her consciousness of the unique dilemma of all women, who must acquiesce in their status as objects after an adolescence in which they experience themselves as free agents. Simone de Beauvoir expresses the question asked by all Austen's heroines: "if I can accomplish my destiny only as the *Other*, how shall I give up my Ego?"[25] Like Emma, Austen's heroines are made to view their adolescent eroticism, their imaginative and physical activity, as an outgrown vitality incompatible with womanly restraint and survival: "how improperly had she been acting.... How inconsiderate, how indelicate, how irrational, how unfeeling, had been her conduct! What blindness, what madness, had led her on!" (III, chap. 11). The initiation into conscious acceptance of powerlessness is always mortifying, for it involves the fall from authority into the acceptance of one's status as a mere character, as well as the humiliating acknowledgment on the part of the witty sister that she must become her self-denying, quiet double. Assertion, imagination, and wit are tempting forms of self-definition which encourage each of the lively heroines to think that she can master or has mastered the world, but this is proven a dangerous illusion for women who must accept the fate of being mastered, and so the heroine learns the benefits of modesty, reticence, and patience.

If we recall Sophia's dying advice to Laura in *Love and Freindship*— "Run mad as often as you chuse; but do not faint"—it becomes clear that Austen is haunted by both these options and that she seems to feel that fainting, even if it only means playing at being dead, is a more viable solution for women who are acceptable to men only when they inhabit the glass coffin of silence, stillness, second-ariness. At the same time, however, Austen never renounces the subjectivity of what her heroines term their own "madness" until the end of each of their stories. The complementarity of the lively and the quiet sisters, moreover, suggests that these two inadequate responses to the female situation are inseparable. We have already seen that Marianne Dashwood's situation when she is betrayed by the man she considers her fiancé is quite similar to her sister's, and many critics have shown that Elinor has a great deal of sensibility, while Marianne has some sense.[26] Certainly Elizabeth and Jane Bennet, like Emma Woodhouse and Jane Fairfax, are confronted with similar dilemmas even as they eventually reach similar strategies for survival. In consistently drawing our attention to the friendship and reciprocity between sisters, Austen holds out the hope that maturity can bring women consciousness of self as subject and object.

Although all women may be, as she is, split between the conflicting desire for assertion in the world and retreat into the security of the home—speech and silence, independence and dependency—Austen implies that this psychic conflict can be resolved. Because the relationship between personal identity and social role is so problematic for women, the emerging self can only survive with a sustained double vision. As Austen's admirers have always appreciated, she does write out accommodations, even when admitting their cost: since the polarities of fainting and going mad are extremes that tempt but destroy women, Austen describes how it is possible for a kind of dialectic of self-consciousness to emerge. While this aspect of female consciousness has driven many women to schizophrenia,

Austen's heroines live and flourish *because* of their contradictory projections. When the heroines are able to live Christian lives, doing unto others as they would be done, the daughters are ready to become wives. Self-consciousness liberates them from the self, enabling them to be exquisitely sensitive to the needs and responses of others. This is what distinguishes them from the comic victims of Austen's wit, who are either imprisoned in officious egoism or incapacitated by lethargic indolence: for Austen selfishness and selflessness are virtually interchangeable.

Only the mature heroines can sympathize and identify with the self-important meddlers and the somnambulant valetudinarians who abound in Austen's novels. But their maturity implies a fallen world and the continual possibility, indeed the necessity, of self-division, duplicity, and double-talk. As the narrator of *Emma* explains, "Seldom, very seldom, does complete truth belong to any human disclosure; seldom can it happen that something is not a little disguised or a little mistaken" (III, chap. 13). Using silence as a means of manipulation, passivity as a tactic to gain power, submission as a means of attaining the only control available to them, the heroines *seem* to submit as they get what they both want and need. On the one hand, this process and its accompanying sense of doubleness is psychologically and ethically beneficial, even a boon to women who are raised by it to real heroism. On the other hand, it is a painful degradation for heroines immersed or immured in what de Beauvoir would call their own "alterity."

The mortifications of Emma, Elizabeth, and Marianne are, then, the necessary accompaniment to the surrender of self-responsibility and definition. While Marianne Brandon, Elizabeth Darcy, and Emma Knightley never exist except in the slightly malevolent futurity of all happily-ever-afters, surely they would have learned the intricate gestures of subordination. And in *Mansfield Park* (1814), where Austen examines most carefully the price of doubleness, the mature author dramatizes how the psychic split so common in women can explode into full-scale fragmentation when reintegration becomes impossible. Nowhere in her fiction is the conflict between self and other portrayed with more sensitivity to the possibility of the personality fragmenting schizophrenically than in this novel in which Austen seems the most conflicted about her own talents.

Fanny Price and Mary Crawford enact what has developed into a familiar conflict in Austen's fiction. Fanny loves the country, where she lives quietly and contentedly, conservative in her tastes, revering old buildings and trees, and acquiescent in her behavior, submitting to indignities from every member of the household with patient humility. But "what was tranquillity and comfort to Fanny was tediousness and vexation to Mary" (II, chap. 11), because differences of disposition, habit, and circumstance make the latter a talented and restless girl, a harpist, a superb card player, and a witty conversationalist capable of parody and puns. In the famous play episode the two are most obviously contrasted: exemplary Fanny refuses to play a part, deeming the theatrical improper in Sir Bertram's absence, while Mary enters into the rehearsals with vivacity and anticipation of the performance precisely because it gives her the opportunity to dramatize, under the cover of the written script, her own amorous feelings toward Edmund. This use of art links Mary to Austen in a way further corroborated by biographical accounts of Austen's delight as a girl in such home theatricals. While many critics agree that Austen sets out to celebrate Fanny's responsiveness to nature,[27] in fact it is Mary who most resembles her creator in seeing "inanimate nature, with little observation; her attention was all for men and women, her talents for the light and lively" (I, chap. 8).

In spite of their antithetical responses, Mary and Fanny, like the other "sisters" in Austen's fiction, have much in common. Both are visitors in the country and virtually parentless outsiders at Mansfield Park. Both have disreputable family histories which they seek to escape in part through their contact with the Bertram household. Both are loving sisters to brothers very much in need of their counsel and support. Both are relatively poor, dependent on male relatives for financial security. While Mary rides Fanny's horse, Fanny wears what she thinks is one of Mary's necklaces. While Fanny loves to hear Mary's music, Mary consistently seeks out Fanny's advice. They are the only two young people aware that Henry is flirting outrageously with both Bertram sisters and thereby creating terrible jealousies. Both see Rushworth as the fool that he is, both are aware of the potential impropriety of the play, and both are in love with

Edmund Bertram. Indeed, each seems incomplete because she lacks precisely the qualities so fully embodied by the other: thus, Fanny seems constrained, lacking nerve and will, while Mary is insensitive to the needs and feelings of her friends; one is too silent, the other too talkative.

Perhaps Fanny does learn enough from Mary to become a true Austen heroine. Not only does she "come out" at a dance in her honor, but she does so in a state "nearly approaching high spirits" (II, chap. 10). She rejects the attempts at persuasion made by Sir Thomas and he accuses her of "wilfulness of temper, self-conceit, and . . . independence of spirit" (III, chap. 1). In defending herself against the unwelcome addresses of Henry Crawford, Fanny also speaks more, and more angrily, than she ever has before. Finally, she does liberate herself from the need for Edmund's approval, specifically when she questions his authority and becomes "vexed into displeasure, and anger, against Edmund" (III, chap. 8). Recently, two feminist critics have persuasively argued that, when Fanny refuses to marry for social advantage, she becomes the moral model for all the other characters, challenging their social system and exposing its flimsy values.[28] And certainly Fanny does become a kind of authority figure for her younger sister Susan, whom she eventually liberates from the noisy confinement of the Portsmouth household.

Yet, trapped in angelic reserve, Fanny can never assert or enliven herself except in extreme situations where she only succeeds through passive resistance. A model of domestic virtue—"dependent, helpless, friendless, neglected, forgotten" (II, chap. 7)—she resembles Snow White not only in her passivity but in her invalid deathliness, her immobility, her pale purity. And Austen is careful to show us that Fanny can only assert herself through silence, reserve, recalcitrance, and even cunning. Since, as Leo Bersani has argued, "nonbeing is the ultimate prudence in the world of *Mansfield Park*,"[29] Fanny is destined to become the next Lady Bertram, following the example of Sir Thomas's corpselike wife. With purity that seems prudish and reserve bordering on hypocrisy, Fanny is far less likeable than Austen's other heroines: as Frank Churchill comments of Jane Fairfax, "There is safety in reserve, but no attraction" (II, chap. 6).

Obedience, tears, pallor, and martyrdom are effective but not especially endearing methods of survival, in part because one senses some pride in Fanny's self-abasement.

If Fanny Price seems unable fully to actualize herself as an authentic subject, Mary Crawford fails to admit her contingency. Because of this, like the Queen who insists on telling and living her own lively stories, she is exorcised from Mansfield Park, both the place and the plot, in a manner that dramatizes Austen's obsessive anxiety over Mary's particular brand of impropriety—her audacious speech. When Mary's liberty deteriorates into license and her self-actualization into selfishness, Edmund can only defend her by claiming that "She does not *think* evil, but she speaks it—speaks it in playfulness—" and he admits this means "the mind itself was tainted" (II, chap. 9). Although Mary's only crimes do, in fact, seem to be verbal, we are told repeatedly that her mind has been "led astray and bewildered, and without any suspicion of being so; darkened, yet fancying itself light" (III, chap. 6). Because she would excuse as "folly" what both Fanny and Edmund term "evil," her *language* gives away her immodesty, her "blunted delicacy" (III, chap. 16). Edmund says in horror, "No reluctance, no horror, no feminine—shall I say? no modest loathings!" (III, chap. 16). It is, significantly, "the manner in which she spoke" (III, chap. 16) that gives the greatest offense and determines Edmund's final rejection.

When, during the episode of the theatricals, Fanny silently plays the role of the angel by refusing to play, Mary Crawford metamorphoses into a siren as she coquettishly persuades Edmund to participate in the very theatricals he initially condemned as improper. Fanny knows that in part her own reticence is caused by fear of exposing herself, but this does not stop her from feeling extremely jealous of Mary, not only because Mary is a fine actress but because she has chosen to play a part that allows her to express her otherwise silent opposition to Edmund's choice of a clerical profession. Heretical, worldly, cynical in her disdain for the institutions of the Church, Mary is a damned Eve who offers to seduce prelapsarian Edmund Bertram in the garden of the green room, when the father is away on a business trip, and she almost succeeds, at least until the absent father reappears to burn all the scripts, to repress this libidinal outbreak in paradise and call for music which "helped conceal the want of real harmony" (II, chap. 2). Since the rehearsals have brought nothing but restlessness, rivalry, vexation, pettiness, and sexual license, *Lover's Vows* illustrates Austen's belief that self-expression and artistry are dangerously attractive precisely because they liberate actors from the rules, roles, social obligations, and familial bonds of every day life.[30]

Mary's seductive allure is the same as her brother Henry's. He is the best actor, both on and off the stage, because he has the ability to be "every thing to every body" (II, chap. 13). But he can "do nothing without a mixture of evil" (II, chap. 13). Attractive precisely because of his protean ability to change himself into a number of attractive personages, Henry is an impersonator who degenerates into an imposter, not unlike Frank Churchill, who is also "acting a part or making a parade of insincere professions" (*E*, II, chap. 6). Indeed, Henry is a good representative of the kind of young man with whom each of the heroines falls briefly in love before she is finally disillusioned: Willoughby, Wickham, Frank Churchill, Henry Crawford, and Mr. Elliot are eminently agreeable because they are self-changers, self-shapers. In many respects they are attractive to the heroines because somehow they act as doubles: younger men who must learn to please, narcissists, they experience traditionally "feminine" powerlessness and they are therefore especially interested in becoming the creators of themselves.

In *Mansfield Park*, however, Austen defines this self-creating spirit as a "bewitching" (II, chap. 13) "infection" (II, chap. 1), and the epidemic restlessness represented by the Crawfords is seen as far more dangerous than Fanny's invalid passivity. Fanny's rejection of Henry represents, then, her censure of his presumptuous attempt to author his own life, his past history, and his present fictional identities. Self-divided, indulging his passions, alienated from authority, full of ambition, and seeking revenge for past injuries, the false young man verges on the Satanic. While he manages to thrive in his own fashion, finding a suitable lover or wife and generally making his fortune in the process, his way cannot be the Austen heroine's. Although his crimes are real actions while hers are purely rhetorical, she is more completely censured because her liberties more seriously defy her social role.

When her Adam refuses to taste the fruit offered by Mary Crawford,

Austen follows the example of Samuel Richardson in her favorite of his novels, *Sir Charles Grandison*, where Harriet draws a complimentary analogy between Sir Charles and Adam: the former would not have been so compliant as to taste the forbidden fruit; instead he would have left it to God to annihilate the first Eve and supply a second.[31] Just as Fanny sees through the play actor, Henry Crawford, to the role-player and hypocrite, Edmund finally recognizes Mary's playfulness as her refusal to submit to the categories of her culture, a revolt that is both attractive and immoral because it gains her the freedom to become whatever she likes, even to choose not to submit to one identity but to try out a variety of voices. For all these reasons, she has to be annihilated. But, unlike Richardson, Austen in destroying this unrepentant, imaginative, and assertive girl is demonstrating her own self-division.

In all six of Austen's novels women who are refused the means of self-definition are shown to be fatally drawn to the dangerous delights of impersonation and pretense. But Austen's profession depends on just these disguises. What else, if not impersonation, is characterization? What is plot, if not pretense? In all the novels, the narrator's voice is witty, assertive, spirited, independent, even (as D. W. Harding has shown) arrogant and nasty.[32] Poised between the subjectivity of lyric and the objectivity of drama, the novel furnishes Austen with a unique opportunity: she can create Mary Crawford's witty letters or Emma's brilliant retorts, even while rejecting them as improper; furthermore, she can reprove as indecent in a heroine what is necessary to an author. Authorship for Austen is an escape from the very restraints she imposes on her female characters. And in this respect she seems typical, for women may have contributed so significantly to narrative fiction precisely because it effectively objectifies, even as it sustains and hides, the subjectivity of the author. Put another way, in the novels Austen questions and criticizes her own aesthetic and ironic sensibilities, noting the limits and asserting the dangers of an imagination undisciplined by the rigors of art.

Using her characters to castigate the imaginative invention that informs her own novels, Austen is involved in a contradiction that, as we have seen, she approves as the only solution available to her heroines. Just as they manage to survive only by seeming to submit, she succeeds in maintaining her double consciousness in fiction that proclaims its docility and restraint even as it uncovers the delights of assertion and rebellion. Indeed the comedy of Austen's novels explores the tensions between the freedom of her art and the dependency of her characters: while they stutter and sputter and lapse into silence and even hasten to perfect felicity, she attains a woman's language that is magnificently duplicitous. In this respect, Austen serves as a paradigm of the literary ladies who would emerge so successfully and plentifully in the mid-nineteenth century, popular lady novelists like Rhoda Broughton, Charlotte Mary Yonge, Home Lee, and Mrs. Craik[33] who strenuously suppressed awareness of how their own professional work called into question traditional female roles. Deeply conservative as their content appears to be, however, it frequently retains traces of the original duplicity so manifest in its origin, even as it demonstrates their own exuberant evasion of the inescapable limits they prescribe for their model heroines.

Although Austen clearly escapes the House of Prose that confines her heroines by making her story out of their renunciation of story-telling, she also dwells in the freer prospects of Emily Dickinson's "Possibility" by identifying not only with her model heroines, but also with less obvious, nastier, more resilient and energetic female characters who enact her rebellious dissent from her culture, a dissent, as we have seen, only partially obscured by the "blotter" of her plot. Many critics have already noticed duplicity in the "happy endings" of Austen's novels in which she brings her couples to the brink of bliss in such haste, or with such unlikely coincidences, or with such sarcasm that the entire message seems undercut[34]: the implication remains that a girl without the aid of a benevolent narrator would never find a way out of either her mortifications or her parents' house.

Perhaps less obvious instances of Austen's duplicity occur in her representation of a series of extremely powerful women each of whom acts out the rebellious anger so successfully repressed by the heroine and the author. Because they so rarely appear and so infrequently speak in their own voices, these furious females remain secret presences in the plots. Not only do they play a less prominent role in the novels than their function in the plot would seem to require; buried or killed or banished at the end of the story, they seem to warrant this punishment by their very unattractiveness. Like Lady Susan, they are mothers or surrogate mothers who seek to destroy their docile children. Widows who are no longer defined by men simply because they have survived the male authorities in their lives, these women can exercise power even if they can never legitimize it; thus they seem both pushy and dangerous. Yet if their energy appears destructive and disagreeable, that is because this is the mechanism by which Austen disguises the most assertive aspect of herself as the Other. We shall see that these bitchy women enact impulses of revolt that make them doubles not only for the heroines but for their author as well.

We have seen Austen at her most conflicted in *Mansfield Park*, so perhaps it is here that we can begin to understand how she quietly yet forcefully undercuts her own moral. Probably the most obnoxious character in the book, Aunt Norris, is clearly meant to be a dark parody of Mary Crawford, revealing—as she does—how easily Mary's girlish liveliness and materialism could degenerate into meddlesome, officious penny-pinching. But, as nasty as she is repeatedly shown and said to be when she tries to manage and manipulate, to condescend to Fanny, to save herself some money, Aunt Norris is in some ways castigated for moral failures which are readily understandable, if not excusable. After all, she is living on a small, fixed income, and if she uses flattery to gain pecuniary help, her pleasures are dependent on receiving it. Like Fanny Price, Aunt Norris knows that she must please and placate Sir Thomas. Even when he gives "advice," both accept it as "the advice of absolute power" (II, chap. 18). Perhaps one reason for her implacable hatred of Fanny is that Aunt Norris sees in her a rival for Sir Thomas's protection, another helpless and useful dependent. Furthermore, like Fanny, Aunt Norris uses submission as a strategy to get her own way: acquiescing to the power in authority, she manages to talk her brother-in-law into all her schemes.

Unlike "good" Lady Bertram, Aunt Norris is an embittered, manipulative, pushy female who cannot allow other people to live their own lives. At least, this is how these sisters first strike us, until we remember that, for all her benign dignity, Lady Bertram does nothing but sit "nicely dressed on a sofa, doing some long piece of needlework, of little use and no beauty, thinking more of her pug than her children" (I, chap. 2). Indeed, the contrast between her total passivity and Aunt Norris's indiscriminate exertions recalls again the options described by Sophia in *Love and Freindship*— fainting or running mad. Like all the other "good" mothers in Austen's fiction who are passive because dead, dying, or dumb, Lady Bertram teaches the necessity of submission, the all-importance of a financially sound marriage, and the empty-headedness that goes with these values. For all her noisy bustling, Aunt Norris is a much more loving mother to Lady Bertram's daughters. If she indulges them, it is in part out of genuine affection and loyalty. And as she herself actively lives her own life and pursues her own ends, Aunt Norris quite naturally identifies with her headstrong nieces. Unlike the figure of the "good" mother, the figure of bad Aunt Norris implies that female strength, exertion, and passion are necessary for survival and pleasure.

Instead of abandoning Maria after the social disgrace of the elopement and divorce, Aunt Norris goes off to live with her as her surrogate mother. Although she is thereby punished and driven from Mansfield Park, Aunt Norris (we cannot help suspecting) is probably as relieved to have escaped the dampening effect of Sir Thomas's sober rule as he is to have rid himself of the one person who has managed to assert herself against his wishes, to evade his control. This shrew is still talking at the end of the book, untamed and presumably untameable. As if to authenticate her completely unacceptable admiration for this kind of woman, Austen constructs a plot which quite consistently finds its impetus in Aunt Norris. It is she, for instance, who decides to take Fanny from her home and bring her to Mansfield; she places Fanny in Sir Thomas's household and allocates her inferior status; she rules Mansfield in Sir Thomas's absence and allows the play to progress; she plans and executes the visit to Southerton that creates the marriage between Maria and Mr. Rushworth. Quite openly dedicated to the pursuit of pleasure and activity, especially the joy of controlling other people's lives, Aunt Norris is a parodic surrogate for the author, a suitable double whose manipulations match those of Aunt Jane.

As vilified as she is, Aunt Norris was the character most often praised and enjoyed by Jane Austen's contemporaries, to the author's delight.[35] Hers is one of the most memorable voices in *Mansfield Park*. She resembles not only the hectic, scheming Queen, stepmother to Snow White, but also the Queen of the Night in Mozart's *The Magic Flute*. Actually, all the angry dowagers in Austen's novels represent a threat to the enlightened reason of the male god who eventually wins the heroine only by banishing the forces of female sexuality, capriciousness, and loquacity. But, as in *The Magic Flute*, where the Queen of the Night is carried offstage still singing her exuberantly strenuous resistence, women like Aunt Norris are never really completely stifled. The despised Mrs. Ferrars of *Sense and Sensibility*, for example, exacts the punishment which Elinor Dashwood could not help but wish on a man who has been selfishly deceiving her for the entire novel. By tampering with the patriarchal line of inheritance, Mrs. Ferrars proves that the very forms valued by Elinor are arbitrary. But even though *Sense and Sensibility* ends with the overt message that young women like Marianne and Elinor must submit to the powerful conventions of society by finding a male protector, Mrs. Ferrars and her scheming protégée Lucy Steele prove that women can themselves become agents of repression, manipulators of conventions, and survivors.

Most of these powerful widows would agree with Lady Catherine De Bourgh in seeing "no occasion for entailing estates from the female lines" (*PP*, II, 6). Opposed to the very basis of patriarchy, the exclusive right of male inheritance, Lady Catherine quite predictably earns the vilification always allotted by the author to the representatives of matriarchal power. She is shown to be arrogant, officious, egotistical, and rude as she patronizes all the other characters in the novel. Resembling Lady Susan in her disdain for her own pale, weak, passive daughter, Lady Catherine delights in managing the affairs of others. Probably most unpleasant when she opposes Elizabeth's right to marry Darcy, she questions Elizabeth's birth and breeding by admitting that Elizabeth is "a gentleman's daughter," but demanding, "who was your mother?" (III, chap. 14).

As dreadful as she seems to be, however, Lady Catherine is herself in some ways an appropriate mother to Elizabeth because the two women are surprisingly similar. Her ladyship points this out herself when she says to Elizabeth, "You give your opinion very decidedly for so young a person" (II, chap. 6). Both speak authoritatively of matters on which neither is an authority. Both are sarcastic and certain in their assessment of people. Elizabeth describes herself to Darcy by asserting, "There is a stubbornness about me that never can bear to be frightened at the will of others" (II, chap. 8), and in this respect too she resembles Lady Catherine, whose courage is indomitable. Finally, these are the only two women in the novel capable of feeling and expressing genuine anger, although it is up to Lady Catherine to articulate the rage against entailment that Elizabeth must feel since it has so rigidly restricted her own and her sisters' lives. When Elizabeth and Lady Catherine meet in conflict, each retains her decided resolution of carrying her own purpose. In all her objections to Elizabeth's match with Darcy, Lady Catherine only articulates what Elizabeth has herself thought on the subject, that her mother is an unsuitable relation for him and her sister an even less appropriate connection. Highly incensed and unresponsive to advice, Elizabeth resembles her interlocutor; it is fitting not only that she takes the place meant for Lady Catherine's daughter when she marries Darcy, but that she also sees to it that her husband is persuaded to entertain his aunt at Pemberley. As Darcy and Elizabeth both realize, Lady Catherine has been the author of their marriage, bringing about the first proposal by furnishing the occasion and place for meetings, and the second by endeavoring to separate them when she actually communicates Elizabeth's renewed attraction to a suitor waiting for precisely such encouragement.

The vitriolic shrew is so discreetly hidden in *Emma* that she never appears at all, yet again she is the causal agent of the plot. Like her predecessors, Mrs. Churchill is a proud, arrogant, and capricious woman who uses all means, including reports of her poor health, to elicit attention and obedience from her family. In fact, only her death—which clears the way for the marriage of Frank Churchill to Jane Fairfax—convinces them that her nervous disorders were more than selfish, imaginary complaints. Actually Mrs. Churchill can be viewed as the cause of all the deceit practiced by the lovers inasmuch as their secret engagement is a response to her disapproval of the match. Thus this disagreeable women with "no more heart than a stone to people in general, and the devil of a temper" (I, chap. 14) is the "invisible presence" which, as W. J. Harvey explains, "enables Jane Austen to embody that aspect of our intuition of reality summed up by Auden—'we are lived by powers we do not understand.' "[36]

But Mrs. Churchill is more than the representative of the unpredictable contingency of reality. On the one hand, she displays an uncanny and ominous resemblance to Jane Fairfax, who will also be a penniless upstart when she marries and who is also subject to nervous headaches and fevers. Mrs. Churchill, we are told by Mr. Weston, "is as thorough a fine lady as anybody ever beheld" (II, chap. 18), so it is quite fitting that polite Jane Fairfax becomes the next Mrs. Churchill and inherits that lady's jewels. On the other hand, Mrs. Churchill seems much like Emma, who is also involved in becoming a pattern lady: selfish in their very imaginings, both have the power of having too much their own way, both are convinced of their superiority in talent, elegance of mind, fortune, and consequence, and both want to be first in society where they can enjoy assigning subservient parts to those in their company.

The model lady haunts all the characters of *Emma*, evoking "delicate plants" to Mr. Woodhouse (II, chap. 16) and the showy finery of Selena for Mrs. Elton. But it is Mrs. Churchill who illustrates the bankruptcy of the ideal, for she is not only a monitory image of what Austen's heroines could be, she is also a double of what they are already fast becoming. If Mrs. Churchill represents Austen's guilt at her own authorial control, she also reminds us that feminine propriety, reserve, and politeness can give way to bitchiness since the bitch is what the young lady's role and values imply from the beginning, built—as we have seen them to be—out of complicity, manipulation, and deceit. At the same time, however, Mrs. Churchill is herself the victim of her own ladylike silences, evasions, and lies: no one takes seriously her accounts of her own ill health, no one believes that her final illness is more than a manipulative fiction, and her death—one of the few to occur in Austen's mature fiction—is an ominous illustration of feminine vulnerability that Austen would more fully explore in her last novel.

It is not only Austen's mad matriarchs who reflect her discomfort with the glass coffin of female submission. Her last completed novel,

Persuasion (1818), focuses on an angelically quiet heroine who has given up her search for a story and has thereby effectively killed herself off. Almost as if she were reviewing the implications of her own plots, Austen explores in *Persuasion* the effects on women of submission to authority and the renunciation of one's life story. Eight years before the novel begins, Anne Elliot had been persuaded to renounce her romance with Captain Wentworth, but this decision sickened her by turning her into a nonentity. Forced into "knowing [her] own nothingness" (I, chap. 6), Anne is a "nobody with either father or sister" so her word has "no weight" (I, chap. 1). An invisible observer who tends to fade into the background, she is frequently afraid to move lest she should be seen. Having lost the "bloom" of her youth, she is but a pale vestige of what she had been and realizes that her lover "should not have known [her] again" (I, chap. 7), their relationship being "now nothing!" Anne Elliot is the ghost of her own dead self; through her, Austen presents a personality haunted with a sense of menace.

At least one reason why Anne has deteriorated into a ghostly insubstantiality is that she is a dependent female in a world symbolized by her vain and selfish aristocratic father, who inhabits the mirrored dressing room of Kellynch Hall. It is significant that *Persuasion* begins with her father's book, the *Baronetage*, which is described as "the book of books" (I, chap. 1) because it symbolizes male authority, patriarchal history in general, and her father's family history in particular. Existing in it as a first name and birth date in a family line that concludes with the male heir presumptive, William Walter Elliot, Esq., Anne has no reality until a husband's name can be affixed to her own. But Anne's name is a new one in the *Baronetage*: the history of this ancient, respectable line of heirs records "all the Marys and Elizabeths they had married" (I, chap. 1), as if calling our attention to the hopeful fact that, unlike her sisters Mary and Elizabeth, Anne may not be forced to remain a character within this "book of books." And, in fact, Anne will reject the economic and social standards represented by the *Baronetage*, deciding, by the end of her process of personal development, that not she but the Dowager Viscountess Dalrymple and her daughter the Honourable Miss Carteret are "nothing" (II, chap. 4). She will also discover that Captain Wentworth is "no longer nobody" (II, chap. 12), and, even more significantly, she will insist on her ability to seek and find "at least the comfort of telling the whole story her own way" (II, chap. 9).

But before Anne can become somebody, she must confront what being a nobody means: "I'm Nobody!" (J. 228), Emily Dickinson could occasionally avow, and certainly, by choosing not to have a story of her own, Anne seems to have decided to dwell in Dickinson's realm of "Possibility," for what Austen demonstrates through her is that the person who has not become anybody is haunted by everybody. Living in a world of her father's mirrors, Anne confronts the several selves she might have become and discovers that they all reveal the same story of the female fall from authority and autonomy.

As a motherless girl, Anne is tempted to become her own mother, although she realizes that her mother lived invisibly, unloved, within Sir Walter's house. Since Anne could marry Mr. Elliot and become the future Lady Elliot, she has to confront her mother's unhappy marriage as a potential life story not very different from that of Catherine Morland's Mrs. Tilney. At the same time, however, since serviceable Mrs. Clay is an unattached female who aspires to her mother's place in the family as her father's companion and her sister Elizabeth's intimate, Anne realizes that she could also become patient Penelope Clay, for she too understands "the art of pleasing" (I, chap. 2), of making herself useful. When Anne goes to Uppercross, moreover, she functions something like Mrs. Clay, "being too much in the secret of the complaints" of each of the tenants of both households (I, chap. 6), and trying to flatter or placate each and all into good humor. The danger exists, then, that Anne's sensitivity and selflessness could degenerate into Mrs. Clay's ingratiating, hypocritical service.

Of course, Mary Musgrove's situation is also a potential identity for Anne, since Charles had actually asked for Anne's hand in marriage before he settled on her younger sister, and since Mary resembles Anne in being one of Sir Walter's unfavored daughters. Indeed, Mary's complaint that she is "always the last of my family to be noticed" (II, chap. 6) could easily be voiced by Anne. Bitter about being nobody, Mary responds to domestic drudgery with "feminine" invalidism that is an extension of Anne's sickening self-doubt, as well as the only means at Mary's disposal of using her imagination to add some drama and importance to her life. Mary's hypochondria reminds us that Louisa Musgrove provides a kind of paradigm for all these women when she literally falls from the Cobb and suffers from a head injury resulting in exceedingly weak nerves. Because incapacitated Louisa is first attracted to Captain Wentworth and finally marries Captain Benwick, whose first attentions had been given to Anne, she too is clearly an image of what Anne might have become.

Through both Mary and Louisa, then, Austen illustrates how growing up female constitutes a fall from freedom, autonomy, and strength into debilitating, degrading, ladylike dependency. In direct contradiction to Captain Wentworth's sermon in the hedgerow, Louisa discovers that even firmness cannot save her from such a fall. Indeed, it actually precipitates it, and she discovers that her fate is not to jump from the stiles down the steep flight of seaside stairs but to read love poetry quietly in the parlor with a suitor suitably solicitous for her sensitive nerves. While Louisa's physical fall and subsequent illness reinforce Anne's belief that female assertion and impetuosity must be fatal, they also return us to the elegiac autumnal landscape that reflects Anne's sense of her own diminishment, the loss she experiences since her story is "now nothing."

Anne lives in a world of mirrors both because she could have become most of the women in the novel and, as the title suggests, because all the characters present her with their personal preferences rationalized into principles by which they attempt to persuade her. She is surrounded by other people's versions of her story and offered coercive advice by Sir Walter, Captain Wentworth, Charles Musgrove, Mrs. Musgrove, Lady Russell, and Mrs. Smith. Eventually, indeed, the very presence of another person becomes oppressive for Anne, since everyone but she is convinced that his or her version of reality is the only valid one. Only Anne has a sense of the different, if equally valid, perspectives of the various families and individuals among which she moves. Like Catherine Morland, she struggles against other people's fictional use and image of her; and finally she penetrates to the secret of patriarchy through absolutely no skill of detection on her own part. Just as Catherine blunders on the secret of the ancestral mansion to understand the arbitrary power of General Tilney, who does not mean what he says, Anne stumbles fortuitously on the secret of the heir to Kellynch Hall, William Elliot,

who had married for money and was very unkind to his first wife.
Mr. Elliot's "manoevres of selfishness and duplicity must ever be
revolting" (II, chap. 7) to Anne, who comes to believe that "the
evil" of this suitor could easily result in "irremediable mischief"
(II, chap. 10).

For all of Austen's heroines, as Mr. Darcy explains, "detection
could not be in [their] power, and suspicion certainly not in [their]
inclination" (II, chap. 3). Yet Anne does quietly and attentively
watch and listen and judge the members of her world and, as Stuart
Tave has shown, she increasingly exerts herself to speak out, only
gradually to discover that she is being heard.[37] Furthermore, in her
pilgrimage from Kellynch Hall to Upper Cross and Lyme to Bath,
the landscapes she encounters function as a kind of psychic geography
of her development so that, when the withered hedgerows and tawny
autumnal meadows are replaced by the invigorating breezes and
flowing tides of Lyme, we are hardly surprised that Anne's bloom is
restored (I, chap. 12). Similarly, when Anne gets to Bath, this woman
who has heard and overheard others has trouble listening because
she is filled with her own feelings, and she decides that "one half of
her should not be always so much wiser than the other half, or always
suspecting the other half of being worse than it was" (II, chap. 7).
Therefore, in a room crowded with talking people, Anne manages
to signal to Captain Wentworth her lack of interest in Mr. Elliot
through her assertion that she has no pleasure in parties at her father's
house. "She had spoken it," the narrator emphasizes; if "she trembled
when it was done, conscious that her words were listened to" (II,
chap. 10), this is because Anne has actually "never since the loss of
her dear mother, known the happiness of being listened to, or encouraged" (I, chap. 6).

The fact that her mother's loss initiated her invisibility and silence
is important in a book that so closely associates the heroine's felicity
with her ability to articulate her sense of herself as a woman. Like
Elinor Tilney, who feels that "A mother could have been always
present. A mother would have been a constant friend; her influence
would have been beyond all others" (*NA*, II, chap. 7), Anne misses
the support of a loving female influence. It is then fitting that the
powerful whispers of well-meaning Mrs. Musgrove and Mrs. Croft
furnish Anne with the cover—the opportunity and the encourage-

ment—to discuss with Captain Harville her sense of exclusion from patriarchal culture: "Men have had every advantage of us in telling their own story. . . . The pen has been in their hands" (II, chap. 11). Anne Elliot will "not allow books to prove anything" because they "were all written by men" (II, chap. 11); her contention that women love longest because their feelings are more tender directly contradicts the authorities on women's "fickleness" that Captain Harville cites. As we have already seen, her speech reminds us that the male charge of "inconstancy" is an attack on the irrepressible interiority of women who cannot be contained within the images provided by patriarchal culture. Though Anne remains inalterably inhibited by these images since she cannot express her sense of herself by "saying what should not be said" (II, chap. 11) and though she can only replace the *Baronetage* with the *Navy Lists*—a book in which women are conspicuously absent—still she is the best example of her own belief in female subjectivity. She has both deconstructed the dead selves created by all her friends to remain true to her own feelings, and she has continually reexamined and reassessed herself and her past.

Finally, Anne's fate seems to be a response to Austen's earlier stories in which girls are forced to renounce their romantic ambitions: Anne "had been forced into prudence in her youth, she learned romance as she grew older—the natural sequel of an unnatural beginning" (I, chap. 4). It is she who teaches Captain Wentworth the limits of masculine assertiveness. Placed in Anne's usual situation of silently overhearing, he discovers her true, strong feelings. Significantly, his first reponse is to drop his pen. Then, quietly, under the cover of doing some business for Captain Harville, Captain Wentworth writes her his proposal, which he can only silently hand to her before leaving the room. At work in the common sitting-room of the White Hart Inn, alert for inauspicious interruptions, using his other letter as a kind of blotter to camouflage his designs, Captain Wentworth reminds us of Austen herself. While Anne's rebirth into "a second spring of youth and beauty" (II, chap. 1) takes place within the same corrupt city that fails to fulfill its baptismal promise of purification in *Northanger Abbey*, we are led to believe that her life with this man will escape the empty elegance of Bath society.

That the sea breezes of Lyme and the watery cures of Bath have revived Anne from her ghostly passivity furnishes some evidence that naval life may be an alternative to and an escape from the corruption of the land so closely associated with patrilineal descent. Sir Walter Elliot dismisses the navy because it raises "men to honours which their fathers and grandfathers never dreamt of" (I, chap. 3). And certainly Captain Wentworth seems almost miraculously to evade the hypocrisies and inequities of a rigid class system by making money on the water. But it is also true that naval life seems to justify Sir Walter's second objection that "it cuts up a man's youth and vigour most horribly." While he is thinking in his vanity only about the rapidity with which sailors lose their looks, we are given an instance of the sea cutting up a man's youth, a singularly unprepossessing man at that: when worthless Dick Musgrove is created by Austen only to be destroyed at sea, we are further reminded of her trust in the beneficence of nature, for only her anger against the unjust adulation of sons (over daughters) can explain the otherwise gratuitous cruelty of her remarks about Mrs. Musgrove's "large fat sighings over the destiny of a son, whom alive nobody had cared for" (I, chap. 8). Significantly, this happily lost son was recognized as a fool by Captain Wentworth, whose naval success closely associates him with a vocation that does not as entirely exclude women as most landlocked vocations do: his sister, Mrs. Croft, knows that the difference between "a fine gentleman" and a navy man is that the former treats women as if they were "all fine ladies, instead of rational creatures" (I, chap. 8). She herself believes that "any reasonable woman may be perfectly happy" on board ship, as she was when she crossed the Atlantic four times and traveled to and from the East Indies, more comfortably (she admits) than when she settled at Kellynch Hall, although her husband *did* take down Sir Walter's mirrors.

Naval men like Captain Wentworth and Admiral Croft are also closely associated, as is Captain Harville, with the ability to create "ingenious contrivances and nice arrangements . . . to turn the actual space to the best possible account" (I, chap. 11), a skill not unrelated to a "profession which is, if possible, more distinguished in its domestic virtue than in its national importance" (II, chap. 12). While Austen's dowagers try to gain power by exploiting traditionally male prerogatives, the heroine of the last novel discovers an egalitarian society in which men value and participate in domestic life, while women contribute to public events, a complementary ideal that presages the emergence of an egalitarian sexual ideology.[38] No longer confined to a female community of childbearing and childrearing, activities portrayed as dreary and dangerous in both Austen's novels and her letters,[39] Anne triumphs in a marriage that represents the union of traditionally male and female spheres. If such a consummation can only be envisioned in the future, on the water, amid imminent threats of war, Austen nonetheless celebrates friendship between the sexes as her lovers progress down Bath streets with "smiles reined in and spirits dancing in private rapture" (II, chap. 11).

When Captain Wentworth accepts Anne's account of their story, he agrees with her highly ambivalent assessment of the woman who advised her to break off their engagement. Lady Russell is one of Austen's last pushy widows, but, in this novel which revises Austen's earlier endorsement of the necessity of taming the shrew, the cautionary monster is one of effacement rather than assertion. If the powerful origin of *Emma* is the psychologically coercive model of the woman as lady, in *Persuasion* Austen describes a heroine who refuses to become a lady. Anne Elliot listened to the persuasions of the powerful, wealthy, proper Lady Russell when she refrained from marrying the man she loved. But finally she rejects Lady Russell, who is shown to value rank and class over the dictates of the heart, in part because her own heart is perverted, capable of revelling "in angry pleasure, in pleased contempt" (II, chap. 1) at events sure to hurt Anne. Anne replaces this cruel stepmother with a different kind of mother surrogate, another widow, Mrs. Smith. Poor, confined, crippled by rheumatic fever, Mrs. Smith serves as an emblem of the dispossession of women in a patriarchal society, and she is, as Paul Zietlow has shown, also the embodiment of what Anne's future could have been under less fortunate circumstances.[40]

While Lady Russell persuaded Anne not to marry a poor man, Mrs. Smith explains why she should not marry a rich one. Robbed of all physical and economic liberty, with "no child . . . no relatives . . . no health . . . no possibility of moving" (II, chap. 5), Mrs. Smith is paralyzed, and, although she exerts herself to maintain good humor in her tight place, she is also maddened. She expresses her rage at the false forms of civility, specifically at the corrupt and selfish double-dealings of Mr. Elliot, the heir apparent and the epitome of patriarchal society. With fierce delight in her revengeful revelations, Mrs. Smith proclaims herself an "injured, angry woman" (II, chap. 9) and she articulates Anne's—and Austen's—unacknowledged fury at her own unnecessary and unrecognized paralysis and suffering. But although this widow is a voice of angry female revolt against the injustices of patriarchy, she is as much a resident of Bath as Lady Russell. This fashionable place for cures reminds us that society *is* sick. And Mrs. Smith participates in the moral degeneration of the place when she selfishly lies to Anne, placing her own advancement over Anne's potential marital happiness by withholding the truth about Mr. Elliot until she is quite sure Anne does not mean to marry him. Like Lady Russell, then, this other voice within Anne's psyche can also potentially victimize her.

It is Mrs. Smith's curious source of knowledge, her informant or her muse, who best reveals the corruption that has permeated and informs the social conventions of English society. A woman who nurses sick people back to health, wonderfully named nurse Rooke resembles in her absence from the novel many of Austen's most important avatars. Pictured perched on the side of a sickbed, nurse Rooke seems as much a vulture as a savior of the afflicted. Her freedom of movement in society resembles the movement of a chess piece which moves parallel to the edge of the board, thereby defining the limits of the game. And she "rooks" her patients, discovering their hidden hoards.

Providing ears and eyes for the confined Mrs. Smith, this seemingly ubiquitous, omniscient nurse is privy to all the secrets of the sickbed. She has taught Mrs. Smith how to knit, and she sells "little thread-cases, pin-cushions and cardracks" not unlike Austen's "little bit (two Inches wide) of Ivory." What she brings as part of her services are volumes furnished from the sick chamber, stories of weakness and selfishness and impatience. A historian of private life, nurse Rooke communicates in typically female fashion as a gossip engaged in the seemingly trivial, charitable office of selling feminine handcrafts to the fashionable world. This and her gossip are, of course, a disguise for her subversive interest in uncovering the sordid realities behind the decorous appearances of high life. In this regard she is a wonderful portrait of Austen herself. While seemingly unreliable, dependent (as she is) for information upon many interactions which are subject to errors of misconception and ignorance, this uniquely female historian turns out to be accurate and revolutionary as she reveals "the manoevers of selfishness and duplicity" (II, chap. 9) of one class to another. Finally, sensible nurse Rooke also resembles Austen in that, despite all her knowledge, she does not withdraw from society. Instead, acknowledging herself a member of the community she nurses, she is a "favourer of matrimony" who has her own "flying visions" of social success (II, chap. 9). Although many of Austen's female characters seem inalterably locked inside Mr. Elton's riddle, nurse Rooke resembles the successful heroines of the author's works in making the best of this tight place.

That Austen was fascinated with the sickness of her social world, especially its effect on people excluded from a life of active exertion, is probably last illustrated through the Parker sisters in *Sanditon*, where officious Diane supervises the application of six leeches a day for ten days and the extraction of a number of teeth in order to cure her disabled sister Susan's poor health. One sister representing "activity run mad" (chap. 9), the other languishing on the sofa, the two remind us of lethargic Lady Bertram, crippled Mrs. Smith, ill Jane Fairfax, fever-stricken Marianne Dashwood, the infected Crawfords, hypochondriacal Mary Musgrove, ailing Louisa Musgrove, and pale, sickly Fanny Price. But, as nurse Rooke's healing arts imply, the diseased shrews and the dying fainters define the boundaries of the state in which Austen's most successful characters usually manage to settle. A few of her heroines do evade the culturally induced idiocy and impotence that domestic confinement and female socialization seem to breed. Neither fainting into silence nor self-destructing into verbosity, Elizabeth Bennet, Emma Woodhouse, and Anne Elliot echo their creator in their duplicitous ability to speak with the tact that saves them from suicidal somnambulism on the one hand and contaminating vulgarity on the other, as they exploit the evasions and reservations of feminine gentility.

III
How Are We Fal'n?:
Milton's Daughters

Illustration on the preceding page: *Milton and His Two Daughters*, by George Romney. From *The Poetical Works of John Milton, with a Life of the Author by William Hayley* (London, 1794).

6

Milton's Bogey: Patriarchal Poetry and Women Readers

I say that words are men and when we spell
In alphabets we deal with living things;
With feet and thighs and breasts, fierce heads, strong wings;
Material Powers, great Bridals, Heaven and Hell.
There is a menace in the tales we tell.

—Anna Hempstead Branch

Torn from your body, furbished from your rib;
I am the daughter of your skeleton,
Born of your bitter and excessive pain . . .

—Elinor Wylie

Patriarchal Poetry their origin and their history their history
patriarchal poetry their origin patriarchal poetry their history
their origin patriarchal poetry their history their origin
patriarchal poetry their history patriarchal poetry their origin
patriarchal poetry their history their origin.

—Gertrude Stein

Adam had a time, whether long or short, when he could wander
about on a fresh and peaceful earth. . . . But poor Eve found him
there, with all his claims upon her, the moment she looked into the
world. That is a grudge that woman has always had against the
Creator [so that some] young witches got everything they wanted
as in a catoptric image [and believed] that no woman should allow
herself to be possessed by any male but the devil. . . . this they got
from reading—in the orthodox witches' manner—the book of
Genesis backwards.

—Isak Dinesen

To resurrect "the dead poet who was Shakespeare's sister," Virginia
Woolf declares in *A Room of One's Own*, literate women must "look

past Milton's bogey, for no human being should shut out the view."[1]
The perfunctory reference to Milton is curiously enigmatic, for the
allusion has had no significant development,[2] and Woolf, in the midst
of her peroration, does not stop to explain it. Yet the context in which
she places this apparently mysterious bogey is highly suggestive.
Shutting out the view, Milton's bogey cuts women off from the
spaciousness of possibility, the predominantly male landscapes of
fulfillment Woolf has been describing throughout *A Room*. Worse,
locking women into "the common sitting room" that denies them
individuality, it is a murderous phantom that, if it didn't actually
kill "Judith Shakespeare," has helped to keep her dead for hundreds
of years, over and over again separating her creative spirit from "the
body which she has so often laid down."

Nevertheless, the mystery of Woolf's phrase persists. For who (or
what) *is* Milton's bogey? Not only is the phrase enigmatic, it is
ambiguous. It may refer to Milton himself, the real patriarchal
specter or—to use Harold Bloom's critical terminology—"Covering
Cherub" who blocks the view for women poets.[3] It may refer to Adam,
who is Milton's (and God's) favored creature, and therefore also a
Covering Cherub of sorts. Or it may refer to another fictitious specter,
one more bogey created by Milton: his inferior and Satanically
inspired Eve, who has also intimidated women and blocked their
view of possibilities both real and literary. That Woolf does not
definitively indicate which of these meanings she intended suggests
that the ambiguity of her phrase may have been deliberate. Certainly
other Woolfian allusions to Milton reinforce the idea that for her,
as for most other women writers, both he and the creatures of his
imagination constitute the misogynistic essence of what Gertrude
Stein called "patriarchal poetry."

As our discussion of the metaphor of literary paternity suggested,
literary women, readers and writers alike, have long been "confused"
and intimidated by the patriarchal etiology that defines a solitary
Father God as the only creator of all things, fearing that such a
cosmic Author might be the sole legitimate model for all earthly
authors. Milton's myth of origins, summarizing a long misogynistic
tradition, clearly implied this notion to the many women writers
who directly or indirectly recorded anxieties about his paradigmatic
patriarchal poetry. A minimal list of such figures would include

Margaret Cavendish, Anne Finch, Mary Shelley, Charlotte and Emily Brontë, Emily Dickinson, Elizabeth Barrett Browning, George Eliot, Christina Rossetti, H. D., and Sylvia Plath, as well as Stein, Nin, and Woolf herself. In addition, in an effort to come to terms with the institutionalized and often elaborately metaphorical misogyny Milton's epic expresses, many of these women devised their own revisionary myths and metaphors.

Mary Shelley's *Frankenstein*, for instance, is at least in part a despairingly acquiescent "misreading" of *Paradise Lost*, with Eve-Sin apparently exorcised from the story but really translated into the monster that Milton hints she is. Emily Brontë's *Wuthering Heights*, by contrast, is a radically corrective "misreading" of Milton, a kind of Blakeian Bible of Hell, with the fall from heaven to hell transformed into a fall from a realm that conventional theology would associate with "hell" (the Heights) to a place that parodies "heaven" (the Grange). Similarly, Elizabeth Barrett Browning's "A Drama of Exile," Charlotte Brontë's *Shirley*, and Christina Rossetti's "Goblin Market" all include or imply revisionary critiques of *Paradise Lost*, while George Eliot's *Middlemarch* uses Dorothea's worship of that "affable archangel" Casaubon specifically to comment upon the disastrous relationship between Milton and his daughters. And in her undaughterly rebellion against that "Papa above" whom she also called "a God of Flint" and "Burglar! Banker—Father," Emily Dickinson, as Albert Gelpi has noted, was "passionately Byronic," and therefore, as we shall see, subtly anti-Miltonic.[4] For all these women, in other words, the question of Milton's misogyny was not in any sense an academic one.[5] On the contrary, since it was only through patriarchal poetry that they learned "their origin and their history"—learned, that is, to define themselves as misogynistic theology defined them—most of these writers read Milton with painful absorption.

Considering all this, Woolf's 1918 diary entry on *Paradise Lost*, an apparently casual summary of reactions to a belated study of that poem, may well represent all female anxieties about "Milton's bogey," and is thus worth quoting in its entirety.

> Though I am not the only person in Sussex who reads Milton,
> I mean to write down my impressions of *Paradise Lost* while I

am about it. Impressions fairly well describes the sort of thing left in my mind. I have left many riddles unread. I have slipped on too easily to taste the full flavour. However I see, and agree to some extent in believing, that this full flavour is the reward of highest scholarship. I am struck by the extreme difference between this poem and any other. It lies, I think, in the sublime aloofness and impersonality of the emotion. I have never read Cowper on the sofa, but I can imagine that the sofa is a degraded substitute for *Paradise Lost*. The substance of Milton is all made of wonderful, beautiful, and masterly descriptions of angels' bodies, battles, flights, dwelling places. He deals in horror and immensity and squalor and sublimity but never in the passions of the human heart. Has any great poem ever let in so little light upon one's own joys and sorrows? I get no help in judging life; I scarcely feel that Milton lived or knew men and women; except for the peevish personalities about marriage and the woman's duties. He was the first of the masculinists, but his disparagement rises from his own ill luck and seems even a spiteful last word in his domestic quarrels. But how smooth, strong and elaborate it all is! What poetry! I can conceive that even Shakespeare after this would seem a little troubled, personal, hot and imperfect. I can conceive that this is the essence, of which almost all other poetry is the dilution. The inexpressible fineness of the style, in which shade after shade is perceptible, would alone keep one gazing into it, long after the surface business in progress has been despatched. Deep down one catches still further combinations, rejections, felicities and masteries. Moreover, though there is nothing like Lady Macbeth's terror or Hamlet's cry, no pity or sympathy or intuition, the figures are majestic; in them is summed up much of what men thought of our place in the universe, of our duty to God, our religion.[6]

Interestingly, even the diffident first sentence of this paragraph expresses an uncharacteristic humility, even nervousness, in the presence of Milton's "sublime aloofness and impersonality." By 1918 Woolf was herself an experienced, widely published literary critic, as well as the author of one accomplished novel, with another in progress. In the preceding pages she has confidently set down judgments of Christina Rossetti ("She has the natural singing power"), Byron ("He has at least the male virtues"), Sophocles' *Electra* ("It's not so fearfully difficult after all"), and a number of other serious literary subjects. Yet Milton, and Milton alone, leaves her feeling puzzled, excluded, inferior, and even a little guilty. Like Greek or metaphysics, those other bastions of intellectual masculinity, Milton is for Woolf a sort of inordinately complex algebraic equation, an insoluble problem that she feels obliged—but unable—to solve ("I have left many riddles unread"). At the same time, his *magnum opus* seems to have little or nothing to do with her own, distinctively female perception of things ("Has any great poem ever let in so little light upon one's own joys and sorrows?"). Her admiration, moreover, is cast in peculiarly vague, even abstract language ("how smooth, strong and elaborate it all is"). And her feeling that Milton's verse (not the dramas of her beloved, androgynous Shakespeare) must be "the essence of which almost all other poetry is the dilution" perhaps explains her dutiful conclusion, with its strained insistence that in the depths of Milton's verse "is summed up much of what men thought of our place in the universe, of our duty to God, our religion." Our? Surely Woolf is speaking here "as a woman," to borrow one of her own favorite phrases, and surely her conscious or unconscious statement is clear: Milton's bogey, whatever else it may be, is ultimately his cosmology, his vision of "what *men* thought" and his powerful rendering of the culture myth that Woolf, like most other literary women, sensed at the heart of Western literary patriarchy.

The story that Milton, "the first of the masculinists," most notably tells to women is of course the story of woman's secondness, her otherness, and how that otherness leads inexorably to her demonic anger, her sin, her fall, and her exclusion from that garden of the gods which is also, for her, the garden of poetry. In an extraordinarily important and yet also extraordinarily distinctive way, therefore, Milton is for women what Harold Bloom (who might here be paraphrasing Woolf) calls "the great Inhibitor, the Sphinx who strangles even strong imaginations in their cradles." In a line even more appropriate to women, Bloom adds that "the motto to English poetry since Milton was stated by Keats: 'life to him would be death to me.'"[7] And interestingly, Woolf herself echoes just this line in speaking of her father years after his death. Had Sir Leslie Stephen lived into his nineties, she remarks, "His life would have entirely ended mine. What would have happened? No writing, no books:— inconceivable."[8] For whatever Milton is to the male imagination, to the female imagination Milton and the inhibiting Father—the Patriarch of patriarchs—are one.

For Woolf, indeed, even Milton's manuscripts are dramatically associated with male hegemony and female subordination. One of the key confrontations in *A Room* occurs when she decides to consult the manuscript of *Lycidas* in the "Oxbridge" library and is forbidden entrance by an agitated male librarian

> like a guardian angel barring the way with a flutter of black gown instead of white wings, a deprecating, silvery, kindly gentleman, who regretted in a low voice as he waved me back that ladies are only admitted to the library if accompanied by a Fellow of the College or furnished with a letter of introduction.[9]

Locked away from female contamination at the heart of "Oxbridge's" paradigmatically patriarchal library—in the very heaven of libraries, so to speak—there is a Word of power, and the Word is Milton's.

Although *A Room* merely hints at the cryptic but crucial power of the Miltonic text and its misogynistic context, Woolf clearly defined Milton as a frightening "Inhibitor" in the fictional (rather than critical) uses she made or did not make of Milton throughout her literary career. Both *Orlando* and *Between the Acts*, for instance, her two most ambitious and feminist re-visions of history, appear quite deliberately to exclude Milton from their radically transformed chronicles of literary events. Hermaphroditic Orlando meets Shakespeare the enigmatic androgyne, and effeminate Alexander Pope— but John Milton simply does not exist for him/her, just as he doesn't exist for Miss La Trobe, the revisionary historian of *Between the Acts*. As Bloom notes, one of the ways in which a poet evades anxiety is to deny even the existence of the precursor poet who is the source of anxiety.

On the other hand, when Woolf does allude to Milton in a novel, as she does in *The Voyage Out*, her reference grants him his pernicious power in its entirely. Indeed, the motto of the heroine, Rachel Vinrace, might well be Keats's "Life to him would be death to me," for twenty-four-year-old Rachel, dying of some unnamed disease mysteriously related to her sexual initiation by Terence Hewet, seems to drown in waves of Miltonic verse. "Terence was reading Milton aloud, because he said the words of Milton had substance and shape, so that it was not necessary to understand what he was saying . . . [But] the words, in spite of what Terence had said, seemed to be laden with meaning, and perhaps it was for this reason that it was painful to listen to them."[10] An invocation to "Sabrina Fair," the goddess "under the glassy, cool, translucent wave," the words Terence reads from *Comus* seek the salvation of a maiden who has been turned to stone. But their effect on Rachel is very different. Heralding illness, they draw her toward a "deep pool of sticky water" murky with images derived from Woolf's own episodes of madness, and ultimately they plunge her into the darkness "at the bottom of the sea."[11] Would death to Milton, one wonders, have been life for Rachel?

Charlotte Brontë would certainly have thought so. Because Woolf was such a sophisticated literary critic, she may have been at once the most conscious and the most anxious heiress of the Miltonic culture myth. But among earlier women writers it was Brontë who seemed most aware of Milton's threatening qualities, particularly of the extent to which his influence upon women's fate might be seen as—to borrow a pun from Bloom—an unhealthy *influenza*.[12] In *Shirley* she specifically attacked the patriarchal Miltonic cosmology, within whose baleful context she saw both her female protagonists sickening, orphaned and starved by a male-dominated society. "Milton was great; but was he good?" asks Shirley Keeldar, the novel's eponymous heroine.

> [He] tried to see the first woman, but . . . he saw her not. . . .
> It was his cook that he saw; or it was Mrs. Gill, as I have seen
> her, making custards, in the heat of summer, in the cool dairy,
> with rose-trees and nasturtiums about the latticed window,
> preparing a cold collation for the rectors,—preserves, and
> "dulcet creams"—puzzled "What choice to choose for delicacy
> best."[13]

Shirley's allusion is to the passage in book 5 of *Paradise Lost* in which housewifely Eve, "on hospitable thoughts intent," serves Adam and his angelic guest an Edenic cold collation of fruits and nuts, berries and "dulcet creams." With its descriptions of mouth-watering seraphic banquets and its almost Victorian depiction of primordial domestic bliss, this scene is especially vulnerable to the sort of parodic wit Brontë has Shirley turn against it. But the alternative that Brontë and Shirley propose to Milton's Eve-as-little-woman is more serious and implies an even severer criticism of *Paradise Lost*'s visionary misogyny. The first woman, Shirley hypothesizes, was not an Eve, "half doll, half angel," and always potential fiend. Rather, she was a Titan, and a distinctively Promethean one at that:

> " . . . from her sprang Saturn, Hyperion, Oceanus; she bore Prometheus. . . . The first woman's breast that heaved with life on this world yielded the daring which could contend with Omnipotence: the strength which could bear a thousand years of bondage,—the vitality which could feed that vulture death through uncounted ages,—the unexhausted life and uncorrupted excellence, sisters to immortality, which . . . could conceive and bring forth a Messiah . . . I saw—I now see—a woman-Titan. . . . she reclines her bosom on the ridge of Stilbro' Moor; her mighty hands are joined beneath it. So kneeling, face to face she speaks with God. That Eve is Jehovah's daughter, as Adam was his son."

Like Woolf's concept of "Milton's bogey," this apparently bold vision of a titanic Eve is interestingly (and perhaps necessarily) ambiguous. It is possible, for instance, to read the passage as a comparatively conventional evocation of maternal Nature giving birth to *male* greatness. Because she "bore Prometheus," the first woman's breast nursed daring, strength, vitality. At the same time, however, the syntax here suggests that "the daring which could content with Omnipotence" and "the strength which could bear a thousand years of bondage" belonged, like the qualities they parallel —"the unexhausted life and uncorrupted excellence . . . which . . . could . . . bring forth a Messiah"—to the first woman herself. Not only did Shirley's Eve bring forth a Prometheus, then, she was herself a Prometheus, contending with Omnipotence and defying bondage.[14] Thus, where Milton's Eve is apparently submissive, except for one moment of disastrous rebellion in which she listens to the wrong voice, Shirley's is strong, assertive, vital. Where Milton's Eve is domestic, Shirley's is daring. Where Milton's Eve is from the first curiously hollow, as if somehow created corrupt, "in outward show / Elaborate, of inward less exact" (*PL* 8. 538–39) Shirley's is filled with "unexhausted life and uncorrupted excellence." Where Milton's Eve is a sort of divine afterthought, an almost superfluous and mostly material being created from Adam's "supernumerary" rib, Shirley's is spiritual, primary, "heaven-born." Finally, and perhaps most significantly, where Milton's Eve is usually excluded from God's sight and, at crucial moments in the history of Eden, drugged and silenced by divinely ordained sleep, Shirley's speaks "face to face" with God. We may even speculate that, supplanted by a servile and destructive specter, Shirley's Eve is the first avatar of that dead poet whom Woolf, in her re-vision of this myth, called Judith Shakespeare and who was herself condemned to death by Milton's bogey.

Besides having interesting descendants, Shirley's titanic woman has interesting ancestors. For instance, if she is herself a sort of Prometheus as well as Prometheus's mother, she is in a sense closer to Milton's Satan than to his Eve. Certainly "the daring which could contend with Omnipotence" and "the strength which could bear a thousand years of bondage" are qualities that recall not only the firm resolve of Shelley's Prometheus (or Byron's or Goethe's or Aeschylus's) but "the unconquerable will" Milton's fiend opposes to "The tyranny of Heav'n." Also, the gigantic size of Milton's fallen angel (" . . . in bulk as huge / As whom the Fables name of monstrous size, / *Titanian*, or *Earth-born*" [*PL* 1. 196–98]) is repeated in the enormity of Shirley's Eve. She "reclines her bosom on the ridge of Stillbro' Moor" just as Satan lies "stretched out huge in length" in book 1 of *Paradise Lost*, and just as Blake's fallen Albion (another neo-Miltonic figure) appears with his right foot "on Dover cliffs, his heel / On Canterbury ruins; his right hand [covering] lofty Wales / His left Scotland," etc.[15] But of course Milton's Satan is himself the ancestor of all the Promethean heroes conceived by the Romantic poets who influenced Brontë. And as if to acknowledge that fact, she has Shirley remark that under her Titan woman's breast "I see

her zone, purple like that horizon: through its blush shines the star
of evening"—Lucifer, the "son of the morning" and the evening
star, who is Satan in his unfallen state.

Milton's Satan transformed into a Promethean Eve may at first
sound like a rather unlikely literary development. But even the briefest
reflection on *Paradise Lost* should remind us that, despite Eve's
apparent passivity and domesticity, Milton himself seems deliberately
to have sketched so many parallels between her and Satan that it is
hard at times for the unwary reader to distinguish the sinfulness of
one from that of the other. As Stanley Fish has pointed out, for
instance, Eve's temptation speech to Adam in book 9 is "a tissue of
Satanic echoes," with its central argument "Look on me. / Do not
believe," an exact duplicate of the anti-religious empiricism embedded in Satan's earlier temptation speech to her.[16] Moreover,
where Adam falls out of uxorious "fondness," out of a self-sacrificing
love for Eve which, at least to the modern reader, seems quite noble,
Milton's Eve falls for exactly the same reason that Satan does: because
she wants to be "as Gods," and because, like him, she is secretly
dissatisfied with her place, secretly preoccupied with questions of
"equality." After *his* fall, Satan makes a pseudo-libertarian speech
to his fellow angels in which he asks, "Who can in reason then or
right assume / Monarchy over such as live by right / His equals, if
in power and splendor less, / In freedom equal?" (*PL* 5. 794–97).
After *her* fall, Eve considers the possibility of keeping the fruit to
herself "so to add what wants / In Female Sex, the more to draw
[Adam's] Love, / And render me more equal" (*PL* 9. 821–23).

Again, just as Milton's Satan—despite his pretensions to equality
with the divine—dwindles from an angel into a dreadful (though
subtle) serpent, so Eve is gradually reduced from an angelic being
to a monstrous and serpentine creature, listening sadly as Adam
thunders, "Out of my sight, thou Serpent, that name best / Befits
thee with him leagu'd, thyself as false / And hateful; nothing wants,
but that thy shape, / Like his, and colour Serpentine may show / Thy
inward fraud" (*PL* 10. 867–71) The enmity God sets between the
woman and the serpent is thus the discord necessary to divide those
who are not opposites or enemies but too much alike, too much
attracted to each other. In addition, just as Satan feeds Eve with the
forbidden fruit, so Eve—who is consistently associated with fruit,

not only as Edenic chef but also as herself the womb or bearer of fruit—feeds the fruit to Adam. And finally, just as Satan's was a fall into generation, its first consequence being the appearance of the material world of Sin and Death, so Eve's (and not Adam's) fall completes the human entry into generation, since its consequence is the pain of birth, death's necessary opposite and mirror image. And just as Satan is humbled and enslaved by his desire for the bitter fruit, so Eve is humbled by becoming a slave not only to Adam the individual man but to Adam the archetypal man, a slave not only to her husband but, as de Beauvoir notes, to the species.[17] By contrast, Adam's fall is fortunate because, among other reasons, from the woman's point of view his punishment seems almost like a reward, as he himself suggests when he remarks that "On mee the Curse aslope / Glanc'd on the ground, with labour I must earn / My bread; what harm? Idleness had been worse . . . " (*PL* 10. 1053–55).

We must remember, however, that as Milton delineates it Eve's relationship to Satan is even richer, deeper, and more complex than these few points suggest. Her bond with the fiend is strengthened not only by the striking similarities that link her to him, but also by the ways in which she resembles Sin, his female avatar and, indeed— with the exception of Urania, who is a kind of angel in the poet's head—the only other female who graces (or, rather, disgraces) *Paradise Lost*.[18] Brontë's Shirley, whose titanic Eve is reminiscent of the Promethean aspects of Milton's devil, does not appear to have noticed this relationship, even in her bitter attack upon Milton's little woman. But we can be sure that Brontë herself, like many other female readers, did—if only unconsciously—perceive the likeness. For not only is Sin female, like Eve, she is serpentine as Satan is and as Adam tells Eve *she* is. Her body, "Woman to the waist, and fair, / But [ending] foul in many a scaly fold / Voluminous and vast, a Serpent arm'd / With mortal sting" exaggerates and parodies female anatomy just as the monstrous bodies of Spenser's Error and Duessa do (*PL* 2. 650–53). Similarly, with her fairness ironically set against foulness, Sin parodies Adam's fearful sense of the tension between Eve's "outward show / Elaborate" and her "inward less exact." Moreover, just as Eve is a secondary and contingent creation, made from Adam's rib, so Sin, Satan's "Daughter," burst from the fallen angel's brain like a grotesque subversion of the Graeco-Roman story of wise

Minerva's birth from the head of Jove. In a patriarchal Christian context the pagan goddess Wisdom may, Milton suggests, become the loathesome demoness Sin, for the intelligence of heaven is made up exclusively of "Spirits Masculine," and the woman, like her dark double, Sin, is a "fair defect / Of Nature" (*PL* 10. 890–93).

If Eve's punishment, moreover, is her condemnation to the anguish of maternity, Sin is the only model of maternity other than the "wide womb of Chaos" with which *Paradise Lost* provides her, and as a model Milton's monster conveys a hideous warning of what it means to be a "slave to the species." Birthing innumerable Hell Hounds in a dreadful cycle, Sin is endlessly devoured by her children, who continually emerge from and return to her womb, where they bark and howl unseen. Their bestial sounds remind us that to bear young is to be not spiritual but animal, a *thing* of flesh, an incomprehensible and uncomprehending body, while their ceaseless suckling presages the exhaustion that leads to death, companion of birth. And Death is indeed their sibling as well as the father who has raped (and thus fused with) his mother, Sin, in order to bring this pain into being, just as "he" will meld with Eve when in eating the apple she ends up "eating Death" (*PL* 9. 792).

Of course, Sin's pride and her vulnerability to Satan's seductive wiles make her Eve's double too. It is at Satan's behest, after all, that Sin disobeys God's commandments and opens the gates of hell to let the first cause of evil loose in the world, and this act of hers is clearly analogous to Eve's disobedient eating of the apple, with its similar consequences. Like both Eve and Satan, moreover, Sin wants to be "as Gods," to reign in a "new world of light and bliss" (*PL* 2. 867), and surely it is not insignificant that her moving but blasphemous pledge of allegiance to Satan ("Thou art my Father, thou my Author, thou / My being gav'st me; whom should I obey / But thee, whom follow?" [*PL* 2. 864–66]) foreshadows Eve's most poignant speech to Adam ("But now lead on ... with thee to go, / Is to stay here; without thee here to stay, / Is to go hence unwilling; thou to mee / Art all things under Heav'n...." [*PL* 12. 614–18]), as if in some part of himself Milton meant not to instruct the reader by contrasting two modes of obedience but to undercut even Eve's "goodness" in advance. Perhaps it is for this reason that, in the grim shade of Sin's Medusa-like snakiness, Eve's beauty, too, begins (to an experienced reader of *Paradise Lost*) to seem suspect: her golden tresses waving in wanton, wandering ringlets suggest at least a sinister potential, and it hardly helps that so keen a critic as Hazlitt thought her nakedness made her luscious as a piece of fruit.[19]

Despite Milton's well-known misogyny, however, and the highly developed philosophical tradition in which it can be placed, all these connections, parallels, and doublings among Satan, Eve, and Sin are shadowy messages, embedded in the text of *Paradise Lost*, rather than carefully illuminated overt statements. Still, for sensitive female readers brought up in the bosom of a "masculinist," patristic, neo-Manichean church, the latent as well as the manifest content of such a powerful work as *Paradise Lost* was (and is) bruisingly real. To such women the unholy trinity of Satan, Sin and Eve, diabolically mimicking the holy trinity of God, Christ, and Adam,[20] must have seemed even in the eighteenth and nineteenth centuries to illustrate that historical dispossession and degradation of the female principle which was to be imaginatively analyzed in the twentieth century by Robert Graves, among others. "The new God," Graves wrote in *The White Goddess*, speaking of the rise of the Judaic-Pythagorean tradition whose culture myth Milton recounts,

> claimed to be dominant as Alpha and Omega, the Beginning and the End, pure Holiness, pure Good, pure Logic, able to exist without the aid of woman; but it was natural to identify him with one of the original rivals of the Theme [of the *White Goddess*] and to ally the woman and the other rival permanently against him. The outcome was philosophical dualism with all the tragic-comic woes attendant on spiritual dichotomy. If the True God, the God of the Logos, was pure thought, pure good, whence came evil and error? Two separate creations had to be assumed: the true spiritual Creation and the false material Creation. In terms of the heavenly bodies, Sun and Saturn were now jointly opposed to Moon, Mars, Mercury, Jupiter and Venus. The five heavenly bodies in opposition made a strong partnership, with a woman at the beginning and a woman at the end. Jupiter and the Moon Goddess paired together as the rulers of the material World, the lovers Mars and Venus paired together as the lustful Flesh, and between the pairs stood Mercury who was the Devil,

the Cosmocrator or author of the false creation. It was these five who composed the Pythagorean *hyle*, or grove, of the five material senses; and spiritually minded men, coming to regard them as sources of error, tried to rise superior to them by pure meditation. This policy was carried to extreme lengths by the Godfearing Essenes, who formed their monkish communities within compounds topped by acacia hedges, from which all women were excluded; lived ascetically, cultivated a morbid disgust for their own natural functions and turned their eyes away from World, Flesh and Devil.[21]

Milton, who offers at least lip service to the institution of matrimony, is never so intensely misogynistic as the fanatically celibate Essenes. But a similar though more disguised misogyny obviously contributes to Adam's espousal of Right Reason as a means of transcending the worldly falsehoods propounded by Eve and Satan (and by his vision of the "Bevy of fair Women" whose wiles betrayed the "Sons of God" [*PL* 11. 582, 622]). And that the Right Reason of *Paradise Lost* did have such implications was powerfully understood by William Blake, whose fallen Urizenic Milton must reunite with his female Emanation in order to cast off his fetters and achieve imaginative wholeness. Perhaps even more important for our purposes here, in the visionary epic *Milton* Blake reveals a sure grasp of the psychohistorical effects he thought Milton's misguided "chastity" had, not only upon Milton, but upon women themselves. While Milton-as-noble-bard, for instance, ponders "the intricate mazes of Providence," Blake has his "six-fold Emanation" howl and wail, "Scatter'd thro' the deep / In torment."[22] Comprised of his three wives and three daughters, this archetypal abandoned woman knows very well that Milton's anti-feminism has deadly implications for her own character as well as for her fate. "Is this our Feminine Portion," Blake has her demand despairingly. "Are we Contraries O Milton, Thou & I / O Immortal! how were we led to War the Wars of Death [?]" And, as if to describe the moral deformity such misogyny fosters in women, she explains that "Altho' our Human Power can sustain the severe contentions . . . our Sexual cannot: but flies into the [hell of] the Ulro. / Hence arose all our terrors in Eternity!"[23]

Still, although he was troubled by Milton's misogyny and was radically opposed to the Cartesian dualism Milton's vaguely Manichean cosmology anticipated, Blake did portray the author of *Paradise Lost* as the hero—the redeemer even—of the poem that bears his name. Beyond or behind Milton's bogey, the later poet saw, there was a more charismatic and congenial figure, a figure that Shirley and her author, like most other female readers, must also have perceived, judging by the ambiguous responses to Milton recorded by so many women. For though the epic voice of *Paradise Lost* often sounds censorious and "masculinist" as it recounts and comments upon Western patriarchy's central culture myth, the epic's creator often seems to display such dramatic affinities with rebels against the censorship of heaven that Romantic readers well might conclude with Blake that Milton wrote "in fetters" and "was of the devil's party without knowing it."²⁴ And so Blake, blazing a path for Shirley and for Shelley, for Byron and for Mary Shelley, and for all the Brontës, famously defined Satan as the real, burningly visionary god—the Los—of *Paradise Lost*, and "God" as the rigid and death-dealing Urizenic demon. His extraordinarily significant misreading clarifies not only the lineage of, say, Shelley's Prometheus, but also the ancestry of Shirley's titanic Eve. For if Eve is in so many negative ways like Satan the serpentine tempter, why should she not also be akin to Satan the Romantic outlaw, the character whom (Harold Bloom reminds us) T. S. Eliot considered "Milton's curly-haired Byronic hero"?²⁵

That Satan is throughout much of *Paradise Lost* a handsome devil and therefore a paradigm for the Byronic hero at his most attractive is, of course, a point frequently made by critics of all persuasions, including those less hostile than Eliot was to both Byron and Milton. Indeed, Satan's Prometheanism, the indomitable will and courage he bequeathed to characters like Shirley's Eve, almost seems to have been created to illustrate some of the crucial features of Romanticism in general. Refusing, like Shelley's Prometheus, to submit to the "tyranny of Heaven," and stalking "apart in joyless revery" like Byron's Childe Harold,²⁶ Milton's Satan is as alienated from celestial society as any of the early nineteenth-century poets *maudit* who made him their emblem. Accursed and self-cursing, paradoxical and mystical ("Which way I fly is hell; myself am Hell . . . Evil be thou my Good" [*PL* 4. 75, 110]), he experiences the guilty double consciousness, the sense of a stupendous self capable of nameless and perhaps criminal enormities, that Byron redefined in *Manfred* and *Cain* as marks of superiority. Moreover, to the extent that the tyranny of heaven is associated with Right Reason, Satan is Romantically antirational in his exploration of the secret depths of himself and of the cosmos. He is anti-rational—and Romantic—too, in his indecorous yielding to excesses of passion, his Byronic "gestures fierce" and "mad demeanor" (*PL* 4. 128–29). At the same time, his aristocratic egalitarianism, manifested in his war against the heavenly system of primogeniture that has unjustly elevated God's "Son" above even the highest angels, suggests a Byronic (and Shelleyan and Godwinian) concern with liberty and justice for all. Thunder-scarred and world-weary, this black-browed devil would not, one feels, have been out of place at Missolonghi.

Significantly, Eve is the only character in *Paradise Lost* for whom a rebellion against the hierarchical status quo is as necessary as it is for Satan. Though he is in one sense oppressed, or at least manipulated, by God, Adam is after all to his own realm what God is to His: absolute master and guardian of the patriarchal rights of primogeniture. Eve's docile speech in book 4 emphasizes this: "My Author and Disposer, what thou bidd'st / Unargu'd I obey; so God ordains, / God is thy Law, thou mine: to know no more / Is woman's happiest knowledge and her praise" (*PL* 4. 635–38). But the dream she has shortly after speaking these words to Adam (reported in book 5) seems to reveal her true feelings about the matter in its fantasy of a Satanic flight of escape from the garden and its oppressions: "Up to the Clouds . . . I flew, and underneath beheld / The Earth out-stretcht immense, a prospect wide / And various. . ." [27] (*PL* 5.86–89), a redefined prospect of happy knowledge not unlike the one Woolf imagines women viewing from their opened windows. And interestingly, brief as is the passage describing Eve's flight, it foreshadowed fantasies that would recur frequently and compellingly in the writings of both women and Romantic poets. Byron's Cain, for instance, disenchanted by what his author called the "politics of paradise," [28] flies through space with his seductive Lucifer like a masculine version of Milton's Eve, and though Shirley's Eve is earthbound—almost earthlike—innumerable other "Eves" of female origin have flown, fallen, surfaced, or feared to fly, as if to acknowledge in a backhanded sort of way the power of the dream Milton let Satan grant to Eve. But whether female dreams of flying escapes are derived from Miltonic or Romantic ideas, or from some collective female unconscious, is a difficult question to answer. For the connections between Satan, Romanticism, and concealed or incipient feminism are intricate and far-reaching indeed.

Certainly, if both Satan and Eve are in some sense alienated, rebellious, and therefore Byronic figures, the same is true for women writers as a class—for Shirley's creator as well as for Shirley, for Virginia Woolf as well as for "Judith Shakespeare." Dispossessed by her older brothers—the "Sons of God"—educated to submission, enjoined to silence, the woman writer, in fantasy if not in reality, must often have "stalked apart in joyless revery," like Byron's heroes, like Satan, like Prometheus. Feeling keenly the discrepancy between the angel she was supposed to be and the angry demon she knew she often was, she must have experienced the same paradoxical double consciousness of guilt and greatness that afflicts both Satan and, say, Manfred. Composing herself to saintly stillness, brooding narcissistically like Eve over her own image and like Satan over her own power, she may even have feared occasionally that like Satan—or Byron's Lara, or his Manfred—she would betray her secret fury by "gestures fierce" or a "mad demeanor." Asleep in the bower of domesticity, she would be unable to silence the Romantic/Satanic whisper— "Why sleepst thou Eve?"—with its invitation to join the visionary world of those who fly by night.

Again, though Milton goes to great lengths to associate Adam, God, Christ, and the angels with visionary prophetic powers, that visionary night-world of poetry and imagination, insofar as it is a *demonic* world, is more often subtly associated in *Paradise Lost* with Eve, Satan, and femaleness than with any of the "good" characters except the epic speaker himself. Blake, of course, saw this quite clearly. It is the main reason for the Satan-God role reversal he postulates. But his friend Mary Wollstonecraft and her Romantic female descendants must have seen it too, just as Byron and Shelley did. For though Adam is magically shown, as in a crystal ball, what the future holds, Satan and Eve are both the real dreamers of *Paradise Lost*, possessed in the Romantic sense by seductive reflections and uncontrollable imaginings of alternative lives to the point where, like Manfred or Christabel or the Keats of *The Fall of Hyperion*, they are so scorched by visionary longings they become fevers of themselves, to echo Moneta's words to Keats. But even this suffering sense of the hellish discrepancy between Satan's (or Eve's) aspiration and position is a model of aesthetic nobility to the Romantic poet and the Romantically inspired feminist. Contemplating the "lovely pair" of Adam and Eve in their cosily unfallen state, Mary Wollstonecraft confesses that she feels "an emotion similar to what we feel when children are playing or animals sporting," and on such occasions "I have, with conscious dignity, or Satanic pride, turned to hell for sublimer subjects." [29] Her deliberate, ironic confusion of "conscious dignity" and "Satanic pride," together with her reverence for the "sublime," prefigure Shelley's Titan as clearly as Shirley's titanic woman. The imagining of more "sublime" alternative lives, moreover, as Blake and Wollstonecraft also saw, reinforces the revolutionary fervor that Satan the visionary poet, like Satan the aristocratic Byronic rebel, defined for women and Romantics alike.

That the Romantic aesthetic has often been linked with visionary politics is, of course, almost a truism. From the apocalyptic revolutions of Blake and Shelley to those of Yeats and D. H. Lawrence, moreover, re-visions of the Miltonic culture myth have been associated with such repudiations of the conservative, hierarchical "politics of paradise." "In terrible majesty," Blake's Satanic Milton thunders, "Obey thou the words of the Inspired Man. / All that can be annihilated must be annihilated / That the children of Jerusalem may be saved from slavery." [30] Like him, Byron's Lucifer offers autonomy and knowledge —the prerequisites of freedom—to Cain, while Shelley's Prometheus, overthrowing the tyranny of heaven, ushers in "Life, Joy, Empire, and Victory" for all of humanity. [31] Even D. H. Lawrence's Satanic snake, emerging one hundred years later from the hellishly burning bowels of the earth, seems to be "one of the lords / Of life," an exiled king "now due to be crowned again," signalling a reborn society. [32] For in the revolutionary cosmologies of all these Romantic poets, both Satan and his other self, Lucifer ("son of the morning"), were emblematic of that liberated dawn in which it *would* be bliss to be alive.

It is not surprising, then, that women, identifying at their most rebellious with Satan, at their least with rebellious Eve, and almost all the time with the Romantic poets, should have been similarly obsessed with the apocalyptic social transformations a revision of Milton might bring about. Mary Wollstonecraft, whose *A Vindication of the Rights of Woman* often reads like an outraged commentary on *Paradise Lost*, combined a Blakeian enthusiasm for the French Revolution—at least in its early days—with her "pre-Romantic" reverence for the Satanic sublime and her feminist anger at Milton's misogyny. But complicated as it was, that complex of interrelated feelings was not hers alone. For not only have feminism and Romantic radicalism been consciously associated in the minds of many women writers, Byronically (and Satanically) rebellious visionary politics have often been used by women as metaphorical disguises for sexual politics. Thus in *Shirley* Brontë not only creates an anti-Miltonic Eve, she also uses the revolutionary anger of the frame-breaking workers with whom the novel is crucially concerned as an image for the fury of its dispossessed heroines. Similarly, as Ellen Moers has noted, English-women's factory novels (like Gaskell's *Mary Barton*) and American women's anti-slavery novels (like Stowe's *Uncle Tom's Cabin*) sub-merged or disguised "private, brooding, female resentment" in ostensibly disinterested examinations of larger public issues.[33] More recently, even Virginia Woolf's angrily feminist *Three Guineas* purports to have begun not primarily as a consideration of the woman question but as an almost Shelleyan dream of transforming the world—abolishing war, tyranny, ignorance, etc.—through the formation of a female "Society of Outsiders."

But of course such a society would be curiously Satanic, since in the politics of paradise the Prince of Darkness was literally the first Outsider. Even if Woolf herself did not see far enough past Milton's bogey to recognize this, a number of other women, both feminists and anti-feminists, did. In late nineteenth-century America, for instance, a well-known journal of Romantically radical politics and feminism was called *Lucifer the Light-bearer*, and in Victorian England Mrs. Rigby wrote of Charlotte Brontë's Byronic and feminist *Jane Eyre* that "the tone of mind and thought which has overthrown authority and violated every code human and divine abroad, and fostered Chartism and rebellion at home"—in other words, a Byronic,

Promethean, Satanic, and Jacobin tone of mind—"is the same which has also written *Jane Eyre*."[34]

Paradoxically, however, Brontë herself may have been less conscious of the extraordinary complex of visionary and revisionary impulses that went into *Jane Eyre* than Mrs. Rigby was, at least in part because, like many other women, she found her own anger and its intellectual consequences almost too painful to confront. Commenting on the so-called condition of women question, she told Mrs. Gaskell that there are "evils—deep-rooted in the foundation of the social system—which no efforts of ours can touch; of which we cannot complain: of which it is advisable not too often to think." Like Mary Elizabeth Coleridge, she evidently had moments in which she saw "no friend in God—in Satan's host no foes."[35] Still, despite her refusal to "complain," Brontë's unwillingness to think of social inequities was more likely a function of her anxiety about her own rebelliously Satanic impulses than a sign of blind resignation to what Yeats called "the injustice of the skies."[36]

The relationship between women writers and Milton's curly-haired Byronic hero is, however, even more complicated than we have so far suggested. And in the intricate tangle of this relationship resides still another reason for the refusal of writers like Brontë consciously to confront their obsessive interest in the impulses incarnated in the villain of *Paradise Lost*. For not only is Milton's Satan in certain crucial ways very much *like* women, he is also (as we saw in connection with Austen's glamorously Satanic anti-heroes) enormously attractive to women. Indeed, both Eliot's phrase and Byron's biography imply that he is in most ways the incarnation of worldly male sexuality, fierce, powerful, experienced, simultaneously brutal and seductive, devilish enough to overwhelm the body and yet enough a fallen angel to charm the soul. As such, however, in his relations with women he is a sort of Nietzschean *Übermensch*, giving orders and expecting homage to his "natural"—that is, masculine—superiority, as if he were God's shadow self, the id of heaven, Satanically reduplicating the politics of paradise wherever he goes. And yet, wherever he goes, women follow him, even when they refuse to follow the God whose domination he parodies. As Sylvia Plath so famously noted, "Every woman adores a Fascist, / The boot in the face, the brute / Brute heart of a brute like you." Speaking of "Daddy," Plath was of course speaking also of Satan, "a man in black with a Mein Kampf look."[37] And the masochistic phenomenon she described helps explain the unspeakable, even unthinkable sense of sin that also caused women like Woolf and Brontë to avert their eyes from their own Satanic impulses. For if Eve is Sin's as well as Satan's double, then Satan is to Eve what he is to Sin—both a lover and a daddy.

That the Romantic fascination with incest derived in part from Milton's portrayal of the Sin-Satan relationship may be true but is in a sense beside the point here. That both women and Romantic poets must have found at least an analog for their relationship to each other in Satan's incestuous affair with Sin is, however, very much to the point. Admiring, even adoring, Satan's Byronic rebelliousness, his scorn of conventional virtues, his raging energy, the woman writer may have secretly fantasized that she *was* Satan— or Cain, or Manfred, or Prometheus. But at the same time her feelings of female powerlessness manifested themselves in her conviction that the closest she could really get to being Satan was to be his creature, his tool, the witchlike daughter/mistress who sits at his right hand. Leslie Marchand recounts a revealing anecdote about Mary Shelley's stepsister, Claire Clairmont, that brilliantly illuminates this movement from self-assertive identification to masochistic self-denial. Begging Byron to criticize her half-finished novel, rebellious Claire (who was later to follow the poet to Geneva and bear his daughter Allegra) is said to have explained that he *must* read the manuscript because "the creator ought not to destroy his creature."[38]

Despite Brontë's vision of a Promethean Eve, even her *Shirley* betrays a similar sense of the difficulty of direct identification with the assertive Satanic principle, and the need for women to accept their own instrumentality, for her first ecstatic description of an active, indomitable Eve is followed by a more chastened story. In this second parable, the "first woman" passively wanders alone in an alienating landscape, wondering whether she is "thus to burn out and perish, her living light doing no good, never seen, never needed" even though "the flame of her intelligence burn[s] so vivid" and "something within her stir[s] disquieted." Instead of coming from that Promethean fire within her, however, as the first Eve's salvation implicitly did, this Eva's redemption comes through a Byronic/Satanic god of the Night called "Genius," who claims her, a "lost atom of life," as his bride. "I take from thy vision, darkness . . . I, with my presence, fill vacancy," he declares, explaining that "Unhumbled, I can take what is mine. Did I not give from the altar the very flame which lit Eva's being?"[39] Superficially, this allegorical narrative may be seen as a woman's attempt to imagine a male muse with whom she can have a sexual interaction that will parallel the male poet's congress with his female muse. But the incestuous Byronic love story in which Brontë embodies her allegorical message is more significant here than the message itself.

It suggests to begin with that, like Claire Clairemont, Brontë may have seen herself as at best a creation of male "Genius"—whether artwork or daughter is left deliberately vague—and therefore a being ultimately lacking in autonomy. Finding her ideas astonishingly close to those of an admired male (Byron, Satan, "Genius"), and accustomed to assuming that male thought is the source of all female thinking just as Adam's rib is the source of Eve's body, she supposes that he has, as it were, invented her. In addition, her autonomy is further denied even by the incestuous coupling which appears to link her to her creator and to make them equals. For, as Helene Moglen notes, the devouring ego of the Satanic-Byronic hero found the fantasy (or reality) of incest the best strategy for metaphorically annihilating the otherness—the autonomy—of the female. "In his union with [his half-sister] Augusta Leigh," Moglen points out, "Byron was in fact striving to achieve union with himself," just as Manfred expresses his solipsistic self-absorption by indulging his forbidden passion for his sister, Astarte. Similarly, the enormity of Satan's ego is manifested in the sexual cycle of his solipsistic production and reproduction of himself first as Sin and later as Death. Like Byron, he seems to be "attempting to become purely self-dependent by possessing his past in his present, affirming a more complete identity by enveloping and containing his other, complementary self. But, as Moglen goes on to remark, "to incorporate 'the other' is also after all to negate it. No space remains for the female. She can either allow herself to be devoured or she can retreat into isolation."[40]

It is not insignificant, then, that the fruit of Satan's solipsistic union with Sin is Death, just as death is the fruit of Manfred's love for

Astarte and ultimately—as we shall see—of all the incestuous neo-Satanic couplings envisioned by women writers from Mary Shelley to Sylvia Plath. To the extent that the desire to violate the incest taboo is a desire to be self-sufficient—self-begetting—it is a divinely interdicted wish to be "as Gods," like the desire for the forbidden fruit of the tree of knowledge, whose taste also meant death. For the woman writer, moreover, even the reflection that the Byronic hero is as much a creature of her mind—an incarnation of her "private, brooding, female resentments"—as she is an invention of his, offers little solace. For if in loving her he loves himself, in loving him she loves herself, and is therefore similarly condemned to the death of the soul that punishes solipsism.

But of course such a death of the soul is implied in any case by Satan's conception of his unholy creatures: Sin, Death, and Eve. As a figure of the heavenly interloper who plays the part of false "cosmocrator" in the dualistic patriarchal cosmology Milton inherited from Christian tradition, Satan is in fact a sort of artist of death, the paradigmatic master of all those perverse aesthetic techniques that pleasure the body rather than the soul, and serve the world rather than God. From the golden palace he erects at Pandemonium to his angelic impersonations in the garden and the devilish machines he engineers as part of his war against God, he practices false, fleshly, death-devoted arts (though a few of them are very much the kinds of arts a Romantic sensualist like Keats sometimes admired). As if following Milton even here, Byron makes the Satanic Manfred similarly the master of false, diabolical arts. And defining herself as the "creature" of one or the other of these irreligious artists, the woman writer would be confirmed not only in her sense that she was part of the "effeminate slackness" of the "false creation" but also in her fear that she was herself a false creator, one of the seductive "bevy of fair women" for whom the arts of language, like those of dance and music, are techniques "Bred only . . . to the taste / Of lustful appetance," sinister parodies of the language of the angels and the music of the spheres (*PL* 11. 618–19). In the shadow of such a fear, even her housewifely arts would begin, like Eve's cookery—her choosing of delicacies "so contriv'd as not to mix / Tastes" (*PL* 5. 334–35)—to seem suspect, while the poetry she conceived might well appear to be a monster birth, like Satan's horrible child Death. Fallen like Anne Finch into domesticity, into the "dull mannage of a servile house"[41] as well as into the slavery of generation, she would not even have the satisfaction Manfred has of dying nobly. Rather, dwindling by degrees into an infertile drone, she might well conclude that this image of Satan and Eve as the false artists of creation was finally the most demeaning and discouraging avatar of Milton's bogey.

What would have made her perception of this last bogey even more galling, of course, would have been the magisterial calm with which Milton, as the epic speaker of *Paradise Lost*, continually calls attention to his own art, for the express purpose, so it seems, of defining himself throughout the poem as a type of the true artist, the virtuous poet who, rather than merely delighting (like Eve and Satan), delights while instructing. A prophet or priestly bard and therefore a guardian of the sacred mysteries of patriarchy, he serenely proposes to justify the ways of God to men, calls upon subservient female muses for the assistance that is his due (and in real life upon slavish daughters for the same sort of assistance), and at the same time wars upon women with a barrage of angry words, just as God wars upon Satan. Indeed, as a figure of the true artist, God's emissary and defender on earth, Milton himself, as he appears in *Paradise Lost*, might well have seemed to female readers to be as much akin to God as they themselves were to Satan, Eve, or Sin.

Like God, for instance, Milton-as-epic-speaker creates heaven and earth (or their verbal equivalents) out of a bewildering chaos of history, legend, and philosophy. Like God, he has mental powers that penetrate to the furthest corners of the cosmos he has created, to the depths of hell and the heights of heaven, soaring with "no middle flight" toward ontological subjects "unattempted yet in Prose or Rhyme" (*PL* 1. 16). Like God, too, he knows the consequence of every action and event, his comments upon them indicating an almost divine consciousness of the simultaneity of past, present, and future. Like God, he punishes Satan, rebukes Adam and Eve, moves angels from one battle station to another, and grants all mankind glimpses of apocalyptic futurity, when a "greater Man" shall arrive to restore Paradisal bliss. And like God—like the Redeemer, like the Creator, like the Holy Ghost—he is male. Indeed, as a male poet justifying the ways of a male deity to male readers he rigorously excludes all females from the heaven of his poem, except insofar as he can beget new ideas upon their chaotic fecundity, like the Holy Spirit "brooding on the vast Abyss" and making it pregnant (*PL* 1. 21–22).

Even the blindness to which this epic speaker occasionally refers makes him appear godlike rather than handicapped. Cutting him off from "the cheerful ways" of ordinary mortals and reducing Satan's and Eve's domain of material nature to "a universal blanc," it elevates him above trivial fleshly concerns and causes "Celestial light" to "shine inward" upon him so that, like Tiresias, Homer, and God, he may see the mysteries of the spiritual world and "tell / Of things invisible to mortal sight" (*PL* 3. 55). And finally, even the syntax in which he speaks of these "things invisible" seems somehow godlike. Certainly the imposition of a Latinate sentence structure on English suggests both supreme confidence and supreme power. *Paradise Lost* is the "most remarkable Production of the world," Keats dryly decided in one of his more anti-Miltonic moments, because of the way its author forced a "northern dialect" to accommodate itself "to greek and latin inversions and intonations."[42] But not only are Greek and Latin the quintessential languages of masculine scholarship (as Virginia Woolf, for instance, never tired of noting), they are also the languages of the Church, of patristic and patriarchal ritual and theology. Imposed upon English, moreover, their periodic sentences, perhaps more than any other stylistic device in *Paradise Lost*, flaunt the poet's divine foreknowledge. When Milton begins a sentence "Him the Almighty" the reader knows perfectly well that only the poet and God know how the sentence—like the verse, the book, and the epic of humanity itself—will come out in the end.

That the Romantics perceived, admired, and occasionally identified with Milton's bardlike godliness while at the same time identifying with Satan's Promethean energy and fortitude is one of the more understandable paradoxes of literary history. Though they might sometimes have been irreligious and radically visionary with Satan, poets like Wordsworth and Shelley were after all fundamentally "masculinist" with Milton, even if they revered Mary Wollstonecraft (as Shelley did) or praised Anne Finch (as Wordsworth did). In this respect, their metaphors for the poet and "his" art are as revealing as Milton's. Both Wordsworth and (as we have seen) Shelley conceive of the poet as a divine ruler, an "unacknowledged legislator" in Shelley's famous phrase and "an upholder and preserver" in Wordsworth's more conservative words. As such a ruler, a sort of inspired patriarch, he is, like Milton, the guardian and hierophant of sacred mysteries, inalterably opposed to the "idleness and unmanly despair" of the false, effeminate creation. More, he is a virile trumpet that calls mankind to battle, a fiercely phallic sword that consumes its scabbard, and—most Miltonic of all—a godlike "influence which is moved not, but moves," modeled upon Aristotle's Unmoved Mover.[43]

No wonder then that, as Joseph Wittreich puts it, the author of *Paradise Lost* was "the quintessence of everything the Romantics most admired . . . the Knower moved by truth alone, the Doer . . . causing divine deeds to issue forth from divine ideas, the Sayer who translates the divine idea into poetry. . . . Thus to know Milton was to know the answers to the indistinguishable questions—What is a poet? What is poetry?"[44] Virginia Woolf, living in a world where the dead female poet who was "Judith Shakespeare" had laid aside her body so many times, made the same point in different words: "This is the essence of which almost all other poetry is the dilution." Such an assertion might seem jubilant if made by a man. But the protean shadow of Milton's bogey seems to darken the page as Woolf writes.

7 Horror's Twin:
Mary Shelley's Monstrous Eve

The nature of a Female Space is this: it shrinks the Organs
Of Life till they become Finite & Itself seems Infinite
And Satan vibrated in the immensity of the Space! Limited
To those without but Infinite to those within . . .
—William Blake

The woman writes as if the Devil was in her; and that is the only
condition under which a woman ever writes anything worth reading.
—Nathaniel Hawthorne, on Fanny Fern

I probed Retrieveless things
My Duplicate—to borrow—
A Haggard Comfort springs

From the belief that Somewhere—
Within the Clutch of Thought—
There dwells one other Creature
Of Heavenly Love—forgot—

I plucked at our Partition
As One should pry the Walls—
Between Himself—and Horror's Twin—
Within Opposing Cells—
—Emily Dickinson

What was the effect upon women writers of that complex of culture
myths summarized by Woolf as Milton's bogey? Surrounded by
"patriarchal poetry," what strategies for artistic survival were they
able to develop? The comments of writers like Brontë, Woolf, and
Wollstonecraft show that intelligent women were keenly conscious
of the problems Milton posed. But they were dizzied by them, too,

for the secret messages of *Paradise Lost* enclosed the poem's female readers like a roomful of distorting mirrors. Keats's wondering remark—"Whose head is not dizzy at the possibly [*sic*] speculations of Satan in the serpent prison"[1]—seems to apply with even greater force to women, imprisoned in the coil of serpentine images that misogynistic myths and traditions constructed for them. On the surface, however, many women writers responded equably, even docilely to Milton and all he represented. Certainly the following dialogue from *Middlemarch* seems to suggest a dutiful and submissive attitude toward patriarchal poetry:

> "Could I not be preparing myself now to be more useful?" said Dorothea to [Casaubon], one morning, early in the time of courtship; "could I not learn to read Latin and Greek aloud to you, as Milton's daughters did to their father, without under-standing what they read?"
>
> "I fear that would be wearisome to you," said Mr. Casaubon smiling; "and, indeed, if I remember rightly, the young women you have mentioned regarded that exercise in unknown tongues as a ground for rebellion against the poet."
>
> "Yes; but in the first place they were very naughty girls, else they would have been proud to minister to such a father; and in the second place they might have studied privately and taught themselves to understand what they read, and then it would have been interesting. I hope you don't expect me to be naughty and stupid?"[2]

Usefulness, reading aloud, "ministering" to a wise father—all these terms and notions reinforce Milton's concept of woman as at best a serviceable second, a penitent Eve bearing children or pruning branches under Adam's thoughtful guidance. Offering herself with "ardent submissive affection" as helpmate to paternal Casaubon, Dorothea Brooke appears as nobly free of Satanic aspirations as George Eliot herself must have wished to be. A closer look at this passage and at its context, however, transforms this interpretation, revealing that with characteristic irony Eliot has found a way of having submissive Dorothea intend, among other things, the very opposite of what she says to Casaubon. Indeed, even the passage's concern with Milton as father (rather than with, say, Milton as politician or Milton as bard) tends paradoxically to sap the strength of the patriarchal associations that accrue around the name "Milton."

To take the last point first, paintings of Milton dictating to his daughters were quite popular at the end of the eighteenth century and throughout the nineteenth. One of Keats's first acts on moving into new lodgings, for instance, was to unpack his books and pin up "Haydon—Mary Queen [of] Scotts, and Milton with his daughters in a row."[3] Representing virtuous young ladies angelically ministering to their powerful father, the picture would seem to hold a mirror up to the nature of one of Western culture's fondest fantasies. At the same time, however, from a female point of view—as the *Middlemarch* passage suggests—the image of the Miltonic father *being ministered to* hints that his powers are not quite absolute, that in fact he has been reduced to a state of dependence upon his female descendents. Blinded, needing tea and sympathy as well as secretarial help, the godlike bard loses at least some of his divinity and is humanized, even (to coin a term) Samsonized. Thus, just as Charlotte Brontë implies that Jane Eyre leading blinded Rochester through the grounds of his own rural seat has found a rather Delilah-ish way of making herself not only useful to him but equal to him, so Eliot, working in the same iconographic tradition, implies that Dorothea secretly desires to make herself the equal of a Romantically weakened Casaubon: "it was not entirely out of devotion to her future husband that she wished to know Latin and Greek. . . . she had not reached that point of renunciation at which she would have been satisfied with having a wise husband: she wished, poor child, to be wise herself."[4]

But this unspoken wish to be as wise as a wise (though weak-eyed) husband is not only made possible by the dramatic situation of Milton and his daughters, it is expressed by Dorothea herself even when she seems merely to be stating her "ardent submissive affection," and it is clarified by Eliot in other passages. Milton's "naughty" daughters, Dorothea says, should have been "proud to minister to such a father." Not to "their" father, not to *any* father, but to a special father whose wisdom they might imbibe from close daily contact, as she herself hopes to imbibe Casaubon's learning. More important, she speculates that "they might have studied privately and taught themselves to understand what they read, and then it

would have been interesting." They might, in other words, have
refused to accept their secondary position, might have made themselves their father's equals in knowledge, might—like Dorothea—
have wished to be wise themselves.

To the extent, however, that Dorothea's wish to be wise is not
only a wish to be equal to her husband but also a wish to penetrate
those forbidden "provinces of masculine knowledge . . . from which
all truth could be seen more truly," it is a longing for intellectual
self-reliance that parodies the Satanic. More, such a wish obviously
subverts the self-effacing rhetoric in which it is couched ("Could
I not be preparing myself now to be more useful?"), making it
possible to impute to Dorothea—of all people—a sort of Satanic
deviousness. And in fact, though any deviousness on her part is
largely unconscious, her Satanic aspirations for power and wisdom
as well as her Eve-like curiosity (itself a function of the Satanic) are
clearly if guardedly defined in several places. Her desire "to arrive
at the core of things," for instance, though ostensibly the result of a
docile wish to "judge soundly on the duties of a Christian," is inextricably bound up with her ambitious plan to renovate her society
by designing new housing for the poor. But "how could she be
confident that one-room cottages were not for the glory of God,"
asks Eliot dryly, "when men who knew the classics appeared to
conciliate indifference to the cottagers with zeal for the glory?
Perhaps even Hebrew might be necessary," she notes, "at least the
alphabet and a few roots—in order to arrive at the core of things"
—and in order, by implication, to defeat the arguments of learned
men on their own terms.[5]

In an earlier passage, in which Dorothea considers together the
problems of education and architecture, Eliot makes the nature
and intensity of her ambition even clearer. Indeed, in its expression
of a will to be "as Gods" this passage seems almost like a direct prose
translation of Eve's musings in Book 9 of *Paradise Lost*.

> "I should learn everything then [married to Casaubon]," she
> said to herself. . . . "It would be my duty to study that I might
> help him the better in his great works. There would be nothing
> trivial about out lives. Everyday things with us would mean the
> greatest things. . . . I should learn to see the truth by the same

> light as great men have seen it by. . . . I should see how it was
> possible to lead a grand life here—now—in England"[6]

Though this Eve may not yet have eaten the apple, her desire to be
both "good" and "wise," together with her longing for "a grand
life here—now," suggest that she may soon succumb to a passion
for such "intellectual food." That the food is also associated in her
mind with freedom makes the point most strongly of all. When
Dorothea fantasizes about the benefits of a marriage with Casaubon,
Eliot remarks that "the union which attracted her was one that
would deliver her from her girlish subjection to her own ignorance,
and give her the freedom of voluntary submission to a guide who
would take her along the grandest path."[7] For clearly this aspiring
scholar imagines Casaubon a connubial guide to whom secret studies
would soon make her equal, "for inferior who is free?"

Interestingly, as a guide along the grandest path Casaubon seems
at first more archangel than Adam, and even more idealized Milton
than archangel. Certainly Eliot's epigraph to chapter 3 of *Middlemarch*
("Say, goddess, what ensued, when Raphael, / The affable . . . ")
portrays the guide of Dorothea's dreams as affable archangel,
heavenly narrator, "winged messenger," and Dorothea herself as
an admiring Eve waiting to be instructed, while other passages
show him metamorphosing into a sort of God: "he thinks a whole
world of which my thought is but a poor two penny mirror."[8] And
as both instructing angel and Godlike master of the masculine
intellectual spheres, this dream-Casaubon would come close, as
Dorothea's daughterly speech implies, to being a sort of reincarnated
Milton.

Behind the dream-Casaubon, however, lurks the real Casaubon,
a point Eliot's irony stresses from the scholar's first appearance in
Middlemarch, just as—the Miltonic parallels continually invite us
to make this connection—the "real" Milton dwelt behind the carefully constructed dream image of the celestial bard. Indeed, Eliot's
real Casaubon, as opposed to Dorothea's idealized Casaubon, is in
certain respects closer to the real author of *Paradise Lost* than his
dream image is to the Miltonic epic speaker. Like Milton, after all,
Casaubon is a master of the classics and theology, those "provinces
of masculine knowledge . . . from which all truth could be seen more

truly." Like Milton's, too, his intellectual ambition is vast, ontological, almost overweening. In a sense, in fact, Casaubon's ambition
is identical with Milton's, for just as Milton's aim was to justify the
ways of God to man by learnedly retelling the central myth of
Western culture, so Casaubon's goal is to "reconcile complete knowledge with devoted piety" by producing a "key to all mythologies."[9]
It is not at all unreasonable of Dorothea, therefore, to hope that as
a dutiful daughter-wife-pupil she might be to Casaubon as Milton's
daughters were to Milton, and that her virtuous example would
criticize, by implication, the vices of her seventeenth-century precursors.

If the passionate reality of Dorothea comments upon the negative
history of Milton's daughters, however, the dull reality of Casaubon
comments even more forcefully upon history's images of Milton. For
Casaubon as the forger of a key to all myths is of course a ludicrous
caricature of Milton as sublime justifier of sublimity. Bonily self-
righteous, pedantic, humorless, he dwindles in the course of *Middlemarch* from heavenly scholar to tiresome Dryasdust to willful corpse
oppressing Dorothea even from beyond the grave, and in his carefully
articulated dissolution he is more like Milton's Satan, minus the
Byronic glamour, than he is like Milton. But his repudiation of the
guilty flesh, his barely disguised contempt for Dorothea's femininity,
his tyranny, and his dogmatism make him the parodic shadow of
the Miltonic misogynist and (at the same time) an early version of
Virginia Woolf's red-faced, ferocious "Professor von X. engaged
in writing his monumental work entitled *The Mental, Moral, and
Physical Inferiority of the Female Sex.*"[10] Uneasily wed to such a man,
ambitious Dorothea inevitably metamorphoses into the archetypal
wretched woman Blake characterized as Milton's wailing six-fold
Emanation, his three wives and three daughters gathered into a
single grieving shape. That she herself had defined the paradigm of
Milton's daughters more hopefully is no doubt an irony Eliot fully
intended.

If the story of Milton's daughters was so useful to both Eliot and
her protagonist, ambiguous iconography and all, it is even more
useful now for critics seeking to understand the relationship between

women and the cluster of misogynistic themes Milton's work brought
together so brilliantly. Since the appearance of *Paradise Lost*—even,
in a sense, before—all women writers have been to some extent
Milton's daughters, continually wondering what their relationship
to his patriarchal poetry ought to be and continually brooding upon
alternative modes of daughterhood very much like those Dorothea
describes. Margaret of Newcastle, for instance, seems to be trying
to explain Milton's cosmos to herself in the following passage:

> . . . although nature has not made women so strong of body and
> so clear of understanding as the ablest of men, yet she has made
> them fairer, softer, slenderer. . . . [and] has laid in tender affec-
> tions, as love, piety, charity, clemency, patience, humility, and
> the like, which makes them nearest to resemble angels, which
> are the most perfect of all her works, where men by their
> ambitions, extortion, fury, and cruelty resemble the devil. But
> some women are like devils too when they are possessed with
> those evils, and the best of men . . . are like to gods.[11]

Similarly, Anne Finch's "How are we fal'n, fal'n by mistaken rules, /
And Education's more than Nature's fools?" defines the Miltonic
problem of the fall as a specifically female dilemma.[12] And the
Elizabethan "Jane Anger," like Milton's "naughty" daughters, in-
veighs against the patriarchal oppression of a proto-Miltonic cosmology in which "the gods, knowing that the minds of mankind
would be aspiring, and having thoroughly viewed the wonderful
virtues wherewith women are enriched, least they should provoke
us to pride, and so confound us with Lucifer, they bestowed the
supremacy over us to man."[13] Even before Milton had thought about
women, it seems, women had thought of Milton.

Following the rise of Romanticism, however, with its simultaneous
canonization of Milton *and* Satan, women writers have been undeniably Milton's daughters. More important, they have even more
obviously claimed for themselves precisely the options Eliot has
Dorothea explain to Casaubon: on the one hand, the option of
apparently docile submission to male myths, of being "proud to
minister to such a father," and on the other hand the option of secret
study aimed toward the achievement of equality. In a large, metaphorical sense, these two courses of action probably define categories

in which almost all writing by women can be subsumed. More narrowly—but still metaphorically—these two alternative patterns describe the main critical responses nineteenth- and twentieth-century women writers have made specifically to their readings, or misreadings, of *Paradise Lost*.

We shall argue here that the first alternative is the one Mary Shelley chooses in *Frankenstein*: to take the male culture myth of *Paradise Lost* at its full value—on its own terms, including all the analogies and parallels it implies—*and rewrite it so as to clarify its meaning*. The way of Milton's more ardently submissive daughters, it is the choice of the woman writer who, like Dorothea, strives to minister to such a father by understanding exactly what he is telling her about herself and what, therefore, he wants of her. But again, like Dorothea's ministrations, this apparently docile way of coping with Miltonic misogyny may conceal fantasies of equality that occasionally erupt in monstrous images of rage, as we shall see in considering *Frankenstein*.

Such guarded fury comes closer (though not completely) to the surface in the writing of women who choose the second alternative of Milton's daughters, the alternative of *rewriting Paradise Lost so as to make it a more accurate mirror of female experience*. This way of coping with Miltonic patriarchy is the modus operandi chosen by, for instance, Emily Brontë (in *Wuthering Heights* and elsewhere), and it is the way of the imaginary daughter who studies Greek and Latin in secret—the woman, that is, who teaches herself the language of myth, the tongue of power, so that she can reinvent herself and her own experience while seeming innocently to read to her illustrious father. We shall see that, resolutely closing their Goethe, these women often passionately reopen their Byron, using Romantic modes and manners to enact subversively feminist reinterpretations of *Paradise Lost*. Thus, though the woman writer who chooses this means of coping with her difficult heritage may express her anger more openly, she too produces a palimpsestic or encoded artwork, concealing female secrets within male-devised genres and conventions. Not only *Wuthering Heights* but more recently such female—even feminist—myths as Christina Rossetti's "Goblin Market," Virginia Woolf's *Orlando*, and Sylvia Plath's *Ariel* are works by women who have chosen this alternative. But of course the connection of such re-visions of *Paradise Lost* to the patriarchal poetry that fathered them becomes increasingly

figurative in the twentieth century, an era whose women have had
an unusually developed female tradition from which they can draw
strength in their secret study of Milton's language. It is in earlier,
lonelier works, in novels like *Frankenstein* and *Wuthering Heights*, that
we can see the female imagination expressing its anxieties about
Paradise Lost most overtly. And *Frankenstein* in particular is a fictionalized rendition of the meaning of *Paradise Lost* to women.

Many critics have noticed that *Frankenstein* (1818) is one of the key
Romantic "readings" of *Paradise Lost*.[14] Significantly, however, as a
woman's reading it is most especially the story of hell: hell as a dark
parody of heaven, hell's creations as monstrous imitations of heaven's
creations, and hellish femaleness as a grotesque parody of heavenly
maleness. But of course the divagations of the parody merely return
to and reinforce the fearful reality of the original. For by parodying
Paradise Lost in what may have begun as a secret, barely conscious
attempt to subvert Milton, Shelley ended up telling, too, the central
story of *Paradise Lost*, the tale of "what misery th' inabstinence of
Eve / Shall bring on men."

Mary Shelley herself claims to have been continually asked "how
I ... came to think of and to dilate upon so very hideous an idea"
as that of *Frankenstein*, but it is really not surprising that she should
have formulated her anxieties about femaleness in such highly
literary terms. For of course the nineteen-year-old girl who wrote
Frankenstein was no ordinary nineteen-year-old but one of England's
most notable literary heiresses. Indeed, as "the daughter of two
persons of distinguished literary celebrity," and the wife of a third,
Mary Wollstonecraft Godwin Shelley was the daughter and later
the wife of some of Milton's keenest critics, so that Harold Bloom's
useful conceit about the family romance of English literature is
simply an accurate description of the reality of her life.[15]

In acknowledgment of this web of literary/familial relationships,
critics have traditionally studied *Frankenstein* as an interesting example
of Romantic myth-making, a work ancillary to such established
Promethean masterpieces as Shelley's *Prometheus Unbound* and Byron's
Manfred. ("Like almost everything else about [Mary's] life," one
such critic remarks, *Frankenstein* "is an instance of genius observed

and admired but not shared."[16]) Recently, however, a number of writers have noticed the connection between Mary Shelley's "waking dream" of monster-manufacture and her own experience of awakening sexuality, in particular the "horror story of Maternity" which accompanied her precipitous entrance into what Ellen Moers calls "teen-age motherhood."[17] Clearly they are articulating an increasingly uneasy sense that, despite its male protagonist and its underpinning of "masculine" philosophy, *Frankenstein* is somehow a "woman's book," if only because its author was caught up in such a maelstrom of sexuality at the time she wrote the novel.

In making their case for the work as female fantasy, though, critics like Moers have tended to evade the problems posed by what we must define as *Frankenstein*'s literariness. Yet, despite the weaknesses in those traditional readings of the novel that overlook its intensely sexual materials, it is still undeniably true that Mary Shelley's "ghost story," growing from a Keatsian (or Coleridgean) waking dream, is a Romantic novel about—among other things—Romanticism, as well as a book about books and perhaps, too, about the writers of books. Any theorist of the novel's femaleness and of its significance as, in Moers's phrase, a "birth myth" must therefore confront this self-conscious literariness. For as was only natural in "the daughter of two persons of distinguished literary celebrity," Mary Shelley explained her sexuality to herself in the context of her reading and its powerfully felt implications.

For this orphaned literary heiress, highly charged connections between femaleness and literariness must have been established early, and established specifically in relation to the controversial figure of her dead mother. As we shall see, Mary Wollstonecraft Godwin read her mother's writings over and over again as she was growing up. Perhaps more important, she undoubtedly read most of the reviews of her mother's *Posthumous Works*, reviews in which Mary Wollstonecraft was attacked as a "philosophical wanton" and a monster, while her *Vindication of the Rights of Woman* (1792) was called "A scripture, archly fram'd for propagating w[hore]s."[18] But in any case, to the "philosophical wanton's" daughter, all reading about (or of) her mother's work must have been painful, given her knowledge that that passionate feminist writer had died in giving life to *her*, to bestow upon Wollstonecraft's death from complications of childbirth the melodramatic cast it probably had for the girl herself. That Mary Shelley was conscious, moreover, of a strangely intimate relationship between her feelings toward her dead mother, her romance with a living poet, and her own sense of vocation as a reader and writer is made perfectly clear by her habit of "taking her books to Mary Wollstonecraft's grave in St. Pancras' Churchyard, there," as Muriel Spark puts it, "to pursue her studies in an atmosphere of communion with a mind greater than the second Mrs. Godwin's [and] to meet Shelley in secret." [19]

Her mother's grave: the setting seems an unusually grim, even ghoulish locale for reading, writing, or lovemaking. Yet, to a girl with Mary Shelley's background, literary activities, like sexual ones, must have been primarily extensions of the elaborate, gothic psychodrama of her family history. If her famous diary is largely a compendium of her reading lists and Shelley's that fact does not, therefore, suggest unusual reticence on her part. Rather, it emphasizes the point that for Mary, even more than for most writers, reading a book was often an emotional as well as an intellectual event of considerable magnitude. Especially because she never knew her mother, and because her father seemed so definitively to reject her after her youthful elopement, her principal mode of self-definition—certainly in the early years of her life with Shelley, when she was writing *Frankenstein*—was through reading, and to a lesser extent through writing.

Endlessly studying her mother's works and her father's, Mary Shelley may be said to have "read" her family and to have been related to her reading, for books appear to have functioned as her surrogate parents, pages and words standing in for flesh and blood. That much of her reading was undertaken in Shelley's company, moreover, may also help explain some of this obsessiveness, for Mary's literary inheritance was obviously involved in her very literary romance and marriage. In the years just before she wrote *Frankenstein*, for instance, and those when she was engaged in composing the novel (1816–17), she studied her parents' writings, alone or together with Shelley, like a scholarly detective seeking clues to the significance of some cryptic text. [20]

To be sure, this investigation of the mysteries of literary genealogy was done in a larger context. In these same years, Mary Shelley recorded innumerable readings of contemporary gothic novels, as well as a program of study in English, French, and German literature that would do credit to a modern graduate student. But especially, in 1815, 1816, and 1817, she read the works of Milton: *Paradise Lost* (twice), *Paradise Regained, Comus, Areopagetica, Lycidas*. And what makes the extent of this reading particularly impressive is the fact that in these years, her seventeenth to her twenty-first, Mary Shelley was almost continuously pregnant, "confined," or nursing. At the same time, it is precisely the coincidence of all these disparate activities—her family studies, her initiation into adult sexuality, and her literary self-education—that makes her vision of *Paradise Lost* so significant. For her developing sense of herself as a literary creature and/or creator seems to have been inseparable from her emerging self-definition as daughter, mistress, wife, and mother. Thus she cast her birth myth—her myth of origins—in precisely those cosmogenic terms to which her parents, her husband, and indeed her whole literary culture continually alluded: the terms of *Paradise Lost*, which (as she indicates even on the title page of her novel), she saw as preceding, paralleling, and commenting upon the Greek cosmogony of the Prometheus play her husband had just translated. It is as a female fantasy of sex and reading, then, a gothic psychodrama reflecting Mary Shelley's own sense of what we might call bibliogenesis, that *Frankenstein* is a version of the misogynistic story implicit in *Paradise Lost*.

It would be a mistake to underestimate the significance of *Franken-stein*'s title page, with its allusive subtitle ("The Modern Prometheus") and carefully pointed Miltonic epigraph ("Did I request thee, Maker, from my clay / To mould me man? Did I solicit thee / From darkness to promote me?"). But our first really serious clue to the highly literary nature of this history of a creature born outside history is its author's use of an unusually *evidentiary* technique for conveying the stories of her monster and his maker. Like a literary jigsaw puzzle, a collection of apparently random documents from whose juxtaposition the scholar-detective must infer a meaning, *Frankenstein* consists of three "concentric circles" of narration (Walton's letters, Victor Frankenstein's recital to Walton, and the monster's speech to Frankenstein), within which are embedded pockets of digression containing other miniature narratives (Frankenstein's mother's story, Elizabeth Lavenza's and Justine's stories, Felix's and Agatha's story, Safie's story), etc.[21] As we have noted, reading and assembling documentary evidence, examining it, analyzing it and researching it comprised for Shelley a crucial if voyeuristic method of exploring origins, explaining identity, understanding sexuality. Even more obviously, it was a way of researching and analyzing an emotionally unintelligible text, like *Paradise Lost*. In a sense, then, even before *Paradise Lost* as a central item on the monster's reading list becomes a literal event in *Frankenstein*, the novel's literary structure prepares us to confront Milton's patriarchal epic, both as a sort of research problem and as the framework for a complex system of allusions.

The book's dramatic situations are equally resonant. Like Mary Shelley, who was a puzzled but studious Miltonist, this novel's key characters—Walton, Frankenstein, and the monster—are obsessed with problem-solving. "I shall satiate my ardent curiosity with the sight of a part of the world never before visited," exclaims the young explorer, Walton, as he embarks like a child "on an expedition of discovery up his native river" (2, letter 1). "While my companions contemplated . . . the magnificent appearance of things," declares Frankenstein, the scientist of sexual ontology, "I delighted in investigating their causes" (22, chap. 2). "Who was I? What was I? Whence did I come?" (113–15, chap. 15) the monster reports wondering, describing endless speculations cast in Miltonic terms. All three, like Shelley herself, appear to be trying to understand their presence in a fallen world, and trying at the same time to define the nature of the lost paradise that must have existed before the fall. But unlike Adam, all three characters seem to have fallen not merely from Eden but from the earth, fallen directly into hell, like Sin, Satan, and—by implication—Eve. Thus their questionings are in some sense female, for they belong in that line of literary women's questionings of the fall into gender which goes back at least to Anne Finch's plaintive "How are we fal'n?" and forward to Sylvia Plath's horrified "I have fallen very far!"[22]

From the first, however, *Frankenstein* answers such neo-Miltonic questions mainly through explicit or implicit allusions to Milton, retelling the story of the fall not so much to protest against it as to clarify its meaning. The parallels between those two Promethean overreachers Walton and Frankenstein, for instance, have always been clear to readers. But that both characters can, therefore, be described (the way Walton describes Frankenstein) as "fallen angels" is not as frequently remarked. Yet Frankenstein himself is perceptive enough to ask Walton "Do you share my madness?" at just the moment when the young explorer remarks Satanically that "One man's life or death were but a small price to pay . . . for the dominion I [wish to] acquire" (13, letter 4). Plainly one fallen angel can recognize another. Alienated from his crew and chronically friendless, Walton tells his sister that he longs for a friend "on the wide ocean," and what he discovers in Victor Frankenstein is the fellowship of hell.

In fact, like the many other secondary narratives Mary Shelley offers in her novel, Walton's story is itself an alternative version of the myth of origins presented in *Paradise Lost*. Writing his ambitious letters home from St. Petersburgh [*sic*], Archangel, and points north, Walton moves like Satan away from the sanctity and sanity represented by his sister, his crew, and the allegorical names of the places he leaves. Like Satan, too, he seems at least in part to be exploring the frozen frontiers of hell in order to attempt a return to heaven, for the "country of eternal light" he envisions at the Pole (1, letter 1) has much in common with Milton's celestial "Fountain of Light" (*PL* 3. 375).[23] Again, like Satan's (and Eve's) aspirations, his ambition has violated a patriarchal decree: his father's "dying injunction" had forbidden him "to embark on a seafaring life." Moreover, even the icy hell where Walton encounters Frankenstein and the monster is Miltonic, for all three of these diabolical wanderers must learn, like the fallen angels of *Paradise Lost*, that "Beyond this flood a frozen Continent / Lies dark and wild . . . / Thither by harpy-footed Furies hal'd, / At certain revolutions all the damn'd / Are brought . . . From Beds of raging Fire to starve in Ice" (*PL* 2. 587–600).

Finally, another of Walton's revelations illuminates not only the likeness of his ambitions to Satan's but also the similarity of his anxieties to those of his female author. Speaking of his childhood, he reminds his sister that, because poetry had "lifted [my soul] to heaven," he had become a poet and "for one year lived in a paradise of my own creation." Then he adds ominously that "You are well-acquainted with my failure and how heavily I bore the disappointment" (2–3, letter 1). But of course, as she confesses in her introduction to *Frankenstein*, Mary Shelley, too, had spent her childhood in "waking dreams" of literature; later, both she and her poet-husband hoped she would prove herself "worthy of [her] parentage and enroll [herself] on the page of fame" (xii). In a sense, then, given the Miltonic context in which Walton's story of poetic failure is set, it seems possible that one of the anxious fantasies his narrative helps Mary Shelley covertly examine is the fearful tale of a female fall from a lost paradise of art, speech, and autonomy into a hell of sexuality, silence, and filthy materiality, "A Universe of death, which God by curse / Created evil, for evil only good, / Where all life dies, death lives, and Nature breeds, / Perverse, all monstrous, all prodigious things" (*PL* 2. 622–25).

Walton and his new friend Victor Frankenstein have considerably more in common than a Byronic (or Monk Lewis-ish) Satanism. For one thing, both are orphans, as Frankenstein's monster is and as it turns out all the major and almost all the minor characters in *Frankenstein* are, from Caroline Beaufort and Elizabeth Lavenza to Justine, Felix, Agatha, and Safie. Victor Frankenstein has not always been an orphan, though, and Shelley devotes much space to an account of his family history. Family histories, in fact, especially those of orphans, appear to fascinate her, and wherever she can include one in the narrative she does so with an obsessiveness suggesting that through the disastrous tale of the child who becomes "an orphan and a beggar" she is once more recounting the story of the fall, the expulsion from paradise, and the confrontation of hell. For Milton's Adam and Eve, after all, began as motherless orphans reared (like Shelley herself) by a stern but kindly father-god, and ended as beggars rejected by God (as she was by *God*win when she eloped). Thus Caroline Beaufort's father dies leaving her "an orphan and a beggar," and Elizabeth Lavenza also becomes "an orphan and a beggar"—the phrase is repeated (18, 20, chap. 1)—with the disappearance of her father into an Austrian dungeon. And though both girls are rescued by Alphonse Frankenstein, Victor's father, the early alienation from the patriarchal chain-of-being signalled by their orphanhood prefigures the hellish fate in store for them and their family. Later, motherless Safie and fatherless Justine enact similarly ominous anxiety fantasies about the fall of woman into orphanhood and beggary.

Beyond their orphanhood, however, a universal sense of guilt links such diverse figures as Justine, Felix, and Elizabeth, just as it will eventually link Victor, Walton, and the monster. Justine, for instance, irrationally confesses to the murder of little William, though she knows perfectly well she is innocent. Even more irrationally, Elizabeth is reported by Alphonse Frankenstein to have exclaimed "Oh, God! I have murdered my darling child!" after her first sight of the corpse of little William (57, chap. 7). Victor, too, long before he knows that the monster is actually his brother's killer, decides that his "creature" has killed William and that therefore he, the creator, is the "true murderer": "the mere presence of the idea," he notes, is "an irresistable proof of the fact" (60, chap. 7). Complicity in the murder of the child William is, it seems, another crucial component of the Original Sin shared by prominent members of the Frankenstein family.

At the same time, the likenesses among all these characters—the common alienation, the shared guilt, the orphanhood and beggary— imply relationships of redundance between them like the solipsistic relationships among artfully placed mirrors. What reinforces our sense of this hellish solipsism is the barely disguised incest at the heart of a number of the marriages and romances the novel describes. Most notably, Victor Frankenstein is slated to marry his "more than sister" Elizabeth Lavenza, whom he confesses to having always considered "a possession of my own" (21, chap. 1). But the mysterious Mrs. Saville, to whom Walton's letters are addressed, is apparently in some sense *his* more than sister, just as Caroline Beaufort was clearly a "more than" wife, in fact a daughter, to her father's friend Alphonse Frankenstein. Even relationless Justine appears to have a metaphorically incestuous relationship with the Frankensteins, since as their servant she becomes their possession and more than sister, while the female monster Victor half-constructs in Scotland will be a more than sister as well as a mate to the monster, since both have the same parent/creator.

Certainly at least some of this incest-obsession in *Frankenstein* is, as Ellen Moers remarks, the "standard" sensational matter of Romantic novels.[24] Some of it, too, even without the conventions of the gothic thriller, would be a natural subject for an impressionable young woman who had just spent several months in the company of the famously incestuous author of *Manfred*.[25] Nevertheless, the streak of incest that darkens *Frankenstein* probably owes as much to the book's Miltonic framework as it does to Mary Shelley's own life and times. In the Edenic cosiness of their childhood, for instance, Victor and Elizabeth are incestuous as Adam and Eve are, literally incestuous because they have the same creator, and figuratively so because Elizabeth is Victor's pretty plaything, the image of an angelic soul or "epipsyche" created from his own soul just as Eve is created from Adam's rib. Similarly, the incestuous relationships of Satan and Sin, and by implication of Satan and Eve, are mirrored in the incest fantasies of *Frankenstein*, including the disguised but intensely sexual waking dream in which Victor Frankenstein in effect couples with his monster by applying "the instruments of life" to its body and inducing a shudder of response (42, chap. 5). For Milton, and therefore for Mary Shelley, who was trying to understand Milton, incest was an inescapable metaphor for the solipsistic fever of self-awareness that Matthew Arnold was later to call "the dialogue of the mind with itself."[26]

If Victor Frankenstein can be likened to both Adam and Satan, however, who or what is he *really*? Here we are obliged to confront both the moral ambiguity and the symbolic slipperiness which are at the heart of all the characterizations in *Frankenstein*. In fact, it is probably these continual and complex reallocations of meaning, among characters whose histories echo and re-echo each other, that have been so bewildering to critics. Like figures in a dream, all the people in *Frankenstein* have different bodies and somehow, horribly, the same face, or worse—the same two faces. For this reason, as Muriel Spark notes, even the book's subtitle "The Modern Prometheus" is ambiguous, "for though at first Frankenstein is himself the Prometheus, the vital fire-endowing protagonist, the Monster, as soon as he is created, takes on [a different aspect of] the role."[27] Moreover, if we postulate that Mary Shelley is more concerned with Milton than she is with Aeschylus, the intertwining of meanings grows even more confusing, as the monster himself several times points out to Frankenstein, noting "I ought to be thy Adam, but I am rather the fallen angel," (84, chap. 10), then adding elsewhere that "God, in pity, made man beautiful . . . after His own image; but my form is a filthy type of yours. . . . Satan had his companions . . . but I am solitary and abhorred" (115, chap. 15). In other words, not only do Frankenstein and his monster both in one way or another enact the story of Prometheus, each is at one time or another like God (Victor as creator, the monster as his creator's "Master"), like Adam (Victor as innocent child, the monster as primordial "creature"), and like Satan (Victor as tormented overreacher, the monster as vengeful fiend).

What is the reason for this continual duplication and reduplication of roles? Most obviously, perhaps, the dreamlike shifting of fantasy figures from part to part, costume to costume, tells us that we are in fact dealing with the psychodrama or waking dream that Shelley herself suspected she had written. Beyond this, however, we would argue that the fluidity of the narrative's symbolic scheme reinforces in another way the crucial significance of the Miltonic skeleton around which Mary Shelley's hideous progeny took shape. For it becomes increasingly clear as one reads *Frankenstein* with *Paradise Lost* in mind that because the novel's author is such an inveterate student of literature, families, and sexuality, and because she is using her novel as a tool to help her make sense of her reading, *Frankenstein* is ultimately a mock *Paradise Lost* in which both Victor and his monster, together with a number of secondary characters, play all the neo-biblical parts over and over again—all except, it seems at first, the part of Eve. Not just the striking omission of any obvious Eve-figure from this "woman's book" about Milton, but also the barely concealed sexual components of the story as well as our earlier analysis of Milton's bogey should tell us, however, that for Mary Shelley the part of Eve *is* all the parts.

On the surface, Victor seems at first more Adamic than Satanic or Eve-like. His Edenic childhood is an interlude of prelapsarian innocence in which, like Adam, he is sheltered by his benevolent father as a sensitive plant might be "sheltered by the gardener, from every rougher wind" (19–20, chap. 1). When cherubic Elizabeth Lavenza joins the family, she seems as "heaven-sent" as Milton's

Eve, as much Victor's "possession" as Adam's rib is Adam's. Moreover, though he is evidently forbidden almost nothing ("My parents [were not] tyrants . . . but the agents and creators of many delights"), Victor hints to Walton that his deific father, like Adam's and Walton's, did on one occasion arbitrarily forbid him to pursue his interest in arcane knowledge. Indeed, like Eve and Satan, Victor blames his own fall at least in part on his father's apparent arbitrariness. "If . . . my father had taken the pains to explain to me that the principles of Agrippa had been entirely exploded. . . . It is even possible that the train of my ideas would never have received the fatal impulse that led to my ruin" (24–25, chap. 2). And soon after asserting this he even associates an incident in which a tree is struck by Jovian thunder bolts with his feelings about his forbidden studies.

As his researches into the "secrets of nature" become more feverish, however, and as his ambition "to explore unknown powers" grows more intense, Victor begins to metamorphose from Adam to Satan, becoming "as Gods" in his capacity of "bestowing animation upon lifeless matter," laboring like a guilty artist to complete his false creation. Finally, in his conversations with Walton he echoes Milton's fallen angel, and Marlowe's, in his frequently reiterated confession that "I bore a hell within me which nothing could extinguish" (72, chap. 8). Indeed, as the "true murderer" of innocence, here cast in the form of the child William, Victor perceives himself as a diabolical creator whose mind has involuntarily "let loose" a monstrous and "filthy demon" in much the same way that Milton's Satan's swelled head produced Sin, the disgusting monster he "let loose" upon the world. Watching a "noble war in the sky" that seems almost like an intentional reminder that we are participating in a critical rearrangement of most of the elements of *Paradise Lost*, he explains that "I considered the being whom I had cast among mankind . . . nearly in the light of my own vampire, my own spirit let loose from the grave and forced to destroy all that was dear to me" (61, chap. 7).

Even while it is the final sign and seal of Victor's transformation from Adam to Satan, however, it is perhaps the Sin-ful murder of the child William that is our first overt clue to the real nature of the bewilderingly disguised set of identity shifts and parallels Mary Shelley incorporated into *Frankenstein*. For as we saw earlier, not just Victor and the monster but also Elizabeth and Justine insist upon responsibility for the monster's misdeed. Feeling "as if I had been guilty of a crime" (41, chap. 4) even before one had been committed, Victor responds to the news of William's death with the same self-accusations that torment the two orphans. And, significantly, for all three—as well as for the monster and little William himself—one focal point of both crime and guilt is an image of that other beautiful orphan, Caroline Beaufort Frankenstein. Passing from hand to hand, pocket to pocket, the smiling miniature of Victor's "angel mother" seems a token of some secret fellowship in sin, as does Victor's post-creation nightmare of transforming a lovely, living Elizabeth, with a single magical kiss, into "the corpse of my dead mother" enveloped in a shroud made more horrible by "grave-worms crawling in the folds of the flannel" (42, chap. 5). Though it has been disguised, buried, or miniaturized, femaleness—the gender definition of mothers and daughters, orphans and beggars, monsters and false creators—is at the heart of this apparently masculine book.

Because this is so, it eventually becomes clear that though Victor Frankenstein enacts the roles of Adam and Satan like a child trying on costumes, his single most self-defining act transforms him definitively into Eve. For as both Ellen Moers and Marc Rubenstein have pointed out, after much study of the "cause of generation and life," after locking himself away from ordinary society in the tradition of such agonized mothers as Wollstonecraft's Maria, Eliot's Hetty Sorel, and Hardy's Tess, Victor Frankenstein has a baby.[28] His "pregnancy" and childbirth are obviously manifested by the existence of the paradoxically huge being who emerges from his "workshop of filthy creation," but even the descriptive language of his creation myth is suggestive: "incredible labours," "emaciated with confinement," "a passing trance," "oppressed by a slow fever," "nervous to a painful degree," "exercise and amusement would . . . drive away incipient disease," "the instruments of life" (39–41, chap. 4), etc. And, like Eve's fall into guilty knowledge and painful maternity, Victor's entrance into what Blake would call the realm of "generation" is marked by a recognition of the necessary interdependence of those complementary opposites, sex and death: "To examine the causes of life, we must first have recourse to death," he observes (36, chap. 4), and in his isolated workshop of filthy creation—filthy because obscenely sexual[29]—he collects and arranges materials furnished by "the dissecting room and the slaughterhouse." Pursuing "nature to her hiding places" as Eve does in eating the apple, he learns that "the tremendous secrets of the human frame" are the interlocked secrets of sex and death, although, again like Eve, in his first mad pursuit of knowledge he knows not "eating death." But that his actual orgasmic animation of his monster-child takes place "on a dreary night in November," month of All Souls, short days, and the year's last slide toward death, merely reinforces the Miltonic and Blakean nature of his act of generation.

Even while Victor Frankenstein's self-defining procreation dramatically transforms him into an Eve-figure, however, our recognition of its implications reflects backward upon our sense of Victor-as-Satan and our earlier vision of Victor-as-Adam. Victor as Satan, we now realize, was never really the masculine, Byronic Satan of the first book of *Paradise Lost*, but always, instead, the curiously female, outcast Satan who gave birth to Sin. In his Eve-like pride ("I was surprised . . . that I alone should be reserved to discover so astonishing a secret" [37, chap. 4]), this Victor-Satan becomes "dizzy" with his creative powers, so that his monstrous pregnancy, bookishly and solipsistically conceived, reenacts as a terrible bibliogenesis the moment when, in Milton's version, Satan "dizzy swum / In darkness, while [his] head flames thick and fast / Threw forth, till on the left side op'ning wide" and Sin, Death's mother-to-be, appeared like "a Sign / Portentous" (*PL* 2: 753–61). Because he has conceived— or, rather, misconceived—his monstrous offspring by brooding upon the *wrong* books, moreover, this Victor-Satan is paradigmatic, like the falsely creative fallen angel, of the female artist, whose anxiety about her own aesthetic activity is expressed, for instance, in Mary Shelley's deferential introductory phrase about her "hideous progeny," with its plain implication that in her alienated attic workshop of filthy creation she has given birth to a deformed book, a literary abortion or miscarriage. "How [did] I, then a young girl, [come] to think of and to *dilate* upon so very hideous an idea?" is a key (if disingenuous) question she records. But we should not overlook her word play upon *dilate*, just as we should not ignore the anxious pun on the word *author* that is so deeply embedded in *Frankenstein*.

If the adult, Satanic Victor is Eve-like both in his procreation and his anxious creation, even the young, prelapsarian, and Adamic

Victor is—to risk a pun—*curiously* female, that is, Eve-like. Innocent and guided by silken threads like a Blakeian lamb in a Godwinian garden, he is consumed by "a fervent longing to penetrate the secrets of nature," a longing which—expressed in his explorations of "vaults and charnelhouses," his guilty observations of "the unhallowed damps of the grave," and his passion to understand "the structure of the human frame"—recalls the criminal female curiosity that led Psyche to lose love by gazing upon its secret face, Eve to insist upon consuming "intellectual food," and Prometheus's sister-in-law Pandora to open the forbidden box of fleshly ills. But if Victor-Adam is also Victor-Eve, what is the real significance of the episode in which, away at school and cut off from his family, he locks himself into his workshop of filthy creation and gives birth by intellectual parturition to a giant monster? Isn't it precisely at this point in the novel that he discovers he is not Adam but Eve, not Satan but Sin, not male but female? If so, it seems likely that what this crucial section of *Frankenstein* really enacts is the story of Eve's discovery not that she must fall but that, having been created female, she *is* fallen, femaleness and fallenness being essentially synonymous. For what Victor Frankenstein most importantly learns, we must remember, is that he is the "author" of the monster—for him alone is "reserved . . . so astonishing a secret"—and thus it is he who is "the true murderer," he who unleashes Sin and Death upon the world, he who dreams the primal kiss that incestuously kills both "sister" and "mother." Doomed and filthy, is he not, then, Eve instead of Adam? In fact, may not the story of the fall be, for women, the story of the discovery that one is not innocent and Adam (as one had supposed) but Eve, and fallen? Perhaps this is what Freud's cruel but metaphorically accurate concept of penis-envy really means: the girl-child's surprised discovery that she is female, hence fallen, inadequate. Certainly the almost grotesquely anxious self-analysis implicit in Victor Frankenstein's (and Mary Shelley's) multiform relationships to Eve, Adam, God, and Satan suggest as much.

The discovery that one is fallen is in a sense a discovery that one is a monster, a murderer, a being gnawed by "the never-dying worm" (72, chap. 8) and therefore capable of any horror, including but not limited to sex, death, and filthy literary creation. More, the discovery that one is fallen—self-divided, murderous, material—is the discovery that one 'has released a "vampire" upon the world, "forced to destroy all that [is] dear" (61, chap. 7). For this reason—because *Frankenstein* is a story of woman's fall told by, as it were, an apparently docile daughter to a censorious "father"—the monster's narrative is embedded at the heart of the novel like the secret of the fall itself. Indeed, just as Frankenstein's workshop, with its maddening, riddling answers to cosmic questions is a hidden but commanding attic womb/room where the young artist-scientist murders to dissect and to recreate, so the murderous monster's single, carefully guarded narrative commands and controls Mary Shelley's novel. Delivered at the top of Mont Blanc—like the North Pole one of the Shelley family's metaphors for the indifferently powerful source of creation and destruction—it is the story of deformed Geraldine in "Christabel," the story of the dead-alive crew in "The Ancient Mariner," the story of Eve in *Paradise Lost*, and of her degraded double Sin—all secondary or female characters to whom male authors have imperiously denied any chance of self-explanation.[30] At the same time the monster's narrative is a philosophical meditation on what it means to be born without a "soul" or a history, as well as an exploration of what it feels like to be a "filthy mass that move[s] and talk[s]," a thing, an other, a creature of the second sex. In fact, though it tends to be ignored by critics (and film-makers), whose emphasis has always fallen upon Frankenstein himself as the archetypal mad scientist, the drastic shift in point of view that the nameless monster's monologue represents probably constitutes *Frankenstein*'s most striking technical *tour de force*, just as the monster's bitter self-revelations are Mary Shelley's most impressive and original achievement.[31]

Like Victor Frankenstein, his author and superficially better self, the monster enacts in turn the roles of Adam and Satan, and even eventually hints at a sort of digression into the role of God. Like Adam, he recalls a time of primordial innocence, his days and nights in "the forest near Ingolstadt," where he ate berries, learned about heat and cold, and perceived "the boundaries of the radiant roof of light which canopied me" (88, chap. 11). Almost too quickly, however, he metamorphoses into an outcast and Satanic figure, hiding in a shepherd's hut which seems to him "as exquisite . . . a retreat as

Pandemonium . . . after . . . the lake of fire" (90, chap. 11). Later,
when he secretly sets up housekeeping behind the De Laceys' pigpen,
his wistful observations of the loving though exiled family and their
pastoral abode("Happy, happy earth! Fit habitation for gods . . . "
[100, chap. 12]) recall Satan's mingled jealousy and admiration of
that "happy rural seat of various view" where Adam and Eve are
emparadised by God and Milton (*PL* 4. 247). Eventually, burning
the cottage and murdering William in demonic rage, he seems to
become entirely Satanic: "I, like the arch-fiend, bore a hell within
me" (121, chap. 16); "Inflamed by pain, I vowed eternal hatred . . .
to all mankind" (126, chap. 16). At the same time, in his assertion
of power over his "author," his mental conception of another creature
(a female monster), and his implicit dream of founding a new,
vegetarian race somewhere in "the vast wilds of South America,"
(131, chap. 17), he temporarily enacts the part of a God, a creator,
a master, albeit a failed one.

As the monster himself points out, however, each of these Miltonic
roles is a Procrustean bed into which he simply cannot fit. Where, for
instance, Victor Frankenstein's childhood really was Edenic, the
monster's anxious infancy is isolated and ignorant, rather than in-
sulated or innocent, so that his groping arrival at self-consciousness—
"I was a poor, helpless, miserable wretch; I knew and could distinguish nothing; but feeling pain invade me on all sides, I sat down and
wept" (87–88, chap. 11)—is a fiercely subversive parody of Adam's
exuberant "all things smil'd, / With fragrance and with joy my heart
o'erflowed. / Myself I then perus'd, and Limb by Limb / Survey'd,
and sometimes went, and sometimes ran / With supple joints, as lively
vigor led" (*PL* 8. 265–69). Similarly, the monster's attempts at
speech ("Sometimes I wished to express my sensations in my own
mode, but the uncouth and inarticulate sounds which broke from
me frightened me into silence again" (88, chap. 11) parody and
subvert Adam's ("To speak I tri'd, and forthwith spake, / My Tongue
obey'd and readily could name / Whate'er I saw" (*PL* 8. 271–72).
And of course the monster's anxiety and confusion ("What was I?
The question again recurred to be answered only with groans"
[106, chap. 13]) are a dark version of Adam's wondering bliss ("who
I was, or where, or from what cause, / [I] Knew not. . . . [But I]
feel that I am happier than I know" (*PL* 8. 270–71, 282).

Similarly, though his uncontrollable rage, his alienation, even his enormous size and superhuman physical strength bring him closer to Satan than he was to Adam, the monster puzzles over discrepancies between his situation and the fallen angel's. Though he is, for example, "in bulk as huge / As whom the Fables name of monstrous size, / *Titanian*, or *Earth-born*, that warr'd on *Jove*," and though, indeed, he is fated to war like Prometheus on Jovean Frankenstein, this demon/monster has fallen from no heaven, exercised no power of choice, and been endowed with no companions in evil. "I found myself similar yet at the same time strangely unlike to the beings concerning whom I read and to whose conversation I was a listener," he tells Frankenstein, describing his schooldays in the De Lacey pigpen (113, chap. 15). And, interestingly, his remark might well have been made by Mary Shelley herself, that "devout but nearly silent listener" (xiv) to masculine conversations who, like her hideous progeny, "continually studied and exercised [her] mind upon" such "histories" as *Paradise Lost*, Plutarch's *Lives*, and *The Sorrows of Werter* [*sic*] "whilst [her] friends were employed in their ordinary occupations" (112, chap. 15).

In fact, it is his intellectual similarity to his authoress (rather than his "author") which first suggests that Victor Frankenstein's male monster may really be a female in disguise. Certainly the books which educate him—*Werter*, Plutarch's *Lives*, and *Paradise Lost*—are not only books Mary had herself read in 1815, the year before she wrote *Frankenstein*, but they also typify just the literary categories she thought it necessary to study: the contemporary novel of sensibility, the serious history of Western civilization, and the highly cultivated epic poem. As specific works, moreover, each must have seemed to her to embody lessons a female author (or monster) must learn about a male-dominated society. Werter's story, says the monster—and he seems to be speaking for Mary Shelley—taught him about "gentle and domestic manners," and about "lofty sentiments . . . which had for their object something out of self." It functioned, in other words, as a sort of Romantic conduct book. In addition, it served as an introduction to the virtues of the proto-Byronic "Man of Feeling," for, admiring Werter and never mentioning Lotte, the monster explains to Victor that "I thought Werter himself a more divine being than I had ever . . . imagined," adding, in a line whose female

irony about male self-dramatization must surely have been intentional, "I wept [his extinction] without precisely understanding it"
(113, chap. 15).

If *Werter* introduces the monster to female modes of domesticity
and self-abnegation, as well as to the unattainable glamour of male
heroism, Plutarch's *Lives* teaches him all the masculine intricacies
of that history which his anomalous birth has denied him. Mary
Shelley, excluding herself from the household of the second Mrs.
Godwin and studying family as well as literary history on her mother's
grave, must, again, have found in her own experience an appropriate
model for the plight of a monster who, as James Rieger notes, is
especially characterized by "his unique knowledge of what it is like
to be born free of history."[32] In terms of the disguised story the novel
tells, however, this monster is not unique at all, but representative,
as Shelley may have suspected she herself was. For, as Jane Austen
has Catherine Morland suggest in *Northanger Abbey*, what is woman
but man without a history, at least without the sort of history related
in Plutarch's *Lives*? "History, real solemn history, I cannot be interested in," Catherine declares " . . . the men all so good for nothing,
and hardly any women at all—it is very tiresome" (*NA* I, chap. 14).

But of course the third and most crucial book referred to in the
miniature *Bildungsroman* of the monster's narrative is *Paradise Lost*,
an epic myth of origins which is of major importance to him, as it is
to Mary Shelley, precisely because, unlike Plutarch, it does provide
him with what appears to be a personal history. And again, even the
need for such a history draws Shelley's monster closer not only to
the realistically ignorant female defined by Jane Austen but also to
the archetypal female defined by John Milton. For, like the monster,
like Catherine Morland, and like Mary Shelley herself, Eve is characterized by her "unique knowledge of what it is like to be born free
of history," even though as the "Mother of Mankind" she is fated to
"make" history. It is to Adam, after all, that God and His angels
grant explanatory visions of past and future. At such moments of
high historical colloquy Eve tends to excuse herself with "lowliness
Majestic" (before the fall) or (after the fall) she is magically put to
sleep, calmed like a frightened animal "with gentle Dreams . . . and
all her spirits compos'd / To meek submission" (*PL* 12. 595–96).

Nevertheless, one of the most notable facts about the monster's ceaselessly anxious study of *Paradise Lost* is his failure even to mention Eve. As an insistently male monster, on the surface of his palimpsestic narrative he appears to be absorbed in Milton's epic only because, as Percy Shelley wrote in the preface to *Frankenstein* that he drafted for his wife, *Paradise Lost* "most especially" conveys "the truth of the elementary principles of human nature," and conveys that truth in the dynamic tensions developed among its male characters, Adam, Satan, and God (xvii). Yet not only the monster's uniquely ahistorical birth, his literary anxieties, and the sense his readings (like Mary's) foster that he must have been parented, if at all, by *books*; not only all these facts and traits but also his shuddering sense of deformity, his nauseating size, his namelessness, and his orphaned, motherless isolation link him with Eve and with Eve's double, Sin. Indeed, at several points in his impassioned analysis of Milton's story he seems almost on the verge of saying so, as he examines the disjunctions among Adam, Satan, and himself:

> Like Adam, I was apparently united by no link to any other being in existence; but his state was far different from mine in every other respect. He had come forth from the hands of God a perfect creature, happy and prosperous, guided by the especial care of his Creator; he was allowed to converse with and acquire knowledge from beings of a superior nature, but I was wretched, helpless, and alone. Many times I considered Satan as the fitter emblem of my condition, for often, like him, when I viewed the bliss of my protectors, the bitter gall of envy rose within me. . . . Accursed creator! Why did you form a monster so hideous that even *you* turned from me in disgust? God, in pity, made man beautiful and alluring, after his own image; but my form is a filthy type of yours, more horrid even from the very resemblance. Satan had his companions, fellow devils, to admire and encourage him, but I am solitary and abhorred. [114–15, chap. 15]

It is Eve, after all, who languishes helpless and alone, while Adam converses with superior beings, and it is Eve in whom the Satanically bitter gall of envy rises, causing her to eat the apple in the hope of adding "what wants / In Female Sex." It is Eve, moreover, to whom deathly isolation is threatened should Adam reject her, an isolation more terrible even than Satan's alienation from heaven. And finally it is Eve whose body, like her mind, is said by Milton to resemble "less / His Image who made both, and less [to express] / The character of that Dominion giv'n / O'er other Creatures . . . " (*PL* 8. 543–46). In fact, to a sexually anxious reader, Eve's body might, like Sin's, seem "horrid even from [its] very resemblance" to her husband's, a "filthy" or obscene version of the human form divine.[33]

As we argued earlier, women have seen themselves (because they have been seen) as monstrous, vile, degraded creatures, second-comers, and emblems of filthy materiality, even though they have also been traditionally defined as superior spiritual beings, angels, better halves. "Woman [is] a temple built over a sewer," said the Church father Tertullian, and Milton seems to see Eve as both temple and sewer, echoing that patristic misogyny.[34] Mary Shelley's conscious or unconscious awareness of the monster woman implicit in the angel woman is perhaps clearest in the revisionary scene where her monster, as if taking his cue from Eve in *Paradise Lost* book 4, first catches sight of his own image: "I had admired the perfect forms of my cottagers . . . but how was I terrified when I viewed myself in a transparent pool. At first I started back, unable to believe that it was indeed I who was reflected in the mirror; and when I became fully convinced that I was in reality the monster that I am, I was filled with the bitterest sensations of despondence and mortification" (98–99, chap. 12). In one sense, this is a corrective to Milton's blindness about Eve. Having been created second, inferior, a mere rib, how could she possibly, this passage implies, have seemed anything but monstrous to herself? In another sense, however, the scene supplements Milton's description of Eve's introduction to herself, for ironically, though her reflection in "the clear / Smooth Lake" is as beautiful as the monster's is ugly, the self-absorption that Eve's confessed passion for her own image signals is plainly meant by Milton to seem morally ugly, a hint of her potential for spiritual deformity: "There I had fixt / Mine eyes till now, and pin'd with vain desire, / Had not a voice thus warn'd me, What thou seest, / What there thou seest fair Creature is thyself . . . " (*PL* 4. 465–68).

The figurative monstrosity of female narcissism is a subtle deformity, however, in comparison with the literal monstrosity many women are taught to see as characteristic of their own bodies. Adrienne Rich's twentieth-century description of "a woman in the shape of a monster / A monster in the shape of a woman" is merely the latest in a long line of monstrous female self-definitions that includes the fearful images in Djuna Barnes's *Book of Repulsive Women*, Denise Levertov's "a white sweating bull of a poet told us / our cunts are ugly" and Sylvia Plath's "old yellow" self of the poem "In Plaster."[35] Animal and misshapen, these emblems of self-loathing must have descended at least in part from the distended body of Mary Shelley's darkly parodic Eve/Sin/Monster, whose enormity betokens not only the enormity of Victor Frankenstein's crime and Satan's bulk but also the distentions or deformities of pregnancy and the Swiftian sexual nausea expressed in Lemuel Gulliver's horrified description of a Brobdignagian breast, a passage Mary Shelley no doubt studied along with the rest of *Gulliver's Travels* when she read the book in 1816, shortly before beginning *Frankenstein*.[36]

At the same time, just as surely as Eve's moral deformity is symbolized by the monster's physical malformation, the monster's physical ugliness represents his social illegitimacy, his bastardy, his namelessness. Bitchy and dastardly as Shakespeare's Edmund, whose association with filthy femaleness is established not only by his devotion to the material/maternal goddess Nature but also by his interlocking affairs with those filthy females Goneril and Regan, Mary Shelley's monster has also been "got" in a "dark and vicious place." Indeed, in his vile illegitimacy he seems to incarnate that bestial "unnameable" place. And significantly, he is himself as nameless as a woman is in patriarchal society, as nameless as unmarried, illegitimately pregnant Mary Wollstonecraft Godwin may have felt herself to be at the time she wrote *Frankenstein*.

"This nameless mode of naming the unnameable is rather good," Mary commented when she learned that it was the custom at early dramatizations of *Frankenstein* to place a blank line next to the name of the actor who played the part of the monster.[37] But her pleased surprise was disingenuous, for the problem of names and their connection with social legitimacy had been forced into her consciousness all her life. As the sister of illegitimate and therefore nameless Fanny Imlay, for instance, she knew what bastardy meant, and she knew it too as the mother of a premature and illegitimate baby girl who died at the age of two weeks without ever having

been given a name. Of course, when Fanny dramatically excised
her name from her suicide note Mary learned more about the
significance even of insignificant names. And as the stepsister of
Mary Jane Clairmont, who defined herself as the "creature" of
Lord Byron and changed her name for a while with astonishing
frequency (from Mary Jane to Jane to Clara to Claire), Mary knew
about the importance of names too. Perhaps most of all, though,
Mary's sense of the fearful significance of legitimate and illegitimate
names must have been formed by her awareness that her own name,
Mary Wollstonecraft Godwin, was absolutely identical with the
name of the mother who had died in giving birth to *her*. Since this
was so, she may have speculated, perhaps her own monstrosity, her
murderous illegitimacy, consisted in her being—like Victor Frankenstein's creation—a reanimation of the dead, a sort of galvanized
corpse ironically arisen from what should have been "the cradle of
life."

This implicit fantasy of the reanimation of the dead in the monstrous and nameless body of the living returns us, however, to the
matter of the monster's Satanic, Sin-ful and Eve-like moral deformity.
For of course the crimes that the monster commits once he has
accepted the world's definition of him as little more than a namelessly
"filthy mass" all reinforce his connection with Milton's unholy
trinity of Sin, Eve/Satan, and Death. The child of two authors
(Victor Frankenstein and Mary Shelley) whose mothers have been
stolen away by death, this motherless monster is after all made from
dead bodies, from loathsome parts found around cemeteries, so that
it seems only "natural" for him to continue the Blakeian cycle of
despair his birth began, by bringing further death into the world.
And of course he brings death, in the central actions of the novel:
death to the childish innocence of little William (whose name is
that of Mary Shelley's father, her half-brother, and her son, so that
one can hardly decide to which male relative she may have been
alluding); death to the faith and truth of allegorically named Justine;
death to the legitimate artistry of the Shelleyan poet Clerval; and
death to the ladylike selflessness of angelic Elizabeth. Is he acting,
in his vile way, for Mary Shelley, whose elegant femininity seemed,
in view of her books, so incongruous to the poet Beddoes and to
literary Lord Dillon? "She has no business to be a woman by her

books," noted Beddoes. And "your writing and your manners are not in accordance," Dillon told Mary herself. "I should have thought of you—if I had only read you—that you were a sort of . . . Sybil, outpouringly enthusiastic . . . but you are cool, quiet and feminine to the last degree. . . . Explain this to me." [38]

Could Mary's coolness have been made possible by the heat of her monster's rage, the strain of her decorous silence eased by the demonic abandon of her nameless monster's ritual fire dance around the cottage of his rejecting "Protectors"? Does Mary's cadaverous creature want to bring more death into the world because he has failed—like those other awful females, Eve and Sin—to win the compassion of that blind and curiously Miltonic old man, the Godlike musical patriarch De Lacey? Significantly, he is clinging to the blind man's knees, begging for recognition and help—"Do not you desert me in the hour of trial!"—when Felix, the son of the house, appears like the felicitous hero he is, and, says the monster, "with supernatural force [he] tore me from his father . . . in a transport of fury, he dashed me to the ground and struck me violently with a stick . . . my heart sank within me as with bitter sickness" (119, chap. 15). Despite everything we have been told about the monster's physical vileness, Felix's rage seems excessive in terms of the novel's overt story. But as an action in the covert plot—the tale of the blind rejection of women by misogynistic/Miltonic patriarchy —it is inevitable and appropriate. Even more psychologically appropriate is the fact that having been so definitively rejected by a world of fathers, the monster takes his revenge, first by murdering William, a male child who invokes his father's name ("My papa is a syndic—he is M. Frankenstein—he will punish you") and then by beginning a doomed search for a maternal, female principle in the harsh society that has created him.

In this connection, it begins to be plain that Eve's—and the monster's—motherlessness must have had extraordinary cultural and personal significance for Mary Shelley. "We think back through our mothers if we are women," wrote Virginia Woolf in *A Room of One's Own*.[39] But of course one of the most dramatic emblems of Eve's alienation from the masculine garden in which she finds herself is her motherlessness. Because she is made in the image of a man who is himself made in the image of a male creator, her unprecedented femininity seems merely a defective masculinity, a deformity like the monster's inhuman body.[40] In fact, as we saw, the only maternal model in *Paradise Lost* is the terrifying figure of Sin. (That Eve's punishment for *her* sin is the doom of agonized maternity—the doom of painfully becoming no longer herself but "Mother of Human Race"—appears therefore to seal the grim parallel.) But all these powerful symbols would be bound to take on personal weight and darkness for Shelley, whose only real "mother" was a tombstone— or a shelf of books—and who, like all orphans, must have feared that she had been deliberately deserted by her dead parent, or that, if she was a monster, then her hidden, underground mother must have been one too.

For all these reasons, then, the monster's attitude toward the possibility (or impossibility) of finding a mother is unusually con-flicted and complex. At first, horrified by what he knows of the only "mother" he has ever had—Victor Frankenstein—he regards his parentage with loathing. Characteristically, he learns the specific details of his "conception" and "birth" (as Mary Shelley may have learned of hers) through reading, for Victor has kept a journal which records "that series of disgusting circumstances" leading "to the production of [the monster's] . . . loathsome person."[41] Later, how-ever, the ill-fated miniature of Caroline Beaufort Frankenstein, Victor's "angel mother," momentarily "attract[s]" him. In fact, he claims it is because he is "forever deprived of the delights that such beautiful creatures could bestow" that he resolves to implicate Justine in the murder of William. His reproachful explanation is curious, though ("The crime had its source in her; be hers the punishment"), as is the sinister rape fantasy he enacts by the side of the sleeping orphan ("Awake, fairest, thy lover is near—he who would give his life but to obtain one look of affection from thine eyes" [127–28, chap. 16]). Clearly feelings of rage, terror, and sexual nausea, as well as idealizing sentiments, accrete for Mary and the monster around the maternal female image, a fact which explains the later climactic wedding-night murder of apparently innocent Elizabeth. In this fierce, Miltonic world, *Frankenstein* says, the angel woman and the monster woman alike must die, if they are not dead already. And what is to be feared above all else is the reanimation of the dead, specifically of the maternal dead. Perhaps that is why a significant pun is embedded in the crucial birth scene ("It was on a dreary night of November") that, according to Mary Shelley, rose "unbidden" from her imagination. Looking at the "demoniacal corpse to which I had so miserably given life," Victor remarks that "A *mummy* again endued with animation could not be so hideous as that wretch" (43, chap. 5). For a similarly horrific (and equally punning) statement of sexual nausea, one would have to go back to Donne's "Loves Alchymie" with its urgent, misogynistic imperative: "Hope not for minde in women; at their best / Sweetnesse and wit, they are but / *Mummy* possest."

Interestingly, the literary group at Villa Diodati received a packet of books containing, among other poems, Samuel Taylor Coleridge's recently published "Christabel," shortly before Mary had her monster-dream and began her ghost story. More influential than "Loves Alchymie"—a poem Mary may or may not have read— "Christabel"'s vision of femaleness must have been embodied for the author of *Frankenstein* not only in the witch Geraldine's withered side and consequent self-loathing ("Ah! What a stricken look was hers!") but also in her anxiety about the ghost of Christabel's dead mother ("Off, wandering mother! Peak and pine!") and in Christabel's "Woe is me / She died the hour that I was born." But even without Donne's puns or Coleridge's Romanticized male definition of deathly maternity, Mary Shelley would have absorbed a keen sense of the agony of female sexuality, and specifically of the perils of motherhood, not just from *Paradise Lost* and from her own mother's fearfully exemplary fate but also from Wollstonecraft's almost prophetically anxious writings.

Maria, or the Wrongs of Woman (1797), which Mary read in 1814 (and possibly in 1815) is about, among other "wrongs," Maria's search for her lost child, her fears that "she" (for the fantasied child is a daughter) may have been murdered by her unscrupulous father, and her attempts to reconcile herself to the child's death. In a suicide scene that Wollstonecraft drafted shortly before her own death, as her daughter must have known, Maria swallows laudanum: "her soul was calm . . . nothing remained but an eager longing . . . to fly . . . from this hell of disappointment. Still her eyes closed not. . . . Her murdered child again appeared to her . . . [But] 'Surely it is better to die with me, than to enter on life without a mother's care!'"[42]

Plainly, *Frankenstein*'s pained ambivalence toward mothers and mummies is in some sense a response to *Maria's* agonized reaching—from beyond the grave, it may have seemed—toward a daughter. "Off, wandering mother! Peak and pine!" It is no wonder if Coleridge's poem gave Mary Wollstonecraft Godwin Shelley bad dreams, no wonder if she saw Milton's "Mother of Human Race" as a sorrowful monster.

Though *Frankenstein* itself began with a Coleridgean and Miltonic nightmare of filthy creation that reached its nadir in the monster's revelation of filthy femaleness, Mary Shelley, like Victor Frankenstein himself, evidently needed to distance such monstrous secrets. Sinful, motherless Eve and sinned-against, daughterless Maria, both paradigms of woman's helpless alienation in a male society, briefly emerge from the sea of male heroes and villains in which they have almost been lost, but the ice soon closes over their heads again, just as it closes around those two insane figure-skaters, Victor Frankenstein and his hideous offspring. Moving outward from the central "birth myth" to the icy perimeter on which the novel began, we find ourselves caught up once more in Walton's naive polar journey, where Frankenstein and his monster reappear as two embattled grotesques, distant and archetypal figures solipstically drifting away from each other on separate icebergs. In Walton's scheme of things, they look again like God and Adam, Satanically conceived. But now, with our more nearly complete understanding of the bewildered and bewildering perspective Mary Shelley adopted as "Milton's daughter," we see that they were Eve and Eve all along.

Nevertheless, though Shelley did manage to still the monster's suffering and Frankenstein's and her own by transporting all three from the fires of filthy creation back to the ice and silence of the Pole, she was never entirely to abandon the sublimated rage her monster-self enacted, and never to abandon, either, the metaphysical ambitions *Frankenstein* incarnated. In *The Last Man* she introduced, as Spark points out, "a new, inhuman protagonist," PLAGUE (the name is almost always spelled entirely in capitals), who is characterized as female and who sees to it that "disaster is no longer the property of the individual but of the entire human race."[43] And of course PLAGUE's story is the one that Mary claims to have found in the Sibyl's cave, a tale of a literally female monster that was merely foreshadowed by the more subdued narrative of "The Modern Prometheus."

Interestingly, PLAGUE's story ends with a vision of last things, a vision of judgment and of paradise nihilistically restored that balances *Frankenstein's* vision of first things. With all of humanity wiped out by the monster PLAGUE, just as the entire Frankenstein family was destroyed by Victor's monster, Lionel Verney, the narrator, goes to Rome, that cradle of patriarchal civilization whose ruins had seemed so majestically emblematic to both Byron and Shelley. But where Mary's husband had written of the great city in a kind of ecstasy, his widow has her disinherited "last man" wander lawlessly about empty Rome until finally he resolves, finding "parts of a manuscript . . . scattered about," that "I also will write a book . . . [but] for whom to read?—to whom dedicated? And then with silly flourish (what so capricious and childish as despair?) I wrote,

DEDICATION

TO THE ILLUSTRIOUS DEAD

SHADOWS, ARISE, AND READ YOUR FALL!

BEHOLD THE HISTORY OF THE LAST MAN.[44]

His hostile, ironic, literary gesture illuminates not only his own career but his author's. For the annihilation of history may well be the final revenge of the monster who has been denied a true place in history: the moral is one that Mary Shelley's first hideous progeny, like Milton's Eve, seems to have understood from the beginning.

8

Looking Oppositely:
Emily Brontë's Bible of Hell

Down from the waist they are Centaurs,
Though women all above:
But to the girdle do the Gods inherit,
Beneath is all the fiend's: there's hell, there's darkness,
There is the sulphurous pit. . .

—*King Lear*

It indeed appear'd to Reason as if Desire was cast out, but the
Devils account is, that the Messiah fell. & formed a heaven of what
he stole from the Abyss

—William Blake

A loss of something ever felt I—
The first that I could recollect
Bereft I was—of what I knew not
Too young that any should suspect

A Mourner walked among the children
I notwithstanding went about
As one bemoaning a Dominion
Itself the only Prince cast out—

Elder, Today, a session wiser
And fainter, too, as Wiseness is—
I find myself still softly searching
For my Delinquent Palaces—

And a Suspicion, like a Finger
Touches my Forehead now and then
That I am looking oppositely
For the site of the Kingdom of Heaven—
—Emily Dickinson

Frankenstein and *Wuthering Heights* (1847) are not usually seen as related works, except insofar as both are famous nineteenth-century literary puzzles, with Shelley's plaintive speculation about where she got so "hideous an idea" finding its counterpart in the position of Heathcliff's creator as a sort of mystery woman of literature. Still, if both Brontë and Shelley wrote enigmatic, curiously unprecedented novels, their works are puzzling in different ways: Shelley's is an enigmatic fantasy of metaphysical horror, Brontë's an enigmatic romance of metaphysical passion. Shelley produced an allusive, Romantic, and "masculine" text in which the fates of subordinate female characters seem entirely dependent upon the actions of ostensibly male heroes or anti-heroes. Brontë produced a more realistic narrative in which "the perdurable voice of the country," as Mark Schorer describes Nelly Dean, introduces us to a world where men battle for the favors of apparently high-spirited and independent women.[1]

Despite these dissimilarities, however, *Frankenstein* and *Wuthering Heights* are alike in a number of crucial ways. For one thing, both works *are* enigmatic, puzzling, even in some sense generically problematical. Moreover, in each case the mystery of the novel is associated with what seem to be its metaphysical intentions, intentions around which much critical controversy has collected. For these two "popular" novels—one a thriller, the other a romance—have convinced many readers that their charismatic surfaces conceal (far more than they reveal) complex ontological depths, elaborate structures of allusion, fierce though shadowy moral ambitions. And this point in particular is demonstrated by a simpler characteristic both works have in common. Both make use of what in connection with *Frankenstein* we called an evidentiary narrative technique, a Romantic story-telling method that emphasizes the ironic disjunctions between different perspectives on the same events as well as the ironic tensions that inhere in the relationship between surface drama and concealed authorial intention. In fact, in its use of such a technique, *Wuthering Heights* might be a deliberate copy of *Frankenstein*. Not only do the stories of both novels emerge through concentric circles of narration, both works contain significant digressions. Catherine Earnshaw's diary, Isabella's letter, Zillah's narrative, and Heathcliff's confidences to Nelly function in *Wuthering Heights* much as Alphonse

Frankenstein's letter, Justine's narrative, and Safie's history do in *Frankenstein*.

Their common concern with evidence, especially with written evidence, suggests still another way in which *Wuthering Heights* and *Frankenstein* are alike: more than most novels, both are consciously literary works, at times almost obsessively concerned with books and with reading as not only a symbolic but a dramatic—plot-forwarding—activity. Can this be because, like Shelley, Brontë was something of a literary heiress? The idea is an odd one to consider, because the four Brontë children, scribbling in Yorkshire's remote West Riding, seem as trapped on the periphery of nineteenth-century literary culture as Mary Shelley was embedded in its God-winian and Byronic center. Nevertheless, peripheral though they were, the Brontës had literary parents just as Mary Shelley did: the Reverend Patrick Brontë was in his youth the author of several books of poetry, a novel, and a collection of sermons, and Maria Branwell, the girl he married, apparently also had some literary abilities.[2] And of course, besides having obscure literary parents Emily Brontë had literary siblings, though they too were in most of her own lifetime almost as unknown as their parents.

Is it coincidental that the author of *Wuthering Heights* was the sister of the authors of *Jane Eyre* and *Agnes Grey*? Did the parents, especially the father, bequeath a frustrated drive toward literary success to their children? These are interesting though unanswerable questions, but they imply a point that is crucial in any consideration of the Brontës, just as it was important in thinking about Mary Shelley: it was the habit in the Brontë family, as in the Wollstonecraft-Godwin-Shelley family, to approach reality through the mediating agency of books, to read one's relatives, and to feel related to one's reading. Thus the transformation of three lonely yet ambitious Yorkshire governesses into the magisterially androgynous trio of Currer, Ellis, and Acton Bell was a communal act, an assertion of family identity. And significantly, even the games these writers played as children prepared them for such a literary mode of self-definition. As most Brontë admirers know, the four young inhabitants of Haworth Parsonage began producing extended narratives at an early age, and these eventually led to the authorship of a large library of minia-ture books which constitutes perhaps the most famous juvenilia in

English. Though in subject matter these works are divided into two groups—one, the history of the imaginary kingdom of Gondal, written by Emily and Anne, and the other, stories of the equally imaginary land of Angria, written by Charlotte and Branwell—all four children read and discussed all the tales, and even served as models for characters in many. Thus the Brontës' deepest feelings of kinship appear to have been expressed first in literary collaboration and private childish attempts at fictionalizing each other, and then, later, in the public collaboration the sisters undertook with the ill-fated collection of poetry that was their first "real" publication. Finally Charlotte, the last survivor of these prodigious siblings, memorialized her lost sisters in print, both in fiction and in non-fiction (*Shirley*, for instance, mythologizes Emily). Given the traditions of her family, it was no doubt inevitable that, for her, writing—not only novel-writing but the writing of prefaces to "family" works—would replace tombstone-raising, hymn-singing, maybe even weeping.[3]

That both literary activity and literary evidence were so important to the Brontës may be traced to another problem they shared with Mary Shelley. Like the anxious creator of *Frankenstein*, the authors of *Wuthering Heights*, *Jane Eyre*, and *The Tenant of Wildfell Hall* lost their mother when they were very young. Like Shelley, indeed, Emily and Anne Brontë were too young when their mother died even to know much about her except through the evidence of older survivors and perhaps through some documents. Just as *Frankenstein*, with its emphasis on orphans and beggars, is a motherless book, so all the Brontë novels betray intense feelings of motherlessness, orphanhood, destitution. And in particular the problems of literary orphanhood seem to lead in *Wuthering Heights*, as in *Frankenstein*, not only to a concern with surviving evidence but also to a fascination with the question of origins. Thus if all women writers, metaphorical orphans in patriarchal culture, seek literary answers to the questions "How are we fal'n, / Fal'n by mistaken rules . . . ?" motherless orphans like Mary Shelley and Emily Brontë almost seem to seek literal answers to that question, so passionately do their novels enact distinctive female literary obsessions.

Finally, that such a psychodramatic enactment is going on in both *Wuthering Heights* and *Frankenstein* suggests a similarity between the two novels which brings us back to the tension between dramatic surfaces and metaphysical depths with which we began this discussion. For just as one of *Frankenstein*'s most puzzling traits is the symbolic ambiguity or fluidity its characters display when they are studied closely, so one of *Wuthering Heights*'s key elements is what Leo Bersani calls its "ontological slipperiness."[4] In fact, because it is a *metaphysical* romance (just as *Frankenstein* is a *metaphysical* thriller) *Wuthering Heights* seems at times to be about forces or beings rather than people, which is no doubt one reason why some critics have thought it generically problematical, maybe not a novel at all but instead an extended exemplum, or a "prosified" verse drama. And just as all the characters in *Frankenstein* are in a sense the same two characters, so "everyone [in *Wuthering Heights*] is finally related to everyone else and, in a sense, repeated in everyone else," as if the novel, like an illustration of Freud's "Das Unheimlische," were about "the danger of being haunted by alien versions of the self."[5] But when it is created by a woman in the misogynistic context of Western literary culture, this sort of anxiously philosophical, problem-solving, myth-making narrative must—so it seems—inevitably come to grips with the countervailing stories told by patriarchal poetry, and specifically by Milton's patriarchal poetry.

Milton, Winifred Gérin tells us, was one of Patrick Brontë's favorite writers, so if Shelley was Milton's critic's daughter, Brontë was Milton's admirer's daughter.[6] By the Hegelian law of thesis/antithesis, then, it seems appropriate that Shelley chose to repeat and restate Milton's misogynistic story while Brontë chose to correct it. In fact the most serious matter *Wuthering Heights* and *Frankenstein* share is the matter of *Paradise Lost*, and their profoundest difference is in their attitude toward Milton's myth. Where Shelley was Milton's dutiful daughter, retelling his story to clarify it, Brontë was the poet's rebellious child, radically revising (and even reversing) the terms of his mythic narrative. Given the fact that Brontë never mentions either Milton or *Paradise Lost* in *Wuthering Heights*, any identification of her as Milton's daughter may at first seem eccentric or perverse. Shelley, after all, provided an overtly Miltonic framework in *Franken-stein* to reinforce our sense of her literary intentions. But despite the absence of Milton references, it eventually becomes plain that

Wuthering Heights is also a novel haunted by Milton's bogey. We may speculate, indeed, that Milton's absence is itself a presence, so painfully does Brontë's story dwell on the places and persons of his imagination.

That *Wuthering Heights* is about heaven and hell, for instance, has long been seen by critics, partly because all the narrative voices, from the beginning of Lockwood's first visit to the Heights, insist upon casting both action and description in religious terms, and partly because one of the first Catherine's major speeches to Nelly Dean raises the questions "What is heaven? Where is hell?" perhaps more urgently than any other speech in an English novel:

> "If I were in heaven, Nelly, I should be extremely miserable. . . .
> I dreamt once that I was there [and] that heaven did not seem to
> be my home, and I broke my heart with weeping to come back to
> earth; and the angels were so angry that they flung me out into
> the middle of the heath on the top of Wuthering Heights, where
> I woke sobbing for joy." [7]

Satan too, however—at least Satan as Milton's prototypical Byronic hero—has long been considered a participant in *Wuthering Heights*, for "that devil Heathcliff," as both demon lover and ferocious natural force, is a phenomenon critics have always studied. Isabella's "Is Mr. Heathcliff a man? If so, is he mad? And if not is he a devil?" (chap. 13) summarizes the traditional Heathcliff problem most succinctly, but Nelly's "I was inclined to believe . . . that conscience had turned his heart to an earthly hell" (chap. 33) more obviously echoes *Paradise Lost*.

Again, that *Wuthering Heights* is in some sense about a fall has frequently been suggested, though critics from Charlotte Brontë to Mark Schorer, Q. D. Leavis, and Leo Bersani have always disputed its exact nature and moral implications. Is Catherine's fall the archetypal fall of the *Bildungsroman* protagonist? Is Heathcliff's fall, his perverted "moral teething," a shadow of Catherine's? Which of the two worlds of *Wuthering Heights* (if either) does Brontë mean to represent the truly "fallen" world? These are just some of the controversies that have traditionally attended this issue. Nevertheless, that the story of *Wuthering Heights* is built around a central fall seems indisputable, so that a description of the novel as in part a *Bildungs-*

roman about a girl's passage from "innocence" to "experience" (leaving aside the precise meaning of those terms) would probably also be widely accepted. And that the fall in *Wuthering Heights* has Miltonic overtones is no doubt culturally inevitable. But even if it weren't, the Miltonic implications of the action would be clear enough from the "mad scene" in which Catherine describes herself as "an exile, and outcast . . . from what had been my world," adding "Why am I so changed? Why does my blood rush into a hell of tumult at a few words?" (chap. 12). Given the metaphysical nature of *Wuthering Heights*, Catherine's definition of herself as "an exile and outcast" inevitably suggests those trail-blazing exiles and outcasts Adam, Eve, and Satan. And her Romantic question—"Why am I so changed?"— with its desperate straining after the roots of identity, must ultimately refer back to Satan's hesitant (but equally crucial) speech to Beelzebub, as they lie stunned in the lake of fire: "If thou be'est he; But O . . . how chang'd" (*PL* 1. 84).

Of course, *Wuthering Heights* has often, also, been seen as a subversively visionary novel. Indeed, Brontë is frequently coupled with Blake as a practitioner of mystical politics. Usually, however, as if her book were written to illustrate the enigmatic religion of "No coward soul is mine," this visionary quality is related to Catherine's assertion that she is tired of "being enclosed" in "this shattered prison" of her body, and "wearying to escape into that glorious world, and to be always there" (chap. 15). Many readers define Brontë, in other words, as a ferocious pantheist/transcendentalist, worshipping the manifestations of the One in rock, tree, cloud, man and woman, while manipulating her story to bring about a Romantic *Liebestod* in which favored characters enter "the endless and shadowless hereafter." And certainly such ideas, like Blake's *Songs of Innocence*, are "something heterodox," to use Lockwood's phrase. At the same time, however, they are soothingly rather than disquietingly neo-Miltonic, like fictionalized visions of *Paradise Lost*'s luminous Father God. They are, in fact, the ideas of "steady, reasonable" Nelly Dean, whose denial of the demonic in life, along with her commitment to the angelic tranquility of death, represents only one of the visionary alternatives in *Wuthering Heights*. And, like Blake's metaphor of the lamb, Nelly's pious alternative has no real meaning for Brontë outside of the context provided by its tigerish opposite.

The tigerish opposite implied by *Wuthering Heights* emerges most dramatically when we bring all the novel's Miltonic elements together with its author's personal concerns in an attempt at a single formulation of Brontë's metaphysical intentions: the sum of this novel's visionary parts is an almost shocking revisionary whole. Heaven (or its rejection), hell, Satan, a fall, mystical politics, metaphysical romance, orphanhood, and the question of origins—disparate as some of these matters may seem, they all cohere in a rebelliously topsy-turvy retelling of Milton's and Western culture's central tale of the fall of woman and her shadow self, Satan. This fall, says Brontë, is not a fall *into* hell. It is a fall *from* "hell" into "heaven," not a fall from grace(in the religious sense) but a fall into grace(in the cultural sense). Moreover, for the heroine who falls it is the loss of Satan rather than the loss of God that signals the painful passage from innocence to experience. Emily Brontë, in other words, is not just Blakeian in "double" mystical vision, but Blakeian in a tough, radically political commitment to the belief that the state of being patriarchal Christianity calls "hell" is eternally, energetically delightful, whereas the state called "heaven" is rigidly hierarchical, Urizenic, and "kind" as a poison tree. But because she was metaphorically one of Milton's daughters, Brontë differs from Blake, that powerful son of a powerful father, in reversing the terms of Milton's Christian cosmogony for specifically feminist reasons.

Speaking of Jane Lead, a seventeenth-century Protestant mystic who was a significant precursor of Brontë's in visionary sexual politics, Catherine Smith has noted that "to study mysticism and feminism together is to learn more about the links between envisioning power and pursuing it," adding that "Idealist notions of transcendence may shape political notions of sexual equality as much as materialist or rationalist arguments do."[8] Her points are applicable to Brontë, whose revisionary mysticism is inseparable from both politics and feminism, although her emphasis is more on the loss than on the pursuit of power. Nevertheless, the feminist nature of her concern with neo-Miltonic definitions of hell and heaven, power and powerlessness, innocence and experience, has generally been overlooked by critics, many of whom, at their most biographical, tend to ask patronizing questions like "What is the matter with Emily Jane?"[9] Interestingly, however, certain women understood Brontë's feminist

mythologies from the first. Speculating on the genesis of A. G. A.,
the fiery Byronic queen of Gondal with whose life and loves Emily
Brontë was always obsessed, Fanny Ratchford noted in 1955 that
while Arthur Wellesley, the emperor of Charlotte Brontë's fantasy
kingdom of Angria, was "an arch-Byronic hero, for love of whom
noble ladies went into romantic decline, . . . Gondal's queen was of
such compelling beauty and charm as to bring all men to her feet,
and of such selfish cruelty as to bring tragedy to all who loved her. . . .
It was as if Emily was saying to Charlotte, 'You think the man is the
dominant factor in romantic love, I'll show you it is the woman.'" [10]
But of course Charlotte herself understood Emily's revisionary tendencies better than anyone. More than one hundred years before
Ratchford wrote, the heroine of *Shirley*, that apotheosis of Emily
"as she would have been in a happier life," speaks the English novel's
first deliberately feminist criticism of Milton—"Milton did not see
Eve, it was his cook that he saw"—and proposes as her alternative
the Titan woman we discussed earlier, the mate of "Genius" and the
potentially Satanic interlocutor of God. Some readers, including most
recently the Marxist critic Terence Eagleton, have spoken scornfully
of the "maundering rhetoric of *Shirley*'s embarrassing feminist mysticism." [11] But Charlotte, who was intellectually as well as physically
akin to Emily, had captured the serious deliberation in her sister's
vision. She knew that the author of *Wuthering Heights* was—to quote
the Brontës' admirer Emily Dickinson—"looking oppositely / For the
site of the Kingdom of Heaven" (J. 959).

Because Emily Brontë was looking oppositely not only for heaven
(and hell) but for her own female origins, *Wuthering Heights* is one of
the few authentic instances of novelistic myth-making, myth-making
in the functional sense of problem-solving. Where writers from
Charlotte Brontë and Henry James to James Joyce and Virginia
Woolf have used mythic material to give point and structure to their
novels, Emily Brontë uses the novel form to give substance—plausibility, really—to her myth. It is urgent that she do so because, as we
shall see, the feminist cogency of this myth derives not only from its
daring corrections of Milton but also from the fact that it is a
distinctively nineteenth-century answer to the question of origins:

it is the myth of how culture came about, and specifically of how nineteenth-century society occurred, the tale of where tea-tables, sofas, crinolines, and parsonages like the one at Haworth came from.

Because it is so ambitious a myth, *Wuthering Heights* has the puzzling self-containment of a *mystery* in the old sense of that word—the sense of mystery plays and Eleusinian mysteries. Locked in by Lockwood's uncomprehending narrative, Nelly Dean's story, with its baffling duplication of names, places, events, seems endlessly to reenact itself, like some ritual that must be cyclically repeated in order to sustain (as well as explain) both nature and culture. At the same time, because it is so prosaic a myth—a myth about crinolines!—*Wuthering Heights* is not in the least portentous or self-consciously "mythic." On the contrary, like all true rituals and myths, Brontë's "cuckoo's tale" turns a practical, casual, humorous face to its audience. For as Lévi-Straus's observations suggest, true believers gossip by the prayer wheel, since that modern reverence which enjoins solemnity is simply the foster child of modern skepticism.[12]

Gossipy but unconventional true believers were rare, even in the pious nineteenth century, as Arnold's anxious meditations and Carlyle's angry sermons note. But Brontë's paradoxically matter-of-fact imaginative strength, her ability to enter a realistically freckled fantasy land, manifested itself early. One of her most famous adolescent diary papers juxtaposes a plea for culinary help from the parsonage housekeeper, Tabby—"Come Anne pilloputate"—with "The Gondals are discovering the interior of Gaaldine" and "Sally Mosely is washing in the back kitchen."[13] Significantly, no distinction is made between the heroic exploits of the fictional Gondals and Sally Mosely's real washday business. The curiously childlike voice of the diarist records all events without commentary, and this reserve suggests an implicit acquiescence in the equal "truth" of all events. Eleven years later, when the sixteen-year-old reporter of "pilloputate" has grown up and is on the edge of *Wuthering Heights*, the naive, uninflected surface of her diary papers is unchanged:

> ... Anne and I went our first long journey by ourselves together, leaving home on the 30th of June, Monday, sleeping at York, returning to Keighley Tuesday evening ... during our excursion we were Ronald Mcalgin, Henry Angora, Juliet Angusteena,

> Rosabella Esmalden, Ella and Julian Egremont, Catharine
> Navarre, and Cordilia Fitzaphnold, escaping from the palaces
> of instruction to join the Royalists who are hard driven at
> present by the victorious Republicans. . . . I must hurry off now
> to my turning and ironing. I have plenty of work on hands, and
> writing, and am altogether full of business.[14]

Psychodramatic "play," this passage suggests, is an activity at once
as necessary and as ordinary as housework: ironing and the exploration of alternative lives are the same kind of "business"—a perhaps
uniquely female idea of which Anne Bradstreet and Emily Dickinson,
those other visionary housekeepers, would have approved.

No doubt, however, it is this deep-seated tendency of Brontë's to
live literally with the fantastic that accounts for much of the critical
disputation about *Wuthering Heights*, especially the quarrels about the
novel's genre and style. Q. D. Leavis and Arnold Kettle, for instance,
insist that the work is a "sociological novel," while Mark Schorer
thinks it "means to be a work of edification [about] the nature of a
grand passion." Leo Bersani sees it as an ontological psychodrama,
and Elliot Gose as a sort of expanded fairytale.[15] And strangely there
is truth in all these apparently conflicting notions, just as it is also
true that (as Robert Kiely has affirmed) "part of the distinction of
Wuthering Heights [is] that it has no 'literary' aura about it," and true
at the same time that (as we have asserted) *Wuthering Heights* is an
unusually literary novel because Brontë approached reality chiefly
through the mediating agency of literature.[16] In fact, Kiely's comment
illuminates not only the uninflected surface of the diary papers but
also the controversies about their author's novel, for Brontë is "unliterary" in being without a received sense of what the eighteenth
century called literary decorum. As one of her better-known poems
declares, she follows "where [her] own nature would be leading,"
and that nature leads her to an oddly literal—and also, therefore,
unliterary—use of extraordinarily various literary works, ideas, and
genres, all of which she refers back to herself, since "it vexes [her]
to choose another guide."[17]

Thus *Wuthering Heights* is in one sense an elaborate gloss on the
Byronic Romanticism and incest fantasy of *Manfred*, written, as
Ratchford suggested, from a consciously female perspective. Heath-

cliff's passionate invocations of Catherine ("Come in! . . . hear me" [chap. 3] or "Be with me always—take any form—drive me mad" [chap. 16]) almost exactly echo Manfred's famous speech to Astarte ("Hear me, hear me . . . speak to me! Though it be in wrath . . . ").[18] In another way, though, *Wuthering Heights* is a prose redaction of the metaphysical storms and ontological nature/culture conflicts embodied in *King Lear*, with Heathcliff taking the part of Nature's bastard son Edmund, Edgar Linton incarnating the cultivated morality of his namesake Edgar, and the "wuthering" chaos at the Heights repeating the disorder that overwhelms Lear's kingdom when he relinquishes his patriarchal control to his diabolical daughters. But again, both poetic Byronic Romanticism and dramatic Shakespearean metaphysics are filtered through a novelistic sensibility with a surprisingly Austenian grasp of social details, so that *Wuthering Heights* seems also, in its "unliterary" way, to reiterate the feminist psychological concerns of a *Bildungsroman* Brontë may never have read: Jane Austen's *Northanger Abbey*. Catherine Earnshaw's "half savage and hardy and free" girlhood, for example, recalls the tomboy childhood of that other Catherine, Catherine Morland, and Catherine Earnshaw's fall into ladylike "grace" seems to explore the tragic underside of the anxiously comic initiation rites Catherine Morland undergoes at Bath and at Northanger Abbey.[19]

The world of *Wuthering Heights*, in other words, like the world of Brontë's diary papers, is one where what seem to be the most unlikely opposites coexist without, apparently, any consciousness on the author's part that there is anything unlikely in their coexistence. The ghosts of Byron, Shakespeare, and Jane Austen haunt the same ground. People with decent Christian names (Catherine, Nelly, Edgar, Isabella) inhabit a landscape in which also dwell people with strange animal or nature names (Hindley, Hareton, Heathcliff). Fairy-tale events out of what Mircea Eliade would call "great time" are given a local habitation and a real chronology in just that historical present Eliade defines as great time's opposite.[20] Dogs and gods (or goddesses) turn out to be not opposites but, figuratively speaking, the same words spelled in different ways. Funerals are weddings, weddings funerals. And of course, most important for our purposes here, hell is heaven, heaven hell, though the two are not separated, as Milton and literary decorum would prescribe, by vast eons of space but by a little strip of turf, for Brontë was rebelliously determined to walk

> . . . not in old heroic traces
> And not in paths of high morality.
> And not among the half-distinguished faces,
> The clouded forms of long-past history.

On the contrary, surveying that history and its implications, she came to the revisionary conclusion that "the earth that wakes *one* human heart to feeling / Can centre both the worlds of Heaven and Hell."[21]

If we identify with Lockwood, civilized man at his most genteelly "cooked" and literary, we cannot fail to begin Brontë's novel by deciding that hell is a household very like Wuthering Heights. Lockwood himself, as if wittily predicting the reversal of values that is to be the story's central concern, at first calls the place "a perfect misanthropist's Heaven" (chap. 1). But then what is the traditional Miltonic or Dantesque hell if not a misanthropist's heaven, a site that substitutes hate for love, violence for peace, death for life, and in consequence the material for the spiritual, disorder for order? Certainly Wuthering Heights rings all these changes on Lockwood's first two visits. Heathcliff's first invitation to enter, for instance, is uttered through closed teeth, and appropriately enough it seems to his visitor to express "the sentiment 'Go to the Deuce.'" The house's other inhabitants—Catherine II, Hareton, Joseph, and Zillah, as we later learn—are for the most part equally hostile on both occasions, with Joseph muttering insults, Hareton surly, and Catherine II actually practicing (or pretending to practice) the "black arts."[22] Their energies of hatred, moreover, are directed not only at their uninvited guest but at each other, as Lockwood learns to his sorrow when Catherine II suggests that Hareton should accompany him through the storm and Hareton refuses to do so if it would please *her*.

The general air of sour hatred that blankets the Heights, moreover, manifests itself in a continual, aimless violence, a violence most particularly embodied in the snarling dogs that inhabit the premises. "In an arch under the dresser," Lockwood notes, "reposed a huge, liver-coloured bitch pointer, surrounded by a swarm of squealing puppies; and other dogs haunted other recesses" (chap. 1). His use of *haunted* is apt, for these animals, as he later remarks, are more like "four-footed fiends" than ordinary canines, and in particular Juno, the matriarch of the "hive," seems to be a parody of Milton's grotesquely maternal Sin, with her yapping brood of hellhounds. Significantly, too, the only nonhostile creatures in this fiercely Satanic stronghold are dead: in one of a series of blackly comic blunders, Lockwood compliments Catherine II on what in his decorous way he assumes are her cats, only to learn that the "cats" are just a heap of dead rabbits. In addition, though the kitchen is separate from the central family room, "a vast oak dresser" reaching "to the very roof" of the sitting room is laden with oatcakes, guns, and raw meat: "clusters of legs of beef, mutton, and ham." Dead or raw flesh and the instruments by which living bodies may be converted into more dead flesh are such distinctive features of the room that even the piles of oatcakes and the "immense pewter dishes . . . towering row after row" (chap. 1) suggest that, like hell or the land at the top of the beanstalk, Wuthering Heights is the abode of some particularly bloodthirsty giant.

The disorder that quite naturally accompanies the hatred, violence, and death that prevail at Wuthering Heights on Lockwood's first visits leads to more of the city-bred gentleman's blunders, in particular his inability to fathom the relationships among the three principal members of the household's pseudo-family—Catherine II, Hareton, and Heathcliff. First he suggests that the girl is Heathcliff's "amiable lady," then surmises that Hareton is "the favoured possessor of the beneficent fairy" (chap. 2). His phrases, like most of his assumptions, parody the sentimentality of fictions that keep women in their "place" by defining them as beneficent fairies or amiable ladies. Heathcliff, perceiving this, adds a third stereotype to the discussion: "You would intimate that [my wife's] spirit has taken the form of ministering angel," he comments with the "almost diabolical sneer" of a Satanic literary critic. But of course, though Lockwood's thinking is stereotypical, he is right to expect some familial relationship among his tea-table companions, and right too to be daunted by the hellish lack of relationship among them. For though Hareton, Heathcliff, and Catherine II are all in some sense related, the primordial schisms that

have overwhelmed the Heights with hatred and violence have divided
them from the human orderliness represented by the ties of kinship.
Thus just as Milton's hell consists of envious and (in the poet's view)
equality-mad devils jostling for position, so these inhabitants of
Wuthering Heights seem to live in chaos without the structuring
principle of heaven's hierarchical chain of being, and therefore
without the heavenly harmony God the Father's ranking of virtues,
thrones, and powers makes possible. For this reason Catherine sullenly
refuses to do anything "except what I please" (chap. 4), the servant
Zillah vociferously rebukes Hareton for laughing, and old Joseph—
whose viciously parodic religion seems here to represent a hellish
joke at heaven's expense—lets the dogs loose on Linton without
consulting his "maister," Heathcliff.

In keeping with this problem of "equality," a final and perhaps
definitive sign of the hellishness that has enveloped Wuthering
Heights at the time of Lockwood's first visits is the blinding snowfall
that temporarily imprisons the by now unwilling guest in the home
of his infernal hosts. Pathless as the kingdom of the damned, the
"billowy white ocean" of cold that surrounds Wuthering Heights
recalls the freezing polar sea on which Frankenstein, Walton, the
monster—and the Ancient Mariner—voyaged. It recalls, too, the
"deep snow and ice" of Milton's hell, "A gulf profound as that
Serbonian Bog . . . Where Armies whole have sunk" and where "by
harpy-footed" and no doubt rather Heathcliff-ish "Furies hal'd / . . .
all the damn'd / Are brought . . . to starve in Ice" (*PL* 2. 592–600).
But of course, as *King Lear* implies, hell is simply another word for
uncontrolled "nature," and here as elsewhere *Wuthering Heights*
follows *Lear*'s model.

Engulfing the Earnshaws' ancestral home and the Lintons', too,
in a blizzard of destruction, hellish nature traps and freezes everyone
in the isolation of a "perfect misanthropist's heaven." And again, as
in *Lear* this hellish nature is somehow female or associated with
femaleness, like an angry goddess shaking locks of ice and introducing
Lockwood (and his readers) to the female rage that will be a central
theme in *Wuthering Heights*. The femaleness of this "natural" hell is
suggested, too, by its likeness to the "false" material creation Robert
Graves analyzed so well in *The White Goddess*. Female nature has
risen, it seems, in a storm of protest, just as the Sin-like dog Juno

rises in a fury when Lockwood "unfortunately indulge[s] in winking and making faces" at her while musing on his heartless treatment of a "goddess" to whom he never "told" his love (chap. 1). Finally, that the storm is both hellish and female is made clearest of all by Lockwood's second visionary dream. Out of the tapping of branches, out of the wind and swirling snow, like an icy-fingered incarnation of the storm rising in protest against the patriarchal sermon of "Jabes Branderham," appears that ghostly female witch-child the *original* Catherine Earnshaw, who has now been "a waif for twenty years."

Why is Wuthering Heights so Miltonically hellish? And what happened to Catherine Earnshaw? Why has she become a demonic, storm-driven ghost? The "real" etiological story of *Wuthering Heights* begins, as Lockwood learns from his "human fixture" Nelly Dean, with a random weakening of the fabric of ordinary human society. Once upon a time, somewhere in what mythically speaking qualifies as pre-history or what Eliade calls "illo tempore," there is/was a primordial family, the Earnshaws, who trace their lineage back at least as far as the paradigmatic Renaissance inscription "1500 Hareton Earnshaw" over their "principal doorway." And one fine summer morning toward the end of the eighteenth century, the "old master" of the house decides to take a walking tour of sixty miles to Liverpool (chap. 4). His decision, like Lear's decision to divide his kingdom, is apparently quite arbitrary, one of those mystifying psychic *données* for which the fictional convention of "once upon a time" was devised. Perhaps it means, like Lear's action, that he is half-consciously beginning to prepare for death. In any case, his ritual questions to his two children—an older son and a younger daughter—and to their servant Nelly are equally stylized and arbitrary, as are the children's answers. "What shall I bring you?" the old master asks, like the fisherman to whom the flounder gave three wishes. And the children reply, as convention dictates, by requesting their heart's desires. In other words, they reveal their true selves, just as a father contemplating his own ultimate absence from their lives might have hoped they would.

Strangely enough, however, only the servant Nelly's heart's desire is sensible and conventional: she asks for (or, rather, accepts the promise of) a pocketful of apples and pears. Hindley, on the other hand, the son who is destined to be next master of the household, does not ask for a particularly masterful gift. His wish, indeed, seems frivolous in the context of the harsh world of the Heights. He asks for a fiddle, betraying both a secret, soft-hearted desire for culture and an almost decadent lack of virile purpose. Stranger still is Catherine's wish for a whip. "She could ride any horse in the stable," says Nelly, but in the fairy-tale context of this narrative that realistic explanation hardly seems to suffice,[23] for, symbolically, the small Catherine's longing for a whip seems like a powerless younger daughter's yearning for power.

Of course, as we might expect from our experience of fairy tales, at least one of the children receives the desired boon. Catherine gets her whip. She gets it figuratively—in the form of a "gypsy brat"—rather than literally, but nevertheless "it" (both whip and brat) functions just as she must unconsciously have hoped it would, smashing her rival-brother's fiddle and making a desirable third among the children in the family so as to insulate her from the pressure of her brother's domination. (That there should always have been three children in the family is clear from the way other fairytale rituals of three are observed, and also from the fact that Heathcliff is given the name of a dead son, perhaps even the true oldest son, as if he were a reincarnation of the lost child.)

Having received her deeply desired whip, Catherine now achieves, as Hillis Miller and Leo Bersani have noticed, an extraordinary fullness of being.[24] The phrase may seem pretentiously metaphysical (certainly critics like Q. D. Leavis have objected to such phrases on those grounds)[25] but in discussing the early paradise from which Catherine and Heathcliff eventually fall we are trying to describe elusive psychic states, just as we would in discussing Wordsworth's visionary childhood, Frankenstein's youth before he "learned" that he was (the creator of) a monster, or even the prelapsarian sexuality of Milton's Adam and Eve. And so, like Freud who was driven to grope among such words as *oceanic* when he tried to explain the heaven that lies about us in our infancy, we are obliged to use the paradoxical and metaphorical language of mysticism: phrases like *wholeness, fullness of being*, and *androgyny* come inevitably to mind.[26] All three, as we shall see, apply to Catherine, or more precisely to Catherine-Heath-cliff.

In part Catherine's new wholeness results from a very practical shift in family dynamics. Heathcliff as a fantasy replacement of the dead oldest brother does in fact supplant Hindley in the old master's affections, and therefore he functions as a tool of the dispossessed younger sister whose "whip" he is. Specifically, he enables her for the first time to get possession of the kingdom of Wuthering Heights, which under her rule threatens to become, like Gondal, a queendom. In addition to this, however, Heathcliff's presence gives the girl a fullness of being that goes beyond power in household politics, because as Catherine's whip he is (and she herself recognizes this) an alternative self or double for her, a complementary addition to her being who fleshes out all her lacks the way a bandage might staunch a wound. Thus in her union with him she becomes, like Manfred in his union with his sister Astarte, a perfect androgyne. As devoid of sexual awareness as Adam and Eve were in the pre-lapsarian garden, she sleeps with her whip, her other half, every night in the primordial fashion of the countryside. Gifted with that in-nocent, unselfconscious sexual energy which Blake saw as eternal delight, she has "ways with her," according to Nelly, "such as I never saw a child take up before" (chap. 5). And if Heathcliff's is the body that does her will—strong, dark, proud, and a native speaker of "gibberish" rather than English—she herself is an "unfeminine" instance of transcendently vital spirit. For she is never docile, never submissive, never ladylike. On the contrary, her joy—and the Coleridgean word is not too strong—is in what Milton's Eve is never allowed: a tongue "always going—singing, laughing, and plaguing everybody who would not do the same," and "ready words: turning Joseph's religious curses into ridicule . . . and doing just what her father hated most" (chap. 5).

Perverse as it may seem, this paradise into which Heathcliff's advent has transformed Wuthering Heights for the young Catherine is as authentic a fantasy for women as Milton's Eden was for men, though Milton's misogynistically cowed daughters have rarely had the revisionary courage to spell out so many of the terms of their dream. Still, that the historical process does yield moments when that feminist dream of wholeness has real consequences is another point Brontë wishes us to consider, just as she wishes to convey her rueful awareness that, given the prior strength of patriarchal misogyny, those consequences may be painful as well as paradisal. Producing Heathcliff from beneath his greatcoat as if enacting a mock birth, old Mr. Earnshaw notes at once the equivocal nature of Catherine's whip: "You must e'en take it as a gift of God, though it's as dark almost as if it came from the devil" (chap. 4). His ambivalence is well-founded: strengthened by Heathcliff, Catherine becomes increasingly rebellious against the parodic patriarchal religion Joseph advocates, and thus, too, increasingly unmindful of her father's discipline. As she gains in rebellious energy, she becomes Satanically "as Gods" in her defiance of such socially constituted authority, and in the end, like a demonic Cordelia (that is, like Cordelia, Goneril, and Regan all in one) she has the last laugh at her father, answering his crucial dying question "Why canst thou not always be a good lass, Cathy?" with a defiantly honest question of her own: "Why cannot you always be a good man, Father?" (chap. 5) and then singing him, rather hostilely, "to sleep"—that is, to death.

Catherine's heaven, in other words, is very much like the place such a representative gentleman as Lockwood would call hell, for it is associated (like the hell of *King Lear*) with an ascendent self-willed female who radiates what, as Blake observed, most people consider "diabolical" energy—the creative energy of Los and Satan, the life energy of fierce, raw, uncultivated being.[27] But the ambiguity Catherine's own father perceives in his "gift of God" to the girl is also manifested in the fact that even some of the authentically hellish qualities Lockwood found at Wuthering Heights on his first two visits, especially the qualities of "hate" (i.e. defiance) and "violence" (i.e. energy), would have seemed to him to characterize the Wuthering Heights of Catherine's heavenly childhood. For Catherine, however, the defiance that might seem like hate was made possible by love (her oneness with Heathcliff) and the energy that seemed like violence was facilitated by the peace (the wholeness) of an undivided self.

Nevertheless, her personal heaven is surrounded, like Milton's Eden, by threats from what she would define as "hell." If, for instance, she had in some part of herself hoped that her father's death would ease the stress of that shadowy patriarchal yoke which was the only cloud on her heaven's horizon, Catherine was mistaken. For paradoxically old Earnshaw's passing brings with it the end to Catherine's Edenic "half savage and hardy and free" girlhood. It brings about a divided world in which the once-androgynous child is to be "laid alone" for the first time. And most important it brings about the accession to power of Hindley, by the patriarchal laws of primogeniture the real heir and thus the new father who is to introduce into the novel the proximate causes of Catherine's (and Heathcliff's) fall and subsequent decline.

Catherine's sojourn in the earthly paradise of childhood lasts for six years, according to C. P. Sanger's precisely worked-out chronology, but it takes Nelly Dean barely fifteen minutes to relate the episode.[28] Prelapsarian history, as Milton knew, is easy to summarize. Since happiness has few of the variations of despair, to be unfallen is to be static, whereas to fall is to enter the processes of time. Thus Nelly's account of Catherine's fall takes at least several hours, though it also covers six years. And as she describes it, that fall—or process of falling—begins with Hindley's marriage, an event associated for obvious reasons with the young man's inheritance of his father's power and position.

It is odd that Hindley's marriage should precipitate Catherine out of her early heaven because that event installs an adult woman in the small Heights family circle for the first time since the death of Mrs. Earnshaw four years earlier, and as conventional (or even feminist) wisdom would have it, Catherine "needs" a mother-figure to look after her, especially now that she is on the verge of adolescence. But precisely because she and Heathcliff are twelve years old and growing up, the arrival of Frances is the worst thing that could happen to her. For Frances, as Nelly's narrative indicates, is a model young lady, a creature of a species Catherine, safely sequestered in her idiosyncratic Eden, has had as little chance of encountering as Eve had of meeting a talking serpent before the time came for her to fall.

Of course, Frances is no serpent. On the contrary, light-footed and fresh-complexioned, she seems much more like a late eighteenth-

century model of the Victorian angel in the house, and certainly her
effect upon Hindley has been both to subdue him and to make him
more ethereal. "He had grown sparer, and lost his colour, and spoke
and dressed quite differently," Nelly notes (chap. 6); he even proposes
to convert one room into a parlor, an amenity Wuthering Heights
has never had. Hindley has in fact become a cultured man, so that
in gaining a ladylike bride he has, as it were, gained the metaphorical
fiddle that was his heart's desire when he was a boy.

It is no doubt inevitable that Hindley's fiddle and Catherine's whip
cannot peaceably coexist. Certainly the early smashing of the fiddle
by the "whip" hinted at such a problem, and so perhaps it would not
be entirely frivolous to think of the troubles that now ensue for
Catherine and Heathcliff as the fiddle's revenge. But even without
pressing this conceit we can see that Hindley's angel/fiddle is a
problematical representative of what is now introduced as the
"heavenly" realm of culture. For one thing, her ladylike sweetness
is only skin-deep. Leo Bersani remarks that the distinction between
the children at the Heights and those at the Grange is the difference
between "aggressively selfish children" and "whiningly selfish children."[29] If this is so, Frances foreshadows the children at the Grange
—the children of genteel culture—since "her affection [toward
Catherine] tired very soon [and] she grew peevish," at which point
the now gentlemanly Hindley becomes "tyrannical" in just the way
his position as the household's new *pater familias* encourages him to be.
His tyranny consists, among other things, in his attempt to impose
what Blake would call a Urizenic heavenly order at the heretofore
anti-hierarchical Heights. The servants Nelly and Joseph, he decrees,
must know their place—which is "the back kitchen"—and Heathcliff, because he is socially nobody, must be exiled from culture:
deprived of "the instruction of the curate" and cast out into "the
fields" (chap. 6).

Frances's peevishness, however, is not just a sign that her ladylike
ways are inimical to the prelapsarian world of Catherine's childhood;
it is also a sign that, as the twelve-year-old girl must perceive it, to
be a lady is to be diseased. As Nelly hints, Frances is tubercular, and
any mention of death causes her to act "half silly," as if in some part
of herself she knows she is doomed, or as if she is already half a ghost.
And she is. As a metaphor, Frances's tuberculosis means that she

is in an advanced state of just that *social* "consumption" which will eventually kill Catherine, too, so that the thin and silly bride functions for the younger girl as a sort of premonition or ghost of what she herself will become.

But of course the social disease of ladyhood, with its attendant silliness or madness, is only one of the threats Frances incarnates for twelve-year-old Catherine. Another, perhaps even more sinister because harder to confront, is associated with the fact that though Catherine may well need a mother—in the sense in which Eve or Mary Shelley's monster needed a mother/model—Frances does not and cannot function as a good mother for her. The original Earnshaws were shadowy but mythically grand, like the primordial "true" parents of fairy tales (or like most parents seen through the eyes of preadolescent children). Hindley and Frances, on the other hand, the new Earnshaws, are troublesomely real though as oppressive as the step-parents in fairy tales.[30] To say that they are in some way like step-parents, however, is to say that they seem to Catherine like transformed or alien parents, and since this is as much a function of her own vision as of the older couple's behavior, we must assume that it has something to do with the changes wrought by the girl's entrance into adolescence.

Why do parents begin to seem like step-parents when their children reach puberty? The ubiquitousness of step-parents in fairy tales dealing with the crises of adolescence suggests that the phenomenon is both deepseated and widespread. One explanation—and the one that surely accounts for Catherine Earnshaw's experience—is that when the child gets old enough to become conscious of her parents as sexual beings they really do begin to seem like fiercer, perhaps even (as in the case of Hindley and Frances) younger versions of their "original" selves. Certainly they begin to be more threatening (that is, more "peevish" and "tyrannical") if only because the child's own sexual awakening disturbs them almost as much as their sexuality, now truly comprehended, bothers the child. Thus the crucial passage from Catherine's diary which Lockwood reads even before Nelly begins her narration is concerned not just with Joseph's pious oppressions but with the cause of those puritanical onslaughts, the fact that she and Heathcliff must shiver in the garret because "Hindley and his wife [are basking] downstairs before a comfortable fire . . .

kissing and talking nonsense by the hour—foolish palaver we should be ashamed of." Catherine's defensiveness is clear. She (and Heathcliff) are troubled by the billing and cooing of her "step-parents" because she understands, perhaps for the first time, the sexual nature of what a minute later she calls Hindley's "paradise on the hearth" and—worse—understands its relevance to her.

Flung into the kitchen, "where Joseph asseverated, 'owd Nick' would fetch us," Catherine and Heathcliff each seek "a separate nook to await his advent." For Catherine-and-Heathcliff—that is, Catherine and Catherine, or Catherine and her whip—have already been separated from each other, not just by tyrannical Hindley, the *deus* produced by time's *machina*, but by the emergence of Catherine's own sexuality, with all the terrors which attend that phenomenon in a puritanical and patriarchal society. And just as peevish Frances incarnates the social illness of ladyhood, so also she quite literally embodies the fearful as well as the frivolous consequences of sexuality. Her foolish if paradisaical palaver on the hearth, after all, leads straight to the death her earlier ghostliness and silliness had predicted. Her sexuality's destructiveness was even implied by the minor but vicious acts of injustice with which it was associated—arbitrarily pulling Heathcliff's hair, for instance—but the sex-death equation, with which Milton and Mary Shelley were also concerned, really surfaces when Frances's and Hindley's son, Hareton, is born. At that time, Kenneth, the lugubrious physician who functions like a medical Greek chorus throughout *Wuthering Heights*, informs Hindley that the winter will "probably finish" Frances.

To Catherine, however, it must appear that the murderous agent is not winter but sex, for as she is beginning to learn, the Miltonic testaments of her world have told woman that "thy sorrow I will greatly multiply / By thy Conception . . . " (*PL* 10. 192–95) and the maternal image of Sin birthing Death reinforces this point. That Frances's decline and death accompany Catherine's fall is metaphysically appropriate, therefore. And it is dramatically appropriate as well, for Frances's fate foreshadows the catastrophes which will follow Catherine's fall into sexuality just as surely as the appearance of Sin and Death on earth followed Eve's fall. That Frances's death also, incidentally, yields Hareton—the truest scion of the Earnshaw clan—

is also profoundly appropriate. For Hareton is, after all, a resurrected version of the original patriarch whose name is written over the great main door of the house, amid a "wilderness of shameless little boys." Thus his birth marks the beginning of the historical as well as the psychological decline and fall of that Satanic female principle which has temporarily usurped his "rightful" place at Wuthering Heights.

Catherine's fall, however, is caused by a patriarchal past and present, besides being associated with a patriarchal future. It is significant, then, that her problems begin—violently enough—when she literally falls down and is bitten by a male bulldog, a sort of guard/god from Thrushcross Grange. Though many readers overlook this point, Catherine does not *go* to the Grange when she is twelve years old. On the contrary, the Grange seizes her and "holds [her] fast," a metaphoric action which emphasizes the turbulent and inexorable nature of the psychosexual *rites de passage Wuthering Heights* describes, just as the ferociously masculine bull/dog—as a symbolic representative of Thrushcross Grange—contrasts strikingly with the ascendancy at the Heights of the hellish female bitch goddess alternately referred to as "Madam" and "Juno."[31]

Realistically speaking, Catherine and Heathcliff have been driven in the direction of Thrushcross Grange by their own desire to escape not only the pietistic tortures Joseph inflicts but also, more urgently, just that sexual awareness irritatingly imposed by Hindley's romantic paradise. Neither sexuality nor its consequences can be evaded, however, and the farther the children run the closer they come to the very fate they secretly wish to avoid. Racing "from the top of the Heights to the park without stopping," they plunge from the periphery of Hindley's paradise (which was transforming their heaven into a hell) to the boundaries of a place that at first seems authentically heavenly, a place full of light and softness and color, a "splendid place carpeted with crimson ... and [with] a pure white ceiling bordered by gold, a shower of glass-drops hanging in silver chains from the centre, and shimmering with little soft tapers" (chap. 6). Looking in the window, the outcasts speculate that if they were inside such a room "we should have thought ourselves in heaven!" From the outside, at least, the Lintons' elegant haven appears paradisaical. But once the children have experienced its Urizenic interior, they know that in their terms this heaven is hell.

Because the first emissary of this heaven who greets them is the bulldog Skulker, a sort of hellhound posing as a hound of heaven, the wound this almost totemic animal inflicts upon Catherine is as symbolically suggestive as his role in the girl's forced passage from Wuthering Heights to Thrushcross Grange. Barefoot, as if to emphasize her "wild child" innocence, Catherine is exceptionally vulnerable, as a wild child must inevitably be, and when the dog is "throttled off, his huge, purple tongue hanging half a foot out of his mouth . . . his pendant lips [are] streaming with bloody slaver." "Look . . . how her foot bleeds," Edgar Linton exclaims, and "She may be lamed for life," his mother anxiously notes (chap. 6). Obviously such bleeding has sexual connotations, especially when it occurs in a pubescent girl. Crippling injuries to the feet are equally resonant, moreover, almost always signifying symbolic castration, as in the stories of Oedipus, Achilles, and the Fisher King. Additionally, it hardly needs to be noted that Skulker's equipment for aggression—his huge purple tongue and pendant lips, for instance—sounds extraordinarily phallic. In a Freudian sense, then, the imagery of this brief but violent episode hints that Catherine has been simultaneously catapulted into adult female sexuality *and* castrated.

How can a girl "become a woman" and be castrated (that is, desexed) at the same time? Considering how Freudian its iconographic assumptions are, the question is disingenuous, for not only in Freud's terms but in feminist terms, as Elizabeth Janeway and Juliet Mitchell have both observed, femaleness—implying "penis envy"—quite reasonably *means* castration. "No woman has been deprived of a penis; she never had one to begin with," Janeway notes, commenting on Freud's crucial "Female Sexuality" (1931).

> But she *has* been deprived of something else that men enjoy: namely, autonomy, freedom, and the power to control her destiny. By insisting, falsely, on female deprivation of the male organ, Freud is pointing to an actual deprivation and one of which he was clearly aware. In Freud's time the advantages enjoyed by the male sex over the inferior female were, of course,

even greater than at present, and they were also accepted to a much larger extent, as being inevitable, inescapable. Women were evident *social* castrates, and the mutilation of their potentiality as achieving human creatures was quite analogous to the physical wound.[32]

But if such things were true in Freud's time, they were even truer in Emily Brontë's. And certainly the hypothesis that Catherine Earnshaw has become in some sense a "social castrate," that she has been "lamed for life," is borne out by her treatment at Thrushcross Grange—and by the treatment of her alter ego, Heathcliff. For, assuming that she is a "young lady," the entire Linton household cossets the wounded (but still healthy) girl as if she were truly an invalid. Indeed, feeding her their alien rich food—negus and cakes from their own table—washing her feet, combing her hair, dressing her in "enormous slippers," and wheeling her about like a doll, they seem to be enacting some sinister ritual of initiation, the sort of ritual that has traditionally weakened mythic heroines from Persephone to Snow White. And because he is "a little Lascar, or an American or Spanish castaway," the Lintons banish Heathcliff from their parlor, thereby separating Catherine from the lover/brother whom she herself defines as her strongest and most necessary "self." For five weeks now, she will be at the mercy of the Grange's heavenly gentility.

To say that Thrushcross Grange is genteel or cultured and that it therefore seems "heavenly" is to say, of course, that it is the opposite of Wuthering Heights. And certainly at every point the two houses are opposed to each other, as if each in its self-assertion must absolutely deny the other's being. Like Milton and Blake, Emily Brontë thought in polarities. Thus, where Wuthering Heights is essentially a great parlorless room built around a huge central hearth, a furnace of dark energy like the fire of Los, Thrushcross Grange has a parlor notable not for heat but for light, for "a pure white ceiling bordered by gold" with "a shower of glass-drops" in the center that seems to parody the "sovran vital Lamp" (*PL* 3. 22) which illuminates Milton's heaven of Right Reason. Where Wuthering Heights, moreover, is close to being naked or "raw" in Lévi-Strauss' sense—its floors uncarpeted, most of its inhabitants barely literate, even the meat on its shelves open to inspection—Thrushcross Grange is clothed and "cooked": carpeted in crimson, bookish, feeding on cakes and tea and negus.[33] It follows from this, then, that where Wuthering Heights is functional, even its dogs working sheepdogs or hunters, Thrushcross Grange (though guarded by bulldogs) appears to be decorative or aesthetic, the home of lapdogs as well as ladies. And finally, therefore, Wuthering Heights in its stripped functional rawness is essentially anti-hierarchical and egalitarian as the aspirations of Eve and Satan, while Thrushcross Grange reproduces the hierarchical chain of being that Western culture traditionally proposes as heaven's decree.

For all these reasons, Catherine Earnshaw, together with her whip Heathcliff, has at Wuthering Heights what Emily Dickinson would call a "Barefoot-Rank."[34] But at Thrushcross Grange, clad first in enormous, crippling slippers and later in "a long cloth habit which she [is] obliged to hold up with both hands" (chap. 7) in order to walk, she seems on the verge of becoming, again in Dickinson's words, a "Lady [who] dare not lift her Veil / For fear it be dispelled" (J. 421) For in comparison to Wuthering Heights, Thrushcross Grange is, finally, the home of concealment and doubleness, a place where, as we shall see, reflections are separated from their owners like souls from bodies, so that the lady in anxiety "peers beyond her mesh— / And wishes—and denies— / Lest Interview— annul a want / That Image—satisfies." And it is here, therefore, at heaven's mercy, that Catherine Earnshaw learns "to adopt a double character without exactly intending to deceive anyone" (chap. 8).

In fact, for Catherine Earnshaw, Thrushcross Grange in those five fatal weeks becomes a Palace of Instruction, as Brontë ironically called the equivocal schools of life where her adolescent Gondals were often incarcerated. But rather than learning, like A. G. A. and her cohorts, to rule a powerful nation, Catherine must learn to rule herself, or so the Lintons and her brother decree. She must learn to repress her own impulses, must girdle her own energies with the iron stays of "reason." Having fallen into the decorous "heaven" of femaleness, Catherine must become a lady. And just as her entrance into the world of Thrushcross Grange was forced and violent, so this process by which she is obliged to accommodate herself to that world is violent and painful, an unsentimental education recorded by a practiced, almost sadistically accurate observer. For the young

Gondals, too, had had a difficult time of it in their Palace of Instruction: far from being wonderful Golden Rule days, their school days were spent mostly in dungeons and torture cells, where their elders starved them into submission or self-knowledge.

That education for Emily Brontë is almost always fearful, even agonizing, may reflect the Brontës' own traumatic experiences at the Clergy Daughters School and elsewhere.[35] But it may also reflect in a more general way the repressiveness with which the nineteenth century educated all its young ladies, strapping them to backboards and forcing them to work for hours at didactic samplers until the more high-spirited girls—the Catherine Earnshaws and Catherine Morlands—must have felt, like the inhabitants of Kafka's penal colony, that the morals and maxims of patriarchy were being embroidered on their own skins. To mention Catherine Morland here is not to digress. As we have seen, Austen did not subject her heroine to education as a gothic/Gondalian torture, except parodically. Yet even Austen's parody suggests that for a girl like Catherine Morland the school of life inevitably inspires an almost instinctive fear, just as it would for A. G. A. "Heavenly" Northanger Abbey may somehow conceal a prison cell, Catherine suspects, and she develops this notion by sensing (as Henry Tilney cannot) that the female romances she is reading are in some sense the disguised histories of her own life.

In Catherine Earnshaw's case, these points are made even more subtly than in the Gondal poems or in *Northanger Abbey*, for Catherine's education in doubleness, in ladylike decorum meaning also ladylike deceit, is marked by an actual doubling or fragmentation of her personality. Thus though it is ostensibly Catherine who is being educated, it is Heathcliff—her rebellious alter ego, her whip, her id—who is exiled to a prison cell, as if to implement delicate Isabella Linton's first horrified reaction to him: "Frightful thing! Put him in the cellar" (chap. 6). Not in the cellar but in the garret, Heathcliff is locked up and, significantly, starved, while Catherine, daintily "cutting up the wing of a goose," practices table manners below. Even more significantly, however, she too is finally unable to eat her dinner and retreats under the table cloth to weep for her imprisoned playmate. To Catherine, Heathcliff is "more myself than I am," as she later famously tells Nelly, and so his literal starvation is symbolic of her more terrible because more dangerous spiritual starvation, just as her literal wound at Thrushcross Grange is also a metaphorical deathblow to *his* health and power. For divided from each other, the once androgynous Heathcliff-and-Catherine are now conquered by the concerted forces of patriarchy, the Lintons of Thrushcross Grange acting together with Hindley and Frances, their emissaries at the Heights.

It is, appropriately enough, during this period, that Frances gives birth to Hareton, the new patriarch-to-be, and dies, having fulfilled her painful function in the book and in the world. During this period, too, Catherine's education in ladylike self-denial causes her dutifully to deny her self and decide to marry Edgar. For when she says of Heathcliff that "he's more myself than I am," she means that as her exiled self the nameless "gipsy" really does preserve in his body more of her original being than she retains: even in his deprivation he seems whole and sure, while she is now entirely absorbed in the ladylike wishing and denying Dickinson's poem describes. Thus, too, it is during this period of loss and transition that Catherine obsessively inscribes on her windowsill the crucial writing Lockwood finds, writing which announces from the first Emily Brontë's central concern with identity: "a name repeated in all kinds of characters, large and small—Catherine Earnshaw, here and there varied to Catherine Heathcliff, and then again to Catherine Linton" (chap. 3). In the light of this repeated and varied name it is no wonder, finally, that Catherine knows Heathcliff is "more myself than I am," for he has only a single name, while she has so many that she may be said in a sense to have none. Just as triumphant self-discovery is the ultimate goal of the male *Bildungsroman*, anxious self-denial, Brontë suggests, is the ultimate product of a female education. What Catherine, or any girl, must learn is that she does not know her own name, and therefore cannot know either who she is or whom she is destined to be.

It has often been argued that Catherine's anxiety and uncertainty about her own identity represents a moral failing, a fatal flaw in her character which leads to her inability to choose between Edgar and Heathcliff. Heathcliff's reproachful "Why did you betray your own heart, Cathy?" (chap. 15) represents a Blakeian form of this moral criticism, a contemptuous suggestion that "those who restrain desire do so because theirs is weak enough to be restrained."[36] The more vulgar and commonsensical attack of the Leavisites, on the other hand—the censorious notion that "maturity" means being strong enough to choose not to have your cake and eat it too—represents what Mark Kinkead-Weeks calls "the view from the Grange."[37] To talk of morality in connection with Catherine's fall—and specifically in connection with her self-deceptive decision to marry Edgar— seems pointless, however, for morality only becomes a relevant term where there are meaningful choices.

As we have seen, Catherine has no meaningful choices. Driven from Wuthering Heights to Thrushcross Grange by her brother's marriage, seized by Thrushcross Grange and held fast in the jaws of reason, education, decorum, she cannot do otherwise than as she does, must marry Edgar because there is no one else for her to marry and a lady must marry. Indeed, her self-justifying description of her love for Edgar—"I love the ground under his feet, and the air over his head, and everything he touches, and every word he says" (chap. 9)—is a bitter parody of a genteel romantic declaration which shows how effective her education has been in indoctrinating her with the literary romanticism deemed suitable for young ladies, the swooning "femininity" that identifies all energies with the charisma of fathers/lovers/husbands. Her concomitant explanation that it would "degrade" her to marry Heathcliff is an equally inevitable product of her education, for her fall into ladyhood has been accompanied by Heathcliff's reduction to an equivalent position of female powerlessness, and Catherine has learned, correctly, that if it is degrading to be a woman it is even more degrading to be *like* a woman. Just as Milton's Eve, therefore, being already fallen, had no meaningful choice despite Milton's best efforts to prove otherwise, so Catherine has no real choice. Given the patriarchal nature of culture, women must fall—that is, they are already fallen because doomed to fall.

In the shadow of this point, however, moral censorship is merely redundant, a sort of interrogative restatement of the novel's central fact. Heathcliff's Blakeian reproach is equally superfluous, except insofar as it is not moral but etiological, a question one part of Catherine asks another, like her later passionate "Why am I so changed?" For as Catherine herself perceives, social and biological forces have fiercely combined against her. God as—in W. H. Auden's words—a "Victorian papa" has hurled her from the equivocal natural paradise she calls "heaven" and He calls "hell" into His idea of "heaven" where she will break her heart with weeping to come back to the Heights. Her speculative, tentative "mad" speech to Nelly captures, finally, both the urgency and the inexorability of her fall. "Supposing at twelve years old, I had been wrenched from the Heights . . . and my all in all, as Heathcliff was at that time, and been converted at a stroke into Mrs. Linton, the lady of Thrushcross Grange, and the wife of a stranger: an exile, and outcast, thenceforth, from what had been my world." In terms of the psychodramatic action of *Wuthering Heights*, only Catherine's use of the word *supposing* is here a rhetorical strategy; the rest of her speech is absolutely accurate, and places her subsequent actions beyond good and evil, just as it suggests, in yet another Blakeian reversal of customary terms, that her madness may really be sanity.

Catherine Earnshaw Linton's decline follows Catherine Earnshaw's fall. Slow at first, it is eventually as rapid, sickening, and deadly as the course of Brontë's own consumption was to be. And the long slide toward death of the body begins with what appears to be an irreversible death of the soul—with Catherine's fatalistic acceptance of Edgar's offer and her consequent self-imprisonment in the role of "Mrs. Linton, the lady of Thrushcross Grange." It is, of course, her announcement of this decision to Nelly, overheard by Heathcliff, which leads to Heathcliff's self-exile from the Heights and thus definitively to Catherine's psychic fragmentation. And significantly, her response to the departure of her true self is a lapse into illness which both signals the beginning of her decline and foreshadows its mortal end. Her words to Nelly the morning after Heathcliff's departure are therefore symbolically as well as dramatically resonant: "Shut the window, Nelly, I'm starving!" (chap. 9).

As Dorothy van Ghent has shown, windows in *Wuthering Heights* consistently represent openings into possibility, apertures through which subversive otherness can enter, or wounds out of which respectability can escape like flowing blood.[38] It is, after all, on the window ledge that Lockwood finds Catherine's different names obsessively inscribed, as if the girl had been trying to decide which self to let in the window or in which direction she ought to fly after making her own escape down the branches of the neighboring pine. It is through the same window that the ghost of Catherine Linton extends her icy fingers to the horrified visitor. And it is a window at the Grange that Catherine, in her "madness," begs Nelly to open so that she can have one breath of the wind that "comes straight down the moor" (chap. 12). "Open the window again wide, fasten it open!" she cries, then rises and, predicting her own death, seems almost ready to start on her journey homeward up the moor. ("I could not trust her alone by the gaping lattice," Nelly comments wisely.) But besides expressing a general wish to escape from "this shattered prison" of her body, her marriage, her self, her life, Catherine's desire now to *open* the window refers specifically back to that moment three years earlier when she had chosen instead to close it, chosen to inflict on herself the imprisonment and starvation that as part of her education had been inflicted on her double, Heathcliff.

Imprisonment leads to madness, solipsism, paralysis, as Byron's *Prisoner of Chillon*, some of Brontë's Gondal poems, and countless other gothic and neo-gothic tales suggest. Starvation—both in the modern sense of malnutrition and the archaic Miltonic sense of freezing ("to starve in ice")—leads to weakness, immobility, death. During her decline, starting with both starvation and imprisonment, Catherine passes through all these grim stages of mental and physical decay. At first she seems (to Nelly anyway) merely somewhat "headstrong." Powerless without her whip, keenly conscious that she has lost the autonomy of her hardy and free girlhood, she gets her way by indulging in tantrums, wheedling, manipulating, so that Nelly's optimistic belief that she and Edgar "were really in possession of a deep and growing happiness" contrasts ironically with the housekeeper's simultaneous admission that Catherine "was never subject to depression of spirits before" the three interlocking events of Heathcliff's departure, her "perilous illness," and her marriage (chap. 10). But Heathcliff's mysterious reappearance six months after her wedding intensifies rather than cures her symptoms. For his return does not in any way suggest a healing of the wound of femaleness that was inflicted at puberty. Instead, it signals the beginning of "madness," a sort of feverish infection of the wound. Catherine's marriage to Edgar has now inexorably locked her into a social system that denies her autonomy, and thus, as psychic symbolism, Heathcliff's return represents the return of her true self's desires without the rebirth of her former powers. And desire without power, as Freud and Blake both knew, inevitably engenders disease.

If we understand all the action that takes place at Thrushcross Grange between Edgar, Catherine, and Heathcliff from the moment of Heathcliff's reappearance until the time of Catherine's death to be ultimately psychodramatic, a grotesque playing out of Catherine's emotional fragmentation on a "real" stage, then further discussion of her sometimes genteelly Victorian, sometimes fiercely Byronic decline becomes almost unnecessary, its meaning is so obvious. Edgar's autocratic hostility to Heathcliff—that is, to Catherine's desirous self, her independent will—manifests itself first in his attempt to have her entertain the returned "gipsy" or "ploughboy" in the kitchen because he doesn't belong in the parlor. But soon Edgar's hatred results in a determination to expel Healthcliff entirely from his house because he fears the effects of this demonic intruder, with all he signifies, not only upon his wife but upon his sister. His fear is justified because, as we shall see, the Satanic rebellion Heathcliff introduces into the parlors of "heaven" contains the germ of a terrible dis-ease with patriarchy that causes women like Catherine and Isabella to try to escape their imprisonment in roles and houses by running away, by starving themselves, and finally by dying.

Because Edgar is so often described as "soft," "weak," slim, fair-haired, even effeminate-looking, the specifically patriarchal nature of his feelings toward Heathcliff may not be immediately evident. Certainly many readers have been misled by his almost stylized angelic qualities to suppose that the rougher, darker Heathcliff incarnates masculinity in contrast to Linton's effeminacy. The returned Heathcliff, Nelly says, "had grown a tall, athletic, well-formed man, beside whom my master seemed quite slender and youthlike. His upright carriage suggested the idea of his having been in the army" (chap. 10). She even seems to acquiesce in his superior maleness. But her constant, reflexive use of the phrase "my master" for Edgar tells us otherwise, as do some of her other expressions. At this point in the novel, anyway, Heathcliff is always merely "Heathcliff" while Edgar is variously "Mr. Linton," "my master," "Mr. Edgar," and "the master," all phrases conveying the power and status he has independent of his physical strength.

In fact, as Milton also did, Emily Brontë demonstrates that the power of the patriarch, Edgar's power, begins with words, for heaven is populated by "*spirits* Masculine," and as above, so below. Edgar does not need a strong, conventionally masculine body, because his mastery is contained in books, wills, testaments, leases, titles, rent-rolls, documents, languages, all the paraphernalia by which patriarchal culture is transmitted from one generation to the next. Indeed, even without Nelly's designation of him as "the master," his notable bookishness would define him as a patriarch, for he rules his house from his library as if to parody that male education in Latin and Greek, privilege and prerogative, which so infuriated Milton's daughters.[39] As a figure in the psychodrama of Catherine's decline, then, he incarnates the education in young ladyhood that has commanded her to learn her "place." In Freudian terms he would no doubt be described as her superego, the internalized guardian of morality and culture, with Heathcliff, his opposite, functioning as her childish and desirous id.

But at the same time, despite Edgar's superegoistic qualities, Emily Brontë shows that his patriarchal rule, like Thrushcross Grange itself, is based on physical as well as spiritual violence. For her, as for Blake, heaven *kills*. Thus, at a word from Thrushcross Grange, Skulker is let loose, and Edgar's magistrate father cries "What prey, Robert?" to his manservant, explaining that he fears thieves because "yesterday was my rent day." Similarly, Edgar, having decided that he has "humored" Catherine long enough, calls for two strong men servants to support his authority and descends into the kitchen to evict Heathcliff. The patriarch, Brontë notes, needs words, not muscles, and Heathcliff's derisive language paradoxically suggests understanding of the true male power Edgar's "soft" exterior conceals: "Cathy, this lamb of yours threatens like a bull!" (chap. 11). Even more significant, perhaps, is the fact that when Catherine locks Edgar in alone with her and Heathcliff—once more imprisoning herself while ostensibly imprisoning the hated master—this apparently effeminate, "milk-blooded coward" frees himself by striking Heathcliff a breathtaking blow on the throat "that would have levelled a slighter man."

Edgar's victory once again recapitulates that earlier victory of Thrushcross Grange over Wuthering Heights which also meant the victory of a Urizenic "heaven" over a delightful and energetic "hell." At the same time, it seals Catherine's doom, locking her into her downward spiral of self-starvation. And in doing this it finally explains what is perhaps Nelly's most puzzling remark about the relationship between Edgar and Catherine. In chapter 8, noting that the love-struck sixteen-year-old Edgar is "doomed, and flies to his fate," the housekeeper sardonically declares that "the soft thing [Edgar] . . . possessed the power to depart [from Catherine] as much as a cat possesses the power to leave a mouse half killed or a bird half eaten." At that point in the novel her metaphor seems odd. Is not headstrong Catherine the hungry cat, and "soft" Edgar the half-eaten mouse? But in fact, as we now see, Edgar all along represented the devouring force that will gnaw and worry Catherine to death, consuming flesh and spirit together. For having fallen into "heaven," she has ultimately—to quote Sylvia Plath—"fallen / Into the stomach of indifference," a social physiology that urgently needs her not so much for herself as for her function.[40]

When we note the significance of such imagery of devouring, as well as the all-pervasive motif of self-starvation in *Wuthering Heights*, the kitchen setting of this crucial confrontation between Edgar and Heathcliff begins to seem more than coincidental. In any case, the episode is followed closely by what C. P. Sanger calls Catherine's "hunger strike" and by her famous mad scene.[41] Another line of Plath's describes the feelings of self-lessness that seem to accompany Catherine's realization that she has been reduced to a role, a function, a sort of walking costume: "I have no face, I have wanted to efface myself."[42] For the weakening of Catherine's grasp on the world is most specifically shown by her inability to recognize her own face in the mirror during the mad scene. Explaining to Nelly that she is not mad, she notes that if she were "I should believe you really *were* [a] withered hag, and I should think I *was* under Penistone Crag; and I'm conscious it's night and there are two candles on the table making the black press shine like jet." Then she adds, "It does appear odd—I see a face in it" (chap. 12). But of course, ironically, there is no "black press" in the room, only a mirror in which Catherine sees and repudiates her own image. Her fragmentation has now gone so far beyond the psychic split betokened by her division from Heathcliff that body and image (or body and soul) have separated.

Q. D. Leavis would have us believe that his apparently gothic episode, with its allusion to "dark superstitions about premonitions of death, about ghosts and primitive beliefs about the soul . . . is a proof of [Emily Brontë's] immaturity at the time of the original conception of *Wuthering Heights*." Leo Bersani, on the other hand, suggests that the scene hints at "the danger of being haunted by alien versions of the self." [43] In a sense, however, the image Catherine sees in the mirror is neither gothic nor alien—though she is alienated from it—but hideously familiar, and further proof that her madness may really equal sanity. Catherine sees in the mirror an image of who and what she has really become in the world's terms: "Mrs. Linton, the lady of Thrushcross Grange." And oddly enough, this image appears to be stored like an article of clothing, a trousseau-treasure, or again in Plath's words "a featureless, fine / Jew linen," [44] in one of the cupboards of childhood, the black press from her old room at the Heights.

Because of this connection with childhood, part of the horror of Catherine's vision comes from the question it suggests: was the costume/face always there, waiting in a corner of the little girl's wardrobe? But to ask this question is to ask again, as Frankenstein does, whether Eve was created fallen, whether women are not Education's but "Nature's fools," doomed from the start to be exiles and outcasts despite their illusion that they are hardy and free. When Milton's Eve is for her own good led away from her own image by a superegoistic divine voice which tells her that "What there thou sees fair creature is thyself"—*merely* thyself—does she not in a sense determine Catherine Earnshaw's fall? When, substituting Adam's superior image for her own, she concedes that female "beauty is excell'd by manly grace / And wisdom" (*PL* 4. 490–91) does not her "sane" submission outline the contours of Catherine Earnshaw's rebelliously Blakeian madness? Such questions are only implicit in Catherine's mad mirror vision of herself, but it is important to see that they are implied. Once again, where Shelley clarifies Milton, showing the monster's dutiful disgust with "his" own self-image, Brontë repudiates him, showing how his teachings have doomed her protagonist to what dutiful Nelly considers an

insane search for her lost true self. "I'm sure I should be myself were
I once more among the heather on those hills," Catherine exclaims,
meaning that only a journey back into the androgynous wholeness
of childhood could heal the wound her mirror-image symbolizes,
the fragmentation that began when she was separated from heather
and Heathcliff, and "laid alone" in the first fateful enclosure of her
oak-panelled bed. For the mirror-image is one more symbol of the
cell in which Catherine has been imprisoned by herself and by society.

To escape from the horrible mirror-enclosure, then, might be to
escape from all domestic enclosures, or to begin to try to escape.
It is significant that in her madness Catherine tears at her pillow
with her teeth, begs Nelly to open the window, and seems "to find
childish diversion in pulling the feathers from the rents she [has]
just made" (chap. 12). Liberating feathers from the prison where
they had been reduced to objects of social utility, she imagines them
reborn as the birds they once were, whole and free, and pictures
them "wheeling over our heads in the middle of the moor," trying
to get back to their nests. A moment later, standing by the window
"careless of the frosty air," she imagines her own trip back across
the moor to Wuthering Heights, noting that "it's a rough journey,
and a sad heart to travel it; and we must pass by Gimmerton Kirk
to go that journey!...But Heathcliff, if I dare you now, will you
venture?...I won't rest till you are with me. I never will!" (chap. 12).
For a "fallen" woman, trapped in the distorting mirrors of patriarchy,
the journey into death is the only way out, Brontë suggests, and the
Liebestod is not (as it would be for a male artist, like Keats or Wagner)
a mystical but a practical solution. In the presence of death, after all,
"The mirrors are sheeted," to quote Plath yet again.[45]

The masochism of this surrender to what A. Alvarez has called
the "savage god" of suicide is plain, not only from Catherine's own
words and actions but also from the many thematic parallels between
her speeches and Plath's poems.[46] But of course, taken together,
self-starvation or anorexia nervosa, masochism, and suicide form a
complex of psychoneurotic symptoms that is almost classically associated with female feelings of powerlessness and rage. Certainly the
"hunger strike" is a traditional tool of the powerless, as the history
of the feminist movement (and many other movements of oppressed
peoples) will attest. Anorexia nervosa, moreover, is a sort of mad

corollary of the self-starvation that may be a sane strategy for survival. Clinically associated with "a distorted concept of body size"—like Catherine Earnshaw's alienated/familiar image in the mirror—it is fed by the "false sense of power that the faster derives from her starvation," and is associated, psychologists speculate, with "a struggle for control, for a sense of identity, competence, and effectiveness."

But then in a more general sense it can surely be argued that all masochistic or even suicidal behavior expresses the furious power hunger of the powerless. Catherine's whip—now meaning Heathcliff, her "love" for Heathcliff, and also, more deeply, her desire for the autonomy her union with Heathcliff represented—turns against Catherine. She whips herself because she cannot whip the world, and she must whip something. Besides, in whipping herself does she not, perhaps, torment the world? Of this she is, in her powerlessness, uncertain, and her uncertainty leads to further madness, reinforcing the vicious cycle. "O let me not be mad," she might cry, like Lear, as she tears off her own socially prescribed costumes so that she can more certainly feel the descent of the whip she herself has raised. In her rebelliousness Catherine has earlier played alternately the parts of Cordelia and of Goneril and Regan to the Lear of her father and her husband. Now, in her powerlessness, she seems to have herself become a figure like Lear, mourning her lost kingdom and suicidally surrendering herself to the blasts that come straight down the moor.

Nevertheless, though her madness and its setting echo Lear's disintegration much more than, say, Ophelia's, Catherine is different from Lear in a number of crucial ways, the most obvious being the fact that her femaleness dooms her to a function as well as a role, and threatens her, therefore, with the death Frances's fate had predicted. Critics never comment on this point, but the truth is that Catherine is pregnant during both the kitchen scene and the mad scene, and her death occurs at the time of (and ostensibly because of) her "confinement." In the light of this, her anorexia, her madness, and her masochism become even more fearsomely meaningful. Certainly, for instance, the distorted body that the anorexic imagines for herself is analogous to the distorted body that the pregnant woman really must confront. Can eating produce such a body? The question, mad as it may seem, must be inevitable. In any case, some psychoanalysts have suggested that anorexia, endemic to pubescent girls, reflects a fear of oral impregnation, to which self-starvation would be one obvious response.[47]

But even if a woman accepts, or rather concedes, that she is pregnant, an impulse toward self-starvation would seem to be an equally obvious response to the pregnant woman's inevitable fear of being monstrously inhabited, as well as to her own horror of being enslaved to the species and reduced to a tool of the life process. Excessive ("pathological") morning sickness has traditionally been interpreted as an attempt to vomit up the alien intruder, the child planted in the belly like an incubus.[48] And indeed, if the child has been fathered—as Catherine's has—by a man the woman defines as a stranger, her desire to rid herself of it seems reasonable enough. But what if she must kill herself in the process? This is another question Catherine's masochistic self-starvation implies, especially if we see it as a disguised form of morning sickness. Yet another question is more general: must motherhood, like ladyhood, kill? Is female sexuality necessarily deadly?

To the extent that she answers yes, Brontë swerves once again from Milton, though rather less radically than usual. For when she was separated from her own reflection, Eve was renamed "mother of human race," a title Milton seems to have considered honorifically life-giving despite the dreadful emblem of maternity Sin provided. Catherine's entrance into motherhood, however, darkly parodies even if it does not subvert this story. Certainly childbirth brings death to her (and eventually to Heathcliff) though at the same time it does revitalize the patriarchal order that began to fail at Wuthering Heights with her early assertions of individuality. Birth is, after all, the ultimate fragmentation the self can undergo, just as "confinement" is, for women, the ultimate pun on imprisonment. As if in recognition of this, Catherine's attempt to escape maternity does, if only unconsciously, subvert Milton. For Milton's Eve "knew not eating Death." But Brontë's does. In her refusal to be enslaved to the species, her refusal to be "mother of human race," she closes her mouth on emptiness as, in Plath's words, "on a communion tablet." It is no use, of course. She breaks apart into two Catherines—the old, mad, dead Catherine fathered by Wuthering Heights, and the

new, more docile and acceptable Catherine fathered by Thrushcross
Grange. But nevertheless, in her defiance Emily Brontë's Eve, like
her creator, is a sort of hunger artist, a point Charlotte Brontë
acknowledged when she memorialized her sister in *Shirley*, that other
revisionary account of the Genesis of female hunger.[49]

Catherine's fall and her resulting decline, fragmentation, and
death are the obvious subjects of the first half of *Wuthering Heights*.
Not quite so obviously, the second half of the novel is concerned with
the larger, social consequences of Catherine's fall, which spread out
in concentric circles like rings from a stone flung into a river, and
which are examined in a number of parallel stories, including some
that have already been set in motion at the time of Catherine's death.
Isabella, Nelly, Heathcliff, and Catherine II—in one way or another
all these characters' lives parallel (or even in a sense contain)
Catherine's, as if Brontë were working out a series of alternative
versions of the same plot.

Isabella is perhaps the most striking of these parallel figures, for
like Catherine she is a headstrong, impulsive "miss" who runs away
from home at adolescence. But where Catherine's fall is both fated
and unconventional, a fall "upward" from hell to heaven, Isabella's
is both willful and conventional. Falling from Thrushcross Grange
to Wuthering Heights, from "heaven" to "hell," in exactly the
opposite direction from Catherine, Isabella patently chooses her own
fate, refusing to listen to Catherine's warnings against Heathcliff
and carefully evading her brother's vigilance. But then Isabella has
from the first functioned as Catherine's opposite, a model of the
stereotypical young lady patriarchal education is designed to produce.
Thus where Catherine is a "stout hearty lass" raised in the raw heart
of nature at Wuthering Heights, Isabella is slim and pale, a daughter
of culture and Thrushcross Grange. Where Catherine's childhood is
androgynous, moreover, as her oneness with Heathcliff implies,
Isabella has borne the stamp of sexual socialization from the first,
or so her early division from her brother Edgar—her future guardian
and master—would suggest. When Catherine and Heathcliff first
see them, after all, Isabella and Edgar are quarreling over a lapdog,
a genteel (though covertly sexual) toy they cannot share. "When

would you catch me wishing to have what Catherine wanted? or
find us [arguing] divided by the whole room?" Heathcliff muses on
the scene (chap. 6). Indeed, so much the opposite of Catherine's is
Isabella's life and lineage that it is almost as if Brontë, in contriving
it, were saying "Let's see what would happen if I told Catherine's
story the 'right' way"—that is, with socially approved characters
and situations.

As Isabella's fate suggests, however—and this is surely part of
Brontë's point—the "right" beginning of the story seems almost as
inevitably to lead to the wrong ending as the wrong or "subversive"
beginning. Ironically, Isabella's bookish upbringing has prepared
her to fall in love with (of all people) Heathcliff. Precisely because she
has been taught to believe in coercive literary conventions, Isabella
is victimized by the genre of romance. Mistaking appearance for
reality, tall athletic Heathcliff for "an honourable soul" instead of
"a fierce, pitiless wolfish man," she runs away from her cultured
home in the naive belief that it will simply be replaced by another
cultivated setting. But like Claire Clairmont, who enacted a similar
drama in real life, she underestimates both the ferocity of the Byronic
hero and the powerlessness of all women, even "ladies," in her society.
Her experiences at Wuthering Heights teach her that hell really is
hellish for the children of heaven: like a parody of Catherine, she
starves, pines and sickens, oppressed by that Miltonic grotesque,
Joseph, for she is unable to stomach the rough food of nature (or hell)
just as Catherine cannot swallow the food of culture (or heaven). She
does not literally die of all this, but when she escapes, giggling like a
madwoman, from *her* self-imprisonment, she is so effectively banished
from the novel by her brother (and Brontë) that she might as well
be dead.

Would Isabella's fate have been different if she had fallen in love
with someone less problematical than Heathcliff—with a man of
culture, for instance, rather than a Satanic nature figure? Would she
have prospered with the love of someone like her own brother, or
Heathcliff's tenant, Lockwood? Her early relationship with Edgar,
together with Edgar's patriarchal rigidity, hint that she would not.
Even more grimly suggestive is the story Lockwood tells in chapter 1
about his romantic encounter at the seacoast. Readers will recall that
the "fascinating creature" he admired was "a real goddess in my

eyes, as long as she took no notice of [me]." But when she "looked a return," her lover "shrunk icily into myself . . . till finally the poor innocent was led to doubt her own senses . . . " (chap. 1). Since even the most cultivated women are powerless, women are evidently at the mercy of all men, Lockwoods and Heathcliffs alike.

Thus if literary Lockwood makes a woman into a goddess, he can unmake her at whim without suffering himself. If literary Isabella makes a man into a god or hero, however, she must suffer—may even have to die—for her mistake. Lockwood in effect kills his goddess for being human, and would no doubt do the same to Isabella. Heathcliff, on the other hand, literally tries to kill Isabella for trying to be a goddess, an angel, a lady, and for having, therefore, a "mawkish, waxen face." Either way, Isabella must in some sense be killed, for her fate, like Catherine's, illustrates the double binds with which patriarchal society inevitably crushes the feet of runaway girls.[50] Perhaps it is to make this point even more dramatically that Brontë has Heathcliff hang Isabella's genteelly named springer, Fanny, from a "bridle hook" on the night he and Isabella elope. Just as the similarity of Isabella's and Catherine's fates suggests that "to fall" and "to fall in love" are equivalents, so the *bridle* or *bridal hook* is an apt, punning metaphor for the institution of marriage in a world where fallen women, like their general mother Eve, are (as Dickinson says) "Born—Bridalled—Shrouded— / In a Day."[51]

Nelly Dean, of course, seems to many critics to have been put into the novel to help Emily Brontë disavow such uniformly dark intentions. "For a specimen of true benevolence and homely fidelity, look at the character of Nelly Dean," Charlotte Brontë says with what certainly appears to be conviction, trying to soften the picture of "perverse passion and passionate perversity" Victorian readers thought her sister had produced.[52] And Charlotte Brontë "rightly defended her sister against allegations of abnormality by pointing out that . . . Emily had created the wholesome, maternal Nelly Dean," comments Q. D. Leavis.[53] How wholesome and maternal *is* Nelly Dean, however? And if we agree that she is basically benevolent, of what does her benevolence consist? Problematic words like *wholesome* and *benevolent* suggest a point where we can start to trace the relationship between Nelly's history and Catherine's (or Isabella's).

To begin with, of course, Nelly is healthy and wholesome because she is a survivor, as the artist-narrator must be. Early in the novel, Lockwood refers to her as his "human fixture," and there is, indeed, a durable thinglike quality about her, as if she had outlasted the Earnshaw/Linton storms of passion like their two houses, or as if she were a wall, a door, an object of furniture meant to begin a narration in response to the conventional sigh of "Ah, if only these old walls could speak, what stories they would tell." Like a wall or fixture, moreover, Nelly has a certain impassivity, a diplomatic immunity to entangling emotions. Though she sometimes expresses strong feelings about the action, she manages to avoid taking sides— or, rather, like a wall, she is related to both sides. Consequently, as the artist must, she can go anywhere and hear everything.

At the same time, Nelly's evasions suggest ways in which her history has paralleled the lives of Catherine and Isabella, though she has rejected their commitments and thus avoided their catastrophes. Hindley, for instance, was evidently once as close to Nelly as Heathcliff was to Catherine. Indeed, like Heathcliff, Nelly seems to have been a sort of stepchild at the Heights. When old Mr. Earnshaw left on his fateful trip to Liverpool, he promised to bring back a gift of apples and pears for Nelly as well as the fiddle and whip Hindley and Catherine had asked for. Because she is only "a poor man's daughter," however, Nelly is excluded from the family, specifically by being defined as its servant. Luckily for her, therefore (or so it seems), she has avoided the incestuous/egalitarian relationship with Hindley that Catherine has with Heathcliff, and at the same time— because she is ineligible for marriage into either family—she has escaped the bridal hook of matrimony that destroys both Isabella and Catherine.

It is for these reasons, finally, that Nelly is able to tell the story of all these characters without herself becoming ensnared in it, or perhaps, more accurately, she is able (like Brontë herself) to use the act of telling the story as a strategy for protecting herself from such entrapment. "I have read more than you would fancy, Mr. Lockwood," Nelly remarks to her new master. "You could not open a book in this library that I have not looked into and got something out of also ... it is as much as you can expect of a poor man's daughter" (59). By this she means, no doubt, that in her detachment she knows about Miltonic fears of falling and Richardsonian dreams of rising, about the anxieties induced by patriarchal education and the hallucinations of genteel romance.[54] And precisely because she has such a keen literary consciousness, she is able ultimately to survive and to triumph over her sometimes unruly story. Even when Heathcliff locks her up, for example, Nelly gets out (unlike Catherine and Isabella, who are never really able to escape), and one by one the deviants who have tried to reform her tale—Catherine, Heathcliff, even Isabella—die, while Nelly survives. She survives and, as Bersani has also noted, she coerces the story into a more docile and therefore more congenial mode.[55]

To speak of coercion in connection with Nelly may seem unduly negative, certainly from the Leavisite perspective. And in support of that perspective we should note that besides being wholesome because she is a survivor, Nelly is benevolent because she is a nurse, a nurturer, a foster-mother. The gift Mr. Earnshaw promises her is as symbolically significant in this respect as Catherine's whip and Hindley's fiddle, although our later experiences of Nelly suggest that she wants the apples and pears not so much for herself as for others. For though Nelly's health suggests that she is a hearty eater, she is most often seen feeding others, carrying baskets of apples, stirring porridge, roasting meats, pouring tea. Wholesomely nurturing, she does appear to be in some sense an ideal woman, a "general mother"—if not from Emily Brontë's point of view, then from, say, Milton's. And indeed, if we look again at the crucial passage in *Shirley* where Charlotte Brontë's Shirley/Emily criticizes Milton, we find an unmistakable version of Nelly Dean. "Milton tried to see the first woman," says Shirley, "but, Cary, he saw her not. . . . It was his cook that he saw . . . puzzled 'what choice to choose for delicacy best. . . .'"

This comment explains a great deal. For if Nelly Dean is Eve as Milton's cook—Eve, that is, as Milton (but not Brontë or Shirley) would have had her—she does not pluck apples to eat them herself; she plucks them to make applesauce. And similarly, she does not tell stories to participate in them herself, to consume the emotional food they offer, but to create a moral meal, a didactic fare that will nourish future generations in docility. As Milton's cook, in fact, Nelly Dean is patriarchy's paradigmatic housekeeper, the man's woman who has traditionally been hired to keep men's houses in order by straightening out their parlors, their daughters, and their stories. "My heart invariably cleaved to the master's, in preference to Catherine's side," she herself declares (chap. 10), and she expresses her preference by acting throughout the novel as a censorious agent of patriarchy.

Catherine's self-starvation, for instance, is notably prolonged by Nelly's failure to tell "the master" what his wife is doing, though in the first place it was induced by tale-bearing on Nelly's part. All her life Catherine has had trouble stomaching the food offered by Milton's cook, and so it is no wonder that in her madness she sees Nelly as a witch "gathering elf-bolts to hurt our heifers." It is not so much that Nelly Dean is "Evil," as Q. D. Leavis scolds "an American critic" for suggesting,[56] but that she is accommodatingly manipulative, a stereotypically benevolent man's woman. As such, she would and does "hurt [the] heifers" that inhabit such an anti-Miltonic heaven of femaleness as Wuthering Heights. In fact, as Catherine's "mad" words acknowledge, there is a sense in which Nelly Dean herself is Milton's bogey, the keeper of the house who closes windows (as Nelly does throughout *Wuthering Heights*) and locks women into the common sitting room. And because Emily Brontë is not writing a revolutionary polemic but a myth of origins, she chooses to tell her story of psychogenesis ironically, through the words of the survivor who helped *make* the story—through "the perdurable voice of the country," in Schorer's apt phrase. Reading Nelly's text, we see what we have lost through the eyes of the cook who has transformed us into what we are.

But if Nelly parallels or comments upon Catherine by representing Eve as Milton's cook, while Isabella represents Catherine/Eve as a bourgeois literary lady, it may at first be hard to see how or why Heathcliff parallels Catherine at all. Though he is Catherine's alter ego, he certainly seems to be, in Bersani's words, "a non-identical double."[57] Not only is he male while she is female—implying many subtle as well as a few obvious differences, in this gender-obsessed book—but he seems to be a triumphant survivor, an insider, a power-usurper throughout most of the novel's second half, while Catherine is not only a dead failure but a wailing, outcast ghost. Heathcliff does love her and mourn her—and finally Catherine does in some sense "kill" him—but beyond such melodramatically romantic connections, what bonds unite these one-time lovers?

Perhaps we can best begin to answer this question by examining the passionate words with which Heathcliff closes his first grief-stricken speech after Catherine's death: "Oh, God! it is unutterable! I cannot live without my life! I cannot live without my soul!" (chap. 16). Like the metaphysical paradox embedded in Catherine's crucial adolescent speech to Nelly about Heathcliff ("He's more myself than I am"), these words have often been thought to be, on the one hand, emptily rhetorical, and on the other, severely mystical. But suppose we try to imagine what they might mean as descriptions of a psychological fact about the relationship between Heathcliff and Catherine. Catherine's assertion that Heathcliff was *herself* quite reasonably summarized, after all, her understanding that she was being transformed into a lady while Heathcliff retained the ferocity of her primordial half-savage self. Similarly, Heathcliff's exclamation that he cannot live without his soul may express, as a corollary of this idea, the "gypsy's" own deep sense of being Catherine's whip, and his perception that he has now become merely the soulless body of a vanished passion. But to be merely a body—a whip without a mistress—is to be a sort of monster, a fleshly thing, an object of pure animal materiality like the abortive being Victor Frankenstein created. And such a monster is indeed what Heathcliff becomes.

From the first, Heathcliff has had undeniable monster potential, as many readers have observed. Isabella's questions to Nelly—"Is Mr. Heathcliff a man? If so, is he mad? And if not is he a devil?" (chap. 13)—indicate among other things Emily Brontë's cool awareness of having created an anomalous being, a sort of "Ghoul" or "Afreet," not (as her sister half hoped) "despite" herself but for good reasons. Uniting human and animal traits, the skills of culture with the energies of nature, Heathcliff's character tests the boundaries between human and animal, nature and culture, and in doing so proposes a new definition of the demonic. What is more important for our purposes here, however, is the fact that, despite his outward masculinity, Heathcliff is somehow female in his monstrosity. Besides in a general way suggesting a set of questions about humanness, his existence therefore summarizes a number of important points about the relationship between maleness and femaleness as, say, Milton representatively defines it.

To say that Heathcliff is "female" may at first sound mad or absurd. As we noted earlier, his outward masculinity seems to be definitively demonstrated by his athletic build and military carriage, as well as by the Byronic sexual charisma that he has for ladylike Isabella. And though we saw that Edgar is truly patriarchal despite his apparent effeminacy, there is no real reason why Heathcliff should not simply represent an alternative version of masculinity, the maleness of the younger son, that paradigmatic outsider in patriarchy. To some extent, of course, this is true: Heathcliff is clearly just as male in his Satanic outcast way as Edgar in his angelically established way. But at the same time, on a deeper associative level, Heathcliff is "female"—on the level where younger sons and bastards and devils unite with women in rebelling against the tyranny of heaven, the level where orphans are female and heirs are male, where flesh is female and spirit is male, earth female, sky male, monsters female, angels male.

The sons of Urizen were born from heaven, Blake declares, but "his daughters from green herbs and cattle, / From monsters and worms of the pit." He might be describing Heathcliff, the "little dark thing" whose enigmatic ferocity suggests vegetation spirits, hell, pits, night— all the "female" irrationality of nature. Nameless as a woman, the gypsy orphan old Earnshaw brings back from the mysterious bowels of Liver/pool is clearly as illegitimate as daughters are in a patrilineal culture. He speaks, moreover, a kind of animal-like gibberish which, together with his foreign swarthiness, causes sensible Nelly to refer to him at first as an "it," implying (despite his apparent maleness) a deep inability to get his gender straight. His "it-ness" or id-ness emphasizes, too, both his snarling animal qualities—his appetites, his brutality—and his thingness. And the fact that he speaks gibberish suggests the profound alienation of the physical/natural/female realm he represents from language, culture's tool and the glory of "spirits Masculine." In even the most literal way, then, he is what Elaine Showalter calls "a woman's man," a male figure into which a female artist projects in disguised form her own anxieties about her sex and its meaning in her society.[58] Indeed, if Nelly Dean is Milton's cook, Heathcliff incarnates that unregenerate natural world which must be metaphorically cooked or spiritualized, and therefore a raw kind of femaleness that, Brontë shows, has to be exorcised if it cannot be controlled.

In most human societies the great literal and figurative chefs, from Brillat-Savarin to Milton, are males, but as Sherry Ortner has noted, everyday "cooking" (meaning such low-level conversions from nature to culture as child-rearing, pot-making, bread-baking) is done by women, who are in effect charged with the task of policing the realm they represent.[59] This point may help explain how and why Catherine Earnshaw becomes Heathcliff's "soul." After Nelly as archetypal house-keeper finishes nursing him, high-spirited Catherine takes over his education because he meets her needs for power. Their relationship works so well, however, because just as he provides her with an extra body to lessen her female vulnerability, so she fills his need for a soul, a voice, a language with which to address cultured men like Edgar. Together they constitute an autonymous and androgynous (or, more accurately, gynandrous) whole: a woman's man and a woman *for herself* in Sartre's sense, making up one complete woman.[60] So complete do they feel, in fact, that as we have seen they define their home at Wuthering Heights as a heaven, and themselves as a sort of Blakeian angel, as if sketching out the definition of an angel D. H. Lawrence would have Tom Brangwen offer seventy-five years later in *The Rainbow*:

> "If we've got to be Angels, and if there is no such thing as a man nor a woman amongst them, then ... a married couple makes one Angel. ... For ... an Angel can't be less than a human being. And if it was only the soul of a man *minus* the man, then it would be less than a human being."[61]

That the world—particularly Lockwood, Edgar, and Isabella—sees the heaven of Wuthering Heights as a "hell" is further evidence of the hellish femaleness that characterizes this gynandrous body and soul. It is early evidence, too, that without his "soul" Heathcliff will become an entirely diabolical brute, a "Ghoul" or "Afreet." Speculating seriocomically that women have souls "only to make them capable of *Damnation*," John Donne articulated the traditional complex of ideas underlying this point even before Milton did. "Why hath the common opinion afforded women soules?" Donne asked. After all, he noted, women's only really "spiritual" quality is their power of speech, "for which they are beholding to their *bodily instruments*: For perchance an *Oxes* heart, or a *Goates*, or a *Foxes*, or a *Serpents* would speak just so, if it were in the *breast*, and could move that *tongue* and *jawes*." [62] Though speaking of women, he might have been defining the problem Isabella was to articulate for Emily Brontë: "Is Mr. Heathcliff a *man*? Or what is he?"

As we have already seen, when Catherine is first withdrawn from the adolescent Heathcliff, the boy becomes increasingly brutish, as if to foreshadow his eventual soullessness. Returning in her ladylike costume from Thrushcross Grange, Catherine finds her one-time "counterpart" in old clothes covered with "mire and dirt," his face and hands "dismally beclouded" by dirt that suggests his inescapable connection with the filthiness of nature. Similarly, when Catherine is dying Nelly is especially conscious that Heathcliff "gnashed ... and foamed like a mad dog," so that she does not feel as if he is a creature of her own species (chap. 15). Still later, after his "soul's" death, it seems to her that Heathcliff howls "not like a man, but like a savage beast getting goaded to death with knives and spears" (chap. 16) His subsequent conduct, though not so overtly animal-like, is consistent with such behavior. Bastardly and dastardly, a true son of the bitch goddess Nature, throughout the second half of *Wuthering Heights* Heathcliff pursues a murderous revenge against patriarchy, a revenge most appropriately expressed by *King Lear's* equally outcast Edmund: "Well, then, / Legitimate Edgar, I must have your land." [63] For Brontë's revisionary genius manifests itself especially in her perception of the deep connections among Shakespeare's Edmund, Milton's Satan, Mary Shelley's monster, the demon lover/animal groom figure of innumerable folktales—and Eve, the original rebellious female.

Because he unites characteristics of all these figures in a single body, Heathcliff in one way or another acts like all of them throughout the second half of *Wuthering Heights*. His general aim in this part of the novel is to wreak the revenge of nature upon culture by subverting legitimacy. Thus, like Edmund (and Edmund's female counterparts Goneril and Regan) he literally *takes* the *place* of one legitimate heir after another, supplanting both Hindley and Hareton at the Heights, and—eventually—Edgar at the Grange. Moreover, he not only replaces legitimate culture but in his rage strives like Frankenstein's monster to end it. His attempts at killing Isabella and Hindley, as well as the infanticidal tendencies expressed in his merciless abuse of his own son, indicate his desire not only to alter the ways of his world but literally to dis-continue them, to get at the heart of patri-archy by stifling the line of descent that ultimately gives culture its legitimacy. Lear's *"hysterica passio,"* his sense that he is being smothered by female nature, which has inexplicably risen against all fathers everywhere, is seriously parodied, therefore, by the suffocating womb/room of death where Heathcliff locks up his sickly son and legitimate Edgar's daughter.[64] Like Satan, whose fall was originally inspired by envy of the celestial legitimacy incarnated in the Son of God, Heathcliff steals or perverts birthrights. Like Eve and her double, Sin, he undertakes such crimes against a Urizenic heaven in order to vindicate his own worth, assert his own energy. And again, like Satan, whose hellish kingdom is a shadowy copy of God's luminous one, or like those suavely unregenerate animal grooms Mr. Fox and Bluebeard, he manages to achieve a great deal because he realizes that in order to subvert legitimacy he must first imper-sonate it; that is, to kill patriarchy, he must first pretend to be a patriarch.

Put another way, this simply means that Heathcliff's charismatic maleness is at least in part a result of his understanding that he must defeat on its own terms the society that has defeated him. Thus, though he began his original gynandrous life at Wuthering Heights as Catherine's whip, he begins his transformed, soulless or Satanic life there as Isabella's bridal hook. Similarly, throughout the extended maneuvers against Edgar and his daughter which occupy him for the twenty years between Isabella's departure and his own death, he impersonates a "devil daddy," stealing children like Catherine II and Linton from their rightful homes, trying to separate Milton's cook from both her story and her morality, and perverting the innocent Hareton into an artificially blackened copy of himself. His understanding of the inauthenticity of his behavior is consistently shown by his irony. Heathcliff knows perfectly well that he is not really a father in the true (patriarchal) sense of the word, if only because he has himself no *sur*name; he is simply acting like a father, and his bland, amused "I want my children about me to be sure" (chap. 29) comments upon the world he despises by sardonically mimicking it, just as Satan mimics God's logic and Edmund mimics Gloucester's astrologic.

On the one hand, therefore, as Linton's deathly father, Heathcliff, like Satan, is truly the father of death (begotten, however, not upon Sin but upon silliness), but on the other hand he is very consciously a mock father, a male version of the terrible devouring mother, whose blackly comic admonitions to Catherine II ("No more runnings away! . . . I'm come to fetch you home, and I hope you'll be a dutiful daughter, and not encourage my son to further disobedience" [chap. 29]) evoke the bleak hilarity of hell with their satire of Miltonic righteousness. Given the complexity of all this, it is no wonder Nelly considers his abode at the Heights "an oppression past explaining."

Since Heathcliff's dark energies seem so limitless, why does his vengeful project fail? Ultimately, no doubt, it fails because in stories of the war between nature and culture nature always fails. But that point is of course a tautology. Culture tells the story (that is, the story is a cultural construct) and the story is etiological: how culture triumphed over nature, where parsonages and tea-parties came from, how the lady got her skirts—and her deserts. Thus Edmund, Satan, Frankenstein's monster, Mr. Fox, Bluebeard, Eve, and Heathcliff all must fail in one way or another, if only to explain the status quo. Significantly, however, where Heathcliff's analogs are universally destroyed by forces outside themselves, Heathcliff seems to be killed, as Catherine was, by something within himself. His death from self-starvation makes his function as Catherine's almost identical double definitively clear. Interestingly, though, when we look closely at the events leading up to his death it becomes equally clear that Heathcliff is not just killed by his own despairing desire for his vanished "soul" but at least in part by another one of Catherine's parallels, the new and cultivated Catherine who has been reborn through the intervention of patriarchy in the form of Edgar Linton. It is no accident, certainly, that Catherine II's imprisonment at the Heights and her rapprochement with Hareton coincide with Heathcliff's perception that "there is a strange change approaching," with his vision of the lost Catherine, and with his development of an eating disorder very much akin to Catherine's anorexia nervosa.

If Heathcliff is Catherine's almost identical double, Catherine II really is her mother's "non-identical double." Though he has his doubles confused, Bersani does note that Nelly's "mild moralizing"

seems "suited to the younger Catherine's playful independence."[65] For where her headstrong mother genuinely struggled for autonomy, the more docile Catherine II merely plays at disobedience, taking make-believe journeys within the walls of her father's estate and dutifully surrendering her illicit (though equally make-believe) love letters at a word from Nelly. Indeed, in almost every way Catherine II differs from her fierce dead mother in being culture's child, a born lady. "It's as if Emily Brontë were telling the same story twice," Bersani observes, "and eliminating its originality the second time."[66] But though he is right that Brontë is telling the same story over again (really for the third or fourth time), she is not repudiating her own originality. Rather, through her analysis of Catherine II's successes, she is showing how society repudiated Catherine's originality.

Where, for instance, Catherine Earnshaw rebelled against her father, Catherine II is profoundly dutiful. One of her most notable adventures occurs when she runs away from Wuthering Heights to get *back* to her father, a striking contrast to the escapes of Catherine and Isabella, both of whom ran purposefully away from the world of fathers and older brothers. Because she is a dutiful daughter, moreover, Catherine II is a cook, nurse, teacher, and housekeeper. In other words, where her mother was a heedless wild child, Catherine II promises to become an ideal Victorian woman, all of whose virtues are in some sense associated with daughterhood, wifehood, motherhood. Since Nelly Dean was her foster mother, literally replacing the original Catherine, her development of these talents is not surprising. To be mothered by Milton's cook and fathered by one of his angels is to become, inevitably, culture's child. Thus Catherine II nurses Linton (even though she dislikes him), brews tea for Heathcliff, helps Nelly prepare vegetables, teaches Hareton to read, and replaces the wild blackberries at Wuthering Heights with flowers from Thrushcross Grange. Literary as her father and her aunt Isabella, she has learned the lessons of patriarchal Christianity so well that she even piously promises Heathcliff that she will forgive both him and Linton for their sins against her: "I know [Linton] has a bad nature . . . he's your son. But I'm glad I've a better to forgive it" (chap. 29). At the same time, she has a genteel (or Urizenic) feeling for rank which comes out in her early treatment of Hareton, Zillah, and others at the Heights.

Even when she stops biblically forgiving, moreover, literary modes dominate Catherine II's character. The "black arts" she tries to practice are essentially bookish—and plainly inauthentic. Indeed, if Heath'cliff is merely impersonating a father at this point in the story, Catherine II is merely impersonating a witch. A real witch would threaten culture; but Catherine II's vocation is to serve it, for as her personality suggests, she is perfectly suited to (has been raised for) what Sherry Ortner defines as the crucial female function of mediating between nature and culture.[67] Thus it is she who finally restores order to both the Heights and the Grange by marrying Hareton Earnshaw, whom she has, significantly, prepared for his new mastery by teaching him to read. Through her intervention, therefore, he can at last recognize the name over the lintel at Wuthering Heights—the name Hareton Earnshaw—which is both his own name and the name of the founder of the house, the primordial patriarch.

With his almost preternatural sensitivity to threats, Heathcliff himself recognizes the danger Catherine II represents. When, offering to "forgive him," she tries to embrace him he shudders and remarks "I'd rather hug a snake!" Later, when she and Hareton have cemented their friendship, Heathcliff constantly addresses her as "witch" and "slut." In the world's terms, she is the opposite of these: she is virtually an angel in the house. But for just those reasons she *is* Urizenically dangerous to Heathcliff's Pandemonium at the Heights. Besides threatening his present position, however, Catherine II's union with Hareton reminds Heathcliff specifically of the heaven he has lost. Looking up from their books, the young couple reveal that "their eyes are precisely similar, and they are those of Catherine Earnshaw" (chap. 33). Ironically, however, the fact that Catherine's descendants "have" her eyes tells Heathcliff not so much that Catherine endures as that she is both dead and fragmented. Catherine II has only her mother's eyes, and though Hareton has more of her features, he too is conspicuously not Catherine. Thus when Edgar dies and Heathcliff opens Catherine's casket as if to free her ghost, or when Lockwood opens the window as if to admit the witch child of his nightmare, the original Catherine arises in her ghostly wholeness from the only places where she can still exist in wholeness: the cemetary, the moor, the storm, the irrational realm of those that fly by night, the realm of Satan, Eve, Sin, and Death. Outside of this realm, the ordinary world inhabited by Catherine II and Hareton is, Heathcliff now notes, merely "a dreadful collection of memoranda that [Catherine] did exist, and that I have lost her!" (chap. 33).

Finally, Catherine II's alliance with Hareton awakens Heathcliff to truths about the younger man that he had not earlier understood, and in a sense his consequent disillusionment is the last blow that sends him toward death. Throughout the second half of the novel Heathcliff has taken comfort not only in Hareton's "startling" physical likeness to Catherine, but also in the likeness of the dispossessed boy's situation to his own early exclusion from society. "Hareton seem[s] a personification of my youth, not a human being," Heathcliff tells Nelly (chap. 33). This evidently causes him to see the illiterate outcast as metaphorically the true son of his own true union with Catherine. Indeed, where he had originally dispossessed Hareton as a way of revenging himself upon Hindley, Heathcliff seems later to want to keep the boy rough and uncultivated so that he, Heathcliff, will have at least one strong natural descendant (as opposed to Linton, his false and deathly descendant). As Hareton moves into Catherine II's orbit, however, away from nature and toward culture, Heathcliff realizes the mistake he has made. Where he had supposed that Hareton's reenactment of his own youth might even somehow restore the lost Catherine, and thus the lost Catherine-Heathcliff, he now sees that Hareton's reenactment of his youth is essentially corrective, a retelling of the story the "right" way. Thus if we can call Catherine II C^2 and define Hareton as H^2, we might arrive at the following formulation of Heathcliff's problem: where C plus H equals fullness of being for both C and H, C^2 plus H^2 specifically equals a negation of both C and H. Finally, the ambiguities of Hareton's name summarize in another way Heathcliff's problem with this most puzzling Earnshaw. On the one hand, Hare/ton is a nature name, like Heathcliff. But on the other hand, Hare/ton, suggesting Heir/ton (Heir/town?) is a punning indicator of the young man's legitimacy.

It is in his triumphant legitimacy that Hareton, together with Catherine II, acts to exorcise Heathcliff from the traditionally legitimate world of the Grange and the newly legitimized world of Wuthering Heights. Fading into nature, where Catherine persists "in every cloud, in every tree," Heathcliff can no longer eat the carefully cooked human food that Nelly offers him. While Catherine II decorates Hareton's porridge with cut flowers, the older man has irreligious fantasies of dying and being unceremoniously "carried to the churchyard in the evening." "I have nearly attained *my* heaven," he tells Nelly as he fasts and fades, "and that of others is . . . uncoveted by me" (chap, 34). Then, when he dies, the boundaries between nature and culture crack for a moment, as if to let him pass through: his window swings open, the rain drives in. "Th' divil's harried off his soul," exclaims old Joseph, *Wuthering Heights'* mock Milton, falling to his knees and giving thanks "that the lawful master and the ancient stock [are] restored to their rights" (chap. 34). The illegitimate Heathcliff/Catherine have finally been re-placed in nature/hell, and replaced by Hareton and Catherine II—a proper couple—just as Nelly replaced Catherine as a proper mother for Catherine II. Quite reasonably, Nelly now observes that "The crown of all my wishes will be the union of" this new, civilized couple, and Lockwood notes of the new pair that "together, they would brave Satan and all his legions." Indeed, in both Milton's and Brontë's terms (it is the only point on which the two absolutely agree) they have already braved Satan, and they have triumphed. It is now 1802; the Heights —hell—has been converted into the Grange—heaven; and with patriarchal history redefined, renovated, restored, the nineteenth century can truly begin, complete with tea-parties, ministering angels, governesses, and parsonages.

Joseph's important remark about the restoration of the lawful master and the ancient stock, together with the dates—1801/1802— which surround Nelly's tale of a pseudo-mythic past, confirm the idea that *Wuthering Heights* is somehow etiological. More, the famous care with which Brontë worked out the details surrounding both the novel's dates and the Earnshaw-Linton lineage suggests she herself was quite conscious that she was constructing a story of origins and renewals. Having arrived at the novel's conclusion, we can now go back to its beginning, and try to summarize the basic story *Wuthering Heights* tells. Though this may not be the book's only story, it is surely a crucial one. As the names on the windowsill indicate, *Wuthering Heights* begins and ends with Catherine and her various avatars. More specifically, it studies the evolution of Catherine Earnshaw into Catherine Heathcliff and Catherine Linton, and then her return through Catherine Linton II and Catherine Heathcliff II to her "proper" role as Catherine Earnshaw II. More generally, what this evolution and de-evolution conveys is the following parodic, anti-Miltonic myth:

There was an Original Mother (Catherine), a daughter of nature whose motto might be "Thou, Nature, art my goddess; to thy law / My services are bound." But this girl fell into a decline, at least in part through eating the poisonous cooked food of culture. She fragmented herself into mad or dead selves on the one hand (Catherine, Heathcliff) and into lesser, gentler/genteeler selves on the other (Catherine II, Hareton). The fierce primordial selves disappeared into nature, the perversely hellish heaven which was their home. The more teachable and docile selves learned to read and write, and moved into the fallen cultured world of parlors and parsonages, the Miltonic heaven which, from the Original Mother's point of view, is really hell. Their passage from nature to culture was facilitated by a series of teachers, preachers, nurses, cooks, and model ladies or patriarchs (Nelly, Joseph, Frances, the Lintons), most of whom gradually disappear by the end of the story, since these lesser creations have been so well instructed that they are themselves able to become teachers or models for other generations. Indeed, so model are they that they can be identified with the founders of ancestral houses (Hareton Earnshaw, 1500) and with the original mother redefined as the patriarch's wife (Catherine Linton Heathcliff Earnshaw).

The nature/culture polarities in this Brontë myth have caused a number of critics to see it as a version of the so-called Animal Groom story, like Beauty and the Beast, or the Frog Prince. But, as Bruno Bettelheim has most recently argued, such tales usually function to help listeners and readers assimilate sexuality into consciousness and thus nature into culture (e.g., the beast is really lovable, the frog really handsome, etc.).[68] In *Wuthering Heights*, however, while culture does require nature's energy as raw material—the Grange needs the Heights, Edgar wants Catherine—society's most pressing need is to exorcise the rebelliously Satanic, irrational, and "female" representatives of nature. In this respect, Brontë's novel appears to be closer to a number of American Indian myths Lévi-Strauss recounts than it is to any of the fairy tales with which it is usually compared. In particular, it is reminiscent of an Opaye Indian tale called "The Jaguar's Wife."

In this story, a girl marries a jaguar so that she can get all the meat she wants for herself and her family. After a while, as a result of her marriage, the jaguar comes to live with the Indians, and for a time the girl's family becomes friendly with the new couple. Soon, however, a grandmother feels mistrust. "The young woman [is] gradually turning into a beast of prey.... Only her face remain[s] human ... the old woman therefore resort[s] to witchcraft and kill[s] her granddaughter." After this, the family is very frightened of the jaguar, expecting him to take revenge. And although he does not do so, he promises enigmatically that "Perhaps you will remember me in years to come," and goes off "incensed by the murder and spreading fear by his roaring; but the sound [comes] from farther and farther away." [69]

Obviously this myth is analogous to *Wuthering Heights* in a number of ways, with alien and animal-like Heathcliff paralleling the jaguar, Catherine paralleling the jaguar's wife, Nelly Dean functioning as the defensive grandmother, and Catherine II and Hareton acting like the family which inherits meat and a jaguar-free world from the departed wife. Lévi-Strauss's analysis of the story makes these likenesses even clearer, however, and in doing so it clarifies what Brontë must have seen as the grim necessities of *Wuthering Heights*.

> In order that all man's present possessions (which the jaguar has now lost) may come to him from the jaguar (who enjoyed them formerly when man was without them), there must be some agent capable of establishing a relation between them: this is where the jaguar's (human) wife fits in.
>
> But once the transfer has been accomplished (through the agency of the wife):
>
> a) The woman becomes useless, because she has served her purpose as a preliminary condition, which was the only purpose she had.
>
> b) Her survival would contradict the fundamental situation, which is characterized by a total absence of reciprocity.
>
> The jaguar's wife must therefore be eliminated.[70]

Though Lévi-Strauss does not discuss this point, we should note too that the jaguar's distant roaring hints he may return some day: obviously culture must be vigilant against nature, the superego must be ready at all times to battle the id. Similarly, the random weakening of Wuthering Heights' walls with which Brontë's novel began— symbolized by old Earnshaw's discovery of Heathcliff in Liverpool— suggests that patriarchal culture is always only precariously holding off the rebellious forces of nature. Who, after all, can say with certainty that the restored line of Hareton Earnshaw 1802 will not someday be just as vulnerable to the onslaughts of the goddess's illegitimate children as the line of Hareton Earnshaw 1500 was to Heathcliff's intrusion? And who is to say that the carving of Hareton Earnshaw 1500 was not similarly preceded by still another war between nature and culture? The fact that everyone has the same name leads inevitably to speculations like this, as though the drama itself, like its actors, simply represented a single episode in a sort of mythic infinite regress. In addition, the fact that the little shepherd boy still sees "Heathcliff and a woman" wandering the moor hints that the powerfully disruptive possibilities they represent may some day be reincarnated at Wuthering Heights.

Emily Brontë would consider such reincarnation a consummation devoutly to be wished. Though the surface Nelly Dean imposes upon Brontë's story is as dispassionately factual as the tone of "The Jaguar's Wife," the author's intention is passionately elegiac, as shown by the referential structure of *Wuthering Heights*, Catherine-Heathcliff's charisma, and the book's anti-Miltonic messages. This is yet another point Charlotte Brontë understood quite well, as we can see not only from the feminist mysticism of *Shirley* but also from the diplomatic irony of parts of her preface to *Wuthering Heights*. In *Shirley*, after all, the first woman, the true Eve, *is* nature—and she is noble and she is lost to all but a few privileged supplicants like Shirley-Emily herself, who tells Caroline (in response to an invitation to go to church) that "I will stay out here with my mother Eve, in these days called Nature. I love her—undying, mighty being! Heaven may have faded from her brow when she fell in paradise; but all that is glorious on earth shines there still."[71] And several years later Charlotte concluded her preface to *Wuthering Heights* with a discreetly qualified description of a literal heath/cliff that might also apply to *Shirley*'s titanic Eve:

... the crag took human shape; and there it stands, colossal, dark, and frowning, half statue, half rock: in the former sense, terrible and goblin-like; in the latter, almost beautiful, for its coloring is of mellow grey, and moorland moss clothes it; and heath, with its blooming bells and balmy fragrance, grows faithfully close to the giant's foot.[72]

This grandeur, Charlotte Brontë says, is what "Ellis Bell" was writing about; this is what she (rightly) thought we have lost. For like the fierce though forgotten seventeenth-century Behmenist mystic Jane Lead, Emily Brontë seems to have believed that Eve had become tragically separated from her fiery original self, and that therefore she had "lost her Virgin Eagle Body ... and so been sown into a slumbering Death, in Folly, Weakness, and Dishonor."[73]

Her slumbering death, however, was one from which Eve might still arise. Elegiac as it is, mournfully definitive as its myth of origin seems, *Wuthering Heights* is nevertheless haunted by the ghost of a lost gynandry, a primordial possibility of power now only visible to children like the ones who see Heathcliff and Catherine.

> No promised Heaven, these wild Desires
> Could all or half fulfil,
> No threatened Hell, with quenchless fire
> Subdue this quenchless will!

Emily Brontë declares in one of her poems.[74] The words may or may not be intended for a Gondalian speech, but it hardly matters, since in any case they characterize the quenchless and sardonically impious will that stalks through *Wuthering Heights*, rattling the windowpanes of ancient houses and blotting the pages of family bibles. Exorcised from the hereditary estate of the ancient stock, driven to the sinister androgyny of their *Liebestod*, Catherine and Heathcliff nevertheless linger still at the edge of the estate, as witch and goblin, Eve and Satan. Lockwood's two dreams, presented as prologues to Nelly's story, are also, then, necessary epilogues to that tale. In the first, "Jabes Branderham," Joseph's nightmare fellow, tediously thunders Miltonic curses at Lockwood, enumerating the four hundred and ninety sins of which erring nature and the quenchless will are guilty. In the second, nature, personified as the wailing witch child "Catherine

Linton," rises willfully in protest, and gentlemanly Lockwood's unexpectedly violent attack upon her indicates his terrified perception of the danger she represents.

Though she reiterated Milton's misogyny where Brontë struggled to subvert it, Mary Shelley also understood the dangerous possibilities of the outcast will. Her lost Eve became a monster, but "he" was equally destructive to the fabric of society. Later in the nineteenth century other women writers, battling Milton's bogey, would also examine the annihilation with which patriarchy threatens Eve's quenchless will, and the witchlike rage with which the female responds. George Eliot, for instance, would picture in *The Mill on the Floss* a deadly androgyny that seems like a grotesque parody of the *Liebestod* Heathcliff and Catherine achieve. "In their death" Maggie and Tom Tulliver "are not divided"—but the union they achieve is the only authentic one Eliot can imagine for them, since in life the one became an angel of renunciation, the other a captain of industry. Significantly, however, their death is caused by a flood that obliterates half the landscape of culture: female nature does and will continue to protest.

If Eliot specifically reinvents Brontë's *Liebestod*, Mary Elizabeth Coleride reimagines her witchlike nature spirit. In a poem that also reflects her anxious ambivalence about the influence of her great uncle Samuel, the author of "Christabel," Coleridge *becomes* Geraldine, Catherine Earnshaw, Lucy Gray, even Frankenstein's monster —all the wailing outcast females who haunt the graveyards of patriarchy. Speaking in "the voice that women have, who plead for their heart's desire," she cries

> I have walked a great while over the snow
> And I am not tall nor strong.
> My clothes are wet, and my teeth are set,
> And the way was hard and long.
> I have wandered over the fruitful earth,
> But I never came here before.
> Oh, lift me over the threshhold, and let me in at the door ...

And then she reveals that "She came—and the quivering flame / Sank and died in the fire."[75]

Emily Brontë's outcast witch-child is fiercer, less dissembling than

Coleridge's, but she longs equally for the extinction of parlor fires and the rekindling of unimaginably different energies. Her creator, too, is finally the fiercest, most quenchless of Milton's daughters. Looking oppositely for the queendom of heaven, she insists, like Blake, that "I have also the Bible of Hell, which the world shall have whether they will or no."[76] And in the voice of the wind that sweeps through the newly cultivated garden at Wuthering Heights, we can hear the jaguar, like Blake's enraged Rintrah, roaring in the distance.

IV
The Spectral Selves of Charlotte Brontë

Illustration on the preceding page: *The Poor Teacher*, by Richard Redgrave. Crown Copyright, Victoria and Albert Museum. Reproduced by permission.

A Secret, Inward Wound:
The Professor's Pupil

> The strong pulse of Ambition struck
>   In every vein I owned;
> At the same instant, bleeding broke
>   A secret, inward wound.
> > —Charlotte Brontë

> I saw my life branching out before me like the green fig tree in the story.
> From the tip of every branch, like a fat purple fig, a wonderful future beckoned and winked. One fig was a husband and a happy home and children, and another fig was a famous poet and another fig was a brilliant professor, and another fig was Ee Gee, the amazing editor. . . .
> I saw myself sitting in the crotch of this fig tree, starving to death, just because I couldn't make up my mind which of the figs I would choose. . . . and, as I sat there, unable to decide, the figs began to wrinkle and go black, and, one by one, they plopped to the ground at my feet.
> > —Sylvia Plath

> There is a pain—so utter—
> It swallows substance up—
> Then covers the Abyss with Trance—
> So Memory can step
> Around—across—upon it—
> As one within a Swoon—
> Goes safely—where an open eye—
> Would drop Him—Bone by Bone.
> > —Emily Dickinson

Charlotte Brontë was essentially a trance-writer. "All wondering why I write with my eyes shut," she commented in her Roe Head journal,[1]

311

and, as Winifred Gérin points out, the irregular lines of her manuscripts indicate that she did write this way, a habit Gérin suggests she adopted "intentionally the better to sharpen the inner vision and shut out her bodily surroundings."[2] Inner vision: the rhetoric is Romantic, and it is Brontë's as much as Gérin's, recalling Wordsworth's "Trances of thought and mountings of the mind," as well as Coleridge's "Close your eyes with holy dread." "All this day," Brontë wrote in the same journal, "I have been in a dream half miserable and half ecstatic—miserable because I could not follow it out uninterruptedly, and ecstatic because it shewed almost in the vivid light of reality the ongoings of the infernal world [the childhood fantasy world of Angria]."[3] This is assuredly Romantic. And yet, we believe, it is distinctively female, too. For though most of Brontë's vocabulary and many of her visions derive from the early nineteenth-century writers in whose work her mind was steeped—Wordsworth, Coleridge, Scott, Byron—the entranced obsessiveness with which she worked out recurrent themes and metaphors seems to have been determined primarily by her gender, her sense of her difficult sexual destiny, and her anxiety about her anomalous, "orphaned" position in the world.

That this was the case is made a little clearer by the following passage from the same Roe Head journal entry:

> The parsing lesson was completed. . . . The thought came over me am I to spend all the best part of my life in this wretched bondage. . . . I crept up to the bed-room to be alone for the first time that day. Delicious was the sensation I experienced as I laid down on the spare bed & resigned myself to the luxury of twilight & solitude. The stream of thought, checked all day, came flowing free & calm along its channel. . . . the toil of the day, succeeded by this moment of divine leisure had acted on me like opium & was coiling about me a disturbed but fascinating spell such as I never felt before. What I imagined grew morbidly vivid. I remember I quite seemed to see with my bodily eyes a lady standing in the hall of a gentleman's house as if waiting for some one. It was dusk & there was the dim outline of antlers with a hat & a rough great-coat upon them. She had a flat candle-stick in her hand & seemed coming from the kitchen or

some such place. . . . As she waited I most distinctly heard the front-door open and saw the soft moonlight disclosed upon the lawn outside, and beyond the lawn at a distance I saw a town with lights twinkling through the gloaming. . . . No more. I have not time to work out the vision. At last I became aware of a heavy weight laid across me—I knew I was wide awake & that it was dark & that moreover the Ladies were now come into the room to get their curl-papers. . . . I heard them talking about me—I wanted to speak, to rise, it was impossible. . . . I must get up I thought, and did so with a start.[4]

The interest of this passage derives in part from the fact that, as Gérin remarks, such a confession is "rare in the annals of literature for its perception of the actual creative processes at work."[5] But surely some of its "morbidly vivid" elements are even more interesting: the gloomy gentleman's house, with its threateningly sexual outlines of antlers and its rough great-coat, the mysterious lady standing in the hall, the front-door opening upon inaccessible and glamorous distances, and (in a later section) the enigmatic figure of the girl Lucy, whose "faded bloom . . . reminded me of one who might . . . be dead and buried under the . . . sod."

"I have not time to work out the vision," Brontë notes, complaining of "a heavy weight laid across me." Nevertheless, we would argue that this is the vision she worked out in most of her novels, a vision of an indeterminate, usually female figure (who has often come "from the kitchen or some such place") trapped—even buried—in the architecture of a patriarchal society, and imagining, dreaming, or actually devising escape routes, roads past walls, lawns, antlers, to the glittering town outside. In this respect, Brontë's career provides a paradigm of the ways in which, as we have suggested, many nineteenth-century women wrote obsessively, often in what could be (metaphorically) called a state of "trance," about their feelings of enclosure in "feminine" roles and patriarchal houses, and wrote, too, about their passionate desire to flee such roles or houses.

Certainly Brontë's Angrian tales use Byronic elements to articulate female fantasies of liberation into an exotic "male" landscape. Written during the novelist's adolescence—from the time she was ten until she was about twenty-two—these stories of the "infernal

world" are as Satanically revisionary in their assessment of patriarchal Miltonic moral categories as any of Charlotte's sister Emily's
Gondalian fictions were. But, as we shall show, Charlotte Brontë
was far more ambivalent than Emily about the dichotomies of
heaven and hell, angel and monster. Thus her famous "Farewell
to Angria," written when she was on the verge of *The Professor*,
was not just a farewell to juvenile fantasies; it was, more importantly,
a farewell to the Satanic rebellion that those fantasies embodied.
Repudiating Angria, Brontë was adopting more elaborate disguises,
committing herself to an oscillation between overtly "angelic" dogma
and covertly Satanic fury that would mark the whole of her professional literary career. On the surface, indeed, she would seem to
have drastically revised her own revisionary impulses in order to
follow Carlyle's advice to "Close thy *Byron*; open thy *Goethe*."
Careful readings of all four of her novels suggest, however, that she
was in a sense reading her Goethe *and* her Byron simultaneously.

We shall see, for example, that *Jane Eyre* parodies both the nightmare confessional mode of the gothic genre and the moral didacticism
of Bunyan's *Pilgrim's Progress* to tell its distinctively female story of
enclosure and escape, with a "morbidly vivid" escape dream acted
out by an apparently "gothic" lunatic who functions as the more
sedate heroine's double. Similarly, *Shirley* uses a judicious, author-
omniscient technique to tell, in the context of a seemingly balanced,
conservative history of the conflict between male frame-breakers
and male mill-owners, a "female" tale of the genesis of female
"starvation." And even *Villette*, the most obviously eccentric of
Brontë's novels, and thus the one that comes closest to openly presenting its readers with an alternative female aesthetic, disguises its
dream narrative of female burial and tentatively imagined resurrection in a complex structure of self-denying parables and severe moral
homilies. Metaphorically speaking, Satan and Gabriel, angel and
monster, nun and witch, engage in an elaborate dialogue throughout
its pages, from its deliberately obscure beginning to its consciously
ambiguous conclusion, as if to distract us from the real point. During
all this, moreover, Lucy Snowe—the novel's narrator—pretends, like
Goethe's Makarie, to be a woman with no story of her own except
that story of repression which gave Makarie (and perhaps Brontë
after her) such terrible headaches.

Of course, like so many other women writers, Brontë was not always entirely conscious of the extent of her own duplicity—the extent, for instance, to which her entranced reveries about escape pervaded even her most craftsmanlike attempts at literary decorum. In her "Farewell to Angria," for instance, preparing herself to master the complexities of the "realistic" Victorian novel, she exclaimed that "I long to quit for a while the burning clime where we [she, Branwell, Emily, and Anne] have sojourned too long—its skies flame—the glow of sunset is always upon it—the mind would cease from excitement and turn now to a cooler region where the dawn breaks grey and sober, and the coming day for a time at least is subdued by clouds."[6] And yet *The Professor* (1846, pub. 1857), the pseudo-masculine *Bildungsroman* to which she turned with, in effect, eyes wide open, develops several crucial elements of the basic female enclosure-escape story. Perhaps more significant, though it appears dutifully to trace a traditional, hero-triumphant pattern, it contains figures whose characterizations seem as obsessive and involuntary as any in the earlier Angrian tales she was repudiating, figures who foreshadow the "morbidly vivid" dream actors in such later novels as *Jane Eyre* and *Villette*: a sensitive, outcast orphan girl; two inexplicably hostile brothers—one tyrannical, the other quietly revolutionary; a sinister and manipulative "stepmother"; and a Byronic ironist whose comments on the action often appear to reflect not just his own Romantic disaffection but also the narrator's—and the author's—secret, ungovernable rage, a rage which asserts itself the minute the novelist closes her eyes and feels again the "heavy weight" of her gender laid across her.

The narrator and the author are more carefully distinguished from each other in *The Professor* than in any of Brontë's other mature novels. Moreover, the use of the male narrator, as much as the book's "plain and homely" style, suggests an attempt by the female novelist to objectify her vision of the story she is telling, to disentangle personal fantasies from its plot and cool the "burning clime" of wish-fulfillment. For this reason, it is understandable that Winifred Gérin, among others, sees the male narrator as "an intrinsic demerit" in the work: Charlotte Brontë as William Crimsworth certainly lacks the apparent directness and confessional intensity of Charlotte Brontë as Jane Eyre or Charlotte Brontë as Lucy Snowe.

Curiously, however, even (or perhaps especially) this apparent objectivity of *The Professor* links it to the earlier, more obviously "entranced" Angrian tales, for those stories, too, were generally told by a male speaker, an "incurably inquisitive" avatar of the fledgling author with the significant name of *Charles* Arthur Florian Wellesley. Younger brother to the ambiguously fascinating Zamorna, Angria's sultanic/Satanic ruler, this early narrator openly fomented revolt against what he considered the insane tyranny of his sibling: "Serfs of Angria! Freeman of Verdopolis!" he exclaims in the preface to "The Spell, An Extravaganza," written when Brontë was eighteen, "I tell you that your tyrant, your Idol is mad! Yes! There are black veins of utter perversion of intellect born with him and running through his whole soul."[7] And while no such accusations are made by William Crimsworth, the sober professor, his restrained account of his own "ascent of the 'Hill of Difficulty' " indicts *his* older brother's "outrageous peculiarities" even more vigorously, though "rather by implication than assertion."[8]

Is there, then, any significant relationship between Brontë's literary male-impersonation (both in the Angrian tales and in *The Professor*) and her "female" proclivity for what we have called trance-writing? As we have seen, many women working in a male-dominated literary tradition at first attempt to resolve the ambiguities of their situation not merely by male mimicry but by some kind of metaphorical male impersonation. Similarly, trance-writing —in the sense in which we are using the phrase to describe Charlotte Brontë's simultaneous enactment and evasion of her own rebellious impulses—is clearly an attempt to allay the anxieties of female authorship. Beyond the fact that both are ways of resolving literary anxieties, however, it seems possible that trance-writing and male impersonation have even deeper connections. For one thing, the woman writer who may shrink from a consciously female appraisal of her female vulnerability in a male society can more easily make such an appraisal in her role of male impersonator. That is, by pretending to be a man, she can see herself as the crucial and powerful Other sees her. More, by impersonating a man she can gain male power, not only to punish her own forbidden fantasies but also to act them out. These things, however, especially the last, are also the things she does in her somnambulistic reiteration of a duplicitous enclosure-escape story, a story which secretly subverts its own ostensible morality. We shall see, though, that infection may breed in the trance-writer's dreaming sentences just as surely as it does in the sentences of the artist who is more fully conscious of her own despair. For the "strong pulse of Ambition" that drives a woman to become a professional writer often opens a "secret, in-ward wound" whose bleeding necessitates complicated defenses, disguises, evasions.

For all its apparent coolness, *The Professor* is just such a tissue of disguises. Lacking the feverish glow of the Angrian tales, the revolu-tionary fervor of *Shirley*, the gothic and mythic integrity of *Jane Eyre* or *Villette*, it nevertheless explores the problem of the literally and figuratively disinherited female in a patriarchal society and attempts (not quite successfully) to resolve the anger and anxiety of its author both by examining her situation through sympathetic male eyes and by transforming her into a patriarchal male professor, an orphaned underling turned master. At the beginning of the book, however, William Crimsworth, the narrator/protagonist, is neither master nor professor, and in recounting the tale of *his* struggles up "the Hill of Difficulty" Brontë found still a third way of confronting her own, distinctively feminine problems.

The Professor opens awkwardly, with an expository letter from Crimsworth to a friend. Although, especially in her late Angrian tales, she had handled technical problems of narration—point of view, time-scheme, transition—with considerable skill, Brontë seems to have felt compelled in her first "real" book to try to master the Richardsonian rigors of the epistolary novel. Her attempt, like her sister Anne's (in *The Tenant of Wildfell Hall*) or Jane Austen's (in *Lady Susan*), was a failure, and she quickly abandoned the letter-mechanism in favor of a more straightforward autobiographical structure. But that, like Anne and Austen, she made the effort in the first place is notable: Richardson, to whose work she alludes several times in *The Professor*, was an obvious master of prose fiction, and—significantly—a master whose images of women had forcefully told his female readers not only what they were but what they ought to be.[11] Now, masquerading as Crimsworth, Brontë seemed to want to reappraise the exemplary Richardsonian image of the young-lady-as-angel.

In his opening letter, for instance, her narrator informs his correspondent that he has cut himself off from his dead mother's family by rejecting both a career in the church and the possibility of marriage with one of his six aristocratic cousins. "How like a nightmare is the thought of being bound for life to one of my cousins!" he exclaims, adding "No doubt they are accomplished and pretty; but . . . to think of passing the winter evenings . . . alone with one of them—for instance, the large and well-modelled statue, Sarah—no . . ." (chap. 1). Later in the letter he describes himself turning "wearily" from his brother Edward's pretty wife, whose soulless and "infantine expression" is disagreeable to him—and, we might add, to Brontë herself, who was to attack the ideal of the perfect "lady" with similar anger in all three of her later novels.

But at the same time as they signal an intention to reexamine culturally accepted images of women, the early parts of Crimsworth's narrative convey an unusually chilling vision of the male world. Here, though, Brontë was on more familiar ground: for if Angrian women were as a rule extraordinarily independent in comparison to the more passive and sardonically drawn ladies who inhabit the pages of *The Professor*, Angrian men were no more unpleasant than William Crimsworth's male relatives. Half Byronic heroes and half crafty politicians drawn from the young Brontës' readings of contemporary newspapers, Zamorna, the Duke of Northangerland, and others seem like exaggerated versions of the "beastly" Englishmen who, Mrs. Sara Ellis explained in the *Family Monitor*, would turn entirely red in tooth and claw without a lady's civilizing touch.[12] But Crimsworth's mean-spirited uncles are just as beastly. These ungentle gentlemen, we learn, repudiated both their sister (for marrying the wrong man) and her son William (for not marrying the right woman). "I grew up," William tells us, "and heard by degrees of the persevering hostility, the hatred till death evinced by them against my father—of the sufferings of my mother—of all the wrongs, in short, of our house" (chap. 1). And the older brother to whom he turns for refuge is, significantly, no better than his uncles; indeed, he is in some respects far worse.

Inexplicably hostile and despotic, Edward Crimsworth is a bad-tempered Captain of Industry whose petty tyrannies prefigure the vicious oppressions of John Reed in *Jane Eyre*, and whose landscape-destroying business, "brooded over" by "a dense permanent vapor," looks forward to the dark Satanic mills in *Shirley*. He beats his horse, enslaves his subordinates, and, comments William's friend Yorke Hunsden, "will some day be a tyrant to his wife" (chap. 6). As for brotherly love, there is no such phrase in the lexicon of his heart. "I shall excuse you nothing on the plea of being my brother," he tells William. "I expect to have the full value of my money out of you" (chap. 2). At the one party to which he invites the young man, he introduces him to no one—so that, the narrator tells us, "I looked weary, solitary, kept down like some desolate tutor or governess; he was satisfied" (chap. 3). Finally, in a violent confrontation, he actually takes his whip to his brother. And yet, though he is the epitome of patriarchal injustice—the domineering older brother, master of Crimsworth Hall and rightful heir of the maternal portrait that William really loves—Edward has a tyrannical vigor which, Brontë shows, is inevitably rewarded in a society dominated by equally "beastly" men: even after his business has failed and he has alienated his rich wife with the beatings Yorke Hunsden predicted, he ends up "getting richer than Croesus by railway speculations" (chap. 25).

In this world of passive, doll-like women and ferociously over-bearing men, Brontë's male narrator plays from the first a curiously androgynous part. In his yearnings toward women he is conventionally masculine. But his judgments of women—his disgust, for instance, with the stereotypical doll-woman—suggest that he is at the least an unusual male, and his sense of the social unacceptability of his own nature qualifies his maleness even further. Similarly, although he seems conventionally male in worldly ambition, his reserve and almost shrinking passivity—the "equability of [his] temper"—are stereotypically female, as is his willingness to let himself be "kept down like some . . . governess." More important, disinherited and orphaned, as women are in a male society, he is powerless like a woman, "wrecked and stranded on the shores of commerce" (chap. 4) as Charlotte Brontë felt herself to be when her own early attempts at financial independence failed.

As in Brontë's later novels and in the works of many other women,

Crimsworth reacts to his perception of his "female" powerlessness
first with claustrophobic feelings of enclosure, burial, imprisonment,
and then with a rebellious decision to escape. "I began to feel like
a plant growing in humid darkness out of the slimy walls of a well"
(chap. 4), he confesses, and when he repudiates his commercial
career after his final quarrel with his brother, he exclaims "I leave
a prison, I have a tyrant," adding that "I felt light and liberated"
(chap. 5). As he embarks for Brussels, he utters a paean to "Liberty,"
foreshadowing Jane Eyre's meditations on that subject. "Liberty
I clasped in my arms for the first time, and the influence of her smile
and embrace revived my life like the sun and the west wind" (chap.
7). But his vision of Liberty as a supportive woman suggests that
the powerless, androgynous Crimsworth, escaping an oppressively
female role, is on the brink of metamorphosis into a more powerful
creature, a decidedly male hero-professor.

   As it will be for Lucy Snowe in *Villette*, the strangeness of Brussels
is important to William Crimsworth. Awaking in "a wide lofty
foreign chamber" heightens his feeling of liberation and intensifies
his sense that he is about to enter into a Vita Nuova. Seeking, like
Jane Eyre, a new "service," he embarks with surprising masterfulness
upon his life in M. Pelet's school for boys. What interests him rather
more than Pelet or his pupils, however, is the "unseen paradise"
next door: a "Pensionnat de Demoiselles" modelled exactly upon
the Pensionnat Héger where Charlotte and Emily Brontë studied
in Brussels. "Pensionnat!" he confides. "The word excited an uneasy
sensation in my mind; it seemed to speak of restraint" (chap. 7).
But clearly the word suggests restraint even more to Crimsworth's
creator than to Crimsworth himself. Indeed, in this middle and
major section of *The Professor* which is devoted to the story of his
career in Brussels, Brontë will use him among other things as a sort
of lens through which to examine the narrow female world of the
pensionnat in which she herself was immured for two extraordinarily
painful years.
   Before he actually visits the girls' school, though, Crimsworth
becomes oddly obsessed with it. A boarded-up window in his room

overlooks the pensionnat garden next door—boarded-up, M. Pelet explains lamely, because "les convenances exigent—" and the young teacher, unable to "get a peep at the consecrated ground," confesses that "it is astonishing how disappointed I felt." Do his feelings mirror Charlotte's own desire to "get a peep" into the "consecrated" realm of men? Probably in part. But they also suggest a characteristically female desire to comprehend the mysteries of femaleness. Crimsworth, like many women novelists, fantasizes becoming a *voyeur*, a scientist of sexual secrets. "I thought it would have been so pleasant to have looked out upon a garden planted with flowers and trees, so amusing to have watched the demoiselles at their play; to have studied female character in a variety of phases, myself the while sheltered from view by a modest muslin curtain" (chap. 7). When he is finally invited to join the staff of the pensionnat, his ecstatic reaction ("I shall now at last see the mysterious garden: I shall gaze both on the angels and their Eden") is not just a parody of male idealizations of women; it is an expression of Brontë's own desire to analyze the walled garden of femininity.

And analyze she does, with—the phrase seems singularly appropriate—a vengeance. "The idea by which I had been awed," Crimsworth explains, as if to reiterate Richardson, "was that the youthful beings before me, with their dark nun-like robes and softly-braided hair, were a kind of half-angels" (chap. 10). But, he continues in a later chapter, "Let the idealists, the dreamers about earthly angels and human flowers, just look here while I open my portfolio and show them a sketch or two, pencilled after nature" (chap. 12). There follows a devastating series of "Characters" (in the seventeenth-century sense) describing the immodesty, the impropriety, the sensuality, and the flirtatiousness of the "respectable" Belgian *jeunes filles* at the pensionnat. "Most ... could lie with audacity.... All understood the art of speaking fair when a point was to be gained ... back-biting and tale-bearing were universal ... [and while] each and all were supposed to have been reared in utter unconsciousness of vice ... an air of bold, impudent flirtation, or a loose silly leer, was sure to answer the most ordinary glance from a masculine eye" (chap. 12).

Because Brontë has taken great pains to establish Crimsworth as a sober, idealistic young man, this censoriousness is not out of keeping with his personality. Yet since "his" observations are sanctioned by the author herself, their extraordinary bitterness is at first somewhat puzzling. Would the old saws about female hostility to other females account for such vicious caricatures of schoolgirls whose average age is hardly more than fourteen? Or is an explanation to be found in Brontë's own English anti-Catholicism? She herself allows Crimsworth to offer this as a reason for his feelings, and certainly Brontë's attacks on the Catholic church in *Villette* and elsewhere in *The Professor* suggest that he may be criticizing the students at the pensionnat not for being girls but for being Catholic girls. But why, then, does he generalize about what he calls "the female character"? His position, he indicates, allows him to penetrate aspects of this enigma that would be opaque to others: indeed, it soon begins to seem that such penetration is the ultimate source of his "mastery." "Know, O incredulous reader!" he explains, "that a master stands in a somewhat different relation towards a pretty, light-headed, probably ignorant girl, to that occupied by a partner at a ball, or a gallant on the promenade. A professor does not . . . see her dressed in satin. . . . he finds her in the schoolroom, plainly dressed, with books before her" (chap. 14). He sees her, in other words, as she really is, preparing in devious and idiosyncratic ways for her female role; sees her in the classroom where she is learning not just the set curriculum of the nineteenth-century pensionnat but, more important, the duplicitous stratagems of femininity. Thus, as master of the classroom, he is really master of the mystery of female identity. He "knows," as other men do not (but as Brontë herself must have feared *she* did) what a female really is.

And what is she? Though Brontë may not have consciously admitted this to herself, through the medium of Crimsworth she suggests that a female is a servile and "mentally depraved" creature, more slave than angel, more animal than flower. And—the book implies, even if Crimsworth/Brontë does not—she is like this because it is her task in a patriarchal society to be such a creature. Lying, "speaking fair when a point [is] to be gained," tale-bearing, backbiting, flirting, leering—all these are, after all, slave traits, ways of not submitting while seeming to submit, ways of circumventing male power. But they are also, of course, morally "monstrous" traits, so that once again the monster-woman emerges from behind the facade of the angelic lady. It is significant, in view of the links between angel and monster she was to examine in *Jane Eyre*, that here in *The Professor* Brontë reacted with almost excessive horror to the characteristics of the female monster/slave.

Nowhere is her aversion to womanly duplicity more clearly delineated, for instance, than in Crimsworth's portrait of Zoraïde Reuter, the directress—and thus in a sense the model female—of the pensionnat. Brontë had strong personal reasons for painting this woman as black as possible. Her original was certainly the hated Madame Héger, who moved so vigorously and with what seemed such sinister duplicity to separate the young Englishwoman from M. Héger, her own beloved "maitre."[13] And in Madame Beck of *Villette* Brontë was to offer an even darker picture of this woman. Nevertheless, beyond the fact of the wounded novelist's undeniable resentment, it seems likely that a larger, more philosophical hostility played an important part in the creation of Zoraïde Reuter.

At first, however, William Crimsworth has nothing but admiration for the "moderate, temperate, tranquil" directress of the pensionnat, whom he admires precisely because her character seems to belie traditional male images of women (though not, like the characters of her students, in a disillusioning way). "Look at this little woman," he remarks. "Is she like the women of novelists and romancers? To read of female character as depicted in Poetry and Fiction, one would think it was made up of sentiment, either for good or bad— [but] here is a specimen, and a most sensible and respectable specimen, too, whose staple ingredient is abstract reason" (chap. 10). Soon, though, he begins to suspect that Zoraïde's reasonableness, her moderation and tranquillity, are signs of duplicity, functions of a manipulative craftiness which works in secret to subvert the abstract reason it dissembles. "Observe her," M. Pelet tells Crimsworth, "when she has some knitting, or some other woman's work in hand, and sits the image of peace.... If gentlemen approach her chair ... a meeker modesty settles over her features ... [but] observe then her eyebrows, et dites-moi s'il n'y a pas du chat dans l'un et du renard dans l'autre" (chap. 11). Clearly Pelet, a suave upholder of the status quo, admires such deft hypocrisy. But Crimsworth is repelled: is the slavish duplicity of the students patterned after the sinister craft of their headmistress?

Another, stronger blow to the young teacher's faith in Zoraïde's trustworthiness is struck when he overhears her and Pelet discussing their forthcoming marriage as they stroll in a "forbidden" alley of the pensionnat garden. Zoraïde's behavior to Crimsworth has been modestly seductive, just the strategy to ensnare this upright young man. Yet all the time, he sees, she has been double-dealing, as the schoolgirls do. Flirting with the idealism Crimsworth represents, she has nevertheless engaged herself to the patriarchal establishment embodied in Pelet. A cynical marriage of convenience, a union of "notaries and contracts" rather than one of love and honesty, is what she apparently contemplates. Brontë's sense of exclusion from the businesslike partnership of the Hégers must have contributed to Crimsworth's rage at his discovery, but after a while one begins to wonder which came first, jealousy of the Hégers or anger at female duplicity? The "something feverish and fiery" that gets into Crimsworth's veins (chap. 12) seems to manifest sexual nausea as much as thwarted passion.

Significantly, the final blow to Crimsworth's admiration for the directress comes when she continues slavishly to woo him, even after he has adopted a manner of "hardness and indifference" in his dealings with her. Here it is clearest of all that what both Brontë and Crimsworth despise in her is her stereotypically female reverence for just those "male" characteristics which are most valued in a patriarchal society. Indeed, the list of traits to which Zoraïde gives her "slavish homage" would best describe William's tyrannical older brother Edward, that apotheosis of male despotism: "it was . . . her tendency to consider pride, hardness, selfishness, as proofs of strength. . . . to violence, injustice, tyranny, she succumbed—they were her natural masters" (chap. 15). Considering all this, it is not only inevitable that Zoraïde must marry the worldly Pelet, but also that her antipathy towards any but assumed humility will be most powerfully expressed in her wicked stepmotherish treatment of the young Swiss-English lacemender Frances Henri, the only character in the novel whose true nature does not violate male idealizations of femininity in an ironic or offensive way.

The Professor is as much about Frances Henri as it is about William Crimsworth. Indeed, the careers of the two are parallel, as though each were shaped to echo the other. Like William, Frances is an impoverished orphan, a Protestant in a Catholic country, an idealist in a materialist society, and finally a self-established success, "Madame the Directress," the professional equal of M. le Professeur. The differences in their personalities, however, are as important as the similarities, and they result partly from their sexual difference and partly from the fact that we experience the "orphanhood" of the two characters at different points in the novel. For if in her narration of Crimsworth's career Brontë acts out a fantasy about the transformation of an orphaned and "womanly" man into a magisterial professor, in her narration of Frances Henri's career she examines from Crimsworth's newly masterful point of view the actual situation of an orphaned woman, a situation that was to become the basis for more elaborate fantasies in *Jane Eyre* and *Villette*. And, interestingly, it is the desolation of Frances Henri which completes Crimsworth's metamorphosis from outcast to master.

Pale, small, thin, and "careworn," Frances is the physical type of Charlotte Brontë herself, and of such later heroines as Jane Eyre and Lucy Snowe. Moreover, like Brontë and Lucy, she occupies an anomalous position in the pensionnat. As a lacemender and a shy, ineffectual, part-time sewing teacher, she ranks near the bottom of the school's hierarchy: a Cinderella who prepares feminine costumes for the other young ladies, she has no socially acceptable costume herself, and like the female figure in Brontë's journal, she has clearly come "from the kitchen or some such place." Later in the novel, indeed, after Zoraïde Reuter has fired her from her job at the pensionnat, Crimsworth finds Frances wandering through the Protestant cemetery at Louvain like "a dusky shade." Mourning the death of the aunt who was her only remaining relative, she seems also to be mourning her own burial alive, for—pacing back and forth the way Jane Eyre will pace at Thornfield—she clearly senses that she has been living through a living death, as Lucy Snowe will in *Villette* and as the mysterious Lucy of Brontë's journal did. Moreover, she lives (at this point, toward the end of the book) in chilly lodgings in the Rue Notre Dame aux Neiges, a real Brussels street whose name has symbolic overtones. Even as a student, however, Frances suffers, as Brontë must have, from being older and less conventionally educated than her classmates. Yet because, like Crimsworth, she is intellectual and idealistic, she quickly reveals her superiority, and as that most anomalous of creatures, an openly intelligent woman, she incurs the hostility of Mademoiselle Reuter while at the same time inspiring the admiration of her idiosyncratic professor.

But Frances Henri is more than an intelligent woman, an orphaned bluestocking. Just as Crimsworth began his career as a misfit in his society because his "true nature" was in a sense androgynous, Frances is a misfit in her world because, as Crimsworth sees, she is an artist: Charlotte Brontë and every other woman writer photographed, as it were, in the midst of the creative process. Her compositions first excite Crimsworth's interest by the English inflection with which their author reads them: hers, he says, "was a voice of Albion" (chap. 15). But soon he is even more impressed by the substance of her "devoirs," seeing in her work "some proofs of taste and fancy" and advising her, rather patronizingly, to "cultivate the faculties that God and nature have bestowed on you, and do not fear ... under any pressure of injustice, to derive ... consolation from the consciousness of their strength and rarity." Her triumphant response is a smile which shows that the oppressed lacemender is well aware of her secret identity. "I am glad," her expression seems to Crimsworth to say, that "you have been forced to discover so much of my nature. ... [but] Do you think I am myself a stranger to myself? What you tell me in terms so qualified, I have known fully from a child" (chap. 16).

Crimsworth's fears about the "pressure of injustice," his patronizing qualifications, and Frances Henri's guarded pride are all of special interest in this passage. Injustice, for instance, surrounds the young artist. It is manifest not only in her poverty, her isolation and orphanhood, but most strikingly in Zoraïde's ever-watchful hostility. "Calmly clipping the tassels of her finished purse," the feline directress is present even while Crimsworth is complimenting Frances, and— we later understand—she is already plotting the lacemender's separation from job, school, and master. An agent of patriarchy, Zoraïde is slavish to men but despotic to women, especially to women who are not themselves slavish.

As for Crimsworth's qualifications, they signal his transformation from servant to master, from a male Frances Henri to a sort of professorial Edward. In part he himself effects this change out of consideration for his pupil. "I perceived that in proportion as my manner grew austere and magisterial, hers became easy and self-possessed" (chap. 17). Though she differs from Zoraïde in so many ways, Frances seems like Zoraïde in desiring male mastery. In part, however, the change in Crimsworth occurs because Frances gives his "true nature" the recognition no one else has given it. Sensing his alienation from the school for duplicity in which they find themselves, she encourages him to teach her to cope with the ways of a world that punishes integrity and rewards tyranny or slavishness. Paradoxically, however, in doing this she substitutes one despotism for another. For loving though he is, as Crimsworth becomes an ever more moralizing master—and Frances always addresses him as "master," even after their marriage—he comes to incarnate a male literary tradition that discourages female writers even while it seems to encourage integrity, idealism, and Romantic rebellion against social hypocrisy. Teaching Frances her art, Crimsworth nevertheless punishes her for wilfulness, "begrudges" praise, and later in her life, though she has already become a successful teacher herself, "doses" her with Wordsworth, whose "deep, serene, and sober mind [and] language" are difficult for her to understand, so that "she had to ask questions, to sue for explanations, to be like a child and a novice, and to acknowledge me as her senior and director" (chap. 25).[14]

Because Brontë is writing in a kind of creative trance, the dynamics of this master/pupil relationship are not fully worked out in *The Professor*. But perhaps that is for the best. Dreams often tell the truth, and the truth told here is ambiguous. Crimsworth, for instance, is also Frances's master because, since she is English on her mother's side, Swiss on her father's, he speaks her "mother tongue." His own matriarchal inclination (another suggestion of his early androgynous nature) has been indicated by his attachment to the portrait of his dead mother, whose possession he begrudges his brother Edward, though he never shows any interest in the portrait of his dead father. And certainly, by instructing Frances in the mother tongue she has forgotten since her mother's death when she was ten, he gives her her true artistic voice—"the voice of Albion"—and hence a place in the very tradition from which her dislike of Wordsworth seems to exclude her.[15]

The voice of Albion: that voice is raised in a "silvery" female register throughout Frances Henri's compositions, and raised to

express, in typically female disguise, the outcast artist's secret pride.
As Crimsworth was at the beginning of *The Professor*, Frances is "kept
down" in Brussels "like some desolate tutor or governess." But in the
lessons and poems she writes for or about her master, she examines
her own situation, as Brontë herself does in all her novels, and
fantasizes, alternatively, resignation and escape. The first full-length
composition we hear about, for instance, is a version of the story of
King Alfred and the cakes. Beginning with "a description of a Saxon
peasant's hut, situated within the confines of a great, lifeless, winter
forest," it vividly portrays the peasant woman's warning to Alfred—
"Whatever sound you hear, stir not ... this forest is most wild and
lonely"—and concludes with a statement of the "crownless king"'s
bleak faith: "though stripped and crushed by thee ... I do not despair,
I cannot despair" (chap. 26). No escape routes are charted for Alfred,
no solutions to his problem imagined, but all the elements of the little
story are related to motifs which recur obsessively throughout the
writings of many women.

The great cold of the wintry forest, for example—a straightforward
image of desolation and lovelessness—looks forward to the cold of
Lowood and of the moors in *Jane Eyre* and is related to the polar cold
in, say, Mary Shelley's *Frankenstein* or Emily Dickinson's poems.
"The old Saxon ghost legends" foreshadow gothic images in *Jane
Eyre* and *Villette*, and remind us of the monsters inhabiting so many
other female imaginations. Indeed, the peasant woman's warning
to Alfred may be seen as, in a sense, symbolic of every woman's
warning to herself, every woman's attempt to repress her own
monstrous rage at confinement: "You might chance to hear, as it
were, a child cry,[16] and on opening the door to afford it succour, a
great black bull, or a shadowy goblin dog, might rush over the
threshold. ... " Most important, the dramatic figure of the dispossessed and crownless king, echoing the story of Milton's Satan,
summarizes once again Frances Henri's—and Charlotte Brontë's—
appraisal of her own situation in the world. Conscious of the kingdom
of imagination she has inherited, she is also bitterly aware that she
has been deprived of her birthright: in a society which encourages
female servility, she must live, as it were, in the house of a serf. At
the same time, Alfred's "courage under calamity" reflects Frances's
own passion for self-determination—"J'ai mon projet," she tells

Crimsworth—and prefigures the quiet defiance implicit in all Brontë's later books.

Frances Henri's next "devoir" is summarized more briefly by Crimsworth, but its elements are equally resonant. "An emigrant's letter to his friends at home," it describes "the scene of virgin forest and great New World river," then hints at "the difficulties and dangers that attend a settler's life," as well as his "indestructible self-respect" (chap. 28). Crimsworth's qualified support has evidently brightened Frances's view of things: where Alfred, locked into the serf's hut, had only the grim consolation of self-knowledge, her emigrant can at least imagine a New World, an escape from the disasters of the past, in which the secret pride of the artist may be rewarded. It is surely significant, however, that after Crimsworth has praised her for writing this composition Zoraïde finally separates Frances from her "master". Must the artist's dream of escape be ruthlessly repressed by the agents of society? At its most gloomy, *The Professor* suggests as much, and in this connection, Frances Henri's final literary achievement—at least the last one we are given in the book—is perhaps her most interesting work: it is the poem "Jane," which Brontë evidently composed before writing *The Professor*, about her own feelings for M. Héger. Nevertheless, it was skillfully assimilated into this fictionalization of their friendship. Arriving at the allegorical Rue Notre Dame aux Neiges, with the plan of proposing marriage to Frances, Crimsworth overhears her reciting the poem as she paces "backwards and forwards, backwards and forwards" in her tiny room. So Brontë herself might have wished to be overheard by Héger, and of herself, too, she might have written that, as Crimsworth says of Frances, "Solitude might speak thus in a desert, or in the hall of a forsaken house."

Going beyond an exploration of "solitude" to an examination of sickness, however, the poem itself tells of "Jane's"—and Frances's and Charlotte Brontë's—love for her master: how, seeing her weaken under the weight of her schoolwork, he liberates her temporarily from "tedious task and rule"; how she "toils" to please him and reads the "secret meaning" of his approval in his face; how she wins the school-prize, "a laurel-wreath," and how at that moment of triumph, as "the strong pulse of Ambition" strikes in her veins, "bleeding broke / A secret, inward wound," ostensibly because she realizes that she must now "cross the sea" and be separated from her teacher (chap. 23). But if on a literal level "Jane" tells the story of Brontë's relationship with Héger (though more perhaps as she wished it had been than as it was), figuratively the poem is of interest because it exactly depicts Brontë's sense of the pain a woman artist must endure, a pain closely related to the profound ambivalence of her relationship with her "master."

It is clearly important, for instance, that Jane becomes aware of her "secret, inward wound" *not* when she realizes she must cross the sea but when, as the laurel-crown of art is bound to her "throbbing forehead," she feels "the strong pulse of Ambition," perhaps for the first time. Is it this pulse—and not the mysterious "they" of the poem ("They call again; leave then my breast")—which impels her to leave her master and cross the sea? In part this seems to be the case. But in another sense the pulse of ambition seems itself to be an impulse of disease, the harbinger of a wound, or at least a headache. For the woman artist, Brontë implies, ambition can only lead to grief, to an inevitable separation from her master—that is, from the literary tradition which has fostered her, sometimes praising her efforts and sometimes dosing her with Wordsworth—and to a consciousness of her own secret sense of inadequacy in comparison to the full adequacy and masterfulness of the male world. The bleeding wound is, of course, a standard Freudian symbol of femininity, representing both the woman's fertility and the apparent imperfection of her body. But Brontë expands its meaning so that in "Jane" it symbolizes not only female physiology but female psychology, not only the woman's bleeding imperfect body but her aching head, her wounded and dispossessed imagination.

Like writers from Anne Finch to Mary Shelley and Emily Brontë, Charlotte Brontë is trying to solve the problem of woman's "fall." But she goes beyond most in charting the ambiguities of the fall and its resultant wound. For while Jane, like, say, the Countess of Winchilsea, suffers from the disease of ambition, she sees the educator who has in a sense prepared her fall, not as a culprit, a disinheriting God, but as a sheltering foster father, a refuge, a home. "They call again; leave then my breast," Frances imagines her master saying at the end of the poem. "Quit thy true shelter, Jane; / But when deceived, repulsed, opprest, / Come home to me again." And unlike Jane, whose fate is left to the reader's imagination, Frances does "come home" to her master. Paternally setting her on his knee, Crimsworth proposes marriage, and when she says "Master, I consent to pass my life with you," he approvingly remarks "Very well, Frances," as if he were grading one of her compositions. Their subsequent marriage and professional success are as charged with ambiguity as everything else about their relationship. Though Crimsworth has become wholly a professor and patriarch, Frances does refuse to remain entirely a dependent pupil. On the one hand, she seems to have abandoned her art (we hear of no more "compositions"). But on the other hand, she insists upon retaining her "employment of teaching," and it is clear that "the strong pulse of Ambition" has not completely deserted her.

After the two have married, the conflict in Frances between "the strong pulse of Ambition" and the "secret, inward wound" finds an equally ambiguous solution, one which looks backward to Austen's duplicitous structures, and forward to the questionable dénouements of many other novels by women. As Mrs. Crimsworth, she develops a sort of schizophrenic personality: "So different was she under different circumstances," Crimsworth tells us, that "I seemed to possess two wives" (chap. 25). During the day she is Madame the Directress, "vigilant and solicitous," with something of the sinister authority of Zoraïde Reuter. In the evening, however, she becomes "Frances Henri, my own little lace-mender," receiving "many a punishment" from Monsieur "for her wilfulness." A "good and dear wife" to her professor, she nevertheless exhibits barely repressed signs of a spirit whose energy Crimsworth encourages only within carefully defined limits.

The issue of Crimsworth's marriage to Frances is a strange child named Victor, about whom we learn that there is "a something in [his] temper—a kind of electrical ardour and power—which [as if to recall the history of Victor Frankenstein] emits now and then ominous sparks." The magisterial professor thinks this "something" should be "if not whipped out of him, at least soundly disciplined." Frances, however, "gives this *something* in her son's marked character no name; but when it appears . . . in the fierce revolt of feeling against disappointment. . . she folds him to her breast" (chap. 25), for his mysterious problem, together with his parents' differing attitudes toward it, seems to summarize all the tensions that Brontë, whether writing with her eyes open or closed, has been considering throughout *The Professor*. Appropriately enough, therefore, the novel ends with an anecdote about Victor, Victor's dog Yorke, and an important third personage, Crimsworth's old acquaintance Hunsden Yorke Hunsden. This last character has appeared frequently throughout the narrative, but his true function is sometimes hard to understand. For one thing, he seems at first to have little or no place in the plot of the novel. For another, Crimsworth, austere and idealistic, seems positively to dislike him, and certainly he has good reasons for doing so. The scion of an old, radical-mercantile family, Hunsden is more of a disaffected Byronic (or Satanic) hero than any other character in *The Professor*, the very opposite, it seems, of the shy and almost girlish Crimsworth. Where Crimsworth is passive, reserved, aristocratic, Hunsden is a troublemaker; where Crimsworth is idealistic and sensitive, Hunsden is cynical; where Crimsworth is magisterial, Hunsden is revolutionary. Neither ever expresses any particular affection for the other. And yet the two seem inextricably bound together in an uneasy partnership that lasts longer than any other relationship in the book.

Is there any reason for this unfriendly friendship, and why does Brontë dramatize it in both the beginning and ending sections of *The Professor*? What comes close to suggesting an explanation is the increasingly obvious parallel between Hunsden's bitterness and (in the beginning) Crimsworth's bitterness, between Hunsden's rebelliousness and (later) Frances's or Victor's rebelliousness. Hunsden, it begins to seem, incarnates much of the disaffection in *The Professor*: he is an involuntary image—like Charles Wellesley, Zamorna, or the Duke of Northangerland—of the anger in Charlotte Brontë's own mind. His name, Hunsden Yorke Hunsden, suggests both barbaric willingness to overturn established institutions, and a deep affinity with the English "motherland" to which Frances Henri and Crimsworth long to return. But besides being an angry "spirit of place," Hunsden is a somewhat androgynous figure. Though at first he appears "powerful and massive," Crimsworth discovers upon closer examination "how small, and even feminine, were his lineaments . . .

[he had] now the mien of a morose bull, and anon that of an arch and mischievous girl; more frequently, the two semblances were blent, and a queer composite countenance they made" (chap. 4). And though he seems contemptuous of William, taking him to task for his aristocratic lineage, his appraisal of William's situation is clearly the young man's own ("You've no power, you can do nothing"), as if his were the voice of the passive clerk's own fury. Acting, as William does not, to expose Edward's tyranny, Hunsden again acts as William's agent. It is his story of the older Crimsworth's misdeeds that precipitates the scene between the brothers which leads to William's liberation. His explanation of his action ("I followed my instinct, opposed a tyrant, and broke a chain") describes what William himself would like to have done. And again, his suggestion to the indecisive, jobless clerk ("Go on to the continent") is accepted with alacrity ("God knows I should like to go!"), as if it betrayed secret knowledge of Crimsworth's own desires.

In a sense, then, besides being a voice of rebellion, Hunsden is a plot-manipulator, a narrator-in-disguise, seeing to it that the action proceeds as it should, and commenting on events as they occur. Presenting Crimsworth with the lost portrait of his mother, he presents him also with a refreshed sense of identity. At the same time, when he argues about patriotism with Frances and Crimsworth, his caustic views counteract the potential sentimentality implicit in their idealization of England, and parodically express the secret disaffection in the novel: "Examine the footprints of our august aristocracy; see how they walk in blood, crushing hearts as they go" (chap. 24). Most interesting of all, his love for the enigmatic Lucia, whose portrait he carries with him everywhere, offers Frances (and thus Brontë herself) a last chance to fantasize escape from the stifling enclosures of patriarchy.

Studying the ivory miniature on which the picture of Lucia's "very handsome and very individual-looking ... face" is drawn, the former lacemaker speculates that "Lucia once wore chains and broke them," adding nervously, "I do not mean matrimonial chains ... but social chains of some sort" (chap. 25). Does this story contain even a germ of truth? Significantly, we never learn; like Hunsden's, Lucia's function in the plot of *The Professor* is more thematic than dramatic, and both Hunsden's and Frances's comments about her are important mainly because they represent half-repressed desires for rebellion, liberation, escape. Like Brontë herself, Hunsden evidently could not bring himself to enact his anger. Frances suggests that Lucia "filled a sphere from whence you would never have thought of taking a wife," and the "individual-looking" woman's image has, we notice, been reduced to a mere miniature. Nevertheless, disaffected commentator that he is, Hunsden consistently speaks rebellion, and if the boy Victor "has a preference" for him it is not surprising: fraught as it is with ambiguities, the union of Frances Henri and William Crimsworth would inevitably produce a child attracted to the dangers and delights of Byronic rebellion.

By the end of *The Professor*, however, Crimsworth himself no longer feels any attraction to such radicalism. About Lucia's flaming spirit, he tells Frances with magisterial irony that "My sight was always too weak to endure a blaze," and when Hunsden's namesake, Victor's beloved mastiff Yorke, is bitten by a rabid dog, Crimsworth shoots his son's pet without delay, though Victor, enraged, points out that "He might have been cured" (chap. 25). If the incident does not advance the story, it does clarify Brontë's symbolism: Crimsworth is anxious not only to kill the dog but to kill what the dog represents. Now fully a patriarch and professor, he sees Yorke Hunsden, as well as the dog Yorke, as a diseased, rabid element in his life.[17]

Earlier in the novel, however, Crimsworth himself had been mysteriously diseased. Even after establishing himself as a professor, even (or perhaps especially) after Frances had agreed to be his wife, he had suffered from an odd seizure of "hypochondria" in another episode which—like Yorke's hydrophobia—did little to advance the plot but much to clarify the symbolism. Personified as a woman, a "dreaded and ghastly concubine," Crimsworth's affliction is also, like Yorke Hunsden and like Brontë herself, a grim narrator/commentator. "What tales she would tell me. . . . What songs she would recite. . . . How she would discourse to me of her own country—the grave. . . . 'Necropolis!' she would whisper. . . . 'It contains a mansion prepared for you'" (chap. 23). Battling against "the dreadful tyranny of my demon," Crimsworth reminds us of the dead-alive Lucy in Charlotte's journal, and of Frances Henri buried alive in the Protestant cemetery or struggling to survive her own bleeding wound. His shooting of the dog Yorke seems part of the same battle. Role adjustments for both professor and pupil, Brontë suggests, entail ruthless self-repression.

But to speak of *The Professor* in terms merely of roles and repressions is in a sense to trivialize the young novelist's achievement in her first full-length book. For even if this novel is not the judicious, "plain and homely" *Bildungsroman* its author hoped it would be, if its plot does not always seem adequate to the complexities of its hidden intentions, it is nevertheless of considerable importance as a preliminary statement of themes which were to be increasingly significant throughout Charlotte Brontë's career. Writing with her eyes metaphorically closed, Brontë explored here her own vocation, her own wound, and tried—gropingly, as if in a dream—to discover the differing paths to wholeness. The hypochondriacal young Crimsworth is, after all, drawn to Frances Henri in the first place because, like paler versions of Heathcliff and Catherine, both are misfits. And just as Heathcliff's dispossession parallels Catherine's wounding fall, Crimsworth's sickness "talks to [Frances's] wound, it corresponds," to quote from Sylvia Plath's poem "Tulips."[18] Thus the diseases and difficulties of both these crucial characters in Charlotte Brontë's first novel correspond to their author's own, paradigmatic female wound, even while they also recall many of the afflictions that beset Jane Austen's society of invalids. At the same time, however, we must observe that, incomplete as they are throughout much of the book, both Crimsworth and Frances have struggled (more than most of Austen's characters) to find a place where they can be fully themselves. Though their literal journeys have been between Switzerland, Belgium, and England, the real goal of their entranced mutual journey has been—as we shall see more clearly in Brontë's other novels— not England, that mythic motherland, and not Angria, that feverish childhood heaven, but a "true home," a land where wholeness is possible for themselves and their creator, a country (to quote from "Tulips" again) "as far away as health."

10 A Dialogue of Self and Soul: Plain Jane's Progress

> I dreamt that I was looking in a glass when a horrible face—the face of an animal—suddenly showed over my shoulder. I cannot be sure if this was a dream, or if it happened.
>
> —Virginia Woolf

> Never mind. . . . One day, quite suddenly, when you're not expecting it, I'll take a hammer from the folds of my dark cloak and crack your little skull like an egg-shell. Crack it will go, the egg-shell; out they will stream, the blood, the brains. One day, one day. . . . One day the fierce wolf that walks by my side will spring on you and rip your abominable guts out. One day, one day. . . . Now, now, gently, quietly, quietly. . . .
>
> —Jean Rhys

> I told my Soul to sing—
>
> She said her Strings were snapt—
> Her bow—to Atoms blown—
> And so to mend her—gave me work
> Until another Morn—
> —Emily Dickinson

If *The Professor* is a somewhat blurred trance-statement of themes and conflicts that dominated Charlotte Brontë's thought far more than she herself may have realized, *Jane Eyre* is a work permeated by angry, *Angrian* fantasies of escape-into-wholeness. Borrowing the mythic quest-plot—but not the devout substance—of Bunyan's male *Pilgrim's Progress*, the young novelist seems here definitively to have opened her eyes to female realities within her and around her: confinement, orphanhood, starvation, rage even to madness. Where the fiery image of Lucia, that energetic woman who probably "once wore chains and broke them," is miniaturized in *The Professor*, in *Jane Eyre* (1847) this figure becomes almost larger than life, the emblem of a passionate, barely disguised rebelliousness.

Victorian critics, no doubt instinctively perceiving the subliminal intensity of Brontë's passion, seem to have understood this point very well. Her "mind contains nothing but hunger, rebellion, and rage," Matthew Arnold wrote of Charlotte Brontë in 1853.[1] He was referring to *Villette*, which he elsewhere described as a "hideous, undelightful, convulsed, constricted novel,"[2] but he might as well have been speaking of *Jane Eyre*, for his response to Brontë was typical of the outrage generated in some quarters by her first published novel.[3] "Jane Eyre is throughout the personification of an unregenerate and undisciplined spirit," wrote Elizabeth Rigby in *The Quarterly Review* in 1848, and her "autobiography . . . is pre-eminently an anti-Christian composition. . . . The tone of mind and thought which has fostered Chartism and rebellion is the same which has also written *Jane Eyre*."[4] Anne Mozley, in 1853, recalled for *The Christian Remembrancer* that "Currer Bell" had seemed on her first appearance as an author "soured, coarse, and grumbling; an alien . . . from society and amenable to none of its laws."[5] And Mrs. Oliphant related in 1855 that "Ten years ago we professed an orthodox system of novel-making. Our lovers were humble and devoted . . . and the only true love worth having was that . . . chivalrous true love which consecrated all womankind . . . when suddenly, without warning, *Jane Eyre* stole upon the scene, and the most alarming revolution of modern times has followed the invasion of *Jane Eyre*."[6]

We tend today to think of *Jane Eyre* as moral gothic, "myth domesticated," *Pamela*'s daughter and *Rebecca*'s aunt, the archetypal scenario for all those mildly thrilling romantic encounters between a scowling Byronic hero (who owns a gloomy mansion) and a trembling heroine (who can't quite figure out the mansion's floor plan). Or, if we're more sophisticated, we give Charlotte Brontë her due, concede her strategic as well as her mythic abilities, study the patterns of her imagery, and count the number of times she addresses the reader. But still we overlook the "alarming revolution"—even Mrs. Oliphant's terminology is suggestive—which "followed the invasion of *Jane Eyre*." "Well, obviously *Jane Eyre* is a feminist tract, an argument for the social betterment of governesses and equal rights for women," Richard Chase somewhat grudgingly admitted in 1948. But like most other modern critics, he believed that the novel's power arose from its mythologizing of Jane's confrontation with masculine sexuality.[7]

Yet, curiously enough, it seems not to have been primarily the coarseness and sexuality of *Jane Eyre* which shocked Victorian reviewers (though they disliked those elements in the book), but, as we have seen, its "anti-Christian" refusal to accept the forms, customs, and standards of society—in short, its rebellious feminism. They were disturbed not so much by the proud Byronic sexual energy of Rochester as by the Byronic pride and passion of Jane herself, not so much by the asocial sexual vibrations between hero and heroine as by the heroine's refusal to submit to her social destiny: "She has inherited in fullest measure the worst sin of our fallen nature—the sin of pride," declared Miss Rigby.

> Jane Eyre is proud, and therefore she is ungrateful, too. It pleased God to make her an orphan, friendless, and penniless— yet she thanks nobody, and least of all Him, for the food and raiment, the friends, companions, and instructors of her helpless youth. . . . On the contrary, she looks upon all that has been done for her not only as her undoubted right, but as falling far short of it.[8]

In other words, what horrified the Victorians was Jane's anger. And perhaps they, rather than more recent critics, were correct in their response to the book. For while the mythologizing of repressed rage may parallel the mythologizing of repressed sexuality, it is far more dangerous to the order of society. The occasional woman who has a weakness for black-browed Byronic heroes can be accommodated in novels and even in some drawing rooms; the woman who yearns to escape entirely from drawing rooms and patriarchal mansions obviously cannot. And Jane Eyre, as Matthew Arnold, Miss Rigby, Mrs. Mozley, and Mrs. Oliphant suspected, was such a woman.

Her story, providing a pattern for countless others, is—far more obviously and dramatically than *The Professor*—a story of enclosure and escape, a distinctively female *Bildungsroman* in which the problems encountered by the protagonist as she struggles from the imprisonment of her childhood toward an almost unthinkable goal of mature freedom are symptomatic of difficulties Everywoman in a patriarchal society must meet and overcome: oppression (at Gateshead), starvation (at Lowood), madness (at Thornfield), and coldness (at Marsh End). Most important, her confrontation, not with Rochester but with Rochester's mad wife Bertha, is the book's central confrontation, an encounter—like Frances Crimsworth's fantasy about Lucia—not with her own sexuality but with her own imprisoned "hunger, rebellion, and rage," a secret dialogue of self and soul on whose outcome, as we shall see, the novel's plot, Rochester's fate, and Jane's coming-of-age all depend.

Unlike many Victorian novels, which begin with elaborate expository paragraphs, *Jane Eyre* begins with a casual, curiously enigmatic remark: "There was no possibility of taking a walk that day." Both the occasion ("that day") and the excursion (or the impossibility of one) are significant: the first is the real beginning of Jane's pilgrim's progress toward maturity; the second is a metaphor for the problems she must solve in order to attain maturity. "I was glad" not to be able to leave the house, the narrator continues: "dreadful to me was the coming home in the raw twilight . . . humbled by the consciousness of my physical inferiority" (chap. 1).[9] As many critics have commented, Charlotte Brontë consistently uses the opposed properties of fire and ice to characterize Jane's experiences, and her technique is immediately evident in these opening passages.[10] For while the world outside Gateshead is almost unbearably wintry, the world within is claustrophobic, fiery, like ten-year-old Jane's own mind. Excluded from the Reed family group in the drawing room because *she* is not a "contented, happy, little child"—excluded, that is, from "normal" society—Jane takes refuge in a scarlet-draped window seat where she alternately stares out at the "drear November day" and reads of polar regions in Bewick's *History of British Birds*. The "death-white realms" of the Arctic fascinate her; she broods upon "the multiplied rigors of extreme cold" as if brooding upon her own dilemma: whether to stay in, behind the oppressively scarlet curtain, or to go out into the cold of a loveless world.

Her decision is made for her. She is found by John Reed, the tyrannical son of the family, who reminds her of her anomalous position in the household, hurls the heavy volume of Bewick at her, and arouses her passionate rage. Like a "rat," a "bad animal," a "mad cat," she compares him to "Nero, Caligula, etc." and is borne away to the red-room, to be imprisoned literally as well as figuratively. For "the fact is," confesses the grownup narrator ironically, "I was [at that moment] a trifle beside myself; or rather *out* of myself, as the French would say. . . . like any other rebel slave, I felt resolved . . . to go all lengths" (chap. 1).

But if Jane was "out of" herself in her struggle against John Reed, her experience in the red-room, probably the most metaphorically vibrant of all her early experiences, forces her deeply into herself. For the red-room, stately, chilly, swathed in rich crimson, with a great white bed and an easy chair "like a pale throne" looming out of the scarlet darkness, perfectly represents her vision of the society in which she is trapped, an uneasy and elfin dependent. "No jail was ever more secure," she tells us. And no jail, we soon learn, was ever more terrifying either, because this is the room where Mr. Reed, the only "father" Jane has ever had, "breathed his last." It is, in other words, a kind of patriarchal death chamber, and here Mrs. Reed still keeps "divers parchments, her jewel-casket, and a miniature of her dead husband" in a secret drawer in the wardrobe (chap. 2). Is the room haunted, the child wonders. At least, the narrator implies, it is realistically if not gothically haunting, more so than any chamber in, say, *The Mysteries of Udolpho*, which established a standard for such apartments. For the spirit of a society in which Jane has no clear place sharpens the angles of the furniture, enlarges the shadows, strengthens the locks on the door. And the deathbed of a father who was not really her father emphasizes her isolation and vulnerability.

Panicky, she stares into a "great looking glass," where her own image floats toward her, alien and disturbing. "All looked colder and darker in that visionary hollow than in reality," the adult Jane explains. But a mirror, after all, is also a sort of chamber, a mysterious enclosure in which images of the self are trapped like "divers parchments." So the child Jane, though her older self accuses her of mere superstition, correctly recognizes that she is doubly imprisoned. Frustrated and angry, she meditates on the injustices of her life, and fantasizes "some strange expedient to achieve escape from insupportable oppression—as running away, or, if that could not be effected, never eating or drinking more, and letting myself die" (chap. 2). Escape through flight, or escape through starvation: the alternatives will recur throughout *Jane Eyre* and, indeed, as we have already noted, throughout much other nineteenth- and twentieth-century literature by women. In the red-room, however, little Jane chooses (or is chosen by) a third, even more terrifying, alternative: escape through madness. Seeing a ghostly, wandering light, as of the moon on the ceiling, she notices that "my heart beat thick, my head grew hot; a sound filled my ears, which I deemed the rushing of wings; something seemed near me; I was oppressed, suffocated: endurance broke down." The child screams and sobs in anguish, and then, adds the narrator coolly, "I suppose I had a species of fit," for her next memory is of waking in the nursery "and seeing before me a terrible red glare crossed with thick black bars" (chap. 3), merely the nursery fire of course, but to Jane Eyre the child a terrible reminder of the experience she has just had, and to Jane Eyre the adult narrator an even more dreadful omen of experiences to come.

For the little drama enacted on "that day" which opens *Jane Eyre* is in itself a paradigm of the larger drama that occupies the entire book: Jane's anomalous, orphaned position in society, her enclosure in stultifying roles and houses, and her attempts to escape through flight, starvation, and—in a sense which will be explained—madness. And that Charlotte Brontë quite consciously intended the incident of the red-room to serve as a paradigm for the larger plot of her novel is clear not only from its position in the narrative but also from Jane's own recollection of the experience at crucial moments throughout the book: when she is humiliated by Mr. Brocklehurst at Lowood, for instance, and on the night when she decides to leave Thornfield. In between these moments, moreover, Jane's pilgrimage consists of a series of experiences which are, in one way or another, variations on the central, red-room motif of enclosure and escape.

As we noted earlier, the allusion to pilgriming is deliberate, for like the protagonist of Bunyan's book, Jane Eyre makes a life-journey which is a kind of mythical progress from one significantly named place to another. Her story begins, quite naturally, at *Gateshead*, a starting point where she encounters the uncomfortable givens of her career: a family which is not her real family, a selfish older "brother" who tyrannizes over the household like a substitute patriarch, a foolish and wicked "stepmother," and two unpleasant, selfish "stepsisters." The smallest, weakest, and plainest child in the house, she embarks on her pilgrim's progress as a sullen Cinderella, an angry Ugly Duckling, immorally rebellious against the hierarchy that oppresses her: "I know that had I been a sanguine, brilliant, careless, exacting, handsome, romping child—though equally dependent and friendless—Mrs. Reed would have endured my presence more complacently," she reflects as an adult (chap. 2).

But the child Jane cannot, as she well knows, be "sanguine and brilliant." Cinderella never is; nor is the Ugly Duckling, who, for all her swansdown potential, has no great expectations. "Poor, plain, and little," Jane Eyre—her name is of course suggestive—is invisible as air, the heir to nothing, secretly choking with ire. And Bessie, the kind nursemaid who befriends her, sings her a song that no fairy godmother would ever dream of singing, a song that summarizes the plight of all real Victorian Cinderellas:

> My feet they are sore, and my limbs they are weary,
>   Long is the way, and the mountains are wild;
> Soon will the twilight close moonless and dreary
>   Over the path of the poor orphan child.

A hopeless pilgrimage, Jane's seems, like the sad journey of Wordsworth's Lucy Gray, seen this time from the inside, by the child herself rather than by the sagacious poet to whom years have given a philosophic mind. Though she will later watch the maternal moon rise to guide her, now she imagines herself wandering in a moonless twilight that foreshadows her desperate flight across the moors after leaving Thornfield. And the only hope her friend Bessie can offer is, ironically, an image that recalls the patriarchal terrors of the

red-room and hints at patriarchal terrors to come—Lowood, Brocklehurst, St. John Rivers:

> Ev'n should I fall o'er the broken bridge passing,
>   Or stray in the marshes, by false lights beguiled,
> Still will my Father, with promise and blessing
>   Take to His bosom the poor orphan child.

It is no wonder that, confronting such prospects, young Jane finds
herself "whispering to myself, over and over again" the words of
Bunyan's Christian: "What shall I do?—What shall I do?" (chap.
4).[11]

What she does do, in desperation, is burst her bonds again and
again to tell Mrs. Reed what she thinks of her, an extraordinarily
self-assertive act of which neither a Victorian child nor a Cinderella
was ever supposed to be capable. Interestingly, her first such explosion
is intended to remind Mrs. Reed that she, too, is surrounded by
patriarchal limits: "What would Uncle Reed say to you if he were
alive?" Jane demands, commenting, "It seemed as if my tongue
pronounced words without my will consenting to their utterance:
something spoke out of me over which I had no control" (chap. 4).
And indeed, even imperious Mrs. Reed appears astonished by these
words. The explanation, "something spoke out of me," is as frightening as the arrogance, suggesting the dangerous double consciousness—"the rushing of wings, something . . . near me"—that brought
on the fit in the red-room. And when, with a real sense that "an
invisible bond had burst, and that I had struggled out into unhoped-
for liberty," Jane tells Mrs. Reed that "I am glad you are no relation
of mine" (chap. 4), the adult narrator remarks that "a ridge of
lighted heath, alive, glancing, devouring, would have been a meet
emblem of my mind"—as the nursery fire was, flaring behind its
black grates, and as the flames consuming Thornfield also will be.

Significantly, the event that inspires little Jane's final fiery words
to Mrs. Reed is her first encounter with that merciless and hypocritical patriarch Mr. Brocklehurst, who appears now to conduct
her on the next stage of her pilgrimage. As many readers have
noticed, this personification of the Victorian superego is—like St.

John Rivers, his counterpart in the last third of the book—consistently described in phallic terms: he is "a black pillar" with a "grim face at the top ... like a carved mask," almost as if he were a funereal and oddly Freudian piece of furniture (chap. 4). But he is also rather like the wolf in "Little Red Riding Hood." "What a face he had.... What a great nose! And what a mouth! And what large prominent teeth!" Jane Eyre exclaims, recollecting that terror of the adult male animal which must have wrung the heart of every female child in a period when all men were defined as "beasts."

Simultaneously, then, a pillar of society and a large bad wolf, Mr. Brocklehurst has come with news of hell to remove Jane to *Lowood*, the aptly named school of life where orphan girls are starved and frozen into proper Christian submission. Where else would a beast take a child but into a wood? Where else would a column of frozen spirituality take a homeless orphan but to a sanctuary where there is neither food nor warmth? Yet "with all its privations" Lowood offers Jane a valley of refuge from "the ridge of lighted heath," a chance to learn to govern her anger while learning to become a governess in the company of a few women she admires.

Foremost among those Jane admires are the noble Miss Temple and the pathetic Helen Burns. And again, their names are significant. Angelic Miss Temple, for instance, with her marble pallor, is a shrine of ladylike virtues: magnanimity, cultivation, courtesy—and repression. As if invented by Coventry Patmore or by Mrs. Sarah Ellis, that indefatigable writer of conduct books for Victorian girls, she dispenses food to the hungry, visits the sick, encourages the worthy, and averts her glance from the unworthy. "'What shall I do to gratify myself—to be admired—or to vary the tenor of my existence' are not the questions which a woman of right feelings asks on first awaking to the avocations of the day," wrote Mrs. Ellis in 1844.

> Much more congenial to the highest attributes of woman's character are inquiries such as these: "How shall I endeavor through this day to turn the time, the health, and the means permitted me to enjoy, to the best account? Is any one sick? I must visit their chamber without delay.... Is any one about

to set off on a journey? I must see that the early meal is spread. . . .
Did I fail in what was kind or considerate to any of the family
yesterday? I will meet her this morning with a cordial welcome."[12]

And these questions are obviously the ones Miss Temple asks herself,
and answers by her actions.

Yet it is clear enough that she has repressed her own share of
madness and rage, that there is a potential monster beneath her
angelic exterior, a "sewer" of fury beneath this temple.[13] Though
she is, for instance, plainly angered by Mr. Brocklehurst's sancti-
monious stinginess, she listens to his sermonizing in ladylike silence.
Her face, Jane remembers, "appeared to be assuming . . . the coldness
and fixity of [marble]; especially her mouth, closed as if it would
have required a sculptor's chisel to open it" (chap. 7). Certainly
Miss Temple will never allow "something" to speak through her,
no wings will rush in her head, no fantasies of fiery heath disturb
her equanimity, but she will feel sympathetic anger.

Perhaps for this reason, repressed as she is, she is closer to a fairy
godmother than anyone else Jane has met, closer even to a true
mother. By the fire in her pretty room, she feeds her starving pupils
tea and emblematic seedcake, nourishing body and soul together
despite Mr. Brocklehurst's puritanical dicta. "We feasted," says
Jane, "as on nectar and ambrosia." But still, Jane adds, "Miss
Temple had always something . . . of state in her mien, of refined
propriety in her language, which precluded deviation into the ardent,
the excited, the eager: something which chastened the pleasure of
those who looked on her and listened to her, by a controlling sense
of awe" (chap. 8). Rather awful as well as very awesome, Miss
Temple is not just an angel-in-the-house; to the extent that her
name defines her, she is even more house than angel, a beautiful
set of marble columns designed to balance that bad pillar Mr.
Brocklehurst. And dispossessed Jane, who is not only poor, plain,
and little, but also fiery and ferocious, correctly guesses that she can
no more become such a woman than Cinderella can become her
own fairy godmother.

Helen Burns, Miss Temple's other disciple, presents a different
but equally impossible ideal to Jane: the ideal—defined by Goethe's

Makarie—of self-renunciation, of all-consuming (and consumptive) spirituality. Like Jane "a poor orphan child" ("I have only a father; and he . . . will not miss me" [chap. 9]), Helen longs alternately for her old home in Northumberland, with its "visionary brook," and for the true home which she believes awaits her in heaven. As if echoing the last stanzas of Bessie's song, "God is my father, God is my friend," she tells Jane, whose skepticism disallows such comforts, and "Eternity [is] a mighty home, not a terror and an abyss" (chap. 7). One's duty, Helen declares, is to submit to the injustices of this life, in expectation of the ultimate justice of the next: "it is weak and silly to say you *cannot bear* what it is your fate to be required to bear" (chap. 7).

Helen herself, however, does no more than *bear* her fate. "I make no effort [to be good, in Lowood's terms]," she confesses. "I follow as inclination guides me" (chap. 7). Labeled a "slattern" for failing to keep her drawers in ladylike order, she meditates on Charles I, as if commenting on all inadequate fathers ("what a pity . . . he could see no farther than the prerogatives of the crown") and studies *Rasselas*, perhaps comparing Dr. Johnson's Happy Valley to the unhappy one in which she herself is immured. "One strong proof of my wretchedly defective nature," she explains to the admiring Jane, "is that even [Miss Temple's] expostulations . . . have no influence to cure me of my faults." Despite her contemplative purity, there is evidently a "sewer" of concealed resentment in Helen Burns, just as there is in Miss Temple. And, like Miss Temple's, her name is significant. Burning with spiritual passion, she also burns with anger, leaves her things "in shameful disorder," and dreams of freedom in eternity: "By dying young, I shall escape great sufferings," she explains (chap. 9). Finally, when the "fog-bred pestilence" of typhus decimates Lowood, Helen is carried off by her own fever for liberty, as if her body, like Jane's mind, were "a ridge of lighted heath . . . devouring" the dank valley in which she has been caged.

This is not to say that Miss Temple and Helen Burns do nothing to help Jane come to terms with her fate. Both are in some sense mothers for Jane, as Adrienne Rich has pointed out,[14] comforting her, counseling her, feeding her, embracing her. And from Miss Temple, in particular, the girl learns to achieve "more harmonious thoughts: what seemed better regulated feelings had become the inmates of my mind. I had given in allegiance to duty and order. I appeared a disciplined and subdued character" (chap. 10). Yet because Jane is an Angrian Cinderella, a Byronic heroine, the "inmates" of her mind can no more be regulated by conventional Christian wisdom than Manfred's or Childe Harold's thoughts. Thus, when Miss Temple leaves Lowood, Jane tells us, "I was left in my natural element." Gazing out a window as she had on "that day" which opened her story, she yearns for true liberty: "for liberty I uttered a prayer." Her way of confronting the world is still the Promethean way of fiery rebellion, not Miss Temple's way of ladylike repression, not Helen Burns's way of saintly renunciation. What she has learned from her two mothers is, at least superficially, to compromise. If pure liberty is impossible, she exclaims, "then . . . grant me at least a new servitude" (chap. 10).

It is, of course, her eagerness for a new servitude that brings Jane to the painful experience that is at the center of her pilgrimage, the experience of *Thornfield*, where, biblically, she is to be crowned with thorns, she is to be cast out into a desolate field, and most important, she is to confront the demon of rage who has haunted her since her afternoon in the red-room. Before the appearance of Rochester, however, and the intrusion of Bertha, Jane—and her readers—must explore Thornfield itself. This gloomy mansion is often seen as just another gothic trapping introduced by Charlotte Brontë to make her novel saleable. Yet not only is Thornfield more realistically drawn than, say, Otranto or Udolpho, it is more metaphorically radiant than most gothic mansions: it is the house of Jane's life, its floors and walls the architecture of her experience.

Beyond the "long cold gallery" where the portraits of alien unknown ancestors hang the way the specter of Mr. Reed hovered in the red-room, Jane sleeps in a small pretty chamber, harmoniously furnished as Miss Temple's training has supposedly furnished her own mind. Youthfully optimistic, she notices that her "couch had no thorns in it" and trusts that with the help of welcoming Mrs. Fairfax "a fairer era of life was beginning for me, one that was to have its flowers and pleasures, as well as its thorns and toils'' (chap. 11). Christian, entering the Palace Beautiful, might have hoped as much.

The equivocal pleasantness of Mrs. Fairfax, however, like the ambiguous architecture of Thornfield itself, suggests at once a way in which the situation at Thornfield reiterates all the other settings of Jane's life. For though Jane assumes at first that Mrs. Fairfax is her employer, she soon learns that the woman is merely a house*keeper*, the surrogate of an absent master, just as Mrs. Reed was a surrogate for dead Mr. Reed or immature John Reed, and Miss Temple for absent Mr. Brocklehurst. Moreover, in her role as an extension of the mysterious Rochester, sweet-faced Mrs. Fairfax herself becomes mysteriously chilling. "Too much noise, Grace," she says peremptorily, when she and Jane overhear "Grace Poole's" laugh as they tour the third story. "Remember directions!" (chap. 11).

The third story is the most obviously emblematic quarter of Thornfield. Here, amid the furniture of the past, down a narrow passage with "two rows of small black doors, all shut, like a corridor in some Bluebeard's castle" (chap. 11), Jane first hears the "distinct formal mirthless laugh" of mad Bertha, Rochester's secret wife and in a sense her own secret self. And just above this sinister corridor, leaning against the picturesque battlements and looking out over the world like Bluebeard's bride's sister Anne, Jane is to long again for freedom, for "all of incident, life, fire, feeling that I . . . had not in my actual existence" (chap. 12). These upper regions, in other words, symbolically miniaturize one crucial aspect of the world in which she finds herself. Heavily enigmatic, ancestral relics wall her in; inexplicable locked rooms guard a secret which may have something to do with *her*; distant vistas promise an inaccessible but enviable life.

Even more importantly, Thornfield's attic soon becomes a complex focal point where Jane's own rationality (what she has learned from Miss Temple) and her irrationality (her "hunger, rebellion and rage") intersect.[15] She never, for instance, articulates her rational desire for liberty so well as when she stands on the battlements of Thornfield, looking out over the world. However offensive these thoughts may have been to Miss Rigby—and both Jane and her creator obviously suspected they would be—the sequence of ideas expressed in the famous passage beginning "Anybody may blame me who likes" is as logical as anything in an essay by Wollstonecraft or Mill. What is somewhat irrational, though, is the restlessness and passion which, as it were, italicize her little meditation on freedom. "I could not help it," she explains,

> the restlessness was in my nature, it agitated me to pain sometimes. Then my sole relief was to walk along the corridor of the third story, backwards and forwards, safe in the silence and solitude of the spot, and allow my mind's eye to dwell on whatever bright visions rose before it.

And even more irrational is the experience which accompanies Jane's pacing:

> When thus alone, I not unfrequently heard Grace Poole's laugh: the same peal, the same low, slow ha! ha! which, when first heard, had thrilled me: I heard, too, her eccentric murmurs; stranger than her laugh. [chap. 12]

Eccentric murmurs that uncannily echo the murmurs of *Jane's* imagination, and a low, slow ha! ha! which forms a bitter refrain to the tale *Jane's* imagination creates. Despite Miss Temple's training, the "bad animal" who was first locked up in the red-room is, we sense, still lurking somewhere, behind a dark door, waiting for a chance to get free. That early consciousness of "something near me" has not yet been exorcised. Rather, it has intensified.

Many of Jane's problems, particularly those which find symbolic expression in her experiences in the third story, can be traced to her ambiguous status as a governess at Thornfield. As M. Jeanne Peterson points out, every Victorian governess received strikingly conflicting messages (she was and was not a member of the family, was and was not a servant).[16] Such messages all too often caused her features to wear what one contemporary observer called "a fixed sad look of despair."[17] But Jane's difficulties arise also, as we have seen, from her constitutional *ire*; interestingly, none of the women she meets at Thornfield has anything like that last problem, though all suffer from equivalent ambiguities of status. Aside from Mrs. Fairfax, the

three most important of these women are little Adèle Varens, Blanche
Ingram, and Grace Poole. All are important negative "role-models"
for Jane, and all suggest problems she must overcome before she can
reach the independent maturity which is the goal of her pilgrimage.

The first, Adèle, though hardly a woman, is already a "little
woman," cunning and doll-like, a sort of sketch for Amy March in
Louisa May Alcott's novel. Ostensibly a poor orphan child, like
Jane herself, Adèle is evidently the natural daughter of Edward
Rochester's dissipated youth. Accordingly, she longs for fashionable
gowns rather than for love or freedom, and, the way her mother
Céline did, sings and dances for her supper as if she were a clockwork
temptress invented by E. T. A. Hoffman. Where Miss Temple's was
the way of the lady and Helen's that of the saint, hers and her mother's
are the ways of Vanity Fair, ways which have troubled Jane since
her days at Gateshead. For how is a poor, plain governess to contend
with a society that rewards beauty and style? May not Adèle, the
daughter of a "fallen woman," be a model female in a world of
prostitutes?

Blanche Ingram, also a denizen of Vanity Fair, presents Jane
with a slightly different female image. Tall, handsome, and well-
born, she is worldly but, unlike Adèle and Céline, has a respectable
place in the world: she is the daughter of "Baroness Ingram of
Ingram Park," and—along with Georgiana and Eliza Reed—Jane's
classically wicked stepsister. But while Georgiana and Eliza are
dismissed to stereotypical fates, Blanche's history teaches Jane ominous lessons. First, the charade of "Bridewell" in which she and
Rochester participate relays a secret message: conventional marriage
is not only, as the attic implies, a "well" of mystery, it is a Bridewell,
a prison, like the Bluebeard's corridor of the third story. Second, the
charade of courtship in which Rochester engages her suggests a grim
question: is not the game of the marriage "market" a game even
scheming women are doomed to lose?

Finally, Grace Poole, the most enigmatic of the women Jane
meets at Thornfield—"that mystery of mysteries, as I considered
her"—is obviously associated with Bertha, almost as if, with her
pint of porter, her "staid and taciturn" demeanor, she were the
madwoman's public representative. "Only one hour in the twenty
four did she pass with her fellow servants below," Jane notes, attempt-

ing to fathom the dark "pool" of the woman's behavior; "all the rest of her time was spent in some low-ceiled, oaken chamber of the third story; there she sat and sewed ... as companionless as a prisoner in her dungeon" (chap. 17). And that Grace is as companionless as Bertha or Jane herself is undeniably true. Women in Jane's world, acting as agents for men, may be the keepers of other women. But both keepers and prisoners are bound by the same chains. In a sense, then, the mystery of mysteries which Grace Poole suggests to Jane is the mystery of her own life, so that to question Grace's position at Thornfield is to question her own.

Interestingly, in trying to puzzle out the secret of Grace Poole, Jane at one point speculates that Mr. Rochester may once have entertained "tender feelings" for the woman, and when thoughts of Grace's "uncomeliness" seem to refute this possibility, she cements her bond with Bertha's keeper by reminding herself that, after all, "*You* are not beautiful either, and perhaps Mr. Rochester approves you" (chap. 16). Can appearances be trusted? Who is the slave, the master or the servant, the prince or Cinderella? What, in other words, are the real relationships between the master of Thornfield and all these women whose lives revolve around his? None of these questions can, of course, be answered without reference to the central character of the Thornfield episode, Edward Fairfax Rochester.

Jane's first meeting with Rochester is a fairytale meeting. Charlotte Brontë deliberately stresses mythic elements: an icy twilight setting out of Coleridge or Fuseli, a rising moon, a great "lion-like" dog gliding through the shadows like "a North-of-England spirit, called a 'Gytrash' which ... haunted solitary ways, and sometimes came upon belated travellers," followed by "a tall steed, and on its back a rider." Certainly the Romanticized images seem to suggest that universe of male sexuality with which Richard Chase thought the Brontës were obsessed.[18] And Rochester, in a "riding-cloak, fur-collared, and steel-clasped," with "a dark face ... stern features and a heavy brow" himself appears the very essence of patriarchal energy, Cinderella's prince as a middle-aged warrior (chap. 12). Yet what are we to think of the fact that the prince's first action is to fall on the ice, together with his horse, and exclaim prosaically "What the deuce is to do now?'' Clearly the master's mastery is not universal. Jane offers help, and Rochester, leaning on her shoulder, admits that "necessity compels me to make you useful." Later, remembering the scene, he confesses that he too had seen the meeting as a mythic one, though from a perspective entirely other than Jane's. "When you came on me in Hay Lane last night, I . . . had half a mind to demand whether you had bewitched my horse" (chap. 13). Significantly, his playful remark acknowledges *her* powers just as much as (if not more than) her vision of the Gytrash acknowledged *his*. Thus, though in one sense Jane and Rochester begin their relationship as master and servant, prince and Cinderella, Mr. B. and Pamela, in another they begin as spiritual equals.

As the episode unfolds, their equality is emphasized in other scenes as well. For instance, though Rochester imperiously orders Jane to "resume your seat, and answer my questions" while he looks at her drawings, his response to the pictures reveals not only his own Byronic broodings, but his consciousness of hers. "Those eyes in the Evening Star you must have seen in a dream. . . . And who taught you to paint wind? . . . Where did you see Latmos?" (chap. 13). Though such talk would bewilder most of Rochester's other dependents, it is a breath of life to Jane, who begins to fall in love with him not because he is her master but in spite of the fact that he is, not because he is princely in manner, but because, being in some sense her equal, he is the only qualified critic of her art and soul.

Their subsequent encounters develop their equality in even more complex ways. Rudely urged to entertain Rochester, Jane smiles "not a very complacent or submissive smile," obliging her employer to explain that "the fact is, once for all, I don't wish to treat you like an inferior . . . I claim only such superiority as must result from twenty years difference in age and a century's advance in experience" (chap. 14). Moreover, his long account of his adventure with Céline —an account which, incidentally, struck many Victorian readers as totally improper, coming from a dissipated older man to a virginal young governess[19]—emphasizes, at least superficially, not his superiority to Jane but his sense of equality with her. Both Jane and Charlotte Brontë correctly recognize this point, which subverts those Victorian charges: "The ease of his manner," Jane comments, "freed me from painful restraint; the friendly frankness . . . with which he treated me, drew me to him. *I felt at* [*these*] *times as if he were my relation rather than my master*" (chap. 15 [ital. ours]). For of course, despite critical suspicions that Rochester is seducing Jane in these scenes, he is, on the contrary, solacing himself with her unseduceable independence in a world of self-marketing Célines and Blanches.

His need for her strength and parity is made clearer soon enough —on, for instance, the occasion when she rescues him from his burning bed (an almost fatally symbolic plight), and later on the occasion when she helps him rescue Richard Mason from the wounds inflicted by "Grace Poole." And that these rescues are facilitated by Jane's and Rochester's mutual sense of equality is made clearest of all in the scene in which only Jane of all the "young ladies" at Thornfield fails to be deceived by Rochester in his gypsy costume: "With the ladies you must have managed well," she comments, but "You did not act the character of a gypsy with me" (chap. 19). The implication is that he did not—or could not—because he respects "the resolute, wild, free thing looking out of" Jane's eyes as much as she herself does, and understands that just as he can see beyond her everyday disguise as plain Jane the governess, she can see beyond his temporary disguise as a gypsy fortune-teller—or his daily disguise as Rochester the master of Thornfield.

This last point is made again, most explicitly, by the passionate avowals of their first betrothal scene. Beginning with similar attempts at disguise and deception on Rochester's part ("One can't have too much of such a very excellent thing as my beautiful Blanche") that encounter causes Jane in a moment of despair and ire to strip away her own disguises in her most famous assertion of her own integrity:

> "Do you think, because I am poor, obscure, plain, and little, I am soulless and heartless? You think wrong!—I have as much soul as you,—and full as much heart! And if God had gifted me with some beauty, and much wealth, I should have made it as hard for you to leave me, as it is now for me to leave you. I am not talking to you now through the medium of custom, conventionalities, or even of mortal flesh:—it is my spirit that addresses your spirit; just as if both had passed through the grave, and we stood at God's feet equal,—as we are!" [chap. 23]

Rochester's response is another casting away of disguises, a confession that he has deceived her about Blanche, and an acknowledgment of their parity and similarity: "My bride is here," he admits, "because my *equal* is here, and my *likeness*." The energy informing both speeches is, significantly, not so much sexual as spiritual; the impropriety of its formulation is, as Mrs. Rigby saw, not moral but political, for Charlotte Brontë appears here to have imagined a world in which the prince and Cinderella are democratically equal, Pamela is just as good as Mr. B., master and servant are profoundly alike. And to the marriage of such true minds, it seems, no man or woman can admit impediment.

But of course, as we know, there is an impediment, and that impediment, paradoxically, pre-exists in both Rochester and Jane, despite their avowals of equality. Though Rochester, for instance, appears in both the gypsy sequence and the betrothal scene to have cast away the disguises that gave him his mastery, it is obviously of some importance that those disguises were necessary in the first place. Why, Jane herself wonders, does Rochester have to trick people, especially women? What secrets are concealed behind the charades he enacts? One answer is surely that he himself senses his trickery is a source of power, and therefore, in Jane's case at least, an evasion of that equality in which he claims to believe. Beyond this, however, it is clear that the secrets Rochester is concealing or disguising throughout much of the book are themselves in Jane's— and Charlotte Brontë's—view secrets of inequality.

The first of these is suggested both by his name, apparently an allusion to the dissolute Earl of Rochester, and by Jane's own reference to the Bluebeard's corridor of the third story: it is the secret of masculine potency, the secret of male sexual guilt. For, like those pre-Byron Byronic heroes the real Restoration Rochester and the mythic Bluebeard (indeed, in relation to Jane, like any experienced adult male), Rochester has specific and "guilty" sexual knowledge which makes him in some sense her "superior." Though this point may seem to contradict the point made earlier about his frankness to Jane, it really should not. Rochester's apparently improper recounting of his sexual adventures *is* a kind of acknowledgment of Jane's equality with him. His possession of the hidden details of sexuality, however—his knowledge, that is, of the *secret* of sex, symbolized both by his doll-like daughter Adèle and by the locked doors of the third story behind which mad Bertha crouches like an animal—qualifies and undermines that equality. And though his puzzling transvestism, his attempt to impersonate a *female* gypsy, may be seen as a semi-conscious effort to reduce this sexual advantage his masculinity gives him (by putting on a woman's clothes he puts on a woman's weakness), both he and Jane obviously recognize the hollowness of such a ruse. The prince is inevitably Cinderella's superior, Charlotte Brontë saw, not because his rank is higher than hers, but because it is *he* who will initiate *her* into the mysteries of the flesh.

That both Jane and Rochester are in some part of themselves conscious of the barrier which Rochester's sexual knowledge poses to their equality is further indicated by the tensions that develop in their relationship after their betrothal. Rochester, having secured Jane's love, almost reflexively begins to treat her as an inferior, a plaything, a virginal possession—for she has now become his initiate, his "mustard-seed," his "little sunny-faced . . . girl-bride." "It is your time now, little tyrant," he declares, "but it will be mine presently: and when once I have fairly seized you, to have and to hold, I'll just—figuratively speaking—attach you to a chain like this" (chap. 24). She, sensing his new sense of power, resolves to keep him "in reasonable check": "I never can bear being dressed like a doll by Mr. Rochester," she remarks, and, more significantly, "I'll not stand you an inch in the stead of a seraglio. . . . I'll [prepare myself] to go out as a missionary to preach liberty to them that are enslaved" (chap. 24). While such assertions have seemed to some critics merely the consequences of Jane's (and Charlotte Brontë's) sexual panic, it should be clear from their context that, as is usual with Jane, they are political rather than sexual statements, attempts at finding emotional strength rather than expressions of weakness.

Finally, Rochester's ultimate secret, the secret that is revealed together with the existence of Bertha, the literal impediment to his marriage with Jane, is another and perhaps most surprising secret of inequality: but this time the hidden facts suggest the master's inferiority rather than his superiority. Rochester, Jane learns, after the aborted wedding ceremony, had married Bertha Mason for status, for sex, for money, for everything but love and equality. "Oh, I have no respect for myself when I think of that act!" he confesses. "An agony of inward contempt masters me. I never loved, I never esteemed, I did not even know her" (chap. 27). And his statement reminds us of Jane's earlier assertion of her own superiority: "I would scorn such a union [as the loveless one he hints he will enter into with Blanche]: therefore I am better than you" (chap. 23). In a sense, then, the most serious crime Rochester has to expiate is not even the crime of exploiting others but the sin of self-exploitation, the sin of Céline and Blanche, to which he, at least, had seemed completely immune.[20]

That Rochester's character and life pose in themselves such substantial impediments to his marriage with Jane does not mean, however, that Jane herself generates none. For one thing, "akin" as she is to Rochester, she suspects him of harboring all the secrets we know he does harbor, and raises defenses against them, manipulating her "master" so as to keep him "in reasonable check." In a larger way, moreover, all the charades and masquerades—the secret messages—of patriarchy have had their effect upon her. Though she loves Rochester the man, Jane has doubts about Rochester the husband even before she learns about Bertha. In her world, she senses, even the equality of love between true minds leads to the inequalities and minor despotisms of marriage. "For a little while," she says cynically to Rochester, "you will perhaps be as you are now, [but] ... I suppose your love will effervesce in six months, or less. I have observed in books written by men, that period assigned as the farthest to which a husband's ardor extends" (chap. 24). He, of course, vigorously repudiates this prediction, but his argument— "Jane: you please me, and you master me [because] you seem to submit"—implies a kind of Lawrentian sexual tension and only makes things worse. For when he asks "Why do you smile [at this], Jane? What does that inexplicable ... turn of countenance mean?" her peculiar, ironic smile, reminiscent of Bertha's mirthless laugh, signals an "involuntary" and subtly hostile thought "of Hercules and Samson with their charmers." And that hostility becomes overt at the silk warehouse, where Jane notes that "the more he bought me, the more my cheek burned with a sense of annoyance and degradation. . . . I thought his smile was such as a sultan might, in a blissful and fond moment, bestow on a slave his gold and gems had enriched" (chap. 24).

Jane's whole life-pilgrimage has, of course, prepared her to be angry in this way at Rochester's, and society's, concept of marriage. Rochester's loving tyranny recalls John Reed's unloving despotism, and the erratic nature of Rochester's favors ("in my secret soul I knew that his great kindness to me was balanced by unjust severity to many others" [chap. 15]) recalls Brocklehurst's hypocrisy. But even the dreamlike paintings that Jane produced early in her stay at Thornfield—art works which brought her as close to her "master" as Helen Graham (in *The Tenant of Wildfell Hall*) was to hers— functioned ambiguously, like Helen's, to predict strains in this relationship even while they seemed to be conventional Romantic fantasies. The first represented a drowned female corpse; the second a sort of avenging mother goddess rising (like Bertha Mason Rochester or *Frankenstein*'s monster) in "electric travail" (chap. 13); and the third a terrible paternal specter carefully designed to recall Milton's sinister image of Death. Indeed, this last, says Jane, quoting *Paradise Lost*, delineates "the shape which shape had none," the patriarchal shadow implicit even in the Father-hating gloom of hell.

Given such shadowings and foreshadowings, then, it is no wonder that as Jane's anger and fear about her marriage intensify, she begins to be symbolically drawn back into her own past, and specifically to reexperience the dangerous sense of doubleness that had begun in the red-room. The first sign that this is happening is the powerfully depicted, recurrent dream of a child she begins to have as she drifts into a romance with her master. She tells us that she was awakened "from companionship with this baby-phantom" on the night Bertha attacked Richard Mason, and the next day she is literally called back into the past, back to Gateshead to see the dying Mrs. Reed, who reminds her again of what she once was and potentially still is: "Are you Jane Eyre? . . . I declare she talked to me once like something mad, or like a fiend" (chap. 21). Even more significantly, the phantom-child reappears in two dramatic dreams Jane has on the night before her wedding eve, during which she experiences "a strange regretful consciousness of some barrier dividing" her from Rochester. In the first, "burdened" with the small wailing creature, she is "following the windings of an unknown road" in cold rainy weather, straining to catch up with her future husband but unable to reach him. In the second, she is walking among the ruins of Thornfield, still carrying "the unknown little child" and still following Rochester; as he disappears around "an angle in the road," she tells him, "I bent forward to take a last look; the wall crumbled; I was shaken; the child rolled from my knee, I lost my balance, fell, and woke" (chap. 25).

What are we to make of these strange dreams, or—as Jane would call them—these "presentiments"? To begin with, it seems clear that the wailing child who appears in all of them corresponds to "the poor orphan child" of Bessie's song at Gateshead, and therefore to the child Jane herself, the wailing Cinderella whose pilgrimage began in anger and despair. That child's complaint—"My feet they are sore, and my limbs they are weary;/ Long is the way, and the mountains are wild"—is still Jane's, or at least the complaint of that part of her which resists a marriage of inequality. And though consciously Jane wishes to be rid of the heavy problem her orphan self presents, "I might not lay it down anywhere, however tired were my arms, however much its weight impeded my progress." In other words, until she reaches the goal of her pilgrimage— maturity, independence, true equality with Rochester (and therefore in a sense with the rest of the world)—she is doomed to carry her orphaned alter ego everywhere. The burden of the past cannot be sloughed off so easily—not, for instance, by glamorous lovemaking, silk dresses, jewelry, a new name. Jane's "strange regretful consciousness of a barrier" dividing her from Rochester is, thus, a keen though disguised intuition of a problem she herself will pose.

Almost more interesting than the nature of the child image, however, is the *predictive* aspect of the last of the child dreams, the one about the ruin of Thornfield. As Jane correctly foresees, Thornfield *will* within a year become "a dreary ruin, the retreat of bats and owls." Have her own subtle and not-so-subtle hostilities to its master any connection with the catastrophe that is to befall the house? Is her clairvoyant dream in some sense a vision of wish-fulfilment? And why, specifically, is she freed from the burden of the wailing child at the moment *she* falls from Thornfield's ruined wall?

The answer to all these questions is closely related to events which follow upon the child dream. For the apparition of a child in these crucial weeks preceding her marriage is only one symptom of a dissolution of personality Jane seems to be experiencing at this time, a fragmentation of the self comparable to her "syncope" in the red-room. Another symptom appears early in the chapter that begins, anxiously, "there was no putting off the day that advanced —the bridal day" (chap. 25). It is her witty but nervous speculation about the nature of "one Jane Rochester, a person whom as yet I knew not," though "in yonder closet . . . garments *said* to be hers had already displaced [mine]: *for not to me appertained that . . . strange wraith-like apparel*" (chap. 25 [ital. ours]). Again, a third symptom appears on the morning of her wedding: she turns toward the mirror and sees "a robed and veiled figure, so unlike my usual self that it seemed almost the image of a stranger" (chap. 26), reminding us of the moment in the red-room when all had "seemed colder and darker in that visionary hollow" of the looking glass "than in reality." In view of this frightening series of separations within the self—Jane Eyre splitting off from Jane Rochester, the child Jane splitting off from the adult Jane, and the image of Jane weirdly separating from the body of Jane—it is not surprising that another and most mysterious specter, a sort of "vampyre," should appear in the middle of the night to rend and trample the wedding veil of that unknown person, Jane Rochester.

Literally, of course, the nighttime specter is none other than Bertha Mason Rochester. But on a figurative and psychological level it seems suspiciously clear that the specter of Bertha is still another—indeed the most threatening—avatar of Jane. What Bertha now *does*, for instance, is what Jane wants to do. Disliking the "vapoury veil" of Jane Rochester, Jane Eyre secretly wants to tear the garments up. Bertha does it for her. Fearing the inexorable "bridal day," Jane would like to put it off. Bertha does that for her too. Resenting the new mastery of Rochester, whom she sees as "*dread but adored*," (ital. ours), she wishes to be his equal in size and strength, so that she can battle him in the contest of their marriage. Bertha, "a big woman, in stature almost equalling her husband," has the necessary "virile force" (chap. 26). Bertha, in other words, is Jane's truest and darkest double: she is the angry aspect of the orphan child, the ferocious secret self Jane has been trying to repress ever since her days at Gateshead. For, as Claire Rosenfeld points out, "the novelist who consciously or unconsciously exploits psychological Doubles" frequently juxtaposes "two characters, the one representing the socially acceptable or conventional personality, the other externalizing the free, uninhibited, often criminal self."[21]

It is only fitting, then, that the existence of this criminal self imprisoned in Thornfield's attic is the ultimate legal impediment to Jane's and Rochester's marriage, and that its existence is, paradoxically, an impediment raised by Jane as well as by Rochester. For it now begins to appear, if it did not earlier, that Bertha has functioned as Jane's dark double *throughout* the governess's stay at Thornfield. Specifically, every one of Bertha's appearances—or, more accurately, her manifestations—has been associated with an experience (or repression) of anger on Jane's part. Jane's feelings of "hunger, rebellion, and rage" on the battlements, for instance, were accompanied by Bertha's "low, slow ha! ha!" and "eccentric murmurs." Jane's apparently secure response to Rochester's apparently egalitarian sexual confidences was followed by Bertha's attempt to incinerate the master in his bed. Jane's unexpressed resentment at Rochester's manipulative gypsy-masquerade found expression in Bertha's terrible shriek and her even more terrible attack on Richard Mason. Jane's anxieties about her marriage, and in particular her fears of her own alien "robed and veiled" bridal image, were objectified by the image of Bertha in a "white and straight" dress, "whether gown, sheet, or shroud I cannot tell." Jane's profound desire to destroy Thornfield, the symbol of Rochester's mastery and of her own servitude, will be acted out by Bertha, who burns down the house and destroys *herself* in the process as if she were an agent of Jane's desire as well as her own. And finally, Jane's disguised hostility to Rochester, summarized in her terrifying prediction to herself that "you shall, yourself, pluck out your right eye; yourself cut off your right hand" (chap. 27) comes strangely true through the intervention of Bertha, whose melodramatic death causes Rochester to lose both eye and hand.

These parallels between Jane and Bertha may at first seem somewhat strained. Jane, after all, is poor, plain, little, pale, neat, and quiet, while Bertha is rich, large, florid, sensual, and extravagant; indeed, she was once even beautiful, somewhat, Rochester notes, "in the style of Blanche Ingram." Is she not, then, as many critics have suggested, a monitory image rather than a double for Jane? As Richard Chase puts it, "May not Bertha, Jane seems to ask herself, be a living example of what happens to the woman who [tries] to be the fleshly vessel of the [masculine] *élan*?"²² "Just as [Jane's] instinct for self-preservation saves her from earlier temptations," Adrienne Rich remarks, "so it must save her from becoming this woman by curbing her imagination at the limits of what is bearable for a powerless woman in the England of the 1840s."²³ Even Rochester himself provides a similar critical appraisal of the relationship between the two. "That is *my wife*," he says, pointing to mad Bertha,

> "And *this* is what I wished to have ... this young girl who stands so grave and quiet at the mouth of hell, looking collectedly at the gambols of a demon. I wanted her just as a change after that fierce ragout.... Compare these clear eyes with the red balls yonder—this face with that mask—this form with that bulk...." [chap. 26]

And of course, in one sense, the relationship between Jane and Bertha is a monitory one: while acting out Jane's secret fantasies, Bertha does (to say the least) provide the governess with an example of how not to act, teaching her a lesson more salutary than any Miss Temple ever taught.

Nevertheless, it is disturbingly clear from recurrent images in the novel that Bertha not only acts *for* Jane, she also acts *like* Jane. The imprisoned Bertha, running "backwards and forwards" on all fours in the attic, for instance, recalls not only Jane the governess, whose only relief from mental pain was to pace "backwards and forwards" in the third story, but also that "bad animal" who was ten-year-old Jane, imprisoned in the red-room, howling and mad. Bertha's "goblin appearance"—"half dream, half reality," says Rochester— recalls the lover's epithets for Jane: "malicious elf," "sprite," "changeling," as well as his playful accusation that she had magically downed his horse at their first meeting. Rochester's description of Bertha as a "monster" ("a fearful voyage I had with such a monster in the vessel" [chap. 27]) ironically echoes Jane's own fear of being a monster ("Am I a monster?... is it impossible that Mr. Rochester should have a sincere affection for me?" [chap. 24]). Bertha's fiendish madness recalls Mrs. Reed's remark about Jane ("she talked to me once like something mad or like a fiend") as well as Jane's own estimate of her mental state ("I will hold to the principles received by me when I was sane, and not mad—as I am now [chap. 27]"). And most dramatic of all, Bertha's incendiary tendencies recall Jane's early flaming rages, at Lowood and at Gateshead, as well as that "ridge of lighted heath" which she herself saw as emblematic of her mind in its rebellion against society. It is only fitting, therefore, that, as if to balance the child Jane's terrifying vision of herself as an alien figure in the "visionary hollow" of the red-room looking glass, the adult Jane first clearly perceives her terrible double when Bertha puts on the wedding veil intended for the second Mrs. Rochester, and turns to the mirror. At that moment, Jane sees "the reflection of the visage and features quite distinctly in the dark oblong glass," sees them as if they were her own (chap. 25).

For despite all the habits of harmony she gained in her years at Lowood, we must finally recognize, with Jane herself, that on her arrival at Thornfield she only "*appeared* a disciplined and subdued character" [ital. ours]. Crowned with thorns, finding that she is, in Emily Dickinson's words, "The Wife—without the Sign," [24] she represses her rage behind a subdued facade, but her soul's impulse to dance "like a Bomb, abroad," to quote Dickinson again,[25] has not been exorcised and will not be exorcised until the literal and symbolic death of Bertha frees her from the furies that torment her and makes possible a marriage of equality—makes possible, that is, wholeness within herself. At that point, significantly, when the Bertha in Jane falls from the ruined wall of Thornfield and is destroyed, the orphan child too, as her dream predicts, will roll from her knee—the burden of her past will be lifted—and she will wake. In the meantime, as Rochester says, "never was anything at once so frail and so indomitable ... consider the resolute wild free thing looking out of [Jane's] eye.... Whatever I do with its cage, I cannot get at it—the savage, beautiful creature" (chap. 27).

That the pilgrimage of this "savage, beautiful creature" must now necessarily lead her away from Thornfield is signalled, like many other events in the novel, by the rising of the moon, which accompanies a reminiscent dream of the red-room. Unjustly imprisoned now, as she was then, in one of the traps a patriarchal society provides for outcast Cinderellas, Jane realizes that this time she must escape through deliberation rather than through madness. The maternal moon, admonishing her ("My daughter, flee temptation!") appears to be "a white human form . . . inclining a glorious brow," a strengthening image, as Adrienne Rich suggests, of the Great Mother.[26] Yet—"profoundly, imperiously, archetypal"[27]— this figure has its ambiguities, just as Jane's own personality does, for the last night on which Jane watched such a moon rise was the night Bertha attacked Richard Mason, and the juxtaposition of the two events on that occasion was almost shockingly suggestive:

> [The moon's] glorious gaze roused me. Awaking in the dead of night, I opened my eyes on her disk. . . . It was beautiful, but too solemn: I half rose, and stretched my arm to draw the curtain.
> Good God! What a cry! [chap. 20]

Now, as Jane herself recognizes, the moon has elicited from her an act as violent and self-assertive as Bertha's on that night. "What was I?" she thinks, as she steals away from Thornfield. "I had injured—wounded—left my master. I was hateful in my own eyes" (chap. 28). Yet, though her escape may seem as morally ambiguous as the moon's message, it is necessary for her own self-preservation. And soon, like Bertha, she is "crawling forwards on my hands and knees, and then again raised to my feet—as eager and determined as ever to reach the road."

Her wanderings on that road are a symbolic summary of those wanderings of the poor orphan child which constitute her entire life's pilgrimage. For, like Jane's dreams, Bessie's song was an uncannily accurate prediction of things to come. "Why did they send me so far and so lonely, / Up where the moors spread and grey rocks are piled?" Far and lonely indeed Jane wanders, starving, freezing, stumbling, abandoning her few possessions, her name, and even her self-respect in her search for a new home. For "men are hard-hearted, and kind angels only / Watch'd o'er the steps of a poor orphan child." And like the starved wanderings of Hetty Sorel in *Adam Bede*, her terrible journey across the moors suggests the essential homelessness—the nameless, placeless, and contingent status—of women in a patriarchal society. Yet because Jane, unlike Hetty, has an inner strength which her pilgrimage seeks to develop, "kind angels" finally do bring her to what is in a sense her true home, the house significantly called *Marsh End* (or Moor House) which is to represent the end of her march toward selfhood. Here she encounters Diana, Mary, and St. John Rivers, the "good" relatives who will help free her from her angry memories of that wicked stepfamily the Reeds. And that the Rivers prove to be literally her relatives is not, in psychological terms, the strained coincidence some readers have suggested. For having left Rochester, having torn off the crown of thorns he offered and repudiated the unequal charade of marriage he proposed, Jane has now gained the strength to begin to discover her real place in the world. St. John helps her find a job in a school, and once again she reviews the choices she has had: "Is it better, I ask, to be a slave in a fool's paradise at Marseilles ... or to be a village schoolmistress, free and honest, in a breezy mountain nook in the healthy heart of England?" (chap. 31). Her unequivocal conclusion that "I was right when I adhered to principle and law" is one toward which the whole novel seems to have tended.

The qualifying word *seems* is, however, a necessary one. For though in one sense Jane's discovery of her family at Marsh End does represent the end of her pilgrimage, her progress toward selfhood will not be complete until she learns that "principle and law" in the abstract do not always coincide with the deepest principles and laws of her own being. Her early sense that Miss Temple's teachings had merely been superimposed on her native vitality had already begun to suggest this to her. But it is through her encounter with St. John Rivers that she assimilates this lesson most thoroughly. As a number of critics have noticed, all three members of the Rivers family have resonant, almost allegorical names. The names of Jane's true "sisters," Diana and Mary, notes Adrienne Rich, recall the

Great Mother in her dual aspects of Diana the huntress and Mary the virgin mother;[28] in this way, as well as through their independent, learned, benevolent personalities, they suggest the ideal of female strength for which Jane has been searching. St. John, on the other hand, has an almost blatantly patriarchal name, one which recalls both the masculine abstraction of the gospel according to St. John ("in the beginning was the *Word*") and the disguised misogyny of St. John the Baptist, whose patristic and evangelical contempt for the flesh manifested itself most powerfully in a profound contempt for the *female*. Like Salome, whose rebellion against such misogyny Oscar Wilde was later also to associate with the rising moon of female power, Jane must symbolically, if not literally, behead the abstract principles of this man before she can finally achieve her true independence.

At first, however, it seems that St. John is offering Jane a viable alternative to the way of life proposed by Rochester. For where Rochester, like his dissolute namesake, ended up appearing to offer a life of pleasure, a path of roses (albeit with concealed thorns), and a marriage of passion, St. John seems to propose a life of principle, a path of thorns (with no concealed roses), and a marriage of spirituality. His self-abnegating rejection of the worldly beauty Rosamund Oliver—another character with a strikingly resonant name—is disconcerting to the passionate and Byronic part of Jane, but at least it shows that, unlike hypocritical Brocklehurst, he practices what he preaches. And what he preaches is the Carlylean sermon of self-actualization through work: "Work while it is called today, for the night cometh wherein no man can work."[29] If she follows him, Jane realizes, she will substitute a divine Master for the master she served at Thornfield, and replace love with labor—for "you are formed for labour, not for love," St. John tells her. Yet when, long ago at Lowood, she asked for "a new servitude" was not some such solution half in her mind? When, pacing the battlements at Thornfield she insisted that "women [need] a field for their efforts as much as their brothers do" (chap. 12), did she not long for some such practical "exercise"? "Still will my Father with promise and blessing, / Take to his bosom the poor orphaned child," Bessie's song had predicted. Is not Marsh End, then, the promised end, and St. John's way the way to His bosom?

Jane's early repudiation of the spiritual harmonies offered by Helen Burns and Miss Temple is the first hint that, while St. John's way will tempt her, she must resist it. That, like Rochester, he is "akin" to her is clear. But where Rochester represents the fire of her nature, her cousin represents the ice. And while for some women ice may "suffice," for Jane, who has struggled all her life, like a sane version of Bertha, against the polar cold of a loveless world, it clearly will not. As she falls more deeply under St. John's "freezing spell," she realizes increasingly that to please him "I must disown half my nature." And "as his wife," she reflects, she would be "always restrained . . . forced to keep the fire of my nature continually low, . . . though the imprisoned flame consumed vital after vital" (chap. 34). In fact, as St. John's wife and "the sole helpmate [he] can influence efficiently in life, and retain absolutely till death" (chap. 34), she will be entering into a union even more unequal than that proposed by Rochester, a marriage reflecting, once again, her absolute exclusion from the life of wholeness toward which her pilgrimage has been directed. For despite the integrity of principle that distinguishes him from Brocklehurst, despite his likeness to "the warrior Greatheart, who guards his pilgrim convoy from the onslaught of Apollyon" (chap. 38), St. John is finally, as Brocklehurst was, a pillar of patriarchy, "a cold cumbrous column" (chap. 34). But where Brocklehurst had removed Jane from the imprisonment of Gateshead only to immure her in a dank valley of starvation, and even Rochester had tried to make her the "slave of passion," St. John wants to imprison the "resolute wild free thing" that is her soul in the ultimate cell, the "iron shroud" of principle (chap. 34).

Though in many ways St. John's attempt to "imprison" Jane may seem the most irresistible of all, coming as it does at a time when she is congratulating herself on just that adherence to "principle and law" which he recommends, she escapes from his fetters more easily than she had escaped from either Brocklehurst or Rochester. Figuratively speaking, this is a measure of how far she has traveled in her pilgrimage toward maturity. Literally, however, her escape is facilitated by two events. First, having found what is, despite all its ambiguities, her true family, Jane has at last come into her inheritance. Jane Eyre is now the heir of that uncle in Madeira whose first intervention in her life had been, appropriately, to define the legal impediment to her marriage with Rochester, now literally as well as figuratively an independent woman, free to go her own way and follow her own will. But her freedom is also signaled by a second event: the death of Bertha.

Her first "presentiment" of that event comes, dramatically, as an answer to a prayer for guidance. St. John is pressing her to reach a decision about his proposal of marriage. Believing that "I had now put love out of the question, and thought only of duty," she "entreats Heaven" to "Show me, show me the path." As always at major moments in Jane's life, the room is filled with moonlight, as if to remind her that powerful forces are still at work both without and within her. And now, because such forces are operating, she at last hears—she is receptive to—the bodiless cry of Rochester: "Jane! Jane! Jane!" Her response is an immediate act of self-assertion. "I broke from St. John. . . . It was *my* time to assume ascendancy. *My* powers were in play and in force" (chap. 35). But her sudden forcefulness, like her "presentiment" itself, is the climax of all that has gone before. Her new and apparently telepathic communion with Rochester, which many critics have seen as needlessly melodramatic, has been made possible by her new independence and Rochester's new humility. The plot device of the cry is merely a sign that the relationship for which both lovers had always longed is now possible, a sign that Jane's metaphoric speech of the first betrothal scene has been translated into reality: "my spirit . . . addresses your spirit, just as if both had passed through the grave, and we stood at God's feet, equal—as we are!" (chap. 23). For to the marriage of Jane's and Rochester's true minds there is now, as Jane unconsciously guesses, no impediment.

Jane's return to Thornfield, her discovery of Bertha's death and of the ruin her dream had predicted, her reunion at Ferndean with the maimed and blinded Rochester, and their subsequent marriage form an essential epilogue to that pilgrimage toward selfhood which had in other ways concluded at Marsh End, with Jane's realization that she could not marry St. John. At that moment, "the wondrous shock of feeling had come like the earthquake which shook the foundations of Paul and Silas' prison; it had opened the doors of the soul's cell, and loosed its bands—it had wakened it out of its sleep" (chap. 36). For at that moment she had been irrevocably freed from the burden of her past, freed both from the raging specter of Bertha (which had already fallen in fact from the ruined wall of Thornfield) and from the self-pitying specter of the orphan child (which had symbolically, as in her dream, rolled from her knee). And at that moment, again as in her dream, she had *wakened* to her own self, her own needs. Similarly, Rochester, "caged eagle" that he seems (chap. 37), has been freed from what was for him the burden of Thornfield, though at the same time he appears to have been fettered by the injuries he received in attempting to rescue Jane's mad double from the flames devouring his house. That his "fetters" pose no impediment to a new marriage, that he and Jane are now, in reality, equals, is the thesis of the Ferndean section.

Many critics, starting with Richard Chase, have seen Rochester's injuries as "a symbolic castration," a punishment for his early profligacy and a sign that Charlotte Brontë (as well as Jane herself), fearing male sexual power, can only imagine marriage as a union with a diminished Samson. "The tempo and energy of the universe can be quelled, we see, by a patient, practical woman," notes Chase ironically.[30] And there is an element of truth in this idea. The angry Bertha in Jane *had* wanted to punish Rochester, to burn him in his bed, destroy his house, cut off his hand and pluck out his overmastering "full falcon eye." Smiling enigmatically, she had thought of "Hercules and Samson, with their charmers."

It had not been her goal, however, to quell "the tempo and energy of the universe," but simply to strengthen herself, to make herself an equal of the world Rochester represents. And surely another important symbolic point is implied by the lovers' reunion at Ferndean: when both were physically whole they could not, in a sense, *see* each other because of the social disguises—master/servant, prince/Cinderella—blinding them, but now that those disguises have been shed, now that they are equals, they can (though one is blind) see and speak even beyond the medium of the flesh. Apparently sightless, Rochester—in the tradition of blinded Gloucester—now sees more clearly than he did when as a "mole-eyed blockhead" he married Bertha Mason (chap. 27). Apparently mutilated, he is paradoxically stronger than he was when he ruled Thornfield, for now, like Jane, he draws his powers from within himself, rather than from inequity, disguise, deception. Then, at Thornfield, he was "no better than the old lightning-struck chestnut tree in the orchard," whose ruin foreshadowed the catastrophe of his relationship with Jane. Now, as Jane tells him, he is "green and vigorous. Plants will grow about your roots whether you ask them or not" (chap. 37). And now, being equals, he and Jane can afford to depend upon each other with no fear of one exploiting the other.

Nevertheless, despite the optimistic portrait of an egalitarian relationship that Brontë seems to be drawing here, there is "a quiet autumnal quality" about the scenes at Ferndean, as Robert Bernard Martin points out.[31] The house itself , set deep in a dark forest, is old and decaying: Rochester had not even thought it suitable for the loathsome Bertha, and its valley-of-the-shadow quality makes it seem rather like a Lowood, a school of life where Rochester must learn those lessons Jane herself absorbed so early. As a dramatic setting, moreover, Ferndean is notably stripped and asocial, so that the physical isolation of the lovers suggests their spiritual isolation in a world where such egalitarian marriages as theirs are rare, if not impossible. True minds, Charlotte Brontë seems to be saying, must withdraw into a remote forest, a wilderness even, in order to circumvent the strictures of a hierarchal society.

Does Brontë's rebellious feminism—that "irreligious" dissatisfaction with the social order noted by Miss Rigby and *Jane Eyre*'s other Victorian critics—compromise itself in this withdrawal? Has Jane exorcised the rage of orphanhood only to retreat from the responsibilities her own principles implied? Tentative answers to these questions can be derived more easily from *The Professor, Shirley*, and *Villette* than from *Jane Eyre*, for the qualified and even (as in *Villette*) indecisive endings of Brontë's other novels suggest that she herself was unable clearly to envision viable solutions to the problem of patriarchal oppression. In all her books, writing (as we have seen) in a sort of trance, she was able to act out that passionate drive toward freedom which offended agents of the status quo, but in none was she able consciously to define the full meaning of achieved freedom—perhaps because no one of her contemporaries, not even a Wollstonecraft or a Mill, could adequately describe a society so drastically altered that the matured Jane and Rochester could really live in it.

What Brontë could not logically define, however, she could embody in tenuous but suggestive imagery and in her last, perhaps most significant redefinitions of Bunyan. Nature in the largest sense seems now to be on the side of Jane and Rochester. *Ferndean*, as its name implies, is without artifice—"no flowers, no garden-beds"—but it is green as Jane tells Rochester he will be, green and ferny and fertilized by soft rains. Here, isolated from society but flourishing in a natural order of their own making, Jane and Rochester will become physically "bone of [each other's] bone, flesh of [each other's] flesh" (chap. 38), and here the healing powers of nature will eventually restore the sight of one of Rochester's eyes. Here, in other words, nature, unleashed from social restrictions, will do "no miracle—but her best" (chap. 35). For not the Celestial City but a natural paradise, the country of Beulah "upon the borders of heaven," where "the contract between bride and bridegroom [is] renewed," has all along been, we now realize, the goal of Jane's pilgrimage.[32]

As for the Celestial City itself, Charlotte Brontë implies here (though she will later have second thoughts) that such a goal is the dream of those who accept inequities on earth, one of the many tools used by patriarchal society to keep, say, governesses in their "place." Because she believes this so deeply, she quite consciously concludes *Jane Eyre* with an allusion to *Pilgrim's Progress* and with a half-ironic apostrophe to that apostle of celestial transcendence, that shadow of "the warrior Greatheart," St. John Rivers. "His," she tells us, "is the exaction of the apostle, who speaks but for Christ when he says—'Whosoever will come after me, let him deny himself and take up his cross and follow me'" (chap. 38). For it was, finally, to repudiate such a crucifying denial of the self that Brontë's "hunger, rebellion, and rage" led her to write *Jane Eyre* in the first place and to make it an "irreligious" redefinition, almost a parody, of John Bunyan's vision.[33] And the astounding progress toward equality of plain Jane Eyre, whom Miss Rigby correctly saw as "the personification of an unregenerate and undisciplined spirit," answers by its outcome the bitter question Emily Dickinson was to ask fifteen years later: "'My husband'—women say—/ Stroking the Melody—/ Is *this*—the way?'"[34] No, Jane declares in her flight from Thornfield, *that* is not the way. *This*, she says—this marriage of true minds at Ferndean—this is the way. Qualified and isolated as her way may be, it is at least an emblem of hope. Certainly Charlotte Brontë was never again to indulge in quite such an optimistic imagining.

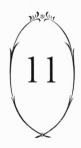

11 The Genesis of Hunger According to *Shirley*

I was, being human, born alone;
I am, being woman, hard beset;
I live by squeezing from a stone
The little nourishment I get.
        —Elinor Wylie

There is nothing to be said against Charlotte's frenzied efforts to counter the nihilism of her surroundings, unless one is among those who would find amusement in the sight of the starving fighting for food.

        —Rebecca West

In times of the most extreme symbols
The walls are very thin,
Almost transparent.
Space is accordion pleated;
Distance changes.
But also, the gut becomes one dimensional
And we starve.
        —Ruth Stone

Where *Jane Eyre* has an Angrian intensity that compelled even the most hostile of its early readers to recognize its story as radical and in some sense "mythic," Charlotte Brontë seems, with *Shirley* (1849), to have retreated to the heavier disguises and more intricate evasions of *The Professor*. But while in that first novel she strove for realism by literally attempting to impersonate a man—and an austere, censorious man at that—in *Shirley*, as if reacting against the flames of rage released in *Jane Eyre*, she seems at first glance to be trying for objectivity, balance, restraint, by writing a novel of private, lonely struggle in an historical setting with public references which seem to dictate that her central characters will lose potency and withdraw rather than advance as the story unfolds.

Brontë herself was ambivalent about her use of this narrative strategy, and astute contemporary readers—G. H. Lewes for one— seem to have perceived her discomfort. "There is no passionate link [in *Shirley*]," Lewes wrote, "nor is there any artistic fusion, or undergrowth by which one part evolves itself from another."[1] While it is true that *Shirley* fails to develop organically, this is at least partially because, in trying to create the calm objectivity she associated specifically with the magisterial omniscience of a "Titan" like Thackeray, Brontë becomes enmeshed in essentially the same male-dominated structures that imprison the characters in all her books.[2] Certainly, in trying to deal historically with a caste denied any public existence, Brontë is committed to exploring the distance between historical change and the seemingly unrelated, lonely struggles of her heroines. When this generic incongruity results in a loss of artistic fusion, as Lewes complained, we can see from our vantage point that the pain of female confinement is not merely her subject in *Shirley*; it is a measure or aspect of her artistry.

Significantly, the novel begins with a distinctively male scene, the sort of scene Jane Austen, for instance, notoriously refused to write. Three clergymen are at a table: complaining that the roast beef is tough and the beer flat, they nevertheless swallow enormous quantities of both, calling for "More bread!" and ordering their landlady to "Cut it, woman."[3] They also consume all her vegetables, cheese, and spice cake. The voracious curates are not, as many of Brontë's critics have claimed, merely a bit of local color, or an irrelevant digression. With them commences a novel very much about the expensive delicacies of the rich, the eccentric cookery of foreigners, the food riots in manufacturing towns, the abundant provisions due soldiers, the scanty dinner baskets of child laborers, and the starvation of the unemployed. Indeed, the hunger of the exploited links them to all those excluded from an independent and successful life in English society: one of the workers lucidly explains that "starving folk cannot be satisfied or settled folk" (chap. 18). And since, as in *Jane Eyre*, hunger is inextricably linked to rebellion and rage, it is hardly surprising that contemporary reviewers discovered in *Shirley* the female identity of Currer Bell. For, despite its omniscient and pseudo-masculine point of view, Charlotte Brontë's third book is far more consciously than either of her earlier works a novel about the "woman question." Set during the wartime crisis in England's depressed mercantile economy of 1811–12, the novel describes how the wrath of the workers does the work of destruction for all those exploited, most especially (as our epigraphs imply) for those women famished for a sense of purpose in their lives.

Describing the same hunger that troubles the dispossessed characters of Jane Austen, Mary Shelley, and Emily Brontë, Charlotte Brontë also implies that women are as famished for food as they are for sustaining fictions of their own devising. Therefore, when introducing the "unromantic" scene of the greedy curates at the beginning of the novel, the narrator explains that "the first dish set upon the table should be one that a good Catholic—ay, even an Anglo-Catholic—might eat on Good Friday in Passion Week: it shall be unleavened bread with bitter herbs, and no roast lamb" (chap. 1). Of course, from Fielding to Barth, novelists have set their fictional repasts before readers whose palates they have tried to tantalize and satiate, but in *Shirley* Brontë begins with so unappetizing a first course because she wants to consider why the curates' feast initiates her heroines' fasts. Indeed, in *Shirley* Brontë portrays not only how the hunger of women is, in the words of Dickinson, "a way / Of Persons outside Windows—," but also why "The Entering—takes away—" desire (J. 579), since the foods and fictions that sustain men are precisely those that have contributed to the sickening of women. The word these "Apostolic" curates furnish is one reason why women are famished, or so Brontë seems to imply in this feminist critique of the biblical myth of the garden.

We have already seen how Shirley's attack on Milton—"Milton was great; but was he good?"—is related to the fictional strategies of Brontë's female predecessors. But Brontë is far more pessimistic about the results of revisionary poetics, although in *Shirley* she is presumably depicting an Emily Brontë born under happier circumstances. Thus, focusing upon a world already inalterably fallen, she suggests that the private broodings of women writers cannot eradicate the powerful effect of public myths. During the writing of *Shirley*,

Brontë witnessed the decline and death of Branwell, Emily, and Anne, and we sense great despair at her own isolation in a novel that attests to her imprisonment within her own narrative structures. Like Elizabeth Barrett, who set her postlapsarian "A Drama of Exile" (1844) directly outside the locked garden gates,[4] Charlotte Brontë studies the self-inflicted punishments of Eve's exiled daughters.

Since *Shirley* is about impotence, Brontë had to solve the problem of plotting a story about characters defined by their very inability to initiate action. As we shall see, every class in this novel has been affected by the inability of the English to win their war against France. In Yorkshire, the manufacturers, the clergy, and the workers suffer because the Orders of Council have cut off the principal markets of trade. To underline this point, the book begins with the curates called away from their meal to help mill-operator Robert Moore, who is waiting for the arrival of machinery that finally appears smashed to pieces by the angry workers. Throughout the novel, Moore waits, hoping to alter his waning fortunes but unable to take any real initiative. Finally he is reduced to the morally reprehensible and pitifully ineffective decision not to marry Caroline Helstone because she is poor, and instead to propose to Shirley Keeldar because she is rich. The novel is centrally concerned with these two young women and the inauspicious roles assigned them. But while none of the characters can initiate effective action because of the contingencies of a costly war abroad, Brontë's heroines are so circumscribed by their gender that they cannot act at all. Though many readers have criticized *Shirley* for a plot which consistently calls attention to its own inorganic development,[5] we shall see that Brontë deliberately seeks to illustrate the inextricable link between sexual discrimination and mercantile capitalism, even as she implies that the coercion of a patriarchal society affects and infects each of its individual members. With this the case, it is not easy to provide or describe escape routes.

The best of the Yorkshire leaders, those most dedicated to shaping their lives through their own exertions, are two men who are bitter political enemies. Hiram Yorke, a rebellious blasphemer, rants against a land "king-ridden, priest-ridden, peer-ridden" while Mr.

Helstone, an ecclesiastic, defends God, king, and "the judgment to come" (chap. 4). Each thinks the other damned. They are barely on speaking terms, yet they share uncommon personal courage and honesty. Yorke's democratic and blunt generosity is as admirable as Helstone's loyal fearlessness. Whig and Tory, manufacturer and clergyman, family man and childless widower, one a wealthy landowner and the other comfortably well-off from a clerical living, these two pillars of the community remain unaffected by the poverty and bankruptcy of their neighbors. Moreover, secure about their future, representative of the best in their society, they share a common past, for early in the novel we discover that they were rivals in their youth for "a girl with the face of a Madonna; a girl of living marble; stillness personified" (chap. 4).

This "monumental angel" is ominously named Mary Cave, reminding us of the parables of the cave that spell out how females have been entrapped in immanence, robbed of all but secondary arts and of their matriarchal genealogy. Indeed, because she was a kind of angel of death, Mary Cave was completely ignored by her clergyman-husband. We are told that, belonging as she did to "an inferior order of existence," she was evidently no companion for Mr. Helstone, and we learn that, after a year or two of marriage, she died, leaving behind a "still beautiful-featured mould of clay . . . cold and white" (chap. 4). Marriage to Yorke, we later learn, would also have led to her suffering, for neither of these men respects or likes the female sex, Helstone preferring women as silly as possible, and Yorke choosing a morose, tyrannical wife to breed and rear his brood. Even the noblest patriarchs are obsessed with delusive and contradictory images of women, Brontë implies, images pernicious enough to cause Mary Cave's death. She is therefore an emblem, a warning that the fate of women inhabiting a male-controlled society involves suicidal self-renunciation.

Understandably, then, she haunts the imagination of Caroline Helstone, who has taken her place in her uncle's house, where she too lives invisibly. Unable to remember her mother, Caroline seems as vulnerable and lonely as her aunt had been. But her life with Helstone is at least calmer than her past existence with her father, who had shut her up day and night, unattended, in an unfurnished garret room where "she waited for his return knowing drink would make him a madman or senseless idiot" (chap. 7). Helstone, at least, merely ignores her, always supplying adequate physical surroundings. And she can visit her cousins, the Moores, until her uncle's political feuding, coupled with Robert's rejection of her, makes these visits impossible.

Caroline's escape into the Moore household is by no means a liberation, however, since she is tortured by her cousin Hortense as she is initiated into the "duties of women," which consist of grammatical problems in French, incessant sewing, and eye-straining stocking-mending, inflicted because Hortense is convinced that this decorous girl is "not sufficiently girlish and submissive" (chap. 5). And certainly, although she seems exceptionally docile, Caroline does know her own mind; she knows, for instance, that she loves Robert Moore. Although demure and neat, moreover, she criticizes Robert's cruelty toward the workers and tries to teach him the evils of pride, drawing lessons from *Coriolanus*. Perhaps because of the examples of Mary Cave and of her own father, Caroline also knows from the first that she would be better off if she were able to earn her own living. Realizing that her cousin is dedicated to getting and spending, so much so that he will not allow himself to marry a portionless girl, she has little difficulty interpreting his mere glance, distant and cousinly, as a rejection of her.

As a female who has loved without being asked to love, therefore, Caroline is chastized by the narrator. Spurned, she is admonished to "ask no questions; utter no remonstrances" (chap. 7). The narrator's comments are pitiless, couched in all the imagery that has developed around the opposition of food and stone, as well as the necessity of self-enclosure and self-containment for women:

> Take the matter as you find it; ask no questions; utter no remonstrances: it is your best wisdom. You expected bread, and you have got a stone; break your teeth on it, and don't shriek because the nerves are martyrised: do not doubt that your mental stomach—if you have such a thing—is strong as an ostrich's: the stone will digest. You held out your hand for an egg, and fate put into it a scorpion. Show no consternation: close your fingers firmly upon the gift; let it sting through your palm. Never mind: in time, after your hand and arm have

> swelled and quivered long with torture, the squeezed scorpion
> will die, and you will have learned the great lesson how to
> endure without a sob. For the whole remnant of your life, if
> you survive the test—some, it is said, die under it—you will
> be stronger, wiser, less sensitive. [chap. 7]

Infection is surely breeding in these sentences spoken by the voice
of repression we might associate with Nelly Dean or Zoraïde Reuter,
for the assurance that "the stone will digest" or "the squeezed
scorpion will die" is contradicted not only by the images themselves,
but also by the grotesque transubstantiation from bread to stone,
from egg to scorpion, which is prescribed as a suitable punishment
for someone "guilty" of loving. Like the ballad heroine of *Puir Mary
Lee*, Caroline can only withdraw into her imprisonment with the
ambiguous solace that comes of being hidden:

> And smoor me up in the snaw fu' fast,
>   And ne'er let the sun me see!
>
> Oh, never melt awa' thou wreath o' snaw
>   That's sae kind in graving me;   [chap. 7]

One of the damned, brought from Miltonic "Beds of raging Fire to
starve in Ice," Caroline is plagued with "pining and palsying faculties," because "Winter seemed conquering her spring; the mind's
soil and its treasures were freezing gradually to barren stagnation"
(chap. 10). Withdrawing first into her room and then, more dangerously, into herself until she begins literally to disappear from lack
of food, Caroline *Hel/stone* is obsessed with a "deep, secret, anxious
yearning to discover and know her mother" (chap. 11). But as a
motherless girl she is helpless against male rejection, and so she
follows the example set by Mary Cave: standing in shadows, shrinking
into the concealment of her own mind, she too becomes "a mere
white mould, or rigid piece of statuary" (chap. 24).

As a ghost of herself, however, Caroline has nothing left but to
attempt the rites and duties of the lady at her uncle's tea table and
Sunday school. To emphasize this fact, the first scene after Robert's
look of rejection pictures Caroline tending the jews-basket, "that
awful incubus" (chap. 7), while entertaining the community's paragons of propriety in her uncle's parlor. Wearied by such pointless

activity, tired of the lethargy caused by the tasteless rattle of the piano and the interminable gossip, Caroline retreats to a quieter room only to be caught unexpectedly in a meeting with Robert. There is something foreboding in her warning that his harshness to the mill laborers will lead to his own destruction. She wants him to know "how the people of this country bear malice: it is the boast of some of them that they can keep a stone in their pocket seven years, turn it at the end of that time, keep it seven years longer, and hurl it and hit their mark at last" (chap. 7). The man who offers stones instead of bread in return for the woman's love will receive as his punishment the rocks and stones cast by the other victims of his competitive egotism, the workers.

That Robert can offer Caroline nothing but stones becomes even clearer when we learn that he is himself "a living sepulchre" dedicated to trade (chap. 8), and that he feels as if "sealed in a rock" (chap. 9). Caroline recognizes the hardness in him that allows him to believe and act as if he and all men should be the free masters of their own and society's future. Priding himself on his own exertions, on work and self-reliance, Robert embodies the faith of English tradesmen and shopkeepers who view all activity except business as "eating the bread of idleness" (chap. 10). Given this credo, he necessarily despises women; but he also condescends to his own workers. With nothing but his own economic interests to guide him, moreover, he even opposes the continuation of a war that he knows must be fought to insure British liberty. Thus Brontë implies through him and the other manufacturers that the work ethic of self-help means selfishness and sexism, and, linking the exploitation of the workers with the unemployment of women, she further indicates that the acquisitive mentality that treats both women and workers as property is directly related to disrespect for the natural resources of the nation.

While Robert Moore is quite sure of his course of action, however —a revengeful attempt to exert control over his mill, the wares in it, his workers, and his women—Caroline must study the "knotty" problem of life (chap. 7). "Where is my place in the world?" is the question she is puzzled to solve (chap. 10). Curbing her remembrances of a romantic past, forcing herself to return to her present lonely condition, she tries to replace visions of feeding Moore berries and nuts in Nunnely Wood with a clear-sighted recognition of her own narrow chamber; instead of the songs of birds, she listens to the rain on her casement and watches her own dim shadow on the wall. Although she knows that virtue does not lie in self-abnegation, there do not seem to be other answers in her world. The bitten who survive will be stronger because less sensitive, like Miss *Mann*, the exemplary spinster Caroline visits in order to learn the secrets of old maids. But what she discovers on that occasion is a Medusa whose gaze turns men to stone, a woman to whom "a crumb is not thrown once a year"; a woman who exists "ahungered and athirst to famine" (chap. 10). And Miss Ainely, the other local spinster, manages to live more optimistically only through religious devotion and self-denial. Scorned by Robert, these lives are not attractive to Caroline either, but she nevertheless sees no other option because "All men, taken singly are more or less selfish; and taken in bodies they are intensely so" (chap. 10). With clenched hands, then, she decides to follow Miss Ainely's example: to work hard at keeping down her anguish, although she is haunted by a "funereal inward cry" (chap. 10).

Just as *Jane Eyre* is a parable about an Everywoman who must encounter and triumph over a series of allegorical, patriarchal perils, Caroline Helstone's case history provides proof that the real source of tribulation is simply the dependent status of women. Unlike Jane, however, Caroline is quite beautiful, and she is protected from penury by the generosity of her uncle, who promises an annuity to provide for her even after his death. But Jane has at least mobility, traveling from Gateshead to Lowood, from Thornfield to Marsh End, and finally to Ferndean, while Caroline never leaves Yorkshire. Caroline, in fact, would welcome what she knows to be an uncomfortable position as governess because it would at least alleviate the inertia that suffocates her. But of course such an option is rejected as improper by her "friends," so that her complete immobility finally begins to make it seem quite probable that her "mental stomach" cannot "digest the stone" nor her hand endure the scorpion's sting. Significantly, it is only at this point of total paralysis that Brontë introduces Shirley Keeldar, a heroine who serves in all ways as a contrast to Caroline.

As brilliant as Caroline is colorless, as outgoing as Caroline is retiring, Shirley is not a dependent inmate or a passive suppliant, not a housekeeper or housewife. She is a wealthy heiress who owns her own house, the ancestral mansion usually allotted to the hero, complete with old latticed windows, a stone porch, and a shadowy gallery with carved stags' heads hung on its walls. Almost always pictured (when indoors) beside a window, she enters the novel that bears her name through the glass doors of the garden. As "lord" of the manor she scorns lap dogs, romping instead with a huge mastiff reminiscent of Emily's hound Keeper. And she clearly enjoys her status as well as its ambiguous effect on her role in society:

> Business! Really the word makes me conscious I am indeed no longer a girl, but quite a woman and something more. I am an esquire! Shirley Keeldar, Esquire, ought to be my style and title. They gave me a man's name; I hold a man's position: it is enough to inspire me with a touch of manhood, and when I see such people as that stately Anglo-Belgian—that Gérard Moore before me, gravely talking to me of business, really I feel quite gentleman-like. [chap. 11]

Part of this is teasing, because Shirley is speaking to Mr. Helstone, who is unsympathetic to her independence. But the passage also reflects Brontë's recurrent and hopeless concern with transvestite behavior: Mr. Rochester dressing up as a gypsy, Shirley preening as a gallant cavalier, Lucy Snowe flirting as a fop for the hand of a coquette in a theatrical production, and Charlotte herself impersonating Charles Wellesley or William Crimsworth—all show a fascination with breaking the conventions of traditional sexual roles to experience the liberating and (especially in Victorian England) tantalizingly mysterious experiences of the other sex. When Shirley plays the captain to Caroline's modest maiden, their coy banter and testing infuses the relationship with a fine, subtle sexuality that is markedly absent from their manipulative heterosexual relationships. Yet, given that Shirley's masculine name was bestowed by

parents who had wished for a son, there is something not a little
foreboding about the fact that independence is so closely associated
with men that it confines Shirley to a kind of male mimicry.

A true Lady Bountiful, strong yet loving, Shirley is never except
playfully a male manqué. Laying out impromptu feasts in the
garden or banquets in the dining room, she owns the dairy cows
that supply the cottagers with milk and butter, and she pays exor-
bitant bills for bread, candles, and soap, although she suspects that
her housekeeper must be cheating her. Shirley manages to give
sustenance to Caroline, not only because she has meat and wine
for Moore's men or sweet cake in her reticule to throw to chickens
and sparrows, but also because she is blessed with the capacity for
delight that poetic imagination can inspire: in moments of "fulness
of happiness," Shirley's "sole book ... was the dim chronicle of
memory, or the sibyl page of anticipation ... round her lips at
moments played a smile which revealed glimpses of the tale or
prophecy" (chap. 13). To Caroline, this gift promises to save Shirley
from the grotesque dependence she herself feels upon men and their
approval, for Caroline is convinced that even extreme misery when
experienced by a poet is dissipated by the creation of literature:
Cowper and Rousseau, for instance, certainly "found relief in writing
... and that gift of poetry—the most divine bestowed on man—
was, I believe, granted to allay emotions when their strength threatens harm" (chap. 12). Such a poet does not need to be loved, "and
if there were any female Cowpers and Rousseaus, I should assert
the same of them" (chap. 12). In other words, Caroline hopes that
in Shirley she has found a woman free from the constraints which
threaten to destroy her own life.

And, certainly, the fact that Shirley emerges only when Caroline
has been completely immobilized through her own self-restraint and
submission is reminiscent of the ways in which Bertha Mason
Rochester offers a means of escape to the otherwise boxed-in Jane
Eyre. But here repression signals the emergence of a free and uninhibited self that is not criminal. That Shirley is Caroline's double,
a projection of all her repressed desire, becomes apparent in the
acts she performs "for" Caroline. What Shirley *does* is what Caroline
would like to do: Caroline's secret hatred for the curates is gratified
when Shirley angrily throws them out of her house after they are

attacked by her dog; Caroline needs to move Helstone, and Shirley bends him to her will; Caroline wishes early in the novel that she could penetrate the business secrets of men, while Shirley reads the newspapers and letters of the civic leaders; Caroline wants to lighten Robert's financial burden and Shirley secures him a loan; Caroline tries to repress her desire for Robert, while Shirley gains his attention and proposal of marriage; Caroline has always known that he needs to be taught a lesson (consider her explication of *Coriolanus*) and Shirley gives it to him in the form of a humilating rejection of his marriage proposal. Caroline wishes above all else for her long-lost mother and Shirley supplies her with just this person in the figure of Mrs. Pryor.

Paradoxically, however, for all the seeming optimism in this depiction of a double, as opposed to the earlier portrait of self-destructive and enraged Bertha, Shirley does not provide the release she first seems to promise Caroline. Instead, she herself becomes enmeshed in a social role that causes her to duplicate Caroline's immobility. For example, she gratuitously flirts, thereby inflicting pain on Caroline, who is tortured by her belief that Shirley is a successful rival for Robert Moore's love. Indeed, Shirley manages to rob Caroline of even a modicum of pleasure from Moore's presence: "Her famished heart had tasted a drop and crumb of nourishment ... but the generous feast was snatched from her, spread before another, and she remained but a bystander at the banquet" (chap. 13). Furthermore, Shirley begins to resemble Caroline in the course of the novel until she finally succumbs to Caroline's fate. And, for all her assertiveness, she is shown to be as confined by her gender, as excluded from male society, as her friend. Brontë traces the origin and nature of this imprisonment through the juxtaposition of two central episodes, the Sunday school feast and the attack on the mill.

Looking "very much like a snow-white dove and gem-tinted bird-of-paradise" (chap. 16), Caroline and Shirley head the Briarfield contingent of women and children in the Whitsuntide celebration. When, in a narrow lane in which only two can walk abreast, they confront an opposition procession of Dissenters, Shirley very accurately terms them "our doubles" (chap. 17). Since Helstone and Shirley force the Dissenters to flee, the final feast becomes more a victory celebration than a Christian rite of piety. Even if Brontë had not linked this scene to the defense of the mill, its military and national overtones would have been apparent: not only is the church an arm of the state; both church and state depend on exclusion and coercion which are economic, social, and sexual. Or so the taking of toast and tea imply, for in the midst of merriment and cheer, Shirley has to resort to the most inane feminine wiles to preserve a seat, while Caroline is silently tortured by her friend's intimacy with the man she secretly loves. Above all the imbibing, suspended in at least twenty cages, sit an incongruous flock of canaries placed there by a clerk who "knew that amidst confusion of tongues they always carolled loudest" (chap. 16). A mocking symbol of the heroines' chatter and finery, the caged birds are just as decorative and irrelevant as Caroline and Shirley, who are excluded from the plans for defense of the mill and only able to watch the historic conflict between mill owners and workers from a nearby hill. When the workers, their "doubles," break down gates and doors, hurling volleys of stones at the windows of the mill, Caroline and Shirley are divided in sympathy between owners and workers and effectively prevented from any form of participation.

To understand the workers' violent wrath at the mill in terms of the women's revenge, it is necessary to recall the meditations of Shirley and Caroline after they refuse to follow the rest of the Sunday school into the church at the close of the day and before the nighttime battle. For it is in this scene that, moved by the beauty of nature, Shirley offers Caroline the alternative to Milton's story of creation that we discussed in our consideration of "Milton's bogey." Shirley describes not the domesticated housekeeper pictured by Milton, but "a woman-Titan" who could conceive and bring forth a Messiah, an Eve who is heaven-born, yet also an Amazon mother originally called "Nature" (chap. 18). And, as we have already observed, Charlotte Brontë's portrait of her sister links Emily to a character who makes Nature her goddess. Throughout *Shirley*, Shirley's green thoughts in a green shade are "the pure gift of God to his creatures," but they are also, significantly, "the free dower of Nature to her child" (chap. 22). Finally, in fact, Shirley's capacity for joy is not unrelated to her intimate awareness of the fertility, the felicity, and the physicality of her own Titan-Eve. But this means that, for Shirley, the goddess of nature supplants the god of

spirit, as she did at times for Emily Dickinson, whose belief that
"'Nature' is what we see—/ . . . Nature is what we know" (J. 668)
resulted in her complementary feeling that "the Bible is an antique
Volume—/Written by faded Men" (J. 1545). At the same time,
however, both Brontë and Dickinson imply that the male-created
word, the book of books, is powerful enough to cause women to
"forget" both their past and their power. Although Eden is only
"a legend—dimly told—" (J. 503), it obscures the tunes women
originally heard, specifically the melodies of their own special glee,
their unfallen nature.

Just in case we have forgotten how radical a departure is Shirley's
Titan from the biblical Eve, Brontë almost immediately introduces
Moore's foreman to remind us. This censorious workman quotes
the second chapter of Saint Paul's first epistle to Timothy: "'Let
the woman learn in silence, with all subjection. . . . For Adam was
first formed, then Eve,'" and when Shirley does not receive the
lesson immediately, he continues: "'Adam was not deceived; but
the woman, being deceived, was in the transgression'" (chap. 18).
Clearly there is a confusion of tongues here, for Shirley can no
more accept this Eve than the foreman could have understood her
Titan-woman. Neither Shirley nor Caroline can really make any
headway with the man, however. Shirley is "puzzled" by the biblical
injunctions, and Caroline can only feebly resist them with the defense
that Dorothea Brooke exploits against her Milton: "if I could read the
original Greek," she speculates hopefully, ". . . It would be possible,
I doubt not, with a little ingenuity, to give the passage quite a
contrary turn" (chap. 18).

It was precisely this "ingenuity" in giving the passage "quite a
contrary turn" that Elizabeth Cady Stanton and her "Revising
Committee" attempted in the nineties in their feminist commentaries
on the word of God. Considered by more than one clergyman the
"work of women and the devil," their *Woman's Bible* begins to
confront Paul's injunctions in the epistles to Timothy by modestly
explaining that "it cannot be that Paul was inspired by infinite
wisdom in this utterance."[6] But Stanton's feminists go on to reveal
how Paul's misogyny is related to male attempts to control not only
women's speech, but their property and their persons.

Although Brontë exposes the ways in which the exploitation of

women that the Bible seems to justify perpetuates mercantile capitalism and its compulsive manipulation of human and physical
nature, her characters cannot escape the confinement of biblical
myth: haunted by Eden, Caroline wants to return to Hollow's Cottage
"as much almost as the first woman, in her exile, must have longed
to revisit Eden" (chap. 13);[7] but she and Shirley, knowing the
power of Paul's use of the story of the garden, also realize that men
imagine women as either angels of submission or monsters of aggression:

> The cleverest, the acutest men are often under an illusion about
> women: they do not read them in a true light: they misappre-
> hend them, both for good and evil: their good woman is a
> queer thing, half doll, half angel; their bad woman almost
> always a fiend. [chap. 20]

Increasingly aware that instead of inhabiting Eden they actually
live on the edge of Nunnwood with its ruins of a nunnery, Shirley
and Caroline feel that men do not read women in a true light and
that the heroines of male-authored literature are false creations.
But Shirley knows as well how subversive her critique of male
authority is, explaining to Caroline that if she were to give her
"real opinion of some [supposedly] first-rate female characters in
first-rate works," she would be "dead under a cairn of avenging
stones in half-an-hour" (chap. 20).

Shirley is also conscious that her own and other women's silent
acquiescence to such debilitating images helps foster female rage.
While planning a trip for herself, her governess, and Caroline,
Shirley describes a mermaid that she dreams of encountering in the
far reaches of the North Atlantic:

> I show you an image, fair as alabaster, emerging from the dim
> wave. We both see the long hair, the lifted and foam-white
> arm, the oval mirror brilliant as a star. It glides nearer: a
> human face is plainly visible; a face in the style of yours, whose
> straight, pure (excuse the word, it is appropriate),—whose
> straight, pure lineaments, paleness does not disfigure. It looks at
> us, but not with your eyes. I see a preternatural lure in its wily

glance: it beckons. Were we men, we should spring at the sign, the cold billow would be dared for the sake of the colder enchantress; being women, we stand safe, though not dreadless. [chap. 13]

Not merely parodying stereotypical male images of women as unnatural (but seductive) monsters, Shirley is also describing the effect such images have on women themselves. Locked into her unnatural, desexed body, the mermaid works her cold enchantment in order to destroy the men who have enslaved such pure women as Caroline and Shirley. A portrait of Gorgon-Medusas like Miss Mann, Miss Moore, and Mrs. Pryor, the mermaid is also a revisionary avatar of Sin, Eve's precursor, and a "monstrous likeness of ourselves" who exacts the revenge of nature against culture; for "the treacherous mermaid," as Dorothy Dinnerstein has shown, is the "seductive and impenetrable female representative of the dark and magic underwater world from which our life comes and in which we cannot live."[8] Unable to become a "female Cowper," since her identification with biological generativity excludes her from cultural creativity, Shirley can only envision a silent oceanic punishment for those castaways who have denied the validity or even the possibility of her self-definition.

Because she so consciously experiences herself as monstrous, deviant, excluded, powerless, and angry, Shirley sees through the coercive myths of her culture that imply and even condone inequality and exploitation. Because she understands the dehumanizing effect of patriarchal capitalism, moreover, she is the only wealthy person in the novel who "cannot forget, either day or night, that these embittered feelings of the poor against the rich have been generated in suffering" (chap. 14), for her experience of her gender as it is circumscribed by available sexual roles gives her insight into the misery of the poor. This does not mean, however, that she has a solution to the class conflict she watches with such ambivalence. Sympathizing with Moore as he defends her property, she knows that his cruelty and the workers' misery have erupted in violence she can only deplore, and although her own rather matriarchal relationship with the laborers allows for more kindness between classes, it too is fraught with potential violence, since she retains economic control over their lives and they, in their masculine pride, are angered by what they see as her unnatural authority.

Still, she alone rejects "all arraying of ranks against ranks, all party hatreds, all tyrannies disguised as liberties" (chap. 21). But her revolt against patriarchal injustice only causes her neighbor, Hiram Yorke, to try to deflate her political ardor by defining it as amorous passion in disguise. Shirley's proud self-defense baffles him since he feels that he cannot read the untranslatable language of her look, which seems to him to be a "fervid lyric in an unknown tongue" (chap. 21). It is during this most interesting impasse that we learn a fact never developed in the novel but highly suggestive: Shirley's father's name was Charles *Cave* Keeldar. Mary Cave, symbol of female protest through suicide, is one of Shirley's ancestors and yet another link with Caroline.

Although Shirley lives a pastoral life of freedom reminiscent of the mythic existence of her own Titan-woman, there *is* something untranslatable not only about her fervid lyrics but about all her gestures and talk. Whether she is the courtly gentleman, the courageous captain, the coy coquette, the Lady Bountiful, the little lady, or the touched bard, Shirley seems condemned to play the roles she parodies. That she is continuously hampered in this way makes less surprising her mysterious decision to invite the Sympson family, with its "pattern young ladies, in pattern attire, with pattern deportment" (chap. 22), into her home. Although neither Caroline nor the reader yet realizes that she is using the Sympsons to obtain the presence of their tutor and her lover, Louis Moore, his appearance is one more step in Shirley's subjugation. When Shirley keeps secret her wiles to gain the presence of a suitor, her lack of freedom affects Caroline's further decline.

Not merely lovesick, Caroline is profoundly discontent, her illness the result of her misery at what she terms her own impotence. Her mentor Mrs. Pryor has already assured her that neither the married state nor a job as governess would offer relief from tedium and loneliness. Into the mouths of the wonderfully named Hardman family (who employed Mrs. Pryor when she was the governess Miss

Grey) are placed all the criticisms leveled against Charlotte Brontë
by the reviewers of *Jane Eyre*. But Miss Grey's story of her governess
days also recalls Anne Brontë's *Agnes Grey*, as if Charlotte needed to
deflate the romantic happy ending envisioned there. In the name
of Christian resignation, Miss Hardman tells Miss Grey what Miss
Rigby had said of Jane Eyre and what Agnes Grey's employers told
her: "You are proud, and therefore you are ungrateful too" (chap.
21). And Mrs. Hardman warns Miss Grey to quell her ungodly
discontent because it can only lead to death in a lunatic asylum
(chap. 21). Both Caroline and Mrs. Pryor agree that this is the
religious faith of an elitist and exploitative pharisee. Yet Caroline
seems to have no alternative except to sit resignedly "still as a
garden statue" (chap. 22). Perceiving the unmarried women she
knows as nuns trapped in close cells, robes straight as shrouds, beds
narrow as coffins, Caroline is repelled by a society that demands
that "old maids, like the houseless and unemployed poor, should
not ask for a place and an occupation in the world" (chap. 22).
It is the "narrowness" of the woman's lot that makes her ill and
causes her to scheme in the "matrimonial market" where she is as
much a commodity as the workers are in the mercantile market.
But Caroline's thoughts about the woman question conclude pitifully, with an impassioned plea directed, of course, to the "Men
of England!" It is they who keep female minds "fettered," and
presumably it is only they who have the power to unlock the chains.

Directly after this outburst, almost as if her own anger is taken
up and expressed in another's voice, Caroline is verbally attacked
by Rose Yorke. Using language that exploits all the imagery of
imprisonment in a context that illustrates how the woman's domestic
lot enlists her as a jailor of herself, Rose proclaims her refusal to
live "a black trance like the toad's buried in marble," for she will
not be "for ever shut up" in a house that reminds her of a "windowed
grave" (chap. 23):

> "And if my Master has given me ten talents, my duty is to
> trade with them, and make them ten talents more. Not in the
> dust of household drawers shall the coin be interred. I will *not*
> deposit it in a broken-spouted tea-pot, and shut it up in a china-
> closet among tea-things. I will *not* commit it to your work-table

to be smothered in piles of woollen hose. I will *not* prison it in the linen press to find shrouds among the sheets; and least of all, mother"—(she got up from the floor)—"least of all will I hide it in a tureen of cold potatoes, to be ranged with bread, butter, pastry, and ham on the shelves of the larder." [chap. 23]

The pun on the word *talent* is a functional one since Rose's point is precisely the connection between the financial dependence of women and the destruction of their creative potential: each and every one of the housekeeper's drawers, chests, boxes, closets, pots, and bags represents the very skill that insures suicidal "feminine" service, self-burial, and silence.

A model "lady" (chap. 9), Caroline Helstone has buried her talents, so she is consumed in the same "well-lit fire" that destroyed Helen Burns, and, as Helen did, she seems to fade away "like any snow-wreath in thaw" (chap. 21). Consumed by sorrow, she cannot eat, reminding us again of the prominence of anorexia nervosa as a female dis-ease and as a theme in women's literature: Caroline has received stones instead of bread, and she has been deprived of maternal care and nourishment, so she denies herself the traditional symbol of that love. But of course, like so many other girls suffering from this disease (all of whose case histories reveal a paralyzing feeling of ineffectiveness), Caroline has good reason to believe that the only control she can exert is over her own body, since she is completely ineffectual at altering her intolerable lot in the world. Like other anorexics, she has been rewarded only for her compliant attractiveness and "feminine" docility, so her self-starvation is, ironically, an acceptance of the ideal of self-denial. And she has also experienced male rejection, which has obviously contributed to a debilitating sense of her own low worth.[9] For Caroline is ashamed at Robert's rejection, not angry or sorry, and her sense of inadequacy becomes therefore a justification for self-punishment, as the initial admonishment to endure meals of stone and the scorpion's sting illustrated.

Caroline's self-starvation is even more symbolically complex than these parallels with contemporary anorexics suggest, however. Earlier in the novel, as we have seen, Brontë carefully associated food with the voracious curates, the Sunday school feast, Mr. Helstone's tea table, and Shirley's supplies for the mill owners. In some ways, then, Caroline's rejection of food is a response not only to these characters but also to their definitions of communion and redemption. Shirley has already attacked the Christian version of Genesis. But now it becomes clearer how that myth of origins, in which a woman is condemned for eating, reflects male hatred of the female and fear of her sustaining or strengthening herself. Caroline has internalized the injunction not to eat, not to speak, and not to be first. And Brontë's portrayal of her self-inflicted torture is strikingly similar to Elizabeth Barrett Browning's dramatization of the guilt of Eve, who asks Adam in "A Drama of Exile" to "put me straight away, / Together with my name! Sweet, punish me!" Admitting that "*I*, also, after tempting, writhe on the ground, / And I would feed on ashes from thine hand," Barrett Browning's Eve resembles Caroline, who also accepts the necessity for feeding on ashes because, like Eve, she feels "twice fallen . . . From joy of place, and also right of wail, / 'I wail' being not for me—only 'I sin.'" [10] In other words, Caroline's silent slow suicide implies all the ways in which she has been victimized by male myths.

On the other hand, like Catherine Earnshaw Linton, Caroline Helstone is also using her hunger strike as a kind of protest. Catherine had rejected her "confinement" as a woman, and her refusal to eat was, we saw, partially a rejection of pregnancy. But anorexia nervosa even more frequently occurs in virgins, and it can be viewed as a protest against growing up female, since self-starvation returns such girls to the physical state of small children, just as it interrupts the menstrual cycle which has been defined for them as a "curse." Finally, Caroline's self-starvation is also a rejection of what her society has defined as nourishing. As an act of revolt, like that of the lady in *Castle Rackrent*, fasting is a refusal to feed on foreign foods. Since eating maintains the self, in a discredited world it is a compromise implying acquiescence. Women will starve in silence, Brontë seems to imply, until new stories are created that confer upon them the power of naming themselves and controlling their world. Caroline's fasting criticizes female providing and male feasting, even as it implies that a Father whose love must be earned by well-invested talents is not worth having.

And so, meaningfully, it is at this point that she begins to question the existence of the other world and the purpose of this one. As Dickinson observed, the precious "Word made Flesh" is often only "tremblingly partook" by women, it seems, since they are far from certain that it is suited "To our specific strength—" (J. 1651). Like Shirley's, Brontë's style becomes more rhapsodic and fervid, more exotic, as her writing progresses and she seeks to create a new word, a new genre for her sex. In *Shirley* as in *Jane Eyre* one heroine silently starves while the other raves. Both are involved in a militant rejection of the old myths and the degrading roles they provide. But unlike *Jane Eyre*, *Shirley* is very consciously an attack on the religion of the patriarchs. Caroline, in her illness, searches for faith in God the Father. She finds instead the encircling arms of her mother.

Mrs. Pryor is a suitable mother. Aloof and withdrawn in public, she has survived the test of "a man-tiger" (chap. 25) whose gentlemanly soft speech hid private "discords that split the nerves and curdled the blood—sounds to inspire insanity" (chap. 24). Formal and reticent, she is the prior woman, prior to Shirley as well as Caroline, because her experience, not the woman-Titan's, is typically female in the society these young women inhabit. Like most girls, Caroline and Shirley will grow into womanhood through marriage, which, Mrs. Pryor warns, is a horrible, shattering experience; although she never details the terror of male potency, it seems all the more dreadful here for remaining so mysterious. Her pain in marriage and eventual flight from it, moreover, are central to the initial split between Caroline and Shirley, the split between suicidal "feminine" passivity and "masculine" self-assertion. Mrs. Pryor has in some sense perpetuated this dichotomy, even as she herself exemplifies it, because her dread of her husband has caused her to reject his daughter, but Caroline is also her daughter and part of herself. Thus Mrs. Pryor contributes to Caroline's passivity because she has withheld from her daughter the love that allows for a strong sense of self. Further, by experiencing men as evil, by seeing herself as a victim who can only submit to male degradation or flee from it, she defines the woman's role as a tragic one. Finally, Shirley's surrogate mother and Caroline's biological mother, she proves that the heroines are similarly circumscribed. At this point, therefore, both heroines—now sisters—are wooed by the brothers Moore, and it seems clear that their initiation into their own sexuality is bound to be humiliating.

After the emergence of Mrs. Pryor, Shirley increasingly shows herself to be as reticent and discreet as that severe lady could have wished. Not only does Shirley refrain from communicating to Caroline her suspicions about Mrs. Pryor's real identity, she is quite secretive about the existence of Caroline's cousin Louis Moore. When Louis does finally appear, Shirley persists in treating him with cold formality, and her reserve reaches its heights when she is bitten by a dog she believes to be mad. Caroline was admonished to show no consternation over the figurative bite of the scorpion, but it is Shirley who fully epitomizes the horror of self-repression when she actually remains silent about her fears of hydrophobia and begins to waste away from sheer anxiety. The cauterized wound is only the outward mark of her pain at this fall which is so similar to the dog bite that initiates Catherine Earnshaw into the prison of gender. For even as she becomes more reserved, Shirley also grows docile in the schoolroom with her old tutor. When she tries to study French, she actually finds "lively excitement in the pleasure of making his language her own" (chap. 27). Returning her, as one chapter title puts it, to "Old Copy-Books," Shirley's fate also recalls Frances Henri's destiny. Gifted as she is with extraordinary visions, Shirley represents one more attempt on Brontë's part to come to terms with the silences of even the most inspired women.

If Shirley, a romantic visionary, had had "a little more of the organ of acquisitiveness in her head—a little more of the love of property in her nature" (chap. 22), the narrator speculates, she might have taken pen to paper. Instead, she will "die without knowing the full value of that spring whose bright fresh bubbling in her heart keeps it green" (chap. 22). Without an adequate language at her disposal, Shirley never experiences "the strong pulse of Ambition." For "Nature is what we know—/Yet have no art to say—," as Dickinson explains, "So impotent Our Wisdom is/To her Simplicity" (J. 668). But Shirley also seems hampered because, like Elizabeth Barrett's Eve, she is afraid to speak again, having spoken "once to such a bitter end."[11] Shirley's final return to the rhetoric of the classroom only confirms and completes her fall. But Brontë does not, as some critics suggest, condone Shirley's submission; instead, she repeatedly calls attention to her buried talents. The Titan-woman has been subdued, and by no one less than the first man. "With animals," Louis declares proudly, "I feel I am Adam's son: the heir of him to whom dominion was given over 'every living thing that moveth upon the earth'" (chap. 26).

As we observed in our discussion of "Milton's bogey," Shirley's old devoir, an essay entitled "La Premiere Femme Savante," differs drastically from her previous descriptions to Caroline of a Promethean Titan-woman since this alternative myth countenances female submission. Here in Shirley's homework for her teacher we find a hungry, cold orphan girl who is first fostered by the earth but who ultimately responds to a male master, called Genius, who finally takes his dying bride into "his home—Heaven," where he "restored her, redeemed, to Jehovah—her Maker" (chap. 27). While Shirley presumably begins by celebrating a sexual union in which the female is infused with the godly power of creativity, she ends up telling what we saw was the embedded myth of *Wuthering Heights*: how the child of physical maternal Nature is seduced or abducted into the Father's deathly realm of spirit. As well as providing a sensitive appreciation of Emily's art, Charlotte's elegy for her sister mourns the diminishment she feels at Emily's absence, even as it pays tribute to Emily's triumphant resistance against the forces that finally seduce Shirley, as they had Catherine Earnshaw before her.

Like Brontë herself, then, Shirley begins with a new story, a female myth of origin; but she too finds herself repeating an old tale of "Eve—and the Anguish—Grandame's story," even as she tries to remember her own melody: "But—I was telling a tune—I heard—" (J. 503). For although Brontë had begun this novel with what seemed like a radical intent, she capitulates to convention. Brontë undercuts traditional expectations by presenting a fair, pale heroine full of rage at the men of England and a dark, romantic woman who is self-contained and silent about her true feelings, but she also seems to describe how Shirley and Louis Moore reverse novelistic conventions. Indeed, these lovers at first seem to reverse the types exploited in *Jane Eyre*: just as Shirley possesses all the accoutrements of the aristocratic hero, Louis Moore—like the young clerk William Crimsworth—is the male counterpart of a governess. A private tutor who is invisible and hungry (chap. 36), he feels his faculties and emotions are pent in, walled up (chap. 26), and in his locked desk he keeps a journal to record a hopeless passion which at one point causes him to fall ill of a fever. He himself refers to this exchange of traditional roles when he remembers "the fable of Semele reversed" (chap. 29). Yet, despite this apparent role reversal, Louis loves Shirley because she requires his mastery, his advice, and his checking. As an older and wiser teacher, he values the perfect lady in her, as well as her need to be curbed. By the end of the novel, therefore, Shirley is a "bondswoman" in the hands of "a hero and a patriarch" (chap. 35).

It looks as if Brontë began *Shirley* with the intention of subverting not only the sexual images of literature but the courtship roles and myths from which they derive. But she could find no models for this kind of fiction; as she explains in her use of the Genesis myth, the stories of her culture actively endorse traditional sexual roles, even as they discourage female authority. In spite of all the rationales Brontë provides, therefore, the absence and inactivity of her heroes seem contrived, just as the problems faced by her heroines seem unrelated to the particular historical framework in which they are set, in spite of the fact that at least one of her major statements in *Shirley* concerns the tragic consequences of the inability of women to shape the public history that necessarily affects their own lives. The tension between Brontë's personal allegiances and the dictates of literary conventions is especially evident when she seeks to write a story of female strength and survival. She has herself explained to the reader in the course of the novel why the only "happy ending" for women in her society is marriage. She gives us that ending, but, like Jane Austen, she never allows us to forget that marriage is a suspect institution based on female subordination, and that women who are not novel heroines probably do not fare even as well as Caroline and Shirley.

More specifically, having recognized that inherited generic conventions assign characters a degree of freedom that contradicts her own sense of the female condition, Brontë can only call attention to this disjunction by describing remarkably improbable escape routes for her heroines. At least part of what makes the ending of *Shirley* seem so unreal is the way in which the plot metes out proper rewards and punishments to all the characters with an almost cynical excess of concession to narrative conventions. Robert Moore, for instance, has erred both in his cruelty to the workers and in his mercenary proposal of marriage to Shirley, so he is shot down "like some wild beast from behind a wall" (chap. 31) by a half-crazed weaver. Robert has made himself into a business machine so he must be taught the limits of self-reliance, the need for charity. Imprisoned at Briarmains, the Yorkes' home, he finds himself at the mercy of a female monster; locked up in an upstairs bedroom, he is taught docility by the terrible Mrs. Horsfalls. Robert's indifference has made Caroline ill; he now wastes away at the hands of a woman who is said to starve him.

The entire episode recalls childhood fantasies and fears that are further emphasized by the introduction of Martin Yorke, a young boy who is enthralled by a contraband volume of fairy tales. An adolescent misogynist, Martin seems endowed with puckish powers since he is able to cast the entire household under a spell, and thereby make possible Caroline's trip upstairs to awaken the sleeping invalid of *Briar*/mains. It is because he is still only a boy that Martin has the sympathy and the imagination to help the lovers. But as a sort of parody of the author, he is corrupt enough to enjoy controlling them with his fictions by viewing them as characters in a romance of his own making. Robert manages to evade Mrs. Horsfalls and Martin only by returning to Caroline, his sister Hortense, and the house he now recognizes for the first time as a home. But by returning to the fairy tale motifs of *Jane Eyre* in this new historically defined context, Brontë marks the redemptive education of the manufacturer as mere wish-fulfillment.

Shirley's path to happiness is no less amazing than Caroline's. Just as Caroline employs Martin, Shirley uses poetic Henry Sympson's admiration to enchant Louis. She rejects three marriage proposals of increasing material advantage, until Louis seems finally transformed from an ugly old duck into a youngish swain. In a set-piece of passion, Shirley rebukes her wicked stepfather Mr. Sympson, who cannot understand why she has rejected all her suitors and questions whether she is really "a young lady." Defiantly she claims to be something a thousand times better—"an honest woman" (chap. 31)—and with the forces of propriety so easily silenced, the time is obviously ripe for union. Presumably Louis's age and intelligence balance off Shirley's wealth and beauty: their only remaining problem is determining who shall speak first. The fact that Louis is the one to break the silence is one more sign of his mastery. "As cool as stone" (chap. 36) even when angry, Louis looks like "a great sand-buried stone head" (chap. 36) of an Egyptian god. By Shirley's own admission he is her "keeper," and she has become a "Pantheress" so that he, the first man, must prove his dominion over her as "She gnaws at the chain" (chap. 36). At the very end of the novel, Brontë qualifies her emphasis on Shirley's submission by quoting her claim that she "acted on system," since Louis "would never have learned to rule, if she had not ceased to govern" (chap. 37). But, whether tactical or obsessive, her submission is the complete and necessary prelude to their marriage.

Brontë calls attention to the ridiculous fantasy that is the novel's end by entitling her final chapter "The Winding-Up." As if that were not enough to qualify the happy ending, she ties up loose ends and proclaims, "I think the varnish has been put on very nicely" (chap. 37). With Shirley on the brink of marriage, it is no surprise that Robert Moore starts perceiving Caroline's resemblance to the Virgin Mary, although for those readers who remember Mary Cave the echo is ominous. Brontë is careful to develop the imagery she has established from the beginning of the novel, most especially the connection between stones and male lovelessness. The scene of the marriage proposal is set near a wall, next to the fragment of a sculptured stone, perhaps the base of a cross, a fitting symbol in this novel of female dispossession. Characteristically, Robert asks, "Is Caroline mine?" He wonders if she can care for him, "as if that rose should promise to shelter from tempest this hard, grey stone" (chap. 37). Still unable to love anyone except himself, he pictures Caroline as the perfect Sunday school mistress for the cottagers he will employ at his expanded mill.

And Robert's is the spirit of the nineteenth century, that "Titan-boy" who "hurls rocks in his wild sport" (chap. 37). The salvation of England has been effected by a similar "demigod," named Wellington. But Brontë implies that the final victory and vision are Robert's. He describes how the "green natural terrace shall be a paved street: there will be cottages in the dark ravine, and cottages on the lonely slopes: the rough pebbled track shall be an even, firm, broad, black, sooty road" (chap. 37). The future has been won by and for men and their industrial patriarchy. The narrator confirms the truth of the prophecy, returning to the Hollow to describe the stones and bricks, the mill as ambitious as a tower of Babel. "His" account ends with a conversation with "his" housekeeper whose mother "had seen a fairish (fairy) in Fieldhead Hollow; and that was the last fairish that ever was seen on this country side" (chap. 37). The absence of fairies, like the repudiation of the fairy tale at the end of this novel, implies that the myth of Mother/Nature has been betrayed in mercantile, postlapsarian England. Happy endings, Brontë suggests, will not be quite so easily arranged in this fallen world, for history replaces mere romance in a world of stony facts.

12 The Buried Life of Lucy Snowe

My very chains and I grew friends,
So much a long communion tends
To make us what we are. . . .
      —Lord Byron

The prisoner in solitary confinement, the toad in the block of
marble, all in time shape themselves to their lot.
      —Charlotte Brontë

One need not be a Chamber—to be Haunted—
One need not be a House—
The Brain has Corridors—surpassing
Material Place—
      —Emily Dickinson

The cage of myself clamps shut.
My words turn the lock
. . . .
I am the lackey who "follows orders."
I have not got the authority.
      —Erica Jong

Villette is in many ways Charlotte Brontë's most overtly and despairingly feminist novel. *The Professor* and *Shirley*, as we have seen, at least pretended to have other intentions, disguising their powerful preoccupations with the anxieties of femaleness behind cool, pseudomasculine façades; and *Jane Eyre*, though rebelliously feminist in its implications, used a sort of fairy tale structure to enable the novelist to conceal even from herself her deepening pessimism about woman's place in man's society. But Lucy Snowe, *Villette's* protagonist-

399

narrator, older and wiser than any of Brontë's other heroines, is from first to last a woman *without*—outside society, without parents or friends, without physical or mental attractions, without money or confidence or health—and her story is perhaps the most moving and terrifying account of female deprivation ever written.

Silent, invisible, at best an inoffensive shadow, Lucy Snowe has no patrimony and no expectations, great or little. Even her creator appears to find her "morbid and weak,"[1] frigid, spiritless: some "subtlety of thought made me decide upon giving her a cold name," she told her publisher.[2] A progressive deterioration in spirit and exuberance from Frances Henri and Jane Eyre, who demand equality and life, to Caroline Helstone, who rarely voices her protest, is completed by Lucy's submission and silence, as if Charlotte Brontë equates maturity with an aging process that brings women only a stifling sense of despair. Indeed the movement of the novels suggests that escape becomes increasingly difficult as women internalize the destructive strictures of patriarchy. Locked into herself, defeated from the start, Lucy Snowe is tormented by the realization that she has bought survival at the price of never fully existing, escaped pain by retreating behind a dull, grave camouflage. Haunted by the persons she might have been, she has been dispossessed not only of meanings and goals, but also of her own identity and power. How can she escape the person she has become?

Villette is of course the last of a series of the writer's fictional attempts to come to terms with her own loveless existence, and specifically with her sorrow at the loss of M. Héger's friendship. Her love for this Brussels schoolteacher ended first in a kind of solitary confinement imposed on Brontë by his wife, and finally in his refusal to respond to Brontë's letters from England. One of her earliest and most plainly autobiographical poems, "Frances," describes not only the desolation that Frances Henri experiences in *The Professor* but Brontë's own profound feelings of exclusion. The heroine's life is a kind of living death:

> For me the universe is dumb,
>   Stone-deaf, and blank, and wholly blind;
> Life I must bound, existence sum
>   In the strait limits of one mind;

> That mind my own. Oh! narrow cell;
>   Dark—imageless—a living tomb!
> There must I sleep, there wake and dwell
>   Content,—with palsy, pain, and gloom.[3]

Lucy Snowe, like Frances in the poem and also, to some extent, like Frances Henri before her marriage, is bound by the limits of her own mind—a dark and narrow cell. Living inside this tomb, she discovers that it is anything but imageless; it is a chamber of terrible visions, not the least of which is that of being buried alive.

That Matthew Arnold, responding to Brontë's hunger, rebellion, and rage, found all this eminently disagreeable is understandable, although—perhaps *because*—the year before the publication of *Villette*, he wrote a poem very much about Lucy's dilemma. "The Buried Life" laments the falseness of an existence divorced from the hidden self. Like Lucy, Arnold knows that many conceal their true feelings for fear they will be met with indifference. Both Arnold and Lucy describe the discrepancy between a dumb, blank life and the hidden, passionate center of being. But the difference between the two views is instructive. For while Lucy's repression is a response to a society cruelly indifferent to women, Arnold claims that the genuine self is buried in all people. Perhaps this explains why the anguished horror of Lucy's experience is absent from Arnold's poem. His is a metaphysical elegy, hers an obsessively personal one. Lucy feels herself confined to a prison cell, while Arnold describes an active life in the world even if it is a life cut off from the forceful river that is the true self. Again, where Lucy rebels against confinement, Arnold philosophically claims that perhaps all is for the best. Fate, he implies, has decreed that the true self be buried so that it cannot be subverted by the conscious will, and thus, he suggests, nature is working benevolently for all.

Arnold is articulating the vague and ultimately optimistic *Weltschmerz* so popular in early and mid-nineteenth-century poetry. Like Byron, Shelley, and Wordsworth, he laments his distance from "the soul's subterranean depth," while holding out the possibility that there are times when "what we mean, we say, and what we would, we know."[4] But as a woman Brontë cannot fully participate in the Romantic conventions of what amounted by her time to a fully developed literary tradition. The male Romantics, having moved independently in society, condemned the trivial world of getting and spending, while Brontë's exclusion from social and economic life precluded her free rejection of it. On the contrary, many of her female characters yearn to enter the competitive market-place reviled by the poets. Thus, where the male Romantics glorified the "buried life" to an ontology, Brontë explores the mundane facts of homelessness, poverty, physical unattractiveness, and sexual dis-crimination or stereotyping that impose self-burial on women. While male poets like Arnold express their desire to experience an inner and more valid self, Brontë describes the pain of women who are restricted to just this private realm. Instead of seeking and celebrating the buried self, these women feel victimized by it; they long, instead, for actualization in the world.

By focusing on a female subject, too, Brontë implicitly criticizes the way in which her male counterparts have found solace for their spiritual yearnings in the limpid look and the tender touch. In "The Buried Life," as in many of his other poems, Arnold implores his female listener to turn her eyes on his so he can read her inmost soul. But the skeptical female reader knows Arnold will see there his own reflection.[5] Thus, confronting and rejecting the egotistical sublime, Brontë questions the tradition Arnold inherits from Words-worth, for both poets seek escape from the dreary intercourse of daily life through the intercession of a girl, image and source of the poets' faith. Brontë's aversion to such a solution explains the numerous echoes in *Villette* of Wordsworth's "Lucy Gray" and of his "Lucy" poems. Living hidden among untrodden ways, wandering alone on a snowy moonlit moor, disappearing in the wild storm, both Lucy and Lucy Gray had functioned for the poet much as his sister did in "Tintern Abbey," as emblems of the calm and peace that nature brings. Here and elsewhere in her fiction, however, Brontë reinter-prets the little-girl-lost story in order to redefine the myth from the lost girl's point of view.

Lucy Snowe is thus in important ways a parody of Lucy or Lucy Gray. Far from being nature's favorite, she seems to be one of those chosen for adversity. Instead of being blessed because she is, as Wordsworth says, "a thing that could not feel,"[6] she is damned: apparently nature *can* betray even those who love her. For in this, her last novel, Brontë explores not the redemptive but the destructive effect of the buried life on women who can neither escape by retreating into the self (since such a retreat is rejected as solipsistic) nor find a solution by dehumanizing the other into a spiritual object. Still, even if there can be no joyous celebration, not even abundant recompense, at least Brontë provides in *Villette* an honest elegy for all those women who cannot find ways out and are robbed of their will to live. At the same time, *Villette* is also the story of the writer's way out. Implying that the female artist is as confined by male conventions as her characters are imprisoned in the institutions of a patriarchal society, Brontë considers the inadequacy of male culture in her search for a female language; her rejection of male-devised arts contributes to her extraordinary depiction of the potential dangers of the imagination for women.

From the very first sentence of *Villette*, which describes the handsome house of Lucy's godmother, it is clear that Brontë has once again created a heroine who is caught in an anomalous family position. The symbolically named Bretton house is the first of a series of female-owned and operated dwellings, an important sign that in some ways Lucy's confinement is self-administered. This is immediately substantiated by her guarded demeanor: even as she journeys from Mrs. Bretton's to Miss Marchmont's house and then to Madame Beck's school, Lucy remains taciturn and withdrawn. Yet, paradoxically, if she is more submissive than her predecessors, she is also more rebellious, refusing to be a governess because her "dimness and depression must both be voluntary."[7] Modern critics of *Villette* recognize the conflict between restraint and passion, reason and imagination within her. But its full significance depends on the ways in which the other characters in the novel are used to objectify what amounts to this protagonist's schizophrenia,[8] for Lucy Snowe exemplifies the truth of Emily Dickinson's "One need not be a Chamber—to be Haunted—" (J. 670).

Instead of participating in the life of the Brettons, Lucy watches it. The appearance of another child-visitor emphasizes her ironic detachment. Not only does Lucy feel contemptuous of six-year-old Polly's need for love and male protection—her dependence first

on her father and then her enthralled attraction to Graham Bretton,
an older boy incapable of returning her love—she ridicules Polly's
fanatic responses and doll-like gestures, and satirizes Polly's refusal
to eat, as well as her need to serve food to her father or his surrogate.
Above such demonstrative displays herself, she proclaims her
superiority: "I, Lucy Snowe, was calm" (chap. 3). While Polly
nestles under her father's cloak or Graham's arms for protection,
Lucy sneers at the girl who must "live, move and have her being in
another" (chap. 3). Yet though Lucy seems determined not to exist
in another's existence, we soon notice that her voyeuristic detachment defines her in terms of others as inexorably as Polly's parasitic
attachments define the younger girl.

Lucy's passive calm contrasts with Polly's passionate intensity;
her withdrawal with Polly's playfulness. But, as is so often the case
in Brontë's fiction, these two antithetical figures have much in
common. Diligent and womanly beyond their years, neat in their
ways, and self-controlled in their verbal expression of emotion, both
are visitors in the Bretton house, inhabiting the same chamber. That
they are intimately connected becomes obvious when Lucy wants
Polly to cry out at a moment of great joy so that she, Lucy, can get
some relief (chap. 2). For, strangely, Lucy has discovered in Polly
a representative of part of herself who "haunts" her (chap. 2) like
"a small ghost" (chap. 3). Finally she takes this ghost into her own
bed to comfort her when she feels bereaved, wondering about the
child's destiny, which, significantly, she imagines in terms of the
humiliations and desolations that are prepared for her *own* life. As
Q. D. Leavis suggests, Polly acts out all those impulses already
repressed by Lucy[9] so that the two girls represent the two sides of
Lucy's divided self, and they are the first of a series of such representative antagonists.

Their fates will be in some ways comparable. As if to stress this,
Polly shows Lucy a book about distant countries which functions
structurally—much like the book of Bewick prints introduced at
the beginning of *Jane Eyre*, or *Coriolanus* in *Shirley*—to hint at future
dangers. As Polly describes the desolate places, the good English
missionary, the Chinese lady's bound foot, and the land of ice and
snow, Lucy listens intently, because these are the trials that await
those split, as she is, between passive acceptance of a limited lot

and rebellious desire for a full life. The book foretells the exile both girls will eventually experience, complete with a godlike healer, specifically foreign forms of repression, and the cold that always endangers female survival. Lucy will have to seek her identity on foreign soil because she is metaphorically a foreigner even in England. Homeless, she is a woman without a country or a community, or so her subsequent status as an immigrant would seem to suggest.

On another level, moreover, Lucy's dilemma is internal, and Brontë dramatizes it again when the girl enters yet another English-woman's house. The elderly invalid Miss Marchmont, a woman whose self-imposed confinement defines the tragic causes and consequences of withdrawal, serves as a monitory image. At the same time, though, alone and in mourning for her lost family, hollow-eyed Lucy already resembles her mistress, a rheumatic cripple confined within two upstairs rooms where she waits for death as a release from pain. Because Lucy prizes the morsel of affection she receives, she is almost content to subsist on an invalid's diet, almost content to *be* Miss Marchmont. Unlike Pip in *Great Expectations*, who would never consider becoming Miss Havisham (even though he pities her the living death caused by the cruel Compeyson), but very much like Anne Elliot, who identifies with the paralyzed Mrs. Smith, Lucy is acquiescent because willing "to escape occasional great agonies by submitting to a whole life of privation and small pains" (chap. 4). Her employer's self-confinement, moreover, is also a response to great pain. Miss Marchmont tells Lucy how, thirty years earlier, on a moonlit Christmas Eve, she watched by the lattice, anxiously awaiting her lover's approaching gallop, and unable to speak when she saw his dead body—"that thing in the moonlight" (chap. 4). Just as Lucy's detachment is a self-sustaining response to the pain endured by the vulnerable Polly, Miss Marchmont has based a life of privation and seclusion on the disappointment of her desire when she saw her lover's corpse in the moonlight.

Nevertheless, even while her predicament implies that self-incarceration is potentially every woman's fate, Miss Marchmont's life-story reverses one of Wordsworth's "Lucy" poems. In "Strange Fits of Passion Have I Known," the speaker, a horseman, gallops under the evening moon to his lover's cot, besieged by the wayward thought that she is dead. Brontë, however, approaches the event from the stationary and enclosed perspective of the waiting woman, whose worst fears are always substantiated. An emblem of the fatality of love, Miss Marchmont lives in confinement, a perpetual virgin dedicated to the memory of the lover she lost on Christmas Eve. She is in effect a nun, but a nun who receives no religious consolation, since she can neither understand nor condone the ways of God. Love, she says, has brought her pain that would have refined an amiable nature to saintliness and turned daemonic an evil spirit (chap. 4). Whether transformed into a nun or a witch, her story suggests, the woman who allows herself to experience love is betrayed and destroyed, for once her best self is buried with her love, she is condemned to endure, alone, in the tomblike cell that is her mind.

What some critics have termed the inflated diction of the Miss Marchmont section[10] is reinforced by the details Brontë uses to depict Lucy's progress on a mythic pilgrimage. It is, ironically, the icy aurora borealis that brings Lucy the energy, after she is released by Miss Marchmont's death, to "Leave this wilderness" (chap. 5). With her desolation rising before her "like a ghost" (chap. 5), Lucy possesses nothing except loathing of her past existence. The watermen fighting over her fare, the black river, the ship named *The Vivid*, the destination Boue-Marine ("ocean mud"), her remembrance of the Styx and of Charon rowing souls to the land of shades —all reflect her anxiety that the trip will end disastrously, even as they mythologize this voyage out through the unconscious toward selfhood. And it is only with this mythic sense of her quest that we can understand the almost surreal details of her arrival in *La/basse/cour*—the canals creeping like half-torpid snakes, the gray and stagnant sky, the single trustworthy Englishman who guides her part of the way through the little city (*Villette*), and the two lecherous men who pursue her, driving her deep into the old, narrow streets. Different as this foreign journey seems to be from Jane Eyre's English pilgrimage, it suggests a similar point about women's disenfranchisement from culture. Also like Jane Eyre, Lucy represents all women who must struggle toward an integrated, mature, and independent identity by coming to terms with their need for love, and their dread of being single, and so, like Jane, Lucy will confront the necessity of breaking through the debilitating roles available to the single women the Victorians termed "redundant."

It is ironic, then, that Harriet Martineau criticized *Villette* on the grounds that the characters think of nothing but love,[11] for that is precisely Brontë's point. Onboard *The Vivid*, Lucy is confronted with several women who are caught in this central female dilemma —a bride (with a husband who looks like an oil-barrel) whose laughter, Lucy decides, must be the frenzy of despair; Ginevra Fanshawe, a frivolous schoolgirl on her way to Villette, who explains that she is one of five sisters who must marry elderly gentlemen with cash; and one Charlotte, the subject of the stewardess's letter, who seems to be on the brink of perpetrating an imprudent match. Although marriage seems no less painful a submission than a life of lonely isolation, Lucy exults on deck, thinking, "Stone walls do not a prison make, / Nor iron bars—a cage." [12] Yet, as always, her moment of triumph is immediately undercut. She too gets ill and must go below like the rest, and the verse remains ambiguous, since the mind which can liberate the caged prisoner can also provide walls and bars for those who are physically free.

On her arrival in Labassecour Lucy is stripped of even the few objects and attributes she possesses. Her keys, her trunk, her money, and her language are equally useless. A stranger in a strange land, she becomes aware that her physical situation reflects her psychic state. With no destination in mind, she catches "at cobwebs," specifically at Ginevra's comment that her schoolmistress wants an English governess. "Accidentally" finding Madame Beck's establishment, she waits inside the salon with her eyes fixed on "a great white folding-door, with gilt mouldings" (chap. 7). It remains closed, but a voice at her elbow unexpectedly begins a symbolic questioning, so that Lucy must assure herself and her reader that "No ghost stood beside me, nor anything of spectral aspect" (chap. 7). But this is not entirely true. The landscape of her passage, as well as its fortuitous end, makes it seem as if Lucy has entered an enchanted dreamland filled with symbolically appropriate details, ruled by extremely improbable coincidences, and peopled by ghosts.

Recent critics of *Villette* frequently ignore these curiosities, focusing instead on the imagery, as if embarrassed by what they consider

inferior or melodramatic plotting.[13] But as intelligent a reader as
George Eliot found the novel's power "preternatural" and majestically testified to her fascination with *Villette* "which we, at least,
would rather read for the third time than most new novels for the
first." Interestingly, Eliot found the novel such a compelling structure for the riskiness of personal growth that she called her elopement
with the already married George Henry Lewes a trip to "Labassecour."[14] What makes the narrative seem authentically "preternatural" or uncanny is Brontë's representation of the psychic life of
Lucy Snowe through a series of seemingly independent characters,
as well as her use of contiguous events to dramatize and mythologize
her imagery by demonstrating its psychosexual meaning. "When
We Dead Awaken," Adrienne Rich explains, "everything outside
our skins is an image / of this affliction."[15] And as Lucy fitfully
awakens from her self-imposed living death, she resembles all those
heroines, from the Grimms' Snow White to Kate Chopin's Edna
Pontellier, whose awakenings are dangerous precisely because they
might very well sense, as Rich does, that "never have we been
closer to the truth / of the lies we were living." In other words, Lucy
accidentally finds her way to Madame Beck's house because it is
the house of her own self. And Madame Beck, who startles her visitor
by entering magically through an invisible door, can effectively spy
on Lucy because she is one of the many voices inhabiting and
haunting Lucy's mind.

A woman whose eyes never "know the fire which is kindled in
the heart or the softness which flows thence" (chap. 8), Madame
Beck haunts the school in her soundless slippers and rules over all
through espionage and surveillance. Lucy compares her to Minos,
to Ignacia, to a prime minister, and a superintendent of police. She
glides around spying at keyholes, oiling the doors, imprinting keys,
opening drawers, carefully scrutinizing Lucy's private memorabilia,
and turning the girl's pockets inside out. She is motivated only by
self-interest, and so her face is a "face of stone" (chap. 8) and her
aspect that of a man (chap. 8). For Madame Beck is a symbol of
repression, the projection and embodiment of Lucy's commitment
to self-control. Calm, self-contained, authoritative, she is alert to
the dangerous passions that she must somehow control lest impropriety give her school a bad name. Her spying is therefore a form

of voyeurism, and though it is deplored by Lucy, it is quickly clear that Lucy is simultaneously engaged in spying on Madame Beck. Like Lucy, Madame Beck dresses in decorous gray; like Lucy, she is attracted to the young Englishman Dr. John; and like Lucy, she is not his choice. In defeat Madame Beck is capable of mastering herself. Not only does Lucy mimic Madame Beck's repressive tactics in the school room, she also applauds the way in which Madame Beck represses her desire for Dr. John: "Brava! once more, Madame Beck. I saw you matched against an Apollyon of a predilection; you fought a good fight, and you overcame!" (chap. 11). And in doing so, Lucy is applauding her own commitment to self-repression, her own impulse toward self-surveillance.

The success of Lucy's self-surveillance, however, is called into question by the number of activities that Madame Beck cannot control by means of *her* spying. Perhaps the most ironic of these involves her own daughter, a child named, appropriately, Desirée. A daemonic parody of Madame Beck, Desirée steals to the attic to open up the drawers and boxes of her *bonne*, which she tears to pieces; she secretly enters rooms in order to smash articles of porcelain or plunder preserves; she robs her mother and then buries the prize in a hole in the garden wall or in a cranny in the garret. Madame Beck's supervision has failed with Desirée, who is a sign that repression breeds revolt, and that revolt (when it comes) will itself involve secrecy, destruction, and deceit. That Lucy herself will rebel is further indicated by the story of the woman whose place she has come to fill, the nurserymaid called Madame "Svini." Actually an Irish Mrs. Sweeny, this alcoholic washerwoman has successfully passed herself off as an English lady in reduced circumstances by means of a splendid wardrobe that was clearly made for proportions other than her own. A counterfeiter, she reminds us that Lucy too hides her passions behind her costume. The split between restraint and indulgence, voyeurism and participation represented in the contrast between Lucy and Polly is repeated in the antagonism between Madame Beck on the one hand and Desirée, Madame Svini, and Ginevra Fanshawe on the other.

Carrying on two secret love affairs right under Madame's nose, it is Ginevra who best embodies Lucy's attraction to self-indulgence and freedom. The resemblance between Ginevra's satiric wit and

Lucy's sardonic honesty provides the basis for Ginevra affectionately calling Lucy her "grandmother," "Timon" and "Diogenes." And Ginevra is aware, as no one else is, that Lucy is "a personage in disguise" (chap. 27). "But *are* you anybody?" (chap. 27) she repeatedly inquires of Lucy. It is Ginevra, too, with her familiar physical demonstrations, who violates Lucy's self-imposed isolation not only when she waltzes Lucy around, but also when she sits "gummed" to Lucy's side, obliging Lucy "sometimes to put an artful pin in my girdle by way of protection against her elbow" (chap. 28). For reasons that she never completely understands, Lucy shares her food with Ginevra, fantasizes about Ginevra's love life, and even admires Ginevra's flagrant narcissism. As their friendship develops, Lucy responds to this girl, who claims that she "*must* go out" (chap. 9) to the garden, where Lucy is actually mistaken for Ginevra.

What makes the garden especially valuable in Lucy's eyes is her knowledge that all else "is stone around, blank wall and hot pavement" (chap. 12). This "enclosed and planted spot of ground" is immediately associated with the illicit, with romantic passion, with every activity Madame Beck cannot control. It is the original Garden, a bit of nature within the city, a hiding place for Desirée's stolen goods, bordered by another establishment, a boy's school, from which rain down billets-doux intended for Ginevra but read by Lucy. When initially described, the garden is an emblem of the buried life:

> ... at the foot of ... a Methuselah of a peartree, dead, all but a few boughs which still faithfully renewed their perfumed snow in spring, and their honeysweet pendants in autumn— you saw, in scraping away the mossy earth between the half-bared roots, a glimpse of slab, smooth, hard, and black. The legend went, unconfirmed and unaccredited, but still propagated, that this was the portal of a vault, imprisoning deep beneath that ground, on whose surface grass grew and flowers bloomed, the bones of a girl whom a monkish conclave of the drear middle ages had here buried alive for some sin against her vow. [chap. 12]

Discovering what Catherine Morland had hoped to find, "some awful memorials of an injured and ill-fated nun" (*NA*, II, chap. 2), Lucy reads her own story in the nun's. However, unlike the convents that spawn erotic adventures in male literature from *Venus in the Cloister; or, the Nun in Her Smock* to Lewis's *The Monk*, the emblem of religious incarceration does not here provide privacy for a liberated sexuality.[16] On the contrary, both Lucy and the nun, when they align themselves with the monk's surveillance, cannot escape the confinement of chastity. Like the buried girl, Lucy haunts the forbidden alley because she is beginning to revolt against the constraints she originally countenanced. "Reason" and "imagination" are the terms she uses to describe the conflict between her conscious self-repression and the libidinal desires she fears and hopes will possess her, but significantly she maintains a sense of herself as separate from both forces and she therefore feels victimized by both.

Under a young crescent moon and some stars (which she remembers shining beside an old thorn in England), while sitting on the hidden seat of "l'allée défendue," Lucy experiences the dangerous feelings she has so long suppressed:

> I had feelings: passive as I lived, little as I spoke, cold as I looked, when I thought of past days, I *could* feel. About the present, it was better to be stoical; about the future—such a future as mine—to be dead. And in catalepsy and a dead trance, I studiously held the quick of my nature. [chap. 12]

She recalls an earlier moment in the school dormitory when she was in a sense obliged to "live." During a storm, while the others began praying to their saints, Lucy crept outside the casement to sit on the ledge in the wet, wild, pitchdark, for "too resistless was the delight of staying with the wild hour, black and full of thunder, pealing out such an ode as language never delivered to man" (chap. 12). The English thorn, the experience of interiority in the garden, the ways in which that experience in tranquility recalls an earlier spot in time when Lucy felt the power of infinitude, all are reminiscent of the poetry of Wordsworth. So too are the diction, the negative syntax, the inverted word order. Unlike the poet, however, Lucy is not in the country but enclosed in a small park at the center of a city; she remembers herself in the wind, not swaying in the boughs of trees, but crouching on a window ledge. The ode she thought she heard was really terrible, not glorious. Like the nun and Lucy herself, the black and white sky was split and Lucy longed for an escape "upwards and onwards" (chap. 12). But like most of her desires, that longing had to be negated, this time because it was suicidal.

In personifying the wish for escape as Sisera, and the repression of it as Jael, Lucy explains how painful her self-division is. In the biblical story, Heber's wife, Jael, persuades the tired warrior to take rest in her tent, where she provides him with milk and a mantle. When Sisera sleeps, Jael takes a hammer and drives a nail through his temple, fastening him to the ground (Judges 4:18–21). On the evening that Lucy remembers her own feelings, her Sisera is slumbering, for he has yet to experience the inevitable moment of horror still to come. But unlike the biblical victim, Lucy's Sisera never fully dies: her longings to escape imprisonment are but "transiently stunned, and at intervals would turn on the nail with a rebellious wrench: then did the temples bleed, and the brain thrill to its core" (chap. 12). The horror of her life, indeed, is the horror of repetition, specifically the periodic bleeding wound so feared by Frances Henri. For Lucy's existence is a living death because she is both the unconscious, dying stranger and the housekeeper who murders the unsuspecting guest. Both Polly and Lucy, both Ginevra and Madame Beck, Lucy is the nun who is immobilized by this internal conflict. No wonder she imagines herself as a snail, a fly caught in Madame Beck's cobwebs, or a spider flinging out its own precarious web. In the conflict within the house of Lucy's self, her antagonistic representatives testify to the fragmentation within that will eventually lead to her complete mental breakdown.

It is significant that all these women are linked, defined, and motivated by their common attraction to Dr. John. He is the bright-haired English missionary of Polly's book, the carrier of the burden of English healing arts, the powerful leopard with the golden mane, and Apollo the sun God, as well as the fearfully powerful lover whom Emily Dickinson was to call "the man of noon." Each woman woos Dr. John in her own way: Madame Beck hires him; Ginevra flirts with him; Lucy quietly helps him protect the woman he loves. In responding to Dr. John, Lucy aids Ginevra, frequents the garden, and experiences her own freedom. But, given the dialectic of her nature—the conflict between engagement with life and retreat from it—her amorous participation arouses the suspicions of Madame

Beck, who opens up all her work boxes and investigates her locked drawers. Torn between what Ginevra and Madame Beck represent to her, Lucy experiences "soreness and laughter, and fire and grief" (chap. 13). She thinks she can resort to her usual remedies of self-restraint and repression; but, having experienced her own emotions, she finds that the casements and doors of the Rue Fossette open out into the summer garden and she acquires a new dress, a sign that she is tempted to participate in her own existence.

The principal sign of Lucy's desire to exist actively, however, is her role-playing in a school theatrical. She participates only after M. Paul commands her, "play you can: play you must" (chap. 14), and since she feels that there are no adequate roles provided for her, she finds her part particularly dreadful: she is assigned the role of an empty-headed fop who flirts to gain the hand of the fair coquette. Lucy fears that self-dramatization will expose her to ridicule, so her part is that of a fool; she fears that imaginative participation is immodest, so her part is masculine. Because she dreads participation, moreover, she must learn her role in the attic, where beetles, cobwebs, and rats cover cloaks said to conceal the nun.

By refusing to dress completely like a man onstage and by choosing only certain items to signify her male character, Lucy makes the role her own. But at the same time she is liberated by the male garments that she does select, and in this respect she reminds us of all those women artists who signal their artistic independence by disguising themselves as men or, more frequently, by engaging in a transvestite parody of symbols of masculine authority. Though cross-dressing can surely signal self-division, paradoxically it can also liberate women from self-hatred, allowing for the freer expression of love for other women. Certainly, dressed in a man's jacket onstage, Lucy actively woos the heroine, played by Ginevra. Unable to attract Dr. John herself, Lucy can stimulate some kind of response from him, even if only anger, by wooing and winning Ginevra. But she can simultaneously appreciate a girl who embodies her own potential gaiety. As if to show that this play-acting is an emblem for all role-playing, after her participation in the theatrical Lucy taunts Dr. John in the garden, in an attempt to deflate the sentimental fictions he has created about Ginevra. Naturally, however, the next morning she decides to "lock up" her relish for theatrical and social acting because "it would not do for a mere looker-on at life" (chap. 14).

Since, as we have seen, the events of the plot chart Lucy's internal drama, the crisis of the play (when Lucy comes out on the stage) can be said to cause the confinement and isolation she experiences during the long vacation when she is left alone in the school with a deformed cretin whose stepmother will not allow her to come home. Lucy feels as if she is imprisoned with some strange untamed animal, for the cretin is a last nightmarish version of herself—unwanted, lethargic, silent, warped in mind and body, slothful, indolent, and angry. Ironically, however, the cretin, luckier than her keeper, is finally taken away by an aunt. Entirely alone, Lucy is then haunted by Ginevra, who becomes her own heroine in a succession of intricately imagined fantasies. Her ensuing illness is her final, anguished recognition of her own life-in-death: she sees the white dormitory beds turned into spectres, "the coronal of each became a deaths-head, huge and sun-bleached—dead dreams of an earlier world and mightier race lay frozen in their wide gaping eyeholes" (chap. 15), and she feels that "Fate was of stone, and Hope a false idol—blind, bloodless, and of granite core" (chap. 15). Lucy is enfolded in a blank despair not far removed from Christina Rossetti's bleak "land with neither night nor day, / Nor heat nor cold, nor any wind nor rain, / Nor hills nor valleys." [17] Finally it is the insufferable thought of being no more loved, even by the dead, that drives Lucy out of the house which is "crushing as the slab of a tomb" (chap. 15).

But she can only escape one confining space for an even more limiting one, the confessional. Nothing is more irritating to some readers than the anti-Papist prejudice of *Villette*. But for Brontë, obsessively concerned with feelings of unreality and duplicity, Catholicism seems to represent the institutionalization of Lucy's internal schisms, permitting sensual indulgence by way of counterpoise to jealous spiritual restraint (chap. 14) and encouraging fervent zeal by means of surveillance or privation. "Tales that were nightmares of oppression, privation and agony" (chap. 13), the saints' lives, make Lucy's temples, heart, and wrist throb with excitement, so repellent are they to her, for she sees Catholicism as slavery. But precisely because Catholicism represents a sort of sanctioned schizophrenia, she finds herself attracted to it, and in her illness she kneels on the stone pavement in a Catholic church. Inhabiting the nun's walk, she has always lived hooded in gray to hide the zealot within (chap. 22). Now, seeking refuge within the confessional, she turns to this opening for community and communication which are as welcome to her "as bread to one in extremity of want" (chap. 15).

But she can only confess that she does not belong in this narrow space which cannot contain her: "mon père, je suis Protestante" (chap. 15). Using the only language at her disposal, a foreign language that persistently feels strange on her lips, Lucy has to experience her nonconformity, her Protestantism, as a sin, the sign of her rejection of any authority that denies her the right to be, whether that authority originates inside or outside herself. The "father" claims that for some there is only "bread of affliction and waters of affliction" (chap. 15), and his counsel reminds us that Brontë's virulent anti-Catholicism is informed by her strong attack on the masculine domination that pervades all forms of Christianity from its myths of origin to its social institutions. Although Lucy is grateful for the kindness of the priest, she would no more contemplate coming near him again than she would think of "walking into a Babylonish furnace." The mercy of the Virgin Mother may make the church seem maternal, as Nina Auerbach has recently argued,[18] but only momentarily for Lucy. She realizes that the priest wants to "kindle, blow and stir up" zeal that would mean she might "instead of writing this heretic narrative, be counting [her] beads in the cell of a certain Carmelite convent." Indeed Lucy will become increasingly certain, as she proceeds to tell her story, that nuns do fret at their convent walls, and that the church is a patriarchal structure with the power to imprison her.

Because she has nowhere else to go, after leaving the confessional she is "immeshed in a network of turns unknown" in the narrow, wind-blown streets. Battered by the storm and pitched "headlong down an abyss," she recalls the fallen angel himself and that poor orphan child sent so far and so lonely, with no sense of her own mission or destiny. While Wordsworth's Lucy experiences the protection of nature—"an overseeing power / To kindle or restrain"—Brontë's Lucy is caught in the horror of her own private dialectic. While Wordsworth's Lucy sports gleefully like a fawn across the lawn, even as she is blessed with the balm of "the silence and the calm/Of mute insensate things," Brontë's Lucy—because she lives unknown, among untrodden ways—is condemned to a wind-beaten expulsion into nowhere or a suffocating burial in her own non-existence.

It is amazing, however, how mysterious Lucy's complaint remains. Indeed, unless one interprets backwards from the breakdown, it is almost incomprehensible: Lucy's conflicts are hidden because, as we have seen, she represents them through the activity of other people. As self-effacing a narrator as she is a character, she often seems to be telling any story but her own. Polly Home, Miss March-mont, Madame Beck, and Ginevra are each presented in more detail, with more analysis, than Lucy herself. The resulting obscurity means that generations of readers have assumed Brontë did not realize her subject until she was half-finished with the book. It means, too, that the work's mythic elements, although recognized, have been generally misunderstood or rejected as unjustifiable. And, after all, why should Lucy's schizophrenia be viewed as a generic problem facing all women? It is this question, with all that it implies, that Brontë confronts in the interlude at the center of *Villette*.

We have already seen that, in telling the stories of other women, Lucy is telling her own tale with as much evasion and revelation as Brontë is in recounting her personal experiences through the history of Lucy Snowe. Just as Brontë alters her past in order to reveal it, Lucy's ambivalence about her "heretic narrative" (chap. 15) causes her to leave much unsaid. Certainly there is a notable lack of specificity in her account. The terrors of her childhood, the loss of her parents, the unreturned love she feels for Dr. John, and the dread of her nightmares during the long vacation are recounted in a curiously allusive way. Instead of describing the actual events, for instance, Lucy frequently uses water imagery to express her feelings of anguish at these moments of suffering. Her turbulent childhood is a time of briny waves when finally "the ship was lost, the crew perished" (chap. 4); Dr. John's indifference makes her feel like "the rock struck, and Meribah's waters gushing out" (chap.

13); during the long vacation, she sickens because of tempestuous and wet weather bringing a dream that forces to her lips a black, strong, strange drink drawn from the boundless sea (chap. 15). This imagery is especially difficult because water is simultaneously associated with security. For example, Lucy remembers her visits to the Brettons as peaceful intervals, like "the sojourn of Christian and Hopeful beside a certain pleasant stream" (chap. 1). This last life-giving aspect of water is nowhere more apparent than in Lucy's return to consciousness after her headlong pitch down the abyss. At this point she discovers herself in the Bretton home, now miraculously placed just outside the city of Villette. Waking in the blue-green room of La Terrasse, she feels reborn into the comfort of a deep submarine chamber. When she has reached this safe asylum (complete with wonderful tea, seedcake, and godmother), she can only pray to be content with a temperate draught of the living stream.

Although she is now willing to drink, however, she continues to fear that once she succumbs to her thirst she will apply too passionnately to the welcome waters. Nevertheless, Lucy is given a second chance: she is reborn into the same conflict, but with the realization that she cannot allow herself to die of thirst. As in her earlier novels, Brontë traces the woman's revolt against paternalism in her heroine's ambivalence about God the Father. Jane Eyre faced the overwhelming "currents" of St. John *Rivers'* enthusiasm which threatened to destroy her as much as the total absence of faith implied by the unredemptive role of *Grace/Poole*. In *Villette*, Lucy Snowe wants to believe that "the waiting waters will stir for the cripple and the blind, the dumb and the possessed" who "will be led to bathe" (chap. 17). Yet, she knows that "Thousands lie round the pool, weeping and despairing, to see it through slow years, stagnant" (chap. 17). If the waters stir, what do they bring? Do the weeping and despairing wait for death or resurrection? Drowning or baptism? Immersion or engulfment? Lucy never departs from the subjunctive or imperative or interrogative when discussing the redemption to come, because her desire for such salvation is always expressed as a hope and a prayer, never as a belief. Aware that life on earth is based on an inequality, which has presumably been countenanced by a power greater than herself, she sardonically, almost sarcastically, admits that His will shall be done, "whether we humble ourselves to resignation or not" (chap. 38).

The very problematic quality of the water imagery, then, reflects Lucy's ambivalence. It is as confusing as it is illuminating, as much a camouflage as a disclosure. Her fear of role-playing quite understandably qualifies the way she speaks or writes, and her reticence as a narrator makes her especially unreliable when she deals with what she most fears. To the consternation of many critics who have bemoaned her trickery,[19] not only does she withhold Dr. John's last name from the reader, she never divulges the contents of his letters, and, until the end of her story, she persistently disclaims warm feelings for him. Furthermore, she consistently withholds information from other characters out of mere perversity. She never, for instance, voluntarily tells Dr. John that he helped her on the night of her arrival in Villette, or that she remembers him as Graham from Bretton days; later, when she recounts an evening at a concert to Ginevra, she falsifies the account; and even when she wishes to tell M. Paul that she has heard his story, she mockingly reverses what she has learned. Indeed, although Lucy is silent in many scenes, when she does speak out, her voice retreats from the perils of self-definition behind sarcasm and irony. "But if I feel, may I *never* express?" she asks herself, only to hear her reason declare, "Never!" (chap. 21). Even in the garden, she can only parody Ginevra and Dr. John (chaps. 14–15), and when her meaning is misunderstood on any of these occasions, she takes "pleasure in thinking of the contrast between reality and [her] description" (chap. 21).

Why would Brontë choose a narrator who purposefully tries to evade the issues or mislead the reader? This is what Lucy seems to do when she allows the reader to picture her childhood "as a bark slumbering through halcyon weather" because "A great many women and girls are supposed to pass their lives something in this fashion" (chap. 4). Why does Brontë choose a voyeur to narrate a fictional biography when this means that the narrator insists on telling the tale as if some other, more attractive woman were its central character? Obviously, Lucy's life, her sense of herself, does not conform to the literary or social stereotypes provided by her culture to define and circumscribe female life. Resembling Goethe's

Makarie in that she too feels as if she has no story, Lucy cannot employ the narrative structures available to her, yet there are no existing alternatives. So she finds herself using and abusing—presenting and undercutting—images and stories of male devising, even as she omits or elides what has been deemed unsuitable, improper, or aberrant in her own experience.

That Lucy feels anxious and guilty about her narrative is evident when she wonders whether an account of her misfortunes might not merely disturb others, whether the half-drowned life-boatman shouldn't keep his own counsel and spin no yarns (chap. 17). At more than one point in her life, she considers it wise, for those who have experienced inner turmoil or madness in solitary confinement, to keep quiet (chap. 24). Resulting sometimes in guilty acquiescence and sometimes in angry revolt, the disparity between what is publicly expected of her and her private sense of herself becomes the source of Lucy's feelings of unreality. Not the little girl lost (Polly), or the coquette (Ginevra), or the male manqué (Madame Beck), or the buried nun (in the garden), Lucy cannot be contained by the roles available to her. But neither is she free of them, since all these women do represent aspects of herself. Significantly, however, none of these roles ascribe to women the initiative, the intelligence, or the need to tell their own stories. Thus Lucy's evasions as a narrator indicate how far she (and all women) have come from silent submission and also how far all must yet go in finding a voice. In struggling against the confining forms she inherits, Lucy is truly involved in a mythic undertaking—an attempt to create an adequate fiction of her own. *Villette* is a novel that falls into two almost equally divided sections: the first part takes Lucy up to the episode of the confessional, and the second recounts her renewed attempt to make her own way in Madame Beck's establishment; but in the interlude at the Brettons' Brontë explores why and how the aesthetic conventions of patriarchal culture are as imprisoning for women as sexist economic, social, and political institutions.

As in her other novels, Brontë charts a course of imprisonment, escape, and exclusion until the heroine, near death from starvation, fortuitously discovers a family of her own. That Lucy has found some degree of self-knowledge through her illness is represented by her coincidental reunion with the Brettons. That she is in some ways healed is made apparent through her quarrel with Dr. John Graham Bretton. Lucy refuses to submit to his view of Ginevra as a goddess, and after calling him a slave, she manages only to agree to differ with him. She sees him as a worshipper ready with the votive offering at the shrine of his favorite saint (chap. 18). In making this charge, she calls attention to the ways in which romantic love (like the spiritual love promulgated by the Catholic church) depends on coercion and slavery—on a loss of independence, freedom, and self-respect for both the worshipper and the one worshipped.

Chapter 19, "The Cleopatra," is crucial in elaborating this point. When Dr. John takes Lucy sight-seeing to a museum, she is struck by the lounging self-importance of the painted heroine of stage and story. To slender Lucy, the huge Egyptian queen looks as absurdly inflated as the manner of her presentation: the enormous canvas is cordoned off, fronted by a cushioned bench for the adoring public. Lucy and her creator are plainly aware of the absurdity of such art, and Lucy has to struggle against the approbation which the monster painting seems to demand as its right. She refuses to treat the portrait as an autonomous entity, separate from reality, just as she defies the rhetoric of the religious paintings of "La vie d'une femme" that M. Paul commends to her attention. The exemplary women in these portraits are "Bloodless, brainless nonentities!" she exclaims, as vapid, interestingly, as "ghosts," because they have nothing to do with life as Lucy knows it. Their piety and patience as young lady, wife, mother, and widow leave her as cold as Cleopatra's voluptuous sensuality.

Of course the paintings are meant to examine the ridiculous roles men assign women, and thus the chapter is arranged to maximize the reader's consciousness of how varying male responses to female images are uniformly produced by the male pride that seeks to control women. In squeamish Dr. John, who deposits and collects Lucy; voyeuristic M. Paul, who turns her away from Cleopatra while himself finding her "Une femme superbe"; and foppish de Hamal, who minces daintily in front of the painting, Brontë describes the range of male responses to the completely sexual Cleopatra and the completely desexed, exemplary girl-wife-mother-widow, as Kate Millett has shown.[20]

In particular, because they parody Lucy's inner conflict between assertive sensuality and ascetic submission, the Cleopatra and "La vie d'une femme" perpetrate the fallacy that one of these extremes can—or should—become an identity. Significantly, the rhetoric of the paintings and of the museum in which they are displayed is commercial, propagandistic, and complacent: the paintings are valuable possessions, each with a message, each presented as a finished and admirable object. Just as commercial are the bourgeois arts at the concert Lucy attends with Dr. John and his mother. Interestingly, it is here that Dr. John decides that Ginevra Fanshawe is not even a pure-minded woman, much less a pure angel. But it is not simply his squeamishness about female sexuality that is illuminated on this occasion, for the very opulence of the concert hall testifies to the smugness of the arts practiced there and the materialism of the people present.

Lucy's imagination, however, is touched by neither the paintings at the museum nor the performances at the civic concert because she resents the manipulation she associates with their magic. These arts are not ennobling because they seem egotistical, coercive, not unlike the grand processions "of the church and the army—priests with relics, and soldiers with weapons" (chap. 36). In fact, declares Lucy, the Catholic church uses its theatrical ceremonies so that "a Priesthood"—an apt emblem of patriarchy—"might march straight on and straight upward to an all-dominating eminence" (chap. 36). Nevertheless, at the concert the illusions perpetrated by the architecture are successfully deceptive: everyone except Lucy seems unaware that the Queen is involved in a tragic drama with her husband, who is possessed by the same ghost that haunts Lucy, "the spectre, Hypochrondria" (chap. 20). The social and aesthetic conventions of the concert appear to cast a spell over the people, who are blinded to the King's actual state by the illusion of state pomp. The arts of the concert, like those of the museum and the church, perpetuate false myths that insure the continuance of patriarchal forms, both secular and sacred, that are themselves devoid of intrinsic power or morality.

Although Dr. John takes Lucy to see the actress Vashti only after she has left La Terrasse for the Rue Fossette, this dramatic performance is a fitting conclusion to Lucy's aesthetic excursions. Once again, the audience is the elite of Villette society. But this time

Lucy's imagination is touched and she experiences the tremendous power of the artist: "in the uttermost frenzy of energy is each maenad movement royally, imperially, incedingly upborne" (chap. 23). Certainly Lucy's description of Vashti is so fervently rhapsodic as to be almost incoherent. But most simply Vashti is a player of parts whose acting is destroying her. Therefore, as many critics have noted, "this woman termed 'plain' "" (chap. 23) is a monitory image for Lucy, justifying her own reticence.[21] Indeed, at least one woman poet was drawn to Vashti because of this biblical queen's determination not to perform. The Black American poet Frances Harper wrote of a "Vashti" who declares "I never will be seen,"[22] and Brontë's Vashti illuminates the impetus behind such a vow by demonstrating the annihilating power of the libidinal energies unleashed by artistic performance. Throughout the novel, Lucy has pleaded guiltless "of that curse, an over-heated and discursive imagination" (chap. 2). But although she has tried to strike a bargain between the two sides of herself, buying an internal life of thought nourished by the "necromantic joys" (chap. 8) of fancy at the high price of an external life limited to drudgery, the imaginative power cannot, Brontë shows, be contained in this way: it resurrects all those feelings that Lucy thought she had so ably put to death. During her mental breakdown, as we saw, her imagination recalled the dead in nightmares, roused the ghosts that haunted her, and transformed the dormitory into a replica of her own mind, a chamber of horrors.

Is the magic of art seen as necromantic for women because it revitalizes females deadened by male myths? After she has returned to Madame Beck's, Lucy finds the release offered by the imagination quite tempting. Reason, the cruel teacher at the front of the room, is associated with frigid beds and barren board; but imagination is the winged angel that appeases with sweet foods and warmth. A daughter of heaven, imagination is the goddess from whom Lucy seeks solace:

> Temples have been reared to the Sun—altars dedicated to the Moon. Oh, greater glory! To thee neither hands build, nor lips consecrecrate: but hearts, through ages, are faithful to thy worship. *A dwelling thou hast, too wide for walls, too high for dome— a temple whose floors are space*—rites whose mysteries transpire in

presence, to the kindling, the harmony of worlds! [chap. 21;
italics ours]

Neither the male sun nor the female moon compare to this androgynous, imaginative power which cannot be contained or confined. But even as she praises the freedom, the expansiveness, of a
force that transcends all limits, Lucy fears that, for her, the power-
that-cannot-be-housed is never to be attained except in the dying
dreams of an exile.

Beyond its representation of Lucy's subjective drama, the Vashti
performance is also an important statement about the dangers of
the imagination for all women. Vashti's passionate acting causes
her to be rejected by proper society. Dr. John, for instance, "judged
her as a woman, not an artist: it was a branding judgment" (chap.
23). But more profoundly important than his societal rejection is
Vashti's own sense of being damned: "Fallen, insurgent, banished,
she remembers the heaven where she rebelled. Heaven's light,
following her exile, pierces its confines, and discloses their forlorn
remoteness" (chap. 23). Lucy had at first thought the presence on
stage "was only a woman." But she "found upon her something
neither of woman nor of man: in each of her eyes sat a devil." These
evil forces wrote "HELL" on her brow. They also "cried sore and
rent the tenement they haunted, but still refused to be exorcised."
The incarnation of "Hate and Murder and Madness" (chap. 23),
Vashti is the familiar figure we saw in *Frankenstein* and in *Wuthering
Heights*, the Satanic Eve whose artistry of death is a testimonial to
her fall from grace and her revolt against the tyranny of heaven
as well as her revenge against the fall and the exile she reenacts with
each performance onstage.

Having experienced the origin of her own passions, Vashti will
be punished for a rebellion that is decidedly futile for women.
Certainly this is what Racine implies in *Phèdre*, which is the most
famous and passionate role played by Vashti's historical prototype,
the great French tragedienne Rachel.[23] But the violence of Vashti's
acting—she stands onstage "locked in struggle, rigid in resistance"
—suggests that she is actually struggling against the fate of the
character she plays, much as Lucy struggles against the uncongenial
roles she plays. Vashti's resistance to "the rape of every faculty"

represents the plight of the female artist who tries to subvert the lessons of female submission implied—if not asserted—by art that damns the heroine's sexuality as the source of chaos and suffering. Because Vashti is portrayed as an uncontainable woman, her power will release a passion that engulfs not only the spectator but Vashti herself as well.

Twice Lucy interrupts her rhapsodic description of this actress to indicate that Vashti puts to shame the artist of the Cleopatra. Unlike the false artists who abound in *Villette*, Vashti uses her art not to manipulate others, but to represent herself. Her art, in other words, is confessional, unfinished—not a product, but an act; not an object meant to contain or coerce, but a personal utterance. Indeed, it is even a kind of strip show, a form of the female suicidal self-exposure that pornographers from Sade to the nameless producers of snuff films have exploited, so that her costly self-display recalls the pained ironic cry of Plath's "Lady Lazarus": "I turn and burn, / Do not think I underestimate your great concern."[24] At the same time, Vashti's performance also inevitably reminds us of the dance of death the Queen must do in her fiery shoes at the end of "Snow White." But while Brontë presents Vashti's suffering, she also emphasizes that this art is a feminist reaction to patriarchal aesthetics, and so Lucy withholds the "real" name of the actress and calls her, instead, "Vashti."

Unlike the queen of Villette, who seeks to solace her lord, or the queen of the Nile, who seems made for male pleasure, Queen Vashti of the Book of Esther refuses to placate King Ahasuerus. Quite gratuitously it seems, on the seventh day, when all patriarchs rest, the king calls on Vashti to display her beauty before the princes of the realm, and she refuses to come. Her revolt makes the princes fear that their wives will be filled with contempt for them. Brontë's actress, like the biblical queen, refuses to be treated as an object, and consciously rejects art that dehumanizes its subject or its audience. By transcending the distinctions between private and public, between person and artist, between artist and art, Vashti calls into question, therefore, the closed forms of male culture. Like that of the biblical queen, her protest means the loss of her estate, banishment from the king's sight. And like sinister Lady Lazarus, who ominously warns that "there is a charge, a very large charge, / For a word or a touch," Vashti puts on an inflammatory performance which so subverts the social order that it actually seems to set the theater on fire and sends all the wealthy patrons rushing outside to save their lives. Even as her drama proposes an alternative to patriarchal culture, then, it defines the pain of female artistry, and the revengeful power of female rebellion.

On a dark, rainy night recalling that similar night "not a year ago" (chap. 20), Lucy arrives for the second time at Madame Beck's and immediately enters into the old conflict—with if anything, greater intensity. Haunted by her desire for a letter from Dr. John, describing it—when it comes—as "nourishing and salubrious meat," she places it unopened into a locked case, within a closed drawer, inside the locked dormitory, within the school. Just as she had previously hidden behind masks and fantastic roles, she now experiences emotions which are represented once again by the bleak, black, cold garret where she reads these concealed letters. In this "dungeon under the leads" (chap. 22), she experiences "a sort of gliding out from the direction of the black recess haunted by the malefactor cloaks" (chap. 22). Once again in Brontë's fiction, the madwoman in the attic emerges as a projection of her heroine's secret desires, in this case Lucy's need for nullity.

As Charles Burkhart explains in *Charlotte Brontë: A Psychosexual Study of Her Novels,* and as both E. D. H. Johnson and Robert Heilman note in perceptive articles, the nun appears to Lucy on five separate occasions, at moments of great passion, when she is an actor in her own life.[25] The apparition embodies her anxiety not only about the imagination and passion, but about her very right to exist. Like Sylvia Plath, who feels her own emptiness "echo[ing] to the least footfall," Lucy is "Nun-hearted and blind to the world."[26] Dr. John is correct, then, in assuming that the nun comes out of Lucy's diseased brain: Lucy has already played the role of de Hamal on the stage, and now *he* is playing her role as the nun in Madame Beck's house. But this psychoanalytic interpretation is limited, as Lucy herself notes.

For one thing, Lucy is haunted by an image that has both attracted and repelled many women before her. Told often enough that they are the source of sin, women may well begin feeling guilty as they accept the necessity for penance. Taught effectively enough that they are irrelevant to the important processes of society, women begin to feel they are living invisibly. Thus the nun is not only a projection of Lucy's desire to submit in silence, to accept confinement, to dress in shadowy black, to conceal her face, to desexualize herself; the nun's way is also symbolic for Lucy of the only socially acceptable life available to single women—a life of service, self-abnegation, and chastity.[27] Her fascinated dread of the nun corresponds, then, to Margaret Fuller's rage at seeing a girl take the veil, a ceremony in which the black-robed sisters look "like crows or ravens at their ominous feasts." A contemporary of Brontë's and an exile, she too is convinced that where the nun's captivity is "enforced or repented of, no hell would be worse."[28]

Yet Lucy's nun is no longer buried. If she is the nun of legend, she haunts the garret, according to the story, as a protest against male injustice. Her refusal to remain buried suggests, therefore, that Lucy may very well be moving toward some kind of rejection of her own conventlike life-in-death. If, unlike condescending Dr. John, we take seriously Lucy's puzzlement over her vision in the garret, we realize that she has become enmeshed in a mystery no less baffling than those faced by Jane Eyre and Caroline Helstone: as a single woman, how can she escape the nun's fate? Haunted by her avatars, Lucy Snowe becomes a detective following clues to piece out an identity, for here, as in *Jane Eyre*, Brontë joins the *Bildungsroman* to the mystery story to demonstrate that growing up female requires vigilant demystification of an enigmatic, male-dominated world.

In this connection it is notable that, in some mysterious way, out of the ice of the garret nun and the fire of Vashti a figure now emerges who is able to combine fire and ice, instead of being split apart by these elements as Lucy is. Polly's "coincidental" appearance at this point in the plot draws our attention to the impossibility of Lucy ever finding a solution through Dr. John. Much as Lucy was reborn at La Terrasse, Polly is born again in the theater: Dr. John opens the dense mass of the crowd, boring through a flesh-and-blood rock—solid, hot, and suffocating—until he and Lucy are brought out into the freezing night and then Polly appears, light as a child (chap. 23). A vital and vestal flame, surrounded by gentle "hoar-frost" (chap. 32), self-contained yet loving, delicate yet strong, Polly remembers the old Bretton days as well as Lucy, and she also receives Dr. John's letters with excitement, carrying them upstairs to secure the treasures under lock and key before savoring them at her leisure. She is, in fact, Lucy Snowe born under a lucky star, and her emergence marks the end of Dr. John's consciousness of Lucy herself as anything but an inoffensive shadow.

When Dr. John's letters to her cease—as cease they now must—Lucy is once again obsessed with images of confinement and starvation. Feeling like a hermit stagnant in his cell, she tries to convince herself that the wise solitary would lock up his own emotions and submit to his snow sepulcher in the hope of a spring thaw. But she knows that the frost might very well "get into his heart" (chap. 24), and for seven weeks, as she awaits a letter, she feels just like a caged and starving animal awaiting food. Reliving the horrors of the long vacation, she finally drops the "tone of false calm which, long to sustain, outwears nature's endurance" (chap. 24), and decides to "Call anguish—anguish, and despair—despair" (chap. 31). In the process of writing her life history, we realize, Lucy has continued the learning process begun by the events she narrates, and the change in her outlook is reflected perhaps most specifically in the way she tells the story of the growing love between Dr. John and Polly.

Painfully, honestly, Lucy tells the story of her rejection of romance. This rejection is forced upon Lucy because, as she says, "the goodly river is bending to another course" (chap. 26). Her response is characteristic: she buries Dr. John's letters in a hermetically sealed jar, in a hole at the base of the pear tree, which she then covers over with slate. The episode, Brontë implies, suggests that worship of the godly male, desire for romantic love and male protection, is so deeply bred into Lucy that, at this point, she can only try to repress it. But the necromantic power of the imagination renders this kind of burial inadequate, and the appearance of the nun at the burial site forecasts the ways in which Dr. John will continue to haunt Lucy: feeling the tomb unquiet she will dream "Strangely of disturbed earth," and (in a strange pre-vision of the story of Lizzie Siddal Rossetti) of hair, "still golden, and living, obtruded through coffin-chinks" (chap. 31). But the burial does allow her to endure, to befriend Polly, to speak with self-possession to Dr. John—refusing to be used by him as an "officious soubrette in a love drama" (chap. 27)—and to be reserved when she is hurt by M. Paul.

Excluded from romance, Lucy discovers that romantic love is itself no panacea. Polly had criticized Schiller's ballad "Das Mädchens Klage" because the summit of earthly happiness is not to love, but to be loved (chap. 26). But Lucy begins to understand that neither loving nor being loved insure against egotism, against, for instance, the insensitivity of Polly's recital of the Schiller poem, which sentimentalizes precisely the suffering Lucy has experienced. Ultimately, it is the recognition of her own self, newly emerged in Polly, that frees Lucy from feeling that she is a nun (none) as a single woman. A delicate dame, a fairy thing, an exquisite imp, a childish sprite who still lisps, a faun, a lamb, and finally a pet puppy, Polly is the paragon of romance—the perfect lady—and Lucy's metaphors demonstrate that she has begun to understand the limits of a role that allows Polly to remain less than an adult. She sees as well the selfishness of Dr. John, who is equally thoughtless, not even realizing, for example, that he has forgotten Lucy's very existence for months, despite his ostensible concern about her hypochrondria. There is, Lucy discovers, "a certain infatuation of egotism" (chap. 37) in lovers, which hurts not only their friends but themselves, for even Polly must be careful to preserve her chaste frost, or she will lose the worship of the fastidious doctor. Finally, there is something malevolent about the amulet Polly makes, the spell to bind her men, since she plaits together her father's gray lock and the golden hairs of Dr. John to prison them in a locket laid at her heart, an object all too reminiscent of Lucy's buried cache (chap. 37).

As if to emphasize the false expectations created by romantic enthrallment, Brontë has Lucy set the glamour of the "romantic" courtship against her own growing friendship with M. Paul, who is emphatically an anti-hero—small, dark, middle-aged, tyrannical, self-indulgent, sometimes cruel, even at times a fool. His very faults, however, make it impossible for Lucy to see him as anything other than an equal. Their relationship, we soon realize, is combative because they are equals, because they are so much alike. Paul, in fact, recognizes Lucy's capacity for passion because of his own fiery nature, and he is convinced that their foreheads, their eyes, even certain tones of voice are similar. They share love of liberty, hatred of injustice, enjoyment of the "allée défendue" in the garden. Paul also, we discover, had a passion that "died in the past—in the present it lies buried—its grave is deep-dug, well-heaped, and many winters old" (chap. 29). Consequently, he too has allowed himself to become a voyeur, peeking through a magic lattice into the garden to spy upon the unwitting inhabitants. For both Paul and Lucy are tainted by the manipulative, repressive ways in which they have managed to lead a buried life, and so both are haunted by the nun, who finally visits them when they stand together under the trees. Together they begin to participate in the joys of food, of story-telling, of walks in the country, of flowered hats and brightly colored clothes. But their relationship is constantly impeded by the haunting which the nun represents and by their common fears of human contact.

The inequality of their relationship, moreover, is dramatized when M. Paul becomes Lucy's teacher, for Paul Carl David Emmanuel only encourages his pupil when her intellectual efforts are marked by "preternatural imbecility." Cruel when she seems to surpass "the limits proper to [her] sex," he causes Lucy to feel the stir of ambition: "Whatever my powers—feminine or the contrary —God had given them, and I felt resolute to be ashamed of no faculty of His bestowal" (chap. 30). Significantly, Paul persists in believing that, "as monkeys are said to have the power of speech if they would but use it" (chap. 30), Lucy is criminally concealing a knowledge of both Greek and Latin. He is convinced that she must be "a sort of 'lusus naturae,'" a monstrous accident, for "he believed in his soul that lovely, placid, and passive feminine mediocrity was the only pillow on which manly thought and sense could find rest for its aching temples" (chap. 30).

Paul, in short, wants Lucy to join the ranks of Milton's dutiful daughters by executing his commands either as a secretary who transcribes his performances or as a writer who will improvise in French on prescribed subjects. Naturally she is horrified at the idea of becoming his creature and writing "for a show and to order, perched up on a platform," in part because she is convinced that "the Creative Impulse," which she imagines as a male muse and the "most maddening of masters," would stand "all cold, all indurated, all granite, a dark Baal with carven lips and blank eye-balls, and breast like the stone face of a tomb" (chap. 30). When, in spite of her remonstrances, she is finally compelled by Paul to submit to an examination, she discovers that his professorial colleagues are the same two men whose lecherous pursuit in the dark streets of Villette had so terrified her on her arrival. This satiric perspective on respectable society liberates her sufficiently so she can express her disdain for M. Paul's petty tyrannies by producing a scathing portrait of "a red, random beldame with arms akimbo" who represents that capriciously powerful bitch goddess, "Human Nature" (chap. 26).

It is interesting, in this regard, that the critics of *Villette* have uniformly ignored one of the most curious episodes of the novel, one which reflects the great anxiety that emerging love produces in Lucy. In the chapter entitled "Malevola," Lucy resembles the typical fairy-tale little girl who must carry a basket of fruit to her grandmother's house. Madame Beck gives her a basket to deliver to Madame Walravens on the occasion of her birthday. In spite of a heavy rain that begins as soon as she enters the old *Basse-Ville* to reach the Rue des *Mages*, in spite of the hostile servant at the door, Lucy manages to enter the old house. In the salon, she stares at a picture that magically rolls back, revealing an arched passageway, a mystic winding stair of cold stone and a most curious figure:

> She might be three feet high, but she had no shape; her skinny hands rested upon each other, and pressed the gold knob of a wand-like ivory staff. Her face was large, set, not upon her shoulders, but before her breast; she seemed to have no neck; I should have said there were a hundred years in her features, and more perhaps in her eyes—her malign, unfriendly eyes, with thick grey brows above, and livid lids all round. How severely they viewed me, with a sort of dull displeasure! [chap. 34]

Madame Walravens curses Madame Beck's felicitations; when she turns to go, a peal of thunder breaks out. Her home seems an "enchanted castle," the storm a "spell-wakened tempest" (chap. 34). Finally she vanishes as mysteriously as she appeared. Her very name illustrates her ancestry: we have already seen that walls are associated repeatedly with imprisonment, while the raven is a traditional Celtic image of the hag who destroys children. And Madame Walravens *has*, we learn, destroyed a child by confining her: Lucy is told that she caused the death of her grandchild, Justine Marie, by opposing her match with the poverty-stricken M. Paul, thereby causing the girl to withdraw into a convent where she had died twenty years ago. With her deformed body, her great age, her malignant look, and her staff, Madame Walravens is clearly a witch.

In fact, coming downstairs from the top of the house, Madame Walravens is yet another vindictive madwoman of the attic, and, like Bertha Mason Rochester, she is malevolently enraged, "with all the violence of a temper which deformity made sometimes daemonic" (chap. 34). Having outlived her husband, her son, and her son's child, she seems especially maddened against those on the brink of matrimonial happiness. Thus, as the terrible mother who seeks to take revenge, she enacts at the end of *Villette* a role which seems to be a final (and most intense) image of Lucy's repressed anger at the injustice of men and male culture, for in journeying to this ancient house in the oldest part of the city, Lucy has met her darkest and most secret avatar. It seems likely, indeed, that it is Lucy's unconscious and unspeakable will that Madame Walravens enacts when she sends Paul on a typically witchy quest for treasure in (of all places) *Basse/terre*. Since, as Anne Ross shows, the hag-raven goddess survives in the folklore of howling *banshees* who wail when death approaches,[29] it seems significant that, as Lucy confesses, she has always feared the gasping, tormented east wind, source of the legend of the Banshee (chap. 4). Furthermore, waiting for Paul to return to her, Lucy—praying, "Peace, Peace, Banshee"—cannot lull the destructive blast of the wind on the stormy sea (chap. 42). Finding M. Paul "more [her] own" after his death, Lucy understandably concludes her narrative with a reference to Madame Walravens's long life.

But if Madame Walravens is the madwoman of Lucy's attic, how is she related to the other vision that haunts Lucy, the nun of the garret? The figure of the hag-raven goddess endures in Christianity, or so Ross argues, in the image of the benign saint, and the Celtic word *cailleach*, meaning "hag," also means "nun." It is significant, then, that decked out in brilliantly colored clothes and rings, the hunchback comes downstairs from the top of the house to emerge *through the portrait of a dead nun*, the lost Justine Marie, Paul's buried love. Lucy is explicit about the picture, which depicts a madonna-like figure in nun's dress with a pale, young face expressing the dejection of grief, ill health, and acquiescent habits. We have already noted the ways in which Bertha Mason Rochester's aggression is a product of Jane Eyre's submission, and the reasons why Shirley Keeldar's masculine power is a result of Caroline Helstone's feminine immobility. In *Villette*, Madame Walraven's malevolence is likewise the other side of Justine Marie's suicidal passivity. As if dramatizing the truth at the center of Dickinson's poetry—"Ourself behind ourself, concealed—/Should startle most—" (J. 670)—Brontë reveals that the witch *is* the nun. Miss Marchmont's early judgment has, we see, been validated: in a patriarchal society those women who escape becoming either witch or nun must be, like Lucy, haunted by both. For Lucy's ambivalence about love and about men is now fully illuminated: she seeks emotional and erotic involvement as the only available form of self-actualization in her world, yet she fears such involvement will lead either to submission or to destruction, suicide or homicide.

As an androgynous "barbarian queen" (chap. 34) possessing demonic powers associated with Eastern enchantment, Madame Walravens resembles Vashti, for she too is an artist, the creator of crafty plots which result in the death of her characters. Her malevolent plotting, however, only solidifies the connection between witchcraft and female artistry, since the source of the witch's power is her image magic, her *buried representations* that cause weakness, disease, and finally death for the represented victim.[30] With all her egotism and energy, Madame Walravens seems to be a black parody of the artist, perhaps of the author herself, because her three-foot height recalls Brontë's own small stature (four feet, nine inches). At the same time, with her silver beard and masculine voice, she is certainly a sort of male manqué, and having attained power by becoming an essential part of patriarchal culture, she uses her arts to further enslave women. In Madame Walravens, then, it is likely that we see Brontë's anxiety about the effect of her creativity on herself and on others. Yet Madame Walravens is not, of course, actually an artist. Her arts are, in fact, just as repressive and manipulative as Madame Beck's magical surveillance was. And although we saw earlier that Madame Beck was the embodiment of Lucy's attempts at repression, now it becomes clear that, as a character in her own right, Madame Beck has "no taste for a monastic life" (chap. 38). Both Madame Beck and Madame Walravens evade the tyranny of Lucy's internal dialectic, but only by becoming like Jael, Heber's wife, custodians of male values, agents of patriarchal culture who enforce the subjugation of others.

In any case, however, some of Lucy's most crucial categories seem to be breaking down at this point, for she is coming to terms finally with a world more complex than her paranoia ever before allowed her to perceive. Even as she rejects Madame Walravens's image magic, then, she realizes that it cannot be equated with the necromantic magic of the woman who rejects patriarchy, seeking power not through the control of others but through her own self-liberation. Power itself does seem to be dangerous, if not fatal, for women: unsupplied with any socially acceptable channel, the independent and creative woman is dubbed crafty, a witch. If she becomes an artist, she faces the possibility of self-destruction; if she does not, she destroys others. But while Vashti embodies the pain of female artistry, Madame Walravens defines the terrible consequences of not becoming an artist, of being contained in a crippling "defeminized" role. The female artist, Brontë implies, must seek to revivify herself. As sibyl, as shaman, as sorceress, she must avoid not only the silence of the nun, but the curse of the witch.

Lucy, who has already employed image magic (in the burial of Dr. John's letters), knows its powers are feeble compared to the fearsome but liberating force of the necromantic imagination (which dreams of their resurrection as golden hairs). Jane Eyre had experimented with these two very different arts in her dreamlike drawings (where we saw her unconscious impulses emerging prophetically) and in her portraits (where she didactically portrays beautiful Blanche Ingram in contrast to her own puny self to prove she has no chance with Rochester). More anxious than Jane about creativity, Lucy practices only the severely limited arts of sewing, tracing elaborate line engravings, and writing satiric sketches. Yet, by the time she describes the climactic park scenes, Lucy is an accomplished author. What has happened? To begin with, in the course of the novel she has learned to speak with her own voice, to emerge from the shadows: she defends her creed successfully against the persuasions of Père Silas and M. Paul; she speaks out for the lovers to Polly's father, and she stands up against Madame Beck's interference. All these advances are followed by moments of eclipse when she withdraws, but the sum progress is toward self-articulation, and self-dramatization.

In the process of writing her story, moreover, Lucy has become less evasive. Her narrative increasingly defines her as the center of her own concerns, the heroine of her own history. Her spirited capsule summaries of Polly's and Ginevra's romantic escapades prove that she sees the limits, even the comic aspects, of romantic love, and that another love, painful and constant and intellectual, is now more interesting to her. In fact, Lucy's plots have led not to burial but to exorcism, for she is in the process of becoming the author not only of her own life story but of her own life. It is for this reason that the subject of the ending of *Villette* is the problematic nature of the imagination. Having delineated the horrors of restraint and repression, Brontë turns to the possibility of a life consecrated to imagination, in part to come to terms with her own commitment to the creation of fictions that will no longer enslave women.

Bringing together all the characters and images in a grand finale, the park scenes are fittingly begun by the failure of Madame Beck's attempts to control Lucy. The administered sleeping potion does not drug but awakens her; escaping from the school that is now openly designated a den, a convent, and a dungeon, Lucy seems to have been roused by the necromantic imagination to sleepwalk through a dreamt, magical masque depicting her own quest for selfhood. Searching for the circular mirror, the stone basin of water in the moonlit, midnight summer park, Lucy discovers an enchanted place illuminated by the symbols of the imagination—a flaming arch of stars, colored meteors, Egyptian architecture. Under a spell, in a magical, hallucinogenic world of apparitions and ghosts, she notes that "on this whole scene was impressed a dream-like character: every shape was wavering, every movement floating, every voice echo-like—half-mocking, half-uncertain" (chap. 38). And the fact that this is a celebration commemorating a struggle for liberty does not destroy the marvel of such sights, because it so clearly reflects her own newly experienced freedom from constraint.[31] The allusions to art, the Eastern settings, the music, and the sense of magic remind us that Lucy's struggle is both psychological and aesthetic. So she refers to the park as a woody theater, filled with actors engaged in discoveries that will lead to a climax (chap. 38) and a denouement (chap. 39).

In fact, the sequence of events in this dreamy midsummer *Walpurgisnacht* furnishes a microcosm of the novel, as Lucy's imagination summons up before her the spirits that have haunted her past and present life. First she sees the Brettons and commemorates her feeling for Graham in typically spatial terms, describing the tent of Peri Banou she keeps for him: folded in the hollow of her hand, it would expand into a tabernacle if released. Admitting for the first time her love for Dr. John, she nevertheless avoids making herself known, moving on to watch the "papist junta" composed of Père Silas, Madame Beck, and Madame Walravens. As they wait for the arrival of Justine Marie, Lucy conjures up a vision of the dead nun. But she sees, instead, M. Paul arriving with his young ward, the niece named for the departed saint. Although she is jealous, Lucy feels that M. Paul's nun has now finally been buried, and at this point of great suffering, she begins to praise the goddess of truth. As she has repeatedly, Lucy is advocating repression, although it requires her to reenact the conflict between Jael and Sisera, the pain of self-crucifixion. When "the iron [has] entered well [her] soul," she finally believes she has been "renovated."

Significantly, on her return to the school Lucy finds what seems to be the nun of the garret sleeping in her bed. Now, however, she can at last defy the specter, for the park scene appears to have liberated her, enabling her to destroy this symbol of her chastity and confinement. Why does the appearance of Paul's nun lead to the surfacing of Lucy's? As always, Brontë uses the plot to suggest an answer. Following her imagination on the night of the park festival, Lucy had escaped the convent and, in doing so, she had

left the door ajar, thus effecting the escape of Ginevra and de Hamal
—the dandy who we now learn has been using the nun's disguise
to court the coquette. We have already seen how Ginevra and de
Hamal represent the self-gratifying, sensual, romantic side of Lucy.
Posturing before mirrors, the fop and the coquette are vacuous but
for the roles they play. Existing only in the "outside" world, they
have no more sense of self than the nun whose life is completely
"internal." Thus, for Lucy to liberate herself from Ginevra and de
Hamal means that she can simultaneously rid herself of the self-
denying nun. In fact, these mutually dependent spirits have been
cast out of her house because, in the park, unable to withdraw into
voyeurism, she experienced jealousy. Hurt without being destroyed,
she has at least temporarily liberated herself from the dialectic of
her internal schism. And to indicate once again how that split is a
male fiction, Brontë shows us how the apparently female image of
the nun masks the romantic male plots of de Hamal.

What is most ironic about this entire sequence, however, is that
Lucy is wrong: Paul is committed to her, not to the memory of the
buried Justine Marie, or to his ward. But, because she is wrong, she
is saved. Imagination has led her astray throughout the park scene
—conjuring up an image of a calm and shadowy park and then
leading her to believe that she can exist invisibly in the illuminated
festival, causing her to picture Madame Beck in her bed and M.
Paul on shipboard, creating the romantic story of Paul and his rich,
beautiful ward. It is with relieved self-mockery that Lucy laughs at
her own panegyric to the so-called goddess of truth, whose message
is really only an imaginative projection of her own worst fears.
Ultimately, indeed, the entire distinction between imagination and
reason breaks down in the park scenes because Lucy realizes that
what she has called "Reason" is really repressive witchcraft or image
magic that would transform her into a nun. Although Lucy leaves
the park thinking that the calm, white, stainless moon triumphs—a
witness of "truth all regnant" (chap. 39)—the next day she cannot
accept the truth. And though she views it as a weakness, this very
inability to acquiesce in silence is a sign of her freedom from the
old internal struggle, for Lucy has emerged from the park a more
integrated person, able to express herself in the most threatening
circumstances. Now she can even defy Madame Beck to catch at

a last chance to speak with Paul, detaining him with her cry: "My heart will break!" (chap. 41).

And, albeit with terrible self-consciousness, Lucy can now ask Paul whether her appearance displeases him. This question climaxes a series of scenes before the mirror, each of which defines Lucy's sense of herself. When, at the beginning of the book, Ginevra shows Lucy an image of herself with no attractive accomplishments, no beauty, no chance of love, the girl accepts the reflection with satiric calm, commending Ginevra's honesty. Midway through the novel, however, at the concert, she experiences a "jar of discord, a pang of regret" (chap. 20) at the contrast between herself in a pink dress and the handsome Brettons. Finally, when she thinks she has lost the last opportunity of seeing Paul, she feelingly perceives herself alone—sodden, white, with swollen and glassy eyes (chap. 38). Instead of seeing the mirror-image as the object of another person's observations, Lucy looks at herself by herself. Increasingly able to identify herself with her body, she is freed from the contradictory and stultifying definitions of her provided by all those who think they know her, and she begins to understand how Dr. John, Mr. Home, Ginevra, and even Polly see her in a biased way. At last, Brontë suggests, Lucy has learned that imaginative "projection" and reasoned "apprehension" of the "truth" are inseparable. The mirror does not reflect reality; it creates it by interpreting it. But the act of interpretation can avoid tyranny when it remains just that—a perceptual act. After all, "wherever an accumulation of small defences is found . . . there, be sure, it is needed" (chap. 27).

It is this mature recognition of the necessity and inadequacy of self-definition—this understanding of the need for fictions that assert their own limits by proclaiming their personal usefulness—that wins for Lucy finally a room of her own, indeed, a house of her own. The school in the Faubourg Clotilde is a fitting conclusion to her struggle and to the struggles of all of Brontë's heroines for a comfortable space. The small house has large, vine-covered windows. The salon is tiny, but pretty, with delicate walls tinged like a blush and a brilliant carpet covering the highly waxed floor. The small furniture, the plants, the diminutive kitchenware please Lucy. Not by any means a dwelling too wide for walls or too high for dome, her tidy house represents on the one hand the lowering of her sights and on the other her willingness to begin making her own way, even if on a small scale.

Both a home and a school, the house represents Lucy's independence: upstairs are two sleeping-rooms and a schoolroom—no attic mentioned. Here, on the balcony overlooking the gardens of the faubourg, near a water-jet rising from a nearby well, Paul and Lucy commemorate their love in a simple meal that consists of chocolate, rolls, and fresh red fruit. Although he is her king, her provider only rents the house himself and she will quickly have to earn her keep: Lucy has escaped both the ancestral mansion and the convent. And so, under the moonlight that is now an emblem of her imaginative power to define her own truths, she is more fortunate than Shirley because she actually experiences the days of "our great Sire and Mother"; she can "taste that grand morning's dew—bathe in its sunrise" (chap. 41).

Unlike Caroline Helstone, moreover, Lucy is given real food, for she is to be sustained by Paul, even in his absence: "he would give neither a stone, nor an excuse—neither a scorpion, nor a disappointment; his letters were real food that nourished, living water that refreshed" (chap. 42). Nevertheless, despite her hope that women can obtain a full, integrated sense of themselves *and* economic independence *and* male affection, Brontë also recognizes that such a wish must not be presented falsely as an accomplished fact. The ambiguous ending of *Villette* reflects Lucy's ambivalence, her love for Paul and her recognition that it is only in his absence that she can exert herself fully to exercise her own powers. It also reflects Brontë's determination to avoid the tyrannical fictions that have traditionally victimized women. Once more, she deflates male romanticism. Although her lover sails off on the *Paul et Virginie*, although her novel—like Bernadin de Saint Pierre's—ends in shipwreck, Brontë insists again that it is the confined woman, Lucy, who waits at home for the adventuring male, but notes that the end of love must not be equated with the end of life. The last chapter of *Villette* begins by reminding us that "Fear sometimes imagines a vain thing" (chap. 42). It ends with Lucy's refusal to end conclusively: "Leave sunny imaginations hope" (chap. 42). Brontë gives us an open-ended, elusive fiction, refraining from any definitive message except to remind us of the continued need for sustaining stories of survival.

The very erratic way Lucy tells the story of becoming the author of her own life illustrates how Brontë produces not a literary object but a literature of consciousness. Just as Brontë has become Lucy Snowe for the writing of *Villette*, just as Lucy has become all her characters, we submit to the spell of the novel, to the sepulchral voice relating truths of the dead revivified by the necromancy of the imagination. Brontë rejects not only the confining images conferred on women by patriarchal art, but the implicitly coercive nature of that art. *Villette* is not meticulously crafted. The very excess of its style, as well as the ambiguous relationship between its author and its heroine, declare Brontë's commitment to the personal processes of writing and reading. In place of the ecstatic or philosophic egotistical sublime, she offers us something closer to the qualified experience of what Keats called "negative capability." Making her fiction a parodic, confessional utterance that can only be understood through the temporal sequences of its plot, Brontë criticizes the artists she considers in *Villette*—Rubens, Schiller, Bernadin de Saint Pierre, Wordsworth, Arnold, and others.

It is ironic that her protest could not save her from being the subject of one of Arnold's poetic complaints on the early death of poets. In "Haworth Churchyard" Arnold recognizes how Brontë's art is lit by intentionality when he describes how she told "With a Master's accent her feign'd History of passionate life." But his insistence on desexing her art—here, by describing her "Master's accent," later by referring to her with a masculine pronoun[32]—shows him to be the first of a long line of readers who could not or would not submit to a reading process and a realization so totally at odds with his own life, his own art and criticism.

It is the act of receptivity that Brontë uses to subvert patriarchal art. Recently some feminists have been disturbed that Brontë did not reject the passivity of her heroines.[33] As we have seen, her books do elaborate on the evils of equating masculinity with power and femininity with submission. But Brontë knew that the habit of submission had bequeathed a vital insight to women—a sympathetic imagination that could help them, in their revolt, from becoming like their masters. Having been obliged to experience themselves as objects, women understand both their need and their capacity for awakening from a living death; they know it is necromancy, not

image magic—a resurrecting confessional art, not a crucifying confessional penance—which can do this without entangling yet another
Other in what they have escaped. Conscious of the politics of poetics,
Brontë is, in some ways, a phenomenologist—attacking the discrepancy between reason and imagination, insisting on the subjectivity
of the objective work of art, choosing as the subject of her fiction
the victims of objectification, inviting her readers to experience with
her the interiority of the Other. For all these reasons she is a powerful
precursor for all the women who have been strengthened by the
haunted and haunting honesty of her art.

V
Captivity and Consciousness in George Eliot's Fiction

Illustration on the preceding page: *Mariage de Convenance*, by William Quiller Orchardson. Courtesy of the Glasgow Art Gallery.

13

Made Keen by Loss:
George Eliot's Veiled Vision

In Eden Females sleep the winter in soft silken veils
Woven by their own hands to hide them in the darksom grave.
But Males immortal live renewed by female deaths.
— William Blake

... good sense and good taste invariably dispose women who have
made extraordinary attainments in any of the abstract sciences,
to draw a veil over them to common observers, as not according
well with the more appropriate accomplishments of their sex ...
— Dugald Stewart

Slow advancing, halting, creeping,
Comes the Woman to the hour!—
She walketh veiled and sleeping,
For she knoweth not her power.
— Charlotte Perkins Gilman

A mask I had not meant
to wear, as if of frost,
covers my face.
Eyes looking out,
a longing silent at song's core.
— Denise Levertov

Charlotte Brontë's fiction clarifies the relationship between imagery
of enclosure and the use of doubles in women's literature: as we
have seen in her work, both are complementary signs of female
victimization. Confined within uncomfortable selves as well as within
uncomfortable spaces, her heroines cannot escape the displaced or
disguised representatives of their own feared impulses. Therefore

443

they are destined to endure the repetition of what Freud called "the return of the repressed," even as they experience that "helplessness in the grip of fate, in the flux of time, helplessness in the face of death, helplessness at the hands of the all-powerful father" that John Irwin has recently explored in male fiction.[1] For women, however, this helplessness is complicated by the fact that it is precisely the solution prescribed as appropriate, if not ideal, to the enigma of female identity, so that Lucy Snowe, for example, can only try to perceive her passivity as a state she has herself chosen.

In this regard, too, Lucy is a suitable model for a uniquely female response to entrapment, as our epigraphs illustrate. Whether they feel veiled like Charlotte Perkins Gilman, or masked like Denise Levertov, women writers describe their sensation of being inescapably removed from the source of their own authority, even as they are tempted to make a special gain out of that sense of loss. Paradoxically, by the middle of the nineteenth century, when women were widening their political, social, and educational spheres of influence and activity,[2] women writers, in retreat from revolt, became concerned with the issue of internalization. Thus although these artists of the mid-century are caught between the twin distinctively female temptations of angelic submission and monstrous assertion, they place a very special emphasis on the problematic role of women in a male-dominated culture. And since all are avid readers of Austen, Wollstonecraft, Mary Shelley, and the Brontës, these women writers consciously participate in a female subculture that explains the intimate bonds we sense between George Eliot and Christina Rossetti in England, Elizabeth Barrett Browning in Italy, and Emily Dickinson and Harriet Beecher Stowe in America, to name but a few of the most prominent.

When Harriet Beecher Stowe was visited by the spectral presence of Charlotte Brontë, for example, she did not seem particularly incredulous that her ghostly guest crossed the Atlantic to speak about her sister Emily, "of whose character she gave a most striking analysis."[3] However, the "weird and Brontëish" dialogue held in Mrs. Stowe's American home only bemused George Eliot. That Eliot placed little faith in spirit-communication comes as no surprise, since her skepticism seems to be a byproduct of her commitment to agnosticism and realism, even as it signals her Victorian compromise in favor of the sweet reasonableness expected of a bona fide Victorian sage. For while, like so many other women writers, Eliot profited from the Romantics' legitimization of the private life of the self as the subject of less than exalted literary forms, she was far from comfortable with what she might have termed the self-indulgence of all the Romantics except for her cherished Wordsworth.

Recently, however, feminist critics have discerned some of the submerged irrational elements in George Eliot's fiction,[4] and, even in her letter of response to Stowe, Eliot admitted, "If there were miserable spirits whom we could help—then I think we should pause and have patience with their trivial-mindedness."[5] Significantly, her admission comes as a typically feminine assumption of responsibility in the nursing of humankind, and it is included in a letter to a woman writer about two other women who shared a sisterly penchant for "female Gothic." For it was primarily because of her ambivalent sense of herself as a woman artist that George Eliot was alternately attracted and repelled by her Romantic precursors, both male and female. Her fascination with the Romanticized figure of Satan (and, by extension, with the Satanic figure of Eve) is probably best approached through a little-read story entitled "The Lifted Veil," which strikingly illustrates her dis-ease with authority as well as her relationship to Mary Shelley and Charlotte Brontë, and her attraction to the Romantic image of the veil. Moreover, although it is not a completely successful work of art, possibly *because* it is not, this story sheds some light on Eliot's less widely studied characters and poems, and on the tensions that continued to inform her life in spite of her successful writing career.

Published anonymously in 1859 in *Blackwood's*, between the success of *Adam Bede* and the writing of *The Mill on the Floss*, "The Lifted Veil" is a novella that has received only scant attention.[6] While we are familiar with George Eliot's sympathetic concern for humanity, her historical representation of English country life, her critique of egoism, and her heroines' fascination with self-sacrifice, we are hardly prepared to have from her a story of gothic secrets, extrasensory powers of perception, and scientific experiments in revivification, all placed in an exotic Continental setting. Further, the involved organic development we have been taught to expect of an Eliot novel is precisely what is violated by a plot in which events are motivated in an arbitary, abrupt manner, and in which the narrator—not at all the omniscient benevolence we usually identify with Eliot—is so disagreeable that it is difficult to determine his relationship to the author.

George Eliot's very hesitations about "The Lifted Veil" make it exceptionally interesting especially because it was actually written when she was about to lift one of her own veils, her pseudonym, and admit authorship of fiction that had already achieved great popularity. Apparently conscious herself that the story contradicts much of her later work, Eliot decided fourteen years after she wrote it that she did not wish it included in a series of *Tales from Blackwood*, although she did prefix a poem to it:

> Give me no light, great Heaven, but such as turns
> To energy of human fellowship;
> No powers beyond the growing heritage
> That makes completer manhood.[7]

Not only does this plea for the redemptive imagination comment directly upon a story about alienation from human fellowship and *in*complete manhood, it also immediately signals that this tale will focus on Eliot's anxiety about the light and power she knows to be hers, although she is just a man in name.

As told by the misanthropic Latimer during the month before the death which he himself has foreseen, "The Lifted Veil" describes the lonely childhood of a second son who first becomes cursed with clairvoyant powers of "prevision" and then with the telepathic ability to "hear" the thoughts of his acquaintances. But rather than contributing to the "energy of human fellowship," Latimer's auditory sensitivity isolates him by revealing the pettiness and selfishness of servants, family, and friends, from whom he becomes increasingly alienated. His visionary insight, moreover, seems less a light from heaven than a curse from hell, since each physical scene he imagines is a horror he feels helpless to avoid: in spite of his first prevision of the city of Prague, his second hallucination of a meeting with the beautiful but cruel woman named Bertha, and his third vision of a married life with her based on mutual hatred, he is unable to avoid pursuing a future he knows to be grotesque. After seeing his presentiments come true, Latimer actively seeks the diminution of his powers to escape the full realization of Bertha's hatred. But a visit from his only childhood companion, a scientist studying revivification, unlocks a terrible secret from a dead maid, his wife's confidante, who returns to life for a moment to reveal that Bertha has plotted to kill him. The horror of this final revelation causes Latimer to separate from Bertha and exile himself until disease limits his wanderings. Eventually, in the ellipsis of the final sentence of his confessional autobiography, his last vision is verified and death intervenes, just in the way and at the time he knew it would.

Both U. C. Knoepflmacher and Ruby Redinger have shown that, in spite of his many disagreeable qualities, Latimer has much in common with George Eliot. Beloved by an angelically ministering mother who dies when he is seven or eight, he is brought up as a second son by a father who is "a firm, unbending, intensely orderly man, in root and stem a banker, but with a flourishing graft of the active landholder, aspiring to country influence" (257). Similarly, George Eliot was sent away from her mother to school at an exceptionally early age and always felt herself to be the daughter of just such an unbending father. Both Latimer and George Eliot feel that their older brothers are heirs to the economic patrimony and the respectful affection of their parents. Both are cursed with feeling second best, and both must struggle against an uncongenial, inadequate education imposed by their fathers in opposition to their wishes. In their revolt against their loveless situation and the fathers they blame for it, both Latimer and George Eliot lose their belief in a heavenly Father and both pay for this loss with a sense of personal shame and isolation. And Latimer's distrust and dislike of strangers is not very different from Eliot's initial responses to new acquaintances, whom she almost always describes in her letters in negative terms.

Like Charlotte Brontë's early male persona, William Crimsworth in *The Professor*, Latimer reflects his author's sense of her own peculiarity. More than the self-consciousness of any of Eliot's women, Latimer's "dislike of [his] own physique" because of its "half-womanish, half-ghostly beauty" (270) probably reveals the sensitivity of a young woman who was not only rejected by men who found her looks masculine, but who described herself as "a hideous hag," and "haggard as an old witch" (*Letters*, 2:11, 25). Both Latimer and

George Eliot suffer from diseases that seem intimately bound up with their "gift" of insight. A number of physical illnesses precipitate Latimer's visions, diseases which emphasize his vulnerability and sensitivity, which are viewed as "defects of [his] organization" (258) by his unsympathetic father, while Latimer himself acknowledges that his present literary endeavors will eventuate in fatal heart disease. Similarly, George Eliot was preoccupied with complaints ranging from fears at night to freezing spells, and she too associates her "crazy body's" ailments (*Letters*, 1: 102) with the melancholic assumption of Latimer that he is isolated from all human sympathy and companionship (255). Throughout her life Eliot was plagued by terrible headaches, but especially when she was beginning a novel, and even when she was the most successful woman novelist living in England, her devoted companion George Henry Lewes could explain his keeping reviews from her: "Unhappily the habitual tone of her mind is distrust of herself, and no sympathy, no praise can do more than lift her out of it for a day or two" (*Letters*, 5: 228).[8]

Both Latimer and George Eliot identify imaginative vision as a kind of illness. Latimer asks whether his powers of insight might not rather be "a disease,—a sort of intermittent delirium, concentrating [his] energy of brain into moments of unhealthy activity" (267), and he associates his previsions with "madness" which brings him "the horror that belongs to the lot of a human being whose nature is not adjusted to simple human conditions" (268). His ability to hear other thinking minds seems a sign of "a morbid organization, framed for passive suffering—too feeble for the sublime resistance of poetic production" (270), and significantly, his "diseased consciousness" (271) becomes entirely preoccupied with the thoughts of those who detest or pity him. Again this recalls a trait of Eliot's, for Latimer's awareness that other people view him as a failure is not very different from George Eliot's constitutional self-doubt. According to Herbert Spencer, she complained of exactly the kind of "double consciousness" (302) she ascribes to Latimer, "a current of self-criticism being an habitual accompaniment of anything she was saying or doing; and this naturally tended toward self-deprecation and self-distrust."[9]

Unable to evade the sights and sounds he imagines, moreover, Latimer is equally unable to articulate them. Consequently, he has "the poet's sensibilities without his voice—the poet's sensibility that finds no vent but in silent tears on the sunny bank" (260). Similarly, George Eliot found no vent for her sensibilities until quite late into her middle age; the victim of what Tillie Olsen calls a "foreground" silence,[10] she too must have felt cursed and voiceless. Thus she associates her own "Hopelessness" in youth with "the chief source of wasted energy with all the consequent bitterness of regret," and she even likens her suffering to the suicidal plans of those who "ran for the final leap, or as Mary Wollstonecraft did, wetted their garments well in the rain hoping to sink the better when they plunged" (*Letters*, 5:160).

This last allusion is useful because it supplies us with a clue to the meaning of Latimer's suffering, for Eliot's depiction of Mary Wollstonecraft adumbrates her later presentation of yet another desperate woman artist, Mirah Cohen in *Daniel Deronda*, who wets her garments in the water in order to sink the better when she plunges. Indeed, Eliot's identification with the "half-womanish, half-ghostly" Latimer's powerlessness, his silence, his secondary status, his weak body and his wounded soul significantly illuminates her own attitudes toward her art and her gender. Driven by an intense need to be loved, motherless in a world of coercive fathers, a female is in a sense a paradigmatic second-born child who must resort to passivity and invalidism to survive. That both Latimer and George Eliot feel surrounded by false appearances veiling the petty, coercive manipulations of indifferent men corresponds, then, to the feeling of so many women who know they must decode mysterious appearances to understand their actual situation in the world. But it also reminds us that women have traditionally played a role "behind the scenes," and that their domestic life with men who inhabit an inaccessible public realm bequeaths to them a unique and implicitly satiric sense of the discrepancy between public assertions and private realities.

The telepathy of Latimer and Eliot can be viewed in part, therefore, as an extension of the woman's traditional role in the home, where she is taught to develop her sensitivity to the unspoken needs and feelings of her family: surely the other side of self-sacrificing renunciation is this schizophrenic sense that one is haunted by alien but familiar voices making demands at odds with one's own interest. Similarly, the ability of Latimer and George Eliot to see into a dreadful future which they are then helpless to avoid corresponds to the feeling among women that they are trapped in stories, unable to evade plots created for them by alien, if not hostile, authors and authorities. Mute despite their extraordinary gifts, Latimer and George Eliot remind us of the powerlessness of, say, Cassandra, whose expressive exertions never alter the events of the past or the future and whose speech is therefore as ineffectual as silence.

Latimer's essentially feminine qualities—his sensitivity, his physical weakness, his secondary status in the family, his dispossession, his passivity, and his intense need to be loved—are a source of anguish because they make it impossible for him actually to become a poet. Granted poetic abilities but denied the power to create, Latimer lives out the classic role of women who are denied the status of artist because they are supposed somehow to become works of art themselves ("You *are* a poem," Will informs Dorothea in *Middlemarch* [chap. 22]), or because they are destined to remain merely artistic, channeling their capabilities into socially acceptable accomplishments, as Mirah Cohen does when she pursues a career as singer and teacher of singing in the private drawing-rooms of London. Eliot describes just such talented women in her review "Women in France," where she explains that the appreciation of a woman like Madame de Sablé "seconded a man's wit with understanding—one of the best offices which womanly intellect has rendered to the advancement of culture" (74). Eliot even advances a biological argument for the female who is always the muse, never the author, explaining that the "larger brain and slower temperament of the English and Germans are, in the womanly organization, generally dreamy and passive" so that "The woman of large capacity can seldom rise beyond the absorption of ideas. . . . the voltaic-pile is not strong enough to produce crystalizations, phantasms of great ideas float through her mind, but she has not the spell which will arrest them, and give them fixity." [11]

Predictably, then, for quite some time Eliot saw herself not as a creator of literature, but only as an editor and translator whose skills in expression were to be subordinate to the meaning of another's words. Despite her prolonged work, her name did not even appear in her edition of David Friedrich Strauss's *The Life of Jesus* (1846). As Gordon Haight explains, "She was quite willing to let Chapman pose as chief editor [of the *Westminster Review*] while she did the real work without public acknowledgment."[12] This association with Chapman was only the last of a series of relationships in which she accepted the office of editorial assistant, secretary, or scribe to men whom she elevated into fatherly gods—even taking the name "Deutera, which *means* second and *sounds* a little like daughter" to a particularly unimpressive Dr. Brabant (*Letters*, 1:164). Moreover, Dorothea Brooke was not the only Eliot heroine to see herself not as Milton but only as one of Milton's dutiful daughters, learning how to read Greek and Latin aloud and transforming that "exercise in unknown tongues" through private study so as to teach herself to understand what she read.[13] Romola also responds to her father's criticism of her "woman's delicate frame, which ever craves repose and variety, and so begets a wandering imagination," with the determination to "study diligently" so as to "be as useful to you as if I had been a boy, and then perhaps some great scholar will want to marry me, and will not mind about a dowry; and he will like to come and live with you, and he will be to you in place of my brother . . . and you will not be sorry that I was a daughter."[14]

Perhaps Eliot's personal anxieties about authorship are in part responsible for her recurrent interest in characters whose passivity, illness, and impotence are directly related to their visionary insight. Like Latimer, these characters are cursed with "the poet's sensibilities without his voice." Jubal, for instance, in the poem named after him, creates the lyre in the home of Cain where the arts began; in his subsequent explorations of the world, however, when new voices come to him, his own "song grows weaker, and the heart must break / For lack of voice, or fingers that can wake / The lyre's full answer."[15] When he returns to his home to hear his name worshipped as divine, he seeks personal recognition, but he is first ridiculed and then cast out by those who cannot believe that he is a God. He can only "shrink and yearn," seeking "the screen / Of thorny thickets" where he falls unseen.

Also like Latimer, who conceives of himself as "an exceptional being, a sort of quiet energumen" (376)—a person possessed by the devil—the visionary son in *Romola* is damned by his father, who considers him "deluded by debasing fanatical dreams, worthy only of an energumen whose dwelling is among tombs" (chap. 5). Endowed with Latimer's passivity and illness, Romola's brother is a clairvoyant whose previsions also warn of a disastrous marriage. Similarly, in Eliot's last completed novel, *Daniel Deronda*, Mordecai is in revolt against a coercive father. Dying with visionary dreams that can only be uttered in fragments because of his labored breath, he speaks a language not understood by English society, "like a poet among people of a strange speech, who may have a poetry of their own, but have no ear for his cadence, no answering thrill to his discovery of latent virtues in his mother tongue." [16] Despite his clairvoyant knowledge about Daniel Deronda's identity and the future of the Jewish race, he is completely passive, unable to exert his will in any way.

All three of these characters are confronted with difficulties about their names that reflect their ambivalence over their visionary role. When he heard his name extolled, but experienced personal deprivation, Jubal "Shrank doubting whether he could Jubal be." Romola's brother transforms himself from "Dino" to "Fra Luca" in his rejection of the values his secular father represents. And Mordecai only regains his family name, Ezra Cohen, when reunited with his sister. All three reflect some of the anxiety that made Eliot herself juggle with names: Mary Ann, Marianne, or Marian Evans, Pollian (a pun on Apollyon, the Angel of Destruction), Clematis (*Mental* Beauty), Deutera, Minie, Polly, Marian Lewes, and Mrs. John W. Cross are the personae assumed by "George Eliot" when she is willing to drop her anonymity. [17] Her fear of invoking her father's or brother's name only reinforces our sense of her guilt about creativity, guilt apparent in the suffering she visits upon her visionary surrogates, all of whom resemble Latimer in his fallen state. All could proclaim with the voice of "Self" in the dialogue between "Self and Life," "Seeing what I might have been / Reproved the thing I was" (205). [18]

Aspiring to divine powers that are never fully achieved, cursed by their distance from paternal grace, possessed by demonic energies, and always in a secondary position, all these figures remind us that Eliot inherited a fascination with the Romanticized figure of Satan, whose revolt and fall had already been made into a paradigm for male artistic exertions by writers she repeatedly quotes—Blake, Byron, Goethe, Coleridge, Shelley, and Keats. We have also seen here, however, that Eve, as an alienated, guilty, passionate, diminished outlaw, becomes Satanic for women writers from Mary Wollstonecraft and Mary Shelley to Charlotte Brontë: Eliot's identification with the fallen Satan in "The Lifted Veil" is clarified by her equally strong sympathies with the Satanic Eve of her verse drama "Armgart" (1871), which describes the presumptuous artistic aspirations and subsequent fall into gender of a successful female artist.

According to her friend and confidante, the ominously named Walpurga, Armgart recognizes that her art legitimizes passionate assertion of self that would otherwise be denied her:

> She often wonders what her life had been
> Without that voice for channel to her soul.
> She says, it must have leaped through all her limbs—
> Made her a Maenad—made her snatch a brand
> And fire some forest, that her rage might mount
> Leaving her still and patient for a while.
> "Poor wretch!" she says, of any murderess—
> "The world was cruel, and she could not sing:
> I carry my revenges in my throat;
> I love in singing, and am loved again."   [92]

Standing in front of the bronze busts of Beethoven and Gluck, Armgart admits that she knows "the oft-taught Gospel" that women "shalt not desire / To do aught best save pure subservience," but she considers her voice a blessing from nature and revels in a performance that will not be judged as "good, nay, wonderful, considering / She is a woman'" (105). Echoing the sentiments of Elizabeth Barrett Browning's *Aurora Leigh*, a poem Eliot had read more than once, Armgart rejects a wealthy suitor because "The man who marries me must wed my Art—/ Honour and cherish it, not tolerate" (110).

Almost as a punishment for her audacious commitment to freedom, Armgart develops an illness which prevents her from pursuing her career. Yet not the illness but its *cure* is the cause of the deterioration of her voice,[19] and her transformation into a "normal" woman. But such normalcy means being buried alive in "films" or "lava-mud" of a "deep, deep tomb, / Crying unheard forever!" "Cured" of her voice, Armgart is "a soul / Made keen by loss" (114), "a self accursed with consciousness of change, / A mind that lives in naught but members lopped, / A power turned to pain—" (115). No longer desired by the wealthy suitor, since she can no longer renounce her gift to his greater glory, she must decline into a normal, genteel, useful female, so she sees her fate as a tale entitled " 'The Woman's Lot: A Tale of Everyday.' "

Although "Prisoned in all the petty mimicries / Called woman's knowledge, that will fit the world / As doll-clothes fit a man" (123), she is Satanically enraged that she must submit to this diminution and drudgery,

> Because Heaven made me royal—wrought me out
> With subtle finish toward pre-eminence,
> Made every channel of my soul converge
> To one high function, and then flung me down,
> That breaking I might turn to subtlest pain.
> An inborn passion gives a rebel's right:
> I would rebel and die in twenty worlds
> Sooner than bear the yoke of thwarted life,
> Each keenest sense turned into keen distaste,
> Hunger not satisfied but kept alive
> Breathing in languor half a century.
> All the world now is but a rack of threads
> To twist and dwarf me into pettiness
> And basely feigned content, the placid mask
> Of women's misery.   [124]

Like Vashti in *Villette* or Catherine Earnshaw in *Wuthering Heights*, she has had a "glimpse of consciousness divine," but now she experiences only separation: "Now I am fallen dark; I sit in gloom, / Remembering bitterly" (125).

Significantly, Armgart's teacher is an artist named Leo, the fictitious composer whose music Mirah in *Daniel Deronda* sings first to Klesmer in her audition and then in the drawing rooms of polite society. Mirah has also realized that her "voice would never be strong enough—it did not fulfill its promise" (chap. 20). Like Latimer, she is taken by her father to Prague, where she is horrified to realize that he is about to sell her to a wealthy count, since she can no longer bring him money with her voice, and finally she runs away. Feeling life closing in upon her "with a wall of fire—everywhere there was scorching that made [her] shrink," Mirah loses her faith in God and man and goes to die in the river (chap. 6). But to George Eliot, in words that look forward to Emily Dickinson's imagery, Mirah is "just a pearl" because her nature is "only to submit" (chap. 20): she is a small and trusting waif who actually finds it a relief not to have to perform any longer on the stage, and so she is rescued from her suicide attempt and given a second chance for achieving happiness. Her angelic resignation is contrasted directly with the demonic ambition of the Princess Halm-Eberstein, Daniel Deronda's mother.

Stricken with the same "double consciousness' (chap. 51) as Latimer, the Princess knows that "every woman is supposed to have the same set of motives, or else to be a monster" (chap. 51). While she claims that she is not a monster for having chosen a career on the stage over a mother's duties, she is introduced by Eliot with a reference to the beauty of Melusina, a kind of lamia, serpent from the hips downward, and therefore an avatar of Sin in *Paradise Lost*, an ally (if not an embodiment) of Sin's father, Satan. With Satanic energy that "at once exalts and deadens" (chap. 51), guilt-ridden, in terrible pain at her revolt against her father's word, the Princess explains to her son that he cannot understand her rebellion against enforced renunciation: "You are not a woman. You may try—but you can never imagine what it is to have a man's force of genius in you, and yet to suffer the slavery of being a girl" (chap. 51). Her dying bitterness consists in her realization that her revolt has been in vain; Daniel will become his grandfather's inheritor. Like Armgart, the Princess at the peak of her powers begins to sing out of tune.[20]

All of this would seem to lead us far afield from "The Lifted Veil," except that this story clearly displays Eliot's consciousness of her place in a tradition of female gothic that is built by Mary Wollstone-craft and Mary Shelley and the Brontës around the close association of the female artist with Satan. Eliot seems to admit her indebtedness to Mary Shelley at the beginning, when Latimer prefaces his confession by proclaiming, "I thirsted for the unknown: the thirst is gone" (254). Latimer resembles Victor Frankenstein, Walton, and the monster in his definition of himself as a student of scientific origins who has been "plentifully crammed with the mechanical powers, the elementary bodies, and the phenomena of electricity and magnetism" (258). Furthermore, Latimer is an investigator, if an unwilling one, into forbidden knowledge of the mysteries of life, and his friendship with Meunier is reminiscent of Frankenstein's friendship with Clerval. Although he begins as a failed poet and lonely outcast who demands our sympathy, moreover, Latimer eventually degenerates into a spiteful Cain. Like Frankenstein's monster, he could complain, "I am solitary and abhorred"; like the monster, he feels defective and mute, and like the monster, unable to win compassion, he ends by exacting revenge and thereby causing more suffering. By locating the early stages of Latimer's story in the Alps of Geneva, by providing him with an English scientific friend who brings a dead corpse back to life, by having the aging Latimer explain that there is "no religion possible, no worship but a worship of devils" (304), and by portraying him finally as a lonely exile, Eliot emphasizes her debt to Mary Shelley.

Scientific overreachers, odd visionaries, revivification experiments, and themes of guilty revolt: these echoes of *Frankenstein* reinforce the impression we get from "The Lifted Veil" that George Eliot apparently identified with the failed aspirations of a fallen Satan because of her own sexually engendered fears of flying and falling, as well as her alienation from a culture she portrays as deathly. In Latimer's first prevision of Prague, a city "arrested in its course," he is plagued with a vision of grim, stony statues, "the real inhabitants and owners of this place," who are "urged by no fear or hope, but compelled by their doom to be ever old and undying, to live on in the rigidity of habit, as they live on in perpetual mid-day, without the repose of night or the new birth of morning" (262–63). Creation is not possible in this world without end where Swift's Struldbrugs or Tennyson's Tithonus would be at home. A city of the living dead where Latimer fittingly meets his bride, Prague resembles the Rome of *Middlemarch* or of Mary Shelley's *The Last Man*. Unlike the Alps, where, at sixteen, Latimer "used to do as Jean Jacques did,—lie down in [his] boat and let it glide where it would" (260), the thirsty, blackened, and unrefreshed city is associated with the grandeur of memories, crowned statues, bridges, churches, courts, and palaces—the paraphernalia of culture. But since its inhabitants live in "the stale repetition of memories, like deposed and superannuated kings" and the statues seem like "the fathers of ancient faded children," this culture announces itself as wearily and overwhelmingly patriarchal.

Elsewhere in Eliot's fiction, the waters of a powerfully providential maternal nature baptize, germinate, destroy, and revivify. But here even the river seems "a sheet of metal." As in the frozen hells of *Paradise Lost* and *Frankenstein*, no regeneration is possible in a world of repetition. Similarly, instead of producing new life, the scientific experiment conducted by Meunier and Latimer provides proof that the masculinist arts of civilization can only reanimate the dead and deaden the living. In a grotesque parody of the final judgment when "*The dead shall live, the living die*" (Dryden, "A Song for St. Cecilia's Day"), the end of "The Lifted Veil" describes the momentary reanimation of Mrs. Archer, whose revelation of Bertha's plot only leads to her own final demise, Bertha's public incrimination, and the continuation of Latimer's deathly existence; for if Latimer is a representative of Eliot's wounded imagination, he is nevertheless also a satiric portrait of the Satanic hero who embodies her concern that this second of God's sons diminishes women by reducing them to mere creatures or, worse still, characters.

Latimer thinks at first that his prevision of Prague is a sign of his poetic nature, manifesting itself in spontaneous creativity: "Surely it was in this way that Homer saw the plain of Troy, that Dante saw the abodes of the departed, that Milton saw the earthward flight of the Tempter" (264). And Latimer's first powers of prophetic insight into "things invisible to mortal sight" do appear after he is afflicted, like Milton, with blindness. Since he cannot control his imaginative vision and cannot create art out of it, Latimer quickly realizes that he is no Milton. But it is curious that in "The Lifted Veil" Eliot does seem to tell Milton's story, as she herself knew it. Like Milton recording "what misery th' inabstinence of Eve / Shall bring on men," Latimer tells the same story as that of *Paradise Lost*. For it is his love for Bertha that causes him a life of pain, and he emphasizes Bertha's likeness to Eve by portraying himself "fondly overcome with Female charm," specifically the charm of a beautiful orphan who keeps secret her plans to obtain independence and power, a narcissistic girl with "great rich coils" of hair who wears a green emerald brooch of a serpent "like a familiar demon on her breast" (300). Like Adam, Latimer would have us believe that he knew what she offered was death, but he was forced to fall because of his love for her.

But Latimer also resembles the Milton that Eliot wrote about four years before the creation of "The Lifted Veil." In an extremely sympathetic treatment of Milton's plea for divorce, she quotes the poet, who she believes is speaking out of his personal experience of marriage: "Who knows not that the bashful muteness of a virgin may oft times hide all the unloveliness and natural sloth which is really unfit for conversation?"[21] She further records Milton bemoaning the fate of a man who finds himself" 'bound fast to an uncomplying discord of nature, or, as it oft happens, to an image of earth and phlegm' " (157). This is not only the story of Latimer's life, it is also the plot Eliot might choose to construct around Lewes's previous marriage. Interestingly, it is also the central focus of a story written by Mary Shelley that has even more in common with "The Lifted Veil" than *Frankenstein* does.

Like many of Shelley's other stories, "The Mortal Immortal" appeared in *The Keepsake*, perhaps even in one of the copies given to Maggie Tulliver in *The Mill on The Floss* or Rosamund Vincy in *Middlemarch*. Its narrator resembles Latimer in considering himself a freak of nature who yearns to die but writes his life's story because he cannot commit suicide.[22] Even more strikingly, Shelley's narrator, who works for an alchemist, was tempted to drink the "Elixir of Immortality" because of his tormented love for a woman named Bertha. His immortality, then, like Latimer's clairvoyance, is a "gift" that is experienced as a curse. In addition, his Bertha shares more than a name with Latimer's: both are wealthy orphans, haughty and teasing coquettes who drive their male admirers mad with jealousy. The mortal immortal has his revenge against his Bertha, however. While he remains vigorous, the wife who originally caused him to participate in the black arts becomes old, ugly, and jealous of him. Although she wishes to share his secret and become with him "as Gods," she cannot. Similarly, Bertha Grant suspects Latimer's superhuman powers of insight but can in no way evade or obtain them. In both tales, female arts remain inadequate and secondary; while the husband is trapped in a world of eternal transcendence, the wife cannot escape the immanence of time.

Looking at "The Lifted Veil" as an instance, like "The Mortal Immortal," of a uniquely female gothicism, we can begin to see the distance between Latimer and George Eliot, a distance signalled by the male gender and role she gives him. As Latimer tells the story of his fascination with a woman he depises, it becomes increasingly clear that he is acting out his fear and hatred of the female sex. Obsessed by a woman who seems like a "fatal-eyed Water-Nixie," a "doubtfully benignant deity" (272), Latimer assumes that Bertha is only playing with his affections. Even after his brother and rival dies and Bertha seems to reciprocate his advances, Latimer's language reveals how deeply he suspects her of disloyalty:

> And she made me believe that she loved me. Without ever quitting her tone of *badinage* and playful superiority, she intoxicated me. . . .It costs a woman so little effort to besot us in this way! A half-repressed word . . . will serve us as *hashish* for a long while. Out of the subtlest web of scarcely perceptible signs, she set me weaving. [292]

Blaming her for his attraction to her, Latimer feels ensnared by the woman he has freely chosen.

Latimer is originally attracted to Bertha because she alone of all his acquaintances remains an enigma to him: he cannot overhear her thoughts, consequently she constitutes a true "other" for him. But while this is the source of his attraction, it is also the origin of his hatred. And so standing before Giorgione's portrait of "the cruel-eyed" Lucrezia Borgia, Latimer has a prevision of married life with a scornful, cruel-eyed Bertha. While he continues to love and pursue the girl Bertha, he fears and loathes the mature wife of his future. The maiden is "a fascinating secret" whose "witchery" he feels in spite of his dread. Yet this "playful sylph" whose "elfish" face possesses his imagination "like a returning siren melody" (288) is inextricably bound to the future fallen female:

> Behind the slim girl Bertha, whose words and looks I watched for, whose touch was bliss, there stood continually that Bertha with the fuller form, the harder eyes, the more rigid mouth,— with the barren selfish soul laid bare; no longer a fascinating secret, but a measured fact, urging itself perpetually on my unwilling sight. [280]

Haunted by this "double consciousness . . . glowing like two parallel streams which never mingle," Latimer—who identifies with Swift— embodies the ways in which the misogynistic imagination endows

the bride with precisely those qualities which will be contradicted
and destroyed by the wife. When, on the night of his father's death,
Latimer's first perception as his father's heir reveals the full force of
Bertha's sin, he is filled with contempt for "the narrow room of this
woman's soul" (296). Significantly, "the terrible moment of complete illumination" comes to him when he sees *himself* in her thoughts
as "a miserable ghost-seer, surrounded by phantoms in the noonday,
trembling under a breeze when the leaves were still, without appetite
for the common objects of human desire, but pining after the moon-
beams" (296). In other words, Latimer's perception of Bertha's evil
seems inescapably part of his fear of her and his loathing of himself.

Associated, as she is, with sirens, serpents, Eve, Cleopatra, Lucrezia
Borgia, water-nixies, and sprites, Bertha is no less a representative of
a popular type in the Romantic mythology of women than Maggie
Tulliver, Rosamund Vincy, and Gwendolen Harleth—fatal females
whose beauty, we shall see, is both sinister and tempting. Explaining
that Cleopatra was one of the first Romantic incarnations of this
fallen woman, Mario Praz outlines the relationship between male
and female that predominates with this type: "he is obscure, and
inferior either in condition or in physical exuberance to the woman,
who stands in the same relation to him as do the female spider, the
praying mantis, etc., to their respective males: sexual cannibalism
is her monopoly."[23] This is exactly the relationship between weak
and ailing Latimer and his blond, strong, Germanic-looking wife.
When, at the end of "The Lifted Veil," Bertha is watching canni-
balistically by the deathbed of her accomplice, afraid that the maid
will reveal the secret plot the two have hatched against Latimer's
life, he wonders "how that face of hers could ever have seemed to me
the face of a woman born of woman" (309–10) because "The features
at that moment seemed so preternaturally sharp, the eyes were so
hard and eager,—she looked like a *cruel immortal*, finding her *spiritual
feast in the agonies of a dying race*" (310; italics ours).

Goethe's *Faust*, Shelley's "Medusa," Keats's "La Belle Dame Sans
Merci," and all of Swinburne's various Ladies of Pain evince the
Romantics' fascination with the fatal female and the deathly principle
she represents, as do the beautiful, dying heroines Poe so admired.
In Coleridge's "The Ancient Mariner," the speaker's breathless
horror at the sight of Life-in-Death and her companion could have

been spoken by Latimer as he watches the dead Mrs. Archer and his wakeful wife: "Is that a DEATH? and are there two?/Is DEATH that woman's mate?" But, as we have seen, Eliot's identification with Latimer is limited, not only by his misogyny, but also by his inflated sense of his own suffering. Latimer might think that he "thirsted for the unknown," but Eliot presents him as a self-indulgent, self-pitying poseur. Hugging his sorrows as a sign of his superiority, creating every possible excuse for inactivity, Latimer seems a parodic version of those passive yet oddly heroic sufferers who populate Romantic literature, figures like the Ancient Mariner, Childe Harold, Wordsworth's beggars, or even Shelley's Prometheus.

Although Eliot shares to some extent Latimer's fascination with female beauty, her early fiction repeatedly cautions against judging the inner being by the outer person. It would be easy to explain Eliot's sensitivity in terms of the repeated rejections she received in young adulthood from men who deemed themselves connoisseurs of female beauty. But probably such personal pain only contributed to her mature recognition that the mystique of female beauty would be especially disabling for women who either could not or would not be reduced to aesthetic objects. That Eliot was also disturbed by the mystique of sexual promiscuity and perversity implicit in so much Romantic poetry is evident in her antagonism to Harriet Beecher Stowe's essay, "The True Story of Lord Byron's Life": Byron and his poetry seemed "repugnant" to her and his story "only worthy to die and rot" (*Letters*, 5:54). Later in her career Eliot had one of her more exemplary heroes, Felix Holt, explain to a girl who cherishes Byronic poetry that Byron was "a misanthropic debauchee ... whose notion of a hero was that he should disorder his stomach and despise mankind. His corsairs and renegades were ever pulled by the strings of lust and pride."[24] Furthermore, while Esther Lyon's "acquaintance with Oriental love was derived chiefly from Byronic poems," she remained deluded, but when "the Giaour concerned was giving her his arm," she discovers to her horror that he has had a wife who was bought *as a slave* (429).

Perhaps we can understand the vehemence of Esther's alienation and Eliot's critique by recalling more specifically her personal victimization as a result of Romantic myths. Living in Chapman's house, for instance, Eliot suffered from his perverse joy at the tangled emotional relationships between his editor, his wife, and his mistress, a taste that might have helped earn him the nickname "Byron." In his house she feels "something like madness which imagines that the four walls are contracting and going to crush one" (*Letters*, 2:54). Eliot might very well have seen Lewes as a double, a victim of the Romantic lives of his friends and lovers, since Lewes had been cruelly burdened by his child-wife, whose devotion to Shelley's doctrine of free love led to her bearing Thornton Hunt's children: Lewes himself had come under the influence of Godwin, Shelley, and Fourier through Leigh and Thornton Hunt. His tolerance for Agnes's conduct—he had condoned her adultery by giving the children his name—made it impossible for him to appeal for divorce by the laws of the day. Although Lewes was possibly the most supportive and loving companion a female author could wish for—he encouraged Eliot to write, took care of publishing details, nursed her through many illnesses, helped with background research—it is nevertheless true that Eliot took the brunt of the social punishment for their illicit life together.

Simultaneously attracted and repelled by Byron, Chapman, Shelley, and the Hunts, both Lewes and Eliot seem to illustrate the conventional Victorian ambivalence that Carlyle tried to resolve with his injunction "Close thy *Byron*; open thy *Goethe*." Living with Goethe's most illustrious biographer, Eliot probably wanted to follow Carlyle's advice, but she knew that in the eyes of the author of *Sartor Resartus* she was herself fallen,[25] and that both Byron's ethic of promiscuity *and* Goethe's principle of the eternal feminine, for that matter, provided her with literary contexts compellingly appropriate to her sense of herself as a woman, yet implicitly misogynist. Eliot's ambivalent response to Romanticism is Victorian, then, but it is also a woman's reaction against her own internalization of a tradition that she recognizes as especially dangerous for females.

As both a critic and an inheritor of the Romantic tradition, Eliot was especially interested in her female precursors, a point which yet another network of echoes in "The Lifted Veil" demonstrates, for if this strange story recalls Mary Shelley's fictions, it also repeatedly evokes the masterpiece of a woman writer whom Eliot praised as the

English George Sand ("only the clothing is less voluptuous" [*Letters*, 2:91]. Charlotte Brontë's fiction is important to the writing of "The Lifted Veil" because it allows Eliot to dramatize the self-division she experiences between the woman-identified woman and the misogynist. The fall into self-division, murderous materiality, and sexuality that haunts the characters of Mary Shelley and Emily Brontë is portrayed by Charlotte Brontë through the madwoman driven to rage that impels her to tear down, burn, and destroy the symbols of male power that have deprived both her and her docile double of ˙ love. Thus, by naming *her* furious madwoman Bertha, Eliot reminds us that "The Lifted Veil" is also a story about the woman's attempt to exact revenge.

Of course, in some sense, all Berthas seem to be symbols of powerful female sexuality.[26] Like the "bad" sister of Elizabeth Barrett Browning's "Bertha in the Lane," whose heat and fire contrast with the pale coldness of the dying angel whose lover she has seduced, Bertha Grant specifically resembles Bertha Mason Rochester not only because of her demonic sexuality but also because she is an orphaned, wealthy heiress whose physical strength and determination are markedly in contrast to prevailing notions of feminine delicacy and compliancy. Eliot strengthens the identification when she portrays Bertha by candlelight as an overwhelmingly malevolent and powerful figure. When Bertha comes to tell Latimer about her new maid, he wonders, "Why did she stand before me with the candle in her hand, with her cruel contemptuous eyes fixed on me?" (300). So too might Rochester or Jane have wondered in the haunting presence of Bertha Mason Rochester. That Bertha Grant's secret plans involve a new maid whose mysterious companionship seems extremely sinister reminds us that Grace Poole also appeared initially complicitous with her strange mistress, and Latimer's shrinking recalls Jane Eyre's anxiety. When he discovers that Mrs. Archer is not being dismissed in spite of insolent behavior, his astonishment parallels Jane's amazement that Grace Poole's destructive behavior has not earned her dismissal from Thornfield. Bertha Grant's fearful dependence on Mrs. Archer is "associated with ill-defined images of candle-light scenes in her dressing room, and the *locking up of something in Bertha's cabinet*" (301; italics ours), scenes which are reminiscent of the fiery walks of Bertha Mason Rochester and the locking up of her attic, especially because we learn that this "something" is poison. When, after being recalled from the dead, Mrs. Archer reveals that the plot is an attempt to murder Bertha's husband, we realize that Eliot is here admitting her indebtedness to the tradition of the madwoman in the attic.

If we wrench ourselves free from Latimer's perspective to consider Bertha's point of view, therefore, it becomes clear how he must represent to her the impoverishment of desire and the renunciation of vitality. Thus, when Latimer withdraws increasingly into passive acceptance of their hellish union, Bertha passionately desires his death as the only way of reclaiming her own life. When she begins suspecting him of clairvoyance, Bertha is "haunted by a terror" of Latimer "which alternated every now and then with defiance. She meditated continually how the incubus could be shaken off her life, —how she could be freed from this hateful bond to a being whom she at once despised as an imbecile, and dreaded as an inquisitor" (298). Bertha's terror is the product of her realization that she has been playing out his plots, that even her resentment of him has been foreseen and created for her by his vision of her as the fatal-eyed lamia.

As the author of Bertha's life, Latimer sits *in his father's library* reading when she appears to play the part he has already imagined for her, and her consciousness of this might very well reduce her in her own eyes to a stage actress or a character. Although Latimer claims to believe that "it might seem wonderful how her hatred toward [him] could grow so intense and active" (298), she has ample reason to fear his "abnormal powers of penetration" (298), so that, as this vocabulary suggests, her attempt to evade male vision is an effort to avoid or negate male potency. It makes perfect sense, then, that when Bertha begins to discover that Latimer's insight has diminished, "she lived in a state of expectation or hopeful suspense" (303). No such suspense has been possible in the closed world of his creation, but now she can presumably move from a sense of herself as a character to a sense of herself as a person. In her search for privacy, this character in flight from an author seems to realize her dilemma when she nicknames Latimer "Tasso" and when she is driven to construct the only plot that can bring her the freedom she desires. Her response to his deathly sublimation, moreover, is inevitably to assert the violence intrinsic in desire, and so the strange psychosexual bond between Bertha and Mrs. Archer develops along with the maturation of the plot to kill Latimer. Having detected the waning of Latimer's clairvoyant powers, Bertha successfully keeps her murderous scheme a secret from him and watches over Mrs. Archer's death "as the sealing of her secret" (310). This secret is the complicity of women—maid and matron—in their search for subversive stories inimical to men. Seeking to undercut the nourishing, nurturing role of the traditionally "feminine" woman, Mrs. Archer and Bertha would get to Latimer's heart *via his stomach*, by poisoning him, thereby proving that—even in their revolt—they find themselves caught in the old structures as they embrace Eve's act of rebellion, offering the apple of death to their man.

In *Jane Eyre* the heroine's prevision and her mad double's act of revenge successfully transform and redeem the male-dominated world, a world seen almost entirely from a female perspective. As a sign of her dissent from Brontë's fiction, George Eliot never allows us to depart from Latimer's consciousness, so that Bertha's female vantage remains silent and relatively inaccessible. Even as she develops the tradition of female gothic, then, Eliot revises it, for while Brontë explores the ways in which women can heal their painful self-divisions, Eliot implies that the divided self can only explode. Latimer and Bertha divorce, recognizing their hatred for each other. Deprived of her accomplice, her secret plot, and her only source of freedom, Bertha's resemblance to "a cunning animal whose hiding-places are surrounded by swiftly advancing flame" (312) even more forcefully recalls the madwoman in Thornfield. By identifying the split within herself as a division between a misogynist male and a misandric female,[27] however, Eliot swerves from the inherited tradition to account for a problem she sees as crucial because it is her own—the issue of self-hatred. Mutually reciprocal characters, both effeminate Latimer and castrating Bertha experience each other as aspects of themselves that rob their lives of freedom. The struggle between Latimer's transcendent insight and Bertha's passionate desire recalls, moreover, the conflict between what Elaine Showalter calls the "feminine" passion of Maggie and the "masculine" repression of Tom Tulliver,[28] and we shall see that it also informs the marital relationships of *Middlemarch*, even as it dramatizes Eliot's sense of paralysis, her guilt at having internalized attitudes at once debilitating and degrading to her sex.

For Eliot, then, the fallen state of consciousness, the secret wound of the female, is not only a subject but also a bind related to the paralysis of self-loathing which is initiated by acceptance of patriarchal values that contradict the woman's inescapable, if unarticulated, sense of her own primacy. It is, after all, significant that in her essay "Margaret Fuller and Mary Wollstonecraft" what Eliot finds to praise in *Woman in the Nineteenth Century* and *Rights of Woman* are passages that deal directly not with the injustice of men but with how the subjugation of women has debased and enfeebled the minds and souls of women. Similarly, she keeps her most impassioned attack as a critic for "the most mischievous form of feminine silliness" in "Silly Novels by Lady Novelists." Eliot's punishment of her heroines, her frequent bouts of illness, her often censorious avuncular tone, and her masculine pseudonym all suggest the depth of her need to evade identification with her own sex.

Seeking to legitimize her efforts and then her success as a writer as an unusual transcendence of the limits of her gender, Eliot resorts frequently in her major novels to pledges of deference and doctrines of feminine renunciation that are directly at odds with her own aggressively pursued career. Therefore, she herself could exclaim, "My own books scourge me" (*Letters*, 5:103–04). Virginia Woolf could just as convincingly claim of Eliot that "for long she preferred not to think of herself at all,"[29] thereby reminding us that George Eliot's headaches, her glorification of "eternal feminine" nobility, as well as her refusal to write her own story, make her into a type of Goethe's Makarie, not the most comfortable of roles for a writer. Further, "The Lifted Veil" shows us how ambivalent Eliot remained about the myth of the fall, the myth of feminine evil. By perpetuating such a myth, Eliot demonstrates her internalization of patriarchal culture's definition of the woman as the "other." We can see the signs of that internalization throughout her career—in her continued guilt over societal disapproval, her avowed preference for male friends, her feminine anti-feminism, her self-deprecatory assumption that all other forms of injustice are more important subjects for her art than female subjugation, her extreme dependence on Lewes for encouragement and approbation, her inability to face the world as a writer and read even the most benevolent reviews of her work.[30]

As the token female in an intellectual circle that included such eminent thinkers as Spencer, Jowett, Froude, and Mazzini, Eliot might have suspected that what she said so vehemently about Mrs. Hannah More could have been thought of her: "She was that most disagreeable of all monsters, a blue-stocking—a monster that can only exist in a miserably false state of society, in which a woman with but a smattering of learning or philosophy is classed along with singing mice and card playing pigs" (*Letters*, 1 : 245). Eliot, of course, had far more than a smattering of learning or philosophy, and she was exceptionally well-read in Greek and Latin. But this could only serve to make her seem even more freakish in her society (a point M. Paul makes to Lucy Snowe). Haight remarks that Eliot's classical education was probably "acquired during the long period of social ostracism when, because of her honest avowal of the union with Lewes, she was not invited to dinner."[31] She knew she was living a life that her own father, for instance, would have condemned as unwomanly, a life her respectable brother found so disagreeable that he refused to acknowledge her existence in any way. "What shall I be without my Father," Eliot had worried early in her life; "It will seem as if a part of my moral nature were gone. I had a vision of myself last night becoming earthly sensual and devilish for want of that purifying restraining influence" (*Letters*, 1 : 283–84).

Certainly the saddest sign of her inability to stand alone—whether or not it is true that the single word *Crisis* in her diary refers to her discovery five and a half months after Lewes's death of his infidelity[32]—is Eliot's precipitous marriage to a man young enough to be her son and troubled enough to need a replacement for the recent death of his mother. The marriage to John Cross just months before her own death points us to the importance of her insight in the novels into the deeply inbred dependence of women. How must this "Beatrice," as he called her, have felt when on their honeymoon her new husband jumped from his balcony in Venice into the Grand Canal below, only to be fished up unharmed by the boatmen?

Yet, whatever her personal insecurities were, she must have known that what she accomplished in her fiction was unprecedented in the history of the novel. Not only were *Adam Bede* and *The Mill on the Floss* extremely popular and financially successful; by the time of the publication of *Middlemarch* Eliot was acclaimed throughout England as a writer who could honestly confront the doubts and despair of her generation and still leave her readers with a heartening sense that profound values of humor, love, and duty would prevail. Her public's enthusiasm was matched by the awe with which her visitors brought their offerings and waited for her words of wisdom. If she was encouraged to play the role of sibyl or muse, however, she made it work for her. While we will explore Eliot's extreme ambivalence over the ideal of female service in her mature fiction, we can see traces of it even in her early translation work, for her anxious interest in Strauss's and Feuerbach's dissection of the story of the Crucifixion is surely related to her determination to preserve the essence of Christian self-sacrifice through the apotheosis of human feeling. But such a discovery would mean that the man/God need no longer be the exclusive symbol of incarnation. Indeed, while usually viewed in terms of her obsessively "feminine" renunciation, Eliot's interest in the Virgin Mother and in Saint Theresa can be seen as an attempt to discover a symbol of uniquely female divinity. Perhaps even her placing of her novels in preindustrial historical settings can be related to her nostalgia for a time when women's work was important to the maintenance of the human community. In any case, Eliot's troubled movement from Evangelical self-denial to a religion of humanity is only one index of the juggling she had constantly to perform between her identification with male culture and her undeniable consciousness of herself as a woman.

One of the most interesting images supplied by "The Lifted Veil" for an understanding of this conflict is the image of the veil itself, for Eliot mediates between its traditionally Romantic meanings and its uniquely female significance. An image of confinement different from yet related to the imagery of enclosure that constantly threatens to stifle the heroines of women's fiction, the veil resembles a wall, but even when it is opaque it is highly impermanent, while transparency transforms it into a possible entrance or exit. Unlike a door, which is either open or shut, however, it is always potentially both—always holding out the mystery of imminent revelation, the promise or the threat that one might be able to see, hear, or even feel through the veil which separates two distinct spheres: the phenomenal and the noumenal; culture and nature; two consciousnesses; life and death; public appearance and private reality; conscious and unconscious impulses; past and present, present and future. Because it is an image of confinement that endows boundaries with a transitory and ambivalent fluidity, and because it takes on special status with respect to images of women, the veil especially fascinated Eliot. She transforms it into a multitude of webs, nets, snares, bandages, shawls, masks, and curtains in her fiction. The veil is, therefore, useful in summarizing her uniquely complex relationship both to Romanticism and to the traditions of women's literature already well established in her day.

That such Romantics as Blake, Wordsworth, Coleridge, Emerson, and Shelley sought to lift the "veil of familiarity" to "see into the life of things" is apparent in their repeated attempts to recapture a time when the countenance divine shone forth upon hills since clouded. Conscious that the veil divides the holy from the most holy place (Exodus 26:33), the Romantic poet seeks the wisdom of a priest/bard to confront the presence of power. Shelley, at the end of *Adonais*, Browning in "By the Fireside," and Swinburne in a number of poems are convinced that they can penetrate to the heavenly harmony behind the veil of mutability. As Kenneth Johnston has shown, however, even when a poet like Wordsworth bemoans his inability to see by more than glimpses, he is fleeing from revelation, reveiling, and retreating from the heightened consciousness that forecasts Apocalypse.[33]

Indeed, although Wordsworth actually wore a veil in his later life to relieve a literal eye problem, it also bespoke his general fear of having and of losing vision. In other words, while they sometimes tore aside the veil, the Romantics also advised themselves to "Lift not the painted veil" because of their common dread of what would be glimpsed behind it. In this respect, they perpetuate a long gothic tradition which embraces the veil as a necessary concealer of grotesque revelations of sin and guilt, past crimes and future suffering. In the stories of Poe ("The Case of M. Valdemar"), Dickens ("The Black Veil"), and Hawthorne ("The Minister's Black Veil"), the veil is a symbol of secret guilt; characters like Young Goodman Brown or the Reverend Mr. Hooper see nothing but evil when the veil separating other minds is rent by their clairvoyant insight.

Clearly Eliot invokes all these associations in her story. Like Shelley's Preacher who lifts the painted veil, Latimer seeks "things to love," and finds instead nothing of which he can approve. When he sees the sun lift "the veil of morning mist" (264), when he penetrates "the curtain of the future" (256), when "the web of [close relations'] characters [is] seen as if thrust asunder by a microscopic vision" (270), when he looks through death which is yet another "dark veil" (310), he discovers nothing that makes any difference at all and learns that "so absolute is our soul's need of something hidden" that he welcomes any kind of screen: "no matter how empty the adytum, so that the veil be thick enough" (291). In other words, "The Lifted Veil" differs from the tales of Poe, Dickens, and Hawthorne in that it never delivers the terrible secret or sustains the sense of evil that it seems originally to promise. Perceiving neither a gothic horror of evil nor a Romantic revelation of divinity behind these veils, Latimer repeatedly finds that "the darkness had hidden no landscape from [him], but only a blank prosaic wall" (296). We readily infer that the true horror is precisely this insipid banality. Accordingly, the return to life of a corpse supplies us with no terrifying vision of the dread gulf that has been bridged, but merely with the confirmation of Latimer's own suspicions that his wife wishes him dead.

If "The Lifted Veil" is a story about the myth of penetrating vision—a critique of gothic and Romantic versions of that myth—it is simultaneously an investigation into the assumptions of the novelist's art. Latimer's ability to see behind or beyond the veil without revealing himself is an emblem of the "omniscient" novelist's claim to perceive the consciousness of characters without being seen herself and presumably without altering the events that will determine her characters' lives. Latimer's imaginative powers endow him with the insight accorded the omniscient narrator, and Eliot shows us that these powers are only alienating. Clairvoyance brings him consciousness of nothing except isolation, distance, impotence, the egoism of his family, the pettiness of his friends, the repetition he is destined to endure. While Eliot expends much of her energy in the rest of her fiction implying or explaining how imaginative identification can redeem life through human sympathy and fellowship, in "The Lifted Veil" imaginative vision seems to rob life of mystery and thereby kills off suspense, preys on the living, destroys even the appearance of beauty, and deprives humankind of all necessary illusions. In order to understand how and why these antithetical attitudes toward imaginative insight continually haunt Eliot, we need to return to the image of the veil as it has been used in male literature to characterize women, because that use perfectly demonstrates the roles offered imaginative women and their resulting conflict between renunciation and rage.

Of course it makes perfect sense that the ambiguity of the veil, its essential mystery as an emblem of obscure potential, should associate it in male minds with that repository of mysterious otherness, the female. As an inspiration and source of imaginative power, the presence behind the veil for many a poet is the female muse. In Shelley's *The Witch of Atlas*, for instance, the creative lady weaves "a subtle veil" to hide her beauty, which is dangerous for mortal sight since it makes "the bright world dim." Inalterably separated by the veil from all that lives, the witch is despite her loveliness a deathly creature who easily modulates into a far more malevolently veiled female, from Keats's Moneta to the sinister Geraldine whose unclothed body is so terrible that Coleridge cannot even describe it: "Behold! her bosom and half her side— / A sight to dream of, not to tell!"[34] In Schiller's poem "The Veiled Image of Saia" the man who dares to look on the face of the female image is found dead before Isis's pedestal.

Whether they embrace or reject the veil, these poets remind us that the angelic muse seems to be just as easily transformed into the monstrous Medusa as she had been in Spenser's dismantling of Duessa or Swift's dressing room poems, or in *The Blithedale Romance*, a book that Eliot definitely read and may have reviewed (*Letters*, 2:56):

> Some upheld that the veil covered the most beautiful countenance in the world; others,—and certainly with more reason, considering the sex of the Veiled Lady,—that the face was the most hideous and horrible, and that this was her sole motive for hiding it. It was the face of a corpse; it was the head of a

skeleton; it was a monstrous visage, with snakey locks, like
Medusa's, and one great red eye in the centre of the forehead.[35]

Whether she is beautiful or hideous, the veiled woman reflects male
dread of women, so that, for example, Milton visited by the spirit of
his dead wife "vested all in white" knows that this ghostly presence
can haunt him as surely as it inspires him.[36]

Eliot's consciousness of this tradition is apparent not only in
Latimer's story of lifting the veil that conceals Bertha's soul, but also
in later references in *Romola* to the beneficent healing of the veiled
Madonna and the blinding powers of the unveiled goddess Minerva.
But as a woman Eliot experiences "only" herself behind the veil and
so she demystifies the revelation of the Muse/Medusa, thereby
deflating both gothic and Romantic myths. Latimer's lifting of the
veil reveals not a monster, but the madwoman Bertha Grant. In
this respect, Eliot extends the tradition established by the Brontës,
for Jane Eyre recognizes her own enraged double when Bertha
Mason Rochester descends, shrouded, to rend the wedding veil,
while Lucy's nun wears narrow black skirts and a white bandage
that veils her face, so Lucy knows the ghostly woman to be another
specter of herself because she, too, remains blanketed in gray, and
eclipsed by shadows. Even rebellious Catherine Earnshaw Linton
places a shawl over her mirror because, pregnant and captive in her
husband's house, she is alienated from the part of herself which is
savage and free. Almost always, it seems, the veil is a symbol for
women of their diminishment into spectral remnants of what they
might have been. Therefore Christina Rossetti, whose role as a
"model" made her extremely sensitive to her entrapment in male
"frames," writes of more than one heroine whose "strength with
weakness is overlaid;/Meek compliances veil her might,"[37] as do
Charlotte Perkins Gilman and Denise Levertov in the epigraphs at
the beginning of this chapter.

That Latimer's lifting of the veil is associated with clairvoyance
reminds us that the veiled lady of male literature is frequently
identified with spiritual powers. The two females in *The Blithedale
Romance* who embody the Madonna and the Medusa aspects of the
veiled lady are both endowed with superhuman powers, so it is hardly
surprising that the feminism of Zenobia and the clairvoyance of

Priscilla are linked by a number of other American novelists. Bayard Taylor's *Hannah Thurston* (1864), William Dean Howells's *The Un-discovered Country* (1880), and James's *The Bostonians* (1884–85) elaborate on the connection made explicit in the title of the pseudonymous Fred Folio's *Lucy Boston: Or Women's Rights and Spiritualism, Illustrating the Follies and Delusions of the Nineteenth Century* (1855).[38] Although such writers probably associate the feminist movement with mediumism, hypnotism, automatic writing, and inspirational speaking in order to discredit the political movement by linking it to "irrational" psychic phenomena, there is also some historical basis for this connection. Elizabeth Cady Stanton, Margaret Fuller, Lucy Stone, Harriet Martineau, Elizabeth Barrett Browning, the Fox sisters, Harriet Beecher Stowe, Victoria Woodhull and many Quaker and Shaker women illustrate the important nexus in the second half of the nineteenth century between feminism and spiritualism that is only strengthened by remembering that Charlotte Brontë wrote with her eyes closed about a heroine who "hears" her lover calling her from miles away, that Gertrude Stein composed an early essay on telepathic communication, and that the heroine of Margaret Atwood's *Lady Oracle* types in a trance that allows her first to enter the other side of the mirror, and then to re-write the ending of *Jane Eyre*.

We have already seen that Latimer's telepathy is a metaphor for his "feminine" qualities—sensitivity to the needs of others, physical weakness, exquisite sensibilities, presumably angelic or demonic powers and shrinking modesty. For women writers like Louisa May Alcott ("Behind a Mask") and Mary Elizabeth Braddon (*Lady Audley's Secret*), the exceptional insight, with resultant duplicity, of a veiled lady becomes a strategy for survival in a hostile, male-dominated world. Denied the freedom to act openly out in the world, their heroines exploit their intuitive understanding of the needs of the male ego in order to provide comfortable places for themselves in society. Similarly, in "The Sullivan Looking-Glass" Harriet Beecher Stowe depicts the clairvoyant powers of a woman who *"hes the gift o' seein'. She was born with a veil over her face!"*[39] Confronting her dispossession, Ruth Sullivan sees in her dressing room mirror a predictive vision of her eventual discovery of a lost will that will return to her a just portion of the ancestral estate. Her clairvoyance, like Jane Eyre's preternatural hearing, illustrates how those cut off from political power may exploit their passivity by becoming instruments compelled by higher forces, even as they are drawn to what constitutes a shortcut to authority through a personal relationship with spiritual powers presumably beyond the control of men. The uniquely female sensitivity of all these heroines becomes a weapon, just as it becomes a means of salvation for the madwomen in Doris Lessing's *Four-Gated City*, where the "sea of sound" Martha hears resembles Latimer's "roar of sound." While prevision and clairvoyance seem first like curses, these women eventually convert such powers into subversive modes of communication, providing escape routes from what George Eliot's most important successor terms "the bourgeois nightmare of repetition."[40]

Finally, then, the recording of what exists behind the veil is distinctively female because it is the woman who exists behind the veil in patriarchal society, inhabiting a private sphere invisible to public view. Thus Eliot determines to explore only the noiseless pain and the unrecorded suffering she appreciated in Wordsworth's poetry. She would reject the ponderously Olympian perspective of a poet like Pope—"Why has not Man a microscopic eye? / For this plain reason, Man is not a Fly."[41]—because she is committed to Latimer's "microscopic vision," which she obtains by applying "a strong lens" to get the otherwise invisible details in focus. Using the woman's traditional place in the home as a vantage revealing the private feebleness behind public posturing, she refutes masculine mythology in a manner that Elizabeth Barrett Browning might have found typically feminine:

> Has paterfamilias, with his oriental traditions and veiled female faces, very successfully dealt with a certain class of evil? What if materfamilias, with her quick sure instincts and honest innocent eyes, do more towards their expulsion by simply looking at them and calling them by their names?[42]

While here it is identified with the honesty of the dispossessed, realism can also become associated with self-renunciation—seeing life from the other person's perspective, appreciating the significance of what might seem trivial from a less sympathetic point of view. But, as "The Lifted Veil" implies, such insight can diminish the self, inundating it in the trivial pettiness of humankind, tainting it with the secret corruption of neighboring souls, and paralyzing it with the experience of contradictory needs and perspectives.

Just as the renunciation of Eliot's heroines frequently leads to their frustration at a sacrifice not worth the making, the self-efface-ment implied by the microscopic eye can yield feelings of impotence and anger. Lifting the veil that separates his consciousness from other consciousnesses means, for Latimer, that the "stream of thought" in other people rushes upon him "like a preternaturally heightened sense of hearing, making audible to one a roar of sound where others find perfect stillness" (276). This is the same faculty that Eliot describes in *Middlemarch*: "If we had a keen vision and feeling of all ordinary human life, it would be like hearing the grass grow and the squirrel's heart beat, and we should die of that roar which lies on the other side of silence" (chap. 20). Because she is able to penetrate "behind the big mask" where "there must be our poor eyes peeking out as usual and our timorous lips more or less under control" (*Middle-march*, chap. 29), Eliot frequently oscillates between pity and disdain.

As a woman writer, moreover, Eliot cannot evade experiencing herself as a veiled lady. Like Latimer, who can read others but who will determinedly hide his own subjectivity out of a sense of shame and fear of self-exposure, Eliot maintains a superiority over her characters that is in part responsible for the overwhelmingly oppres-sive sense we sometimes have that her characters will constantly be tested, evaluated ethically, and found wanting. Whether she becomes a mellow clergyman or a gentleman on horseback watching the scene in the valley below from a hilltop or a disembodied voice which summarizes all the thoughts of the community, Eliot is no less reticent than Latimer, and her plots hide her personal sense of herself as effectively as his conversations do. Emily Dickinson calls shame "The elemental Veil," and surely George Eliot—whose pose of omniscient transcendence makes her inaccessible to her readers—wraps herself in this "shawl of Pink" (J. 1412). But, like Dickinson, Eliot transforms what she experiences as a loss—her alienation from the human community—into a gain: since she is an outsider, a fallen female viewing respectable society, an insect watching provincial life, her unique perspective gains by its obliqueness because "The Thought beneath so slight a film— / Is more distinctly seen—" (J. 210), because "By a departing light / We see acuter, quite" (J. 1714), because "Sunset that screens, reveals— / Enhancing what we see" (J. 1609). A perspective qualified by screens and cracks is a form of renunciation that Dickinson enacts because she would rather veil her own eyes than blind others with her glance. For "it is terrible— the keen bright eye of a woman when it has once been turned with admiration on what is severely true; but then, the severely true rarely comes within its range of vision" (*Felix Holt*, chap. 43). Dis-ease at asserting oneself as an "I" therefore leads not only to "eye" diseases but also to the hiding of one's "eyes." And because a microscopic eye is not worth crushing, it can be overlooked. No wonder, then, that Dickinson, sensing her kinship with Eliot, wrote, "What do I think of *Middlemarch*? What do I think of glory? ... The mysteries of human nature surpass the 'mysteries of redemption.'"[43]

According to Saint Paul, only the veiled woman can prophesy in the temple because the head of every man is identified with Christ and the spirit, while the head of every woman is associated with the body and therefore must be covered (1 Corinthians 11). As in purdah, acceptance of the veil becomes a symbol of the woman's submission to her shame: the unveiled Salome will damn and destroy men, but the Virgin Mother remains a veiled goddess whose purity is shared by religious Jewish women who shave their hair the better to cover their heads, and by nuns who, as the brides of Christ, perpetually wear the veil because they will never degenerate into the wives of Christ. Wearing the mantle of invisibility conferred by her omniscience and the veil of the Madonna conferred by her message of feminine renunciation, Eliot survives in a male-dominated society by defining herself as the Other. But the woman whom Lewes was overheard to call "Madonna" or "Mutter" and whom female friends called "Our Lady"[44] was not unaware that genuine intersubjectivity may threaten the autonomy and, as we shall see, even the life of at least one self.

Although until quite recently she has been viewed almost exclusively in terms of male literary history,[45] Eliot shows in "The Lifted Veil" that she is part of a strong female tradition: her self-conscious relatedness to other women writers, her critique of male literary conventions, her interest in clairvoyance and telepathy, her imagery of confinement, her schizophrenic sense of fragmentation, her self-hatred, and what Emily Dickinson might have called her "Covered Vision" (J. 745) place Eliot in a tradition that still survives today.

Like Sylvia Plath, Louise Bogan, and May Sarton, Eliot looked at the female monster only to find herself:

> I turn your face around! It is my face.
> That frozen rage is what I must explore—
> Oh secret, self-enclosed, and ravaged place!
> This is the gift I thank Medusa for.

May Sarton entitled this poem "The Muse as Medusa," seeing what is implied in Eliot's art, that female power has been subverted into self-hatred which has deformed female creativity. We are unaccustomed to think of Eliot exploring the secret, self-enclosed, and ravaged place of her own self, but "The Lifted Veil" is not nearly so idiosyncratic as she would have us believe. Indeed, like the dead face that unexpectedly springs out of the movable panel to haunt Gwendolen Harleth, "The Lifted Veil" informs the major fiction of Eliot's maturity, although she would do as Maggie Tulliver and Rosamund Vincy did and reject the *Keepsake* of female gothic, if only she could.

14 George Eliot as the Angel of Destruction

Thus *Tapestry* of old, the Walls adorn'd,
Ere noblest Dames the artful *Shuttle* scorn'd:
Arachne, then, with Pallas did contest,
And scarce th'Immortal Work was judg'd the Best.
Nor valorous Actions, then, in Books were fought;
But all the Fame, that from the Field was brought,
Employ'd the *Loom*, where the kind *Consort* wrought:
Whilst sharing in the Toil, she shar'd the Fame,
And with the *Heroes* mixt her interwoven Name.
No longer, *Females* to such Praise aspire,
And serfdom now We rightly do admire.
So much, All Arts are by the *Men* engross'd,
And Our few Talents unimprov'd or cross'd.

—Anne Finch

... a Web, dark & cold, throughout all
The tormented element stretch'd
From the sorrows of Urizens soul.
And the Web is a Female in embrio.
None could break the Web, no wings of fire.

So twisted the cords, & so knotted
The meshes: twisted like to the human brain.

And all called it, The Net of Religion.

—William Blake

"... and the evil longings, the evil prayers, came again and blotted everything else dim, till, in the midst of them—I don't know how it was—... I know nothing—I only know that I saw my wish outside me."

—George Eliot

478

"Will there never be a being to combine a man's mind and woman's heart, and who yet finds life too rich to weep over?" Margaret Fuller once asked in anguish. "Never?"[1] While George Eliot could never have lived Fuller's Byronic life, she might have prided herself on fulfilling that ideal of combining a man's mind with a woman's heart. In her major novels Eliot tries to resolve the conflict she had confronted most bleakly in the miserable marriage of "The Lifted Veil." Yet the Latimer-Bertha marriage serves as a kind of model for many others in Eliot's fiction, even as it illustrates the tension between her detached narrative voice and her commitment to heart and hearth. For, as an agnostic setting out to write about the virtues of clerical life, a "fallen" woman praising the wife's service, a childless writer celebrating motherhood, an intellectual writing what she called "experiments in life" (*Letters*, 6:216) in celebration of womanly feeling, Eliot becomes entangled in contradictions that she can only resolve through acts of vengeance against her own characters, violent retributions that become more prominent when contrasted with her professed purposes as a novelist. This tension between mind and heart reflects her dedication to enacting the role of one of her earliest pen-names—Pollian, the Angel of Destruction—and also illuminates her attraction to two very different American contemporaries, Margaret Fuller and Harriet Beecher Stowe, who seem to embody for her the warring impulses at work in her own art.

Although their achievements differ radically, George Eliot and Margaret Fuller shared anxieties about female power; the two also shared a number of intellectual and personal goals, as Eliot herself seemed to recognize when she remarked that this American's life had been "a help" in her own (*Letters*, 2:15). Brought up by a father who was in his way as formidable and exacting as Eliot's, Fuller had neither wealth nor social standing, and she often found herself writing for money. Considered abnormal because of her extraordinary learning, she was treated like a sibyl, as Eliot was. And like Eliot, she became an expert on German culture, especially the works of Goethe. A friend of Mazzini and an admirerer of Harriet Martineau and George Sand, Fuller wrote essays for a leading intellectual journal and became famous for her close relationship with the married editot. Like Eliot, Fuller was not considered physically

attractive, and she too did not meet the man who could reciprocate
her love until relatively late in her life. Like Eliot, Fuller was much
more interested in theological, scientific, political, and economic
issues than in feminism. Unlike the ladylike novelists they both
scorned, both women travelled, read, and reviewed widely. What
Ann Douglas views as Fuller's special quality, her "invincible
historicism," [2] is also Eliot's. And indeed, what many women (including Eliot) must have found most refreshing about Fuller's work
is precisely this widened perspective on reality, a perspective Eliot's
heroines repeatedly strive to attain and that Emily Dickinson
appreciated in "Mrs. Lewes" herself: "She is the Lane to the Indes,
Columbus was looking for." [3]

Like Eliot, Fuller identified her presumptuous ambition with the
aspiration to transcend the limits of her sex: "I have always thought
that I could not [write], that I would keep all that behind the curtain,
that I would not write like a woman, of love and hope and disappointment, but like a man, of the world of intellect and action." [4]
Fuller found womanhood "too straightly-bounded" to give her
"scope," and she never did write the fiction her female contemporaries
were (by their great numbers, as well as by their success) making a
distinctly feminine vocation. But she also felt she would "stifle" or
even "palsy," should she write like a man, for then she would only
succeed at "play [ing] the artist." [5] In this respect, too, she resembles
Eliot, who feared that inauthentic women's art would seem "an
absurd exaggeration of the masculine style, like the swaggering gait
of a bad actress in male attire." [6] Wanting to surpass her sex by
living a life of significant action, Fuller found it far easier to be
eloquent as a speaker than as an author because "formerly the pen
did not seem to me an instrument capable of expressing the spirit of
a life like mine." [7] Since it seemed "more native to inspire and receive
the poem, than to create it," Fuller recorded dreams in which her
body was a dungeon from which a beautiful angel escaped at the
head; she described her attraction to Goethe's Makarie, who was
"born of the stars," only to bemoan her inability to see such lights
herself except "from the mouth of my damp cave"; lamenting the
terrible migraines and eyestrain that tormented her, she mockingly
complained, "it is but a bad head, as bad as if I were a great man!" [8]

Fuller's sense of paralysis and pain led her to counsel women to develop the "masculine" side of their nature, or what she called the "Minerva" role. Yet at other times she argued that women cannot escape their spiritual destiny: "Through Woman Man was lost, so through Woman must Man be redeemed."[9] It makes perfect sense, then, for Fuller to praise Elizabeth Barrett Browning's "true woman's heart" in her review of *A Drama of Exile: And Other Poems*, even as she defines Barrett Browning's faults in terms of her gender, arguing that a deficiency in the shaping power of poetic energy incapacitates the "poetess" from seeing the angelic hosts as Milton did. For Fuller is quite sure that Barrett Browning "cannot, like Milton, marshall the angels so near the earth as to impart their presence other than by sympathy."[10] Paradoxically, however, after Fuller's untimely death, Elizabeth Barrett Browning was herself quick to understand that Fuller had confronted "the usual difficulties and sadnesses which await a woman in literary life." Honoring Fuller's truth and boldness, she observes how the very problems that beset her own art tragically prevented the American from actually producing the literature her genius seemed to promise: *"Don't read her writings,"* she warns a friend, "because they are quite below and unworthy of her."[11] At the same time, she does exhort her correspondents to read the fiction of a very different contemporary:

> Not read Mrs. Stowe's book! But you *must*. Her book is quite a sign of the times, and has otherwise an intrinsically considerable power. For myself, I rejoice in the success both as a woman and a human being. Oh, and is it possible that you think a woman has no business with questions like the question of slavery. Then she had better use a pen no more. She had better subside into slavery and concubinage herself, I think, as in the times of old, shut herself up with the Penelopes in the "women's apartment," and take no rank among thinkers and speakers.[12]

Barrett Browning seems to be locating the source of the power that might have been responsible for Emily Dickinson's pleasure in *Uncle Tom's Cabin* (1852), which the American poet read in spite of her father's emphatic dislike of fiction.[13]

Eliot praised Fuller for precisely what she believed Stowe's writing lacked—the portrayal of "the most terribly tragic element ... the Nemesis lurking in the vices of the oppressed"—but she was nevertheless drawn to Stowe's portrayal of the virtues of the oppressed. "Why can we not have pictures of religious life among the industrial classes in England, as interesting as Mrs. Stowe's pictures of religious life among the negroes?"[14] Eliot asked the readers of the *Westminster Review* in 1856, and the book she herself would begin to write eleven days later can be viewed as a response to this challenge. She shared with Stowe an interest in history viewed from the bottom up, social life comprehended through the feelings that Stowe identifies with female strengths and roles. Early in her intellectual life, Eliot was drawn to the possibility of a uniquely female tradition in literature, characterized by love rather than by anger, because in art "the entire being" is engaged and women's "sensations and emotions—the maternal ones—" might well produce distinctive forms.[15] Where Fuller had asserted the necessity of women acquiring "masculine" powers of intellect, Eliot seems, therefore, to have preferred Stowe's emphasis on the need for men to develop "feminine" receptivity, specifically that of female nurturance.

As if they constitute the material upon which Eliot founded her hypothesis, Stowe's revolutionary books insist that maternal sensations and feminine powerlessness alone can save a world otherwise damned by masculine aggression. Uncle Tom, for example, has recently been identified as "a stereotypical Victorian heroine: pious, domestic, self-sacrificing, emotionally uninhibited in response to people and ethical questions."[16] His secret prayers and suicidal passivity constitute, moreover, a distinctively feminine response to coercion, a response illuminated by Stowe's critique of slavery as a patriarchal institution in which both slaves and wives—and especially slaves who function as wives and wives who function like slaves—are used and abused. Writing not about an Eve who falls and thereby condemns men to death, but about a little Eva who brings eternal life through self-sacrifice, Stowe insists that Christian love resides especially in the powerless, and there is ultimately, therefore, a sense in which even her Christ is female. As an ethical touchstone, then, the mother-child bond becomes for Stowe a model of what social community should be. Not only are all the characters in *Uncle Tom's Cabin* judged by their attitude toward this bond; the author makes it clear in her "Concluding Remarks" that she is writing to "you,

Mothers of America," who pity "those mothers that are constantly made childless by the American slave trade!"[17]

What Eliot must have learned from these two American female models is that, while Margaret Fuller solved the problem of what we have been calling "the anxiety of authorship" by living an ambitious life that she could not write about because it could not be contained within traditional literary genres, Harriet Beecher Stowe was able to solve the same problem by excluding any portrait of herself from the fictional world she created. Even as Eliot implicitly pays tribute to Stowe by identifying the special strength of women with their maternal capacity for sympathy, her own fiction repeatedly demonstrates her fear that Stowe's appreciation of feminine virtues could degenerate into self-congratulatory sentimentality that would finally sustain the very coercion Stowe deplored. Both Fuller and Stowe were thus clearly hampered by the Muse / Mother ideal that haunted their sense of what they ought to be. Anxious not only about the pain of the individual attempting to combine a man's mind with a woman's heart, but also the resulting conflicts in a society where men and women are so categorized, both doubt "whether the heart does consent with the head, or only obeys its decrees with a passiveness that precludes the exercise of its natural powers, or a repugnance that turns sweet qualities to bitter, or a doubt that lays waste the fair occasions of life."[18]

The tension for these women between masculine and feminine roles typifies the frustration that informs the writing of so many of their contemporaries. Louisa May Alcott, for example, clearly preached the benefits of feminine socialization in *Little Women* (1869), although she depicted the terrible cost of feminine submission through Beth's prolonged suicide. But Alcott also revealed in her paradigmatic Marmee how submission and service could never eradicate (and might even breed) silent, savage rage. When gentlemanly Jo worries that her temperamental flare-ups will eventually result in her killing someone, Marmee admits that she too has a temper which she has been unable to cure for forty years: "I am angry nearly every day of my life," she explains to Jo, "but I have learned not to show it; and I still try to hope to learn not to feel it, though it may take me another forty years to do it."[19]

As domestic a novelist as Mrs. Gaskell could also complain of feeling "deep hatred to my species about whom I [am] obliged to write as if I loved 'em."[20] Interestingly, Mrs. Gaskell very much appreciated George Eliot's early fiction, especially praising "Janet's Repentence" in a letter to Eliot which concludes with the admission, "I should not be quite true . . . if I did not say . . . that I wish you *were* Mrs. Lewes."[21] The patient author of *Scenes of Clerical Life* managed to write back a letter of thanks for Mrs. Gaskell's "assurance of fellow-feeling" that politely refrained from responding to what must have been a particularly painful hint. But Eliot's self-control, like Fuller's and Stowe's and Alcott's, must have required her not infrequently to follow Marmee's advice and fold her lips tightly together; for, like Jo, Eliot experiences her own anger as potentially murderous.

"But, my dear madam," the narrator of *Scenes of Clerical Life* (1857) occasionally cautions, "you would gain unspeakably if you would learn with me to see some of the poetry and the pathos, the tragedy and the comedy, lying in the experience of a human soul that looks out through dull grey eyes, and that speaks in a voice of quite ordinary tones."[22] His condescension is not unrelated to his determination to reform his audience's corrupt taste for melodrama. And certainly Eliot is centrally concerned in her earliest published fiction with sensitizing her readers to common human frailties. As in her later work, she wants to expand our faith in the redemptive possibilities of compassion. In addition, here, as elsewhere in her fiction, she portrays the impact of historical forces, such as Evangelicalism, on provincial life. But while the narrator calls our attention to the ordinary tones and everyday events he has substituted for the excitement and sentiment craved by readers steeped in too many silly novels by lady novelists, these *Scenes* only partly deal with three representative mild-mannered clergymen, since their drama actually depends upon quite extraordinary women. The stories told by Eliot are ignored by most critics in favor of the morals she expounds, in part because these plots are almost embarrassingly melodramatic. But such plots reveal a striking pattern of authorial vengeance in the service of female submission that informs Eliot's later fiction. If we focus

exclusively on this pattern in the *Scenes*, to the exclusion of the philosophic, moralistic, and humorous bent of her narrator, it is partially
to redress this imbalance and partially to understand what compels
the emergence and the modulation of this voice as her fiction matures.

The first story, "Amos Barton," introduces a churchman who is
"superlatively middling, the quintessential extract of mediocrity"
(chap. 5), a man who gains our interest only because of his astonishingly virtuous wife, "a large, fair, gentle Madonna, with . . . large,
tender, short-sighted eyes" (chap. 2) not unlike those of Dorothea
Brooke, the "Blessed Virgin" of *Middlemarch*. The narrator exclaims
over Milly Barton's virtues, "Soothing, unspeakable charm of gentle
womanhood! which supersedes all acquisitions, all accomplishments.
. . . You would even perhaps have been rather scandalized if she had
descended from the serene dignity of *being* to the assiduous unrest of
doing" (chap. 2). He even goes so far as to assert that she is suitably
matched to a husband who reminds the narrator of "mongrel ungainly
dogs" because "her sublime capacity of loving will have all the more
scope" (chap. 2) with such a man. Plagued by a disreputable female
houseguest and an insensitive husband, this angel in the house keeps
her troubles to herself even when her "delicate body was becoming
daily less fit for all the many things that had to be done," and she
continues to mend the clothes and arrange the dinners because "A
loving woman's world lies within the four walls of her own home"
(chap. 7). Actually the trouble that Barton's mediocrity in his
professional vocation makes for Milly suggests an implicit rejection
of his canons of conduct. But it is Milly's death in childbirth which
really represents her superiority to him; its message is the in-
significance of the public world and the importance of private acts
of love. Indeed, her family's helplessness at her deathbed only intensifies her authority as a spiritual guide for their lives after her
death. Like funereal Aunt Pullet (in *The Mill on the Floss*) who always
wears weeds, or lugubrious Liddy, whose predictions of imminent
death serve as a chorus to Esther and Felix Holt, Milly Barton reveals
Eliot's understanding that such female fascination with decline is a
means of obtaining power, if only the power to predict catastrophe.

Since Milly's death is, after all, the logical extension of a life of
being instead of doing, it also serves as a model for feminine submission, which is finally attained by the heroine of "Mr. Gilfil's

Love-Story," but only after she has fully experienced the depth and futility of her own feelings. The Italian ward of Sir Christopher Cheverel is picked up like an *objet d'art* to furnish a plain brick English family house that Sir Christopher is transforming into a gothic mansion. She is one more foreign oddity among the clutter of "Greek statues and busts of Roman emperors; low cabinets filled with curiosities, natural and antiquarian" (chap. 2). Indeed, Sir Christopher calls her his "monkey" or "songbird." That his house is the same ancestral mansion we continually encounter is made clear by the inscription over the fireplace in the housekeeper's room: *Fear God and honour the King*. An orphan with no legitimate place here, Caterina is left to exercise her "only talent [which] lay in loving" (chap. 4), by falling in love with Captain Wybrow, a man who "always did the thing easiest and most agreeable to him from a sense of duty" (chap. 4), and whose lazy egotism therefore adumbrates that of all the later heirs in Eliot's novels: Arthur Donnithorne, Stephen Guest, Harold Transome, Tito Melema, Fred Vincy, and Mr. Grandcourt.

When Captain Wybrow ignores his own implicit promises to Caterina and brings the haughty Beatrice Assher home to woo her as a bride before the petite dependent, the echoes of *Jane Eyre* are hard to ignore. Forced to watch the man she loves courting a wealthy, large-limbed, dark-haired beauty, Caterina is described as a "poor bird ... beginning to flutter and faintly dash its soft breast against the hard iron bars of the inevitable" (chap. 3). Like Jane or like Rochester's ward Adèle, Caterina experiences "gleams of fierce resistance" to any harsh discipline. She even displays a "certain ingenuity in vindictiveness" not unrelated to her financial and spiritual poverty. But it is her resemblance to Catherine of *Wuthering Heights* that helps explain the depth of Caterina's passion. Desiring her unobtainable relative, the captain, Caterina finds a dagger which "she will plunge ... into his Heart" because she decides "in the madness of her passion that she can kill the man whose very voice unnerves her" (chap. 13). But before she has an opportunity to use the knife (to which Eliot's publisher strongly objected), Caterina is inalterably separated from her childhood lover when she finds him dead of a heart attack in the garden. Like Catherine Earnshaw, Caterina Sarti finally marries her more civilized suitor, Mr. Gilfil, and dies in childbirth. Only then is she fully possessed by her husband, who keeps a locked room full of miniature mementos: her little dressing table, her dainty looking glass, her small black kerchief, and so forth.

Although childbirth has so far brought nothing but death, the masculine narrator continues to announce in "Janet's Repentence," as he had in the former stories, that motherhood "stills all anxiety into calm content: it makes selfishness become self-denial, and gives even to hard vanity the glance of admiring love" (chap. 13). But while this encomium comes as an explanation of how Janet Dempster would be less sorrowful about her lot were she a mother, her lot is a life with "a drunken tyrant of a midnight house" (chap. 7), a lawyer she was driven to marry because she "had nothing to look to but being a governess" (chap. 3). "Gypsy," as her husband calls her, is herself driven to secret drinking by his physical brutality:

> Every feverish morning, with its blank listlessness and despair, seemed more hateful than the last; every coming night more impossible to brave without arming herself in leaden stupor. The morning light brought no gladness to her: it seemed only to throw its glare on what had happened in the dim candle-light— on the cruel man seated immovable in drunken obstinacy by the dead fire and dying lights in the dining-room, rating her in harsh tones, reiterating old reproaches—or on a hideous blank of something unremembered, something that must have made that dark bruise on her shoulder, which ached as she dressed herself. [chap. 13]

In her suffering she can only ask her mother why she was allowed to marry: "Why didn't you tell me mother?" she asks; "You knew what brutes men could be; and there's no help for me—no hope" (chap. 14). She is later echoed by Mrs. Transome's heartfelt protest in *Felix Holt*: "Men are selfish. They are selfish and cruel. What they care for is their own pleasure and their own pride" (chap. 5), and by Gwendolen Harleth's useless lament in *Daniel Deronda*: "I don't care if I never marry any one. There is nothing worth caring for. I believe all men are bad, and I hate them" (chap. 14).

Unable to leave her husband because she is incapable of facing "the blank that lay for her outside her married home," Janet is living with

a man whom the servants believe capable of murdering her and shutting her up in a closet. But actually all Dempster need do to demonstrate his power over Janet is literally put her out on the street in her
night-clothes one cold midnight. While we are told that Janet would
be less sorrowful at this kind of treatment if she were a mother, it is
really clear that "Cruelty, like every other vice, requires no motive
outside itself—it only requires opportunity" (chap. 13), because "an
unloving, tyrannous, brutal man needs no motive to prompt his
cruelty; he needs only the perpetual presence of a woman he can call
his own" (chap. 13), and marriage provides precisely this presence. In
spite of the distaste of her publisher, John Blackwood, for the subject,
Eliot insisted on writing about wife abuse and female alcoholism, but
she does this very tactfully, from her description of Janet's "wounded"
consciousness of "the riddle of her life" (chap. 13) to a factual
explanation that her husband "had all her little property in his
hands, and that little was scarcely enough to keep her in comfort
without his aid" (chap. 16). Like all the other marriages in *Scenes of
Clerical Life*, this one is no happier than Bertha and Latimer's in
"The Lifted Veil."

Eliot is concerned in "Janet's Repentence," as she is in "The
Lifted Veil," to show us that "Our daily familiar life is but a hiding
of ourselves from each other behind a screen of trivial words and
deeds, and those who sit with us at the same hearth are often the
farthest off from the deep human soul within us, full of unspoken evil
and unacted good" (chap. 16). Indeed, she seems to have written
about clerical characters in her earliest fiction at least in part because
these men are somehow "feminine." Inhabiting an emotional, moral,
private sphere in which they are supposed to be exemplary, they are
nevertheless profoundly aware of what goes on behind the veil, and
they invite confessions from all who "tremble to let in the daylight on
a chamber of relics which we have never visited except in curtained
silence" (chap. 18). Janet's repentence comes about, in fact, because
of the "fellowship in suffering" she attains with Mr. Tryan, a model
of submission himself (chap. 12). Confessing a sin similar to that
committed by Captain Wybrow—inducing a girl below his station
to an attachment that he fails to honor—he explains to Janet how
only a sense of helpless guilt can prepare for salvation: "There is

nothing that becomes us but entire submission, perfect resignation"
(chap. 18).

Reconciled with her mother, Janet even begins to believe that she
must return to her husband since "There were things in me that were
wrong, and I should like to make up for them if I can" (chap. 20).
And when, on his deathbed, her husband does need her, she gives
unstintingly. Finally, her confidence in the human sympathy of Mr.
Tryan constitutes for her a faith in divine love that allows her to fight
her temptation to drink. The fact that Janet Dempster is saved from
drink and despair and is "changed as the dusty, bruised, and sun-
withered plant is changed when the soft rains of heaven have fallen
on it" (chap. 26) testifies to the saintliness of Mr. Tryan, as does his
early death in the snug red-brick house Janet had furnished for him,
and in her loving embrace. Indeed Janet's devoted nursing of the
dying Mr. Tryan reminds us that Eliot referred to the time when she
nursed her father on his deathbed as the "happiest days of life to me"
(*Letters*, 1:283–84).

The unintentional irony of this phrase is further illuminated by
"Janet's Repentence." For this man who dies in Janet's arms, with
her kiss on his lips, reminds us that another man has also died in
her embrace with the belief that her kiss is deadly and her embrace
will kill. On his deathbed, the brutal misogynist Dempster suffers
from frightening visions of his wife's revenge. He thinks he sees

> "her hair is all serpents ... they're black serpents ... they
> hiss ... they hiss ... let me go ... she wants to drag me with
> her cold arms ... her arms are serpents ... they are great white
> serpents ... they'll twine round me ... she wants to drag me
> into the cold water ... her bosom is cold ... it is black ... it is all
> serpents. ... " [chap. 23]

Nothing less than a female monster to her husband's sickened
imagination, the repentant Janet has been transformed into an image
which suggests that Dempster is simply mad with guilt over his
mistreatment of her. At the same time, however, his death does seem
fully connected with her agency, since she does wish him dead, and
with ample reason, and since his death is so fortuitous a release for
her from otherwise inescapable imprisonment. We are told, further-

more, about a female power that is definitively involved in causing Dempster's death: "Nemesis is lame, but she is of colossal stature, like the gods; and sometimes, while her sword is not yet unsheathed, she stretches out her huge left arm and grasps her victim. The mighty hand is invisible, but the victim totters under the dire clutch" (chap. 13). The huge left arm of Nemesis, which recalls the great white serpent arms of Janet, rewards the repression of the suffering wife's murderous wish by enacting it.

Mr. Tryan articulates the protest against resignation that we sense in all of Eliot's heroines when he admits, "if my heart were less rebellious, and if I were less liable to temptation, I should not need that sort of self-denial" (chap. 11). Certainly Milly Barton, Caterina Sarti, and Janet Dempster all attain angelic submission only after considerable inward struggle against resentment and anger. Indeed, because they are too good for the kind of life they have to lead, all three are saved by death and thereby curiously linked to the forces of destruction. Having "killed" themselves into ladylike docility and selflessness, all three heroines are instances of what Alexander Welsh calls the "angel of death."[23] Even their submission to death can be viewed, however, as a rejection of life. Not only ministering to the dying, these angels of destruction actually bring death, "saving" their patient/victims by killing them off. Or, if they do not actually bring death to those they have every right to resent, the author does. Indeed, the angelic purity of the heroines seems to release the melodramatic response of their author. Thus Milly Barton's death allows her to live out her Madonna role and provides her with the only possible escape from a life of domestic drudgery, even as it punishes her husband for his neglect of her; the invisible left arm of Nemesis sends death to Captain Wybrow in the garden, thereby saving Caterina from killing him herself; and it frees Janet from a miserable marriage by dragging her husband "into the cold water." While each heroine represses her anger and submits to the necessity for renunciation, the author as the goddess Nemesis acts "for" her in much the same way that Frankenstein's monster acted "for" his creator or Bertha Mason Rochester acted "for" Jane Eyre. Thus, interestingly enough, in *Scenes of Clerical Life*, it is the novelist—not as the male narrator, but as the female author behind the scenes—who plays the part of the madwoman.

The contradiction between Marian Evans as historical author and George Eliot as fictive narrator helps explain, then, how a title like *Scenes of Clerical Life* (which Eliot repeatedly insisted on with Blackwood) functions as a kind of camouflage or Austenian "cover" to conceal the dramatic focus of the plot. Insisting on the primacy of male spheres of activity, Eliot aspires to the "masculine" scientific detachment of an essayist reproducing and analyzing "slices of life." And in this respect, as in so many others, *Scenes of Clerical Life* forecasts the camouflages of her later fiction. *Adam Bede*, with its masculine title, relies on the story of fallen and female Hetty Sorel for its suspense, just as *Felix Holt the Radical* maps the mental and moral development of Esther Lyon, while both *The Mill on the Floss* and *Middlemarch* announce themselves as sociological studies of provincial life, though they were originally conceived and still come across as portraits of female destiny. And at the end of her literary career Eliot wrote *Daniel Deronda*, a book that could as easily be entitled "Gwendolen Harleth."[24]

But *Scenes of Clerical Life* is also typical of Eliot's lifelong fascination with the angel of destruction, for the pattern we have seen in this early book—the contradiction between feminine renunciation countenanced by the narrator and female (even feminist) vengeance exacted by the author—remains an important one in Eliot's fiction, as Carol Christ has shown in her very useful essay on the function of providential death in Eliot's fiction.[25] But while Christ explains how Eliot's heroines are saved from performing acts of rage, she neither studies how all the heroines are nevertheless implicated in the author's violence, nor how the author is involved in punishing male characters who specifically symbolize patriarchal power. *The Mill on the Floss* (1860), possibly Eliot's most autobiographical work, illustrates this point more clearly than almost any other novel, showing Maggie Tulliver to be most monstrous when she tries to turn herself into an angel of renunciation.[26]

Described as a child who looks "like a small Medusa with her snakes cropped" (I, chap. 10) and a whirling "pythoness" (I, chap. 4), Maggie fittingly pursues her anger in the attic of her father's house, where she punishes a fetish, a wooden doll "defaced by a long career of vicarious suffering. Three nails driven into the head commemorated as many crises in Maggie's nine years of earthly struggle, that luxury of vengeance having been suggested to her by the picture of Jael destroying Sisera in the old Bible" (I, chap. 4). Like Lucy Snowe, Maggie is both Jael and Sisera, both a Satanic inflictor of pain who pushes her pretty cousin Lucy Deane into the mud and a repentent follower of Thomas à Kempis who associates love with self-inflicted martyrdom. In addition, besides being both Madonna and Medusa, Maggie is nature's child, for her rapt, dreamy feelings constantly carry her away in floods of feeling suggestive of the rhythms of the river that empowers the mill. But the brother to whom she is so passionately devoted inherits the mill itself and is thereby associated with the grinding, crushing process that transforms primordial matter into civilized stuff fit for consumption, much as Nelly Dean in *Wuthering Heights* is identified with the secondary, socializing arts of cooking.

Indeed, in such incidents as the episode of the dead rabbits, the children's feast in the attic, and Maggie's flight to the gypsies, the sibling love between Maggie and Tom recalls the passionate union of Catherine Earnshaw and Heathcliff, but Eliot could be said to be retelling Emily Brontë's story to undercut that earlier vision of gynandrous bliss. Maggie's neglect of the rabbits, resulting in Tom's fury at their death, and Maggie's thoughtless enjoyment of the best piece of cake, followed by Tom's censorious severity, reveal the pain and division between brother and sister even during the brief period of time identified by the narrator as Edenic, as does Maggie's pathetically inadequate search for a "refuge from all the blighting obloquy that had pursued her in civilized life" (I, chap. 11) when she runs away from Tom to become the Queen of the Gypsies: she had, after all, often been told that she was "like a Gypsy and 'half wild'" (I, chap. 11). While Catherine Earnshaw and Heathcliff had romped in joyous union on the heath, "half savage, and hardy, and free," Eliot's siblings are born into a gendered world where girls are driven by an intense need for male approval and boys are locked into a harsh, self-justifying code of honor.

When the mill is entangled in unintelligible but inexorable legal battles over water rights, it becomes clear that the forces of culture are inalterably opposed to those of nature, as if they were enacting on a grand scale the conflict between brother and sister. Excluded from the schooling Tom receives, and closely associated with her bullish father and her earth-motherish Aunt *Moss*, "Miss Spitfire" (as Tom calls her) sees her own status as subhuman, even imagining herself as "a poor uneasy white bear" at a circus show who had gotten "so stupid with the habit of turning backwards and forwards in that narrow space that he would keep doing it if they set him free" (VI, chap. 2). At the same time, Maggie is filled with resentment of Tom, precisely because she hungers for his love. But, if she is paralyzed by constraints imposed because of her sex, Tom is just as unsuccessful as an autonomous person, especially when his boyhood sense of justice degenerates into vindictive self-righteousness and he is filled with loathing for his sister. Even more miserably matched than Catherine and Edgar or Heathcliff and Isabella, Maggie and Tom are completely stymied in their parallel romances with Stephen Guest and Lucy Deane, the legitimate heir and his proper wife, whose survival and union imply a return to the principles of property and propriety.

In some ways, then, when Maggie surreptitiously meets the girlish, crippled Philip Wakem, with his proferred gifts of books and songs, in the symbolic Red Deeps, she is trying to confront her own stunted nature in order to give birth to a healthier self. She even admits imagining a new kind of fiction: tired of books "where the blond-haired women carry away all the happiness," Maggie would like some story "where the dark woman triumphs," because "it would restore the balance" (V, chap. 4). Maggie understands that she cannot triumph in her world except through a man, yet she is kept from Philip Wakem by their fathers' joint injunctions, even as she is inhibited from more than a temporary triumph over Lucy by her own terror of hurting others and by her brother's disapproval of her romance with Stephen Guest.

When the waters break, then, there can be no rebirth for Maggie. Many readers have praised her virtuous attempt to save her brother's life and Tom's ultimate appreciation of her self-sacrificing love. But, though she rides the flood like the Blessed Virgin of St. Ogg's boat, Maggie's miraculous voyage on the water reminds us that she also resembles a figure straight out of one of her childhood fantasies: the "woman in the water's a witch" (I, chap. 3). The brother who has oppressed her by taking first place in their parents' esteem, by sneering at her intellectual ambition, by curtailing her freedom to live or even imagine her own life, and by condemning her harshly in the light of his restrictive moral standards is finally punished when she goes to "save" him from the rising tides only to drag him down into the dark deep in her "embrace" of death. Though the narrator assures us both in the epigraph and in the concluding sentence of the novel, "In their deaths they were not divided," throughout their lives Tom and Maggie *were* divided: only in the fatal fusion of their incestuous *Liesbestod* can Eliot heal their breach.

What Eliot described in her essay on a new edition of *Antigone* as the "struggle between elemental tendencies and established laws" constitutes only a small part of her interest in Maggie Tulliver's tragedy: Eliot was profoundly drawn to Antigone's revolt against the misogynist King Creon because it is motivated by loyalty to a brother, Polynices, and because it takes the form of a rejection of marriage. Indeed, Antigone's revolt *is* her virginal, voluntary self-entombment.[27] By uniting Creon and Polynices in one figure, that of Tom, Eliot uses the story to analyze female enthrallment, born of women's complete dependence on men for self-definition and self-esteem. This is certainly the case for the heroine of *Romola* (1862–63) —who sits for a portrait of Antigone at Colonos—and so it is for Dorothea of *Middlemarch* (1871–72)—who looks like a Christian Antigone—and "So it has been since the days of Hecuba and of Hector," the narrator of *The Mill on the Floss* reasons; the women "inside the gates . . . watching the world's combat from afar, filling their long, empty days with memories and fear; outside, the men, in fierce struggle with things divine and human" (V, chap. 2). Not only dedicated to the private bonds of the family over the legal claims of the state, such modern-day Antigones are lonely, ineffective creatures whose acts of loyalty are invariably suicidal.

Like Maggie, who is excluded from the study of Latin—which fascinates her "like strange horns of beasts and leaves of unknown plants, brought from some far-off region" (II, chap. 1)—Romola is judged "quick and shallow" as a girl and so, unable to help her father with his classical studies, she marries a man who can. When her husband betrays both her father and herself, Romola feels "something like a Bacchante possessed by a divine rage" (chap. 32), but she transforms herself into "a gray phantom" (chap. 37) of resignation, her long white wedding veil becoming a sign of her submission to her spiritual advisor's dictum that she has no vocation but as a wife. She does manage to keep secret her alienation from Tito. But his betrayal of his marriage vows is matched by his disavowal of responsibility for his foster father, Baldassarre, who therefore functions as Romola's double. Indeed, Baldassarre represents a Satanic response to Romola's situation: fallen from grace, cursed with amnesia which makes it impossible for him to read Greek, exiled in a foreign country, filled with resentment, "a man with a double identity" (chap. 38), he seeks the revenge that Romola has been given every reason to desire. Significantly, just at the moment when he does find and murder Tito, Romola also decides that she can no longer live with her husband, so she lies down in a boat to float to her death. The same dark river that providentially brings "salvation" to Baldassarre in the shape of Tito, whom he then kills, "baptizes" Romola by bringing her to "a village of the unburied dead" where she is taken for the Holy Mother (chap. 68). Only these two responses —angelic passivity or Satanic revenge—seem possible given the self-satisfied self-promotion of Tito Melema, whose smugness matches that of Tom Tulliver.

Like Gwendolen in *Daniel Deronda* (1876), who finds herself married to a man whose "words had the power of thumbscrews and the cold touch of the rack," these heroines are "afraid of [their] own wishes" and "afraid of [their] own hatred" (chap. 54). Both Romola and Gwendolen are especially aware that their husbands' selfishness has victimized other women: as the legal wives of men whose mistresses have born children invisible because illegitimate, both Romola and Gwendolen identify with the dispossessed women, as if Eliot were obsessively considering her own ambiguous "wifehood." Just as Romola helps Tessa, eventually establishing a kind of matriarchal family for her children by Tito, Gwendolen feels "a sort of terror" of Lydia Glasher, "as if some ghastly vision had come to her in a dream and said, 'I am a woman's life'" (chap. 14) and her desire for Grandcourt's death is in part attributable to her desire to right the wrongs he has done and specifically to make Lydia Glasher's children his inheritors, thereby simultaneously returning Sir Hugo's estate to its rightful female owners. Like Caterina Sarti, Gwendolen cherishes murderous designs in the shape of a secret knife, but she forces herself to drop in deep water the key to the cabinet holding this knife. Since Grandcourt fortuitously falls out of the boat and drowns—in other words, since the invisible left arm of Nemesis

clearly works Gwendolen's will—her guilt at his death seems
warranted: Daniel Deronda is shown to be at least partially justified
in his choice of the angelically submissive Mirah over the fallen
Gwendolen: "I did kill him in my thoughts," Gwendolen admits
(chap. 56).

All the women in Eliot's novels who cannot find what Maggie and
Romola and Gwendolen seek, "something to guarantee [them] from
more falling" (*MF*, VII, chap. 2), are driven by their anger to murderous thoughts and acts, as Eliot shows in *Adam Bede* (1859), a
revision of one of Wordsworth's ballads: the thorn that knocks on
the window as an omen of Thias Bede's death, the round pool where
Hetty Sorrel wishes to murder herself or her child, her degeneration
into a wandering, sorrow-crazed madwoman—all are clues that point
to the ways in which this novel can be viewed as a retelling of "The
Thorn," as is Arthur Donni/thorne's self-proclaimed dislike of the
Lyrical Ballads. Hetty, whom we first see in the dairy and then gathering fruit in the garden, declines after her fall in the chase into a kind of
Lilith who must wander outside the human community, until she
is banished to the very outskirts of civilization for Lilith's crime, the
killing of her own baby. Infanticide figures too in *Felix Holt the Radical*
(1866): Mrs. Transome is driven by "a hungry desire, like a black
poisonous plant feeding in the sunlight,—the desire that her first,
rickety, ugly, imbecile child should die" (chap. 1). Both these
Liliths are replaced by angelic Marys, by Dinah Morris redeeming
Edenic Adam and Esther Lyon saving Adamic Felix.

Yet, even in books dedicated to dramatizing the discrepancy
between the antithetical faces of Eve, Eliot seems to provide subversive evidence that the fallen murderess is inalterably linked to
the angelic Madonna. In *Adam Bede*, for example, the two Poyser
nieces are orphans, occupying neighboring rooms, and Hetty actually
dresses up as Dinah, even as Dinah seems to haunt Hetty (chap. 15).
Similarly, in *Felix Holt* Esther is "haunted by an Eve gone gray with
bitter memories of an Adam who had complained, 'The woman . . .
she gave me of the tree, and I did eat'" (chap. 49). Determined
not to repeat Mrs. Transome's mistakes, Esther nevertheless realizes
that for all "poor women . . . power lies solely in their influence"
(chap. 34). The frustration this breeds lends credence to Mrs.

Transome's assertion that Esther cannot evade her own miserable fate:

> A woman's love is always freezing into fear. She wants every-thing, she is secure of nothing. This girl has a fine spirit— plenty of fire and pride and wit. Men like such captives, as they like horses that champ the bit and paw the ground; they feel more triumph in their mastery. What is the use of a woman's will?—if she tries, she doesn't get it, and she ceases to be loved. God was cruel when he made women. [chap. 39]

What the passage recalls, of course, is the plight of Gwendolen Grandcourt, whose husband was attracted to her spirit because he wanted to tame her. Like his horses, she becomes just one of his "symbols of command and luxury" (chap. 27). The measure of his success at mastery comes when she admits that "To resist was to act like a stupid animal unable to measure results" (chap. 54).

If Gwendolen feels controlled by bit and bridle, Hetty is associated with kittens, chicks, and ducks, while Maggie is a pony, a puppy, a mass of snakes, a bear, and Caterina is a monkey or bird. Even when it is domestic and tame, the animal familiar reminds us that throughout Eliot's novels the female is closely linked with the forces of nature. As she does in *Scenes of Clerical Life* and "The Lifted Veil," Eliot suggests that relations between men and women are a struggle between the transcendent male and the immanent female, whose only powers are demonic ones deriving from her pact with the physical world. Thus Maggie's affinity with the water that kills Tom resembles Romola's trust in the river that brings life to her and death to her husband. As if justifying Dempster's conviction that his wife's snakey arms will drag him "into the cold water," Dinah Morris defends her right as a woman to preach by explaining that "It isn't for men to make channels for God's Spirit, as they make channels for the water-courses, and say, 'Flow here, but flow not there'" (chap. 8).

All Eliot's novels prove Dinah right. An irresponsible father like Thias Bede is given every reason to fear death by water. When Gwendolen's husband goes on the sea in the firm belief that "he could manage a sail with the same ease that he could manage a horse" (chap. 54) he finds he can manage neither and is punished for his presumption. As Eliot explains in *The Mill on the Floss*, "nature has the deep cunning which hides itself under the appearance of openness, so that small people think they can see through her quite well, and all the while she is secretly preparing a refutation of their confident prophecies" (I, chap. 5). Like Nemesis, female nature here is another word for the author's inflexible purposes, which have been so secretly prepared and cunningly hidden behind her insistent rhetoric of renunciation.

And yet this rhetoric can neither be ignored nor denigrated. While the anger of the fallen female is dramatized in such a way as to link the madwoman with the Madonna in the concealed dialectic of the author's plots, it is the altruistic Madonna who survives as the narrator's heroine. Most readers realize that, in the narrator's view, Dinah (not Hetty), Romola (not Baldassarre), Mirah (not Gwendolen), Esther (not Mrs. Transome), and the chastened, humbled Maggie (not the maddened child) struggle to attain the renunciation that alone can redeem human life from suffering. What distinguishes the heroine from her double is her deflection of anger from the male she is shown justifiably to hate back against herself so that she punishes herself, finding in self-abasement a sign of her moral superiority to the man she continues to serve. While these angels of renunciation are partly a function of the self-hatred we explored in the previous chapter, they also represent a shift in Eliot's attitude toward the conditions of women in a male world, as if through them she is considering how the injustice of masculine society bequeaths to women special strengths and virtues, specifically a capacity for feeling born of disenfranchisement from a corrupt social order.

Significantly, every negative stereotype protested by Charlotte Brontë is transformed into a virtue by George Eliot. While Brontë curses the fact that women are denied intellectual development, Eliot admits the terrible effects of this malnourishment but also implies that emotional life is thereby enriched for women. While Brontë shows how difficult it is for women to be assertive, Eliot dramatizes the virtues of a uniquely female culture based on supportive camaraderie instead of masculine competition. While Brontë dramatizes the suffocating sense of imprisonment born of female confinement, Eliot celebrates the ingenuity of women whose love can, in the words of Donne quoted at the end of *Middlemarch*, make "one little room, an everywhere" (chap. 83). And while Brontë envies men the freedom of their authority, Eliot argues that such authority actually keeps men from experiencing their own physical and psychic authenticity.

Though the danger of this shift in perspective is that it can be used to justify keeping women in "one little room," it can also serve as a means of criticizing masculine values. It is, in other words, a compensatory and conservative aspect of Eliot's fiction that associates women with precisely the traits she felt industrial urbanized England in danger of losing: a commitment to others, a sense of community, an appreciation of nature, and a belief in nurturing love. Thus in *Scenes of Clerical Life* all meaningful relationships are based on the mother-child bond because, "in the love of a brave and faithful man there is always a strain of maternal tenderness; he gives out again those beams of protecting fondness which were shed on him as he lay on his mother's knee" (II, chap. 19). Similarly, Adam Bede becomes feminized by his continued love for the suffering Hetty, for "the mother's yearning, that completest type of the life in another life which is the essence of real human love, feels the presence of the cherished child even in the debased, degraded man" (chap. 43). But while the rejection of a public world of politics and property for a private world of feeling may be redemptive for men like Philip Wakem and Harold Transome, the very virtues born of power-lessness can threaten more fully to imprison the female. Eliot balances the narrator's reverence for gentle heroines with the author's venge-ful impulses throughout her later fiction, but perhaps we can see the full significance of this struggle in her greatest novel, *Middlemarch*.

One of the more curious episodes in *Middlemarch* concerns the amatory history of Tertius Lydgate before his entrance into pro-vincial society. We are told that one night, when studying galvanic experiments in Paris, he left his frogs and rabbits and went to the theater, attracted not by the melodrama, but by an actress whose role was to stab her lover after mistaking him for the villain of the piece. Playing the scene with her real-life husband (who acted the

part of the doomed character), "the wife veritably stabbed her husband, who fell as death willed" (chap. 15). Assured of the accidental
nature of the crime, the youthful Lydgate asks this actress, Madame
Laure, to marry him. Her response is first to tell him confidentially,
"My foot really slipped." Then, however, she pauses and more
slowly explains, two times, "*I meant to do it.*" Protesting against
Lydgate's sentimental explanation that her husband must have
abused her, Madame Laure insists that he only "wearied" her,
observing quite simply, "I do not like husbands."

The inclusion of this singular incident, which is far more violent
than Rochester's account to Jane Eyre of his experience in Paris with
a French actress of dubious morality and far less necessary for the
development of the plot, provides an interesting approach both to
the marital relationships described in *Middlemarch* and to Eliot's
view of the implicitly murderous nature of female acting. As in "The
Lifted Veil" and *Scenes of Clerical Life*, she is fundamentally concerned
with the potential for violence in the two conflicting sides of herself
that she identifies as the masculine mind and the feminine heart.
And it would seem that she too could declare, like Madame Laure,
that "I do not like husbands." Or, as Mr. Brooke says of marriage,
using an important image, "it *is* a noose, you know. Temper, now.
There is temper. And a husband likes to be master" (chap. 4). Even
the admirably decorous Lady Chettam remembers the case of Mrs.
Beevor: "'They said Captain Beevor dragged her about by the hair,
and held up loaded pistols at her'" (chap. 55). While nothing quite
this melodramatic is actually dramatized in *Middlemarch*, the novel
is centrally concerned with the tragic complicity and resulting violence of men and women inhabiting a culture defined as masculine.

The first man to become a husband in *Middlemarch* is, of course,
Edward Casaubon, the Miltonesque father worshiped by near-
sighted Dorothea. As we have already seen, Eliot's emphasis on
seemingly trivial domestic details results in a potentially radical
critique of patriarchal culture, for "even Milton, looking for his
portrait in a spoon, must submit to having the facial angle of a
bumpkin" (chap. 10). As described by clear-sighted Celia and her
provincial neighbors—from the moles on his face to his manner of
eating soup—Edward Casaubon has precisely this aspect of Milton
domesticated and diminished, but he is also closely identified with

Rome, with the English clergy, with scholarship, with Greek and Roman classical texts, and with the best of what has been thought and said by philosophers from Cicero to Locke. Moreover, sitting for a picture of Saint Thomas Aquinas, who rejected the doctrine of the Immaculate Conception, implying that the Virgin was tainted by original sin, Casaubon incarnates patriarchial belief in feminine evil, and thereby demonstrates the inextricable link between male culture and misogyny. And so he only perceives Dorothea as a decorous complement to his own existence, a moon "to adorn the remaining quadrant of his course" (chap. 11), a secretary and scribe, an appreciative representative of the public, even an apostle to carry on his mission after his demise.

Ironically, however, this sun god is surrounded by gloom, not only because his own eyesight is failing, but because everything about him is dying. His iron-gray hair, pale complexion, and deep eye-sockets are only "lit up by a smile like pale wintry sunshine" (chap. 3). "Lean, dry, ill-coloured . . . and all through immoderate pains and extraordinary studies," he is afflicted with "all such diseases as come by over-much sitting," as Burton describes them in the section of *Anatomy of Melancholy* quoted by Eliot. His house of melancholy, of "greenish stone . . . in the old English style, not ugly, but small windowed and melancholy-looking" (chap. 9), is fittingly called Lo/wick and reminds us that all this man does and says seems, to the adoring Dorothea, "like a specimen from a mine, or the inscription on the door of a museum" (chap. 3). Far from being what Dorothea Brooke thought, a lake compared to her pool, Casaubon is a drought compared to her brook. Significantly, then, he is himself haunted by "that chilling ideal which crowded his laborious un-creative hours with the vaporous pressure of Tartarean shades" (chap. 10).

By his own admission, Casaubon lives too much with the dead, and his "mind is something like the ghost of an ancient" (chap. 2). "Buried in books" (chap. 4), he is almost a book himself, at least in the metaphors of his neighbors. He looks like "a dried bookworm" or pamphlet or "a death's head" (chap. 10); his capacity for thought and feeling is "shrunk to a sort of dried preparation, a lifeless embalm-ment of knowledge" (chap. 20). Indeed, "no better than a mummy" (chap. 6), the man himself is "a sort of parchment code" (chap. 8);

under a microscope his blood is "all semicolons and parentheses" (chap. 8). Casaubon reminds us of Borges's description of "the Man of the Book": some superstitious people believe, Borges explains, that "there must exist a book which is the cipher and perfect compendium of *all the rest*: some librarian had perused it, and it is analogous to a god."[28] Not only is Casaubon's undertaking an attempt to write the cipher and perfect compendium of all other books; he is himself "the Man of the Book," Eliot's extremely subversive portrait of male authority.

At the same time, of course, Casaubon, who is "sensitive without being enthusiastic," resembles Latimer of "The Lifted Veil," if only because his soul goes on "fluttering in the swampy ground where it was hatched, thinking of its wings and never flying" (chap. 29). And his inability to actually fulfill his sense of his own vocation—like that of almost all the characters in *Middlemarch*—at least in part reflects Eliot's own fear of failure, specifically her anxiety of authorship. Since genius consists "in a power to make or do, not anything in general, but something in particular" (chap. 10), Casaubon can never fully evade his consciousness of his failure, a consciousness that makes him morbidly reticent and defensive about exposing himself by publishing his writing. Even if he were to complete his book, however, Casaubon would remain a deathly influence, for The Key to All Mythologies would kill myth into history by viewing all Greek, African, and South Sea myths as perverted copies or mere shadows of a single source, namely, biblical revelation. Not only is his work egocentric, then, it is ethnocentric. Further, by reducing all history to a linear progression from a single, discrete point of origin, Casaubon perpetuates a hierarchical genealogy whereby an original Text fathers forth subsidiary and subordinate texts, all of which are reduced to the derivative status of his own work. Through him, as many readers have noticed, Eliot confronts the potentially destructive effects of her own biblical criticism; it was at the time of translating Strauss' *Das Leben Jesu* that she signed herself as Pollian. But actually the thrust of her critical efforts was in the opposite direction from Casaubon's: she sought to rescue the mythic value of the Bible from its historical origins, and to dissect traditional forms of faith only to resurrect reverence for them.

Because Casaubon is so closely associated with authorship and authority, books, dryness, and sterility, Eliot makes it seem as if the very provinces of masculine knowledge that he embodies to Dorothea kill on contact. While Dorothea mistakenly assumes that her marriage to Casaubon will bring her "room for the energies which stirred uneasily under the dimness and pressure of her own ignorance" (chap. 5), and while she hopes to substitute "new vistas" for "that toy-box history of the world adapted to young ladies" (chap. 10), she finds herself instead locked "in a dark closet of his verbal memory" along with his notes. Dorothea had believed that she could dutifully learn from this author, even become wise in his service, but her sister had known from the beginning of the engagement that "there was something funereal in the whole affair, and Mr. Casaubon seemed to be the officiating clergyman, about whom it would be indecent to make remarks" (chap. 5). Unwittingly substantiating Celia's vision of the deathliness of their marriage, Casaubon contrasts his previous life without Dorothea to his hopes for their future: "'I have been little disposed to gather flowers that would wither in my hand, but now I shall pluck them with eagerness, to place them in your bosom'" (chap. 5). The withered flowers plucked for Dorothea's bosom seem a warning of Casaubon's deathly touch, as does his response to her architectural projects for the poor, when he diverted the talk "to the extremely narrow accommodation which was to be had in the dwellings of the ancient Egyptians" (chap. 3).

Although Casaubon explains to Dorothea that the hyperbole "see Rome and die" has to be altered in her case to "see Rome as a bride, and live henceforth as a happy wife" (chap. 20), clearly this is no emendation: to be a happy wife to a dead man is to be buried alive. While Saint Dorothea was a martyr who went to her death as a bride,[29] Dorothea is a martyr *because* she is a bride. Thus Rome becomes for Dorothea the symbol of culture as it is represented by her husband. Observing this "city of visible history, where the past of a whole hemisphere seems moving in funereal procession with strange ancestral images and trophies gathered from afar," she is exhausted by the unintelligibility of what seems a "vast wreck of ambitious ideas" (chap. 20), a "masquerade of ages, in which her own life seemed to become a masque with enigmatical costumes" (chap. 20). From the vast dome of Saint Peter's to the red drapery hung for Christmas which seems to be "spreading itself everywhere like a disease of the retina" (chap. 20), Rome makes Dorothea feel as if her honeymoon itself is an unspeakable illness. Nor does her return home bode well: Will is quite sure that at Lowick Dorothea will be "shut up in that stone prison . . . buried alive" (chap. 22).

At Lowick Dorothea *is*, of course, locked "in a moral imprisonment" so that the shrunken landscape and the stale interiors come to represent her state of mind. The "large vistas and wide fresh air" she had dreamt of finding in her husband's mind are "replaced by anterooms and winding passages which seemed to lead nowhither" (chap. 20). Once past "the door-sill of marriage," she discovers "the sea is not in sight" and instead she is "exploring an enclosed basin" (chap. 20), so that she stops expecting to "see any wide opening where she followed him. Poor Mr. Casaubon himself was lost among small closets and winding stairs . . . he forgot the absence of windows, and . . . [became] indifferent to the sunlight" (chap. 20). Like Thumbelina in Mr. Mole's underground wedding hall, Dorothea experiences a living burial when she becomes a wife. "Born—Bridalled—Shrouded—," she resembles the figure Antigone calls on when she goes to her bridal tomb—Persephone, whose marriage transforms her into the Queen of Non-Being.

Women writers from Mary Shelley (*Proserpine*) to H. D. ("Demeter"), Virginia Woolf (*To the Lighthouse*), Sylvia Plath ("Two Sisters of Persephone"), Muriel Rukeyser ("In the Underworld"), and Toni Morrison (*The Bluest Eye*) have described female sexual initiation in terms of the myth of Persephone, with its themes of abduction, rape, the death of the physical world, and sorrowful separation from female companions. The story of Persephone and her mother also addresses itself to the uniquely female powers of procreation, explaining the seasonal death of nature in terms of the mother's grief over her daughter's enthrallment to the King of the Underworld.[30]

It is interesting, then, that when the setting of Dorothea's life seems most theatrical and unreal to her, she feels, as Madame Laure did, that marriage means being forced to renounce her native land. That Dorothea will be entrapped in sterile submission to male force is what disturbs Will when he is obsessed with her marriage as "the most horrible of virgin-sacrifices" and irritated by visions of "beautiful lips kissing holy skulls" (chap. 37). Similar visions of a marriage of death are accurately predicted by Fra Luca to warn Romola of her future with Tito Melema:

> the priest who married you had the face of death; and the graves opened, and the dead in their shrouds rose and followed you like a bridal train. . . . And thou, Romola, didst wring thy hands and seek for water, and there was none. And the bronze and marble figures seemed to mock thee and hold out cups of water, and when thou didst grasp them and put them in my father's lips they *turned to parchment.* [chap. 15; italics ours]

Significantly, Gwendolen Harleth feels that her engagement to Grandcourt means clothing herself in the gems "sawed from cramped finger-bones of women drowned" (*DD*, chap. 14).

Not only does Dorothea's married life make her feel as if she had "shut her best soul in prison, paying it only hidden visits, that she might be petty enough to please him" (chap. 42), she is especially haunted by that "thin papery feeling" so well documented by Sylvia Plath,[31] the feeling of physical unreality that results from trying to shape herself into Casaubon's rather uncongenial image of what he wants her to be as his wife. Casaubon, after all, lacks "ardour" and "energy," two qualities associated, as U. C. Knoepflmacher has shown, with imagination;[32] but these two words are also frequently used by the Victorians as euphemisms for passion. Casaubon's "frigid rhetoric" seems no less impotent than his "stream of feeling" which is "an exceedingly shallow rill" (chap. 7). Dorothea is understandably repelled by the thought of living in Casaubon's thrall, even after his literal demise, "in a virtual tomb, where there was the apparatus of a ghastly labour producing what would never see the light" (chap. 48), sorting "shattered mummies, and fragments of a tradition" as "food for a theory which was already withered in the birth like an elfin child" (chap. 48).

The book is Casaubon's child, and the writing of it is his marriage, or so Dorothea believes as she realizes how completely textuality has been substituted for sexuality in her married life. But while Eliot follows the myth of Persephone by identifying male coercion with sterility—literary labors, paper mummies, and bookish children —she describes a marriage of death initiated not by rape but by female complicity. In her analysis of the issues surrounding female internalization, Dorothea's own worship of the false male god is at least partially responsible for her plight. The eroticism of inequality —the male teacher and the enamored female student, the male master and the admiring female servant, the male author and the acquiescent female scribe or character—illustrates both how dependent women are upon male approval and how destructive such dependence is.

Since, unlike Persephone, Dorothea herself sought her marriage, and since she is motherless, she is overwhelmed by her feelings of entrapment. Overlooking "the still, white enclosure which made her visible world," her bow-windowed room at Lowick, with its faded furniture and tapestries, thin-legged chairs, and volumes of polite literature that look like imitation books, symbolizes Dorothea's sense of oppression at the gentlewoman's "liberty." In this room, even remembrances of happier times past are "deadened as an unlit transparency." Lost in the labyrinth of Casaubon's version of reality, Dorothea identifies with a miniature portrait of Will's grandmother, and Casaubon's Aunt Julia, whose "delicate woman's face . . . yet had a headstrong look, a peculiarity difficult to interpret" (chap. 28). Having been left in poverty for the crime of marrying a poor man, this Aunt Julia quickens Dorothea's doubts "as to the historical, political reasons why eldest sons had superior rights and why land should be entailed." Within "the chill, colourless, narrowed landscape, with the shrunken furniture, the never-read books, and the ghostly stag in a pale fantastic world that seemed to be vanishing from the daylight," Dorothea is inevitably haunted by a feeling of "new companionship" with the girl who ran away. It is telling that her first defiance of Casaubon's deathly will is made to right the wrong done Aunt Julia, whose disinheritance represents her own dispossession, powerlessness, and invisibility. Like Frances Henri looking at the portrait of Lucia, or Aurora Leigh looking at the painting of her mother, however, Dorothea finds in Aunt Julia's face—framed and miniaturized, as it is—the promise of a different life story.

In a sense the images of entrapment, disease, and sterility that haunt Dorothea when she becomes Casaubon's wife and sees into his soul only prove that she is still condemned to the same labyrinthine maze she inhabited before the marriage, for Dorothea's life with Casaubon is not so very different from what it had been with her uncle Brooke, when she was "struggling in the bands of a narrow teaching, hemmed in by a social life which seemed nothing but a labyrinth of petty courses, a walled-in-maze of small paths that led no whither" (chap. 3). Indeed, with his smattering of unconnected information, his useless classicism, and his misogynistic belief in the biological inferiority of Dorothea's brain, Brooke is a dark parody of Casaubon. His classical allusions, literary gossip, and scientific platitudes are as dated and undigested as Casaubon's notes. As the reform candidate for Parliament and the owner-operator of *The Pioneer*, moreover, he parodies political provinciality the way Casaubon parodies literary provinciality. Thus he is well represented by the buff-colored rag effigy of himself that echoes his words at the political rally, for his own repetitive, derivative, and basically unintelligible speech is also a kind of echo that makes him as much a puppet as Casaubon is a wooden, bald doll (chap. 20).

Dorothea is imprisoned not just by Casaubon, or Brooke, then, but by a "walled-in maze" of relationships in a society controlled by men who are very much like both these men. Actually several professional men in *Middlemarch* seem to be variations of Casaubon. Most critics, for example, have recognized Peter Featherstone as Casaubon's foil: on his deathbed, this sick man also tries to place his "Dead Hand" on the living through his will. Fittingly, in the dying world of Stone Court, Featherstone keeps his documents, codicils, last wills and testaments, as well as his money, locked up in hidden iron chests to which only he has the keys. And, finally, it turns out that his heir—the frog-faced legatee Rigg—would turn himself not into a prince but into a pawnbroker at the happy conclusion of his life story. Rigg's garden of earthly delights takes the form of a money-changer's shop: he wants "to have locks all round him of which he held the keys, and to look sublimely cool as he handled the breeding coins of all notions, while helpless Cupidity looked at him enviously from the other side of an iron lattice" (chap. 53). As sexually sterile as the dried-out Casaubon, who had "not yet succeeded in issuing copies of his mythological keys" (chap. 29), Rigg works with Featherstone and Bulstrode to represent the financial system of England. But Peter Featherstone and his heir are what their names imply, lightweights, compared to a less likely and probably more oppressive embodiment of patriarchal provinciality, for if Casaubon represents the intellectual bankrupcy of criticism and the arts, Tertius Lydgate tells us as much about the moral mediocrity of the sciences.

At twenty-seven, with his heavy eyebrows, dark eyes, straight nose, solid white hands, thick dark hair, and "exquisite cambric pocket handkerchief" (chap. 12), Lydgate looks like the antithesis of Casaubon; his "fearless expectations of success," as well as his "contempt for petty obstacles" and his altruistic goals as a doctor seem further to distinguish him from the fearful, self-pitying pedant. Yet, as W. J. Harvey has shown, Lydgate resembles Casaubon in his search for a key to all living things, the "primitive tissues from which life begins" (chap. 15), "the homogeneous origin of all tissues" (chap. 5).[33] And also like Casaubon, "Lydgate held it one of the prettiest attitudes of the feminine mind to adore a man's preeminence without too precise knowledge of what it consisted in" (chap. 27). Like Casaubon, who looks at the fable of Cupid and Psyche as a "romantic invention" which "cannot ... be reckoned a genuine mythical product" (chap. 20), Lydgate looks for "some common basis from which [tissues] all started, as your sarsnet, gauze, net, satin and velvet from the raw cocoon" (chap. 15), as if Eliot were considering through these representatives of biology and mythology how men demystify and devalue such stories of female divinity as the transformation of Psyche, such mysteries of nature as the transformation of the worm within the cocoon into the butterfly.

Like Dr. Frankenstein and Dr. John and all the other doctors who haunt the works of women writers from Charlotte Perkins Gilman's "The Yellow Wallpaper" to Sylvia Plath's *The Bell Jar*, Lydgate threatens to usurp control of women's bodies and therefore endangers their deepest selves: the landlady of the Tankard believes that "he would recklessly cut up their dead bodies" (chap. 45); Rosamond is disgusted with the body snatching of his hero, Vesalius, as well as with Lydgate's own scientific subjects, which seem to her "like a morbid vampire's taste" (chap. 64); Lady Chettam and Mrs. Talt are robbed by him of their traditionally acknowledged spheres of influence. That Lydgate "cared not only for 'cases,' but for John and Elizabeth, especially Elizabeth" (chap. 15) seems slightly ominous, since he values women mainly as a relaxing diversion or a subject of inquiry: "Plain women he regarded as he did other severe facts of life, to be faced with philosophy and investigated by science" (chap. 11). Certainly the close association between this physician of the body and Bulstrode, the self-proclaimed healer of souls, is also sinister.

Since so "many things would be easier to Lydgate if it would turn out that Mr. Bulstrode was generally justifiable" (chap. 16), Farebrother is hardly exaggerating when he speaks of Bulstrode as Lydgate's "arsenic-man" (chap. 17): Lydgate does act "hand-and-glove" (chap. 67) with Bulstrode in his vote for Mr. Tyke as chaplain, his furnishing Bulstrode with lethal knowledge, his taking Bulstrode's money, and his publicly and physically supporting Bulstrode at the height of the banker's humiliation. If most of Middlemarch feels that Lydgate would cut up their dead bodies, not a few citizens are convinced that Bulstrode—who looks as deathly as Casaubon feels— eats and drinks so little because "he must have a sort of vampire's feast in the sense of mastery" (chap. 16). Identifying his personal will with God's, defining his financial success as a sign of his spiritual election, Bulstrode resembles Lydgate and Casaubon in his failure to achieve his original calling, having given up the ministry in his youth for lucrative dealing in stolen goods.[34] Trying desperately and unsuccessfully to maintain the fiction of his respectability, as Casaubon does and as Lydgate will do, Bulstrode finally is driven to decide to kill the man who haunts him like a guilty conscience.

Finally, then, the image of the key, from Casaubon's mythical Key to Featherstone's and Rigg's physical keys, becomes a symbol of acquisitive and reductive monism which is all the more closely associated with coercion when we are shown Bulstrode handing a key to his servant and thereby empowering her to kill Raffles: Bulstrode knows that the liquor in his cabinet will probably be fatal, but he allows the unwitting woman to administer brandy because he wants to stifle this voice that might reveal his past iniquity. It is easy enough to give the image of the key in *Middlemarch* a Freudian reading. But if Eliot makes a point about male aggression, it is to show that the key unlocking death is inextricably linked with all these men's common obsession with origins: "In attempting to push oneself further and further back to what is only a beginning, a point that is stripped of every use but its categorization in the mind as beginning," Edward Said remarks, "one is caught in a tautological circuit of beginnings about to begin." All the professional men of Middlemarch seem caught in what Eliot shows to be the deathliness of nonbeing; they cannot experience the present moment but grasp instead at past or future through what Said calls "the absolute's felt absence."[35] Bulstrode's origins, shrouded in obscurity, are more real to him than his present success, even as they continually motivate and justify it, just as Peter Featherstone experiences himself more completely as a future dead man than as a breathing dying one. For Lydgate and Casaubon too, contemporary presence is lost in the search for origins.

But the word *key*, which means taxonomy as well as cipher and signature, implies that the key to all mythologies is what, in a discussion of the provisional and unoriginal nature of all origins, Gayatri Chakravorty Spivak has recently identified as the futility of "humankind's . . . common desire for a stable center, and for the assurance of mastery—through knowing or possessing."[36] Casaubon's and Lydgate's will to truth is no less a commitment to a central presence than Featherstone's and Bulstrode's will to power. Through these men, Eliot calls into question the possibility of such a stable origin, end, or identity, not only for these men and their projects, but also, by extension, for her own text as well. What concerns her is the compulsion of pattern and its resulting coercion. "We have lost something," Margaret Atwood exclaims in a poem about this nostalgia, as if voicing the anxious strivings of all these Middlemarchers, "some key to these things / which must be writings." For surely there must be something "that informs, holds together / this confusion, this largeness and dissolving."[37] But the quest for the lost or hidden key seems doomed to sterility and failure. "What bird sings that song / Key, key [?]" Diane Wakoski asks in a poem punningly called "Sun." Only "A bird made out of keys."[38]

At the beginning of *Middlemarch* Dorothea is searching for the keys not only to her mother's casket of jewels, the beauty of which promises revelations, but also for the way out of a "walled-in maze" of prospective identities as Mrs. Cadwallader's future Lady Chettam, the narrator's Saint Theresa, or a self-defined architect for the poor. Like Maggie Tulliver, who wanted "some key that would enable her to understand," Dorothea associates this key "with real learning and wisdom, such as great men knew," (*MF*, IV, chap. 3), so she chooses the role of Milton's daughter. But she quickly realizes that Casaubon will be unable to provide her with the learning and wisdom she had hoped to gain. In spite of her frustration and disappointment, Dorothea discovers that it is easier "to quell emotion than to incur the consequences of venting it" (chap. 29), so she begins to see as intelligible images of "saints with architectural models in their hands, or knives accidentally wedged in their skulls," whereas before such figures had always seemed monstrous (chap. 20).

Nevertheless, although Dorothea searches for "something better than anger and despondency" (chap. 21), throughout her married life with Casaubon, even in her humility, she causes him pain, even robbing him of the illusion of professional dignity with her urging that he actually begin to write the book he has so studiously planned. These words are "among the most cutting and irritating to him that she could have been impelled to use" (chap. 20). To Casaubon she is "a spy watching everything with a malign power of inference" (chap. 20), and he correctly judges her silences as "suppressed rebellion" (chap. 42). Her outward compliancy masks her indignation, superiority, and scorn; when expressed, these feelings result in Casaubon's collapse on the library steps; "the agitation caused by her anger might have helped to bring on" the attack of illness (chap. 30). When Dorothea's identification with Aunt Julia brings her to question the economic basis of patriarchy, specifically Casaubon's right to determine his own will and fix the line of succession in spite of his past familial obligations, she causes the most damage. Angry yet terrified about the murderous potential of her emotion, she is "wretched—with a dumb inward cry for help to bear this nightmare of a life in which every energy was arrested by dread" (chap. 37). Her marriage becomes "a perpetual struggle of energy with fear" (chap. 39). When Casaubon rejects the pity she expresses upon discovering that he suffers from the (metaphorically perfect)

"degeneration of the heart," Dorothea is "in the reaction of a rebellious anger" (chap. 42). "In such a crisis as this," we are told by the
narrator, "some women begin to hate" (chap. 42).

Dorothea's physical and emotional situation is similar to Maggie
Tulliver's:

> Somehow, when she sat at the window with her book, [Maggie's]
> eyes *would* fix themselves blankly on the outdoor sunshine; then
> they would fill with fears, and sometimes . . . she rebelled against
> her lot, she fainted under its loneliness; and fits even of anger and
> hatred . . . would flow out over her affections and conscience
> like a lava stream, and frighten her with a sense that it was not
> difficult for her to become a demon. [*MF*, IV, chap. 3].

Dorothea's strong need to struggle against "the warm flood" of her
feelings (chap. 20) is proof of the strength of her rebellion, and she
finds in repression "the thankfulness that might well up in us if we
had narrowly escaped hurting a lamed creature" (chap. 42). But,
again like Maggie Tulliver, she realizes that "we have no master-key"
for the "shifting relations between passion and duty" (*MF*, VII,
chap. 2). Deciding to resign herself to the life-in-death scenario
Casaubon constructs for her, Dorothea bends to "a new yoke" in the
belief that she is "going to say 'Yes' to her own doom" (chap. 48);
however, her hesitation through the night before acquiescing fully in
Casaubon's stipulation that she dedicate herself to his research after
his death implicates her in that death, at least in her own mind.

Dorothea's dilemma is eerily echoed in the plight of a woman
whose family almost represents the humanities in America during
the second half of the nineteenth century. Alice James remembers
her feelings as she "used to sit immoveable,"

> reading in the library with waves of violent inclination suddenly
> invading my muscles taking some one of their myriad forms such
> as throwing myself out the window, or knocking off the head of
> the benignant pater as he sat with his silver locks, writing at his
> table, it used to seem to me that the only difference between
> me and the insane was that I had not only all the horrors and
> suffering of insanity but the duties of doctor, nurse, and strait-
> jacket imposed on me, too. [39]

Eliot liberates Dorothea from her oscillations between murderous anger and suicidal self-punishment. Yet, paradoxically, by granting her heroine's secret wish, she actually reinforces the lesson of patriarchal morality, for the result of Casaubon's fortuitous death is Dorothea's guilt. Finally, in other words, Eliot does not countenance female renunciation because she believes it to be appropriately feminine, but because she is intensely aware of the destructive potential of female rage. Thus she simultaneously demonstrates the necessity of renouncing anger and the absolute impossibility of genuinely doing so. Perhaps it is for this reason that Eliot leaves Alice James with "the impression, morally and physically, of mildew, or some morbid growth—a fungus of a pendulous shape, or as of something damp to the touch."[40]

To make Dorothea's complicity clearer, Eliot supplies her with a series of foils. Mary Garth, for example, stands by the bedside of the dying Featherstone and decides to fulfill her role as a nurse as patiently as she can, although we are told she is not naturally saintly. Constantly filled with "anger . . . of no use" (chap. 25), Mary nevertheless manages to restrain herself until Featherstone awakens one night and with unusual clarity demands her help. When he orders her to open a box so he can burn one of his last testaments, however, she refuses to comply: "I will not touch your key or your money sir" (chap. 33). Waiting, reminiscent of Dorothea in her decision that "by-and-by she would go to him with the cordial" (chap. 33), Mary also discovers her patient dead "with his right hand clasping the keys, and his left hand lying on the heap of notes and gold" (chap. 33). In the process of defying the old man, she does not consider that she might precipitate his death. But she does realize that, like Dorothea, she has unwittingly cut off an attractive young man from any possible inheritance, thereby paradoxically saving him from both money and the deathly keys. By shaping Fred's life and values, in fact, she demonstrates the elevating effect of a woman's influence, even as she reminds us of the deceit practiced by the woman who functions as a power behind the scenes.

It is Mr. Trumbull who observes Mary Garth as she "has been mixing medicine in drops. She minds what she is doing, sir. That is a great point in a woman. . . . A man whose life is of any value should think of his wife as a nurse" (chap. 32). But perhaps because her patience is such an effort of will, the Christian nurse modulates into those "Christian Carnivora" who watch at all the deathbeds in Middlemarch (chap. 35). When we see that most effeminate man, the pale and sickly Bulstrode, who asks only to be "a vessel ... consecrated by use" (chap. 61), nursing Raffles to death, Eliot exposes the bad faith involved in Christian resignation. That ultimately she chooses to manage such an exposure with a male rather than a female character is indicative of her belief that men are more completely damned than women by precisely their license to act out impulses necessarily restricted in women. In some sense, then, as an outsider whose class status is ambiguous, a religious person who can only establish his piety through words of self-abasement rather than through actual deeds of altruism, Bulstrode is a demonic parody of Dorothea, one who reveals both the deathly implications and the potential bad faith of this heroine's saintly renunciation.

But it is with Rosamond that we must associate Eliot's most important study of female rebellion. The Lilith to Dorothea's Mary, Rosamond is associated early in the novel with sirens, serpents, and devilishly alluring charms. She entangles Lydgate into courtship and then covertly rebels against his mastery, harboring secret designs and willfully asserting her right to enjoy herself. Because Rosamond threatens her father to go into a decline if she cannot have her own way, because her wilful persistence in going horseback riding during her pregnancy against her husband's orders causes her to miscarry, most critics considered her an example of that egoism which Eliot condemns as narcisstic, and certainly we might be tempted to accept Lydgate's view of her as a kind of Madame Laure who would kill him because he wearied her, while we define Dorothea as another sort of woman altogether (chap. 56). But we have already seen that Dorothea is involved in a "form of feminine impassibility" that Rosamond more overtly typifies (chap. 56). Both, moreover, are called angels, each achieving her own perfect standard of a perfect lady, and both are considered beautiful. Both are victims of a miseducation causing them not to "know Homer from slang" (chap. 11), and neither, therefore, shows "any unbecoming knowledge" (chap. 27). Experiencing the frustrating truth of Mrs. Cadwallader's remark, "A woman's choice usually means taking the only man she can get" (chap. 54), Dorothea and Rosamond can only express their dissatisfaction with provincial life by choosing suitors who seem to be possible means of escaping confinement and ennui.

For both, then, marriage is soon associated "with feelings of disappointment" (chap. 64). Oppressed by the gentlewoman's "liberty" (chap. 28), both are resentful that their husbands perceive them only as graceful yet irrelevant accoutrements and both presumptuously attempt to recreate their respective husbands in their own images. Like Dorothea, Rosamond feels that her girlish dreams of felicity are quickly deflated by the inflexible reality of intimacy and while both women struggle to repress their resentment, both find some consolation in the visits of Will. Indeed, when his visits cease, both find themselves looking wearily out the windows of their husbands' houses, oppressed by boredom. Dorothea in Lowick and Rosamond in Lowick Gate try to ease their loneliness in part by writing to their husbands' relatives.

As their common marriage struggles suggest, these women are tied to men who increasingly resemble each other, not only in their careers but in their conjugal lives. When Rosamund expresses her opinion about debts that will affect her life as much as his, Lydgate echoes Casaubon: "You must learn to take my judgment on questions you don't understand" (chap. 58). Lydgate contemptuously calls Rosamond "dear," as Casaubon does Dorothea when he is most annoyed with her presumption. The narrator expresses sympathy for Lydgate's need to bow under "the yoke," but then goes on to explain that he does this "like a creature who had talons" (chap. 58). Lydgate begins to act and speak "with that excited narrow consciousness which reminds one of an animal with fierce eyes and retractile claws" (chap. 66). Like Casaubon, Lydgate will "shrink into unconquerable reticence" (chap. 63) out of personal pride when help is offered. And like Casaubon he experiences the discontent "of wasted energy and a degrading preoccupation" (chap. 64). Fallen into a "swamp" of debt (chap. 58), he feels his life as a mistake "at work in him like a recognized chronic disease, mingling its uneasy importunities with every prospect, and enfeebling every thought" (chap. 58).

Lydgate had dreamed of Rosamond as "that perfect piece of womanhood who would reverence her husband's mind after the fashion of an accomplished mermaid, using her comb and looking-glass and singing her song for the relaxation of his adored wisdom alone" (chap. 58)—a dream not appreciably different from Casaubon's. But this suitor whose distinction of mind "did not penetrate his feeling and judgment about furniture, or women" (chap. 15)— as if these are interchangeable goods—ends up in a losing struggle with his wife about furniture. Admitting that he has gotten an inexperienced girl into trouble (chap. 58), he knows that "she married [him] without knowing what she was going into, and it might have been better for her if she had not" (chap. 76). Lydgate attacks Rosamond's attachment to their house, thinking "in his bitterness, what can a woman care about so much as house and furniture" (chap. 64), but she has been given nothing else to care about. She "could not have imagined" during her courtship that she would "take a house in Bride Street, where the rooms are like cages" (chap. 64).

Having no overt means of escape at her disposal and a husband who refuses to hear or take her advice, Rosamond enacts her opposition as silently as does Dorothea; she is "particularly forcible by means of that mild persistence which, as we know, enables a white living substance to make its way in spite of opposing rock" (chap. 36). Always able to frustrate him by stratagem, Rosamond becomes Lydgate's basil plant, "flourishing wonderfully on a murdered man's brains" (Finale). She fulfills Gwendolen Harleth's vision of women and plants that must look pretty and be bored, which is "the reason why some of them have got poisonous" (*DD*, chap. 13). Rosamond *has* been imprisoned by her marriage, as Eliot's final reference to her married life suggests: "instead of the threatened cage in Bride Street," Lydgate "provided one all flowers and gilding" (Finale). In spite of the narrator's condemnation of her narrow narcissism, then, it is clear that Rosamond enacts Dorothea's silent anger against a marriage of death, Mary Garth's resentment, Bertha Grant's plot, Gwendolen Grandcourt's secret longing, and Janet Dempster's desire, as well as Maggie Tulliver's "volcanic upheavings" (*MF*, IV, chap. 3), even as she reminds us of Emily Dickinson, that "Vesuvius at Home"[41] in America who read these novels with such passionate interest, and whose explosive images of herself as a gun or a bomb are not dissimilar from Eliot's characterization of Rosamond's power as a "torpedo" (chap. 64).

Dorothea discovers her love for Will after she witnesses what she thinks is a love scene between Will and Rosamond, and she feels "like the heart of a mother who seems to see her child divided by the sword, and presses one bleeding half to her breast while her gaze goes forth in agony toward the half which is carried away by the lying woman that has never known the mother's pang" (chap. 80). Interestingly, however, although she continues to feel pain over the divided child, Will, Dorothea does not continue to think of Rosamond as "the lying woman." Instead, she quickly becomes conscious of the scene "as bound up with another woman's life—" (chap. 80), a woman whose plight reminds her of her own before the death of Casaubon. Dorothea had previously explained to Will that she "used to despise women a little for not shaping their lives more, and doing better things" (chap. 54). But once she is herself forced to experience the constraints imposed by her gender, her sympathy for other women expands until it even encompasses someone who appears to be a successful rival.

Eliot always, in fact, associates such an act of sympathetic identification between women—like Dinah and Hetty, Lucy and Maggie, Esther and Mrs. Transome, Romola and Tessa, Mirah and Gwendolen—with a perspective on life that widens as the heroine escapes what the novelist depicts as the ultimate imprisonment, imprisonment within the cell of the self. Like the mad queen in "Snow White" staring at her own fair face, Hetty, Mrs. Transome, Tessa, and Gwendolen sit blindly before their mirrors seeing only themselves, but Dinah, Esther, Romola, and Mirah, looking through this frame to the world outside, resemble the good queen who sews by the window. While Mrs. Transome sees herself as a hag in her glass, for example, Esther draws up the blinds, "liking to see the grey sky, where there were some veiled glimmerings of moonlight, and the lines of the for-ever running river, and the bending movement of the trees." What she obtains is a sense of "the largeness of the world" (chap. 49).

Like the two queens, what these women share is their potential for becoming each other, and it is their recognition of this potential that defines the heroism of sisterhood within patriarchy. Maggie

Tulliver sits "without candle in the twilight with the window wide open toward the river . . . struggling to see still the sweet face," when Lucy actually opens the door; Dinah comes to be a sister to Hetty within the locked prison cell. Watching, waiting receptively, emptied of personal expectations, each of these women has a capacity for experiencing her own nothingness that allows her to be inhabited by another person's being. Dorothea exerts herself not "to sit in the narrow cell of her calamity, in the besotted misery of a consciousness that sees another's lot as an accident of its own" (chap. 80). Like Maggie Tulliver, she sees "the possibility of shifting the position from which she looked at the gratification of her own desires, of taking her stand out of herself and looking at her own life as an insignificant part of a divinely guided whole" (*MF*, IV, chap. 3). And she is not driven mad, as Latimer was, by such an imaginative reconstruction of pain because it wins her a vision from her window when she opens the curtains to see the road: "a man with a bundle on his back and a woman carrying her baby. . . . Far off in the bending sky was the pearly light; and she felt the largeness of the world and the manifold wakings of men to labour and endurance" (chap. 80). Finally, in fact, Dorothea's realization that she is herself a part of "that involuntary, palpitating life" frees her from solipsism and allows her "to see and save Rosamond" (chap. 80).

The meeting between Rosamond and Dorothea is therefore the climax of *Middlemarch*. Both women seem childish because both have been denied full maturity by their femininity. Each is pale from a night of crying, believing that she has "buried a private joy." Each is jealous of the other, yet self-forgetful. Dorothea speaks in what sounds "like a low cry from some suffering creature in the darkness" and Rosamond feels a pang "as if a wound within her had been probed" (chap. 81). Holding hands, they sit talking of love which "murders our marriage" and marriage which "stays with us like a murder" (chap. 81). While Dorothea goes to save Rosamond by an act of self-sacrifice, Rosamond actually makes the sacrifice and thereby saves Dorothea. While Dorothea thinks Rosamond has been her rival, Rosamond had actually acted for Dorothea by informing Will of Casaubon's codicil. While Rosamond's confession to Dorothea is "a reflex of [Dorothea's] own energy" (chap. 81), Rosamond acts independently later to inform Will that Dorothea knows the truth about his love.

Lydgate seems to glimpse the solidarity the two have achieved in their brief moment of sisterhood when he returns, haunted by their pale faces. And when he helps Dorothea to the door, we are reminded how well suited these two might have been. Dorothea, with her need to find a cause to which she can dedicate her energies and her money, might have found a high purpose through Lydgate's aspirations, just as with her support he might have found the time and the belief he needed to pursue his research, a consummation many contemporary reviewers of *Middlemarch* devoutly wished. Eliot's development of this expectation and her subsequent disappointment of it demonstrate exactly how imprisoned both Dorothea and Lydgate are in sexual categories. Significantly, when Lydgate turns from the door to face Rosamond, he realizes that "he had chosen this fragile creature, and had taken the burden of her life upon his arms. He must walk as he could, carrying that burden pitifully" (chap. 81). Just as Dorothea needed to reinterpret the scene between Will and Rosamond, we need to revise our reading of the vision from the window; "no story is the same to us after a lapse of time; or rather, we who read it are no longer the same interpreters" (*AB*, chap. 54). When Dorothea's "flowing tones," her "rising sobs," and her "great wave of sorrow" wash over Rosamond like a "warm stream," these two women clasp each other "as if they had been in a shipwreck" because both realize "how hard it is to walk always in fear of hurting another who is tied to us." Dorothea's window vision of "a man with a bundle on his back, and a woman carrying her baby" evokes Lydgate bearing the burden of Rosamond and Dorothea carrying Will, the man she thinks of as her baby. Perfectly matched, these two couples travel to their separate destinies without ever joining or touching. How different their pilgrimage is from that of Saint Theresa of the "Prelude," who walks "hand-in-hand" with her brother in quest of an epic life.

Nevertheless, while the narrator repeatedly expresses regret over Rosamond's unremitting pettiness, the fact that it is Rosamond who actually saves Will and Dorothea is only one of several hints that she is what Mary Ellmann calls "the daemonic center" of *Middlemarch*.[42] Many readers assume that Rosamond is a vindictive portrait impelled by Eliot's tormented jealousy of pretty women, yet such critics have neglected the clues that align the author with her blonde temptress. Like Madame Laure, Rosamond is a brilliant strategist, "by nature an actress of parts" who "even acted her own character, and so well, that she did not know it to be precisely her own" (chap. 12). Like Eliot, Rosamond is not terribly good at comic parts, but she rarely takes them. This star pupil of Mrs. Lemon's school is "clever with that sort of cleverness which catches every tone" (chap. 16). She is a fine musician who plays the piano and sings with accomplishment. Significantly, moreover, she is always either literally or figuratively sewing: when she does not actually have lacing, netting or tatting in her hands, she plaits her hair, embroiders her linens, and engages for her petticoats to be thickened, her handkerchiefs to be mended, and her hosiery made. And she is constantly plotting, devising futures for herself which she sometimes manages to actualize. In short, like Eliot, she is a spinner of yarns, a weaver of fictions.

Rosamond's sewing is in some ways a sign of her acceptance of her role as a female. In this respect she contrasts markedly with most of Eliot's heroines, who must struggle with their distaste for what they view as a secondary and decidedly compensatory art. As in all those fairy tales in which three drops of blood from a needle or spinning wheel symbolize a fall into female gender and with it either sleep or pregnancy, sewing signals woman's domestic confinement and diminishment. In spite of her disdain for tearing up little pieces of cloth in order to quilt them together, Maggie Tulliver does finally perfect her plain-sewing, but only in her zeal for self-mortification, while Gwendolen Harleth remains horrified by the thought of working with her mother and sisters on a tablecloth or communion cloth. In their rebellion against feminine art done for and in the parlor, Maggie and Gwendolen resemble Dorothea, who is "shut out" from believing that she would be able to find felicity in "the perusal of 'Female Scripture Characters,' . . . and the care of her soul over her embroidery in her own boudoir" (chap. 3).

The "trivial chain-work" done by Rosamond that manages to engage Lydgate in spinning "the mutual web of courtship" (chap. 3) seems airy and vulnerable, a pretty illusion not unlike Rosamond herself. Its flimsiness suggests that "a woman's hopes are woven of sunbeams; a shadow annihilates them"; as Eliot explains in *Felix Holt the Radical*, this shadow is "the presentiment of . . . powerlessness" (chap. 1). Actually, it is powerlessness that leads to womanly wiles like Rosamond's, for "a woman's wiles are a net," as H. D. explains in *Helen in Egypt:*

> if a woman fights,
> she must fight by stealth,
>
> with invisible gear;
> no sword, no dagger, no spear
> in a woman's hands
>
> can make wrong, right:[43]

For all the girls in fairy tales who resent their initiation into such powerlessness, there are many older women like "The Three Spinners,"[44] who manage to spin the flax left by the queen for the girl who cannot or will not spin it herself. Interestingly, these spinners are grotesque, one with a broad foot which she got by treading, one with a falling lip which she got by licking, and one with a broad thumb gotten by twisting the thread. Like the Fates or the Norns, such powerful weaving women remind us of figures like Philomel and Penelope, both of whom also exercise their art subversively and quietly in order to control the lives of men. But they also resemble the spinning crones in de Beauvoir's cave, as well as Helen Diner's mother goddesses who "weave the world tapestry out of genesis and demise."[45] As different as ladylike Rosamond first seems from them, she too weaves what turns out to be a chain strong enough to trap and hold a rather large man. And Rosamond is no less interested in quietly getting her way than the demure seamstress Celia Brooke (who considers notions and scruples in the light of "spilt needles, making one afraid of treading, or sitting down, or even eating" [chap. 2]), or the knitter Mrs. Garth, or Lisbeth Bede, or Mrs. Poyser, that "terrible woman" who is actually "made of needles!" (*AB*, chap. 53). All of these women are, in fact, needlers, querulous about their derivative status but adamant about asserting their influence in even the most inauspicious situations.

Many critics have noticed that Middlemarch society is described as if it were a web woven from different interrelated lives. The history of the town, for example, is described in terms of "fresh threads of connection" made between municipal town and rural parish (chap. 11), while the personal relationships of provincial life likewise become a kind of spun creation. "Who can know," the narrator asks, "how much of this most inward life is made up of the thoughts he believes other men to have about him, until that fabric of opinion is threatened with ruin?" (chap. 64).[46] But what has been less obvious, perhaps, is that it is women who are associated with spinning this fabric of opinion that constitutes the community, because it is they who sew together the threads of connection.

As Eliot explains in *The Mill on the Floss*, "public opinion . . . is always of the feminine gender" (VII, chap. 2). In *Middlemarch* it is women like Mrs. Plyndale, Mrs. Bulstrode, Mrs. Vincy, Mrs. Cadwallader, Mrs. Dollop, Mrs. Hackbutt, and Mrs. Tom Tuller who visit and swap stories: when "wives, widows and single ladies took their work and went out to tea oftener than usual" (chap. 71), they record what "knits together" the community (*MF*, VI, chap. 14). Like gossipy nurse Rooke in *Persuasion*, such female historians of private life are extraordinarily insightful, and so it is hardly surprising that someone like "Mrs. Taft, who was always counting stitches and gathered her information in misleading fragments caught between the rows of her knitting, had got into her head that Mr. Lydgate was a natural son of Bulstrode's, a fact which seemed to justify her suspicions of evangelical laymen" (chap. 26).

There can be no doubt that the social fabric spun by such women is hampering and trivializing to the individual with high aspirations or ideals. Romola feels that "the vision of any great purpose . . . was utterly eclipsed for her now by the sense of a confusion in human things which made all effort a mere dragging at tangled threads" (chap. 61); Mr. Tulliver, like Swift's Gulliver, is "entangled in the meshes of a net" (*MF*, III, chap. 7), in part because "for getting a strong impression that a skein is tangled, there is nothing like snatching at a single thread" (I, chap. 8). Not a few individuals discover that "the finest threads, such as no eye sees, if bound cunningly about the sensitive flesh, so that the movement to break them bring torture, may make a worse bondage than any fetters" (*FH*, chap. 8). Armgart, as we have already seen, feels herself twisting in a "wrack of threads," and many other characters find their "thoughts entangled in metaphors and act fatally on the strength of them" (chap. 10).

Understandably, then, the narrator is presented as someone who is scientifically unravelling the social fabric in order to study how it came into being: "I at least have so much to do in unravelling certain human lots," this narrator reasons, "and seeing how they were woven and interwoven, that all the light I can command must be concentrated on this particular web, and not dispersed over that tempting range of relevancies called the universe" (chap. 15). Like Lydgate or Casaubon, this narrator is searching for the hidden structure that gives coherence and meaning to the whole. Yet, just as interlacing and entwining belong to the female realm, so does unravelling, which is done at night not only by Penelope but also by nature herself, so as to insure the eternal freshness of things. And certainly the overtly masculine narrators of *Scenes of Clerical Life* and *Adam Bede* have been transfigured in *Middlemarch* into a more neutral presence. Whether this narrator is a man involved in an "effort of totalization" jeopardized by the text, as J. Hillis Miller argues, or Quentin Anderson's "Wise Woman," or U. C. Knoepflmacher's "male mother,"[47] the detachment of Eliot's narrative voice is surely born of the same grief that caused Maggie and Dorothea to seek a shift in perspective as the only possible escape from their deathly entrapment. Distance is a source of solace in *Middlemarch*.

Meditative, philosophical, humorous, sympathetic, moralistic, scientific, the narrator presents her/himself as so far above and beyond the ordinary classifications of our culture that s/he transcends gender distinctions. Doing in a woman's way a traditionally male task of knowing, combining "a man's mind and woman's heart," Eliot makes such gender-based categories irrelevant. Because her voice sympathetically articulates opposed perspectives, because it is highly provisional and tentative even as it risks generalizations, this narrator becomes an authentic "we," a voice of the community that is committed to accepting the indeterminacy of meaning, as well as the complex kinship of people and things. But this triumph of transcending the definitions of the culture as well as the limits of selfhood does not displace the reality of female characters forced to live within conventional roles. And, while the narrator presents her /

himself as objectively unravelling webs, it is the author, after all, who has knit these plots together in the first place.

Not a few of Eliot's characters dwell in a fictional world "in which destiny disguises her cold awful face behind a hazy radiant veil, encloses us in warm downy wings, and poisons us with violet-scented breath" (*AB*, chap. 12). Like the lawyer Jermyn in *Felix Holt The Radical*, Eliot can "hold all the threads" and either "use the evidence or . . . nullify it" (chap. 21). And like "nature, that great tragic dramatist, [who] knits us together by bone and muscles, and divides by the subtler web of our brains" (*AB*, chap. 4), the author of *Middlemarch* has given us this sample of a web in which, like Rosamond, she has worked "for" the female community by entangling the representatives of patriarchal culture—Casaubon, Bulstrode, Featherstone, and Lydgate—and by calling into question their authority.

Significantly, Bulstrode believes that the clue that causes Raffles to find him is "a providential thing" (chap. 53), and in a way he is right. If "Nemesis can seldom forge a sword for herself out of our consciences," then "she is apt to take part against us" (*AB*, chap. 29) by means of her punishing plots. As the knitting Mrs. Farebrother explains to Dorothea, "They say Fortune is a woman and capricious. But sometimes she is a good woman and gives to those who merit" (chap. 54). "More bitter than death [is] the woman whose heart is snares and nets," the author of Ecclesiastes warns; "whoso pleaseth God shall escape from her, but the sinner shall be taken by her" (7:26). Although Eliot seems to substitute female Fate for the biblical Father, deeds do have an inexorable effect in her novels because "there is a terrible Nemesis following on some errors, [so] that it is always possible for those who like it to interpret them into a crime" (chap. 72). While her characters remain unaware for the most part of their entrapment,

> any one watching keenly the stealthy convergence of human
> lots, sees a slow preparation of effects from one life on another,
> which tells like a calculated irony on the indifference or the
> frozen stare with which we look at our unintroduced neighbour.
> Destiny stands by sarcastic with our *dramatis personae* folded in
> her hand. [chap. 11].

Caught "in the slow preparation of effects," Eliot's characters might very well feel, with Tito Melema, that "the web had gone on spinning in spite of him, like a growth over which he had no power" (*R*, chap. 34). As we have seen, Lydgate, who receives so much of the narrator's sympathetic attention, is being prepared for "the hampering threadlike pressure of small social conditions" (chap. 18) because "Middlemarch, in fact, counted on swallowing Lydgate and assimilating him very comfortably" (chap. 15). To Bulstrode, moreover, it seems as if "the years had been perpetually spinning" his elaborate justifications "into intricate thickness, like masses of spider-webs, padding the moral sensibility" (chap. 60).

We will explore how Emily Dickinson "fights by stealth / with invisible gear" when she imagines herself as a spider silently spinning out her subversive spells. Working almost invisibly inside the smallest cracks and crevices, the figure of such a spider also dominates Maggie Tulliver's early speculations about the magical lacework created inside the fertile, white-powdered mill on the Floss. And indeed a spider's web is an example of nature's art, much like floss—the silk of the cocoon, the natural fiber of a cornsilk—which, when it is used by Eliot as the name of a river, calls our attention to the metaphorical connection between currents and threads. But of course the web was an important symbol long before Eliot and Dickinson exploited it, as our epigraph from Anne Finch suggests. And as a symbol the web is closely associated with the female fall from authority. Margaret Cavendish actually prefaces her poems with the admission that "True it is, spinning with the fingers is more proper to our sex than studying or writing poetry, which is the spinning with the brain," so it is not at all surprising that she writes a poem describing how "The Spider's housewifery no webs doth spin / To make her clothes, but ropes to hang flies in." [48]

Just as Cavendish seems to spin a story specifically against those who condemn her to physical spinning, Eliot calls attention to the difference between her subtle snares and the intellectual work of the men she entangles. Like "Erinna with the thick-coiled mat" who "held the spindle as she sat," Eliot spins "the byssus drearily / In insect-labour, while the throng / Of gods and men wrought deeds that poets wrought in song" (*DD*, chap. 51). Unlike Casaubon's text and Lydgate's tissue, in other words, Eliot's fictional fabric is a kind of tapestry that fully illustrates the etymological roots of the Latin *texere*, to weave. More, her web is very much like the fretwork or paperhanging in which every form can be found, "from Jupiter to Judy, if you only look with creative inclination" (chap. 32), and it also resembles the famous pier glass of polished steel multitudinously scratched in all directions: "place now against it a lighted candle as a centre of illumination, and lo! the scratches will seem to arrange themselves in a fine series of concentric circles around that little sun" (chap. 27). Like the tapestry, the fretwork, or the pierglass, *Middlemarch* cannot be reduced to a coherent or stable pattern. Labyrinthine in its intricacy, the web which resembles the embroidery, knitting, cross-stitching, and netting of her female characters, reveals exactly how problematic any kind of interpretative act remains—be it literary, political, social, medical, technological, or amatory.

Not only does Eliot's web remain indecipherable because it is infinitely decipherable, not only does it work the revenge of nature against culture, it also represents the female community in its conservative standards. Aunt Glegg of *The Mill on the Floss* is terribly harsh on Maggie's aspirations to transcend societal conventions until the girl needs help, but then the woman who bargained so energetically for a bit of net defends her niece against those who accuse her. By virtue of their very confinement to the domestic sphere, women like Harriet Bulstrode are exceptionally sensitive to the network of obligations and duties that link families together into a community. In the context of this holistic appreciation of social responsibilities, therefore, the greatest heroism is that of Dorothea, who feels another life "bound up" with her own, while the greatest villainy is Bulstrode's, not only because he has misrepresented himself to his wife and neighbors, but also because such misrepresentation is adequately symbolized by his having sold the dyes which rotted Mr. Vincy's silk (chap. 61). If a woman can spin a "web of folly" that produces a "rancorous poisoned garment" or a "Nessus shirt" that threatens to weaken its wearer (*AB*, chap. 22), she can also "thread life by a fresh clue," the clue of renunciation (*R*, chap. 41), and thereby be identified, as Romola and Dorothea and Rosamond are, with Ariadne.[49]

Tito Melema's wedding present to Romola is, curiously, a miniature wooden case which he uses to lock up her brother's cross and on which he has had painted a triptych of the triumph of Bacchus and Ariadne. Significantly, he has revised the myth told by Ovid about the little boy Bacchus on his way home to Naxos: in *Metamorphoses* Bacchus proves his godhood to disbelieving sailors by becalming the ship, winding the oars with ivy and creating the fierce illusion of sea beasts that cause the crew to leap overboard to their deaths; Tito places the wedding of Bacchus and Ariadne on board this ship. His revision reveals his self-satisfied view of himself and his self-deceptive desire to look on only the brighter side of things, even if such vision falsifies reality. But Romola recognizes this vision of the "bower of paradise" as a "lying screen" (chap. 37)—indeed, a locked box— because she undoubtedly remembers the complete myth: the story of Ariadne's aid to Theseus (who needs her thread to find his way through the labyrinth), his killing of the Minotaur, his subsequent abandonment of her, and the god's union with her on the island of Naxos. But Romola also learns that she will resemble the Ariadne abandoned by Theseus far more than the Ariadne crowned by Bacchus since, "instead of taking a long, exciting journey, she was to sit down in her usual place" (chap. 41). Indeed, although Tito enjoys thinking of himself as Bacchus, the rescuer, the part he plays is closer to that of Theseus, the betrayer.

Rewriting abduction as seduction into a marriage of death, the Ariadne myth is an especially compelling version of Persephone's story for Eliot. Both the fact that Ariadne alone has the clue that will thread a way through the labyrinth and the fact that she is still unable to effect her own escape make her an important symbol to Eliot of female helplessness and the resilience, supportiveness, and endurance such helplessness paradoxically engenders. Women are distinguished in Eliot's fiction by their capacity for experiencing those "supreme moments in life when all we have hoped or delighted in, all we can dread or endure, falls away from our regard as insignificant—is lost like a trivial memory in that simple, primitive love which knits us to the beings who have been nearest us, in their times of helplessness or of anguish" (*MF*, III, chap. 1).

In Rome Dorothea stands next to "the reclining Ariadne, then called the Cleopatre" (chap. 19); her rather ironic double, Rosamond, is described "as forlorn as Ariadne—as a charming stage Ariadne left behind with all her boxes full of costumes and no hope of a coach" (chap. 31). For the woman caught in the maze of relationships that constitutes society, Ariadne's gift of the thread, even though it seems destined to be offered to the wrong man, represents what George Eliot sees as women's special capacity for altruism. There can be little doubt that such a characterization of women is conservative; perhaps it is even a way of fending off the advocates of feminism. But the identification of social community and moral intensity with women in Eliot's fiction also lends them primacy. The kind of consciousness that drove Latimer mad endows Eliot's heroines with resources for sympathetic identification that transform the vindictive noose or knot of the author's revengeful plot into a kind of lifeline held out to other creatures threading their various ways through the labyrinth.

Not surprisingly, then, the virtues of a man like Fare/brother are defined by his "feminine" renunciation, his sensitivity, and domestic responsibility for a household of single women. A preacher who speaks without a book (that symbol in *Middlemarch* of masculine authority), Farebrother collects small insects, even spiders. And he tells a story illustrative of the microscopic perspective Eliot explores in "The Lifted Veil," "about the ants whose beautiful house was knocked down by a giant named Tom" who "thought they didn't mind because he couldn't hear them cry, or see them use their pocket-handkerchiefs" (chap. 63). Living within a matriarchal family not unlike Mr. Irwine's in *Adam Bede* or Hans Meyrick's in *Daniel Deronda*, Farebrother accepts his responsibility for a number of female dependents, including his wonderful aunt, Miss Noble, "a tiny old lady of meeker aspect" than his mother, "with frills and kerchief decidedly more worn and mended" (chap. 17), "a wonder-fully quaint picture of self-forgetful goodness" (chap. 50) who sneaks bits of sugar from Mr. Farebrother's tea table to give to those even more needy than herself. Significantly, just as the efforts of Mr. Farebrother bring together Fred Vincy and Mary Garth, it is the spin-ster Miss Noble who helps gain Will a place in Dorothea's sympathy and finally in her house.

While critics like Henry James have castigated Will Ladislaw as a lady's man, Will is Eliot's radically anti-patriarchal attempt to create an image of masculinity attractive to women. Early associated with the winged horse Pegasus (chap. 9), who was created from the blood of Medusa's decapitated head and presented by Minerva to the Muses, Will is thus mythically linked with female power and female inspiration. The Bacchus to Dorothea's Ariadne, he is also feminine because he is an outsider in his society, a man without an inheritance, without an English name. Closely associated with Byron and Shelley, this "slim young fellow with his girl's complexion" (chap. 50) is "a creature who entered into everyone's feelings, and could take the pressure of their thought instead of urging his own with iron resistance" (chap. 50). Just the knowledge of his love for her makes Dorothea feel "as if some hard icy pressure had melted, and her consciousness had room to expand" (chap. 62).

It is Will's dispossession that reveals most strikingly his feminine strength for survival, as well as his matrilineal genealogy. Before Dorothea meets Will, she learns to know him through the miniature of Aunt Julia in Casaubon's bow-windowed room. While she identifies Aunt Julia with herself, she also sees Will's lineaments in Aunt Julia, who is Will's grandmother on his paternal side, a woman dispossessed for marrying the man she loved. On his maternal side too, Will's family history is significant, for his mother also ran away from her family when it became involved in a disreputable pawnbroking business, and she too was dispossessed. A victim of Bulstrode's manipulations, she was lost to the mother who eventually tried to reclaim her: "Bulstrode had never said to himself beforehand, 'The daughter shall not be found'—nevertheless when the moment came he kept her existence hid" (chap. 61). Will's family, therefore, symbolizes the economic dispossession of women in patriarchy.

Ridiculed as an exotic outcast of Polish or Jewish origins, an outsider with no status and an eminently curious name, Will seems like "a sort of gypsy, rather enjoying the sense of belonging to no class" (chap. 46). When he is associated with Hobbes, Milton, and Swift, it is to underline his similarity to Dorothea, not Casaubon, since he too is a secretary, not an author. Thus in his romance with Dorothea Eliot substitutes the equality of a brother/sister model for the hierarchical inadequacy of father/daughter relationships, and some of the dislike of Will might very well be related to the erotic sibling relationship which is here (as elsewhere in Eliot's

fiction) made to function as an alternative to the power struggles
of heterosexuality. In spite of Will's rather literary adoration of
Dorothea, in spite of the deficiency of the troubadour images with
which he is surrounded,[50] he is the man Adrienne Rich has identified
as "The phantom of the-man-who-would-understand, / The lost
brother, the twin—."[51] Making "beaver-like noises" as she "unconsciously drew forth the [tortoise-shell lozenge-box] which she
was fingering" (chap. 83)—a box given to her by Will—Miss Noble
brings Will into Casaubon's library, thereby joining the lovers.
The quasi-allegorical level of the plot implies that Dorothea has at
last united with her own noble will.

While it is true that her life is absorbed in another's and that she
must be satisfied not with great work but with an "incalculably
diffusive" influence (Finale), her marriage is still the most subversive
act available to her within the context defined by the author, since
it is the only act prohibited by the stipulations of the dead man, and
by her family and friends as well. Dorothea utters Lucy Snowe's
words, "My heart will break" (chap. 83); while not renouncing
Lucy's need for male approval, she does extricate herself from an
entanglement with the male teacher and chooses instead a student
for her second husband. By choosing a man she thinks of as a baby,
moreover, Dorothea gains a sense of her own control over the relationship. By choosing Will, associated as he is with southern sunshine,
fresh air, open windows, and intoxicating spirit, Dorothea accepts
the dispossession of Aunt Julia and finds her way out of the deathly
underworld in which she had been so painfully shut up. If she still
does not escape the confining maze of social duties and definitions,
this is because no such transcendence seems possible or even necessarily desirable in Eliot's world.

But this last echo of *Villette*, spoken by Dorothea when she is as
desperate at the prospect of losing Will's love as Lucy is at the
thought of losing M. Paul's, also serves to remind us that George
Eliot is no less a literary heiress than Mary Shelley or Emily Brontë.
Indeed, written after Eliot's apprenticeship as book reviewer for
the *Westminster Review* and during her long personal relationship
with England's foremost literary critic, *Middlemarch* is understandably
a self-conscious literary text. Every chapter is prefaced by a quotation,
from writers like Cervantes, Blake, Shakespeare, Bunyan, Goldsmith,

Scott, and Browne, almost as if Eliot were obsessively stating her credentials. Yet, curiously, not a few of these epigraphs are subversive and witty quotations of her own creation, as if she were ridiculing the convention of citing authorities. As it should be in a book obsessed with literacy, writing is also an important plot device. The letters of Will, Casaubon, Brooke, and Sir Godwin cause the fatal misunderstandings that arouse jealousy and rivalry in all the characters, just as a bit of writing on a scrap of paper stuck in a flask provides Raffles with the clue to Bulstrode's whereabouts. As we have seen, Dorothea wishes to marry to learn how to read Greek and Latin, while Rosamond accepts Lydgate by rejecting Ned Plimdale's *Keepsake*.

Since male authority is associated so closely with writing (through Casaubon's Key, Lydgate's decision "to do worthy the writing,— and to write out myself what I have done" [chap. 45], Featherstone's wills, Brooke's newspaper, Fred's IOUs, Mr. Garth's signature, and Bulstrode's letters of certification), it is hardly surprising that the one woman who teaches reading and writing in *Middlemarch*, Mrs. Garth, is "apt to be a little severe toward her own sex, which in her opinion was formed to be entirely subordinate" (chap. 23), even as she teaches her daughter Letty the necessity of submitting to a brother who can, after all, grow up to become the hero of the story, Cincinnatus, as she cannot. That the book Mary Garth finally writes is attributed to Fred because he "had been to the University, 'where the ancients were studied'" (Finale) is no less ridiculous than that his book on crops and cattle feeding should be ascribed to her. But Mary's *Stories of Great Men, taken from Plutarch*, written for her sons, implies continuing, treacherous contradictions for women, contradictions that ironically adumbrate the treatment Eliot's own reputation would undergo when she became the subject of Sir Leslie Stephen's antagonistic biography for the English Men of Letters series and when she was rejected by women writers from Mrs Oliphant and Eliza Lynn Linton to Dorothy Richardson and Elizabeth Robbins for writing "like a man."[52]

While Mary's *Plutarch*, like Eliot's pseudonym, helps us understand these contradictions, *Middlemarch* itself is a Satanically ambitious book, a "home epic" (Finale) which tells the story not of Great Men but of a "foundress of nothing" (Prelude). Eliot is unafraid to face the dispossession of women who have been given that one talent which

is death to hide. From her earliest discussion of women artists looking
like actresses in male attire, to her description of Maggie Tulliver's
passionate life, which was "a drama for her, in which she demanded
of herself that her part should be played with intensity" (*MF*, IV,
chap. 3), and then to the brief but crucial portrait of Madame Laure,
Eliot employs theatrical metaphors to illustrate that women without
the definition supplied by work have no stable self, no single center.
Only the ontological insecurity born of this terrible emptiness explains
why the very best of her women characters, those who fear the lure
of impersonation, are fatally drawn—as are Antigone, Persephone,
and Ariadne—to the equally dangerous attractions of thralldom: "If
you can do nothing," Tom Tulliver advises Maggie, "submit to
those that can" (*MF*, V, chap. 6). Yet, even in the act of submission,
feminine playing or dissimulation breaks down the masculine style
of knowing and possessing. At the same time, precisely because they
do submit, women experience "resignation to individual nothingness"
(*Letters*, 2:49) more directly than men. Alterity—otherness—or absence structures the lives of Eliot's heroines, who thereby attain a privileged perspective purged from the deathly quest for origins or presence.

But any consideration of Eliot as a literary heiress necessarily
returns us to the two Americans with whom we began, because
Margaret Fuller and Harriet Beecher Stowe also struggled with the
unreality bestowed by the secondary status of women. As pained as
she was by what she sometimes managed to see as her own "temporary
tragedy," Margaret Fuller could imagine integration: "The Woman
in me kneels and weeps in tender rapture; the Man in me rushes forth,
but only to be baffled. Yet the time will come, when, from the union
of this tragic king and queen, shall be born a radiant sovereign self." [53]
Similarly, Harriet Beecher Stowe, whose full life as sister, wife, and
mother along with her successful career as a writer, placed her in
marked contrast to Fuller, also envisioned the ways in which women
could be reborn into radiant sovereign selves.

Perhaps it was Stowe's ability to live a full life within traditional
female roles that first caused George Eliot to write so plaintively to
her, admitting her own misery as a writer and explaining that
Stowe's letters "made me almost wish that you could have a momen-

tary vision of the discouragement, nay, paralyzing despondency in which many days of my writing life have been past, in order that you might fully understand the good I find in such sympathy as yours—" (*Letters*, 5:28). Refusing in this correspondence, which began after her fame was well established in 1869 and continued until her death, to dwell "on any mental sickness of mine," Eliot repeatedly identifies Stowe as a "dear friend and fellow labourer" who has "longer experience than I as a writer, and fuller experience as a woman, since you have borne children and known the mother's history from the beginning" (5:31). She cannot, she explains, send a picture of herself because "I have *no* photograph of myself, having always avoided having one taken" (5:281), but she persistently hopes that Stowe and her husband will "continue to be interested in my spiritual children" and reminds them that she makes "a delightful picture of [Stowe's] life in your orange-grove—taken care of by dear daughters" (6:246).

In Stowe, then, Eliot seems to have found a model of womanly authorship, sufficient to balance her vision of Milton taken care of by dear daughters. But Eliot might have also been conscious that Stowe managed to depict the possibility of women enacting their rage without becoming consumed by it. She read *Uncle Tom's Cabin* long before Stowe sent her a copy, and perhaps she appreciated the end of that novel as much as Charlotte Brontë would have, for it is there that Stowe explores one way in which women can escape the confinement of the ancestral mansion without becoming either suicidal or murderous. Not involuntary enactment but conscious impersonation was the strategy that must have fascinated Eliot, who sought comprehension without coercion throughout her career. More than Bertha Mason Rochester or Bertha Grant, more than Dorothea Casaubon or Rosamond Lydgate, the woman who most successfully exacts female retribution is the maddened slave who dominates the final chapters of *Uncle Tom's Cabin*. Just as Eliot works beyond rage and beyond her early appropriation of male roles in *Middlemarch*, in *Uncle Tom's Cabin* Stowe depicts a uniquely female mode of liberation.

Cassy is Simon Legree's chattel concubine, a woman who has been crazed by the treatment she has experienced at the hands of a white slaveholder who possessed her sexually and legally and sold her two small children, a grief that results in her "saving" her next baby by killing it herself. Living directly below a garret in which "some years before, a negro woman, who had incurred Legree's displeasure, was confined" (401), Cassy decides to take advantage of a rumor that developed in Legree's household, after the woman was brought down dead, that "oaths and cursings, and the sound of violent blows, used to ring through that old garret, and mingled with wailings and groans of despair" (401). First she moves out of her room beneath the garret, implying that the angry spirits make it too noisy for sleep. Next, she leaves ghost books around the house and places the neck of an old bottle in a knothole of the garret so that the wind produces lugubrious wails and shrieks in the night. Legree becomes terrified by her "game" (406). What she is doing, quite clearly, is manipulating a familiar fiction: a madwoman herself, she plans to liberate herself and the girl Emmeline, who is meant to be her successor as Legree's mistress, by exploiting the story of the madwoman in the attic.

It is, in other words, the enactment of a uniquely female plot that enables Cassy to escape. She stores provisions and clothing in the garret so that, after she and Emmeline ostentatiously flee, they can backtrack to hide out in the one spot Legree would never dare search. Using his garret as a sanctuary, while Legree scours the countryside looking for runaways, the two women read and eat and sleep quite safely at the top of his house. Just as Madame Laure of *Middlemarch* used an impersonated murder to camouflage an actual murder, Cassy exploits impersonation of madness and confinement to escape maddening confinement. But, while Madame Laure acts out what is thought to be an impersonation, Cassy impersonates what is thought to be an act, and so she is freed from the guilt of actually exacting her rage. Then, after Uncle Tom dies for his heroic refusal to reveal the attic hideout, Cassy decides to punish the guilty master by haunting him.

In a chapter entitled "An Authentic Ghost Story," Cassy glides around the ancestral mansion, able to enter even locked doors and passageways, "a tall figure in a white sheet" (425). Diminished as Cassy has been by the suffering she has endured, she *is* in a sense the ghost of her own dead self, the self Legree killed by his abuse, but the black woman dressed in white also illustrates the bond between all women who are enslaved by what Stowe has depicted as an overwhelmingly patriarchal slave economy. Legree sees Cassy's "ghost" as his "mother's shroud." And he is right, for this veiled woman represents his denial of his mother, of mother love, and mother right. Guilty of matricide, sick and dying, Legree never can forget that deathly angel: "at his dying bed, stood a stern, white, inexorable figure, saying 'Come! come! come!'" (426). This woman in white, this wife without the sign, testifies to the truth of Stowe's assertion that Charlotte Brontë's spirit had dictated words to her, even as she illuminates the entangled threads of renunciation and rage spun by George Eliot's angels of destruction.

VI
Strength in Agony:
Nineteenth-Century Poetry by
Women

Illustration on the preceding page: *Sketch of an Idea for Crazy Jane*, by Richard Dadd. Courtesy of Bethlem Royal Hospital.

15 The Aesthetics of Renunciation

Thy woman's hair, my sister, all unshorn,
Floats back dissheveled strength in agony,
Disproving thy man's name . . .
     —Elizabeth Barrett Browning

It seemed to me, reviewing the story of Shakespeare's sister as I had
made it . . . that any woman born with a great gift in the sixteenth
century would certainly have gone crazed. . . . For it needs little
skill in psychology to be sure that a highly gifted girl who had
tried to use her gift for poetry would have been so thwarted and
hindered . . . that she must have lost her health and sanity to a
certainty.

     —Virginia Woolf

England has had many learned women . . . and yet where are the
poetesses? . . . I look everywhere for grandmothers and see none.[1]
     —Elizabeth Barrett Browning

Had Mrs. Dickinson been warm and affectionate . . . Emily Dickinson early in life would probably have identified with her, become
domestic, and adopted the conventional woman's role. She would
then have become a church member, active in community affairs,
married, and had children. The creative potentiality would of
course still have been there, but would she have discovered it?
What motivation to write could have replaced the incentive given
by suffering and loneliness?

     —John Cody

"Who shall measure the heat and violence of the poet's heart when
caught and tangled in a woman's body?" Virginia Woolf exclaims
halfway through *A Room of One's Own.* She has been telling the

story of her imaginary but paradigmatic woman poet, "Judith Shakespeare," the great male bard's "wonderfully gifted sister." Like her brother Will, Woolf speculates, Judith would have run off to London to become a poet-playwright, for "the birds that sang in the hedge were not more musical than she was." Unlike Will, however, Judith would quickly have found that her only theatrical future lay in the exploitation of her sexuality. Woolf reminds us that Nick Greene, the Elizabethan actor-manager, said "a woman acting put him in mind of a dog dancing," and obviously a woman writing was even more ludicrously unnatural. The same Nick Greene, however—or so Woolf's story runs—would have been very willing to use Judith Shakespeare sexually. He "took pity on her," Woolf notes dryly; "she found herself with child by [him] and so—who shall measure the heat and violence of the poet's heart when caught and tangled in a woman's body?—she killed herself one winter's night and lies buried at some crossroads where the omnibuses now stop outside the Elephant and Castle." [2]

In this miniature novella of literary seduction and betrayal, Woolf defines a problem that is related to, but not identical with, the subject of "women and fiction" which triggers her extended meditation on the woman question in *A Room*. As she points out and as we have seen throughout our study, England has had—to use Barrett Browning's words—"many learned women, not merely readers but writers of the learned languages." [3] More specifically, both English and American literary histories record the accomplishments of numerous distinguished women prose writers—essayists, diarists, journalists, letter-writers, and (especially) novelists. Indeed, beginning with Aphra Behn and burgeoning with Fanny Burney, Anne Radcliffe, Maria Edgeworth, and Jane Austen, the English novel seems to have been in good part a female invention. Certainly Austen suggested as much in *Northanger Abbey*, and though Woolf mourns the exclusion of women from that weighty male tradition represented by "Thackeray and Dickens and Balzac," she too is able to tell over the names of "sister novelists" as if they were beads on some shimmering feminist rosary. And yet, as Barrett Browning mournfully inquired, "where are the poetesses," the Judith Shakespeares? It is "the poetry that is still denied outlet," Woolf herself notes sorrowfully,[4] and the only hope she expresses is that Mary Carmichael, the imaginary modern novelist who has replaced Judith Shakespeare, "will be a poet . . . in another hundred years."[5]

Woolf wrote these words in 1928, at a time when there had already been, of course, many women poets—or at least many women who wrote poetry. She herself traced the careers of Anne Finch and Margaret Cavendish, admired the "wild poetry" of the Brontës, noted that Elizabeth Barrett Browning's verse-novel *Aurora Leigh* had poetic virtues no prose work could rival, and spoke almost with awe of Christina Rossetti's "complex song."[6] Why, then, did she consider poetry by women somehow problematic in its essence? Why did she feel that Judith Shakespeare was "caught and tangled," "denied," suffocated, self-buried, or not yet born? We can begin to find answers to these questions by very briefly reviewing some of the ways in which male readers and critics, from Nick Greene to John Crowe Ransom and R. P. Blackmur, have reacted to poetry by women like Barrett Browning, Rossetti, and Emily Dickinson, a poet whose work one hopes (but cannot be sure) Woolf read.

Introducing the *Selected Poems of Emily Dickinson* in 1959, James Reeves quoted "a friend" as making a statement which expresses the predominant attitude of many male literati toward poetry by women even more succinctly than Woolf's story did: "A friend who is also a literary critic has suggested, not perhaps quite seriously, that 'woman poet' is a contradiction in terms."[7] In other words, from what Woolf would call the "masculinist" point of view, the very nature of lyric poetry is inherently incompatible with the nature or essence of femaleness. Remarks by other "masculinist" readers and critics elaborate upon the point. In the midst of favorably reviewing the work of his friend (and sometime mistress) Louise Bogan, for instance, the poet Theodore Roethke detailed the various "charges most frequently levelled against poetry by women." Though his statement begins by pretending objectivity, it soon becomes clear that he himself is leveling such charges.

> Two of the [most frequent] charges . . . are lack of range—in subject matter, in emotional tone—and lack of a sense of humor. And one could, in individual instances among writers of real talent, add other aesthetic and moral shortcomings: the spinning out; the embroidering of trivial themes; a concern with the

mere surfaces of life—that special province of the feminine
talent in prose—hiding from the real agonies of the spirit;
refusing to face up to what existence is; lyric or religious
posturing; running between the boudoir and the altar; stamping
a tiny foot against God or lapsing into a sententiousness that
implies the author has re-invented integrity; carrying on
excessively about Fate, about time; lamenting the lot of the
woman; caterwauling; writing the same poem about fifty
times, and so on.[8]

Even a cursory reading of this passage reveals its inconsistency:
women are taxed for both triviality and sententiousness, for both
silly superficiality and melodramatic "carrying on" about profound
subjects. Even more significant, however, is the fact that Roethke
attacks female poets for doing just what male poets do—that is, for
writing about God, fate, time, and integrity, for writing obsessively
on the same themes or subjects, and so forth. But his language suggests
that it is precisely the sex of these literary women that subverts their
art. Shaking a Promethean male fist "against God" is one perfectly
reasonable aesthetic strategy, apparently, but stamping a "tiny"
feminine foot is quite another.

Along similar lines, John Crowe Ransom noted without disapproval in a 1956 essay about Emily Dickinson that "it is common
belief among readers (among men readers at least) that the woman
poet as a type ... makes flights into nature rather too easily and
upon errands which do not have metaphysical importance enough
to justify so radical a strategy."[9] Elsewhere in the same essay, describing Dickinson as "a little home-keeping person," he speculated
that "hardly ... more" than "one out of seventeen" of her 1,775
poems are destined to become "public property," and observed that
her life "was a humdrum affair of little distinction," although "in
her Protestant community the gentle spinsters had their assured
and useful place in the family circle, they had what was virtually a
vocation."[10] (But how, he seemed to wonder, could someone with
so humdrum a social destiny have written great poetry?) Equally
concerned with the problematic relationship between Dickinson's
poetry and her femaleness—with, that is, what seemed to be an
irreconcilable conflict between her "gentle" spinsterhood and her

fierce art—R. P. Blackmur decided in 1937 that "she was neither a professional poet nor an amateur; she was a private poet who wrote indefatigably, as some women cook or knit. Her gift for words and the cultural predicament of her time drove her to poetry instead of anti-macassars."[11]

Even in 1971, male readers of Dickinson brooded upon this apparent dichotomy of poetry and femininity. John Cody's *After Great Pain* offers an important analysis of the suffering that most of Dickinson's critics and biographers have refused to acknowledge. But his conclusion, part of which we have quoted as an epigraph, emphasizes what he too sees as the incompatibility between womanly fulfillment and passionate art. "What motivation to write could have replaced the incentive given by suffering and loneliness? If, in spite of her wifely and motherly duties, [Dickinson] had still felt the need to express herself in verse, what would her subject matter have been? Would art have sprung from fulfillment, gratification, and completeness as abundantly as it did from longing, frustration, and deprivation?" Interestingly, these questions restate an apparently very different position taken by Ransom fifteen years earlier: "Most probably [Dickinson's] poems would not have amounted to much if the author had not finally had her own romance, enabling her to fulfill herself like any other woman."[12] Though Ransom speaks of the presence and "fulfillment" of "romance," while Cody discusses its tormenting absence, neither imagines that poetry itself could possibly constitute a woman's fulfillment. On the contrary, both assume that the art of a woman poet must in some sense arise from "romantic" feelings (in the popular, sentimental sense), arise either in response to a real romance or as compensation for a missing one.

In view of this critical obsession with womanly "fulfillment"— clearly a nineteenth-century notion redefined by twentieth-century thinkers for their own purposes—it is not surprising to find that when poetry by women *has* been praised it has usually been praised for being "feminine" or, conversely, blamed for being deficient in "femininity." Elizabeth Barrett Browning, for instance, the most frequently analyzed, criticized, praised, and blamed woman poet of her day, was typically admired "because of her understanding of the depth, tenderness, and humility of the love which is given by women,"[13] and because "she was a poet in every fibre of her but adorably feminine."[14] As the "Shakespeare of her sex,"[15] moreover, she was especially respected for being "pure and lovely" in her "private life," since "the lives of women of genius have been so frequently sullied by sin ... that their intellectual gifts are [usually] a curse rather than a blessing."[16] Significantly, however, when Barrett Browning attempted unromantic, "unfeminine" political verses in *Poems Before Congress*, her collection of 1860, at least one critic decided that she had been "seized with a ... fit of insanity," explaining that "to bless and not to curse is woman's function; and if Mrs. Browning, in her calmer moments, will but contrast the spirit which has prompted her to such melancholy aberrations with that which animated Florence Nightingale, she can hardly fail to derive a profitable lesson for the future."[17]

Throughout the nineteenth century, prose fiction by women was also frequently criticized in this way, as Elaine Showalter has definitively shown.[18] But in general the attacks of male critics on women novelists seem less heated—or perhaps, more accurately, less personal. There is evidently something about lyric poetry by women that invites meditations on female fulfillment or, alternatively, on female insanity. In devising a story for Judith Shakespeare, Woolf herself was after all driven to construct a violent plot that ends with her suicidal heroine's burial beneath what was to become a bus-stop near the Elephant and Castle. Symbolically speaking, Woolf suggests, modern London, with its technological fumes and its patriarchal roar, grows from the grim crossroads where this mythic woman poet lies dead. And as if to reinforce the morbid ferocity of such imagery, Woolf adds that whenever, reading history or listening to gossip, we hear of witches and magical wise women, "I think we are on the track of ... a suppressed poet ... who dashed her brains out on the moor or mopped and mowed about the highways crazed with the torture that her gift had put her to."[19] For though "the original [literary] impulse was to poetry," and "the 'supreme head of song' was a poetess," literary women in England and America have until recently almost universally elected to write novels rather than poems for fear of precisely the madness Woolf attributes to Judith Shakespeare. "Sure the poore woman is a little distracted," she quotes a contemporary of Margaret Cavendish's as remarking: "Shee could never be soe rediculous else as to venture at writeing book's and in verse too, if I should not sleep this fortnight I should not come to that." [20] In other words, while the woman novelist may evade or exorcise her authorship anxieties by writing *about* madwomen and other demonic doubles, it appears that the woman poet must literally *become* a madwoman, enact the diabolical role, and lie melodramatically dead at the crossroads of tradition and genre, society and art.

Without pretending to exhaust a controversial subject around which whole schools of criticism swim, we should note that there are a number of generic differences between novel-writing and verse-writing which do support the kinds of distinctions Woolf makes, as well as her conclusions about the insanity of suppressed (or even unsuppressed) women poets. For one thing, novel-writing is a *useful* occupation, almost—*pace* Blackmur—like baking or knitting. Novels have always been commercially valuable because they are entertaining and therefore functional, utilitarian, whereas poetry (except for the narrative poetry of Byron and Scott) has traditionally had little monetary value, for reasons we will examine subsequently. Significantly, then, it was *poetry* that Charlotte Brontë sent to Robert Southey, eliciting the famous reply "Literature cannot be the business of a woman's life, and it ought not to be." [21] Apparently the laureate meant business in the noble sense of Jesus' "I must be about my Father's business," not in the more vulgar sense of the Stock Exchange and Grub Street. For though literature by women was not encouraged, it was generally understood in the nineteenth century that under conditions of pressing need a woman might have to live by her pen, just as her less gifted sisters might have to go out into the world as governesses. A talented but impoverished woman might in fact have to rescue herself, and maybe even her whole starving family, by writing novels.

That novel-writing was (and is) conceivably an occupation to *live by* has always, however, caused it to seem less intellectually or spiritually valuable than verse-writing, of all possible literary occupations the one to which the nineteenth century assigned the highest status. Certainly when Walter Pater defined the disinterested ecstasy of art for his contemporaries by noting that "art comes to you proposing frankly to give nothing but the highest quality to your moments as they pass, and simply for those moments' sake,"[22] he was speaking of what he earlier called "the poetic passion," alluding to works like the odes of Keats rather than the novels of Thackeray or George Eliot. Verse-writing—associated with mysterious "inspiration," divine afflatus, bardic ritual—has traditionally been a holy vocation. From the Renaissance to the nineteenth century the poet had a privileged, almost magical role in most European societies, and "he" had a quasi-priestly role after Romantic thinkers had appropriated the vocabulary of theology for the realm of aesthetics. But in Western culture women cannot be priests; there has only been a minor (and hotly debated) Episcopalion exception to this rule. How then—since poets are priests—can women be poets? The question may sound sophistic, but there is a good deal of evidence that it was and has been consciously or unconsciously asked by men and women alike as often as women suffering from "the poetic passion" have appeared in the antechambers of literature.

As Woolf shows, though, novel-writing is not just a "lesser" and therefore more suitably female occupation because it is commercial rather than aesthetic, practical rather than priestly. The novel, until the twentieth century a genre subservient to physical and social "reality," most often requires reportorial observation instead of aristocratic education. On the other hand, "Learn . . . for ancient rules a just esteem; / To copy Nature is to copy them,"[23] Alexander Pope admonished aspiring critics and (by implication) poets, noting that "Nature and Homer" are "the same." As if dutifully acquiescing, even the fiery iconoclast Percy Bysshe Shelley assiduously translated Aeschylus and other Greek "masters." As Western society defines "him," the lyric poet must have aesthetic models, must in a sense speak the esoteric language of literary forms. He (or she) cannot simply record or describe the phenomena of nature and society, for in poetry nature must be mediated through tradition—that is, through an education in "ancient rules." But of course, as Woolf (and Milton's daughters) learned with dismay, the traditional classics of Greek and Latin—meaning the distilled Platonic essence of Western literature, history, philosophy—constituted "spheres of masculine learning" inalterably closed to women except under the most extraordinary circumstances. In "our" ignorance of Greek, Woolf once suggested, we women "should be at the bottom of any class of schoolboys."[24] Interestingly, only Elizabeth Barrett Browning, of all the major women poets, was enabled—by her invalid seclusion, her sacrifice of ordinary pleasures—to make a serious attempt at studing "the ancients." Like Shelley, she translated Aeschylus's *Prometheus Bound*, and she went even further, producing an unusually learned study of the little-known Greek Christian poets. What is most interesting about her skill as a classicist, however, is the fact that her familiarity with "the ancients" was barely noticed in her own day and has been almost completely forgotten in ours.

Obviously, there is a sort of triple bind here. On the one hand, the woman poet who learns a just esteem for Homer is ignored or even mocked—as, say, the eighteenth-century Bluestockings were. On the other hand, the woman poet who does not study Homer—because she is not allowed to—is held in contempt. On the third hand, however, whatever alternative tradition the woman poet attempts to substitute for "ancient rules" is subtly denigrated. Ransom, for instance, asserts that Dickinson's meters, learned from "her father's hymnbook," are all based upon "Folk Line, the popular form of verse and the oldest in our language," adding that "the great classics of this meter are the English Ballads and Mother Goose." Our instinctive sense that this is a backhanded compliment is confirmed when the critic remarks that "Folk Line is disadvantageous . . . if it denies to the poet the use of English Pentameter when that would be more suitable," for "Pentameter is the staple of what we may call the studied or 'university' poetry, and it is capable of containing and formalizing many kinds of substantive content which would be too complex for Folk Line. Emily Dickinson appears never to have tried it."[25] If we read "pentameter" here as a substitute for "classical studies," then we can see that once again "woman" and "poet" are being defined as mutually contradictory terms.

Besides the fact that novel-writing does not seem to require the severely classical education poets and critics have traditionally thought verse-writing entails, the writing of prose fiction is in a sense a far more selfless occupation than the composition of lyric poetry. This has perhaps been the crucial factor in causing literary women to choose one genre over another. Bred to selflessness, most women

were continually conscious of the feelings of others, of "personal
relations," as Woolf reminds us. Indeed, Woolf notes, "all the
literary training that a woman had in the early nineteenth century
was training in the observation of character, in the analysis of
emotion."[26] It is almost inevitable, then, that a talented woman
would feel more comfortable—that is, less guilty—writing novels
than poems. The novelist in a sense says "they": she works in a third
person form even when constructing a first person narrative. But the
poet, even when writing in the third person, says "I." Artists from
Shakespeare to Yeats and T. S. Eliot have of course qualified this
"I," often emphasizing, as Eliot does, the "depersonalization" or
"extinction of personality" involved in the poet's construction of an
artful, masklike persona, or insisting, as Dickinson herself did, that
the speaker of poems is a "supposed person."[27] Nevertheless, the
lyric poem acts as if it is an "effusion" (in the nineteenth-century
sense) from a strong and assertive "I," a central self that is forcefully
defined, whether real or imaginary. The novel, on the other hand,
allows—even encourages—just the self-effacing with'drawal that
society fosters in women. Where the lyric poet must be continually
aware of herself as a *subject*, the novelist must see herself in some sense
as an object, if she casts herself as a participant in the action. In
constructing a narrative voice, moreover, she must as a rule disguise
or repress her subjectivity. Jane Austen may have been, as Ellen
Moers suggests, a powerful narrative presence in her works, but she
was also a relatively unobtrusive one, deviously manipulating events,
in stereotypically "feminine" fashion, from behind the scenes or
beneath the blotter.[28]

That women have had to manipulate events rather than participate in them—have had, that is, to speak indirectly rather than
directly—leads us finally to yet another reason for their long avoid-
ance of verse as well as for their notable history of novelistic success,
and it is a reason that brings us full circle back to Woolf's agonizing
tale of Judith Shakespeare. For as we noted earlier, in the pages of
a novel a woman may exorcise or evade precisely the anxieties and
hostilities that the direct, often confessional "I" of poetry would
bring her closer to enacting in real life. If, as Joyce Carol Oates once
suggested, fiction is a kind of structured daydreaming, lyric poetry is

potentially, as Keats said, like "Adam's dream—he awoke and found it truth." [29] Even if the poet's "I," then, is a "supposed person," the intensity of her dangerous impersonation of this creature may cause her to take her own metaphors literally, enact her themes herself: just as Donne really slept in his coffin, Emily Dickinson really wore white dresses for twenty years, and Sylvia Plath and Anne Sexton really gassed themselves. Because of such metaphoric intensity, Woolf postulates, Judith Shakespeare—"who shall measure the heat and violence of a poet's heart when caught and tangled in a woman's body?"—lies dead at a literary crossroads in the center of *A Room of One's Own.* Yet she is not inalterably dead. For, as we shall see, many women poets have resurrected her unquiet spirit.

If the extraordinary difficulty of conceiving and sustaining living poetry in a woman's body is made clear when we read the pronouncements of "masculinist" critics, it is made even clearer when we compare the self-images of the women who did manage to become poets with those of similarly situated male poets. At the age of nineteen, Christina Rossetti wrote a prose narrative that is extremely interesting in this connection, a semi-autobiographical novella entitled *Maude*, into which she set a number of her most accomplished verses. Rossetti's protagonist, fifteen-year-old Maude Foster, is certainly a surrogate self: she is a precocious poet who would have been "very pretty" except for "a fixed paleness, and an expression . . . languid and preoccupied to a painful degree." Perhaps, however (or so Rossetti implies), this expression of anxiety is caused by Maude's knowledge that "people thought her clever, and that her little copies of verses were handed about and admired," even though "it was the amazement of every one what could make her poetry so broken-hearted as was mostly the case." [30]

Certainly a number of Maude's poems *are* broken-hearted— mysteriously so, it seems at first. In some the girl longs for death or sleep, in others she admonishes lilies and roses to fade, and in still others she rebukes herself for "vanity" or "wrath." In fact, Maude produces only one comparatively cheerful verse in the whole novella, this as part of a *bouts rimés* sonnet contest with her cousin Agnes and

Agnes's friend Magdalen, the predetermined *bouts rimés* end words being given by her other cousin Mary. Yet cheerful though it is, this sonnet is also a peculiarly hostile piece:

> Some ladies dress in muslin full and white,
> Some gentlemen in cloth succinct and black;
> Some patronize a dog-cart, some a hack,
>   Some think a painted clarence only right.
>   Youth is not always such a pleasing sight,
> Witness a man with tassels on his back;
> Or woman in a great-coat like a sack
>   Towering above her sex with horrid height.
> If all the world were water fit to drown
>   There are some whom you would not teach to swim,
> Rather enjoying if you saw them sink;
> Certain old ladies dressed in girlish pink,
> With roses and geraniums on their own:—
>   Go to the Bason, poke them o'er the rim.—[31]

Could Maude's comical desire to drown "certain old ladies dressed in girlish pink" be somehow associated with her perpetual and otherwise inexplicable melancholy? What about her cringing dislike of that grotesque woman "towering above her sex with horrid height"? Of course all participants concede that she has won the *bouts rimés* contest, though her competitors' verses have also been notably revealing. Her cousin Agnes produces a sonnet whose gist is that its author would do anything—freeze, drown, be transformed into a donkey or a turnip or a "miserable hack / Dragging a cab from left to right," even wear "a hideous yellow satin gown"—rather than have to write another sonnet. Agnes's more spiritual friend Magdalen, on the other hand, writes a dutifully spiritual poem, declaring that "I fancy the good fairies dressed in white . . . To foster embryo life." [32]

Plainly, the very act of poetic assertion, with its challenge to attempt self-definition or at least self-confrontation, elicits evasions, anxieties, hostilities, in brief "painful preoccupation," from all competitors, so that the jolly poetry game paradoxically contains the germ of just that gloom it seems designed to dispel. Later in the story Maude's gloom thickens, and broadens too, to threaten also the innocently unpoetic Agnes, Mary, and Magdalen. That these girls are all doubles or alternative selves for Maude is indicated in a number of poems, including one of Rossetti's better-known early works, "She sat and sang alway," in which two girls act out the complementary anxieties of female adolescence:

> She sat and sang alway
> By the green margin of a stream,
> Watching the fishes leap and play
> Beneath the glad sun-beam.
>
> I sat and wept alway
> Beneath the moon's most shadowy beam,
> Watching the blossoms of the may
> Weep leaves into the stream.
>
> I wept for memory;
> She sang for hope that is so fair;—
> My tears were swallowed by the sea;
> Her songs died on the air.[33]

"Her songs died on the air": what Maude evidently sees, and what evidently "breaks her heart," is that there will not or cannot be any real blossoming for her talent. Her songs are doomed to die on the air.

But why? As the story unfolds and each girl meets with her symbolic fate, we begin to understand. Mary gets married and becomes wholly, humiliatingly absorbed in her new husband. Magdalen enters a convent and gives "all for this Cross I bear." Serious-minded Agnes seems destined to become a sensible and useful spinster, perhaps one of the gentle sisterhood Ransom so admired. And Maude, unable to love or pray, suddenly refuses to go to church, explaining that she is incorrigibly wicked—for "No one will say that I cannot avoid putting myself forward and displaying my verses."[34] Then, on her way to Mary's wedding, she is severely injured in a strange cab accident: "She had been overturned; and, though no limb was broken, had neither stirred nor spoken since." Obviously the catastrophe of *overturning* is psychically necessary, as much for Rossetti herself as for her young poet, and our sense of this is reinforced by Maude's death, which comes calmly but inexorably, three weeks later. She appoints her anti-literary and superego-like cousin Agnes as her literary executrix, enigmatically instructing her to "destroy what I evidently never intended to be seen," and Agnes has no trouble carrying out these vague directions. She instantly consigns Maude's locked workbook / journal, unopened, to the girl's coffin, and then, though she is "astonished at the variety of Maude's compositions ... piece after piece she commit[s] them to the flames, fearful lest any should be preserved which were not intended for general perusal: but it cost[s] her a pang to do so; and to see how small a number remained for [Maude's mother]." [35]

As several commentators have observed, the moral of this story is that the Maude in Christina Rossetti—the ambitious, competitive, self-absorbed and self-assertive poet—must die, and be replaced by either the wife, the nun, or, most likely, the kindly useful spinster. Rossetti says of Maude that "Whatever might employ her tongue and to a certain extent her mind, had always an undercurrent of thought intent upon herself," [36] and here is the worst, the most unforgivable sin, the ultimate female sin of vanity. Whether literally or figuratively, a woman must never become enamored of her own image in nature or art. On the contrary, as Rossetti demonstrated in her Lewis Carroll-esque children's story *Speaking Likenesses*, and as she wrote in a much later poem,

> All things that pass
>   Are woman's looking-glass;
> They show her how her bloom must fade,
>   And she herself be laid
> With withered roses in the shade;
> Unlovely, out of reach
> Of summer joy that was.[37]

After all this, it hardly seems necessary to point out that when John Keats (whom Rossetti and both her brothers much admired) was nineteen years old, he had already committed himself seriously and passionately to his own artistic career. By the time he was twenty-one, in fact, he had planned a formidable program of self-development: "O for ten years, that I may overwhelm / Myself in poesy; so I may do the deed / That my own soul has to itself decreed." [38] Significantly, the image of self-immolation suggested by the word *overwhelm* is balanced here by the fiercely assertive and "masculine" notion of verse-writing or "soul-making" as a "deed." Of course Keats understood the need for proper modesty, even humility. How else, after all, could truly effective self-education proceed? At the same time, however, he saw even his ignorance as ambiguously "giant,"[39] and he did not hesitate to declare his intuitive sense that he might be "among the English poets" after his death; no considerations of "vanity" appear to have troubled him in this self-appraisal. Like Maude, he entered a verse-writing contest (with Leigh Hunt, in 1816) and like her, too, he projected his deepest concerns into the sonnet he wrote swiftly, jovially, on a set theme. "The poetry of earth is never dead" was his opening sentence (as opposed to Maude's "Some ladies dress in muslin full and white"), and the health and joy of his certainty that poetry was everywhere, in him as in all of nature, must have been at least in part made possible by his masculine certainty that he was a lord of creation. By contrast, Maude / Rossetti obviously sees herself as a fragile, vainly costumed lady, no ruler of nature at all but a tormented servant.

Like Rossetti's heroine, too, Keats died at an absurdly early age. Where Maude was inexplicably "overturned" by her anxious author, however, Keats—despite Byron's jests and Shelley's suspicions—was killed by no force more inimical than his own heredity. Though Maude dies willingly, Keats struggled hard against extinction, fighting even his own pained half-love for "easeful death." When he died, to be sure, his friends buried several letters from his fianceé, Fanny Brawne, with his body, but they certainly did not destroy a single word *he* had written. That Rossetti may have gotten from Keats the idea of burying Maude's own journal with the dead writer herself suggests, then, just how masochistically a woman poet may transform male metaphors into female images of anxiety or guilt.[40]

Finally, where Maude's last poem stresses her vanity and her need for the constraining cross inflicted by a patriarchal God who "Knoweth when thou art weak, and will control / The powers of darkness" (and presumably vanity) so "that thou needst not fear," Keats's bitter epitaph—"Here lies one whose name was writ in water"—ironically emphasizes the poet's passionate commitment to himself, to his art, and thus to what he believes should rightly be the immortality of his name. In fact, in an early sonnet entitled "On Keats," Rossetti herself quoted this epitaph precisely so that she might refute it by declaring that unto this "strong man" a "goodly lot / Hath fallen in fertile ground; there thorns are not, / But his own daisies," and "His name, in every humble heart that sings, / Shall be a fountain of love, verily."[41] But of course Keats also refuted his own disingenuous epitaph, for the poem generally thought to be his last reaches with raging, masterful passion even from beyond the grave:

> This living hand, now warm and capable
> Of earnest grasping, would, if it were cold
> And in the icy silence of the tomb,
> So haunt thy days and chill thy dreaming nights
> That thou wouldst wish thine own heart dry of blood
> So in my veins red life might stream again,
> And thou be conscience-calmed—see here it is—
> I hold it towards you.

While Maude lies passively, angelically, dutifully dead—and the living Christina Rossetti takes up her pen to spend a lifetime writing "Amen for us all"—dead John Keats refuses to die, shaking an angry fist at the living world that threatens to forget him. More genially but only half-mockingly, he confesses in the last sentence of his last letter that he is impolite: he hesitates to leave the warm room of life because "I always made an awkward bow."[42]

If we look a little more briefly but with equal attention at the lives and works of Emily Dickinson and Walt Whitman, two American poets who are roughly contemporary with each other and who are both iconoclastic in analogous ways, we find the same pattern of female self-effacement and male self-assertion even more strikingly formulated. "I'm Nobody! Who are you?" Dickinson wrote in 1861, adding defensively "How dreary—to be—Somebody! / How public —like a Frog—/ To tell one's name—the livelong June—/ To an admiring Bog!" A year later she wrote the first of her famous letters to Thomas Wentworth Higginson, a note (accompanying four poems) in which she modestly asked the busy editor if he was "too deeply occupied to say if my verse is alive?"[43] And as if to indicate here, too—even while she was taking a diffident first step toward self-publicity—that she saw herself, however ironically, as "Nobody," she left the note itself unsigned, revealing her name only on a card which she included with the letter and poems in a separate sealed envelope. The world, this story tells us, may have written Keats's name in water, but Dickinson herself locked her own name up in a symbolic paper coffin.

Besides reminding us of Keats's epitaph and Dickinson's "I'm Nobody," however, this anecdote recalls Fanny Imlay's more melodramatic excision of her signature from her suicide note. Indeed, biographers have offered similar explanations for the reticence of both women: Imlay, Muriel Spark suggested, may have acted "out of respect for Godwin's name,"[44] and Dickinson, says Richard Sewall, may have felt "genuine worry about involving the Dickinson name in ways that might have brought embarrassment to her family or the town."[45] What such explanations emphasize, however, is the fundamental alienation a woman (especially, perhaps, a woman poet) feels from her "own" name: it is not hers to risk, not hers to publicize, not even hers to immortalize. Rather, it is her father's, her stepfather's, "the town's." In herself, she is—must be—"Nobody," for "A modesty befits the soul / That bears another's—name —/ A doubt—if it be fair—indeed—/ To wear that perfect—pearl—/ The Man—upon the woman—binds—/ To clasp her soul—for all—" (J. 493). But such determined modesty must inevitably pose serious problems for a poet's art, even when it is shored up by the defensive certainty that it would be "dreary" or vulgarly "public" to be Somebody. In Dickinson's case, as we shall see later in greater detail, the literary consequences of being Nobody were far-reaching indeed, ranging from a sometimes grotesquely childlike self-image to a painfully distorted sense of size, a perpetual gnawing hunger, and even, finally, a deep confusion about identity. Moreover, being Nobody had worldly consequences, and these may ultimately have been even more serious. Certainly Dickinson's inability to persist in seeking publication, with her attendant rationalization that "Publication is the auction of the Mind of man," must have come from a conviction that Nobody probably should *not* publish poetry. The double negatives are significant, for multiple negatives seem to have built a formidable wall of societal grammar around this poet, a wall she herself almost completely sealed up when she decided, around 1866, to spend the rest of her life in her "smallest" room with "just the door ajar" between her and the forbidding world outside.

Seven years before Representative Edward Dickinson's modest daughter sat down to write her note to T. W. Higginson, however, another strikingly original—even "peculiar"—American poet had made his literary debut, for in 1855 Walt Whitman published his earliest version of *Leaves of Grass*, a work he was to revise for the rest of his life. As most readers know, the cornerstone of Whitman's epic meditation is a powerful assertion of identity now entitled "Song of Myself" and in that first edition called "Walt Whitman." Because the 1855 edition of *Leaves of Grass* appeared without its author's name on the title page, some critics have spoken of the work's near "anonymity," and perhaps, by comparison with those later editions of Whitman's masterpiece which were decorated not only with the poet's name and photograph but with facsimiles of his signature, this early version was unusually reticent.[46] But of course what was unusual modesty for Whitman would have been mad self-assertion for Dickinson. Not only did Whitman publish his "nearly anonymous" poem himself, he used a daguerreotype of himself as the book's frontispiece, titled his most important poem by his own name, and in addition, integrated his name into the heart of his verse, proclaiming that he was "Walt Whitman, an American, one of the roughs, a Kosmos."[47] He didn't need to put his name on the title page of his poem, because he and his poem were coextensive: the poem itself *was* in a sense his name, writ large and bold.

Whitman's expansive lines, moreover, continually and swaggeringly declared the enormity of his cosmic/prophetic powers. "I celebrate myself and sing myself," his poem begins magisterially, "And what I assume, you shall assume," promising in bardic self-confidence that if you "Stop this day and night with me . . . you shall possess the origin of all poems." While Dickinson, the "slightest in the House," reconciles herself to being Nobody, Whitman genially inquires "Do I contradict myself? / Very well then, I contradict myself, / (I am large, I contain multitudes)." While Dickinson trembles in her room, with the door just ajar, Whitman cries "Unscrew the locks from the doors! / Unscrew the doors themselves from their jambs!" While Dickinson shrouds herself in emblematic white and notes that "I could not bear to live—aloud—/The racket shamed me so—," Whitman exclaims "Through me forbidden voices, / Voices of sexes and lusts, voices veil'd and I remove the veil, / Voices indecent by me clarified and transfigur'd." And as Dickinson, aging, shrinks into herself—shrinks even the length and width of her poems, as if literally trying to make herself invisible—Whitman's masterpiece fattens, and Whitman himself, prospering, indefatigably self-publicizing despite painful rejections and attacks, becomes the "Unofficial Laureate of America," the "good gray" prophet of Camden, New Jersey, to whose cottage multitudes of admirers make pilgrimages. Indeed, as Leslie Fiedler notes, "the very portrait of the author which faced the frontispiece of *Leaves of Grass* grew old along with him and his book, changed in character with the mask or *persona* through which Whitman chose to speak in succeeding editions of the work." This during a twenty-year period in which Dickinson not only refused to be photographed but even required that seamstresses "fit" her and doctors examine her while she walked quickly past them at a safe distance.[48]

Of course, Fiedler's mention of Whitman's "mask or *persona*" constitutes a salutary reminder that, as Ransom also comments, "the aggressive masculinity which [Whitman] asserted so blatantly in the poems was only assumed"[49]—was, in fact, as much a mask or persona as Dickinson's inoffensive, little "woman in white" was a "supposed person." Nevertheless, the distinction between the agonized Nobody who wrote Dickinson's poems and the "turbulent, fleshy, sensual" Somebody who wrote Whitman's is significant in itself. Many critics have suggested that Dickinson's reclusiveness was good for her because good for her poetry. (The passage we have quoted from Cody is fairly representative of this view.) But though the game of literary "what if"—what if Keats had lived longer, what if Shakespeare had died young, what if Dickinson had been "better adjusted" —is not usually a fruitful one, the conclusion that Dickinson's isolation and literary failure were necessarily beneficial begins after a while to sound even more like a rationalization than her own laborious delight in being Nobody. Considering how brilliantly she wrote under extraordinarily constraining circumstances, we might more properly wonder what she would have done if she had had Whitman's freedom and "masculine" self-assurance, just as we might

reasonably wonder what kind of verse Rossetti would have written
if she had not defined her own artistic pride as wicked "vanity."
Of Dickinson, at any rate, we must say that, even posing as Nobody,
she came closer than anyone to being Judith Shakespeare. But
perhaps if she had let herself be Somebody, that Somebody would
have *been* Judith Shakespeare.

We must concede here what Cody does frequently point out:
Dickinson was not *forced* to lock herself into her room; indeed, there
were many alternative life patterns she might have followed, including
a number of relatively rewarding literary careers for women. To
begin with, almost any moderately intelligent young woman seeking
independence in nineteenth-century New England could, for
instance, become the American equivalent of an English governess,
a "schoolmarm." This course, Cody reminds us, was followed by
Susan Gilbert, Emily Dickinson's close friend and, later, Austin
Dickinson's wife. A more talented girl—a Helen Fiske Hunt (later
to become famous as Helen Hunt Jackson) or a Louisa May Alcott—
could try her luck at journalism, fiction-writing, even poetry.
Albert Gelpi has recently noted that

> in nineteenth-century America there were many women poets—
> I should better say, lady poets—who achieved popular success
> and quite lucrative publishing careers by filling newspaper
> columns, gift-books, and volumes of verse with the conventional
> pieties concerning mortality and immortality. . . . Mrs. Lydia
> Sigourney, known as "the Sweet Singer of Hartford," is the
> type, and Mark Twain's Emmeline Grangerford is the parodic,
> but barely parodic recreation.[50]

Rufus Griswold's *Female Poets of America* (1848) and Caroline May's
American Female Poets (1869), two representative anthologies, are
packed with this sort of lucrative genteel verse, verse mostly devoted
to the proposition that "in the sacred retirement of home 'love is an
unerring light / And joy its own security!'"[51] Samuel Bowles's
Springfield Republican, where Dickinson did manage to publish several
of her poems, featured similar "blossoms of woman's genius," to use

Caroline May's phrase.[52] But of course, while struggling to establish herself in newspaper columns and gift-books, a young woman poet like Dickinson could also study the works of a few brilliant and iconoclastic women of letters, chiefly English or French writers like Barrett Browning, Sand, Eliot, and the Brontës, in the hope of finding what we would now call "role-models."

Our purpose in giving this summary history of literary careers for women in nineteenth-century America may seem wholly ironic, but in fact it is only partly so. There can be no doubt that Dickinson wrote her diffident letter to Higginson, as she wrote intermittently all her life to other literary people like Samuel Bowles, Helen Hunt Jackson, Josiah Holland, and later Thomas Niles of the publishing firm Roberts and Son, because despite her defensive demurrers she *did* want to establish herself in just the kind of literary career that swept Helen Hunt, George Eliot, and the Brontës—and Lydia Sigourney and, as Richard Sewall notes, the "Fanny Ferns and the Minny Myrtles"—to fame and fortune. Pictures of George Eliot and Charlotte Brontë hung in her not-so-small room, according to her niece Martha Dickinson Bianchi, and Ruth Miller has suggested that a number of her poems seem to be variations on pieces she read in periodicals, as if she were testing her own skill against that of more "successful" versifiers.[53]

As a matter of fact, Dickinson's problem may have been not that she was repelled by the mercenary "auction of the mind of man," but that she was, if anything, more professional than those Fanny Ferns, Minny Myrtles, and Emmeline Grangerfords who were her female contemporaries. In this connection, even the term "lady poet," used pejoratively by critics and biographers from the magisterial Sewall to the feminist Gelpi, has a sinister significance. Women in nineteenth-century America (and England) were not in fact discouraged from writing verse in the way that Woolf notes seventeenth- and eighteenth-century women were. On the contrary, verse-writing became a genteel accomplishment in the Victorian period, an elegant hobby like sketching, piano-playing, or needlepoint. But, as Jack Capps informs us,[54] Dickinson seems to have marked some lines of *Aurora Leigh* that "italicize" the rebellious kinship she felt for iconoclastic Elizabeth Barrett Browning:

> By the way
> The works of women are symbolical.
> We sew, sew, prick our fingers, dull our sight,
> Producing what? A pair of slippers, Sir,
> To put on when you're weary—or a stool
> To stumble over, and vex you . . . "Curse that stool!" [55]

The lines that come just before these are equally revealing, and must have inspired almost equally intense feelings of kinship in Emily Dickinson. Speaking of her education, supervised by a censorious maiden aunt, Aurora says that she "washed in"

> Landscapes from nature (rather say, washed out).
> I danced the polka and Cellarius,
> Spun glass, stuffed birds, and modelled flowers in wax,
> Because she liked accomplishments in girls.
> I read a score of books on womanhood,
> To prove, if women do not think at all,
> They may teach thinking (to a maiden aunt,
> Or else the author),—books that boldly assert
> Their right of comprehending husband's talk
> When not too deep, and even of answering
> With pretty "may it please you," or "so it is;"
> Their rapid insight and fine aptitude
> Particular worth and general missionariness,
> As long as they keep quiet by the fire,
> And never say "no" when the world says "aye."

She adds, in a particularly witty reminiscence, that she "learnt cross-stitch" and embroidered a shepherdess "leaning lovelorn, with pink eyes / To match her shoes, when I mistook the silks, / Her head uncrushed by that round weight of hat / So strangely similar to the tortoise-shell / Which slew the tragic poet." What such a passage subtly conveys, among other things, is that cross-stitching "slew the tragic poet," a point which would undoubtedly have aroused Dickinson's worst fears as she meditated on her likeness not just to Elizabeth Barrett Browning and Fanny Fern but to John Keats, William Shakespeare, and Thomas Carlyle, the "kosmos" (as Whitman would have called him) whose portrait hung next to Barrett Browning's in her room.

That ladylike verse as a drawing-room accomplishment was disturbing or offensive to just those people whom we would now consider the most serious women poets of their day is definitively indicated in one of the most effective—and satirical—scenes in Rossetti's *Maude*. Maude, whose supportive cousins are "indisposed with colds," has had to go alone to a tiresome tea at one Mrs. Strawdy's. Her worst moments come when the entertainment commences, beginning with a young lady "favouring" the party with some songs, and the crux of her annoyance consists in the fact that her poetry is seen as the equivalent of the other young lady's "music."

> Seated between Miss Savage and Sophia Mowbray, [Maude] was attacked on either hand with questions concerning her verses. In the first place, did she continue to write? Yes. A flood of exstatic compliments followed this admission: she was so young, so much admired, and, poor thing, looked so delicate. It was quite affecting to think of her lying awake at night meditating those sweet verses—("I sleep like a top," Maude put in dryly,)—which so delighted her friends and would so charm the public, if only Miss Foster could be induced to publish. At last the bystanders were called upon to intercede for a recitation.
>
> Maude coloured with displeasure; a hasty answer was rising to her lips, when the absurdity of her position flashed across her mind so forcibly that, almost unable to check a laugh in the midst of her annoyance, she put her handkerchief to her mouth. Miss Savage, impressed with a notion that her request was about to be complied with, raised her hand, imploring silence; and settled herself in a listening attitude.
>
> "You will excuse me," Maude at last said very coldly; "I could not think of monopolizing every one's attention. Indeed, you are extremely good, but you must excuse me."[56]

Such drawing-room adulation was of course designed for "lady" poets—Mrs. Sigourneys and Emmeline Grangerfords—who were not only trained to cross-stitch pink-eyed verses but who demanded such poems of themselves. But the very eagerness of such women to live up to genteel expectations must have raised yet another wall around women poets like Dickinson and Rossetti, a wall as formidable as the mass of double negatives that also walled them in. For clearly the verse that Mrs. Strawdy et al. hope Maude will recite would be *bad* verse, verse designed, as Gelpi says, to perpetuate "conventional pieties" and "most especially [to enshrine] the domestic role of wife and mother in tending her mortal charges and conveying them to immortality." As late as 1928 D. H. Lawrence revealed his belief that his own early poems were terrible—mawkishly sentimental, clumsy, pseudo-genteel—by confessing that "Any young lady might have written them."[57] Of course all his readers in that year, even all his readers now, knew and know exactly what he meant. It would be a mistake to suppose, however, that "young ladies" as talented as Rossetti and Dickinson would not also have known. They would have "known" in the nineteenth century exactly what Louise Bogan "knew" one hundred years later when, internalizing the strictures Roethke was to express, she told John Wheelock that she had turned down the "pretty job" of editing "an anthology of female verse" because "the thought of corresponding with a lot of female songbirds made me acutely ill."[58]

But of course such knowledge was shared in some sense by all women, even though it was especially painful only to a few. Another small, apparently minor literary phenomenon that would have perpetuated everyone's consciousness of the significance of the phrase "lady poet" has to do specifically with the naming of women writers, still a problem for some critics and scholars. Certainly women like Dickinson and Rossetti would have noticed that female writers were not usually spoken of in the same way that male writers were. "Jane Austen" was sometimes "Jane," but John Milton was never "John". As the twentieth century began, with its backslapping familiarities and its psychoanalytic prurience, this practice must have become even more depressing to women poets, because even more widespread. As recently as last week, no doubt, Emily Dickinson was, somewhere, "Emily," and Elizabeth Barrett Browning was, to someone, "Mrs. Browning." Both forms of naming emphasize the anomalous situation of the person who is named, and both stress not the womanhood but the ladyhood—that is, the social dependency, the matrimonial respectability or vulnerable virginity —of women poets.

That the problem of names for women writers still persists should remind us, too, of the trouble women have had not only in asserting their own identity as poets but in preserving whatever precariously conceived body of verse they inherited from their foremothers. Woolf saw the lack of a viable female tradition as a key problem for Judith Shakespeare and her poetic descendents, and to some extent it has also been a problem for women novelists, but not nearly so formidable a difficulty as for poets. On the one hand, it is true that women have often been the most fervent in recognizing each other's achievements. Of all the readers Dickinson had in her own lifetime only Helen Hunt Jackson was completely supportive, assuring her reclusive friend that "you are a great poet—and it is a wrong to the day you live in, that you will not sing aloud."[59] On the other hand, however, the absurd tangle of intrigue surrounding the posthumous publication of Dickinson's poems—lawsuits, different editions, biographies, counterbiographies—seems symbolically significant. For the fierce "War between the Houses"—the struggle for control of the poems to which Richard Sewall devotes half a volume of his two-volume biography of Dickinson—was essentially a war of women.

The combatants in this war were not just women of the poet's own generation—her sister Vinnie and her sister-in-law Sue—but their juniors: Austin's young mistress Mabel Loomis Todd, Mrs. Todd's daughter Millicent Todd Bingham, and Sue Gilbert Dickinson's daughter Martha Dickinson Bianchi. One is struck by wonder, reading Sewall's account of the hostilities. As Ruth Miller puts it, "how strange it is to contemplate these young women continuing a battle on behalf of their mothers, with the poems of Emily Dickinson falling always into a greater state of hopeless confusion."[60] But as much as anything else, such confusion seems to be symptomatic of the problems "Judith Shakespeare" faced—and faces. For where there is no nurturing of poetry, there is no tradition of poetry, and where there is no tradition, there is no clear procedure of preservation to follow. Woolf assumed that all intelligent young women would join in the resurrection of Judith Shakespeare. What she was not cynical or sorrowful enough to foresee was that, when one of Judith Shakespeare's avatars appeared, her female descendents might fall

in fury upon each other, divided by the same old swords patriarchal
society has always set between women, while the poet's *corpus* lay
bloody and unnoticed, not at a crossroads but in a corner.

Given the maze of societal constraints by which women poets
have been surrounded since Anne Finch's day, it is no wonder that
some of the finest of these writers have made whole poetic careers
out of the virtue of necessity. We might define this virtue as, at its
most intensely articulated, a passionate renunciation of the self-
assertion lyric poetry traditionally demands, and at its most ironic
a seemingly demure resignation to poetic isolation or obscurity.
Dickinson, of course, wrote many poems praising the paradoxical
pleasures of such painful renunciation—so many, indeed, that a
number of readers (Richard Wilbur, for instance) have seen "Sumptuous Destitution" as the key motif of her art.[61] And certainly it is
one key motif in her verse, as it also is in the verse of Emily Brontë
and George Eliot. But at the same time that she is an inebriate of
air—or perhaps because she is an *inebriate* of air—Dickinson is
greedy, angry, secretly or openly self-assertive, as we shall see. The
very phrase *"sumptuous* destitution" expresses the ambivalently
affirmed sensuality she is determined to indulge even in her poverty.
By comparison, Christina Rossetti and, to a lesser extent, Elizabeth
Barrett Browning build their art on a willing acceptance of passionate
or demure destitution. They and not Dickinson are the great nineteenth-century women singers of renunciation as necessity's highest
and noblest virtue.

Rossetti's *Maude* was an early attempt at exploring the landscape
of destitution in which a ladylike fifteen-year-old poet ought (the
writer implies) to condemn herself to dwell. But besides being
exaggerated and self-pitying, it was cast in a form uncongenial to
Rossetti, who was never very good at sustaining extended story lines
or explaining complex plots. Her extraordinary "Goblin Market,"
however, was written ten years later at the height of her powers,
and it is a triumphant revision of *Maude*, an impassioned hymn of
praise to necessity's virtue.

Like *Maude*, "Goblin Market" (1859) depicts multiple heroines,
each representing alternative possibilities of selfhood for women.

Where *Maude*'s options were divided rather bewilderingly among Agnes, Mary, Magdalen, and Maude herself, however, "Goblin Market" offers just the twinlike sisters Lizzie and Laura (together with Laura's shadowy precursor Jeanie) who live in a sort of sur-realistic fairytale cottage by the side of a "restless brook" and not far from a sinister glen. Every morning and evening, so the story goes, scuttling, furry, animal-like goblins ("One had a cat's face, / One whisked a tail, / One tramped at a rat's pace, / One crawled like a snail") emerge from the glen to peddle magically delicious fruits that "Men sell not . . . in any town"—"Bloom-down-cheeked peaches, / Swart-headed mulberries, / Wild free-born cranberries," and so forth.[62] Of course the two girls know that "We must not look at goblin men, / We must not buy their fruits: / Who knows upon what soil they fed / Their hungry thirsty roots?" But of course, nevertheless, one of the two—Laura—does purchase the goblin fruit, significantly with "a lock of her golden hair," and sucks and sucks upon the sweet food "until her lips [are] sore."

The rest of the poem deals with the dreadful consequences of Laura's act, and with her ultimate redemption. To begin with, as soon as she has eaten the goblin fruit, the disobedient girl no longer hears the cry of the tiny "brisk fruit-merchant men," though her more dutiful sister does continue to hear their "sugar-baited words." Then, as time goes by, Laura sickens, dwindles, and ages unnaturally: her hair grows "thin and grey," she weeps, dreams of melons, and does none of the housework she had shared with Lizzie in the old fruitless days when they were both "neat like bees, as sweet and busy." Finally, Lizzie resolves to save her sister by purchasing some fruit from the goblin peddlers, who still do appear to her. When she does this, however, they insist that she herself eat their wares on the spot, and when she refuses, standing motionless and silent like "a lily in a flood" or "a beacon left alone / In a hoary roaring sea," they assault her with the fruit, smearing her all over with its pulp. The result is that when she goes home to her sick sister she is able to offer herself to the girl as almost a sacramental meal: "Eat me, drink me, love me . . . make much of me." But when Laura kisses her sister hungrily, she finds that the juice is "wormwood to her tongue, / She loathed the feast; / Writhing as one possessed she leaped and sung." Finally she falls into a swoon. When she wakens, she is her old, girlish self again: "Her gleaming locks showed not one thread of gray, / Her breath was sweet as May." In after years, when she and her sister, now happy wives and mothers, are warning their own daughters about the fruit-merchant men, she tells them the tale of "how her sister stood / In deadly peril to do her good. . . . 'For there is no friend like a sister, / In calm or stormy weather; / To cheer one on the tedious way, / To fetch one if one goes astray, / To lift one if one totters down, / To strengthen whilst one stands.'"

Obviously the conscious or semi-conscious allegorical intention of this narrative poem is sexual/religious. Wicked men offer Laura forbidden fruits, a garden of sensual delights, in exchange for the golden treasure that, like any young girl, she keeps in her "purse," or for permission to "rape" a lock of her hair. Once she has lost her virginity, however, she is literally valueless and therefore not worth even further seduction. Her exaggerated fall has, in fact, intensified the processes of time which, for all humanity, began with Eve's eating of the forbidden fruit, when our primordial parents entered the realm of generation. Thus Laura goes into a conventional Victorian decline, then further shrinks and grays, metamorphosing into a witchlike old woman. But at this point, just as Christ intervened to save mankind by offering his body and blood as bread and wine for general spiritual consumption, so Laura's "good" sister Lizzie, like a female Saviour, negotiates with the goblins (as Christ did with Satan) and offers herself to be eaten and drunk in a womanly holy communion. And just as Christ redeemed mankind from Original Sin, restoring at least the possibility of heaven to Eve's erring descendents, so Lizzie rehabilitates Laura, changing her back from a lost witch to a virginal bride and ultimately leading her into a heaven of innocent domesticity.

Beyond such didacticism, however, "Goblin Market" seems to have a tantalizing number of other levels of meaning—meanings about and for women in particular—so that it has recently begun to be something of a textual crux for feminist critics. To such readers, certainly, the indomitable Lizzie, standing like a lily, a rock, a beacon, a "fruit-crowned orange tree" or "a royal virgin town / Topped with gilded dome and spire," may well seem almost a Victorian Amazon, a nineteenth-century reminder that "sisterhood is powerful." Certainly, too, from one feminist perspective "Goblin Market," with its evil and mercantile little men and its innocent, high-minded women, suggests that men *hurt* while women redeem. Significantly, indeed, there are no men in the poem other than the unpleasant goblins; even when Laura and Lizzie become "wives and mothers" their husbands never appear, and they evidently have no sons. Rossetti does, then, seem to be dreamily positing an effectively matrilineal and matriarchal world, perhaps even, considering the strikingly sexual redemption scene between the sisters, a covertly (if ambivalently) lesbian world.

At the same time, however, what are we to think when the redeemed Eden into which Lizzie leads Laura turns out to be a heaven of domesticity? Awakening from her consumptive trance, Laura laughs "in the innocent old way," but in fact, like Blake's Thel withdrawing from the pit of Experience, she has retreated to a psychic stage prior even to the one she was in when the poem began. Living in a virginal female world and rejecting any notions of sexuality, of self-assertion, of personal pleasure (for men are beasts, as the animal-like goblins proved), she devotes herself now entirely to guarding the "tender lives" of her daughters from dangers no doubt equivalent to the one with which the fruit-merchants threatened her. For her, however, the world no longer contains such dangers, and a note of nostalgia steals into Rossetti's verse as she describes Laura's reminiscences of "Those pleasant days long gone / Of not-returning time," the days of the "haunted glen" and the "wicked quaint fruit-merchant men." Like Lizzie, Laura has become a true Victorian angel-in-the-house—selfless and smiling—so naturally (we intuitively feel the logic of this) the "haunted glen" and the "quaint" goblins have disappeared.

But why is it natural that the glen with its merchants should vanish when Laura becomes angelically selfless? Do the goblins incarnate anything besides beastly and exploitative male sexuality? Does their fruit signify something more than fleshly delight? Answers to these questions may be embedded in the very Miltonic imagery Rossetti exploits. In *Paradise Lost*, we should remember, the Satanic serpent persuades Eve to eat the apple not because it is delicious but because it has brought about a "Strange alteration" in him, adding both "Reason" and "Speech" to his "inward Powers." But, he argues, if he, a mere animal, has been so transformed by this "Sacred, Wise,

and Wisdom-giving Plant," the fruit will surely make Eve, a human
being, "as Gods," presumably in speech as in other powers.[63]
Rossetti's goblin men, more enigmatic than Milton's snake, make
no such promises to Laura, but "Goblin Market's" fruit-eating scene
parallels the *Paradise Lost* scene in so many other ways that there
may well be a submerged parallel here too.

Certainly Eve, devouring the garden's "intellectual food," acts
just like her descendent Laura. "Intent now wholly on her taste,"
she regards "naught else," for "such delight till then . . . In Fruit
she never tasted . . . Greedily she ingorg'd without restraint," until
at last she is "hight'n'd as with Wine, jocund and boon." [64] But
though she is pleasuring herself physically, Eve's true goal is intellectual divinity, equality with or superiority to Adam (and God),
pure self-assertion. Her first resolve, when she is finally "Satiate,"
is to worship the Tree daily, "Not without Song." Given this Miltonic
context, it seems quite possible that Laura too—sucking on the
goblin fruit, asserting and indulging her own desires "without
restraint"—is enacting an affirmation of intellectual (or poetic) as
well as sexual selfhood. There is a sense, after all, in which she is
metaphorically eating *words* and enjoying the taste of *power*, just as
Eve before her did. "A Word made Flesh is seldom / And tremblingly
partook / Nor then perhaps reported," wrote Emily Dickinson. She
might have been commenting on "Goblin Market"'s central symbolism, for she added, as if to illuminate the dynamics of Laura's
Satanically unholy Communion,

> But have I not mistook
> Each one of us has tasted
> With ecstasies of stealth
> The very food debated
> To our specific strength—   [J. 1651]

Both the taste and the "Philology" of power are steeped in guilt, she
seems to be saying. And as we have seen, for women like Eve and
Laura (and Rossetti herself), they can only be partaken "with
ecstasies of stealth."

Such connections between female pleasure and female power,
between assertive female sexuality and assertive female speech, have
been traditional ones. Both the story of Eve and Dickinson's poem

make such links plain, as do the kinds of attacks that were leveled against iconoclastic feminists like Mary Wollstonecraft—the accusation, for instance, that *The Rights of Woman* was "a scripture archly fram'd for propagating whores."[65] (Richard Polwhele, one of Wollstonecraft's most virulent critics, even associated "bliss botanic" with the "imperious mien" and "proud defiance" of Wollstonecraft's "unsex'd" female followers.)[66] We should remember, too, that Barrett Browning was praised for her blameless sexual life, since "the lives of women of genius have so frequently been sullied by sin ... that their intellectual gifts are [usually] a curse rather than a blessing." In this last remark, indeed, the relationship between sexuality and female genius becomes virtually causal: female genius triggers uncontrollable sexual desires, and perhaps, conversely, uncontrollable sexual desires even cause the disease of female genius.

That genius and sexuality *are* diseases in women, diseases akin to madness, is implied in "Goblin Market" both by Laura's illness and by the monitory story of Jeanie, "who should have been a bride;/ But who for joys brides hope to have / Fell sick and died / In her gay prime." For though Rossetti's allusion to bridal joys does seem to reinforce our first notion that the forbidden goblin fruit simply signifies forbidden sexuality, an earlier reference to Jeanie renders the fruit symbolism in her case just as ambiguous as it is in Laura's. Jeanie, Lizzie reminds Laura, met the goblin men "in the moonlight,/ Took their gifts both choice and many,/ Ate their fruits and wore their flowers / Plucked from bowers / Where summer ripens at all hours." In other words, wandering in the moonlight and trafficking with these strange creatures from the glen, Jeanie became a witch or madwoman, yielding herself entirely to an "unnatural" or at least unfeminine life of dream and inspiration. Her punishment, therefore, was that decline which was essentially an outer sign of her inner disease.[67]

That the goblins' fruits and flowers are unnatural and out-of-season, however, associates them further with works of art—the fruits of the mind—as well as with sinful sexuality. More, that they do not reproduce themselves in the ordinary sense and even seem to hinder the reproduction of ordinary vegetation reinforces our sense of their curious and guilty artificiality. Jeanie and Laura are both cursed with physical barrenness, unlike most Victorian fallen women, who almost always (like Eliot's Hetty Sorel or Barrett Browning's Marian Erle) bear bastard children to denote their shame. But not even daisies will grow on Jeanie's grave, and the kernelstone Laura has saved refuses to produce a new plant. Sickening and pining, both Jeanie and Laura are thus detached not only from their own healthful, child-oriented female sexuality, but also from their socially ordained roles as "modest maidens." The day after her visit to the goblin men Laura still helps Lizzie milk, sweep, sew, knead, and churn, but while Lizzie is content, Laura is already "Sick in part," pining for the fruits of the haunted glen, and eventually, like Jeanie, she refuses to participate in the tasks of domesticity.

Finally, while the haunted glen itself is on one level a female sexual symbol, it becomes increasingly clear that on another, equally significant level it represents a chasm in the mind, analogous to that enchanted romantic chasm Coleridge wrote of in "Kubla Khan," to the symbolic Red Deeps George Eliot described in *The Mill on the Floss*, or to the mental chasms Dickinson defined in numerous poems. When we realize this we can more thoroughly understand the dis-ease—the strange weeping, the dreamy lassitude, the sexual barrenness, and witchlike physical deformity—that afflicts both Laura and Jeanie. The goblin men were not, after all, real human-sized, sexually charismatic men. Indeed, at every point Rossetti distinguishes them from the *real* men who never do appear in the poem. Instead, they are—were all along—the desirous little creatures so many women writers have recorded encountering in the haunted glens of their own minds, hurrying scurrying furry ratlike *its* or *ids*, inescapable *incubi*. "Cunning" as animal-like Bertha Rochester, "bad" as that "rat" or "bad cat" the nine-year-old Jane Eyre, they remind us too of the "it" goblin-dark Heathcliff was to Catherine Earnshaw, and the "it" Dickinson sometimes saw herself becoming, the "sweet wolf" she said "we all have inside us." Out of an enchanted but earthly chasm in the self, a mossy cave of the unconscious, these it-like inner selves, "mopping and mowing" with masculine assertiveness, arise to offer Jeanie, Laura, Lizzie, and Rossetti herself the unnatural but honey-sweet fruit of art, fruit that is analogous to (or identical with) the luscious fruit of self-gratifying sensual pleasure.

As *Maude* predicted, however, either Rossetti or one of the surrogate selves into whom she projected her literary anxieties would have to reject the goblin fruit of art. With its attendant invitation to such solipsistic luxuries as vanity and self-assertion, such fruit has "hungry thirsty roots" that have fed on suspicious soil indeed. "From House to Home," one of Rossetti's other major poems of renunciation, was written in the same year as "Goblin Market," and it makes the point more directly. She had inhabited, the poet-speaker confides, "a pleasure-place within my soul; / An earthly paradise supremely fair."[68] But her inner Eden "lured me from the goal." Merely "a tissue of hugged lies," this paradise is complete with a castle of "white transparent glass," woods full of "songs and flowers and fruit," and a muse-like male spirit who has eyes "like flames of fire ... Fulfilling my desire." Rossetti's "pleasure-place" is thus quite clearly a paradise of self-gratifying art, a paradise in which the lures of "Goblin Market"'s masculine fruit-merchants are anticipated by the seductions of the male muse, and the sensual delights of the goblin fruit are embodied in an artfully arranged microcosmos of happy natural creatures. Precisely because this inner Eden *is* a "pleasure-place," however, it soon becomes a realm of banishment in which the poet-speaker, punitively abandoned by her muse, is condemned to freeze, starve, and age, like Laura and Jeanie. For again like Laura and Jeanie, Rossetti must learn to suffer and renounce the self-gratifications of art and sensuality.

As a representative female poet-speaker, moreover, Rossetti believes she must learn to sing selflessly, despite pain, rather than selfishly, in celebration of pleasure. A key passage in "From House to Home" describes an extraordinary, masochistic vision which strikingly illuminates the moral aesthetic on which "Goblin Market" is also based.

> I saw a vision of a woman, where
>   Night and new morning strive for domination;
> Incomparably pale, and almost fair,
>   And sad beyond expression.
>
> . . . .
>
> I stood upon the outer barren ground,
>   She stood on inner ground that budded flowers;
> While circling in their never-slackening round
>   Danced by the mystic hours.

But every flower was lifted on a thorn,
   And every thorn shot upright from its sands
To gall her feet; hoarse laughter pealed in scorn
   With cruel clapping hands.

She bled and wept, yet did not shrink; her strength
   Was strung up until daybreak of delight:
She measured measureless sorrow toward its length,
   And breadth, and depth, and height.

Then marked I how a chain sustained her form,
   A chain of living links not made nor riven:
It stretched sheer up through lightning, wind, and storm,
   And anchored fast in heaven.

One cried: "How long? Yet founded on the Rock
   She shall do battle, suffer, and attain."—
One answered: "Faith quakes in the tempest shock:
   Strengthen her soul again."

I saw a cup sent down and come to her
   Brimful of loathing and of bitterness:
She drank with livid lips that seemed to stir
   The depth, not make it less.

But as she drank I spied a hand distil
   New wine and virgin honey; making it
First bitter-sweet, then sweet indeed, until
   She tasted only sweet.

Her lips and cheeks waxed rosy-fresh and young;
   Drinking she sang: "My soul shall nothing want";
And drank anew: while soft a song was sung,
   A mystical slow chant.

What the female poet-speaker must discover, this passage suggests, is that for the woman poet only renunciation, even anguish, can be a suitable source of song. Bruised and tortured, the Christ-like poet of Rossetti's vision drinks the bitterness of self-abnegation, and *then* sings. For the pure sweetness of the early "pleasure-place," Rossetti implies, is merely a "tissue of lies." The woman artist can be strengthened "to live" only through doses of paradoxically bittersweet pain.

Like the sweet "pleasaunce" of "From House to Home," the fruit of "Goblin Market" has fed on the desirous substrata of the psyche, the childishly self-gratifying fantasies of the imagination. Super-egoistic Lizzie, therefore, is the agent of necessity and necessity's "white and golden" virtue, repression. When Laura returns from eating the forbidden fruit, Lizzie meets her "at the gate / Full of wise upbraidings: 'Dear, you should not stay so late, / Twilight is not good for maidens; / Should not loiter in the glen / In the haunts of goblin men.'" Although, as we noted earlier, the goblin men are not "real" men, they are of course integrally associated with masculinity's prerogatives of self-assertion, so that what Lizzie is telling Laura (and what Rossetti is telling herself) is that the risks and gratifications of art are "not good for maidens," a moral Laura must literally assimilate here just as the poet-speaker had to learn it in "From House to Home." Young ladies like Laura, Maude, and Christina Rossetti should not loiter in the glen of imagination, which is the haunt of goblin men like Keats and Tennyson—or like Dante Gabriel Rossetti and his compatriots of the Pre-Raphaelite Brotherhood.

Later, becoming a eucharistic Messiah, a female version of the patriarchal (rather than Satanic) Word made flesh, Lizzie insists that Laura must devour her—must, that is, ingest her bitter repressive wisdom, the wisdom of necessity's virtue, in order to be redeemed. And indeed, when Laura does feast on Lizzie, the goblin juice on her repressive sister's skin is "wormwood to the tongue." As in "From House to Home," the aesthetic of pleasure has been transformed by censorious morality into an aesthetic of pain. And, again, just as in "From House to Home" the female hero bleeds, weeps, and *sings* because she suffers, so in "Goblin Market" Laura does at last begin to leap and sing "like a caged thing freed" at the moment in which she learns the lesson of renunciation. At this moment, in other words, she reaches what Rossetti considers the height of a woman poet's art, and here, therefore, she is truly Rossetti's surrogate. Later, she will lapse into childlike domesticity, forgoing all feasts, but here, for a brief interval of ecstatic agony, she "stems the light / Straight toward the sun" and gorges "on bitterness without a name," a masochistic version of what Dickinson called "the banquet of abstemiousness." Then, having assimilated her repressive but sisterly superego, she dies utterly to her old poetic / sexual life of self-assertion.

Once again a comparison with Keats seems appropriate, for just as he was continually obsessed with the same poetic apprenticeship that concerned Rossetti in *Maude*, he too wrote a resonantly symbolic poem about the relationship of poetry and starvation to an encounter with interior otherness incarnated in a magical being of the opposite sex. Like Rossetti's goblin men, Keats's "belle dame" fed his vulnerable knight mysterious but luscious food—"roots of relish sweet, / And honey-wild, and manna dew—" and, cementing the connection between food and speech, she told him "in language strange . . . 'I love thee true.'" Like Rossetti's Laura (and like the speaker of "From House to Home"), Keats's knight was also inexplicably deserted by the muselike lady whom he had met in the meads and wooed in an eerie "elfin grot" analogous to the goblin's haunted glen, once she had had her will of him. Like Laura, too, he pined, starved, and sickened on the cold hillside of reality where his *anima* and his author abandoned him. Yet in Keats's case, unlike Rossetti's, we cannot help feeling that the poet's abandonment is only temporary, no matter what the knight's fate might be. Where her betrayal by goblin men (and the distinction between a beautiful queen and rat-faced goblin men is relevant here too) persuades Laura / Rossetti that her original desire to eat the forbidden fruit of art was a vain and criminal impulse, the knight's abandonment simply enhances our sense of his tragic grandeur.

Art, Keats says, is ultimately worth any risk, even the risk of alienation or desolation. The ecstasy of the beautiful lady's "kisses sweet" and "language strange" is more than worth the starvation and agony to come. Indeed, the ecstasy of the kisses, deceptive though they are, itself constitutes the only redemption possible for both Keats and his knight. Certainly any redemption of the kind Lizzie offers Laura, though it might return the knight to the fat land where "the squirrel's granary is full," would destroy what is truly valuable to him—his memory of the elfin grot, the fairy's song, the "honey wild"—just as Laura's memory of the haunted glen and the "fruits like honey to the throat" is ultimately destroyed by her ritual consumption of repressive domesticity. And that "Goblin Market" is not just an observation of the lives of other women but an accurate account of the aesthetics Rossetti worked out for herself helps finally to explain why, although Keats can imagine asserting himself from beyond the grave, Rossetti, banqueting on bitterness, must bury herself alive in a coffin of renunciation.

As we noted earlier, Elizabeth Barrett Browning also made most of her finest poetry out of her reconciliation to that graceful or passionate self-abnegation which, for a nineteenth-century woman, was necessity's highest virtue. But because she had little natural taste for the drastic asceticism Rossetti's temperament and background seem to have fostered, Barrett Browning ultimately substituted a more familiar Victorian aesthetic of service for the younger woman's somewhat idiosyncratic aesthetic of pain. Her masterpiece, *Aurora Leigh* (1856), develops this aesthetic most fully, though it is also in part an epic of feminist self-affirmation. *Aurora Leigh* is too long to analyze here in the kind of detail we have devoted to "Goblin Market," but it certainly deserves some comment, not only because (as Virginia Woolf reports having discovered to her delight)[69] it is so much better than most of its nonreaders realize, but also because it embodies what may well have been the most reasonable compromise between assertion and submission that a sane and worldly woman poet could achieve in the nineteenth century. Indeed, as we shall see, Emily Dickinson's implicit rejection of Barrett Browning's compromise no doubt indicates just how "mad" and unworldly the "myth" of Amherst was.

Briefly, *Aurora Leigh* is a *Künstlerroman* in blank verse about the growth of a woman poet and the education of her heart through pride, sympathy, love, and suffering. Born in Florence to an Englishman and the Italian bride he has been disinherited for marrying, its heroine comes to England as a thirteen-year-old orphan, to be initiated into the torments of feminine gentility by her censorious maiden aunt, an ungentle spinster who acts (like so many women in novels by women) as patriarchy's agent in "breeding" young ladies for decorous domesticity. Partly perhaps because of her un-English and therefore unconventional childhood, Aurora refuses to submit to her aunt's strictures; early, studying her dead father's books, she decides to become a poet. When her highminded, politically ambitious cousin Romney Leigh—a sort of reincarnated St. John Rivers—

asks her to become his wife and helpmate, she proudly declines his offer, explaining that she has her vocation, too: art, which is at least as necessary as social service.[70]

Here, although the specific polarities of self-developing art and self-abnegating "work" recall the prototypical Victorian polarities Tennyson described in, say, "The Palace of Art," Barrett Browning gives the girl's self-justifying speech a feminist dimension that sets her rejection of Romney into precisely the tradition of rebellious self-affirmation that Jane Eyre so notoriously pioneered when she rejected St. John's marriage proposal. Repudiating Romney's patronizing insinuation that women "play at art as children play at swords, / To show a pretty spirit, chiefly admired / Because true action is impossible," she refuses also his invitation to "love and work with me," to work "for uses, not / For such sleek fringes (do you call them ends, / Still less God's glory?) as we sew ourselves / Upon the velvet of those baldoquins / Held 'twixt us and the sun." As passionately assertive as Jane, she insists that "every creature, female as the male, / Stands single in responsible act and thought ... [and] I, too, have my vocation,—work to do, ... Most serious work, most necessary work."[71] At this point in the book, she is "all glittering with the dawn-dew, all erect" and, in a metaphor Dickinson was later to convert to her own uses, "famished for the noon." For this reason, it seems to her, as with masculine aggressiveness she seeks "empire and much tribute," that it is both contemptible and contemptuous for someone to say "I have some worthy work for thee below. / Come, sweep my barns, and keep my hospitals, / And I will pay thee with a current coin / Which men give women."

Significantly, however, *Aurora Leigh* begins where *Jane Eyre* leaves off. Jane rejects St. John's invitation to a life of self-denying work, and enters instead a self-gratifying earthly paradise about which Brontë is unable to give us many details; but Aurora has a whole career ahead of her, and a career—poetry—whose perils are precisely those dangers of hyperbolic self-aggrandizement associated with the prideful "it" that she revealingly calls "the devil of my youth." Thus where Jane's assertion was the product of a long struggle for identity, Aurora's is the postulate with which a long renunciation (or repression) of identity must begin. Jane had to learn to be herself. Aurora has to learn not to be herself.

The particular agent of Aurora's education is Marian Erle, a "woman of the people" who functions as a sisterly double, showing her the way to act and suffer, first by loving and serving Romney, and then by (not quite intentionally) sacrificing her virginity for him. Romney is about to marry Marian Erle as a political gesture toward social equality but Marian is persuaded to renounce him by Lady Waldemar, a self-indulgent and "bitchy" aristocrat who is in love with him herself. Packed off to France under the care of one of this "lady's" servants, Marian—in properly Richardsonian fashion—is trapped in a whorehouse, drugged, raped, impregnated, and driven temporarily mad. What Aurora has to learn from all this is, first, sympathy, and then service. Tormented by her belief that Romney (whom she really loves) plans to marry Lady Waldemar, Aurora goes to Paris, where she encounters the abused Marian and her illegitimate child. By this time Aurora Leigh is a famous and quite formidable poet. But she quickly decides to make a home in her "motherland" of Florence for Marian and the child, a decision that does seem to strike a happy feminist balance between service and "selfishness." Aurora will continue to write her ambitious poems, yet Marian and her child will be secure.

Watching Marian tend the baby, however, the proud poet has learned more than the pleasures of humility. She has learned to envy that "extremity of love" in which a woman is "self-forgot, cast out of self." At this point, Romney appears in Florence and reveals that he has no intention of marrying Lady Waldemar, and moreover that he has been blinded while attempting to rescue Marian's drunken father from a conflagration that destroyed the Leighs' ancestral mansion. On the surface, therefore, he seems to have metamorphosed from a stonily righteous St. John Rivers to a seductively vulnerable Rochester. Softened by her affection for Marian and chastened by this news, Aurora finally concedes to her Victorian audience that "Art is much; but love is more," especially for a woman.

> Art symbolizes heaven; but love is God
> And makes heaven. I, Aurora, fell from mine,
> I would not be a woman like the rest,
> A simple woman who believes in love,

And owns the right of love because she loves,
And, hearing she's beloved, is satisfied
With what contents God: I must analyze,
Confront, and question, just as if a fly
Refused to warm itself in any sun
Till such was *in leone*. . . . [72]

The imagery of her confession is significant, suggesting that in her love Aurora is as unlike Jane Eyre as Romney, despite his blindness, is unlike Rochester. For a woman not to love is to "fall" from heaven like Satan or Eve; to love, on the other hand, is to be like a contented fly, basking in the noontide sun without rivalrously seeking to displace it.

Married to blind Romney, Aurora will be both as wife and as artist her husband's helpmeet. She will not so much desire the sun (the way she did when younger) as she will study it, harvest it, benefit from it. "Gaze on, with inscient vision, toward the sun," Romney admonishes her, "And from his visceral heat pluck out the roots of light beyond him," for "Art's a service, mark: / A silver key is given to thy clasp, / And thou shalt stand unwearied, night and day, / And fix it in the hard, slow-turning wards." [73] In other words, the artist, and specifically the woman poet, is neither a glittering and inspired figure nor a passionately self-assertive Jane Eyre. Rather, she is a modest bride of Apollo who labors for her glorious blind master —and for humanity too—in an "unwearied" trance of self-abnegation almost as intense as the silent agony Rossetti's dream queen endured in "From House to Home."

As her name indicates, therefore, Aurora becomes the dawn goddess who ministers to the god Dickinson was to call "the man of noon" by laying "the first foundations" of *his* reconstructed house. As Romney feeds his "blind majestic eyes / Upon the thought of perfect noon," his artist-wife describes the biblical stones of light she sees in the east—jasper, sapphire, chalcedony, amethyst—from which the visionary walls are being built. Like Dorothea ministering to Casaubon, she enacts Milton's daughter's idealized role: the role of dutiful handmaiden to a blind but powerful master. And just as sightless but still severely patriarchal Romney now seems to be half Rochester and half St. John Rivers, she and her author appear to have achieved a perfect compromise between the docility required by Victorian marriage and the energy demanded by poetry. They have redefined the relationship between the poet's "inspiration" and the poet herself so that it reflects the relationship of a Victorian sage and his submissive helpmeet.

At the same time, however, just as George Eliot's allusion to Milton's daughters hints at secret fantasies of rebellion even while ostensibly articulating a patriarchal doctrine of female servitude, Barrett Browning's compromise aesthetic of service conceals (but does not obliterate) Aurora Leigh's revolutionary impulses. For though the chastened Aurora vows to work *for* Romney, the work Barrett Browning imagines her doing is violent and visionary. As if to mute the shock value of her imaginings, Barrett Browning has Romney rather than Aurora describe Aurora's task. Part of this poet's compromise consists in her diplomatic recognition that Victorian readers might be more likely to accept millenarian utterances from a male character. But the millenarian program Romney outlines is not, of course, his own; it is the revolutionary fantasy of his author—and of her heroine, his wife-to-be—discreetly transferred from female to male lips. He himself concedes this point, though he also elaborates upon the tactful notion that a loving Victorian marriage will sanctify even revolution.

> Now press the clarion on thy woman's lip,
> (Love's holy kiss shall still keep consecrate)
> And breathe thy fine keen breath along the brass,
> And blow all class-walls level as Jericho's . . .

he cries, adding, so there should be no mistake about the sweeping nature of his program, that

> . . . the old world waits the time to be renewed,
> Toward which new hearts in individual growth
> Must quicken, and increase to multitude
> In new dynasties of the race of men,
> Developed whence shall grow spontaneously
> New churches, new economies, new laws
> Admitting freedom, new societies
> Excluding falsehood: HE shall make all new.[74]

The fact that a divine patriarch, aided by a human patriarch and his helpmeet, shall "make all new" does not, finally, conceal the more startling fact that all must and shall, in Barrett Browning's scheme, be *made new*.

Emily Dickinson, who wrote that she experienced a "Conversion of the Mind" when she first read "that Foreign Lady" Elizabeth Barrett Browning, must have perceived the Romantic rage for social transformation concealed behind the veil of self-abnegating servitude with which *Aurora Leigh* concludes.[75] She must have noticed, too, that the celestial city Aurora sees in the sunrise at the end of the poem is, after all, Aurora's and not blind Romney's to see, perhaps because it is that shining capital, the *new* Jerusalem. If the "heat and violence" of Aurora Leigh's heart have been tamed, then, at least her dawn-fires have not been entirely extinguished. It is for this reason, no doubt, that Barrett Browning, while looking everywhere for "grandmothers," became herself the grand mother of all modern women poets in England and America. Certainly she was the spiritual mother of Emily Dickinson who, as we shall see, rejected her compromises but was perpetually inspired by the "inscient vision" with which she solved the vexing "problem" of poetry by women.

16 A Woman—White: Emily Dickinson's Yarn of Pearl

Even among the North American Indians . . . celibacy in Women
. . . was excused in the following instance. . . . A woman dreamt in
youth that she was betrothed to the Sun. She built her a wigwam
apart, filled it with emblems of her alliance, and means of an independent life. There she passed her days, sustained by her own
exertions, and true to her supposed engagement.

In any tribe, we believe, a woman, who lived as if she was
betrothed to the Sun, would be tolerated, and the rays which made
her youth blossom sweetly would crown her with a halo in age.

—Margaret Fuller

A step like a pattering child's in entry & in glided a little plain
woman with two smooth bands of reddish hair . . . in a very plain &
exquisitely clean white pique & a blue net worsted shawl. She
came to me with two day lilies which she put in a sort of childlike
way into my hand & said "These are my introduction" in a soft
frightened breathless childlike voice—& added under her breath
Forgive me if I am frightened; I never see strangers & hardly
know what I say—but she talked soon & thenceforward continuously. . . .

—Thomas Wentworth Higginson

No Romance sold unto
Could so enthrall a Man
As the perusal of
His Individual One—
'Tis Fiction's—to dilute to Plausibility
Our Novel—when 'tis small enough
To Credit—'Tisn't true!

—Emily Dickinson

Emily Dickinson evidently never wrote an extended narrative poem, never attempted to write a prose tale or novel or romance. These facts of omission immediately set her apart from her most distinguished female contemporaries. For in attempting to solve what we have defined as the "problem" of lyric poetry by women, both Elizabeth Barrett Browning and Christina Rossetti dramatized and distanced their anxieties about female art in a series of narratives in which lyric outbursts were safely—that is, unobtrusively—embedded. Thus two of Rossetti's most successful works are "Goblin Market" and "From House to Home," both of which are essentially gothic/romantic tales of a kind women had long written in prose. (The verse of "Goblin Market," moreover, sounds more like *Mother Goose* than like, say, "The Eve of St. Agnes.") And though Barrett Browning may at first seem to have been considerably more assertive than Rossetti in her conception of a verse narrative on as large a scale as *Aurora Leigh*, her own description of the work as a *novel*-poem undercuts the ambition implied by its length. A *Jane Eyre* in iambic pentameter is considerably less grandiose than a traditional epic would have been. An epic, after all, like Wordsworth's *Prelude* or Milton's *Paradise Lost*, would have had truly cosmic goals, relating "man" to "God," while *Aurora Leigh* merely relates woman to man, just as any novel of manners would. Indeed, even at its most mystical, Aurora's betrothal to Romney seems designed (on the surface, anyway) to illustrate Milton's hierarchical "Hee for God only, shee for God in him" (*PL* 4. 299).

None of this is meant to belittle the achievement of either Rossetti or Barrett Browning. Despite their equivocal aesthetics of renunciation, these two artists must still be admired both as successful poets and as women who became successful in their repressive society through the adoption of a protective camouflage that disguised but did not conceal their talent. What these comments are meant to suggest, however, is the magnitude of the poetic self-creation Emily Dickinson achieved through working in a genre that has been traditionally the most Satanically assertive, daring, and therefore precarious of literary modes for women: lyric poetry.

How did Dickinson, who seemed to Thomas Wentworth Higginson so timid, even so neurotically withdrawn, manage such spectacular poetic self-achievement? How did this apparently "gentle spinster," as Ransom calls her, come so close to being "Judith Shakespeare"? In the word *being* inheres, we believe, one key to Dickinson's success. The fantasies of guilt and anger that were expressed in the entranced reveries of the fiction-maker by writers like Rossetti and Barrett Browning, and by all the novelists we have considered, were literally enacted by Dickinson in her own life, her own being. Where George Eliot and Christina Rossetti wrote about angels of destruction and renunciation, Emily Dickinson herself became such an angel. Where Charlotte Brontë projected her anxieties into images of orphan children, Emily Dickinson herself enacted the part of a child. Where almost all late eighteenth- and nineteenth-century women writers from Maria Edgeworth in *Castle Rackrent* to Charlotte Brontë in *Jane Eyre*, Emily Brontë in *Wuthering Heights*, and George Eliot in *Middlemarch*, secreted bitter self-portraits of madwomen in the attics of their novels, Emily Dickinson herself became a madwoman—became, as we shall see, both ironically a madwoman (a deliberate impersonation of a madwoman) and truly a madwoman (a helpless agoraphobic, trapped in a room in her father's house).

Dickinson's life itself, in other words, became a kind of novel or narrative poem in which, through an extraordinarily complex series of maneuvers, aided by costumes that came inevitably to hand, this inventive poet enacted and eventually resolved both her anxieties about her art and her anger at female subordination. Her terse, explosive poems are therefore, in a sense, the speech of a fictional character, for as she told Higginson, "When I state myself, as the Representative of the Verse—it does not mean—me—but a supposed person."[1] Indeed, understood as an elaborate set of dramatic monologues, her poems constitute the "dialogue" in an extended fiction whose subject is the life of that supposed person who was originally called Emily Dickinson but who also christened herself, variously, Emilie, Daisy, Brother Emily, Uncle Emily, and simply Dickinson.

Critics have often, of course, defined Emily Dickinson as one of American literature's most expert poseurs. R. B. Sewall, for instance, asserts that the hyperbole and melodrama of what he calls the Dickinson family "rhetoric" played a crucial part in "the wit, the whimsey, the turn for drama and exaggeration" which characterize so much of this poet's work.[2] At the same time, however, because most critics have not confronted either the nature or the magnitude of the problem Dickinson had to solve as a *woman* poet, they have misunderstood both the nature and the purpose of her "posing." Biographical scholars have concentrated on the mystery of her lover/ master's identity, or on the question of her religious commitment, or both; literary critics have addressed themselves to the linguistic and metaphysical ambiguities of her art. Almost all have concluded, with Sewell, that "as poet [Dickinson] worked from specific to general, concrete to universal. . . . She became preoccupied with essence; the accidents did not concern her."[3] And her posing, her "turn for drama," according to almost all these critics and scholars, was merely one of the "accidents" of Dickinson's life.

We will argue here, however, that Dickinson's posing was not an accident of but essential to her poetic self-achievement, specifically because—as we have suggested—the verse-drama into which she transformed her life enabled her to transcend what Suzanne Juhasz has called the "double bind" of the woman poet: on the one hand, the impossibility of self-assertion for a woman, on the other hand, the necessity of self-assertion for a poet.[4] In the context of a dramatic fiction, Dickinson could metamorphose from a real person (to whom aggressive speech is forbidden) into a series of characters or supposed persons (for whom assertive speeches must be supplied). Even more specifically, we will suggest that the fictional shape Dickinson gave her life was a gothic and romantic one, not just (or even primarily) because of the family "rhetoric" of exaggeration but because the gothic/romantic mode was so frequently employed by all the women writers whom this poet admired more than almost any other literary artists. Significantly, just as critics have tended to define her self-dramatization as "mere" girlish posing, they have ignored or dismissed Dickinson's reading of fiction, especially fiction by women, as irrelevant to her poetry. The closest thing to a serious influence study in this direction has been Ellen Moers's discussion of *Aurora Leigh*'s effect on Dickinson's metaphors, but it is primarily the imagery of Barrett Browning's poem, rather than its plot, that concerns Moers. Otherwise, such explorations of Dickinson's reading as those by Jack Capps and Ruth Miller concentrate almost entirely on her familiarity with male poets from Shakespeare and Quarles to Keats and Emerson.[5]

Like many literate nineteenth-century women, however, Emily Dickinson most often and most passionately read novels, and especially novels by women. She loved Dickens but thought of *Middlemarch* as "glory," eulogized the Brontës, and (though her father disapproved of popular fiction, recommending instead "lonely and rigorous books") read the works of these women and their contemporaries with the kind of secret passion that marks, say, Catherine Morland's hunger for the novels of Mrs. Radcliffe. Indeed, there is a sense in which, just as Catherine is trying to find her own story in the fictionalized corridors of Northanger Abbey, Dickinson was trying to find metaphoric equivalents of her life in the female gothic she covertly read in her "Father's house" and overtly dramatized in her own verse.[6]

We have seen that, from Austen's parodic Laura and Sophia to Emily Brontë's A.G.A., the heroines of fiction by women obsessively and self-consciously enact precisely the melodramatic romances and gothic plots that their reclusive authors deny themselves (or are denied) in their own lives. We have seen, too, that the female author increasingly moves from a position of "objectivity" and indifference, or even one of ironic amusement, toward her protagonists—exemplified by, say, Austen's attitude toward Laura and Sophia—to an open identification with her heroine, like what seems to have been Emily Brontë's immersal in A.G.A. Not surprisingly, then, in the work of Emily Dickinson, the latest and most consciously radical of these artists, we see the culmination of this process, an almost complete absorption of the characters of the fiction into the persona of their author, so that this writer and her protagonist(s) become for all practical purposes one—one "supposed person" achieving the authority of self-creation by enacting many highly literary selves and lives.

That Dickinson was herself quite conscious of this interdependence of self-dramatization, self-creation, and literary creation becomes clear in a number of poems and letters. "Nature is a Haunted House —but Art—a House that tries to be haunted," she once told Higginson,[7] and though the remark is often seen as an Emersonian analysis of the relationship between the Me and the Not-Me, its gothic metaphor, together with its frank admission of dependence upon such metaphors, tells us otherwise, tells us that the self-hauntings of (female) gothic fiction are in Dickinson's view essential to (female) art. For Dickinson, indeed, art is not so much *poesis*—making—as it is *mimesis*—enactment, and this because she believes that even consciousness is not so much reflective as it is theatrical. A poem that Thomas Johnson dates as having been written around 1863 makes this point in greater detail than her letter to Higginson.

> Drama's vitallest Expression is the Common Day
> That arise and set about Us—
> Other Tragedy
>
> Perish in the Recitation—
> This—the best enact
> When the Audience is scattered
> And the Boxes shut—
>
> "Hamlet" to Himself were Hamlet—
> Had not Shakespeare wrote—
> Though the "Romeo" left no Record
> Of his Juliet,
>
> It were infinite enacted
> In the Human Heart—
> Only Theatre recorded
> Owner cannot shut—   [J. 741]

Life is enactment, art the outward manifestation of the scenes performed on an inner stage, and thus an author and her characters are one: they are, as we have said, one "supposed person," or rather a series of such persons, interacting in a romantic drama or (as our epigraph from Dickinson suggests) a gigantic and incredible "Novel" which, "when tis small enough / To credit—Tisn't True!" In the following pages, we will trace the modes and metaphors of some of the supposed persons whom Dickinson "becomes" as her inner novel unfolds, and we shall see that, despite the pain many of her impersonations entailed, the aesthetic on which they depend helped her to free herself from social and psychological constraints which might otherwise have stifled or crippled her art. In particular, we shall see that, by literally and figuratively impersonating "a woman—white," Dickinson wove her life into a gothic "Yarn of Pearl" that gave her exactly the "Amplitude" and "Awe" she knew she needed in order to write great poetry.[8]

As many critics have observed, Dickinson began her poetic career by consciously enacting the part of a child—both by deliberately prolonging her own childhood and by inventing a new, alternative childhood for herself. At the same time, however, her child mask was inseparable from her even more famously self-defining role as the inoffensive and invisible soul of "I'm Nobody! Who are you?" (J. 288). In keeping with this early yet toughly enduring version of herself, Dickinson insistently described herself as a tiny person, a wren, a daisy, a mouse, a child, a modest little creature easily mastered by circumference and circumstance. Like Barrett Browning, whose poetry she much admired, she seems at first to have assuaged the guilt verse-writing aroused by transforming Romantic poetic self-assertion into an aesthetic of female service modeled on Victorian marriage. Certainly something like the relationship between a master-ful husband and a self-abnegating wife appears to be at the heart of much of her poetry, where it is also pictured, variously, as the en-counter of lover and mistress, king and queen. On closer examination, however, we can see that—in keeping with this poet's persistent child pose—the male-female relationship is "really" that of father and daughter, master and scholar/slave, ferocious "man of noon" and vulnerable flower of dawn, reverent or rebellious Nobody and (to borrow a useful neologism from William Blake) omnipotent omnipresent Nobodaddy.[9]

But the fact that Dickinson's poetry suggests such complicated relationships between the female Self and the male Other immediately suggests also the complexity of her art as well as the insistent ambiguity with which even at her most humble and "innocent" she reconciled those apparent opposites of feminine submission and poetic assertion. Disguised or oblique as they sometimes seem, Christina Rossetti's aesthetic of renunciation and Barrett Browning's aesthetic of service are clearcut in comparison to such a darkly self-defining poetics. For though Mrs. Browning's American disciple described herself as No-body, admired *Aurora Leigh*, and seemed on occasion to preach the "piercing virtue" of a Rossettiesque renunciation, many of her most modest and "feminine" remarks were undercut by a steel blade of irony that transformed service into subversion and renunciation into the "Royal Seal" of a "White Election."[10]

Still, despite her secret sense of election, Dickinson understood the social requirements, masquerading as cosmic laws, which obliged every woman in some sense to enact the role of Nobody. Her accurate perceptions are expressed in various poems and letters devoted to what she ironically described as "the honorable Work" of women. For this "gentle spinster" often observed her female contemporaries with almost clinical objectivity, noting that "Gentlewomen" were by turns "Brittle Ladies," "Soft—Cherubic Creatures," veiled images, or even simply "Plushes"—cushiony *things* as passive as sofas.[11] But it was specifically the "soft Eclipse" of marriage, she seems to have speculated, that immobilized most of these women, for marriage (as Emily Brontë suggested in *Wuthering Heights*, a novel Dickinson especially admired) transforms a "half savage, and hardy, and free" girl into a woman and wife by annuling the girl's "first Prospective" of energy and imagination.[12] Dickinson's most famous pronouncement on the subject makes the point succinctly:

> She rose to His Requirement—dropt
> The Playthings of Her Life
> To take the honorable Work
> Of Woman, and of Wife—
>
> If ought She missed in Her new Day
> Of Amplitude, or Awe—
> Or first Prospective—Or the Gold
> In using, wear away,
>
> It lay unmentioned—as the Sea
> Develop Pearl, and Weed,
> But only to Himself—be known
> The Fathoms they abide—   [J. 732]

The irony of the woman/wife's situation as it is described here is that in "rising" to the rigorous "Requirement" of a husband she has (like Catherine Earnshaw Linton) been cast out of the holy, Wordsworthian sea of imagination where she had dwelt as a girl. Even more ironic is the fact that her new husband and master, like all the Nobodaddys of a Puritan-Victorian society, evidently defines products of the sea of imagination—pearly Amplitude, seaweedy Awe—as Playthings. From Dickinson's point of view, however,

Amplitude and Awe are the only absolute necessities. "I always ran home to Awe when a child, if anything befell me," she told Higginson once, adding mysteriously, "He was an awful Mother but I liked him better than none." [13] Like the sea, in other words, Awe is the strong Mother of the poet's imagination, so strong indeed as to require a masculine pronoun. And it is from this powerfully assertive parentage that the woman and wife must "rise." Striving to renounce her*self* in the tradition of Barrett Browning and Rossetti, she rationalizes her decision as a choice of heavenly security and regal maturity:

> I'm "wife"—I've finished that—
> That other state—
> I'm Czar—I'm "Woman" now—
> It's safer so—
>
> How odd the Girl's life looks
> Behind this soft Eclipse—
> I think that Earth feels so
> To folks in Heaven—now—
>
> This being comfort—then
> That other kind—was pain—
> But why compare?
> I'm "Wife"! Stop there!   [J. 199]

The stops and steps of the mind that give this dramatic monologue its strength clearly indicate Dickinson's ironic view of her speaker's anxious rationalizations. "This being comfort—then" one must *infer* that "That other kind—was pain," since there never was (or so the poem implies) any real evidence of pain. The equally anxious question "But why compare?" reinforces our sense that a comparison might indeed be odious, with the wrong term coming out ahead. Hence the speaker who has taken up her "honorable Work" must almost forcibly restrain herself from letting her thoughts—or maybe even her life—go further: "I'm 'Wife'! Stop there!"

But of course, as "She rose to His Requirement" notes, the sea of imagination does *not* stop there. Irrepressible, inexorable, it silently produces pearl and weed, though such objects (like poems in a bureau drawer) are secrets known only to the strong, assertively

masculine part of the woman that must be called *Him*self in a
patriarchal culture. The fact that in some poems Dickinson analyzes
this female double life of surface requirements and sea-deep pearl
with surgical calm does not mean she is unsympathetic to the women
who endure the psychic splits she describes. Nor does it mean that
she supposed herself exempt from such problems because she never
officially undertook the work of wife. On the contrary, both her
irony and her objectivity were intensified by her sense that she
herself was trapped in the Requirements by which all women were
surrounded, a tangled set of implicit laws that had to be described
not as a single rock (which one could tunnel through) but as "A
Cobweb—wove in Adamant—/ A Battlement—of Straw / / A limit
like the Veil / Unto the Lady's face— / But every Mesh—a Citadel—
/ And Dragons—in the Crease" (J. 398). Behind such a battlement
of straw, she must have felt, she and the sea were buried alive, for—
pearl and weed notwithstanding—her life too had been "shaven /
And fitted to a frame" somewhere in the beginning of history, when
women like her were assigned the "smallest" rooms in her father's
house.[14]

It is particularly catastrophic, however, for a poet's sea of Awe
to be hidden and unmentionable. Obviously Dickinson would have
to devise some aesthetic strategies that would give her access to her
secret self. As we have shown, Christina Rossetti made her finest
art out of her paradoxical renunciation of that desirous inner being
who asserted herself in verse, and Elizabeth Barrett Browning made
hers out of her metamorphosis of aesthetic ambition into wifely duty.
For Dickinson, though, the impossibility of anything but a duplicitous renunciation was built into the very imagery with which she
defined her problem. Neither an inner sea nor a mother named
Awe can be renounced: both are facts of the blood, inescapable
inheritances. In a sense, then, Dickinson was a Laura without a
restraining Lizzie, an Aurora Leigh without a chastening Romney.
But what if Lizzies and Romneys were unnecessary? What if the
great playthings of Amplitude and Awe remained appropriate?
Rather early in her life as an artist, Dickinson must have half-
consciously perceived that she could avoid the necessity of renouncing
her art by renouncing, instead, that concept of womanliness which
required self-abnegating renunciation. Or, to put it another way,

she must have decided that to begin with she could try to solve the problem of being a woman by refusing to admit that she was a woman. Though she might then lack the crowning title that is the "sign" of achieved womanliness or wifehood, she would glow with the "White Election" of art.[15] Her garden, as she wrote in a poem to her sister-in-law, might face the icy north, but it would offer the ambiguous consolation of oceans "on every side" (J. 631). By remaining in her father's house, a childlike Nobody (rather than becoming a wifely Nobody in a husband's house), she would have at least a chance of negotiating with Awe for the rank of Somebody. "I dwell in Possibility— / A fairer House than Prose" she wrote in 1862 (J. 657), and surely, as Barbara Clarke Mossberg has pointed out, she meant that the asexual "Possibility" of childhood was far more awesome and amplitudinous than the suffocating "Prose" of female adulthood.[16]

The consequences of Dickinson's early impersonation of childhood and her concomitant fascination with its solemn playthings as opposed to the work "Of Woman, and of Wife" were far-reaching indeed. On the one hand, her initially strong commitment to an elaborately contrived (and from the world's point of view "partially cracked") child mask enabled her not only to write a great deal of poetry but to write a great deal of astonishingly innovative poetry—poetry full of grammatical "mistakes" and stylistic eccentricities such as only a mad child could write.[17] On the other hand, while freeing her from the terrors of marriage and allowing her to "play" with the toys of Amplitude, the child mask (or pose or costume) eventually threatened to become a crippling self, a self that in the crisis of her gothic life fiction locked her into her father's house in the way that a little girl is confined to a nursery. What was habit in the sense of costume became habit in the more pernicious sense of addiction, and finally the two habits led to both an inner and outer in*habit*ation —a haunting interior other *and* an inescapable prison.

In the beginning, however, Dickinson's yearning for childhood was high-spirited and playful. Even as an adolescent, she impersonated a harum-scarum little girl with a delighted understanding of what she was doing and why she was doing it. "I love so to be a child," she wrote to her close friend Abiah Root, when she was twenty, explaining—as if to make the connection with gender as explicit as possible—that in her self-elected childishness she knew she took a very "different view" of life from another friend who was "more of a woman than I am." [18] "God keep me from what they call *households*," she exclaimed elsewhere. Because her mother was sick, she comically noted, she was trying to cope with the overwhelming trivia of a housewife's day. Though she obviously disliked the chore, her exploration of her distaste is exuberant and witty: "Wouldn't you love to see me in these bonds of great despair, looking around my kitchen, and praying for kind deliverance, and declaring by 'Omar's beard' I never was in such a plight. *My* kitchen, I think I called it—God forbid that it was, or shall, be my own—" [19] Wholly identifying herself with childhood irresponsibility and the playthings of life, she does not seriously expect to have to take what she later called a "Station in the Day." [20]

In a number of her early poems, therefore, she plays an "irresponsible" part—that of a rosy-cheeked, busy, ironically old-fashioned little person looking at the adult world with wide-eyed wonder. The piece that begins "'Arcturus' is his other name—/ I'd rather call him 'Star,'" for example, makes witty use of this child's amazement at the matter-of-fact vocabulary with which science has replaced the traditional metaphors of religion and poetry. Thus "What once was 'Heaven' / Is '*Zenith*' now," and it may follow from this that even Heaven itself is changed.

> Perhaps the "Kingdom of Heaven's" changed—
> I hope the "Children" there
> Won't be "new fashioned" when I come—
> And laugh at me—and stare—
>
> I hope the Father in the skies
> Will lift his little girl—
> Old fashioned—naughty—everything—
> Over the stile of "Pearl."   [J. 70]

This last stanza may seem at first almost cloying, with its image of a kindly Victorian Father God and a sweetly naughty little maid in pinafore and petticoats, but it soon becomes clear that, as in her letter to Abiah Root, Dickinson is deliberately parodying both the sentimental pieties of Victorian households and her own carefully created childishness. The excessive, almost sardonic cuteness of her fantasy is one sign that she is doing this. The quotation marks she has placed around all the key words in the poem are another sign. They suggest that she is questioning not only scientific terms like "Zenith" but even traditional phrases like "Kingdom of Heaven," "new fashioned," and "Pearl." The impersonation of a child's naiveté can be put to more than one good use, we see here. Not only can a child play at verse but (since from the child's perspective all language is fresh or strange) all words can become a child's shiny toys, to be examined, handled, tasted, fondled with ironic Awe.

"'Arcturus' is his other name," which Johnson dates 1859, is an exceptionally lighthearted example of what Dickinson could do with an ironically childlike perspective, just as her confessions to Abiah that she loved to be a child and hated households were essentially lighthearted. It is as if at that point, just beginning to assemble the costumes of her life, she hardly suspected the drastic uses to which her childish pinafore would be put. Nineteen years after her letter to Abiah, however, she was informing Higginson unequivocally that "I do not cross my Father's ground to any house in town,"[21] and only fourteen years after the letter to Abiah she was hinting to her cousin Louise Norcross that her family had given her some household chores as occupational therapy. "I make the yellow to the pies, and bang the spice for the cake.... They say I am a Help."[22] And just as her engagement with the business of households remained childlike but darkened, so her poetic questionings of language and experience remained childlike in their perspective of Awe but darkened and became severer.

Even in another poem probably written in 1859, for example, Dickinson assumes the mask of an anxious "little Pilgrim" to question "some Wise Man from the skies": "Will there really be a 'Morning'?/Is there such a thing as 'Day'?... Has it feet like Water lilies?/Has it feathers like a Bird?" (J. 101). The "Wise Man from the skies" here is like "the Father in the Skies" of the Arcturus poem, and the speaker's misconceptions about "Morning" and "Day" are half-comical and naively coquettish (as the young Emily Dickinson sometimes seems herself to have been).[23] But the irony of this poem is tenser, more pained, as though some wire, somewhere, were beginning to tighten. For a skeptic like Dickinson to joke about the pearly gates was one thing; for an inebriate of air to forget the meaning of morning was quite another, so that in her deferential questions we can see there is now little laughing matter; instead shadows are beginning to cloud the poet's eyes. Eventually such shadows will lead to the great bewildered lyrics of the 1860s which assert agony by insisting, childlike, on the impossibility of definitions. "It was not Death, for I stood up,/And all the Dead, lie down—" (J. 510) and "Struck, was I, not yet by Lightning—" (J. 925) are perhaps the two definitive examples of Dickinson's work in this genre, but many other related poems could be named. At the same time, in its confession of childish confusion about even such elementary orderings of experience as night and day, "Will there really be a 'Morning'?" looks forward to the apparently naive mistakes of usage and the deliberately childish eccentricities of personification that give force to a poem like "Good Morning— Midnight" (which was also written in the 'sixties). Only, after all, by acting the part of a polite but bewildered child can Dickinson bring off unconventional stanzas like "Good Morning—Midnight— /I'm coming Home—/Day—got tired of Me—/How could I—of Him?" (J. 425). And only, too, by enacting the weariness of a rejected child can she convey what she defines as her rejection by that masterful male adult world of "Day" to whose Requirements she has, with conscious and distinctly unchildish obstinacy, refused to rise.

Dickinson's attitude toward the powerful male Other who ruled women's days and lives is at the heart of the gothic "Novel" into which she transformed her own life, and it is strikingly ambivalent. On the one hand, the archetypal patriarch whom she called "Burglar! Banker—Father" (J. 49) sounds very like that sinister divinity Blake described as Nobodaddy, the tyrannical God who created "the old Anything." On the other hand, the nameless Master whom Dickinson loved with theatrical fervor is essential to the glamorous mystery Ransom describes as the "romance" that enabled her to "fulfil herself like any other woman."[24] Thus—even leaving aside biographical questions—her ambivalence toward the male Other leads to one of the central paradoxes of her art. In poem after poem, as we have seen, this "gentle spinster" enacts the part of a defiant childwoman who resents her tyrannical husband/father and longs to be delivered from his fierce Requirements. At the same time, in poem after poem, she depicts her beloved Master/Father as a glowing Apollo, confessing that there is a "sweet wolf"[25] inside her that craves his approval, his love, his golden warmth. As a girl, Dickinson had begged to be kept from "what they call households," but ironically, as she grew older, she discovered that the price of her salvation was her agoraphobic imprisonment in her father's household, along with a concomitant exclusion from the passionate drama of adult sexuality. Similarly, she had feared "the burning noon," but when her vision was literally dimmed by a mysterious eye ailment which may even have been "hysterical blindness"[26] she longed literally and figuratively for the light—for "Morning's Amber Road" and for "As much of Noon as I could take / Between my finite eyes" (J. 327).

"As much of Noon as I could *take*": the ambiguities in the word *take*, together with the paradoxical pleasure/pain associated with the noon sun, summarize Dickinson's ambivalence toward the powerful male who plays (in different guises) so important a part in the theater of her verse. In the context of the elaborate drama she was enacting, therefore, her metaphorical (and perhaps occasionally literal) blindness seems to have functioned in part as a castration metaphor, the way Catherine Earnshaw's wounded foot does in *Wuthering Heights*. For, like Catherine, as Dickinson grew into that inescapable sexual consciousness which her little girl pose postponed but did not evade, she realized that she must move away from the androgynous freedom of childhood and began, therefore, to perceive the symbolic castration implicit in female powerlessness. Looking into the scorching dazzle of the patriarchal sun—the enormous "masculine" light that controls and illuminates all public things-as-they-are—she must have felt blinded by its intensity, made aware, that is, both of her own comparative weakness and of her own ambivalence about *looking*. She notes an almost masochistic sexual fascination with "As much of Noon as I could take / Between my finite eyes," even as she describes a passionately self-protective desire not to look for fear that the enormity of the patriarchal noon will "strike me dead." "Before I got my eye put out, I liked as well to see— / As other Creatures . . ." she confides in this poem that is chilling in its enactment of ambivalence.

That the intimidatingly brilliant sun does signify a sort of patriarchal God of light to Dickinson is made clear in the extraordinary meditation on the "man of noon" that she included in a letter she wrote Susan Gilbert in 1852. In its searching examination of the meaning of wifehood, moreover, this letter reveals, more frankly than most of the poems do, the poet's keen consciousness of her own warring feelings about that solar Nobodaddy who was both censorious "Burglar! Banker—Father," and idealized Master/Lover.

> How dull our lives must seem to the bride and the plighted maiden, whose days are fed with gold . . . but to the *wife*, Susie . . . our lives perhaps seem dearer than all others in the world; you have seen flowers at morning, satisfied with the dew, and these same sweet flowers at noon with their heads bowed in anguish before the mighty sun; think you these thirsty blossoms will *now* need nought but—*dew*? No, they will cry for sunlight, and pine for the burning noon, though it scorches them, scathes them; they have got through with peace—they know that the man of noon is *mightier* than the morning and their life is henceforth to him. Oh Susie . . . it does so rend me . . . the thought of it when it comes, that I tremble lest at sometime I, too, am yielded up.[27]

What is almost shocking in this superbly honest letter is its relentlessly elaborated imagery of male power and female powerlessness. The "man of noon" is mighty, burning with fierce vitality, and pitiless in potency. The woman become wife—the sexually realized woman—is as helplessly rooted in her gender as a flower is trapped in the earth and in its need for the energizing sunlight which nevertheless beats it into submission so that it bows its head in anguish. "Daisy," significantly, was one of Dickinson's own nicknames for herself, and obviously, even at the age of twenty-two when she wrote this letter, she had begun apprehensively to define herself as an ambivalently light-loving/sun-fearing flower. Thus, just as the imagery of mother Awe and an inner sea implied that renunciation would be impossible for Dickinson, so an inescapable yielding up of even the old-fashioned little girl is implicit in the imagery of this letter. The sun ascends and a morning flower must helplessly trace his course, if not as his bride then as his impassioned slave.

As a number of biographers have shown, Dickinson's own father provided many of the essential features of this necessary but fearful solar Nobodaddy who was so central in her fiction of her life. A vigorous and austere lawyer, the leading citizen of Amherst, Edward Dickinson was the epitome of an almost ruthlessly public, masterful man. No doubt he inherited much of his Puritan rigor from generations of Amherst ancestors born, as his son Austin later wrote, "within the sound of the old meeting-house bell, all earnest, God-fearing men."[28] But there is no doubt, either, that he was temperamentally as well as culturally a remote, powerful, and grim patriarch. "Edward seems very sober and says very little," his sister Catherine once remarked, and he himself, preparing for marriage, wrote his wife-to-be in tones more censorious than sensual, more righteous than romantic: "Let us prepare for a life of rational happiness. I do not expect or wish for a life of pleasure."[29]

Such severities at first make Edward Dickinson sound like an American St. John Rivers, a grimly righteous pillar of society against whom a young woman of Emily Dickinson's keen wit should have found it quite possible to rebel. But besides being an "earnest God-fearing" citizen of Amherst, the poet's father was a classic American entrepeneur, a boldly—even Satanically—ambitious man whose passion for self-advancement must have been simultaneously attractive and frightening to a daughter steeped in Romantic poetry. "I must make some money in some way, and if I don't speculate in the lands, at the 'East,' I must at the 'West,'" he wrote to his wife in 1835, "and when the fever next attacks me—nothing human shall stop me from making one desperate attempt to make my fortune. . . . I must spread myself over more ground—half a house, and a rod square for a garden, won't answer my turn."[30] In a sense, then, Emily Dickinson had two fathers. One was a scorchingly intense man, almost a Byronic hero, who "read lonely and rigorous books," who "never played," whose "Heart was pure and terrible," and who longed to spread himself over "more ground."[31] The other was a pompous public man who attacked "the women's Suffrage people"

and who struck T. W. Higginson as "thin dry and speechless" so
that he "saw what [Emily's] life had been." [32]

It is clearly from the Requirements of this second father, the
righteous and punctual patriarch, that the poet continually attempts
to escape. In "Where bells no more affright the morn" she even
expresses her willingness to escape into death, "where tired Children
placid sleep / Thro' Centuries of noon," so that "nor Father's bells—
nor Factories / Could scare us any more" (J. 112). Yet just as her
Byronically heroic father was so charismatic that even after his
death Dickinson wrote "I dream about father every night, always
a different dream, and forget what I am doing daytimes, wondering
where he is," [33] so her righteous and punctual public father is so
powerful that, ironically, her prayer for escape must be addressed
to him—the very person she wishes to escape. Describing death as
Edenic—"This place is Bliss—this town is Heaven—"—she girlishly
exclaims "Please, Pater, pretty soon!" (J. 112). For *this* father—the
public patriarch—has gradually metamorphosed from "thin dry
and speechless" Edward Dickinson into God the Father, the celestial
Patriarch.

This metamorphic blurring of the lines between daddy and Nobodaddy happens regularly throughout Dickinson's versified life as a
supposed person. In the early "Papa above!," for instance, the
speaker's heavenly *Pater* is clearly a glorified Victorian *pater familias*,
and the poet, like that bad animal the nine-year-old Jane Eyre,
identifies herself with a subhuman creature.

> Papa above!
> Regard a Mouse
> O'erpowered by the Cat!
> Reserve within thy Kingdom
> A "Mansion" for the Rat!
>
> Snug in seraphic Cupboards
> To nibble all the day,
> While unsuspecting Cycles
> Wheel solemnly away!   [J. 61]

Obviously Dickinson's association of her earthly papa with a
heavenly Papa, like her own identification with a dead mouse,
represents what she genuinely believed was the power ratio between

her father and herself, or even between all fathers and all daughters. At the same time, however, her comically coy exaggeration of daddy into Nobodaddy and herself into a mouse (or a mouse's friend) suggests the artfulness with which she dramatized her problems so as to give extra intensity—extra chiaroscuro, as it were—to the fiction she understood herself to be enacting. Her ironic hyperbole suggests, in addition, her lucid awareness of the literary and theological paradigms she might find for her relationship with her father, and finally it suggests her consciousness of the extent to which she herself desired to destroy or subvert that relationship. Those solemn but unsuspecting celestial cycles are curiously reminiscent, after all, of the six generations of "earnest God-fearing men" who represented the Dickinson family every sabbath in the old meeting house, and the snug poetic mouse is a tiny but subversive force in seraphic cupboards. What foundations might she be undermining, in her childlike "innocence"?

That Dickinson not only understood the revolutionary nature of some of her own feelings about her father but also recognized their literary implications becomes, finally, quite clear from two faint lines she evidently drew in the margin of her copy of *Jane Eyre*, the only two marginal marks in the book. The first appears beside the following passage:

> St. John was a good man; but I began to feel he had spoken truth of himself when he said he was hard and cold. The humanities and amenities of life had no attraction for him— its peaceful enjoyments no charm.

The second appears a few lines away, next to a passage from the same paragraph:

> I saw he [St. John] was of the material from which nature hews her heroes—Christian and Pagan—her lawgivers, her statesmen, her conquerors; a steadfast bulwark for great interests to rest upon; but, at the fireside, too often a cold cumbrous column, gloomy and out of place.[34]

Dickinson's own consciousness of the sort of literary figure her father cut should help us to understand both the rebellion she enacted and the imprisonment she could not escape. Even Jane Eyre, after all, found it difficult to free herself from the iron shroud of principle in which St. John enclosed her. Yet Jane had Rochester to call her from her trance. For Dickinson, however, both St. John and Rochester, both the pillar of society and the charismatic hero, were implicit in the single figure of her Father/Master/Lover, as if God and Satan should unite in the shape of one Nobodaddy.

To be sure, a number of Dickinson's love poems to her mysterious Master seem as passionately affirmative as any tribute Jane might have composed for Rochester in the first flush of her love for him. Just as the works we might call Dickinson's "Nobodaddy" poems are products of a highly literary process of exaggeration, however, these love poems are usually stylized, literary, and ironic. Indeed, their irony frequently bespeaks concealed tensions and hostilities not unlike those that mark Jane's relationship with Rochester, while their self-conscious rhetoric indicates that, as Clark Griffith puts it, the poet is working through "an eminently public literary convention."[35] The elegant "The Daisy follows soft the Sun," for instance, seems to be both an intensely felt address to the patriarchal sun as Father/Master/Lover and a careful elaboration of a courtly conceit. Thus, like many of John Donne's early poems, it mediates sexual passion through an original but stylized use of literary convention.

> The Daisy follows soft the Sun—
> And when his golden walk is done—
> Sits shyly at his feet—
> He—waking—finds the flower there—
> Wherefore—Marauder—art thou here?
> Because, Sir, love is sweet!
>
> We are the Flower—Thou the Sun!
> Forgive us, if as days decline—
> We nearer steal to Thee!
> Enamored of the parting West—
> The peace—the flight—the Amethyst—
> Night's possibility!   [J. 106]

Besides being an interesting example of the way in which Dickinson could make deliberate and ironic use of her helpless need for a

Master/Lover, this poem is (for her) a notably happy fantasy of romantic "fulfillment," a fact that is also indicated by its conscious dependence on conventional structures. The mini-aubade/dialogue between the sun and the daisy literally dramatizes the daydreaming poet's hope, while her rather unusual recourse to a literary "thou" in the explanatory peroration perhaps emphasizes her awareness of the artifice of her own imaginings. In the intensity of her final longing, however, for "The peace—the flight—the Amethyst—/ Night's possibility!" Dickinson not only brings her narrative conceit to a satisfactorily romantic conclusion, she also confesses more openly than elsewhere in the poem the depth of her own sexual need for a fiery Master/Lover.

If we pursue all the metaphorical implications of Dickinson's feared and adored sun, however, "Night's possibility" begins to seem a curiously ambiguous phrase. Since the solar god is withdrawn at night, night's possibility, though triumphantly sensual for a human being, can only be abandonment for a flower. At the same time, if night is the interval when the repressive solar Nobodaddy relaxes his constraints, its possibility for a poet may be self-assertion. That all these problems and rewards are implicit for Dickinson both in the phrase "Night's possibility" and in her fantasy relationship to her solar Master/Lover becomes clearer in some of the other poems that dramatize this relationship.

"The Sun—*just touched* the Morning—," for instance, seems almost like a darkened revision of "The Daisy follows soft the Sun." Beginning optimistically, as the earlier poem did, this verse describes with increasingly bitter irony the way "The *Morning*—Happy thing —/ Supposed that He had come to *dwell*—/ And Life would be all *Spring*!" But small as well as large cycles solemnly wheel, and Dickinson observes that they are not controllable by even the most defiant "Morning," Daisy, mouse, or woman. Thus "Her wheeling King" majestically moves away, leaving the poet, costumed as "Morning," with "a *new necessity*!/ The *want* of *Diadems*!"

> The Morning—*fluttered—staggered*—
> *Felt feebly*—for Her *crown*—
> Her *unanointed forehead*—
> *Henceforth*—Her *only* One!   [J. 232]

Even this poem's appearance on the page shows, just as its sad story does, how far the poet has moved from the cheerfully courtly fantasy of "The Daisy follows soft the Sun." If abandonment was one of night's possibilities, it is here enacted with all the paraphernalia of woe we associate with Dickinson's greatest pain: the halting and breathless speech punctuated by dashes that read almost like gasps, the explosive italics that seem to express a desire to communicate meanings for which there are no words but only tones of voice, the slangy but condensed syntax, the unorthodox versification. For by 1861, when this poem was written, nine years had wheeled by and the anxious twenty-two-year-old girl who had written to Susan Gilbert with virginal objectivity about the mighty "man of noon" *had* been "yielded up" and "rended" by what she represented as a masochistic, almost self-annihilating passion for that mysterious Master who seems to have incarnated, among other things, the worldly and artistic Amplitude she herself secretly desired. But now the child pose designed to save her from a censorious Nobodaddy's Requirements made her, ironically, more vulnerable to a romantic Master's seductions. Because she viewed the world with childlike Awe, her imaginary lover became larger than life, a solar colossus to scorch and then blind her when he abandoned her to night's possibilities of loneliness, coldness, darkness. More, because she had so often dramatically defined herself as the "slightest" in the house, she now imagined herself dwindling further into a wilted daisy, a small whimpering animal, a barely visible "it"—the ultimate Nobody.

Even more than the dashes and italics of "The *Sun—just touched* the Morning—", the hectic rhetoric of Dickinson's notorious "Master letters" suggests in rough draft the style of disrupted syntax, pronoun confusion, and rapid elliptical free association to which such imaginings drove her. The mental state this style implies, moreover, is surely in itself far more significant than the biographical enigma of the "Master's" identity that has obsessed so many scholars: "Oh did I offend it—" she writes in her final, painfully incoherent Master letter. "[Didn't it want me to tell it the truth] Daisy—Daisy— offend it—who bends her smaller life to his [it's] meeker (lower) every day...."[36] And though "he"—the Master—is an "it" here, Dickinson herself, the childlike Daisy, usually is (or contains) an "it," as in poems like "What shall I do—it whimpers so—/This little Hound within the Heart" (J. 186) or "Why make it doubt—it hurts it so—" (J. 462).

The second of these poems, in particular, attests to the fearful power with which the dreaded and adored man of noon has rended Dickinson's mind, shattering logic, syntax, and order. In its entirety the poem reads as follows:

> Why make it doubt—it hurts it so—
> So sick—to guess—
> So strong—to know—
> So brave—upon its little Bed
> To tell the very last They said
> Unto Itself—and smile—And shake—
> For that dear—distant—dangerous—Sake—
> But—the Instead—the Pinching fear
> That Something—it did do—or dare—
> Offend the Vision—and it flee—
> And They no more remember me—
> Nor ever turn to tell me why—
> Oh Master, This is Misery—

"They," "it," "Itself," and "me" continually shift meanings here, and are at the same time held both together and apart by the writer's characteristic dashes, each of which seems now to become a sort of chasm over which the poem leaps only with the greatest difficulty. Significantly, too, there is neither a "he" nor a "you" anywhere present in the verse, except by implication. It is as if the masterful man of noon now rules Dickinson's life so completely that she can hardly confront him face to face. As the ambiguous reality of Dickinson's own father predicted, the glorious Lover/Master has now openly fused with the censorious patriarch, so that here the male Other is himself not just the "distant stately lover" men call God and Blake called Nobodaddy, but the "Missing All" Dickinson had at one time thought she didn't need. Her refusal to be "yielded up" and "rended" by this man of noon's Requirements seems merely to have constituted what she described later as a "not admitting of the wound / Until it grew so wide / That all [her] Life had entered it / And there were troughs beside" (J. 1123).

Indeed, at this point in the fiction of her life, a wound has become Dickinson's ontological home, symbolic of her guilt (her "Pinching fear" of having offended "the Vision"), her powerlessness ("upon [her] little Bed"), and her retributive fate (her "Misery"). Now, therefore, she finds herself imprisoned not in night's ambiguous possibility of fulfillment but in midnight's certainty of abandonment, and she asserts that

> Doom is the House without the Door—
> 'Tis entered from the Sun—
> And then the Ladder's thrown away
> Because Escape—is done—   [J. 475]

Under the blinding gaze of noon, agoraphobia (meaning the desire for walls, for reassurance, for love and certainty) becomes claustrophobia (meaning inescapable walls, "love" transformed to limits), and the old-fashioned little girl is locked into one of the cells of darkness her God/Father seems to have prepared for her.

Buried alive, like Lucy Snowe, in the "sod gown" into which all the fantasied costumes of romance revert, Dickinson also characterizes herself as entombed, like Jane Eyre, in that "iron shroud of principle" Urizenic Nobodaddys weave for female overreachers.[37] No wonder her despairing Master letters uncannily echo Charlotte Brontë's letters to *her* "Master." We know the identity of Brontë's correspondent, and of course we know that Dickinson could not ever have read the Brontë letters. But the Englishwoman's *cris de coeur*, ostensibly addressed to Constantin Héger, a schoolmaster in Brussels, appear to be directed also, like Dickinson's letters, to that larger-than-life male Other who seemed to both these Victorian women to be the Unmoved Mover of women's fates. "To forbid me to write to you, to refuse to answer me would be to tear from me my only joy on earth, to deprive me of my last privilege—a privilege I never shall consent willingly to surrender," Brontë told Héger, and she went on to describe the ways in which her need of her master rended her.

> Believe me, *mon maitre*, in writing to me it is a good deed that you will do. So long as I believe you are pleased with me, so long as I have hope of receiving news from you, I can be at

rest and not too sad. But when a prolonged and gloomy silence seems to threaten me with the estrangement of my master— when day by day I await a letter and when day by day disappointment comes to fling me back into overwhelming sorrow, and the sweet delight of seeing your handwriting and reading your counsel escapes me as a vision that is vain, then fever claims me—I lose appetite and sleep—I pine away.[38]

Compared to Dickinson's, her prose is "unromantic as Monday morning," to quote her own description of *Shirley*'s style.[39] But though Dickinson tells the truth of her desperation more "slant," she has almost exactly the same truth to tell. Guilty, fearful, anxiously dependent on her master's approval, she too wastes and pines in its absence.

Low at the knee that bore her once unto [royal] wordless rest [now] Daisy [stoops a] kneels a culprit—tell her her [offence] fault—Master—if it is [not so] small eno' to cancel with her life, [Daisy] she is satisfied—but punish [do not] don't banish her—shut her in prison, Sir—only pledge that you will forgive —sometime—before the grave, and Daisy will not mind—She will awake in [his] your likeness.

Wonder stings me more than the Bee—who did never sting me—but made gay music with his might wherever I [may] [should] did go—Wonder wastes my pound, you said I had no size to spare.[40]

Like Brontë's, Dickinson's case seems to be hopeless, for both women are suffering from what is for an artist the worst anguish: the psychological constriction of mental slavery. It is profoundly humiliating, Brontë wrote, "to be unable to control one's own thoughts, to be the slave of a regret, of a memory, the slave of a fixed and dominant idea which lords it over the mind"[41]—the slave, in short, of romance and its plots.

Yet as both Brontë and Dickinson knew very well, those plots often signify inescapable toils for women in patriarchy. A "Master letter" by a third nineteenth-century woman writer reveals the extent to which all these talented artists were conscious of romantic coercions. Though Margaret Fuller was in 1852 to claim as "a vulgar error that love, *a* love, to Woman is her whole existence,"[42] in 1843 she drafted a fantasy letter to Beethoven, a Master letter not unlike Dickinson's drafts to her mysterious love and Brontë's letters to Constantin Héger. Here, insisting that "my lot is accursed, yes, my friend, let me curse it. . . . I have no art, in which to vent the swell of a soul as deep as thine," she went on to analyze with terrible clarity not only her imprisonment in romantic plots but the patriarchal structures she knew those plots reflected.

> Thou wouldst forgive me, Master, that I have not been true to my eventual destiny, and therefore have suffered on every side "the pangs of despised love." Thou didst the same ... but thou didst borrow from those errors the inspiration of thy genius. Why is it not thus with me? Is it because, as a woman, I am bound by a physical law, which prevents the soul from manifesting itself? Sometimes the moon seems mockingly to say so,—to say that I, too, shall not shine, unless I can find a sun. O cold and barren moon; tell a different tale, and give me a son of my own.[43]

Interestingly, the pun on *sun* and *son* which Fuller embeds in her letter illuminates imagery that was to obsess Dickinson some twenty years later. Clearly, if Dickinson had been a *son* she would not have had to enact this melodramatic and ambivalent romance with her "man of noon."

For a self-aware and volcanic talent like Dickinson's, however, as for Brontë's or Fuller's, no imprisonment could be permanent. Her claustrophobia alternated (as John Cody has suggested) with agoraphobia—or, rather, the two were necessary complements.[44] Beyond this, however, hers was a soul whose "Bandaged moments" were frequently supplanted by "moments of Escape" when, violently transcending sexual limits, "it" danced "like a Bomb, abroad," fleeing from the shadowy enclosure of female submission, passivity, and self-abnegation to the virile self-assertion of "Noon, and Paradise" (J. 512). And, as we shall see, the poet's strategies for such escape were as varied and inventive as the masks of her defeat had been. In many cases, in fact, the masks of defeat were transformed into the faces of victory.

Though Dickinson's child mask, for instance, helped imprison her in the unadmitted wound of her own life, it did at the same time save her from the unconsciousness that she saw as sealing the soul of the honorably eclipsed wife. Mothered by Awe, the childish little Pilgrim might sometimes abase herself to her distant Master in a fever of despair, but she could also transform him into a powerful muse who served *her* purposes. "Captivity is Consciousness,/So's Liberty," she noted in one poem (J. 384), and for her this was true because even in her most claustrophobic moments of defeat she refused to abandon her "first Prospective" on things. Thus in "I have a King, who does not speak" (J. 103) or "My Life had stood —a Loaded Gun" (J. 754) she celebrates the poetic inspiration her distant stately lover provides. Though he is withdrawn during the day, and though in a poem like "Why make it doubt—it hurts it so" she could not speak *to* him, in "I have a King" she triumphs by encountering him in dreams where she "peep[s]" into regal "parlors, shut by day." In "To My small Hearth His fire came" (J. 638), moreover, she describes the doorless house of "Doom"— the house of the locked-in child—transfigured by inspiration: "all my House aglow/Did fan and rock, with sudden light—" she exclaims, in a poem that transmutes emotional defeat into spiritual victory through a depiction of the poetic process. For in the light of the Master/Muse's sacred fire "Twas Noon—without the News of Night—"—what theologians would call eternity. And energized by such immortal fire, Dickinson at times sloughs off her child mask entirely and confesses—in, say, "My Life had stood—a Loaded Gun—"—that she actually speaks *for* her fiery but silent Master/ Muse, her "King who does not speak." And she speaks with Vesuvian intensity.

If Dickinson's Master is silent while she speaks, however, who is really the master and who the slave? Here her self-effacing pose as Nobody suggests levels of irony as intricately layered as the little bundles of speech that lay hidden all her life in her bureau drawer. It is of course these booklets of poetry which were the real playthings of her life, the ones she refused to drop, no matter what Requirements were imposed upon her. Our awareness of her refusal must qualify our reading of her anguished addresses to Nobodaddy, the man of noon. "Have you the little chest to put the Alive in?" she asks in the second Master letter,[45] and the childlike question is at least in part an ironic one, for it was Dickinson herself who had a modest chest full of live poems. But doesn't a little girl who "plays" by creating a whole garden of verses secretly triumph over the businesslike world of fathers and teachers and households? If so, is not the little girl really, covertly an adult, one of the Elect, even an unacknowledged queen or empress?

At times, confronting the tension between her helpless and dependent child-self (that old fashioned little girl named "Daisy") and her "Adequate—Erect" queenly self (the "woman—white" she once entitled the "Empress of Calvary") Dickinson meditated quietly upon her obscure triumph:

> And then—the size of this "small" life
> The Sages—call it small—
> Swelled—like Horizons—in my vest—
> And I sneered—softly—"small"!   [J. 271]

At other times, however, her almost inaudible sneers were replaced by angry fantasies of more thunderous speech. In "My Life had stood—a Loaded Gun—", for instance, the murderous energy of which the Gun/speaker boasts is at least as significant as the fact that she (or "it") speaks for a silent Master.

> My Life had stood—a Loaded Gun—
> In Corners—till a Day
> The Owner passed—identified—
> And carried Me away—
>
> And now We roam in Sovereign Woods—
> And now We hunt the Doe—
> And every time I speak for Him—
> The Mountains straight reply—
>
> And do I smile, such cordial light
> Upon the Valley glow—
> It is as a Vesuvian face
> Had let its pleasure through—
>
> And when at Night—Our good Day done—
> I guard My Master's Head—
> 'Tis better than the Eider-Duck's
> Deep Pillow—to have shared—

> To foe of His—I'm deadly foe—
> None stir the second time—
> On whom I lay a Yellow Eye—
> Or an emphatic Thumb—
>
> Though I than He—may longer live
> He longer must—than I—
> For I have but the power to kill,
> Without—the power to die—   [J. 754]

Certainly there is a suggestion of autonomous power in the fierce but courtly braggadocio of this smiling Gun/speaker's "Vesuvian face," and in the sinister wit of her understated "None stir the second time—/ On whom *I* lay a Yellow Eye—/ Or an emphatic Thumb—."

This Gun clearly is a poet, and a Satanically ambitious poet at that. In fact, it seems here as if the muselike Master or "Owner" may be merely a catalyst in whose presence the deadly vocabulary of the Gun/poet is activated. The irony of the riddling final quatrain, moreover, hints that it is the Gun and not the Master, the poet and not her muse, who will have the last word. For, enigmatic though these lines are, they do imply that in his humanity the Master is subject to necessities which do not control the Gun's existence. The Master, being human, *must* live, for instance, whereas the Gun, living only when "it" speaks/kills, may or may not be obliged to "live." And in his fleshliness, of course, the Master has the "power" (for which read "weakness," since power in this line means not strength but capacity) to die, while the Gun, inhumanly energized by rage and flame, has "but the power to kill"—only, that is, the immortality conferred by "its" own Vesuvian fury.

The indecorous, Satanic ferocity of this poem is illuminated when we consider the work's relationship to a verse that may possibly have been one of its sources: Sir Thomas Wyatt's "The Lover Compareth His Heart to the Overcharged Gun."

> The furious gun, in his most raging ire,
> When that the bowl is rammed in too sore,
> And that the flame cannot part from the fire,
> Cracks in sunder, and in the air do roar
> The shevered pieces. So doth my desire,
> Whose flame encreaseth ay from more to more;

Which to let out I dare not look nor speak;
So inward force my heart doth all to-break.[46]

Here, too, the conceit of the passionate self-as-gun has volcanically and angrily sexual connotations. The gun is a phallus; its explosion implies orgasm; its sexual energy is associated with "raging ire." But, interestingly enough, in Wyatt's verse the gun's fury is turned against itself. "Overcharged" (as the poem's title indicates), its "flame encreaseth ay from more to more," and eventually it becomes akin to an "inward force [which] my heart doth all to-break."

For Dickinson, on the other hand, the Gun's Vesuvian smile is directed outward, impartially killing the timid doe (a female who rose to patriarchal Requirements?), all the foes of the Muse/Master, and perhaps even, eventually, the vulnerably human Master himself. Dancing "like a Bomb" abroad, exploding out of the "sod gown," the "frame" of darkness to which her life had been "shaven and fitted," the enraged poet becomes her own weapon, her instrumentality transferred from "His Requirements" to her own needs. In a sense, the Master here is no more than the explanation or occasion for the poet's rage. Her voice, we realize, speaks sentences of death that she herself conceives. Like George Eliot's Armgart, she carries her "revenges in [her] throat," and in uttering death, dealing out "words like blades" and laying the "emphatic Thumb" of power on her Master's foes, she attains, herself, a masculine authority or, to use Simone de Beauvoir's existentialist terminology, a kind of "transcendence." For as we saw in chapter 1, de Beauvoir has perceptively commented that in those primitive societies upon which modern patriarchal civilization is still patterned "the worse curse that was laid upon woman was that she should be excluded from [the] warlike forays [of the men, since] superiority has been accorded in humanity not to the sex that brings forth but to that which kills." [47] And in this connection, in a brilliant analysis of "My Life had stood," Albert Gelpi has pointed out the intricate parallels between Dickinson's Gun and the Keatsian Romantic poet who—as in, for example, the "Ode on a Grecian Urn"—"kills" life into art.[48] Taken together, his comments and de Beauvoir's suggest that there are many ways in which this enigmatically powerful poem is an astounding assertion of "masculine" artistic freedom.

Finally, all these poems as a group suggest that the cycle of Dickinson's relationship with "Nobodaddy" is oddly similar to what Northrop Frye has called "The Orc cycle" in William Blake's poetry.[49] As in Blake's "The Mental Traveler," master and slave continually trade places, while the years wheel. At the point in the cycle represented by such poems as "My Life had stood," even Dickinson's overwhelming and previously engulfing "wound" becomes a weapon. "A *Wounded* Deer—leaps highest," she had insisted in one of her earliest verses. "'Tis but the Ecstasy of *death*—/ And then the Brake is still!" (J. 165). Her identification, then, had been with the wounded animal. In "My Life had stood," however, she turns upon that passive and suffering doe in herself and hunts her down. Yet even in the earlier poem, in the second stanza, she had spoken of "the *Smitten* Rock that gushes!/ The *trampled* Steel that springs!" In a sense, therefore, her metamorphosis into a loaded gun was to be expected. Wounds *cause* explosions: the injured deer becomes an enraged "sweet wolf," and the abused earth hisses, sooner or later, its volcanic rage. Not long after writing "A *Wounded* Deer," in fact, Dickinson noted that "those old—phlegmatic mountains / Usually so still—// Bear within—appalling Ordnance, / Fire, and smoke, and gun" (J. 175), and compared their sinister immobility to the "Volcanic" stillness "In the human face / When upon a pain Titanic / Features keep their place—." Later, transforming the human / inhuman volcano into a poet as deadly as the loaded Gun, she described an unmistakably female and violently sexual Vesuvius as

> The Solemn—Torrid—Symbol—
> The lips that never lie—
> Whose hissing Corals part—and shut—
> And Cities—ooze away—   [J. 601]

That she, Emily Dickinson—the supposed person whose history she was narrating in all these verses—had herself experienced the turbulence of the wound-as-volcano, the wound-as-Gun, is made definitively plain in "Dare you see a Soul *at the White Heat*," one of her purest and fiercest boasting poems. "Dare you see a Soul *at the White Heat*?" she challenges her reader, and commands imperiously "then crouch within the door—." Obviously "within the door" signifies, to begin with, both inside the room of the poem and inside

the room of the poet's mind. But that "smallest room" of her little
girl self has now become not just a wound, not just Nobody's claustrophobic house of Doom, like the red-room where Jane Eyre was
imprisoned, but the fiery chamber of a Loaded Gun, a bomb with
a volcano's blazing interiority. From the center of this cave of flame
the poet speaks with a priestess's oracular voice, through the "lips
that never lie," describing the smithy in which her art and her soul
are purified:

> Dare you see a Soul *at the White Heat?*
> Then crouch within the door—
> Red—is the Fire's common tint—
> But when the vivid Ore
> Has vanquished Flame's conditions,
> It quivers from the Forge
> Without a color, but the light
> Of unanointed Blaze.
> Least Village has its Blacksmith
> Whose Anvil's even ring
> Stands symbol for the finer Forge
> That soundless tugs—within—
> Refining these impatient Ores
> With Hammer, and with Blaze
> Until the Designated Light
> Repudiate the Forge—   [J. 365]

The fiery process of self-creation is painful, this poem concedes.
The forge "tugs," the flame "quivers." But significantly, Dickinson's
real emphasis here is not upon her pain but upon her triumph. The
vivid and impatient ore of which her soul is made vanquishes "Flame's
conditions," and finally, as a "Designated" or chosen light, scornfully
"repudiates" even the forge itself, as it explodes into a victory which
is both spiritual and aesthetic. For though this poem incorporates
elements of Christian allegory (the body as a purgatorial furnace
through which the soul must pass; the soul as purifying itself through
a "refiner's fire" of tribulation), Dickinson clearly intends, in the
Romantic tradition, to put the vocabulary of religion to the uses of
poetry. Like Blake's Los, she is a prophet of Imagination whose brain
is a furnace in which the gross materials of life are transformed into

both the products (the refined ore) and the powers (the designated light) of art. And that her brain's blaze is "unanointed" suggests not only that it is uncolored but that, again like Los's blaze, it is passionately secular—or at least unsanctified by traditional religion. At the same time, glowing above the forge with ghostly brilliance, Dickinson's white blaze is the sign of her soul's triumph. White is the halo she imagines around herself, and white, finally, the hue of all her costumes. For "when the vivid ore / Has vanquished Flame's conditions"—when the soul in victory generates its own light, its own art—"Bolts of Melody" quiver from its Forge with the absolute intensity of their own pure and "unanointed" energy. It is this self-creating poetic energy which makes possible what Dickinson elsewhere calls "the White Election."

The white election. The white heat. There is a sense in which the color (or uncolor) white is the key to the whole metaphorical history of Emily Dickinson as a supposed person. Certainly its ambiguities of meaning constitute a central strand in the yarn of pearl which is her life fiction. Some time in the early or mid-sixties, possibly during that equivocal *annus mirabilis* of 1862, she took to wearing her famous white dress, perhaps at first intermittently, as a costume of special import for special occasions; then constantly, so that this extraordinary costume eventually became an ordinary habit. Even before Dickinson literally dressed in white, however, she had written poems in which she figuratively clad herself in white. In 1861, for instance, she created the following self-definition:

> A solemn thing—it was—I said—
> A woman—white—to be—
> And wear—if God should count me fit—
> Her blameless mystery—
>
> A hallowed thing—to drop a life
> Into the purple well—
> Too plummetless—that it return—
> Eternity—until—
>
> I pondered how the bliss would look—
> And would it feel as big—

> When I could take it in my hand—
> As hovering—seen—through fog—
>
> And then—the size of this "small" life—
> The Sages—call it small—
> Swelled—like Horizons—in my vest—
> And I sneered—softly—"small"!   [J. 271]

Dickinson had long associated white, in other words, with size, specifically with theatrical *largesse*. And as early as 1859 she commented that although "to fight aloud, is very brave" it is "*gallanter*" to "charge within the bosom / The Cavalry of Woe—," adding that in honor of this latter, essentially female private drama (rather than in honor of a male public battle) "the Angels go— / Rank after Rank, with even feet— / And Uniforms of Snow" (J. 126).

Today a dress that the Amherst Historical Society assures us is *the* white dress Dickinson wore—or at least one of her "Uniforms of Snow"—hangs in a drycleaner's plastic bag in the closet of the Dickinson homestead. Perfectly preserved, beautifully flounced and tucked, it is larger than most readers would have expected this self-consciously small poet's dress to be, and thus reminds visiting scholars of the enduring enigma of Dickinson's central metaphor, even while it draws gasps from more practical visitors, who reflect with awe upon the difficulties of maintaining such a costume. But what exactly did the literal and figurative whiteness of this costume represent? What rewards did it offer that would cause an intelligent woman to overlook those practical difficulties? Comparing Dickinson's obsession with whiteness to Melville's, William R. Sherwood suggests that "it reflected in her case the Christian mystery and not a Christian enigma . . . a decision to announce . . . the assumption of a worldly death that paradoxically involved regeneration." This, he adds, her gown—"a typically slant demonstration of truth"—should have revealed "to anyone with the wit to catch on." [50]

We might reasonably wonder, however, if Dickinson herself consciously intended her wardrobe to convey any one message. The range of associations her white poems imply suggests, on the contrary, that for her, as for Melville, white is the ultimate symbol of enigma, paradox, and irony, "not so much a color as the visible absence of color, and at the same time the concrete of all colors." Melville's question might, therefore, also be hers: "is it for these reasons that there is such a dumb blankness, full of meaning, in a wide landscape of snows—a colorless, all-color of atheism from which we shrink?" And his concluding speculation might be hers too, his remark "that the mystical cosmetic which produces every one of [Nature's] hues, the great principle of light, for ever remains white or colorless in itself, and if operating without medium upon matter, would touch all objects . . . with its own blank tinge." [51] For white, in Dickinson's poetry, frequently represents both the energy (the white heat) of Romantic creativity, and the loneliness (the polar cold) of the renunciation or tribulation Romantic creativity may demand, both the white radiance of eternity—or Revelation—and the white terror of a shroud.

Dickinson's white is thus a two-edged blade of light associated with both flame and snow, both triumph and martyrdom. Absolute as the "universal blanc" Milton "sees" in *Paradise Lost* (3.48), it paradoxically represents both a divine intensity and a divine absence, both the innocence of dawn and the iciness of death, the passion of the bride and the snow of the virgin. From this it follows, too, that for Dickinson white also suggests both the pure potential of a *tabula rasa*, a blank page, an unlived life—"the Missing All"—and the sheer fatigue of winter, the North, a "polar expiation," that wilderness of ice where Satan's legions journey and Mary Shelley's unholy trinity meet. [52] In addition, therefore, white implies the glory of heaven and the ghastliness of hell united in a single creative/destructive principle, as in Percy Shelley's "Mont Blanc." Dramatically associated with both babies and ghosts, it is the color of the lily's foot and of the spider's thread, of the tender Daisy's petals and of the experienced Pearl's tough skin. Last, despite its importance for Melville, white was in the nineteenth century a distinctively female color, frequently chosen as emblematic by or of women for reasons Dickinson seems to have understood quite well.

The Victorian iconography of female whiteness is to begin with, most obviously related to the Victorian ideal of feminine purity. The angel in the house is a woman in white, like Milton's "late espoused saint," her dutiful chastity manifested by her virginal pallor, her marble forehead, and the metaphorical snowiness of the wings Victorian poetry imagines for her. Passive, submissive, unawakened, she has a pure white complexion which betrays no self-assertive consciousness, no desire for self-gratification. If her cheeks glow pink, they glow with the blush of innocence rather than the flush of sensuality. Ideally, even her hair (as Leslie Fiedler has noted) is celestially golden, as if to relate her further to the whiteness of heaven, that city of glitter and pearls where puritan renunciation is rewarded with spiritual silver and gold.[53]

As we have already seen, Snow White is one prototype of this angelic virgin, and, as in so many fairy tales, her name goes to the heart of the matter. For her snowiness is not just a sign of her purity but the emblem of her death, her entranced indifference to the self-assertion necessary for "real" life. Cold and still in her glass coffin, Snow White is a dead *objet d'art*, and similarly, her metaphorical cousin the snow maiden/angel in the house, as Alexander Welsh has proposed, is an angel of death, a messenger of otherness, a spirit guide who mediates between the realms of the Above and the Below.[54]

Even while the angel virgin's snowy whiteness symbolizes her purity, however, her inhuman superiority to "beastly" men, it also hints tantalizingly at her female vulnerability. In its absence of color, her childish white dress is a blank page that asks to be written on just as her virginity asks to be "taken," "despoiled," "deflowered." Thus her white dress implies that she exists only and completely for the man who will remove it. In her bridal costume she bears herself as a gift to her groom: her whiteness, vulnerability made palpable, presents itself to be stained, her intactness—her self-enclosure—to be broken, her veil to be rent.

How can a woman transcend the weakness implicit in such whiteness? As many myths and tales (including a number of Victorian novels) make clear, one way is through a further deployment of the complex symbolism of whiteness itself. For although in one sense whiteness implies an invitation, in another, it suggests a refusal, just as passivity connotes both compliance and resistance. Snow may be vulnerable to the sun but it is also a denial of heat, and the word *virginity*, because its root associates it with the word *vir*, meaning manliness or power, images a kind of self-enclosing armor, as the mythic moon-white figure of Diana the huntress tells us. For such a snow maiden, virginity, signifying power instead of weakness, is not a gift she gives her groom but a boon she grants to herself: the boon of androgynous wholeness, autonomy, self-sufficiency.

It is no wonder, then, that just as Rossetti's Maude wears white to signify her devotion to her art, Barrett Browning's Aurora Leigh wears both a self-woven crown of laurels and a maidenly white dress when she rejects her cousin Romney's marriage proposal in favor of a life dedicated to self-assertive art. "All glittering with the dawn-dew, all erect / And famished for the noon"—in Barrett Browning's cosmology as in Dickinson's a symbol of male authority—she incarnates that East which Dickinson often saw as the locus of a female paradise. Her cousin Romney mistakes her white dress for a costume of demure virginity. When he speaks of her poetic ambitions he warns her that for women such aspirations bring "headaches" and defile "the clean white morning dresses." But years later, seeing more clearly in his blindness, he recalls how at that moment "your white dress and your burnished curls / Went greatening round you in the still blue air, / As if an inspiration from within / Had blown them all out when you spoke."[55] His original "misconception" of Aurora is corrected, as it were, in his re-vision of her white dress.

But the ambiguities of the Victorian white dress extend even beyond the tension between virginal vulnerability and virginal power, though they are implicit in that tension. It is surely significant that doomed, magical, half-mad, or despairing women ranging from Hawthorne's snow-image to Tennyson's Lady of Shalott, Dickens' Miss Havisham, and Collins's Anne Catherick all wear white. Even more interestingly, each of these male-imagined fictional figures is in one way or another as analogous to the "real" Emily Dickinson as Aurora Leigh is. Certainly, if Aurora represents the healthy and assertive artist Dickinson longed to be, the Lady of Shalott seems like the mad, alienated artist—the poet *maudit*—she must at times have feared she was. Stranded on her "silent isle," the Lady is as obscure as any Massachusetts Nobody, for "who hath seen her wave her hand? / Or at the casement seen her stand? / Or is she known in all the land, / The Lady of Shalott?" Moreover, brooding beside the mirror of her art and weaving "a magic web" not unlike Dickinson's "Yarn of Pearl," the Lady becomes "half sick of shadows" and, like her New England parallel, the Myth of Amherst, she falls in love with a masterful Sir Lancelot, at which point the mirror of her art cracks "from side to side" and she lapses into a depression comparable with the state in which Dickinson wrote her despairing Master letters. "Singing her last song," therefore, she floats herself like mad Ophelia down the river to Camelot, where she is found "Lying, robed in snowy white," a *memento mori* of female helplessness, aesthetic isolation, and virginal vulnerability carried to deadly extremes.[56]

If the Lady's uniform of snow suggests the suicidal passivity implicit in Victorian femininity, the magical white gown in which Hawthorne's snow-image is clad clearly represents the garment of imagination, which inexplicably gives life even to inanimate nature in the dead of winter. Half "flying snow drift," half little girl, the imaginary child that Hawthorne's "real" children, Peony and Violet, shape out of snow bears also a distinct family relationship to Wordsworth's Lucy Gray, who dissolved *into* a snowstorm to signal her natural magic. From a female point of view, however, what is most striking about both these snowy maidens is that ultimately they are merely snow: enchanted and inanimate as their ancestress Snow White. Because this is so, they are powerless in the face of the male will that rules the public, actual world to which they simply present a charming but insubstantial alternative.

Sensitive as she was to the scorching onslaughts of her own solar Nobodaddy, Dickinson would have found the snow-image's fate particularly horrifying—a warning, perhaps, of the fate to which all female garments of imagination might sometimes seem doomed. Imprisoned in a hot parlor by an ostensibly benevolent Victorian *pater familias*, Hawthorne's snow-image melts helplessly into the hearth rug. Despite her suspicion that the snow child incarnates "what we call a miracle," the family's Victorian *mater* is just as helpless to prevent this dénouement as the image herself is. To her tactful "Husband! dear husband! . . . there is something very singular in all this," the father replies, laughing, "My dear wife . . . you are as much a child as Violet and Peony."[57] Finally, Victorian female readers must even, themselves, have begun to feel at the mercy of the male narrator, who ruthlessly puts such powerlessness to the uses of allegory. Ironically, the sadness of the "drooping and reluctant" snow child trapped beside the fiery stove of his art seems as much a matter of indifference to this aesthetic patriarch as it was to the bland and affable father his story depicted. Where one man wanted to "help" the snow girl by killing her, the other wants to help her by moralizing her. In either case, her female uniform of snow is a sign that, as a symbol of nature's magic, she is an object or problem rather than a person.

Miss Havisham's tattered bridal gown and Anne Catherick's strange white dress symbolize other phases of female vulnerability and madness that are inextricably connected with the color white. Miss Havisham, moldering in her satin wedding dress, suggests the corrupting power of romance, which entraps the yearning maiden in white satin, only, sometimes, to abandon her to imprisonment and death in that costume. (This is a fate Dickinson was to satirize in "Dropped into the Ether Acre," [J. 665] in which the white gown becomes a "Sod Gown" and the heroic "Earl" is death himself.) Like the Lady of Shalott (and like Emily Dickinson herself), Miss Havisham is suffering from unrequited love and from the overwhelming rage that inevitably accompanies the lover's rejection. Her great bridal cake, significantly, is crawling with spiders, as if to provide the dreamlike proto-Freudian imagery for such a Dickinson poem as "Alone and in a Circumstance" (J. 1167). And pacing her gloomy mansion in ghostly white, she is also strikingly like Dickinson in suffering from what seems to be severe agoraphobia: immured in her white costume, a mad nun of romance, she has "not seen the sun" for twenty years. That her dress eventually explodes into a pillar of fire suggests, finally, still another grotesque parallel with a poet who imagined herself dancing like a bomb abroad or burning with volcanic white heat.

Where Miss Havisham's costume signifies a mad clinging to romance, Anne Catherick's white dress, which gives Wilkie Collins's *The Woman in White* its title, suggests the pathos of the Victorian child-woman who clings to infancy because adulthood has never become a viable possibility. Even more than her half-sister and double, Laura Fairlie, Anne is completely dependent and naive, so much so that she falls a victim to the machinations of that imposter-patriarch Sir Percival Glide, who imprisons her (and then Laura disguised as Anne) in a madhouse. Thus, just as the snow-image's frosty garment was the key term in an elaborate allegory of female vulnerability, Anne's white dress tells a realistic story of female powerlessness—the same story Samuel Richardson told in *Clarissa*, Mary Wollstonecraft in *Maria*, Mrs. Radcliffe in *The Mysteries of Udolpho*, Maria Edgeworth in *Castle Rackrent*, Jane Austen in *Northanger Abbey*, and Emily Dickinson in her own life.

Could Dickinson's anxiety about madness—expressed in poems like "I felt a Funeral in my Brain" (J. 280)—owe anything to the madness of fictional characters like Anne Catherick, Miss Havisham, and the Lady of Shalott? Was her white dress in any sense modeled on the white costumes nineteenth-century novelists and poets assigned to such women? It seems unlikely that scholars will ever be able to establish whether Dickinson made a deliberate choice of whiteness, both as dress and metaphor, in the sense that Sherwood suggests she did. But the literary associations that clung to her metaphorical garment must have been at least as significant as the theological ones. For like Charlotte Brontë's Lucy Snowe (whose name suggests still another source for Dickinson's imagery) or like Brontë's Frances Henri (whose dwelling on the *Rue Notre Dame aux Neiges* seems equally significant), Amherst's woman in white was more a secular than a religious nun; and like both Lucy and Frances, she sometimes believed that, figuratively speaking, she was buried alive in her own society.

Finally, this concept of living burial and its corollary notion of the "living dead," both ideas encountered as often in Dickinson's mortuary poems as Poe's horror stories, suggest one further aspect of that Victorian iconography of whiteness which underlies Dickinson's metaphorical white dress. Not only in the nineteenth century, but especially in the nineteenth century, with its melodramatic elaboration of the gothic, white is the color of the dead, of ghosts and shrouds and spiritual "visitors." As Harriet Beecher Stowe sardonically noted in *Uncle Tom's Cabin*, "the common family peculiarity of the ghost tribe [is] the wearing of *a white sheet.*" And, as we saw earlier, Stowe arranges for her Cassy and Emmeline to escape from Simon Legree's oppressions by wrapping themselves in white sheets and impersonating not madwomen but the ghosts of madwomen. Might not an ironist like Dickinson have consciously or unconsciously attempted a similar impersonation? Dressing all in white, might she not have meant to indicate the death to the world of an old Emily and the birth of another Emily, a supposed person or a series of supposed persons who escaped the Requirements of Victorian reality by assuming the eccentricities of Victorian fiction? Enacting a private Apocalypse, might she not, like Aurora Leigh, be taking her "part" with "God's dead, who afford to walk in white" in order to practice the art of self-creation?[58]

Certainly, considering the proliferation of fictional Victorian women in white, there must be a sense in which Dickinson was acting out both her reading and its implications. Partly, no doubt, she did this to come to terms with the pain of that white dress in which so many nineteenth-century women were imprisoned. At the same time, however, her insistence upon her "White Election" emphasizes her feeling that she has not only been chosen by whiteness but has freely chosen it herself. Like the subject of Christina Rossetti's sonnet "A Soul"—yet another woman in white—she has chosen to stand "as pale as Parian statues stand," to stand like "a wonder deathly-white . . . patient nerved with inner might, / Indomitable in her feebleness, / Her face and will athirst against the light."[59] And like Rossetti's mysterious heroine, by defiantly gathering all the implications of Victorian whiteness into a single shape of white around her own body Dickinson announces that she herself incarnates the paradox of the Victorian woman poet—the Self disguised as the Other, the creative subject impersonating the fictionalized object—and as such she herself enacts the enigma that she perceives at the heart of her culture, just as Melville's "albino Whale" embodies the enigma nineteenth-century culture saw in nature. At the same time, paradoxically, she escapes her culture's strictures by ironically imposing them on herself. For the *eiron*, who both impersonates and stands apart from her impersonation, always triumphs over her naive interlocutors—over, for instance, the readers whom she challenges to see her self-generating soul *"at the white heat."*

That Dickinson's white dress implies not a single supposed person but a series of characters suggests, however, not just the artful complexity of her strategy for escaping Requirements but also the dangers implicit in that strategy. Impersonating simultaneously a "little maid" in white, a fierce virgin in white, a nun in white, a bride in white, a madwoman in white, a dead woman in white, and a ghost in white, Dickinson seems to have split herself into a series of incubae, haunting not just her father's house but her own mind, for, as she wrote in one of her most openly confessional poems, "One need not be a Chamber—to be Haunted" (J. 670). The ambiguities and discontinuities implicit in her white dress became, therefore, as much signs of her own psychic fragmentation as of her society's multiple (and conflicting) demands upon women. As such, they objectified the enigma of the poet's true personality—for if she was both Daisy and Empress, child and ghost, who was she "really"? In addition, and perhaps most frighteningly, they dramatized an ongoing quarrel within that enigmatic self which became the subject of much of Dickinson's most pained and painful poetry.

" 'Twas like a Maelstrom" (J. 414) and "The Soul has Bandaged Moments" (J. 512) both fictionalize this quarrel in the supposed Emily Dickinson's self as a series of confrontations with a quite gothic-sounding "Goblin." In the first, the helpless and paralyzed "You" of the poem is being tortured by a "Fiend" or "Goblin with a Gauge" until "A Creature gasped 'Reprieve'!" In the second, the "Soul" is again paralyzed and "too appalled to stir," when

> She feels some ghastly Fright come up
> And stop to look at her—
>
> Salute her—with long fingers—
> Caress her freezing hair—
> Sip, Goblin, from the very lips
> The Lover—hovered—o'er—

In both poems, but especially in the second, the "Goblin" seems to incarnate unspeakable dark ideas, "a thought so mean" in "The Soul has bandaged Moments" and "The Agony" in " 'Twas like a Maelstrom." But significantly, in both cases these ideas are embodied in a double, a goblin self within the self, not unlike the "Goblin" Bertha Mason Rochester who accosts Jane Eyre on her wedding night. And indeed, as Charlotte Brontë did in *Jane Eyre*, Dickinson indicates the integral relationship of the apparently innocent "Soul" and its goblin tormentor by noting their likeness: the "Soul" of "the Soul Has Bandaged Moments" is inexplicably a "Felon" just as the "you" of " 'Twas like a Maelstrom" seems to deserve its equally inexplicable punishment and to suffer, therefore, as much in its reprieve as it did in its tribulation. As in so many nineteenth-century gothic tales, criminal and victim, tormentor and tormented are in some sense essentially one.

That this is so, and that Dickinson herself at times consciously identified as much with the "Goblin" as with the "Soul," is made clearest in one of her most chilling dramatic monologues:

> 'Tis Sunrise—Little Maid—Hast Thou
> No Station in the Day?
> 'Twas not thy wont, to hinder so—
> Retrieve thine industry—
>
> 'Tis Noon—My little Maid—
> Alas—and art thou sleeping yet?
> The Lily—waiting to be Wed—
> The Bee—Hast thou forgot?
>
> My little Maid—'Tis Night—Alas
> That Night should be to thee
> Instead of Morning—Had'st thou broached
> Thy little Plan to Die—
> Dissuade thee, if I could not, Sweet,
> I might have aided—thee—   [J. 908]

Here the poet, as if to confess her kinship with the goblin, speaks not as the vulnerable victim she usually pretends to be but, ironically, as the murderous madwoman whom she ordinarily fears. Her tone is sepulchrally "kind," as if to parody the sinister and patronizing benevolence with which Victorian little maids were addressed by well-intentioned relatives and clergymen. Even her formal diction further impersonates and subverts Victorian pomposity, with its "thees" and "thous," its reiterated "Alas's" and its sententious circumlocutions ("Retrieve thine industry"). To this extent, indeed, the poem might have been uttered by a Brocklehurst or a St. John Rivers. But the surprise of its grotesquely suicidal/homicidal conclusion is as bleakly comical as Bertha Mason Rochester's "low, slow ha! ha!" For a parallel, we would have to look ahead one hundred years to "Lady Lazarus," Sylvia Plath's equally sardonic vignette of self-annihilation.

Considering the interior schisms Dickinson dramatizes in poems like these, it is no wonder that she felt herself the victim to be haunted by herself the villain, herself the empress haunted by herself the ghost, herself the child haunted by herself the madwoman. Confronting a murderous or, at least, inexplicably grim interior Other, she wrote a poem about her supposed self which seems almost to paraphrase Stowe's description of Simon Legree during that villain's "haunting" by Cassy and Emmeline. Here is Stowe: "What a fool is he, who locks his door to keep out spirits, who has in his own bosom a spirit he dare not meet alone."[60] And here is Dickinson, on an equally terrible haunting:

> One need not be a Chamber—to be Haunted—
> One need not be a House—
> The Brain has Corridors—surpassing
> Material Place—
>
> Far safer, of a Midnight Meeting
> External Ghost
> Than its interior Confronting—
> That Cooler Host.
>
> Far safer, through an Abbey gallop,
> The Stones a'chase—
> Than Unarmed, one's a'self encounter—
> In lonesome Place—
>
> Ourself behind ourself, concealed—
> Should startle most—
> Assassin hid in our Apartment
> Be Horror's least.
>
> The Body—borrows a Revolver—
> He bolts the Door—
> O'erlooking a superior spectre—
> Or More—   [J. 670]

Besides being confessional in the ways we have suggested, this poem is notable as literary criticism, for it indicates Dickinson's keen awareness that she was living (or, more accurately, constructing) her life as if it were a gothic romance, and it comments upon the real significance of the gothic genre, especially for women: its usefulness in providing metaphors for those turbulent psychological states into which the divided selves of the nineteenth century so often fell. In noting this, however, Dickinson also reaffirms her strong belief that a life of true poetic intensity is far more dramatic than any novelistic fiction. For "'Tis Fiction's—to dilute to Plausibility. / Our Novel— When 'tis small enough / To credit—'tisn't true!"

Certainly, as John Cody's *After Great Pain* suggests, there were agonies far more serious than any gothic thrill of horror implicit in the self-division that for a time became a major episode in Dickinson's yarn of pearl, the life story her poems narrate. Whether or not she suffered from actual psychotic breakdowns, as Cody asserts she did, she enacted the part of a madwoman in a good many poems, and over and over again her "madness" took the form we would expect it to take in a person tormented by self-haunting: the form of a chasm or gap or crack, an inexplicable spatial or temporal discontinuity, felt at the very center of being. In the enigmatic confession that begins "The first Day's Night had come," this heart of darkness actually becomes an incapacitating gulf between one self and another. "I told my Soul to sing," the poet notes, but

> She said her Strings were snapt—
> Her bow—to atoms blown—
> And so to mend her—gave me work
> Until another Morn—

But despite the attempt at mending, the Soul's fragmentation seems here to be complete, leading Dickinson finally to articulate her fears of madness:

> My Brain—begun to laugh—
> I mumbled—like a fool—
> And tho' 'tis years ago—that Day—
> My Brain keeps giggling—still.
>
> And Something's odd—within—
> That person that I was—
> And this One—do not feel the same—
> Could it be Madness—this?   [J. 410]

As in so much of Dickinson's verse of 1862, the psychic rending
described in this poem is mirrored in a style heavily interrupted by
ambiguous punctuation marks, each seeming to represent a chasm
of breath between one phrase and the next. Defining herself as a
madwoman, "Horror's twin," the speaker hesitates to tell all, then
blurts out her fears in a rhythm indicated by those enigmatic dashes
which dot her monologue almost like notations on an actress' rehearsal
script. As in the Master letters, they seem to indicate rending pauses,
silences like wounds in the midst of speech, critical "fracture
within." [61] But here the rending results from a series of interior explosions rather than from injuries inflicted by an indifferent or
malevolent Nobodaddy.

In "I felt a Funeral in my Brain" Dickinson tries more precisely
to define the process whereby "that person that I was" was ripped
away from "this One." To begin with, she describes her brain being
invaded by a host of alien beings, much as her life and art had been
invaded. Here, however, instead of representing the range of roles
she had assigned herself (the virgin bride, the little maid, the empress,
etc.), all are mourners, as if to emphasize what she perceives as the
terrible reiteration of defeat in her own experience. Finally she hears
these mourning doubles "lift a Box / And creak across my Soul" and
"Then Space—began to toll,"

> As all the Heavens were a Bell,
> And Being, but an Ear,
> And I, and Silence, some strange Race
> Wrecked, solitary, here—
>
> And then a Plank in Reason, broke,
> And I dropped down, and down—
> And hit a World, at every plunge,
> And Finished knowing—then—   [J. 280]

Besides being all the mourners, this conclusion implies, she is the
occupant of the box, the dead and therefore alienated representative
of the Race of Silence, and thus as in the more famous "I heard a
Fly buzz—when I died" (J. 465), which also treats this theme, she
enacts now that ultimate moment of separation for which all her
life's severings have been merely preparations. Where "I heard a
Fly buzz" imagines that moment as the instant of death, however,

"I felt a Funeral," in the gothic tradition, images it as the moment of living burial. As the box is lowered—bells tolling, boots creaking, silence invading the crevices—the dead-alive soul drops "down and down" into oblivion. Significantly, its final descent is triggered by the breaking of "a Plank in Reason." Death, here as in much of Dickinson's other poetry, is ultimately a metaphor for madness, specifically for the madness attendant upon psychic alienation and fragmentation.

To the extent that this is so, however, the image of living burial Dickinson elaborates here, like Charlotte Brontë's image of living burial in *Villette*, like some of Emily Brontë's dungeon poems, or like Dickinson's own "One need not be a Chamber—to be Haunted," again conveys a highly conscious literary comment upon the gothic tradition and its psychic implications.[62] At the same time, moreover, the metaphorical equation of death/fragmentation/madness comments upon a form nineteenth-century mortuary verse took over and over again, what we might call the "Voice from beyond the grave" convention, upon which so many Victorian "lady" poets in particular relied. Such poetry, Dickinson seems to be suggesting here, really speaks of the condition of the living rather than that of the dead, for it describes the living burial of those who have been denied a viable place in the life of their society. Excluded, alienated, like a tragic version of Austen's Anne Elliot in *Persuasion*, such a person experiences the profound anomie which in moments of metaphysical anxiety we suppose must be the feeling of the dead. She speaks and no one listens. She falls and no one notices. She buries herself and no one cares. Nameless, invisible, shrouded in snow, she is once again the ultimate Nobody, for—having "Finished knowing" —she imagines that she has lost even the minimal signs of life a body provides.

That such an apparently gothic narrative of living burial as "I felt a Funeral" really tells a story of psychic fragmentation is made clearer when we compare this poem to "I felt a Cleaving in my Mind," a kind of revisionary companion piece apparently written three years later.

> I felt a Cleaving in my Mind—
> As if my Brain had split—

> I tried to match it—Seam by Seam—
> But could not make them fit.
>
> The thought behind, I strove to join
> Unto the thought before—
> But Sequence ravelled out of Sound
> Like Balls—upon a Floor.   [J. 937]

In addition to the parallel structure of their opening lines and their common use of a mental landscape, images of breaking ("My Brain had split," "A Plank in Reason broke") and symbolic dramatizations of silence ("Sequence ravelled out of Sound," "I and Silence some strange Race") link these two poems. But the later work is far more frank in its admission that madness is its true subject, and that psychic fragmentation—an inability to connect one self with another—is the cause of this madness. Here, too, Dickinson's use of both spatial and temporal terminology most openly confronts the overwhelming, all-pervasive nature of the internal discontinuity she is describing. The supposed person who speaks this confession is split because she perceives herself as having several simultaneous personalities, which do not "fit" or "match" each other. But she is also split because she cannot join past and present thoughts: "that person" that she was and "this One" do not "feel the same—." Like Catherine Earnshaw Linton, she does not recognize her original self in the mirror of her own life. No longer what she was, she cannot act the part of the person she supposedly is.

Finally, then, in "This Chasm, Sweet, upon my Life," an extraordinary, almost surrealistic narrative, Dickinson examines the heart of darkness itself, that gap or chasm at the center of her being which widens with each cleaving of the mind, each funeral in the brain, over and over again separating self from self, past from present, sequence from reason. But where "I felt a Cleaving" and "I felt a Funeral" were both hectic, even melodramatic in their approach to this chasm, her tone here is both ironic and sinister, even, as in " 'Tis Sunrise—Little Maid," bleakly comic. If " 'Tis Sunrise—Little Maid" subtly parodied the sermonizing of a Brocklehurst or St. John Rivers, however, "This Chasm" sardonically parodies the saccharine love poetry that ladies were expected to write. Indeed, addressing a mysterious interlocutor as "Sweet" and "Darling," the speaker might even be the dead Little Maid herself, now transformed into a dutiful but suicidal bride, demurely replying to her Master/Lover's censorious questions.

> This Chasm, Sweet, upon my life
> I mention it to you,
> When Sunrise through a fissure drop
> The Day must follow too.
>
> If we demur, its gaping sides
> Disclose as 'twere a Tomb
> Ourself am lying straight wherein
> The Favorite of Doom.
>
> When it has just contained a Life
> Then, Darling, it will close
> And yet so bolder every Day
> So turbulent it grows
>
> I'm tempted half to stitch it up
> With a remaining Breath
> I should not miss in yielding, though
> To Him, it would be Death—
>
> And so I bear it big about
> My Burial—before
> A Life quite ready to depart
> Can harass me no more—   [J. 858]

What specifically is the chasm this poem describes? To begin with, it is a fissure into which "Sunrise" drops, like the morning on which the Little Maid is found dead. Thus, too, it is a metaphorical well or pool of despair that swallows such hopes as the one that dawn-goddess Aurora Leigh represented. Indeed, if the speaker in any of her avatars attempts to escape its devouring darkness ("if we demur") it yawns wider to disclose "Ourself"—that is, the many selves of the poet, packed into one dead figure—"lying straight wherein / The Favorite of Doom."

To be the Favorite of Doom, however, is to be the mistress or beloved of that ultimate Nobodaddy, Death, the "supple Suitor" whose "pallid innuendos" suggest, among other things, Victorian patriarchy's urge to silence women, to dress them in uniforms of snow and bury them alive in mansions of shadow.[63] Rage is therefore the speaker's response to her discovery that all her selves have been locked into a single chasm, paradoxically both containing and contained by her being. No matter how she tries to silence the protesting "Life" within her (that is, within the chasm that is within her), it grows bolder and more turbulent every day, like some monstrous embryo that continually increases in strength and autonomy. And indeed, one of the extraordinary features of this extraordinary and dreamlike narrative is its elaboration of what seems quite clearly to be a conceit of pregnancy. For in a sort of sexual congress with his "Favorite," Doom or Death does appear to have engendered a bold and turbulent child, a child whose burial in the chasm of the poet's flesh objectifies the poet/speaker's own living death, so that she "bear[s] it big about / My Burial—before." She bears before her, in other words, in place of a healthily fruitful womb, a womb that contains the ambiguous burden of a turbulent dead-alive child-self which represents both a burden she must carry *until* she is buried and her own untimely burial *before* her death.[64]

In one sense, the speaker of "This Chasm" is, again, analogous to Catherine Earnshaw Linton, this time in carrying a child/double whose final birth will signal her own death. In another sense, she is like Jane Eyre in being doomed to carry everywhere a wailing orphan self which "I might not lay . . . down anywhere . . . however much its weight impeded my progress."[65] Unlike both Jane and Catherine, though, this demure Little Maid has a mad "little plan" for closing the rift in her life that her child/double inhabits: she is tempted to "stitch" up the hole in her being with a "remaining Breath" she herself "should not miss in yielding" although to her child/double "it would be Death." For it seems to her here that the only way she can both abort her monstrous pregnancy and heal her own terrifying fragmentation is by committing suicide, since in death itself, as opposed to death-in-life, she believes there would be a return to oneness, an escape from the rending consciousness of interior turbulence, and a silence of those hissing, volcanic "lips that never lie." A life that has departed the anxious flesh, she suggests ironically, like an embryo "quite ready to depart" from its mother's body, can no longer "harass" its owner.

The chasm in being that Dickinson perceives turns out, then, to be her own life, and specifically the female body in which she is helplessly (but turbulently) embedded. She herself is "Doom ... the House without the Door," for it is in her own body, her own self, that her many selves are imprisoned or buried; she is their grave, tomb, and prison. Finally, because she sees herself as such a tomb or prison, a sort of personified Chillon, she imagines herself in poem after poem inhabited by "Dilapidation's processes," by cobwebs "on the soul," and by—besides her various human selves—the many scuttling and furtive creatures of decay: the rat ("the concisest Tenant"), the mouse ("Grief is a Mouse"), the worm ("Pink, lank, and warm"), and the spider (the "Neglected Son of Genius").[66] Like Byron's prisoner, she sometimes grimly diverts herself with the antics of these creatures (in, for instance, early poems like "Papa above"). But often, like Poe, she becomes a raconteur of disgust, as she describes her encounters with horrifyingly inhuman incubi.

"Alone and in a Circumstance" is the most chilling of her narratives on this subject. Noting that once when she was "Alone and in a Circumstance / Reluctant to be told / A spider on my reticence / Assiduously crawled," she reveals that her "late abode" has since become "a Gymnasium" in which these sinister, silently spinning "inmates of the Air / Perpetual presumption took / As each were special Heir." Worse still, she confesses, she can find no way to evict these unwanted tenants, for—as we might suspect—their invasion represents an injustice too profound to be redressed:

> If any take my property
> According to the Law
> The Statute is my Learned friend
> But what redress can be
> For an offense nor here nor there
> So not in Equity—
> That Larceny of time and mind
> The marrow of the Day
> By spider, or forbid it Lord
> That I should specify.   [J. 1167]

Like that "slipping" toward death, that "ruin" which is "crash's Law," Dickinson's spiders represent here a natural process or law against which human decrees are powerless. In addition, as the inhabitants of a chasm upon the life of "a woman—white," they are akin to the monstrous child/double who was the "Favorite of Doom." At the same time, however, they are themselves the messengers of a particularly female doom: the doom of sterility which is the price virgin whiteness exacts.

That Dickinson was consciously or unconsciously using spiders in this poem to symbolize such a fatal "Larceny of time and mind" is suggested by the strength of the longstanding mythic tradition which associates virgin women—women who spin, or spin/sters—with spinning spiders. As spinsters, indeed, such women are often defined as themselves being spiders, duplicitous witchlike weavers of webs in which to ensnare men (like Circe), metaphysical spinners of Fate (like the Norns), and fictionalizing weavers or plotters of doom (like so many of George Eliot's characters and, as we have seen, like Eliot herself). But also, as virgins of long standing, free from male attachments, such women have often been seen as empty vessels (or chasms) filled with disquieting shadows. Meditating on myths about the second sex, Simone de Beauvoir brilliantly summarizes this folkloric tradition which depicts the transformation of a "woman —white" from a little maid into an old maid by peopling her body with spiders and spiderlike presences:

> ... virginity has ... erotic attraction only if it is in alliance with youth; otherwise its mystery again becomes disturbing. Many men of today feel a sexual repugnance in the presence of maidenhood too prolonged; and it is not only psychological causes that are supposed to make "old maids" mean and embittered females. The curse is in their flesh itself, that flesh which is object for no subject, which no man's desire has made desirable, which has bloomed and faded without finding a place in the world of men; turned from its proper destination, it becomes an oddity, as disturbing as the incommunicable thought of a madman. Speaking of a woman of forty, still beautiful, but presumably virgin, I have heard a man say coarsely: "It must be full of spiderwebs inside." And, in truth, cellars and attics, no longer entered, of no use, become full of unseemly mystery; phantoms will likely haunt them; abandoned by people, houses become the abode of spirits. Unless feminine virginity has been

dedicated to a god, one easily believes that it implies some kind of marriage with the demon. Virgins unsubdued by man, old women who have escaped his power, are more easily than others regarded as sorceresses; for the lot of women being bondage to another, if she escapes the yoke of man she is ready to accept that of the devil.[67]

As the "Wife—without the Sign," Dickinson evidently kept her virgin snow "intact," and so she was "Born—Bridalled—Shrouded—In a Day." Dead to the world, she seems often to have imagined the house of Doom that was her self as alternately roaring with explosive fragments and veiled in silent cobwebs. But at the same time, despite the stress of her conflicting fictions, it was finally a spiderlike sorcery that helped her sew her scattered selves together into a single yarn of pearl. For if the spinster/spider symbolized sexual decay, she/he was also, for Dickinson, a crucial if "neglected" emblem of art, and of the artist as the most triumphant secret self.

It is, of course, the spider who unwinds a yarn of pearl, as J. 605 tells us:

> The Spider holds a Silver Ball
> In unperceived Hands—
> And dancing softly to Himself
> His Yarn of Pearl—unwinds—

That he has "unperceived Hands" (meaning unperceived *art*) associates this insect artist with Nobody, who tells her name in silence to herself alone, rather than pompously declaring it to "an admiring Bog." Because his achievement is unperceived, therefore—given the terms of Dickinson's world—the spider is as female in reticence as "he" is in his "insubstantial Trade" of spinning. That he dances softly to himself again emphasizes his reticence, and reminds us also that dancing, like spinning or weaving, was another one of Dickinson's metaphors for art, and especially for female art. Not long before she described the spider's dance, she wrote of her own in very similar terms:

> I cannot dance upon my Toes—
> No Man instructed me—
> But oftentimes among my mind,
> A Glee possesseth me,
>
> That had I Ballet Knowledge—
> Would put itself abroad
> In Pirouette to blanch a Troupe—
> Or lay a Prima, mad.

Like the spider, this poem says, she is a virtually invisible dancer; but like his, her dancing represents the secret triumph of her art. For, unlike the dance of the Queen in "Little Snow White," Dickinson's "ballet" is not suicidal but gleeful, not public and humiliating, but private and proud:

> Nor any know I know the Art
> I mention—easy—Here—
> Nor any Placard boast me—
> It's full as Opera—   [J. 326]

Again, the fact that the spider's yarn is of pearl suggests in Dickinson's symbol-system both the paradoxical secrecy of his triumph and the female nature of his trade. For when the dutiful girl of "She rose to His Requirements" took up "the honorable Work / Of Woman, and of Wife," we should remember, the part of her that yearned for Amplitude and Awe was carefully associated with a silent, secretive sea which develops "Pearl and Weed," though "only to Himself—be known / The Fathoms they abide." Taken together, then, all these poems seem to say that, as Dickinson defines it, female art must almost necessarily be secret art; mental pirouettes silently performed in the attic of Nobodaddy's house, the growth of an obscure underwater jewel, or, especially, a spider's unobtrusively woven yarn of pearl.[68]

That in J. 605 the spider "plies from Nought to Nought— / In insubstantial Trade" and finally dangles "from the Housewife's Broom— / His boundaries forgot," suggests, however, the ambiguous nature of his enterprise and the female art it represents. On the one hand, connecting nothing with nothing, he weaves an "insubstantial" spiritual net—a "Continen[t] of Light"—that holds the fragmented world together, if only for a moment of pearly epiphany. On the other hand, the evanescence of his tapestry, its enclosure in a parenthesis of Noughts, and its vulnerability to the censorious "Housewife's Broom," indicate a flicker of Dickinsonian pessimism, or at least of irony, about the immortality of the art her spider's web represents. The continents of light spun out in secret poems are meant to be discovered and admired, after all. What, then, if unsympathetic male editors and female heirs should sweep them efficiently away with all the other detritus of a forgotten, unimportant life?

Though she did have moments of literary uncertainty, even of despair, Dickinson seems to have been fundamentally sure that this would not be so. Despite (or perhaps, as we shall see, because of) the psychic fragmentation implicit in the many costumes she wore as "a woman—white," she was profoundly confident that the spider-artist spinning his yarn of pearl in the dark chasm of her life would triumph in mysterious ways:

> A Spider sewed at Night
> Without a Light
> Upon an Arc of White.
>
> If Ruff it was of Dame
> Or Shroud of Gnome
> Himself himself inform.
>
> Of Immortality
> His Strategy
> Was Physiognomy.   [J. 1138]

As Albert Gelpi has pointed out in an excellent discussion of this poem's American context, the spider here, like the spider who "holds a Silver Ball," "is Emily Dickinson's emblem for the craftsman spinning from within himself his sharply defined world." [69] But as in the earlier poem, Dickinson's emblem is specifically of a crafts-*woman*, a spin/ster or seamstress or tapestry weaver. In striking ways, moreover, this seamstress corresponds precisely to Dickinson herself. In fact, we might speculate that in this poem, more than in any other, Dickinson casts off disguises to reveal the true artist behind the "woman—white." This artist, spider-silent, sews in the privacy and obscurity of the night, partly, we might guess, because s/he has "no Station in the day." Since she has been rended and rejected by the man of noon, midnight is her home. In addition, however, she sews at night because it is chiefly in dreams, and in the visionary night-world of madness and imagination, that she encounters the muse who is her ultimate Master, her "King who does not speak." And finally, because s/he is a denizen of the night, this spider artist can sew fine stitches in the dark, without even a light, except perhaps the inner radiance s/he herself casts upon the "Arc of White" that is her material.

That "Arc of White" hardly needs analysis here, since it is so plainly the material out of which Dickinson created her own character as a woman white. Thus it has all the connotations that we noted earlier in connection with whiteness: it is snow and *tabula rasa*, tribulation and triumph, pearl and—here—paradoxical light in darkness. But what garment does the spider sew from this insubstantial substance? A uniform of snow? A spangled gown? Here Dickinson reveals the strategy of her own yarn of pearl. Hers, she suggests, is a fiction of multiplicity which artistically adopts numerous roles and, even more artfully, settles for none.

Nevertheless, the particular costumes she mentions are significant, for of all her guises they may be the two about which she felt most intensely: "Ruff of Dame" and "Shroud of Gnome." Over and over again, in poems and letters, Dickinson defined herself as a *grande dame*, a queen, an empress. In a sense, then, her poetry—the web of art she wove at night—constituted the Elizabethan ruff that distinguished her costume from those less royal. Even in her queenliness, however, she saw herself also as a tiny enigma, a magical Nobody, an elfin messenger from seas of Amplitude and Awe—that is, as a gnome. "Your Gnome," indeed, was how she signed one of her letters to Higginson.[70] Fearing, therefore, that her often gnomic poetry would be lost, misunderstood, undervalued, she might well have worried that rather than a royal ruff of light for her queenly self, it might become merely a shroud of obscurity for her gnomic self.

That neither she nor her spider artist chooses to choose aloud between shroud and ruff does not mean, however, that poet and spider do not know the purpose of their sewing. The spider knows at every moment which disguise he quite consciously chooses to assume. He himself continually informs himself of his plans. Informing himself in the ordinary sense of the word, moreover, he also, as Gelpi points out, punningly informs himself "in the sense of 'giving form' to a projected image of himself." Or, more accurately, herself. For as Gelpi also notes, "there are two poets" present in this fable of the spider artist, poets whom we would define as, on the one hand, the public poet—the ever-changing "woman—white" clad in that flux of pearl she herself weaves out of words—and the changeless private poet—the silent and deliberate spider who weaves a ruff or shroud of language for her supposed self.[71]

It is about this latter poet that Dickinson is surely speaking when she asserts that "Of Immortality / His strategy / Was Physiognomy," although, like the rest of this crucial poem, that last assertion is significantly ambiguous. Most obviously, the spider's strategy for capturing immortality—the net "he" casts to catch a divine wind— is made of that yarn of pearl he draws from his own body, "the design spun of and from himself to outwit night and death."[72] In this sense, the spider artist is like the bird in "Sang from the Heart, Sir" (J. 1059) whose "Tune" may "drip too much / Have a tint too Red" because she dipped her beak into her own heart to find color for her song. But where the "confessional" bird dramatically bleeds and suffers (and is thus another public version of the poet), the spider is private, silent, and barely visible. Where the bird flutteringly admits to errors—like "a tint too Red"—the spider is a master tactician whose strategy no doubt includes (but is not limited to) the self-deprecations of the bird.

For, as "Physiognomy," the spider's strategy differs, of course, from mere "physiology," which is what the bird's bloody song depends upon. Besides arising from the body or physique, "physiognomy," punning upon "gnome" and "gnomic," suggests enigmas and mysteries; it hints at a "slant" embodiment of the self, a deliberate reliance upon the ambiguous clothing of ruffs which may also be shrouds. According to official definitions, moreover, "Physiognomy" is the science of character, as expressed in outward and especially facial features:

1. the practice of trying to judge character and mental qualities by observation of bodily, esp. facial features. 2. the face; facial features and expression, especially as supposedly indicative of character. 3. apparent characteristics; outward features or appearances.[73]

The spider artist's use of this externalization of character is not to help him/her judge the characters of others; rather—or so the poem implies—his strategy for immortality is to weave a web of varying characters, a net of masks, to attract and entrap lasting fame. In this respect, therefore, he is most like Emily Dickinson, the private poet, carefully contriving a multitude of different fictional faces for her "woman—white," all designed to entangle and devour the attention of the future. "I have a horror of death; the dead are so soon forgotten," Dickinson supposedly once said. "But when I die, they'll have to remember me." What they would have to remember, she must have meant, was the elaborate, fictionalized tapestry of her life that she wove in her poems, a tapestry in which each poem was in a sense a face prepared to meet the faces she imagined she might meet. What they would have to remember, she must have meant too, was the way in which, as a woman artist, she used—to paraphrase William Blake—the productions of time to seduce eternity.

If Dickinson's female spider artist suggests her deliberate elaboration of an aesthetic of artifice, that same spider implies also her commitment to another central female metaphor: sewing. And like almost all the Dickinson symbols and figures we have been examining, this metaphor is ambiguous, simultaneously positive and negative, like the spider's ruff and shroud. Suicidally stitching up the chasm of her life "with a breath," for instance, was one kind of sewing Dickinson imagined. But, as a strategy for mending fragmentation, that was closer to the bleeding bird's public melodrama than to the spider's careful plotting. Angrily sardonic, such a stitching would be a theatrical gesture performed "in broad daylight," like the magical self-immolation of Plath's Lady Lazarus. By contrast, the spider's sewing really does function to mend or heal fragmentation in a positive way. Where the stitching of suicide simply gathers the poet's scattered selves into the uniform snow of death, the spider artist's artful stitching connects those fragments with a single self-developed and self-developing yarn of pearl. The stitch of suicide is a stab or puncture, like a "stitch in the side." The stitch of art is provident and healing, "a stitch in time." Stabbing, wounding, the stitch of suicide paradoxically represents not just a unifying but a further rending. Healing, the stitch of art is a bridge. The death that precipitated the funeral of "I felt a Funeral in my Brain" may well have been caused by the stabbing stitch of suicide or despair, "a weight with Needles on the pounds," as Dickinson characterizes it in another poem. But the cleaving of "I felt a Cleaving in my Mind" and the chasm of "This Chasm, Sweet," are patched and mended, seam to seam, by the magical stitchery of art.

In a sense, indeed, we might say that as a private spider artist Dickinson employs her yarn of pearl to resolve her quarrelsomely fragmented public selves—the nun and the gnome, the virgin and the empress—into a single woman pearly white. But in addition the filaments of thought flung out by what Whitman would have called her "noiseless patient spider" self must also have helped her bridge the gap between the polar loneliness of that privacy in which she invented her selves, and the more populous and tropical air in which she enacted the melodramatic fictions those selves embodied. Finally, as the principal activity through which her creative demon expressed itself, it was the metaphorical sewing of art—a single, all absorbing process—which contrived all the superficially different costumes in which those selves clad themselves for their encounter with immortality.

Not all Dickinson's sewing was metaphorical, however. Like almost all women, always, but especially like all nineteenth-century women in England and America, she must have been as proficient with needle and thread as she was with spoon and pot. Then, more than now, spinsters might often actually spin; matrons really represented the "distaff side"; young girls worked "samplers," old women knitted, and talented women of all ages embroidered, quilted, made lace, did needlepoint, and other "fancy work," maybe even—like some women in the Middle Ages—wove tapestries. The motherless Brontë girls, Winifred Gérin tells us, were kept at their sewing many hours a day every day by their puritanical Aunt Branwell. Similarly, as if to mirror that episode, Barrett Browning has mother-less Aurora Leigh's aunt insist that she learn "cross-stitch, because she did not like / To see me wear the night with empty hands." And in 1862, Emily Dickinson, perhaps beginning to experience the mysterious eye trouble that sent her to Boston for treatment in 1864 and 1865, wrote a poem that began

> Don't put up my Thread and Needle—
> I'll begin to Sew
> When the Birds begin to Whistle—
> Better stitches—so—
>
> These were bent—my sight got crooked—
> When my mind—is plain
> I'll do seams—a Queen's endeavor
> Would not blush to own—   [J. 617]

The poem goes on to discuss "Hems—too fine for lady's tracing" and "Tucks—of dainty interspersion." But literal seams, hems, and tucks were not the only notable products of Dickinson's thread and needle. Far more notable, indeed, are the fascicles into which she literally sewed and bound her poems themselves. As we suggested earlier, these were in one sense modest play books, a little girl's toy imitations of the "real" works male writers produced, like those tiny books the Brontë children contrived.[74] But even the modesty of the Brontës' childish volumes was deceptive. Angria and Gondal, after all, concealed volcanic fantasies of autonomous power. How much more deceptive, then, were Dickinson's slim booklets! As an adult and highly conscious literary seamstress, she knew exactly what she was sewing, and why. She knew, for instance, that when "a Spider sewed at Night," the ruff or shroud into which "he" stitched "an Arc of White" was not only figuratively her poetry but actually the packets into which she stitched her finished verses.

That those verses *were* finished, and that Dickinson herself regarded her sewing as an arcane but viable form of self-publication, becomes very clear to anyone who examines the packet manuscripts them-selves. To say, as Thomas Johnson does, that all of them contain "fair copies" is to understate the case,[75] so smoothly flowing and tidy is their holograph, so professional are the marginal notes that indicate variant readings. Even those famous dashes—meant, we have speculated, to indicate rifts and rendings, hesitations and pauses—appear neater and more soigné in manuscript than in type. Tiny and clear, they are elegant as "Tucks—of dainty interspersion," fine stitches joining split thoughts seam to seam. It is almost as if, in the absence of editor or printer, Dickinson had both edited and printed herself, like some late-blooming scribe. Thus her definitive editorial mark is her needle's mark, the mark that says the scribe's work is completed and the poem has been chosen for binding and storage—that is, for posterity—and chosen, perhaps, as Ruth Miller has argued, to take a specific place in a coherently conceived sequence.[76] In a sense, sewn upon an arc of white, each of these sequences may have been intended, also, as an ark of white to bear the poet's thoughts out upon the flood of immortality, for as she herself noted, "There is no Frigate like a Book" (J. 1263) to carry the soul to survival.

That male editors and female heirs undid Dickinson's stitching and thus, in effect, refragmented the fragments she had made whole is one of the ironies of literary history, but it is an irony the poet herself might have foreseen. Not only her sewing but her poems about sewing indicate she was a conscious literary artist, anxious to communicate, though on her own terms. But she was troubled by the imperfect stitches she feared she made when her sight got "crooked" and her mind was no longer "plain." Refusing to abandon her apparently irregular meters, the "bells whose jingling cooled my tramp," she nevertheless ruefully admitted to Higginson that "all men say 'what' to me," and "I have no Tribunal."[77]

As we have seen throughout this volume, such failures of comprehension have more often than not been the fate of women writers in England and America. That, like Dickinson, many of these women responded to male "whats" by turning to such a silently subversive art as Dickinson's literal and figurative stitchery implies a further irony of literary history. For the art that began as a defense against misunderstanding or hostility often, in the end, became a screen obscuring meaning. Nevertheless, both in the subtle subversiveness of her sewing and in the striving toward wholeness her sewing expressed, Dickinson was enacting and exploiting a traditional metaphor for the female artist. Like Ariadne, Penelope, and Philomela, women have used their looms, thread, and needles both to defend themselves and silently to speak of themselves. Like Mary Shelley, gathering the Sibyl's scattered leaves in *The Last Man*, they have sewed to heal the wounds inflicted by history. Like Mrs. Ramsay in *To the Lighthouse*, they have knitted to fend off the onslaughts of Urizen. Like Mrs. Dalloway, they have sewed "hems too fine for Lady's tracing" to hide the pain at the heart of their lives. Like Adrienne Rich, they have worked to mend "this trailing knitted thing, this cloth of darkness / This woman's garment, trying to save the skein."[78]

For all these women, though, sewing both conceals and reveals a vision of a world in which such defensive sewing would not be necessary. This was especially true of Emily Dickinson. To take her spider metaphor one step further, we might say that inside the brain of the spider artist who dwelt inside the chasm in Dickinson's life, there was a vision of a magic place, a "Tapestry of Paradise" (J. 278), whose image she knew she was weaving with her pearly sorcery. In this paradise, the woman artist would not be a subversive spider who disguises herself and her meaning in webs of obscurity, but a naked and shining figure. Here, no longer obliged to sew at night in the polar loneliness of "the North," she would finally "live aloud," singing and dancing in the dawn sun of "the East." In poem after poem Dickinson notes that male poets, whose "Summer—lasts a Solid Year," have always inhabited such a realm of gold (J. 569). But the female spider artist's "Continents of Light" were inevitably swept away by puritanical brooms. Concealed in "Lady's drawer," however, the spinster's packets continue to express the perfume of her longing. Secretly triumphing, they will "Make Summer—When the Lady lie / In Ceaseless Rosemary—" (J. 675).

The paradise her packets shadowily depict, however, is one Emily Dickinson yearned to inhabit openly, from the silent beginning of her elaborately camouflaged poetic career to its silent end. One of the earliest poems she chose to sew into a packet speaks in greatest detail about the place and its inhabitants:

> There is a morn by men unseen—
> Whose maids upon remoter green
> Keep their Seraphic May—
> And all day long, with dance and game,
> And gambol I may never name—
> Employ their holiday.
>
> Here to light measure, move the feet
> Which walk no more the village street—
> Nor by the wood are found—
> Here are the birds that sought the sun
> When last year's distaff idle hung
> And summer's brows were bound.
>
> Ne'er saw I such a wondrous scene—
> Ne'er such a ring on such a green—
> Nor so serene array—
> As if the stars some summer night
> Should swing their cups of Chrysolite—
> And revel till the day—
>
> Like thee to dance—like thee to sing—
> People upon the mystic green—
> I ask, each new May Morn.
> I wait thy far, fantastic bells—
> Announcing me in other dells—
> Unto the different dawn!   [J. 24]

If, as Simone de Beauvoir convincingly speculates, a virgin woman like Emily Dickinson may seem to be inhabited by spiders and sorcery, this powerful vision explains her commitment to virginity, "the marriage with the demon" within herself that is the strength behind her sorcery.

Other women artists also had such visions of a natural paradise. Emily Brontë wrote of "rocky dells" and "silent moors." Jane Austen gave her Catherine Morland a wild, free, romping girlhood in green meadows. Charlotte Brontë's Lucy Snowe dreamed in a secret garden. And Elizabeth Barrett Browning imagined a room of her own for the adolescent Aurora Leigh which suggested such a garden and which indirectly explained the girl's growth into passionate poetry. "I had a little chamber in the house," Aurora confides,

> As green as any privet-hedge a bird
> Might choose to build in, though the nest itself
> Could show but dead-brown sticks and straws. The walls
> Were green; the carpet was pure green; the straight
> Small bed was curtained greenly; and the folds
> Hung green about the window, which let in
> The outdoor world with all its greenery.
> You could not push your head out, and escape
> A dash of dawn-dew from the honeysuckle,
> But so you were baptized into the grace
> And privilege of seeing. . . .

Similarly, in "From House to Home," Christina Rossetti imagined herself dwelling in a paradisal mystic green place that was even closer to Dickinson's in being a muse-inhabited haunt of song, an innocent interior Eden.

> My pleasaunce was an undulating green,
>   Stately with trees whose shadows slept below,
> With glimpses of smooth garden-beds between,
>   Like flame or sky or snow.
>
> Swift squirrels on the pastures took their ease,
>   With leaping lambs safe from the unfeared knife;
> All singing-birds rejoicing in those trees
>   Fulfilled their careless life.
>
>   . . . .
>
> My heath lay farther off, where lizards lived
>   In strange metallic mail, just spied and gone;
> Like darted lightnings here and there perceived
>   But nowhere dwelt upon.
>
> Frogs and fat toads were there to hop or plod
>   And propagate in peace, an uncouth crew,
> Where velvet-headed rushes rustling nod
>   And spill the morning dew.

. . . .

Ofttimes one like an angel walked with me,
   With spirit-discerning eyes like flames of fire,
But deep as the unfathomed endless sea
   Fulfilling my desire:
. . . .

We sang our songs together by the way,
   Calls and recalls and echoes of delight;
So communed we together all the day,
   And so in dreams by night.[79]

Both Barrett Browning and Rossetti, however, felt that they must renounce these paradises, which seemed to them to be Edens of aesthetic self-indulgence. Only Dickinson refused such renunciation. Professing martyrdom, claiming an affinity for "sumptuous destitution," she nevertheless clung stubbornly to her vision of a green paradise in which the female poet, like her male counterpart, could dance naked in naked light. The shadows of compromise in which she had to sew were only temporary, she seems to have told herself. They were like the realm of incarnate "experience" through which Blake thought the soul had to pass in order to attain the ultimate freedom of "organiz'd innocence." Persisting in her definition of her own whiteness, she imagined herself, sometimes, as nakedly white rather than whitely garmented, and identified her own passion for a paradise of mystic green with a flower's urge to bloom:

> Through the Dark Sod—as Education—
> The Lily passes sure—
> Feels her white foot—no trepidation—
> Her faith—no fear—
>
> Afterward—in the Meadow—
> Swinging her Beryl Bell—
> The Mold-life—all forgotten—now—
> In Ecstasy—and Dell—   [J. 392]

In one sense, as the flower of the Resurrection, the blossoming Lily implies that this is a Christian allegory, a traditional Easter poem. But considering that Dickinson's mystic green is so defiantly female, we have to suspect that the festival she is secretly imagining, like the "holiday" of "There is a Morn," is a female Easter, an apocalyptic day of resurrection on which women would rise from the grave of gender in which Victorian society had buried them alive, and enter a paradise of "Ecstasy—and Dell—".

Ecstasy and dell. The terms of Dickinson's mystic green paradise are significantly different from the terms of many male-imagined aesthetic heavens. The Byzantium of Yeats's "Sailing to Byzantium," for instance, is a city of pure art, where no green comes: exorcising nature with its processes of pain, his poet/speaker sheds heart and body to take on the eternal metal clothing of a golden bird. Keats, more equivocal, also flirts with eternal marble, nature ruled and ordered. Even Milton, imagining the primordial paradise of nature, has his Adam and Eve constantly toiling to prune and trim Eden's unruly growth. To use the medieval terminology, his loyalty is to *natura naturata* rather than *natura naturans*.

For Dickinson, however, the mystic green is a wholly exuberant and untrammeled place. Like Emily Brontë, whom she much admired, she seems to have consciously or unconsciously felt that if, as woman, she equalled Nature, then both as general and as particular woman she should *be* Nature, free and fierce. The lilies—and Daisies—of the field toil not, nor do they spin. Liberated from the spider's exhausting task of self-concealment/self-generation, they simply dance their joy, uttering themselves over and over again in ecstasy and dell. Mountains surround them, and goddesses, .not hissing sinister volcanos but sure strong female presences whose gaze, "by men unseen," strengthens the flowers' living dance. As we have seen, the deity Dickinson usually described in poems was fiercely male: a golden Master or a patriarchal Nobodaddy, whose reign reflected the social realities of her life. But at least twice in her poetic career she cast off her customary disguises to write openly about the nature goddesses who ruled the mystic green she longed to inhabit. Once she wrote about "Sweet Mountains," not volcanos:

> Sweet Mountains—Ye tell Me no lie—
> Never deny Me—Never fly—
> Those same unvarying Eyes
> Turn on Me—when I fail—or feign,

> Or take the Royal names in vain—
> Their far—slow—Violet Gaze—
>
> My Strong Madonnas—Cherish still—
> The Wayward Nun—beneath the Hill—
> Whose service—is to You—
> Her latest Worship—When the Day
> Fades from the Firmament away—
> To lift her Brows on You—   [J. 722]

Surely these "Strong Madonnas" are sisters of that mother Awe to whom, Dickinson told Higginson, she ran home as a child, and surely it was such mothers who enabled (and empowered) this poet to escape her Nobodaddy's requirements, if only in secret. It was these strong Madonnas and yet another Mother, a muse/goddess whose white presence suggests the image of the chaste moon goddess Diana, about whom she wrote once that

> Her face was in a bed of hair,
> Like flowers in a plot—
> Her hand was whiter than the sperm
> That feeds the sacred light.
> Her tongue more tender than the tune
> That totters in the leaves—
> Who hears may be incredulous,
> Who witnesses, believes.   [J. 1722]

Neither sentimentality nor madness, these poems suggest, motivated Dickinson to introduce herself to Higginson by handing him "two day lilies" and, upon occasion, to offer guests "the unlikely choice of a glass of wine or a rose." Guarded, disguised, fictionalizing herself, she nevertheless must have been trying symbolically to convey one bare truth about her private religion.

That religion, she confesses in another one of her few statements on this subject, began with her reading of a "Foreign Lady" who was almost certainly Elizabeth Barrett Browning:

> I think I was enchanted
> When first a sombre Girl—
> I read that Foreign Lady—
> The Dark—felt beautiful—

> And whether it was noon at night
> Or only Heaven—at Noon—
> For very Lunacy of Light
> I had not power to tell—

Transfigured by undisguised, unconcealed female art, even female
Nature becomes a kind of epic poem:

> The Days—to Mighty Metres stept—
> The Homeliest—adorned
> As if unto a Jubilee
> 'Twere suddenly confirmed—

At the same time, the enchantment of this conversion was subtle,
indefinable and Romantically mad:

> I could not have defined the change—
> Conversion of the Mind
> Like Sanctifying in the Soul—
> Is witnessed—not explained—
>
> 'Twas a Divine Insanity—
> The Danger to be Sane
> Should I again experience—
> 'Tis Antidote to turn—
>
> To Tomes of Solid Witchcraft—
> Magicians be asleep—
> But Magic—hath an Element
> Like Deity—to keep—   [J. 593]

Having been converted to this secret sect of art, however, and to
the "Strong Madonnas" who were its goddesses, Dickinson never
again experienced "the Danger to be Sane." Always conscious that
for a spider artist spinning in the shadows of her father's house
"Much Madness is divinest Sense," she clung obstinately and silently
to that "Lunacy of Light" Aurora Leigh had taught her to envision.
When what her world called "sanity" threatened, she steadied her
hold on the mystic green where she could "live aloud" by enacting
"Titanic Operas" in which she imagined fierce flights of escape like
the one Milton's Eve takes in book 5 of *Paradise Lost*, or the ones
Sylvia Plath enacts in *Ariel*. In poems that embody the divine

insanity that comes in dreams, Dickinson dances like a bomb abroad, swings upon the hours, and revels in a "Noon, and Paradise" that may have been covertly female all along. Unbandaged, she escapes the attic and discards the ladylike costumes she had to wear as "a woman—white." Flying into the dawn light like the queen she always suspected she was, she flings off "Shame," that "shawl of Pink" (J. 1412) along with even her pearl-white dress. Having transcended her Nobodaddy's Requirements, she can return at least in thought to that "Mother Country" where she will no longer need her yarn of pearl: the fictions of her life can be discarded like the "old whore petticoats" that Sylvia Plath once called her own conflicting selves.[80]

Finally, at her frankest, Dickinson admits that the power "patriarchal poetry" defines as Satanic but that she knows is really her own accosts her often, accosts her unbidden, accosts her—as Romantic tradition would have it—during those waking and sleeping dreams, those moments of epiphany, that are the Romantic poet's reason for being. And it is for the recurrence of such power that Dickinson most earnestly prays: for power that can transform her "smallest Room" into an Edenic, female continent of light. "There is a morn by men unseen" was one of her earliest prayers for such transfiguration. "Sweet Mountains—Ye tell me no lie" was a prayer she wrote in mid-career. But toward the end of her life her plea to what we must, perhaps, call her goddess was unchanged:

> Let me not mar that perfect Dream
> By an auroral stain
> But so adjust my daily Night
> That it will come again.

> Not when we know, the Power accosts—
> The Garment of Surprise
> Was all our timid Mother wore
> At Home—in Paradise.   [J. 1335]

What this last poem, in particular, suggests is that the uniquely female Awe which energized Dickinson's art was a product not only of romantic fantasies but of Romantic inspiration. For as Dickinson herself knew, the truth that underlies all her fictions is an apocalyptic yearning for "Ecstasy—and Dell," for a transfigured universe in which even the most "old-fashioned" little girl can "live aloud." Guarded and disguised as they are, her self-dramatizations tell us this, tell us—as she once remarked to Higginson about his own art— that if her versified autobiography could "cease to be Romance, it would be Revelation, which is the Seed—of Romance—"[81]

Notes

Epigraphs on page v: George MacDonald, *Lilith* (1895; reprinted New York: Ballantine, 1969), pp. 220–21; Laura (Riding) Jackson, "Eve's Side of It," *Chelsea* 35 (New York, 1976):88–93; first published in *Progress of Stories* (London: Seizin-Constable, 1935).

CHAPTER 1

Epigraphs: "In the End," in *Chelsea* 35:96; "The Introduction," in *The Poems of Anne Countess of Winchilsea,* ed. Myra Reynolds (Chicago: University of Chicago Press, 1903), pp. 4–5; *The Diary of Anaïs Nin, Vol. Two, 1934–1939,* ed. Gunther Stuhlmann (New York: The Swallow Press and Harcourt, Brace, 1967), p. 233.

1 *The Correspondence of Gerard Manley Hopkins and Richard Watson Dixon,* ed. C. C. Abbott (London: Oxford University Press, 1935), p. 133.

2 Edward W. Said, *Beginnings: Intention and Method* (New York: Basic Books, 1975), p. 83.

3 Ibid., p. 162. For an analogous use of such imagery of paternity, see Gayatri Chakravorty Spivak's "Translator's Preface" to Jacques Derrida, *Of Grammatology* (Baltimore: Johns Hopkins University Press, 1976), p. xi: "to use one of Derrida's structural metaphors, [a preface is] the son or seed ... caused or engendered by the father (text or meaning)." Also see her discussion of Nietzsche where she considers the "masculine style of possession" in terms of "the stylus, the stiletto, the spurs," p. xxxvi.

4 James Joyce, *Ulysses* (New York: Modern Library, 1934), p. 205.

5 Ibid. The whole of this extraordinarily relevant passage develops this notion further: "Fatherhood, in the sense of conscious begetting, is unknown to man," Stephen notes. "It is a mystical estate, an apostolic succession, from only begetter to only begotten. On that mystery and not on the madonna which the cunning Italian intellect flung to the mob of Europe the church is founded and founded irremovably because founded, like the world, macro- and microcosm, upon the void. Upon incertitude, upon unlikelihood. *Amor matris,* subjective and objective genitive, may be the only true thing in life. Paternity may be a legal fiction" (pp. 204–05).

6 Coleridge, *Biographia Literaria,* chapter 13. John Ruskin, *Modern Painters,* vol. 2, *The Works of John Ruskin,* ed. E. T. Cook and Alexander Wedderburn (London: George Allen, 1903), pp. 250–51. Although Virginia Woolf noted in *A Room of One's Own* that Coleridge thought "a great mind is androgynous" she added dryly that "Coleridge certainly did not mean ... that it is a mind that has any special sympathy with women" (*A Room of One's Own* [New York: Harcourt Brace, 1929], p. 102). Certainly the imaginative power Coleridge describes does not sound "man-womanly" in Woolf's sense.

7 Shelley, "A Defense of Poetry." Keats to John Hamilton Reynolds, 3 February 1818; *The Selected Letters of John Keats*, ed. Lionel Trilling (New York: Doubleday, 1956), p. 121.

8 See E. R. Curtius, *European Literature and the Latin Middle Ages* (New York: Harper Torchbooks, 1963), pp. 305, 306. For further commentary on both Curtius's "The Symbolism of the Book" and the "Book of Nature" metaphor itself, see Derrida, *Of Grammatology*, pp. 15–17.

9 "Timon, A Satyr," in *Poems by John Wilmot Earl of Rochester*, ed. Vivian de Sola Pinto (London: Routledge and Kegan Paul, 1953), p. 99.

10 Bridget Riley, "The Hermaphrodite," *Art and Sexual Politics*, ed. Thomas B. Hass and Elizabeth C. Baker (London: Collier Books, 1973), p. 82. Riley comments that she herself would "interpret this remark as expressing his attitude to his work as a celebration of life."

11 Norman O. Brown, *Love's Body* (New York: Vintage Books, 1968), p. 134.; John T. Irwin, *Doubling and Incest, Repetition and Revenge* (Baltimore: Johns Hopkins University Press, 1975), p. 163. Irwin also speaks of "the phallic generative power of the creative imagination" (p. 159).

12 Harold Bloom, *The Anxiety of Influence* (New York: Oxford University Press, 1973), pp. 11, 26.

13 All references to *Persuasion* are to volume and chapter of the text edited by R. W. Chapman, reprinted with an introduction by David Daiches (New York: Norton, 1958).

14 Anne Finch, *Poems of Anne Countess of Winchilsea*, pp. 4–5.

15 Southey to Charlotte Brontë, March 1837. Quoted in Winifred Gérin, *Charlotte Brontë: The Evolution of Genius* (Oxford: Oxford University Press, 1967), p. 110.

16 Finch, *Poems of Anne Countess of Winchilsea*, p. 100. Otto Weininger, *Sex and Character* (London: Heinemann, 1906), p. 286. This sentence is part of an extraordinary passage in which Weininger asserts that "women have no existence and no essence; they are not, they are nothing," this because "woman has no relation to the idea ... she is neither moral nor anti-moral," but "all existence is moral and logical existence."

17 Richard Chase speaks of the "masculine *élan*" throughout "The Brontës, or Myth Domesticated," in *Forms of Modern Fiction*, ed. William V. O'Connor (Minneapolis: University of Minnesota Press, 1948), pp. 102–13. For a discussion of the "female eunuch" see Germaine Greer, *The Female Eunuch* (New York: McGraw Hill, 1970). See also Anthony Burgess, "The Book Is Not For Reading," *New York Times Book Review*, 4 December 1966, pp. 1, 74, and William Gass, on Norman Mailer's *Genius and Lust*, *New York Times Book Review*, 24 October 1976, p. 2. In this connection, finally, it is interesting (and depressing) to consider that Virginia Woolf evidently defined *herself* as "a eunuch." (See Noel Annan, "Virginia Woolf Fever," *New York Review*, 20 April 1978, p. 22.)

18 Rufus Griswold, Preface to *The Female Poets of America* (Philadelphia: Carey & Hart, 1849), p. 8.

19 Roland Barthes, *Sade/Fourier/Loyola*, trans. Richard Miller (New York: Hill & Wang, 1976), p. 182; Hopkins, *Correspondence*, p. 133.

20 Finch, *Poems of Anne Countess of Winchilsea*, p. 5.

21 Leo Bersani, *A Future for Astyanax* (Boston: Little, Brown, 1976), p. 194.

22 Jean-Paul Sartre, *The Words*, trans. Bernard Frechtman (Greenwich, Conn.: Braziller, 1964), p. 114.

23 Marjorie Grene, *Sartre* (New York: New Viewpoints, 1973), p. 9.

24 Quoted by Cornelia Otis Skinner in her 1952 theater piece, *Paris '90.*

25 Norman O. Brown, "Daphne," in Joseph Campbell, ed., *Mysteries, Dreams, and Religion* (New York: Dutton, 1970), p. 93.

26 Lewis Carroll, *Through the Looking Glass*, chapter 6, "Humpty Dumpty."

27 Albert Gelpi, "Emily Dickinson and the Deerslayer," in *Shakespeare's Sisters*, ed. Sandra Gilbert and Susan Gubar (Bloomington: Indiana University Press, 1979), pp. 122–134.

28 Simone de Beauvoir, *The Second Sex* (New York: Knopf, 1953), p. 58.

29 D. H. Lawrence, *The Plumed Serpent*, chapter 23, "Huitzilopochtli's Night."

30 See Wolfgang Lederer, M. D., *The Fear of Women* (New York: Harcourt Brace Jovanovich, 1968); also H. R. Hays, *The Dangerous Sex* (New York: G. P. Putnam's Sons, 1964); Katharine Rogers, *The Troublesome Helpmate* (Seattle: University of Washington Press, 1966); and Dorothy Dinnerstein, *The Mermaid and the Minotaur* (New York: Harper & Row, 1976).

31 Lederer, *Fear of Women*, p. 42.

32 Mary Elizabeth Coleridge, "The Other Side of a Mirror," in *Poems by Mary E. Coleridge* (London: Elkin Mathews, 1908), pp. 8–9.

33 See The Wife's Prologue, lines 1–3: "Experience, though noon auctoritee / Were in this world, were right ynough to me / To speke of wo that is in mariage." See also Arlyn Diamond and Lee Edwards, ed., *The Authority of Experience* (Amherst: University of Massachusetts Press, 1977), an anthology of feminist criticism which draws its title from the Wife's speech.

34 In acknowledgment of a point similar to this, Edward Said follows his definition of "authority" with a definition of an accompanying, integrally related concept of "molestation," by which he says he means "that no novelist has ever been unaware that his authority, regardless of how complete, or the authority of a narrator, is a sham" (*Beginnings*, p. 84). For a fascinating discussion of the way in which one woman was driven to try to defy male literary / patriarchal authority, see Mitchell R. Breitweiser, "Cotton Mather's Crazed Wife," in *Glyph 5*. This madwoman literally dis-continued her husband's power by "molesting"—blotting and stealing!—his manuscripts.

35 Virginia Woolf, "Professions for Women," *The Death of the Moth and Other Essays* (New York: Harcourt, Brace, 1942), pp. 236–38.

36 Plath, *Ariel* (New York: Harper & Row, 1966), p. 8.

37 Christina Rossetti, "In an Artist's Studio," in *New Poems by Christina Rossetti*, ed. William Michael Rossetti (New York: Macmillan, 1896), p. 114.

38 "A Woman's Poem," *Harper's Magazine* (February 1859), p. 340.

39 Elizabeth Barrett Browning, *The Poetical Works of Elizabeth Barrett Browning* (New York: Crowell, 1891), pp. 3–4.

40 In a letter to John Kenyon in August 1844 Barrett Browning declared that the

difference between her early, derivative poems (like her "Essay on Mind") and her mature work was "not merely the difference between two schools, nor even the difference between immaturity and maturity; but ... the difference between the dead and the living, between a copy and individuality, between what is myself and what is not myself" (*The Letters of Elizabeth Barrett Browning*, ed Frederic G. Kenyon [2 vols. in 1, New York: Macmillan, 1899], 1:187).

41 Ortner, "Is Female to Male as Nature Is to Culture?" in *Woman, Culture, and Society*, ed. Michelle Zimbalist Rosaldo and Louise Lamphère (Stanford: Stanford University Press, 1974), p. 86.

42 Susan Braudy, "A Day in the Life of Joan Didion," *Ms.* 5 (8 February 1977):109.

43 See, for instance, Rogers, *The Troublesome Helpmate*; Kate Millett, *Sexual Politics* (New York: Avon, 1971).

44 Hans Eichner, "The Eternal Feminine: An Aspect of Goethe's Ethics," in Johann Wolfgang van Goethe, *Faust*, Norton Critical Edition, trans. Walter Arndt, ed. Cyrus Hamlin (New York: Norton, 1976), pp. 616, 617. Significantly, even when talk (rather than silence) is considered specifically feminine, it is "only" talk and not action, as the motto *Fatti maschi, parole femine* implies: Deeds are masculine, words are feminine.

45 Ibid., p. 620. Obviously Makarie's virtues foreshadow (besides those of Patmore's Honoria) those of Virginia Woolf's Mrs. Ramsay, in *To the Lighthouse*, for Mrs. Ramsay is also a kind of "lighthouse" of sympathy and beauty.

46 Coventry Patmore, *The Angel in the House* (London: George Bell & Son, 1885), p. 17.

47 Ibid., p. 73.

48 "The Everlasting Yea," *Sartor Resartus*, book 2, chap. 9.

49 Abbé d'Ancourt, *The Lady's Preceptor* (3rd ed. London: J. Walts, 1745), p. 8.

50 Mrs. Sarah Ellis, *The Women of England* (New York, 1844), pp. 9–10.

51 Mrs. Ellis, *The Family Monitor and Domestic Guide* (New York: Henry G. Laugley, 1844), p. 35.

52 John Ruskin, "Of Queens' Gardens," *Sesame and Lilies* (New York: Charles E. Merrill, 1899), p. 23.

53 Alexander Welsh, *The City of Dickens* (London: Oxford University Press, 1971), p. 184.

54 Ibid., pp. 187, 190.

55 Ann Douglas, *The Feminization of American Culture* (New York: Knopf, 1977), "The Domestication of Death," pp. 200–26.

56 "The Philosophy of Composition," *The Complete Poems and Stories of Edgar Allan Poe, with Selections from his Critical Writings*, ed. A. H. Quinn (New York: Knopf, 1951), 2:982.

57 Douglas, *Feminization of American Culture*, p. 202.

58 Welsh, *City of Dickens*, pp. 182–83.

59 Patmore, *Angel in the House*, pp. 175–76.

60 Oswald Doughty, *A Victorian Romantic: Dante Gabriel Rossetti* (London: Frederick Muller, 1949), p. 417.

61 Quoted in Doughty, p. 418. For a thorough examination, from another per-

spective, of the ambiguous beauty/terror of the dead woman, see Mario Praz, *The Romantic Agony* (London: Oxford, 1970), esp. "The Beauty of the Medusa," pp. 23–45.

62 Patmore, *Angel in the House*, p. 91.

63 Thackeray, *Vanity Fair*, ed. Geoffrey and Kathleen Tillotson (Boston: Houghton Mifflin, 1963), p. 617.

64 Adrienne Rich, *Poems, Selected and New, 1950–1974* (New York: Norton, 1975), p. 146.

65 *King Lear*, 4.4.142–43; *The Faerie Queene*, 1.2.361.

66 John Gay, Alexander Pope, and John Arbuthnot, *Three Hours After Marriage*, ed. Richard Morton and William M. Peterson, Lake Erie College Studies, vol. 1 (Painesville, Ohio: Lake Erie College Press, 1961), p. 22.

67 Walpole to Hannah More, 24 January 1795.

68 *The Poems of Jonathan Swift*, ed. Harold Williams, 3 vols. (Oxford: Clarendon Press, 1937), 2:383, ll. 67–68.

69 "A Beautiful Young Nymph," 2:583, ll. 67–68.

70 Swift, "The Progress of Beauty," 1:228, ll. 77–78.

71 "Epistle II. To a Lady," *The Poems of Alexander Pope*, ed. John Butt (New Haven: Yale University Press, 1963), p. 560, l. 219, l. 3.

72 *Three Hours After Marriage*, pp. 14, 54–56.

73 Jonathan Swift, *A Tale of a Tub, to Which Is Added the Battle of the Books and the Mechanical Operations of the Spirit*, ed. A. C. Guthkelch and D. Nichol Smith (Oxford: Clarendon Press, 1920), p. 240.

74 Pope, *The Rape of the Lock*, canto 4, ll. 58–60, in *The Poems of Alexander Pope*, p. 234.

75 Pope, *The Dunciad in Four Books* (1743), canto 1, ll. 311–18 in *The Poems of Alexander Pope*, p. 734.

76 Simone de Beauvoir, *The Second Sex*, p. 138.

77 Karen Horney, "The Dread of Woman," in *Feminine Psychology* (New York: Norton, 1973), pp. 133–46; Dorothy Dinnerstein, *The Mermaid and the Minotaur*, pp. 124–54. For discussions of the "Medusa Complex" and its misogynistic messages see also Philip Slater, *The Glory of Hera* (Boston: Beacon, 1968) and R. D. Laing, *The Divided Self* (London: Penguin Books, 1965).

78 For discussions of Lilith see *A Dictionary of the Bible*, ed. James Hustings (Edinburgh, 1950); also Louis Ginzberg, *The Legends of the Jews* (Philadelphia: The Jewish Publication Society of America, 1961), pp. 65–66; and T. H. Gaster, *Orientalia* 11 (1942):41–79. Also see George MacDonald, *Lilith*, and Laura Riding, "Eve's Side of It."

79 "Little Snow White." All references are to the text as given in *The Complete Grimm's Fairy Tales* (New York: Random House, 1972).

80 Bruno Bettelheim, *The Uses of Enchantment: The Meaning and Importance of Fairy Tales* (New York: Knopf, 1976), pp. 202–03.

81 Bettelheim, p. 205.

82 See Ellen Moers, *Literary Women* (New York: Doubleday, 1976), pp. 211–42.

83 Bettelheim, p. 211.

84 See "The Juniper Tree" in *The Complete Grimm's Fairy Tales.*
85 Geoffrey Hartman, "The Voice of the Shuttle," in *Beyond Formalism* (New Haven: Yale University Press, 1970), pp. 337–55.
86 *The Poems of Gerard Manley Hopkins,* ed. W. H. Gardner and N. H. MacKenzie (Oxford: Oxford University Press, 1970), p. 133.
87 See Matthew Arnold, "Philomela," in *Poetry and Criticism of* Matthew Arnold, ed. A. Dwight Culler (Boston: Houghton Mifflin, 1961), p. 144, l. 7.

CHAPTER 2

Epigraphs: Doctor on Patient (Philadelphia: Lippincott, 1888), quoted in Ilza Veith, *Hysteria: The History of a Disease* (Chicago: University of Chicago Press, 1965), pp. 219–20; *The Living of Charlotte Perkins Gilman* (New York: Harper & Row, 1975; first published 1935), p. 104; J. 1261 in *The Poems of Emily Dickinson,* ed. Thomas Johnson, 3 vols. (Cambridge, Mass.: The Belknap Press of Harvard University Press, 1955: all subsequent references are to this edition); "The Red Shoes," *The Book of Folly* (Boston: Houghton Mifflin, 1972), pp. 28–29.
 1 In "Tradition and the Individual Talent," T. S. Eliot of course considers these matters. In addition, in *Mimesis* Erich Auerbach traces the ways in which the realist includes what has been previously excluded from art in the name of ever-larger slices of life. Similarly, in *The Sense of an Ending* Frank Kermode shows how poets and novelists lay bare the literariness of their predecessors' forms in order to explore the dissonance between fiction and reality, paradigmatic (inherited) forms and contingency.
 2 J. Hillis Miller, "The Limits of Pluralism, III: The Critic as Host," *Critical Inquiry* (Spring 1977):446.
 3 See Harold Bloom, *The Anxiety of Influence.*
 4 Juliet Mitchell, *Psychoanalysis and Feminism* (New York: Vintage, 1975), p. xiii.
 5 Ibid., pp. 404–05.
 6 Adrienne Rich, "When We Dead Awaken: Writing as Re-Vision," in *Adrienne Rich's Poetry,* ed. Barbara Charlesworth Gelpi and Albert Gelpi (New York: Norton, 1975), p. 90.
 7 Mitchell, *Psychoanalysis and Feminism,* p. 402.
 8 See Elaine Showalter, *A Literature of Their Own* (Princeton: Princeton University Press, 1977).
 9 Annie Gottlieb, "Feminists Look at Motherhood," *Mother Jones* (November 1976):53.
10 *The Letters of Emily Dickinson,* ed. Thomas Johnson, 3 vols. (Cambridge, Mass.: The Belknap Press of Harvard University Press, 1958), 2:475; 2:518.
11 See Jessie Bernard, "The Paradox of the Happy Marriage," Pauline B. Bart, "Depression in Middle-Aged Women," and Naomi Weisstein, "Psychology Constructs the Female," all in Vivian Gornick and Barbara K. Moran, ed., *Woman in Sexist Society* (New York: Basic Books, 1971). See also Phyllis Chesler, *Women and Madness* (New York: Doubleday, 1972), and—for a summary of all these matters—Barbara Ehrenreich and Deirdre English, *Complaints and*

Disorders: The Sexual Politics of Sickness (Old Westbury: The Feminist Press, 1973).

12 In *Hints on Insanity* (1861) John Millar wrote that "Mental derangement frequently occurs in young females from Amenorrhoea, especially in those who have any strong hereditary predisposition to insanity," adding that "an occasional warm hipbath or leeches to the pubis will ... be followed by complete mental recovery." In 1873, Henry Mauldsey wrote in *Body and Mind* that "the monthly activity of the ovaries ... has a notable effect upon the mind and body; wherefore it may become an important cause of mental and physical derangement." See especially the medical opinions of John Millar, Henry Maudsley, and Andrew Wynter in *Madness and Morals: Ideas on Insanity in the Nineteenth Century,* ed. Vieda Skultans (London and Boston: Routledge & Kegan Paul, 1975), pp. 230–35.

13 See Marlene Boskind-Lodahl, "Cinderella's Stepsisters: A Feminist Perspective on Anorexia Nervosa and Bulimia," *Signs* 2, no. 2 (Winter 1976): 342–56; Walter Blum, "The Thirteenth Guest," (on agoraphobia), in *California Living, The San Francisco Sunday Examiner and Chronicle* (17 April 1977): 8–12; Joan Arehart-Treichel, "Can Your Personality Kill You?" (on female rheumatoid arthritis, among other diseases), *New York* 10, no. 48 (28 November 1977): 45: "According to studies conducted in recent years, four out of five rheumatoid victims are women, and for good reason: The disease appears to arise in those unhappy with the traditional female-sex role."

14 More recent discussions of the etiology and treatment of anorexia are offered in Hilde Bruch, M. D., *The Golden Cage: The Enigma of Anorexia Nervosa* (Cambridge, Mass.: Harvard University Press, 1978), and in Salvador Minuchin, Bernice L. Rosman, and Lester Baker, *Psychosomatic Families: Anorexia Nervosa in Context* (Cambridge: Harvard University Press, 1978).

15 Quoted by Ehrenreich and English, *Complaints and Disorders,* p. 19.

16 Eichner, "The Eternal Feminine," Norton Critical Edition of *Faust,* p. 620.

17 John Winthrop, *The History of New England from 1630 to 1649,* ed. James Savage (Boston, 1826), 2:216.

18 Wendy Martin, "Anne Bradstreet's Poetry: A Study of Subversive Piety," *Shakespeare's Sisters,* ed. Gilbert and Gubar, pp. 19–31.

19 "The Uncensored Poet: Letters of Anne Sexton," *Ms.* 6, no. 5 (November 1977): 53.

20 Margaret Atwood, *Lady Oracle* (New York: Simon and Schuster, 1976), p. 335.

21 See *Northanger Abbey,* chapter 10: "You will allow, that in both [matrimony and dancing], man has the advantage of choice, woman only the power of refusal."

22 See Dickinson, *Poems,* J. 579 ("I had been hungry, all the Years"), J. 709 ("Publication—is the Auction"), and J. 891 ("To my quick ear the Leaves— conferred"); see also Christina Rossetti, "Goblin Market."

23 See Dickinson, *Poems,* J. 327 ("Before I got my eye put out"), George Eliot, *Middlemarch,* book 2, chapter 20, and M. E. Coleridge, "Doubt," in *Poems by Mary E. Coleridge,* p. 40.

24 See Dickinson, *Poems,* J. 101.

25 *The Poetical Works of Christina G. Rossetti*, 2 vols. (Boston: Little, Brown, 1909), 2:11.

26 Griswold, *The Female Poets of America*, p. 7.

27 Austen, *Persuasion*, chapter 23.

28 Finch, *Poems of Anne Countess of Winchilsea*, p. 250.

29 See Showalter, *A Literature of their Own*, "The Double Critical Standard and the Feminine Novel," pp. 73–99.

30 Anne Killigrew, "Upon the Saying that My Verses Were Made By Another," in Louise Bernikow, ed., *The World Split Open* (New York: Vintage, 1974), p. 79.

31 Bradstreet, "The Prologue," in Bernikow, pp. 188–89.

32 Joan Goulianos, ed., *By A Woman Writt* (Baltimore: Penguin, 1973), pp. 55–56. See also *The Living of Charlotte Perkins Gilman*, p. 77: "It takes supernal strength / To hold the attitude that brings the pain; / And there are few indeed but stoop at length / To something less than best, / To find, in stooping, rest."

33 Virginia Woolf, *A Room of One's Own* (New York: Harcourt, Brace, and World, 1929), pp. 64–65.

34 "Epilogue," *Sir Patient Fancy* in *The Works of Aphra Behn*, ed. Montague Summers (New York: Benjamin Blom, 1967), 6 vols., 4:115.

35 See Winifred Gérin, *Charlotte Brontë*, pp. 110–11.

36 Dickinson, *Letters*, 2:408.

37 Woolf, *A Room*, p. 77.

38 Quoted in Linda Nochlin, "Why Are There No Great Women Artists?" in Gornick and Moran, *Woman in Sexist Society*, p. 507.

39 Ibid., p. 506.

40 "Preface," *The Lucky Chance* in *The Works of Aphra Behn*, 3:187.

41 Elizabeth Barrett Browning, *Poetical Works of Elizabeth Barrett Browning*, p. 363. On the other hand, compare Margaret Fuller's comment on Sand, which also sees sexual ambiguity as essential to her creativity, but in a very different way: "I am astonished at her insight into the life of thought. She must know it through some man. ... No Sibyls have existed like those of Michelangelo" (Bell Gale Chevigny, *The Woman and the Myth: Margaret Fuller's Life and Writings* [Old Westbury: The Feminist Press, 1976], p. 58).

42 In *Toward a Recognition of Androgyny* (New York: Harper Colophon, 1973), Carolyn Heilbrun does point out that, especially in Greece, there was a "hidden" tradition of androgyny, embodied in such tragic heroines as Antigone and Medea (pp. 1–16). In the last four or five hundred years, however, this tradition has become so hidden as to be invisible.

43 Joyce Carol Oates, *The Hostile Sun: The Poetry of D. H. Lawrence* (Los Angeles: Black Sparrow Press, 1973), p. 44.

44 Joanna Russ, "What Can a Heroine Do? Or Why Women Can't Write," in *Images of Women in Fiction*, ed. Susan Koppelman Cornillon (Bowling Green: Bowling Green University Popular Press, 1972), p. 10.

45 John Keats to Richard Woodhouse, 27 October 1818, *Selected Letters*, pp. 165–67.

46 Harriet Beecher Stowe, *My Wife and I: or, Harry Henderson's History* (New York: Fords, Howard & Hulbert, 1871).

47 See *The Poetical Works of Elizabeth Barrett Browning*, p. 252: "O poet-woman! none foregoes / The leap, attaining the repose."

48 Quoted (and discussed) in Lynn Sukenick, "On Women and Fiction," in Diamond & Edwards, eds., *The Authority of Experience*, p. 31.

49 Quoted in Chevigny, *The Woman and the Myth*, p. 63.

50 See George Eliot, "Silly Novels by Lady Novelists," *Westminster Review* 64 (1856):442–61.

51 Dickinson, *Poems*, J. 1129.

52 See, for instance, Barbara Charlesworth Gelpi, "A Common Language: The American Woman Poet," in *Shakespeare's Sisters*, ed. Gilbert and Gubar, pp. 269–79.

53 Judy Chicago, *Through the Flower: My Struggle as a Woman Artist* (New York: Doubleday, 1977), p. 40.

54 Dickinson, *Poems*, J. 512 ("The Soul has Bandaged moments—").

55 Patricia Meyer Spacks, *The Female Imagination* (New York: Knopf, 1975), p. 317; Carolyn Heilbrun and Catharine Stimpson, "Theories of Feminist Criticism: A Dialogue," in Josephine Donovan, ed., *Feminist Literary Criticism* (Lexington: The University Press of Kentucky, 1975), p. 62; Elaine Showalter, "Review Essay," *Signs* 1, no. 2 (Winter 1975):435. See also Annis V. Pratt, "The New Feminist Criticisms: Exploring the History of the New Space," in *Beyond Intellectual Sexism: A New Woman, A New Reality*, ed. Joan I. Roberts (New York: David McKay, 1976). On p. 183 Pratt describes what she calls her "drowning theory," which "comes from a phenomenon in black culture: You have a little black church back in the marsh and you're going to sing 'Go Down Moses' [but] Every now and then the members of the congregation want to break loose and sing 'Oh Freedom' . . . Whenever they sing that, they've got this big old black pot in the vestibule, and as they sing they pound the pot. That way, no white folks are going to hear. The drowning effect, this banging on the pot to drown out what they are actually saying about feminism, came in with the first woman's novel and hasn't gone out yet. Many women novelists have even succeeded in hiding the covert or implicit feminism in their books from themselves. . . . As a result we get explicit cultural norms superimposed upon an authentic creative mind in the form of all kinds of feints, ploys, masks and disguises embedded in the plot structure and characterization."

56 De Beauvoir, *The Second Sex*, p. 132; Kizer, "Three," from "Pro Femina," in *No More Masks!*, ed. Florence Howe and Ellen Bass (New York: Doubleday, 1973), p. 175.

57 Plath, "Elm," *Ariel*, p. 16; Sarton, "Birthday on the Acropolis," *A Private Mythology* (New York: Norton, 1966), p. 48.

58 *The George Eliot Letters*, 7 vols., ed. Gordon S. Haight (New Haven: Yale University Press, 1954–55), 5:58.

59 Eliot, *Poems*, 2 vols. (New York: Croscup, 1896), p. 124.

60 Rukeyser, "Myth," *Breaking Open* (New York: Random House, 1973), p. 20.

61 For "complex vibration," see Elaine Showalter, "Review Essay," p. 435. For reinventions of mythology, see Mona Van Duyn, "Leda" and "Leda Reconsidered," in *No More Masks!*, pp. 129–32, and Margaret Atwood, "Circe/Mud Poems," in *You Are Happy* (New York: Harper & Row, 1974), pp. 71–94. A poet like H. D. continually reinvents Persephone, Medusa, and Helen in her uniquely female epics, for example in *Helen in Egypt* (New York: New Directions, 1961).

62 Marge Piercy, "Unlearning to not speak," *To Be Of Use* (New York: Doubleday, 1973), p. 38.

63 "I am in danger—sir—," *Adrienne Rich's Poetry*, pp. 30–31.

64 Ellen Moers, *Literary Women*, pp. 90–112.

65 *The Living of Charlotte Perkins Gilman*, p. 77.

66 Dickinson, *Poems*, J. 512 ("The Soul has Bandaged moments—").

67 Boskind-Lodahl, "Cinderella's Stepsisters."

68 Dickinson, *Letters*, 2:460; Byron, "The Prisoner of Chillon," lines 389–92; Brontë, *Shirley* (New York: Dutton, 1970), p. 316; see also Brontë to W. S. Williams, 26 July 1849.

69 Gaston Bachelard, *The Poetics of Space*, trans. Maria Jolas (Boston: Beacon, 1970), p. xxxii.

70 *Adrienne Rich's Poetry*, p. 12: "A thinking woman sleeps with monsters./The beak that grips her, she becomes" ("Snapshots of a Daughter-in-Law," #3).

71 Charlotte Perkins Gilman, *The Yellow Wallpaper* (Old Westbury: The Feminist Press, 1973). All references in the text will be to page numbers in this edition.

72 *The Living of Charlotte Perkins Gilman*, p. 121.

73 "Stings," *Ariel*, p. 62.

CHAPTER 3

Epigraphs: The Republic, trans. W. H. D. Rouse (New York: Mentor, 1956), p. 312 (Book VII); "The Key-Note," *The Poetical Works of Christina G. Rossetti*, 2:11; *A Fountain of Gardens Watered by the River of Divine Pleasure, and Springing Up in all Variety of Spiritual Plants* ... (London, 1697–1701), 1:18. We are grateful to Catherine Smith for introducing us to the writings of Jane Lead.

1 Although see Helen Diner, *Mothers and Amazons: The First Feminine History of Culture* (New York: Anchor Books, 1973-reprint), for a comment on the parable of reincarnation at the end of *The Republic*: "Through Plato's earth gullet, roaring with birth, the souls rise and set, moving down when they come from Life and moving back up with a new destiny that they have been allotted" (p. 6).

2 Edgar Allan Poe, "The Fall of the House of Usher"; Sylvia Plath, "Nick and the Candlestick" ("black bat airs") and "Lady Lazarus" ("grave cave"), *Ariel*, pp. 6, 33.

3 De Beauvoir, *The Second Sex*, pp. 77–78.

4 Ibid., p. 137.

5 Helen Diner, *Mothers and Amazons*, pp. 16–18. Blake, *For The Sexes: The Gates of Paradise* (from "The Keys ... of the Gates," 15 & 16, lines 44–50).

6 Mary Shelley, "Author's Introduction" to *The Last Man* (Lincoln: University

of Nebraska Press, 1965), pp. 1–4.

7 Ibid., p. 4.

8 Northrop Frye, "The Revelation to Eve," in *Paradise Lost: A Tercentenary Tribute*, ed. Balachandra Rajan (Toronto: University of Toronto Press, 1969), p. 46.

9 Rich, "Re-Forming the Crystal," in *Poems: Selected and New*, p. 228.

10 Dickinson, *Poems*, J. 492. See also J. 24 ("There is a morn by men unseen") for the metaphor of the "mystic green," and J. 486 ("I was the slightest in the House") for "I could not bear to live—aloud— / The Racket shamed me so—".

11 *The Poetical Works of Christina G. Rossetti*, 1:116.

12 Dickinson, *Letters*, 1:210 ("man of noon"); J. 891 ("To my quick Ear the leaves conferred . . . Creation seemed a mighty Crack").

13 Rebecca Harding Davis, *Life in the Iron Mills, with a Biographical Interpretation by Tillie Olsen* (Old Westbury: Feminist Press Reprint, 1972), pp. 24, 32–33, 65; "Living in the Cave," *Adrienne Rich's Poetry*, p. 72; Plath, "Nick and the Candlestick," *Ariel*, pp. 33–34.

14 Ursula K. Le Guin, "The New Atlantis," in *The New Atlantis and Other Novellas of Science Fiction*, ed. Robert Silverberg (New York: Hawthorn, 1975), p. 75.

15 Dickinson, *Poems*, J. 278.

16 Willa Cather, *My Antonia* (Boston: Houghton Mifflin, 1918), pp. 337–39.

17 "An Island," *The Poetical Works of Elizabeth Barrett Browning*, pp. 332–35.

CHAPTER 4

Epigraphs: Jane Austen, *Love and Freindship* in *The Works of Jane Austen*, ed. R. W. Chapman, vol. 6 (London: Oxford University Press, 1954), p. 102; *Poems*, J. 613; "Have They Attacked Mary. He Giggled. (A Political Caricature)," in *Selected Writings of Gertrude Stein*, ed. Carl Van Vechten (New York: Vintage, 1962), p. 533; *The Second Sex*, p. 279.

1 *The Autobiography, Times, Opinions and Contemporaries of Sir Egerton Brydges* (London, 1834), vol. 2, chap. 3, p. 41, quoted by Frank Bradbrook, *Jane Austen and Her Predecessors* (Cambridge: Cambridge University Press, 1967), p. 401.

2 To Ann Austen, 9 September 1814, *Jane Austen's Letters to Her Sisters Cassandra and Others*, ed. R. W. Chapman (2d ed. London: Oxford University Press, 1952), p. 401.

3 To J. Edward Austen, 16 December 1816, *Austen's Letters*, pp. 468–69.

4 To Cassandra Austen, 4 February 1813, *Austen's Letters*, p. 299.

5 Quoted by Anne Katharine Elwood, *Memoirs of the Literary Ladies of England* (London, 1843), 2:216.

6 Gaston Bachelard, *The Poetics of Space*, p. 161.

7 Only recently have such traditionally "feminine" arts of women as drawn threadwork, crochet, lace-making, embroidery, and china-painting been rescued from devaluation by the artists working with Judy Chicago in her "Dinner Party Project." See the interview with Chicago in *Chrysalis* 4 (1977):89–101.

8 Walter Scott, unsigned review of *Emma* in *Quarterly Review* (March 1816), reprinted in *Jane Austen: The Critical Heritage*, ed. B. C. Southam (New York:

Barnes & Noble, 1968), p. 68.

9 Charlotte Brontë to G. H. Lewes, 1 January 1848, reprinted in *Critical Heritage*, p. 126.

10 The remark by Fitzgerald is quoted by John Halperin in his fine analysis "Jane Austen's Nineteenth-Century Critics," in *Jane Austen: Bicentenary Essays*, ed. John Halperin (Cambridge: Cambridge University Press, 1975), p. 23 and footnoted there to the *Letters of Edward Fitzgerald*, vol. 2 (London, 1894), p. 131. Elizabeth Barrett Browning's remark is found in a letter to Ruskin, 5 November 1855, *Letters of Elizabeth Barrett Browning*, 2:217.

11 *Journals of Ralph Waldo Emerson: 1856–1863*, ed. E. W. Emerson and W. E. Forbes (Boston: Houghton Mifflin, 1913), 9:336–37.

12 Mark Twain to William Dean Howells, January 18, 1909, reprinted in *The Portable Mark Twain*, ed. Bernard DeVoto (New York: Viking, 1946), p. 785.

13 D. H. Lawrence, "A Propos of Lady Chatterley's Lover," in *Sex, Literature and Censorship*, ed. Harry T. Moore (New York: Twayne Publishers, 1953), p. 119. This remark resembles the comment of Kingsley Amis, who claims that Austen's "judgment and her moral sense were corrupted," in *What Became of Jane Austen? and Other Questions* (London: Jonathan Cape, 1970), p. 17.

14 Henry James, "The Lesson of Balzac," *The Future of the Novel: Essays on the Art of Fiction*, ed. Leon Edel (New York: Vintage, 1956), pp. 100–01.

15 Rudyard Kipling, "The Janeites," *The Writings in Prose and Verse of Rudyard Kipling* (New York: Scribner's, 1926), vol. 31, pp. 159–91.

16 Jane Austen, *Persuasion*, ed. R. W. Chapman (New York: Norton, 1958), vol. I, chap. 11. Volume and chapter numbers will appear parenthetically in the text. Readers with texts where the chapters are consecutively numbered can convert their chap. 13 to Chapman's vol. II, chap. 1.

17 Donald Greene asks whether there is "not a good deal of machismo—our old friend 'male chauvinism'—built into the critical values that would downgrade Jane Austen's novels" in an interesting essay, "The Myth of Limitation" in *Jane Austen Today*, ed. Joel Weinscheimer (Athens, Ga.: University of Georgia Press, 1975), p. 168.

18 W. H. Auden, "Letter to Lord Byron," *Collected Longer Poems* (New York: Random House, 1969), p. 41.

19 Jane Austen, *Love and Freindship* in *Minor Works, The Works of Jane Austen*, ed. R. W. Chapman (London: Oxford University Press, 1954), vol. VI, p. 79. Subsequent quotations of the minor works are taken from this volume.

20 Virginia Woolf, "Jane Austen," *The Common Reader* (New York: Harcourt, Brace and World, 1925), p. 140.

21 Mary Lascelles, *Jane Austen and Her Art* (Oxford: Clarendon Press, 1939), p. 60.

22 "A Letter from a Young Lady, whose feelings being too strong for her Judgement led her into the commission of Errors which her Heart disapproved," *Minor Works*, p. 175.

23 To Cassandra Austen, 7 January 1807, *Austen's Letters*, p. 48.

24 To Cassandra Austen, 24 January 1809, *Austen's Letters*, p. 256.

25 Frank Bradbrook, *Jane Austen and Her Predecessors*, pp. 24–27.

26 Mary Wollstonecraft, *A Vindication of the Rights of Woman*, ed. Carol H. Poston (New York: Norton, 1975), p. 22. Also see Lloyd W. Brown, "Jane Austen and the Feminist Tradition," *Nineteenth-Century Fiction* 28 (1973):321–38.

27 "A Collection of Letters: Letter the Second," *Minor Works*, p. 154.

28 *Sense and Sensibility*, in *The Novels of Jane Austen*, ed. R. W. Chapman (London: Oxford University Press, 1943), vol. I, chap. 10. Subsequent references to volume and chapter will appear parenthetically in the text. Readers using editions where chapters are consecutively numbered can key into Chapman's system by converting chapters 23 to 36 into vol. II chapters 1–14, and chapters 37–50 into vol. III, chapters 1–14.

29 A. Walton Litz, *Jane Austen: A Study of Her Artistic Development* (New York: Oxford University Press, 1965), p. 50.

30 De Beauvoir, *The Second Sex*, p. 277.

31 Karen Horney, "The Overvaluation of Love," *Female Psychology* (New York: Norton, 1967), pp. 182–213.

32 *Sanditon*, in *Minor Works*, p. 390, chap. 6. Subsequent references to chapter numbers appear parenthetically in the text.

33 To Cassandra Austen, 5 March 1814, *Austen's Letters*, p. 379.

34 Jane Austen, *Mansfield Park* in *The Novels of Jane Austen*, ed. R. W. Chapman (London: Oxford University Press, 1923), vol. I, chap. 10. Subsequent references to chapter and volume will appear parenthetically in the text. Chapman's vol. I includes chapters 1–18; II, chapters 1–13, and III, chapters 1–17.

35 Mary Ellmann, *Thinking About Women* (New York: Harcourt Brace Jovanovich, 1968), p. 199.

36 Lascelles, *Jane Austen and Her Art*; Mudrick, *Jane Austen: Irony as Defense and Discovery* (Berkeley: University of California Press, 1968); Butler, *Jane Austen and the War of Ideas* (Oxford: Clarendon Press, 1975).

37 Nina Auerbach, "Austen and Alcott on Matrimony," *Novel* 10, no. 1 (Fall 1976): 6–26.

38 Jane Austen, "Jack and Alice," *Minor Works*, p. 24.

39 "The Three Sisters: A Novel," *Minor Works*, p. 66.

40 "A Tour Though Wales—in a Letter from a Young Lady," *Minor Works*, p. 177.

41 "Letter the Third From a Young Lady in distressed Circumstances to her friend," *Minor Works*, pp. 156–60.

42 Jane Austen, *Northanger Abbey* in *The Works of Jane Austen*, ed. R. W. Chapman (London: Oxford University Press, 1943), vol. I, chap. 10. Subsequent references to volume and chapter will appear parenthetically in the text. Chapman's edition divides the novel into two volumes, the first ending with chapter 15.

43 Mary Wollstonecraft, *A Vindication*, p. 151.

44 Jane Austen, *Pride and Prejudice* in *The Works of Jane Austen*, ed. R. W. Chapman (London: Oxford University Press, 1940), vol. II, chap. 6. Subsequent references to volume and chapter will appear parenthetically in the text. Volume I includes chapters 1 to 34; volume II, chapters 1 to 19; volume III, chapters 1 to 19.

45 Adrienne Rich, *Of Woman Born* (New York: Norton, 1976), p. 235; Lynn Sukenick, "Feeling and Reason in Doris Lessing's Fiction," *Contemporary*

Literature 14 (Fall 1974): 519; Judith Kegan Gardiner, "A Wake for Mothers: The Maternal Deathbed in Women's Fiction," *Feminist Studies* 4 (June 1978): 146–65.

46 "Jack and Alice," p. 13 and p. 28.

47 Jane Austen, *Emma* in *The Works of Jane Austen*, ed. R. W. Chapman (London: Oxford University Press, 1933), vol. II, chap. 17. Subsequent references to volume and chapter will appear parenthetically in the text. Volume I includes chapters 1 to 18; II, chapters 1 to 18; III, chapters 1 to 19.

48 "Jack and Alice," *Minor Works*, p. 24.

49 "Frederic and Elfrida," *Minor Works*, p. 4; "Lesley Castle," p. 111, and "Catharine," p. 199.

50 See the objections to the villainy of the General voiced by Maria Edgeworth and by the *British Critic*, in *Critical Heritage*, p. 17.

51 Samuel Richardson, *Clarissa* (New York: Everyman, 1962), 1:226–27.

52 Darrel Mansell, *The Novels of Jane Austen* (New York: Barnes and Noble, 1973) discusses the false suitor in all of Austen's novels, and Jean Kennard discusses the two-suitor convention in nineteenth-century fiction in *Victims of Convention* (Hamden, Conn.: Archon Books, 1978).

53 "The History of England," *Minor Works*, pp. 139–50.

54 To James Stanier Clarke, 1 April 1816, *Austen's Letters*, pp. 452–53.

55 To James Stanier Clarke, 11 Dec. 1815, *Austen's Letters*, p. 443.

56 Quoted in an extremely useful essay by Irene Tayler and Gina Luria, "Gender and Genre: Women in British Romantic Literature," in *What Manner of Woman: Essays on English and American Life and Literature*, ed. Marlene Springer (New York: New York University Press, 1977), p. 102.

57 George Eliot, *Daniel Deronda* (Baltimore: Penguin, 1967), p. 160.

58 Virginia Woolf, *Three Guineas* (New York: Harcourt Brace and World, 1966), p. 9.

59 Litz, *Jane Austen*, p. 64.

60 Robert Hopkins, "General Tilney and the Affairs of State: The Political Gothic of *Northanger Abbey*," *Philological Quarterly*, forthcoming. Alistair M. Duckworth also explains how Henry Tilney's ironical reconstruction of his sister's irrational fears of a riot is actually a description of the Gordon Riots of 1780; thus the passage ironically illustrates how well founded Elinor's fears are. See *The Improvement of the Estate* (Baltimore: Johns Hopkins University Press, 1971), p. 96.

61 Ellen Moers, *Literary Women*, p. 67.

62 In this letter to Fanny Knight, Austen goes on to admit the obvious, that this "is one very strong argument in favour of Matrimony," 13 March 1817, *Austen's Letters*, p. 483.

63 Mary Burgan, "Mr. Bennet and the Failures of Fatherhood in Jane Austen's Novels," *Journal of English and German Philology* (Fall 1975): 536–52.

64 Katrin Ristkok Burlin, "'The Pen of the Contriver': The Four Fictions of *Northanger Abbey*," in Halperin, *Bicentenary Essays*, pp. 89–111.

65 George Levine, "Translating the Monstrous: *Northanger Abbey*," *Nineteenth-Century Fiction* (December 1975): 335–50; also see Donald Greene, "Jane Austen's Monsters," in *Bicentenary Essays*, pp. 262–78.

66 Florence Rush, "The Freudian Cover-Up: The Sexual Abuse of Children," *Chrysalis* 1 (1977):31–45. Rush describes how young girls are made to feel responsible for parental abuse, much as rape victims have been made to feel guilty for the crimes perpetrated against them.

CHAPTER 5

Epigraphs: Memoirs, vol. 3, p. 259, quoted by Marilyn Butler, *Maria Edgeworth* (Oxford: Clarendon Press, 1972), p. 9; *Poems*, J. 657; *The Girls' Book of Diversions*, quoted in C. Willett Cunnington, *Feminine Attitudes in the Nineteenth Century*, p. 124; From "Pro Femina," *Knock upon Silence* (Garden City, N.Y.: Doubleday, 1965), p. 41, lines 1–2.

1 Virginia Woolf, "Jane Austen," *The Common Reader*, p. 144. Whether or not Edgeworth's comment, like Canning's whom she echoes, is parodying Southey or Coleridge, her view of herself as a needy knifegrinder comes as part of her refusal to supply her readers further information on her life and art.

2 Maria Edgeworth, *The Life and Letters of Maria Edgeworth*, ed. Augustus J. C. Hare, 2 vols. (Freeport, N.Y.: Books for Libraries' Press, 1894, repr. 1971), 1:260. In a letter to Anna Austen, Wednesday 28 September 1814, Jane Austen writes, "I have made up my mind to like no Novels really, but Miss Edgeworth's, Yours & my own," *Austen's Letters*, p. 405.

3 Quoted by Butler, p. 413.

4 Its meticulous research and its fine insight into Edgeworth's literary and pedagogic writings notwithstanding, Marilyn Butler's literary biography seems dedicated to justifying Richard Lovell Edgeworth against the charges of female Victorian biographers who cast him in the role of a villain.

5 Bertha Coolidge Slade, *Maria Edgeworth: A Bibliographical Tribute* (London: Constable, 1937), p. 11, quotes a letter to Sophy Ruxton, 23 February 1794.

6 Maria Edgeworth, *Letters for Literary Ladies, to which is added An Essay on the Noble Science of Self-Justification*. 2nd ed. (London: J. Johnson in St. Paul's Churchyard, 1799), p. 75. This revised edition is prefaced by Edgeworth's admission that "In the first edition the *Second Letter* upon the advantage of cultivating the female understanding, was thought to weaken the cause it was intended to support.—That letter has been written over again; no pains have been spared to improve it and to assert more distinctly the female right to literature," p. iv–v.

7 Maria Edgeworth to Sophy Ruxton, May 1805, quoted by Butler, p. 207.

8 Maria Edgeworth to Sophy Ruxton, 26 February 1805, quoted by Butler, p. 209.

9 Maria Edgeworth, *Castle Rackrent*, ed. George Watson (London: Oxford University Press, 1964), p. 26. Subsequent page references will appear parenthetically in the text.

10 J. H. Plumb, *The First Four Georges* (New York: Wiley, 1967), p. 39.

11 Donald Davie, *The Heyday of Sir Walter Scott* (London: Routledge & Kegan Paul, 1961), p. 68. George Watson, "Introduction," *Castle Rackrent*, pp. x—xiv.

12 For opposing critical arguments on the conscious subversiveness or loyalty of Thady, see James Newcomer, *Maria Edgeworth the Novelist* (Fort Worth: Texas

Christian University Press, 1967), p. 147–51, and Gerry H. Brookes, "The Didacticism of Edgeworth's *Castle Rackrent*," *Studies in English Literature* 17 (Autumn 1977):593–605.

13 Maria Edgeworth to Francis Jeffry, 18 December 1806, quoted by Butler, p. 272.
14 Maria Edgeworth to Etienne Dumont, 18 September 1813, quoted by Butler, p. 289.
15 Ibid., pp. 207, 210, 278, 289.
16 Ibid., p. 403.
17 Mark D. Hawthorne, *Doubt and Dogma in Maria Edgeworth* (Gainesville: University of Florida Press, 1967).
18 *A Memoir of Maria Edgeworth*, edited by her children (privately printed: London, 1867), 3:265–66, quoted by Vineta Colby, *Yesterday's Women: Domestic Realism in the English Novel* (Princeton: Princeton University Press, 1974), pp. 89–90.
19 Woolf, *A Room of One's Own*, pp. 69–70. James Edward Austen-Leigh explains that Austen objected to having the creaking door fixed "because it gave her notice when anyone was coming," in *Memoirs of Jane Austen*, ed. R. W. Chapman (Oxford: Clarendon Press, 1967), p. 102.
20 Sir William Blackstone, *Commentaries of the Laws of England, Book The First* (Oxford, 1765), p. 442.
21 Woolf, "Jane Austen," pp. 142, 146.
22 A. Walton Litz, p. 43, and Margaret Drabble, "Introduction," *Lady Susan/The Watsons/Sanditon* (London: Penguin, 1974), pp. 13–14.
23 James Edward Austen-Leigh, *Memoir of Jane Austen*, p. 157.
24 Robin Lakoff, *Language and Woman's Place* (New York: Harper Colophon, 1975), p. 19.
25 Simone de Beauvoir, *The Second Sex*, p. 315.
26 See, for example, the most recent presentation of this argument by Everett Zimmerman, "Admiring Pope no more than is Proper: *Sense and Sensibility*," in *Jane Austen: Bicentenary Essays*, ed. Halperin, pp. 112–22.
27 Fanny Price's love for Mansfield Park as a place of peace and tranquility is discussed by Tony Tanner, "Jane Austen and 'The Quiet Thing,'" in *Critical Essays on Jane Austen*, ed. B. C. Southam (New York: Barnes and Noble, 1968), pp. 136–61. See also Alistair M. Duckworth, *The Improvement of the Estate*, pp. 71–80.
28 Irene Tayler and Gina Luria, "Gender and Genre: Women in British Romantic Literature," p. 113.
29 Leo Bersani, *A Future for Astyanax*, p. 77. That Fanny disavows the role of angel assigned her by Henry Crawford as "an office of high responsibility" (347) is no contradiction, for her very disavowal certifies her exemplary, Christian humility.
30 Lionel Trilling's influential essay, "*Mansfield Park*," in *Jane Austen: A Collection of Critical Essays*, ed. Ian Watt (Englewood Cliffs, N.J.: Prentice-Hall, 1963), pp. 124–40, has been restated most effectively by Stuart M. Tave, *Some Words of Jane Austen* (Chicago: University of Chicago Press, 1973), pp. 158–204.
31 Samuel Richardson, *Sir Charles Grandison*, 6 vols. (Oxford: Shakespeare Head, 1931), 4:302.

32 D. W. Harding, "Regulated Hatred: An Aspect of the Work of Jane Austen," *Scrutiny* 8 (March 1940):346–62.

33 Wendy Kolmar at Indiana University is currently writing a dissertation on these and lesser-known Victorian women novelists, entitled "Women Writing for Women: Victorian Middle-Class Fiction in the 1860s and 70s."

34 The most sustained discussion of Austen's ironic undercutting of her own endings appears in Lloyd W. Brown, *Bits of Ivory: Narrative Techniques in Jane Austen's Fiction* (Baton Rouge: Louisiana State University Press, 1973), pp. 220–29.

35 Jane Austen's family were almost all delighted with Aunt Norris, as their collected opinions show. See *Jane Austen: A Casebook on "Sense and Sensibility," "Pride and Prejudice," "Mansfield Park,"* ed. B. C. Southam (New York: Macmillan, 1976), pp. 200–03.

36 W. J. Harvey, "The Plot of *Emma*," in *Emma*, A Norton Critical Edition, ed. Stephen M. Parrish (New York: Norton, 1972), p. 456.

37 Stuart Tave, *Some Words of Jane Austen*, pp. 256–87.

38 Michelle Zimbalist Rosaldo suggests that the most egalitarian societies are those in which men participate in domestic life. See "Women, Culture, and Society: A Theoretical Overview," in *Women, Culture, and Society*, ed. Michelle Zimbalist Rosaldo and Louise Lamphere (Princeton: Princeton University Press, 1974), p. 41.

39 From Mrs. Palmer's fear of red-gum in her newborn infant (*Sense and Sensibility*) to Mrs. Musgrove's noisy and selfish household of siblings (*Persuasion*), Austen portrays the discomforts of motherhood. See also the letters in which she laments, "poor Woman! how can she be honestly breeding again?" (to Cassandra, 1 October 1808, *Letters*, p. 210); "poor Animal, she will be worn out before she is thirty" (to Fanny Knight, 23 March 1817, *Letters*, p. 488); "by not beginning the business of Mothering quite so early in life, you will be young in Constitution, spirits, figure & countenance, while Mrs. Wm Hammond is growing old by confinement & nursing" (to Fanny Knight, 13 March 1817, *Letters*, p. 483).

40 Paul Zietlow, "Luck and Fortuitous Circumstance in *Persuasion*: Two Interpretations," *ELH* 32 (1965):179–95, argues that Mrs. Smith is a "goddess who descends on stage at a crucial moment to avert catastrophe" (p. 193).

CHAPTER 6

Epigraphs: Sonnet XXXI, "Sonnets from a Lock Box," in Louise Bernikow, ed., *The World Split Open*, p. 246; Sonnet: "In our content, before the autumn came," in *The World Split Open*, p. 284; *Bee Time Vine* (New Haven: Yale University Press, 1953), p. 263; "The Old Chevalier," *Seven Gothic Tales* (New York: Modern Library, 1934), p. 88.

1 Virginia Woolf, *A Room of One's Own*, p. 118.

2 On p. 7 of *A Room* Woolf recounts an incident involving the MS of "Lycidas." On p. 39 she refers to "the large and imposing figure of a gentleman, which Milton recommended for my perpetual adoration."

3 Harold Bloom, *The Anxiety of Influence*, p. 35. The *OED* gives three meanings

for the word *bogey* or *bogy*, all relevant here: "1. As quasi-proper name: the evil one, the devil. 2. A bogle or goblin; a person much dreaded. 3. *fig.* An object of terror or dread; a bugbear."

4 Albert Gelpi, *Emily Dickinson: The Mind of the Poet* (Cambridge, Mass.: Harvard University Press, 1965), p. 40. Commenting upon Dickinson's girlhood rebelliousness, Gelpi adds that "As with Byron, too, her combativeness cast her in the role of the devil; she told Abiah: 'I have come from "*to* and *fro*, and walking up, and down" the same place that Satan hailed from, when God asked him where he'd been ... ' Neither she nor Byron could escape the sense that the thrust of the will, however magnificent, was not only foolhardy but demonic." (p. 41).

5 This question has most recently been debated in *Milton Studies* by Marcia Landy and Barbara K. Lewalski, both of whom are solely concerned with Milton's own intentions and assertions regarding women (whereas we are just as interested in defining the implications of Milton's ideas for women themselves). See Marcia Landy, "Kinship and the Role of Women in *Paradise Lost*," *Milton Studies IV* (Pittsburgh: University of Pittsburgh Press, 1972), pp. 3–18, and Barbara K. Lewalski, "Milton on Women—Yet Once More," *Milton Studies VI* (Pittsburgh: University of Pittsburgh Press, 1974), pp. 3–20.

6 Woolf, *A Writer's Diary* (New York: Harcourt, Brace, 1954), pp. 5–6. Read in isolation, this passage may strike some as an example of Woolfian irony, but in the context of the diary it is really quite a straightforward expression of Woolf's thoughts and feelings about Milton.

7 Bloom, *The Anxiety of Influence*, p. 32.

8 *A Writer's Diary*, p. 135.

9 *A Room of One's Own*, pp. 7–8.

10 *The Voyage Out* (New York: Harcourt, Brace, 1920), p. 326.

11 Ibid., p. 341.

12 See Bloom, *The Anxiety of Influence*, p. 95: "Influence is *Influenza*—an astral disease."

13 Charlotte Brontë, *Shirley*, chap. 18.

14 In his "The Revelation to Eve" Northrop Frye discusses the relationship between Eve as representative female and "the myth of a great mother-goddess from whom all deified principles in nature have ultimately descended, even though their fathers are fallen angels," thus hinting at the connection between the "Earth-born" Titans, Eve, and—as we shall see—Satan. As Frye notes, however, this relationship, which Brontë makes explicit, is only implicit in Milton, whose patriarchal cosmology necessitates the subordination of the "mother-goddess" Nature. The essay is collected in *Paradise Lost: A Tercentenary Tribute*, ed. Balachandra Rajan (Toronto: University of Toronto Press, 1969); see especially pp. 20–24, 46–47.

Interestingly, Brontë herself seems tentatively to have begun to redefine Eve as a titanic mother-goddess quite early in her career. *Paradise Lost* appears in a crucial scene in chapter 19 of *The Professor*, Brontë's first novel. Reunited with her "master" (and lover) after a painful separation, Frances Henri reads him

"Milton's invocation to that heavenly muse, who on the 'secret top of Oreb or Sinai' had taught the Hebrew shepherd how in the womb of chaos, the conception of a world had originated and ripened." In connection with our earlier argument about the metaphor of literary paternity, it seems significant here that Brontë emphasizes the female creative powers of Milton's muse, calling attention to his images of conception rather than his images of generation and alluding to the authority of the maternal womb rather than that of the paternal "Idea."

15 William Blake, *Milton*, book 2, plate 39, lines 40–42.

16 See Stanley Fish, *Surprised by Sin* (New York: St. Martin's, 1967), pp. 249–53.

17 See de Beauvoir, *The Second Sex*, especially chap. 17, "The Mother."

18 In a letter to Sandra Gilbert, however, Ross Woodhouse has argued interestingly that Urania offers Milton a "matriarchal dictation" and thus a sketchy possibility of androgyny. We are indebted to him for calling her significance to our attention.

19 See "On the Character of Milton's Eve," in *The Complete Works of William Hazlitt*, ed. P. P. Howe (London, 1930–34), 4:105–11. For another discussion of the parallels between Eve and Sin, see William Empson, "Milton and Bentley," in *Some Versions of Pastoral* (New York: New Directions, 1950), pp. 172–78. Commenting on Milton's "Eve-baiting," Empson also notes that "Eve ... has curled hair, modest but 'requiring,' that clutches at Adam like the tendrils of a vine. Eve now then is herself the forbidden tree; the whole face of Hell has become identical with her face; it is filled, as by the mockery of the temptress, with her hair that entangled him; all the beauty of nature, through her, is a covering, like hers, for moral deformity. But at least now we have exposed her; her hair is corpse worms; she is the bitter apple of her own crime, kind as the Eumenides" (pp. 176–77).

20 Of course the negative trinity of Satan, Sin, and Death parodies the "official" Holy Trinity of God, Christ, and the Holy Ghost. But, as *Paradise Lost* is structured, Adam does seem to participate in another, patriarchal trinity along with God and Christ, while Eve belongs metaphorically to a trinity with Satan and Sin.

21 Robert Graves, *The White Goddess* (New York: Creative Age Press, 1948). Graves's understanding of the specific influence this misogynistic tradition had upon John Milton—and especially upon Milton's relationships with women—is clearly articulated in his *Wife to Mr. Milton: The Story of Marie Powell* (New York: Creative Age Press, 1944).

22 *Milton*, book 1, plate 2, lines 19–20. Joseph Wittreich notes that "Ololon is the spiritual form of Milton's sixfold emanation, the truth underlying his errors about women. Milton's three wives and three daughters—all of whom, according to Blake, Milton treated abusively—constitute his emanation." (Joseph Antony Wittreich, Jr., ed., *The Romantics on Milton* [Cleveland: The Press of Case Western Reserve University, 1970], p. 99.) Discussing Blake's view of Milton, Northrop Frye observes that "one is struck by the fact that Milton never sees beyond this sinister 'female will.' His vision of women takes in only the hostility and fear which it is quite right to assume toward the temptress ... but which is by no means the only way in which women can be visualized." (Northrop Frye, *Fearful Symmetry: A Study of William Blake* [Boston: Beacon, 1962], p. 352.) Along

the same lines, Wittreich also comments in his recent *Angel of Apocalypse* that "Blake's point [in *Milton*] is [that] ... because Milton exhibits contempt for this world, precisely because he donned the robes of chastity, holding his soul distinct from his body, he remained isolated, for most of his life, from the divine vision." However "Milton's doctrine of chastity, which had oppressed him, his wives, and his daughters, is, in his moment of triumph, overcome, Milton annihilating the tyranny of the law (Urizen), one of whose tyrannies is 'the Chain of Jealousy' that binds Orc." (*Angel of Apocalypse: Blake's Idea of Milton* [Madison: University of Wisconsin Press, 1975], pp. 37 and 247.)

23 *Milton*, book 2, plate 41, lines 30, 32–33, 35–36.

24 Blake, *The Marriage of Heaven and Hell*, plate 6.

25 Bloom, *The Anxiety of Influence*, p. 23.

26 See Shelley, *Prometheus Unbound*, 3. 1. 57, and Byron, *Childe Harold's Pilgrimage*, canto 1, stanza 6. For a further elaboration of this point, see Mario Praz, "The Metamorphoses of Satan," *The Romantic Agony*, pp. 55–94. On Satan as a handsome devil, moreover, cf. Baudelaire's remark that "le plus parfait type de Beauté virile est Satan—à la manière de Milton" (Baudelaire, *Journaux Intimes*, quoted by Praz, p. 53).

27 In this connection, Frye relates the explosive imagery of Eve's dream-flight both to the volcanic rebelliousness of the enchained Titans and to the Gunpowder Plot. See "The Revelation to Eve," p. 24.

28 Byron to Moore, 19 September 1821, quoted in *Byron, Selected Works*, ed. Edward E. Bostetter (New York: Holt, Rinehart & Winston, 1972), editor's footnote, p. 285.

29 Mary Wollstonecraft, *A Vindication of the Rights of Woman*, ed. Carol H. Poston (New York: Norton, 1975), note by Wollstonecraft, p. 25.

30 Blake, *Milton*, book 2, plate 40, lines 29–31.

31 Shelley, *Prometheus Unbound*, 4:578.

32 "Snake," *The Complete Poems of D. H. Lawrence*, ed. Vivian de Sola Pinto and Warren Roberts (New York: Viking, 1964), vol. 1, pp. 349–51.

33 Ellen Moers, *Literary Women*, p. 19.

34 Review of *Jane Eyre*, *Quarterly Review* 84 (December 1848):173–74. Notably clear statements of the connection between visionary feminist politics and theology, especially *Genesis* (one of Milton's major sources, after all), may also be found in *The Woman's Bible* (first pub. 1895; reprinted as *The Original Feminist Attack on the Bible* [New York: Arno Press, 1974]), esp. pp. 23–27.

35 Letter of 27 August, 1850, quoted in Mrs. Gaskell, *The Life of Charlotte Brontë* (New York: Everyman, 1974), p. 313; "Doubt," *Poems of Mary E. Coleridge*, p. 40; see also Coleridge's "The Devil's Funeral," *Poems*, pp. 32–33.

36 W. B. Yeats, "The Cold Heaven," *Collected Poems of William Butler Yeats* (New York: Macmillan, 1955), pp. 122–23.

37 "Daddy," *Ariel* (New York: Harper & Row, 1966), pp. 50–51.

38 Leslie Marchand, *Byron: A Biography* (New York: Knopf, 1957), vol. 2, p. 591.

39 See *Shirley*, chap. 27.

40 Helene Moglen, *Charlotte Brontë: The Self Conceived* (New York: Norton, 1976), p. 32.

41 "The Introduction," *The Poems of Anne Countess of Winchilsea*, pp. 4–6.

42 Letter to George and Georgiana Keats, 24 September 1819, quoted in Wittreich, *The Romantics on Milton*, p. 562.

43 See Wordsworth, Preface to *Lyrical Ballads*, and Shelley, "A Defence of Poetry."

44 Wittreich, *The Romantics on Milton*, p. 12. A small but striking instance of Milton's role as paradigmatic Poet (and perhaps as "great Inhibitor") occurs in the first draft of Elizabeth Barrett Browning's "A Vision of Poets." Barrett Browning's original list of the greatest poets of all time began as follows (we have bracketed cancelled phrases):

> Here's Homer with the broad suspence (*sic*)
> [That face was Homer's by the sign]
> Of thundrous brows,—lips [infantine] intense
> With garrulous god-innocence—
> Here, Milton—piercingly if blind
> His eyes   the world to find
> The Light of light in heights of mind.
> Here Shakespeare, on whose forehead climb
> The crowns of the world—Oh eyes sublime
> With tears and laughter for all time.

Evidently, before she thought of Shakespeare (though after she thought of Homer), Barrett Browning thought of Milton as a kind of primordial poet. She seems to have had unusual trouble in composing her encomium to him, however, and significantly, in revising the manuscript she excised this reference; in the final version of "A Vision of Poets" Shakespeare follows Homer, and Milton is not mentioned until almost a hundred lines later, as if E. B. B. were trying to put him in his proper place. (The lines quoted above are from the holograph MS in the Berg Collection of the New York Public Library. See also "A Vision of Poets" in *The Poetical Works of Elizabeth Barrett Browning*, pp. 247–60.)

CHAPTER 7

Epigraphs: Milton, book 1, plate 10, lines 6–9; Hawthorne (on Fanny Fern), quoted in Caroline Ticknor, *Hawthorne and His Publishers* (Boston: Houghton Mifflin, 1913), p. 142; *Poems*, J. 532.

1 From Keats's annotations to *Paradise Lost*, quoted by Wittreich in *The Romantics on Milton*, p. 560.

2 George Eliot, *Middlemarch* (1871/1872; Cambridge, Mass.: Riverside Edition, 1956), book 1, chap. 7. All subsequent citations will be from this edition.

3 Letter to J. H. Reynolds, 17 April 1817, in *The Letters of John Keats*, ed. Hyder E. Rollins (Cambridge, Mass.: Harvard University Press, 1958), 1:130. See also Wittreich, p. 563, note 9.

4 *Middlemarch*, I, chap. 7.

5 Ibid.

6 Ibid., I, chap. 3.

7 Ibid.

8 Ibid.

9 Ibid. Interestingly, in deciding that Casaubon's work "would reconcile complete knowledge with devoted piety," Dorothea thinks at this point that "Here was something beyond the shallows of ladies'-school literature."

10 *A Room of One's Own,* p. 31.

11 Preface to *The World's Olio,* in *By a Woman writt,* ed. Joan Goulianos (Baltimore: Penguin Books, 1973), p. 60.

12 Anne Finch, "The Introduction," *Poems of Anne Countess of Winchilsea.*

13 From *Jane Anger her Protection for Women,* in Goulianos, p. 26.

14 See, for instance, Harold Bloom, "Afterword," *Frankenstein* (New York and Toronto: New American Library, 1965), p. 214.

15 Author's introduction to *Frankenstein* (1817; Toronto, New York, London: Bantam Pathfinder Edition, 1967), p. xi. Hereafter page references to this edition will follow quotations, and we will also include chapter references for those using other editions. For a basic discussion of the "family romance" of literature, see Harold Bloom, *The Anxiety of Influence.*

16 Robert Kiely, *The Romantic Novel in England* (Cambridge, Mass.: Harvard University Press, 1972), p. 161.

17 Moers, *Literary Women,* pp. 95–97.

18 See Ralph Wardle, *Mary Wollstonecraft* (Lincoln, Neb.: University of Nebraska Press, 1951), p. 322, for more detailed discussion of these attacks on Wollstonecraft.

19 Muriel Spark, *Child of Light* (Hodleigh, Essex: Tower Bridge Publications, 1951), p. 21.

20 See *Mary Shelley's Journal,* ed. Frederick L. Jones (Norman, Okla.: University of Oklahoma Press, 1947), esp. pp. 32–33, 47–49, 71–73, and 88–90, for the reading lists themselves. Besides reading Wollstonecraft's *Maria,* her *Vindication of the Rights of Women,* and three or four other books, together with Godwin's *Political Justice* and his *Caleb Williams,* Mary Shelley also read parodies and criticisms of her parents' works in these years, including a book she calls *Anti-Jacobin Poetry,* which may well have included that periodical's vicious attack on Wollstonecraft. To read, for her, was not just to read her family, but to read *about* her family.

21 Marc A. Rubenstein suggests that throughout the novel "the act of observation, passive in one sense, becomes covertly and symbolically active in another: the observed scene becomes an enclosing, even womb-like container in which a story is variously developed, preserved, and passed on. Storytelling becomes a vicarious pregnancy." "'My Accursed Origin': The Search for the Mother in *Frankenstein,*" *Studies in Romanticism* 15, no. 2 (Spring 1976): 173.

22 See Anne Finch, "The Introduction," in *The Poems of Anne Countess of Winchilsea,* pp. 4–6, and Sylvia Plath, "The Moon and the Yew Tree," in *Ariel,* p. 41.

23 Speaking of the hyperborean metaphor in *Frankenstein,* Rubenstein argues that Walton (and Mary Shelley) seek "the fantasied mother locked within the ice . . . the maternal Paradise beyond the frozen north," and asks us to consider the

pun implicit in the later meeting of Frankenstein and his monster on the *mer* (or *Mère*) *de Glace* at Chamonix (Rubenstein "'My Accursed Origin,'" pp. 175– 76).

24 See Moers, *Literary Women*, pp. 99.

25 In that summer of 1816 Byron had in fact just fled England in an attempt to escape the repercussions of his scandalous affair with his half-sister Augusta Leigh, the real-life "Astarte."

26 Matthew Arnold, "Preface" to *Poems, 1853*.

27 Spark, *Child of Light*, p. 134.

28 See Moers, *Literary Women*, "Female Gothic"; also Rubenstein, "'My Accursed Origin,'" pp. 165–166.

29 The *OED* gives "obscenity" and "moral defilement" among its definitions of "filth."

30 The monster's narrative also strikingly echoes Jemima's narrative in Mary Wollstonecraft's posthumously published novel, *Maria, or The Wrongs of Woman*. See *Maria* (1798; rpt. New York: Norton, 1975), pp. 52–69.

31 Harold Bloom does note that "the monster is . . . Mary Shelley's finest invention, and his narrative . . . forms the highest achievement of the novel." ("Afterword" to *Frankenstein*, p. 219.)

32 James Rieger, "Introduction" to *Frankenstein*, (*the 1818 Text*) (Indianapolis: Bobbs-Merrill, 1974), p. xxx.

33 In Western culture the notion that femaleness is a deformity or obscenity can be traced back at least as far as Aristotle, who asserted that "we should look upon the female state as being as it were a deformity, though one which occurs in the ordinary course of nature." (*The Generation of Animals*, trans. A. L. Peck [London: Heinemann, 1943], p. 461.) For a brief but illuminating discussion of his theories see Katharine M. Rogers, *The Troublesome Helpmate*.

34 See de Beauvoir, *The Second Sex*, p. 156.

35 Adrienne Rich, "Planetarium," in *Poems: Selected and New* (New York: Norton, 1974), pp. 146–48; Djuna Barnes, *The Book of Repulsive Women* (1915; rpt. Berkeley, Calif., 1976); Denise Levertov, "Hypocrite Women," *O Taste & See* (New York: New Directions, 1965); Sylvia Plath, "In Plaster," *Crossing the Water* (New York: Harper & Row, 1971), p. 16.

36 See *Mary Shelley's Journal*, p. 73.

37 Elizabeth Nitchie, *Mary Shelley* (New Brunswick, N.J.: Rutgers University Press, 1953), p. 219.

38 See Spark, *Child of Light*, pp. 192–93.

39 Woolf, *A Room*, p. 79.

40 In "The Deluge at Norderney," Isak Dinesen tells the story of Calypso, niece of Count Seraphina Von Platen, a philosopher who "disliked and mistrusted everything female" and whose "idea of paradise was . . . a long row of lovely young boys . . . singing his poems to his music." "Annihilated" by her uncle's misogyny, Calypso plans to chop off her own breasts with a "sharp hatchet." See *Seven Gothic Tales*, pp. 43–51.

41 Marc Rubenstein speculates that as a girl Shelley may actually have read (and

been affected by) the correspondence that passed between her parents around the time that she was conceived.

42 *Maria*, p. 152.

43 Spark, *Child of Light*, p. 205.

44 *The Last Man*, p. 339.

CHAPTER 8

Epigraphs: King Lear, 4.6.126–30; *The Marriage of Heaven and Hell*, plates 5–6; *Poems*, J. 959.

1 Mark Schorer, "Fiction and the Analogical Matrix," in William M. Sale, Jr., ed., Norton Critical Edition of *Wuthering Heights* (New York: Norton, 1972, revised), p. 376.

2 Winifred Gérin notes, for instance, that Mrs. Brontë wrote a "sprightly essay," entitled "The Advantages of Poverty in Religious Concerns," which her husband noted that he had "sent for insertion in one of the periodical publications" (Gérin, *Emily Brontë* [Oxford: The Clarendon Press, 1971], p. 3). See also Annette Hopkin, *The Father of the Brontës* (Baltimore: Johns Hopkins Press for Goucher College, 1958), passim.

3 Published instances of the Brontë juvenilia include Charlotte Brontë, *The Twelve Adventurers and Other Stories*, ed. C. W. Hatfield (London: Hodder, 1925); Charlotte Brontë, *The Spell*, ed. G. E. MacLean (London: Oxford University Press, 1931); Charlotte Brontë, *Tales from Angria*, ed. Phyllis Bentley (London: Collins, 1954); Charlotte Brontë, *Five Novelettes*, ed. Winifred Gérin (London: The Folio Press, 1971); Charlotte Brontë, *Legends of Angria*, compiled by Fannie E. Ratchford and William Clyde De Vane (New Haven: Yale University Press, 1933); and Emily Jane Brontë, *Gondal's Queen: A Novel in Verse*, arranged by Fannie E. Ratchford (Austin: University of Texas Press, 1955). Charlotte Brontë's most notable criticism of her sisters' work appeared in *Wuthering Heights, Agnes Grey, together with a selection of Poems by Ellis and Acton Bell*, Prefixed with a Biographical Memoir of the authors by Currer Bell (London: Smith, Elder, 1850).

4 Leo Bersani, *A Future for Astyanax*, p. 203.

5 Ibid., pp. 203, 208–09.

6 Gérin, *Emily Brontë*, p. 47.

7 Norton Critical Edition of *Wuthering Heights*, p. 72. All references will be to this edition.

8 Catherine Smith, "Jane Lead: The Feminist Mind and Art of a Seventeenth-Century Protestant Mystic," forthcoming in Rosemary Ruether, ed., *Women and Religion*.

9 See Thomas Moser, "What is the matter with Emily Jane? Conflicting Impulses in *Wuthering Heights*," *Nineteenth-Century Fiction* 17 (1962):1–19.

10 Fannie E. Ratchford, *Gondal's Queen*, p. 22. As Ratchford shows, many of Brontë's best poems were written as dramatic monologues for A.G.A. In addition, a number of critics have seen A.G.A. as a model for the first Catherine.

11 Terence Eagleton, *Myths of Power* (London and New York: Macmillan, 1975), p. 58.

12 See Claude Lévi-Strauss, *Tristes Tropiques* (New York: Atheneum, 1965), pp. 214–16: "There is something almost scandalous, to a European observer, in the ease with which the (as it seems to us) almost incompatible activities of the men's house are harmonized. Few people are as deeply religious as the Bororo. . . . But their spiritual beliefs and their habits of every day are so intimately mingled that they seem not to have any sensation of passing from one to the other."

13 Ratchford, *Gondal's Queen*, p. 186.

14 Ibid., pp. 192–93.

15 See Q. D. Leavis, "A Fresh Approach to *Wuthering Heights*," Norton Critical Edition, p. 313; Mark Schorer, "Fiction and the Analogical Matrix," p. 371; Leo Bersani, *A Future for Astyanax*, p. 203; Elliot Gose, *Imagination Indulg'd* (Montreal: McGill, Queen's University Press, 1972), p. 59.

16 Robert Kiely, *The Romantic Novel in England* (Cambridge, Mass.: Harvard University Press, 1972), p. 233.

17 Emily Jane Brontë, "Often rebuked, yet always back returning," in C. W. Hatfield, ed., *The Complete Poems of Emily Jane Brontë* (New York: Columbia University Press, 1941), pp. 255–56. Hatfield questions Emily's authorship of this poem, suggesting that Charlotte may really have written the piece to express her own "thoughts about her sister" (*loc. cit.*), but Gérin discusses it unequivocally as a piece by Emily (Gérin, *Emily Brontë*, pp. 264–65).

18 Byron, *Manfred*, 2.4.134–48; see also Gérin, *Emily Brontë*, p. 46.

19 As we noted in discussing Austen, in a letter to G. H. Lewes (12 January 1848) Charlotte remarked that she had never read *Pride and Prejudice* until he advised her to, so it is unlikely that Emily had read any Austen, especially not the comparatively obscure *Northanger Abbey*.

20 Mircea Eliade, *The Myth of the Eternal Return* (New York: Pantheon, 1954).

21 *The Complete Poems of Emily Jane Brontë*, pp. 255–56.

22 To distinguish the second Catherine from the first without obliterating their similarities, we will call Catherine Earnshaw Linton's daughter Catherine II throughout this discussion.

23 The realistically iconoclastic nature of Catherine's interest in riding, however, is illuminated by this comment from a nineteenth-century conduct book: "[Horseback riding] produces in ladies a coarseness of voice, a weathered complexion, and unnatural consolidation of the bones of the lower part of the body, ensuring a frightful impediment to future functions which need not here be dwelt upon; by overdevelopment of the muscles equitation produces an immense increase in the waist and is, in short, altogether masculine and unwomanly" (Donald Walker, *Exercises for Ladies*, 1837, quoted in Cunnington, *Feminine Attitudes in the Nineteenth Century*, p. 86).

24 See Bersani, *A Future for Astyanax*, and J. Hillis Miller, *The Disappearance of God* (Cambridge, Mass.: Belknap Press of Harvard University Press, 1963), pp. 155–211.

25 Q. D. Leavis, "A Fresh Approach to *Wuthering Heights*," p. 321.

26 For a brief discussion of androgyny in *Wuthering Heights*, see Carolyn Heilbrun, *Toward a Recognition of Androgyny* (New York: Knopf, 1973), pp. 80–82.

27 There are thus several levels of irony implicit in Nelly's remark that "no parson in the world ever pictured heaven so beautifully as [Catherine and Heathcliff] did, in their innocent talk" (p. 48).

28 C. P. Sanger, "The Structures of *Wuthering Heights*," Norton Critical Edition, pp. 296–98.

29 Bersani, *A Future for Astyanax*, p. 201.

30 Even in his way of speaking—laconic, old-fashioned, oracular—old Mr. Earnshaw seems like a fairy-tale character, whereas Hindley and Frances talk more like characters in a "realistic" novel.

31 Eagleton does discuss the Lintons' dogs from a Marxist perspective; see *Myths of Power*, pp. 106–07.

32 Elizabeth Janeway, "On 'Female Sexuality,'" in Jean Strouse, ed., *Women and Analysis* (New York: Grossman, 1974), p. 58.

33 See Claude Lévi-Straus, *The Raw and the Cooked: Introduction to a Science of Mythology*, vol. 1 (New York: Harper & Row, 1969).

34 Dickinson, *Letters*, 2:408.

35 Charlotte Brontë elaborated upon the terrors of "ladylike" education in *The Professor*, *Jane Eyre*, and *Villette*. For a factual account of the Cowan Bridge experience, see also Gérin, *Charlotte Brontë*, pp. 1–16.

36 Blake, *The Marriage of Heaven and Hell*, plate 5.

37 Mark Kinkead-Weekes, "The Place of Love in *Jane Eyre* and *Wuthering Heights*," in *The Brontës: A Collection of Critical Essays*, ed. Ian Gregor (Englewood Cliffs: Prentice-Hall, 1970), p. 86.

38 See Dorothy van Ghent, *The English Novel: Form and Function* (New York: Harper & Row, 1961), pp. 153–70.

39 As we noted in discussing the metaphor of literary paternity, Jean-Paul Sartre thought of books as embodiments of power, and it seems relevant here that he once called his grandfather's library "the world caught in a mirror" (Marjorie Grene, *Sartre*, p. 11).

40 Sylvia Plath, "The Stones," in *The Colossus* (New York: Vintage, 1968), p. 82.

41 Sanger, "The Structures of *Wuthering Heights*," p. 288.

42 Plath, "Tulips," *Ariel*, p. 11.

43 Leavis, "A Fresh Approach to *Wuthering Heights*," p. 309; Bersani, *A Future for Astyanax*, pp. 208–09.

44 Plath, "Lady Lazarus," *Ariel*, p. 6.

45 Plath, "Contusion," *Ariel*, p. 83.

46 See A. Alvarez, *The Savage God* (London: Weidenfeld & Nicolson, 1971).

47 Marlene Boskind-Lodahl, "Cinderella's Stepsisters," p. 352.

48 Ibid., pp. 343–44.

49 For a comment on this phenomenon as it may really have occurred in the life of Emily's sister Charlotte, see Helene Moglen, *Charlotte Brontë: The Self Conceived*, pp. 241–42.

50 See Maxine Hong Kingston, *The Woman Warrior* (New York: Knopf, 1976), p. 48: "Even now China wraps double binds around my feet."

51 Dickinson, *Poems*, J. 1072 ("Title divine—is mine!/The Wife—without the Sign!").

52 Charlotte Brontë, "Editor's Preface to the New Edition of *Wuthering Heights* (1850)," Norton Critical Edition, p. 11.

53 Q. D. Leavis, "A Fresh Approach to *Wuthering Heights*," p. 310.

54 Interestingly, even in this speech the characteristic obsession of "Milton's daughters" with Greek and Latin recurs. The only books in the library she *hasn't* read, Nelly notes, are in "that range of Greek and Latin, and that of French," and even about those she can say that "those I know one from another" (p. 59).

55 Bersani, *A Future for Astyanax*, pp. 221–22.

56 Q. D. Leavis, "A Fresh Approach to *Wuthering Heights*," p. 321.

57 Bersani, *A Future for Astyanax*, pp. 208–09.

58 Showalter, *A Literature of Their Own*, pp. 133–52.

59 Ortner, "Is Female to Male as Nature is to Culture?" in *Women, Culture, and Society*, p. 80.

60 The concept of "androgyny," as some feminist critics have recently noted, usually "submerges" the female within the male, but Emily Brontë's vision is notably gynandrous, submerging the male, as it were, within the female.

61 *The Rainbow*, "Wedding at the Marsh," chap. 5.

62 John Donne, "Problemes," VI, "Why Hath the Common Opinion Afforded Women Soules?"

63 *Lear*, 1.2.15–16.

64 Ibid, 2.4.57.

65 Bersani, *A Future for Astyanax*, pp. 221–22.

66 Ibid.

67 Ortner, "Is Female to Male as Nature Is to Culture?"

68 Bettelheim, *The Uses of Enchantment*, pp. 277–310.

69 Lévi-Straus, *The Raw and the Cooked*, pp. 82–83.

70 Ibid.

71 Charlotte Brontë, *Shirley*, chap. 18.

72 Charlotte Brontë, "Editor's Preface," p. 12.

73 Jane Lead, *A Fountain of Gardens*, 2:105–07.

74 "Enough of thought, Philosopher," in *The Complete Poems of Emily Jane Brontë*, p. 220.

75 "The Witch," *Poem by Mary E. Coleridge*, pp. 44–45.

76 Blake, *The Marriage of Heaven and Hell*, plate 24.

CHAPTER 9

Epigraphs: The Professor, chap. 23; *The Bell Jar* (New York: Bantam, 1972), pp. 62–63; *Poems*, J. 599.

1 Charlotte Brontë, undated entry, "Roe Head Journal," unpublished MS #98/7, Bonnell Collection, Brontë Parsonage Museum, Haworth, England.

2 Winifred Gérin, "General Introduction" to Gérin, ed., Charlotte Brontë, *Five Novelettes* (London: The Folio Press, 1971), p. 16.

3 Charlotte Brontë, 14 October 1836, "Roe Head Journal."

4 Ibid.

5 Gérin, General Introduction, p. 17.

6 Quoted by Gérin, ibid., p. 20.

7 Charlotte Brontë, "The Spell," unpublished MS. # Addi. 34255, British Museum, London. See *The Shakespeare Head* Brontë*: The Miscellaneous and Unpublished Writings of Charlotte and Patrick Branwell Brontë*, in two volumes (Oxford: Blockwell, 1936) pp. 377–406, for a facsimile edition. Also, see George MacLean, ed., *The Spell* (Oxford: Oxford University Press, 1931).

8 "Rather by implication than assertion": "C. A. F. Wellesley" claims that in "The Spell" he will prove his brother to be "an ungovernable fiery fool . . . rather by implication than assertion." Charlotte Brontë refers to Crimsworth's "ascent of 'the Hill of Difficulty'" in her preface to *The Professor*, The Haworth Edition, including Poems by Charlotte, Emily, and Anne Brontë, and the Rev. Patrick Brontë, etc., with an Introduction by Mrs. Humphrey Ward (New York and London: Harper & Brothers, 1900), p. 3.

9 Winifred Gérin, *Charlotte Brontë*, p. 312.

10 Southey to Charlotte Brontë, March 1837; quoted in Gérin, *Charlotte Brontë*, p. 110.

11 See, for instance, p. 248.

12 See Mrs. Sarah Ellis, *The Family Monitor and Domestic Guide* (New York: Henry G. Langley, 1844), pp. 17–18: "To men belongs the potent (I had almost said the *omnipotent*) consideration of worldly aggrandizement; and it is constantly misleading their steps, closing their ears against the voice of conscience, and beguiling them. . . . Long before the boy has learned to exult in the dignity of the man, his mind has become familiarized to the habit of investing with supreme importance, all considerations relating to the acquisition of wealth. . . . There is no union in the great field of action to which he is engaged; but envy, and hatred, and opposition, to the close of the day,—every man's hand against his brother, and each struggling to exalt himself . . . by usurping the place of his weaker brother, who faints by his side."

13 See Gérin, *Charlotte Brontë*, chapters 14, "The Black Swan: Brussels, 1843," and 15, "A Slave to Sorrow."

14 Thomas Medwin's *Life of Shelley* records Byron as remarking that "Shelley, when I was in Switzerland, used to dose me with Wordsworth physic even to nausea" (quoted in Leslie Marchand, *Byron: A Biography* [New York: Knopf, 1957], 2:624 note). Brontë's repetition of the figure may be coincidental, but considering her passion for Byron (and the chance that she might have read Medwin) it is possible that we have here another instance of a female reinterpretation of a male metaphor.

15 Interestingly, Brontë associates the first reunion of Crimsworth and Frances with the redefinition of Milton we mentioned in note 14 of chapter 6. Bringing Crimsworth back (to the Rue Notre Dame aux Neiges) to tea, Frances asks him if her tea-service reminds him of England, their mutual "mother country," and reads to him from *Paradise Lost*, "Milton's invocation to [the] heavenly muse" (180). Thus, regaining her master and her life, she begins to regain her "mothers," both muse and country. And soon after this, as if to show that in a just world spiritual revival is accompanied by material prosperity, she

gets a teaching job at the best English school in Brussels.

16 It seems significant that the image of a crying child, hinting at irrepressible rage and/or anxiety, is repeated and elaborated upon in *Jane Eyre*, during the Thornfield episode, when Jane also has her prophetic dream about the destruction of her master's house.

17 Not only does this episode look forward to a crucial episode in *Shirley*, it also echoes Edward Crimsworth's early treatment of William: when he tried to whip William in the counting-house Edward cried that "I wish you were a dog! I'd set to this minute, and never stir from this spot till I'd cut every strip of flesh from your bones with this whip" (43).

18 Sylvia Plath, *Ariel* (New York: Harper & Row, 1966), pp. 10–12.

CHAPTER 10

Epigraphs: Moments of Being (New York: Harcourt Brace Jovanovich, 1977), p. 69; *Good Morning, Midnight* (New York: Vintage, 1974), p. 52; *Poems*, J. 410.

1 Matthew Arnold, *Letters of Matthew Arnold*, ed. George W. E. Russell (New York and London: Macmillan, 1896), 1:34.

2 Matthew Arnold, *The Letters of Matthew Arnold to Arthur Hugh Clough*, ed. Howard Foster Lowry (London and New York: Oxford University Press, 1932), p. 132.

3 Significantly, in view of comments by other contemporary critics, Arnold added in the same letter that "Religion or devotion or whatever it is to be called may be impossible for such people now: but they have at any rate not found a substitute for it, and it was better for the world when they comforted themselves with it." It should of course be noted, however, that *Jane Eyre* (like *Villette*) was warmly praised by many reviewers, usually for what George Henry Lewes, writing in *Fraser's Magazine* 36 (December 1847), called its "deep, significant reality."

4 *Quarterly Review* 84 (December 1848):173–74.

5 *The Christian Remembrancer* 25 (June 1853):423–43.

6 *Blackwood's Magazine* 77 (May 1855):554–68.

7 Richard Chase, "The Brontës, or Myth Domesticated," in *Jane Eyre*, ed. Richard J. Dunn (New York: Norton, 1971), pp. 468 and 464.

8 *Quarterly Review* 84 (December 1848):173–74. That Charlotte Brontë was herself quite conscious of the "revolutionary" nature of many of her ideas is clearly indicated by the fact that, as we shall see, she puts some of Miss Rigby's words into the mouth of the unpleasant and supercilious Miss Hardman in *Shirley*.

9 All references to *Jane Eyre* are to the Norton Critical Edition, ed. Richard J. Dunn (New York: Norton, 1971).

10 See, for instance, David Lodge, "Fire and Eyre: Charlotte Brontë's War of Earthly Elements," in *The Brontës*, ed. Ian Gregor, pp. 110–36.

11 Cf. *The Pilgrim's Progress:* "behold I saw a man clothed with rags . . . he brake out with a lamentable cry, saying, 'What shall I do?'" Charlotte Brontë made even more extensive references to *Pilgrim's Progress* in *Villette*, and in her use of Bunyan she was typical of many nineteenth-century novelists, who—from

Thackeray to Louisa May Alcott—relied on his allegory to structure their own fiction. For comments on Charlotte Brontë's allusions to *Pilgrim's Progress* in *Villette*, see Q. D. Leavis, "Introduction" to *Villette* (New York: Harper & Row, 1972), pp. vii–xli.

12 Mrs. Sarah Ellis, *The Family Monitor*, pp. 9–10.

13 See de Beauvoir (on Tertullian), *The Second Sex*, p. 156.

14 Adrienne Rich, "Jane Eyre: The Temptations of a Motherless Woman," *Ms.* 2, no. 4 (October 1973):69–70.

15 In *The Poetics of Space* Gaston Bachelard speaks of "the rationality of the roof" as opposed to "the irrationality of the cellar." In the attic, he notes, "the day's experiences can always efface the fears of the night," while the cellar "becomes buried madness, walled-in tragedy" (pp. 18–20). Thornfield's attic is, however, in his sense both cellar and attic, the imprisoning lumber-room of the past and the watch-tower from which new prospects are sighted, just as in Jane's mind mad "restlessness" coexists with "harmonious" reason.

16 See M. Jeanne Peterson, "The Victorian Governess: Status Incongruence in Family and Society," in *Suffer and Be Still: Women in the Victorian Age*, ed. Martha Vicinus (Bloomington, Ind.: Indiana University Press, 1972), pp. 3–19.

17 See C. Willet Cunnington, *Feminine Attitudes in the Nineteenth Century*, p. 119.

18 Chase, "The Brontës, or Myth Domesticated," p. 464.

19 See, for instance, Mrs. Oliphant, *Women Novelists of Queen Victoria's Reign* (London: Hurst & Blackett, 1897), p. 19: "The chief thing . . . that distressed the candid and as yet unaccustomed reader in "Jane Eyre" . . . was the character of Rochester's confidences to the girl whom he loved . . . that he should have talked to a girl so evidently innocent of his amours and his mistresses."

20 In a sense, Rochester's "contemptible" prearranged marriage to Bertha Mason is also a consequence of patriarchy, or at least of the patriarchal custom of primogeniture. A younger son, he was encouraged by his father to marry for money and status because sure provisions for his future could be made in no other way.

21 Claire Rosenfeld, "The Shadow Within: The Conscious and Unconscious Use of the Double," in *Stories of the Double*, ed. Albert J. Guerard (Philadelphia: J. B. Lippincott, 1967), p. 314. Rosenfeld also notes that "When the passionate uninhibited self is a woman, she more often than not is dark." Bertha, of course, is a Creole—swarthy, "livid," etc.

22 Chase, "The Brontës, or Myth Domesticated," p. 467.

23 Rich, "Jane Eyre: The Temptations of a Motherless Woman," p. 72. The question of what was "bearable for a powerless woman in the England of the 1840s" inevitably brings to mind the real story of Isabella Thackeray, who went mad in 1840 and was often (though quite mistakenly) thought to be the original of Rochester's mad wife. Parallels are coincidental, but it is interesting that Isabella was reared by a Bertha Mason-like mother of whom it was said that "wherever she went, 'storms, whirlwinds, cataracts, tornadoes' accompanied her," and equally interesting that Isabella's illness was signalled by mad inappropriate laughter and marked by violent suicide attempts, alternating with Jane

Eyre-like docility. That at one point Thackeray tried to guard her by literally *tying* himself to her ("a riband round her waist, & to my waist, and this always woke me if she moved") seems also to recall Rochester's terrible bondage. For more about Isabella Thackeray, see Gordon N. Ray, *Thackeray: The Uses of Adversity, 1811–1846* (New York: McGraw-Hill, 1955), esp. pp. 182–85 (on Isabella's mother) and chap. 10, "A Year of Pain and Hope," pp. 250–77.

24 See Emily Dickinson, *Poems*, J. 1072, "Title divine—is mine!/The Wife—without the Sign!"

25 See Emily Dickinson, *Poems*, J. 512, "The Soul has Bandaged Moments."

26 Rich, "Jane Eyre; The Temptations of a Motherless Woman," p. 106.

27 Ibid.

28 Ibid.

29 *Sartor Resartus*, chap. 9, "The Everlasting Yea."

30 Chase, "The Brontës, or Myth Domesticated," p. 467.

31 Robert Bernard Martin, *The Accents of Persuasion: Charlotte Brontë's Novels* (New York: Norton, 1966), p. 90.

32 *The Pilgrim's Progress* (New York: Airmont Library, 1969), pp. 140–41.

33 It should be noted here that Charlotte Brontë's use of *The Pilgrim's Progress* in *Villette* is much more conventional. Lucy Snowe seems to feel that she will only find true bliss after death, when she hopes to enter the Celestial City.

34 See Emily Dickinson, *Poems*, J. 1072, "Title divine—is mine!"

CHAPTER 11

Epigraphs: "Let No Charitable Hope," *Black Armour* (New York: George H. Doran, 1923), p. 35; "Charlotte Brontë," in *Rebecca West: A Celebration* (New York: Viking, 1977), p. 433; "As Now," *Cheap* (New York: Harcourt Brace Jovanovitch, 1972), p. 36.

1 *Edinburgh Review* 91 (January 1850): 84.

2 Charles Burkhart, *Charlotte Brontë: A Psychosexual Study of Her Novels* (London: Victor Gollancz Ltd., 1973), pp. 80–82. As well as exploring how Lewes himself influenced Brontë's decision to undertake a historical novel, Burkhart explains that *Shirley* is an attempt on her part to imitate the "big, detailed world picture" of Thackeray's novels. See also Moglen, *Charlotte Brontë*, pp. 152–53.

3 All citations here are from Charlotte Brontë, *Shirley* (New York: Dutton, 1970). Subsequent chapter references will appear parenthetically in the text.

4 "A Drama of Exile," *The Poetical Works of Elizabeth Barrett Browning*, pp. 179–211.

5 See, for instance, Patricia Beer, *Reader I Married Him* (London: MacMillan, 1974), pp. 106–9; Burkhart, *Charlotte Brontë*, pp. 80–82; Terence Eagleton, *Myths of Power: A Marxist Study of the Brontës* (New York: Knopf, 1975), pp. 58–63; Patricia Meyer Spacks, *The Female Imagination* (New York: Knopf, 1975), pp. 58–63.

6 Elizabeth Cady Stanton and the Revising Committee, *The Woman's Bible* (Seattle: Coalition Task Force on Women and Religion, 1974), p. 163. The editors of this edition quote Stanton's response to the clergyman who felt the

work was done by women for the devil: "his 'Satanic Majesty' was not invited to join the Revising Committee which consists of women alone" (p. viii).

7 In "Charlotte Brontë, Feminist Manquée," *Bucknell Review* 21, no. 1 (1973): 87–102, M. A. Blom discusses the Genesis myth in *Shirley* and the ways in which all of Brontë's novels explore male dread of female sexuality a'nd its result, the creation of the positive image of the doll and the negative image of the fiend.

8 Dorothy Dinnerstein, *The Mermaid and The Minotaur* (New York: Harper Colophon, 1977), p. 5.

9 Marlene Boskind-Lodahl, "Cinderella's Stepsisters: A Feminist Perspective on Anorexia Nervosa and Bulimia," 350. Her patients fast "in order to accommodate to some mysterious standard of perfection men held."

10 "A Drama of Exile," pp. 185 and 197.

11 Ibid., p. 196.

CHAPTER 12

Epigraphs: The Prisoner of Chillon, lines 389–91; letter to W. S. Williams, 26 July 1849; *Poems*, J. 670; "The Prisoner," *Here Comes and Other Poems* (New York: Signet, 1975), p. 229.

1 Letter to W. S. Williams, 6 November, 1852, in *The Brontës: Their Lives, Friendships and Correspondence*, ed. T. J. Wise and J. Alexander Symington (Oxford: Blackwell, 1932), 4:18.

2 Ibid.

3 "Frances," in *Poems of Charlotte and Branwell Brontë*, ed. T. J. Wise and J. Alexander Symington (Oxford: Shakespeare Head, 1934), pp. 20–28.

4 Matthew Arnold, "The Buried Life," lines 73 and 87.

5 This is precisely the irony that Anthony Hecht exploits in his parody "The Dover Bitch."

6 William Wordsworth, "A Slumber Did My Spirit Seal," line 3. The other Wordsworth poems to which we allude in the text are: "She Dwelt Among the Untrodden Ways," "I Travelled Among Unknown Men," "Strange Fits of Passion Have I Known," "Three Years She Grew in Sun and Shower," and "Lucy Gray."

7 Charlotte Brontë, *Villette* (New York: Harper Colophon, 1972), chap. 26. All subsequent references will be to this edition.

8 While most critics refer to a struggle between reason and imagination that remains abstract and oddly devoid of psychological meaning, Margot Peters persuasively places this antithesis in the larger debate over asserting one's identity in a hostile world. See *Charlotte Brontë: Style in the Novel* (Madison: University of Wisconsin Press, 1973), pp. 119–21. Also Andrew D. Hook, "Charlotte Brontë, the Imagination, and *Villette*," in *The Brontës: A Collection of Critical Essays*, ed. Ian Gregor, pp. 137–56.

9 In her introduction to the Harper Colophon *Villette*, Q. D. Leavis argues that "little Polly is an externalization of [Lucy's] inner self," p. xxvi.

10 See, for example, Robert Martin, *The Accents of Persuasion*, (New York: Norton, 1966), p. 153.

11 In her review of *Villette* in the *Daily News*, 3 February 1853, Harriet Martineau complains that "All the female characters, in all their thoughts and lives, are full of one thing, or are regarded by the reader in the light of that one thought —love." This review is reprinted in *The Brontës: The Critical Heritage*, ed. Miriam Allott (London and Boston: Routledge & Kegan Paul, 1974), pp. 171–74.

12 Richard Lovelace, "To *Althea*, from Prison," lines 25–26.

13 Even as brilliant a critic as Q. D. Leavis considers the nun only a "bogus supernatural theme," used by Brontë to maintain suspense and to get the book published. See her introduction to the Harper Colophon *Villette*, p. xxiii. Also, Nina Auerbach, "Charlotte Brontë: The Two Countries," *University of Toronto Quarterly* 42 (Summer 1973):339, argues in an otherwise insightful essay that the plot is unrelated to Lucy's struggle for identity. Of course there have been several important critical responses to these attacks; probably the most important is still Robert B. Heilman's "Charlotte Bronte's 'New' Gothic," in *From Jane Austen to Joseph Conrad*, ed. Robert C. Rathburn and Martin Steinmann, Jr. (Minneapolis: University of Minnesota Press, 1958), pp. 118–32.

14 George Eliot, *Westminster Review* 65 (January 1856):290–312.

15 Barbara Charlesworth Gelpi and Albert Gelpi, eds., "When We Dead Awaken," *Adrienne Rich's Poetry* (New York: Norton, 1975), p. 59.

16 Max Byrd, "The Madhouse, The Whorehouse and the Convent," *Partisan Review* (Summer 1977), discusses depictions of incest within convents by "Monk" Lewis, E. T. A. Hoffman, and Diderot.

17 Christina Rossetti, "Cobwebs," in Lona Mask Packer, *Christina Rossetti* (Berkeley and Los Angeles: University of California Press, 1963), p. 99.

18 Nina Auerbach, *Communities of Women: An Idea in Fiction* (Cambridge, Mass.: Harvard University Press, 1978), p. 109.

19 E. M. Forster, *Aspects of the Novel* (New York: Harcourt, Brace, 1964), pp. 92–93.

20 Kate Millett, *Sexual Politics* (New York: Avon, 1971), p. 198.

21 Martin, *Accents of Persuasion*, pp. 166–60; See Andrew D. Hook, "Charlotte Brontë, the Imagination, and *Villette*" for an excellent discussion of Lucy's incoherence in describing Vashti, p. 151. Vashti's story appears in the Book of Esther, 1:1 to 2:18.

22 Frances Harper, "Vashti," in *Early Black American Poets*, ed. William Robinson (Iowa: Wm. C. Brown Co., 1969), pp. 34–36.

23 In *Charlotte Brontë*, p. 481, Winifred Gérin explains that Rachel was most famous for her passionate role in *Phèdre*, but that Charlotte Brontë saw her act the "milder" roles of Camille in Corneille's *Les Trois Horaces* and Adrienne in *Adrienne Lecouvreur*.

24 Sylvia Plath, "Lady Lazarus," *Ariel*, pp. 6–9.

25 Charles Burkhart, *Charlotte Brontë: A Psychosexual Study of Her Novels* (London: Victor Gollancz Ltd., 1973), pp. 113–17; Heilman, "Brontë's 'New' Gothic"; E. D. H. Johnson, "'Daring the dread Glance': Charlotte Brontë's Treatment

of the Supernatural in *Villette*," *Nineteenth-Century Fiction* 20 (March 1966): 325–36.

26 Sylvia Plath, "Small Hours," *Crossing the Water* (New York: Harper & Row, 1971), p. 28.

27 The most recent feminist exploration of the nun as a symbol of female self-abnegation appears in Mona Isabel Barreno, Maria Teresa Horta and Maria Velho da Costa, *The Three Marias*, trans. Helen R. Lane (New York: Bantam, 1975).

28 Bell Gale Chevigny, *The Woman and the Myth: Margaret Fuller's Life and Writings* (Old Westbury, N.Y.: The Feminist Press, 1976), p. 440.

29 Anne Ross, "The Divine Hag of the Pagan Celts," in *The Witch Figure*, ed. Venetia Newall (London: Routledge & Kegan Paul, 1973), p. 162.

30 George Lyman Kittredge, *Witchcraft in Old and New England* (New York: Russell & Russell, 1929), pp. 73–103.

31 Earl A. Knies, *The Art of Charlotte Brontë* (Athens, Ohio: Ohio University Press, 1969), p. 194.

32 Matthew Arnold's "Haworth Churchyard" originally appeared in *Fraser's Magazine*, May 1855, and is reprinted in *The Brontës*, ed. Allott, pp. 306–10.

33 Patricia Beer, *"Reader, I Married Him,"* pp. 84–126, and Patricia Meyer Spacks, *The Female Imagination*, pp. 70–72.

CHAPTER 13

Epigraphs: "The Four Zoas" ("Vala: Night the First"); *Elements of the Philosophy of the Human Mind* (New York: Garland Publishers, 1971; reprint of 1792 edition, first pub. Edinburgh), IV, 242 (we are grateful to Michael Kearns for calling this passage to our attention); "She Walketh Veiled and Sleeping," in *The World Split Open*, ed. Bernikow, p. 224; "A Cloak," *Relearning the Alphabet* (New York: New Directions, 1970), p. 44.

1 John T. Irwin, *Doubling and Incest/Repetition and Revenge*, p. 96.

2 Martha Vicinus, ed., *The Widening Sphere* (Bloomington: Indiana University Press, 1977).

3 *The George Eliot Letters*. This quotation appears in a footnote in vol. 5, p. 280, with a reference to CA Stonehill, Inc. Catalogue, April 1934, item 108. Unless otherwise noted, subsequent references to Eliot's letters will appear parenthetically in the text.

4 Nina Auerbach, "The Power of Hunger: Demonism and Maggie Tulliver," *Nineteenth-Century Fiction* 30 (September 1972): 150–171; Carol Christ, "Aggression and Providential Death in George Eliot's Fiction," *Novel* (Winter 1976): 130–40; and Ellen Moers, *Literary Women*, pp. 45–52, 154.

5 Eliot explains that, unless there are such things as "miserable spirits," she doesn't feel bound to study them" (*Letters*, 5:281).

6 Most useful are the studies by U. C. Knoepflmacher, *George Eliot's Early Novels: The Limits of Realism* (Berkeley: University of California Press, 1968), pp. 128–61 and Ruby V. Redinger, *George Eliot: The Emergent Self* (New York: Knopf,

1975), pp. 400–05. For an earlier appreciation of how "The Lifted Veil" relates to the theme of failure and unfulfillment in Eliot's major fiction see Elliot L. Rubinstein, "A Forgotten Tale by George Eliot," *Nineteenth-Century Fiction* 17 (September 1962):175–83. The most recent study of Latimer's imprisonment within his own consciousness as an aspect of the novelist's dilemma is Gillian Beer's "Myth and the Single Consciousness: *Middlemarch* and *The Lifted Veil*," in *This Particular Web: Essays on Middlemarch*, ed. Ian Adams (Toronto and Buffalo: University of Toronto Press, 1975), pp. 91–115.

7 George Eliot, "The Lifted Veil," in *Silas Marner, "The Lifted Veil" and "Brother Jacob"* (Boston: Eates and Lauriat, 1895), p. 252. Subseuqent page references appear parenthetically in the text.

8 In her last completed book, *Impressions of Theophrastus Such* (New York: Harper & Brothers, n.d.), pp. 170–81, Eliot includes a sketch about a minor female author who forces her visitors to read and discuss in great detail an elegantly bound album of the critical reception her novel received. Essay xv is fittingly entitled "Diseases of Small Authorship."

9 Herbert Spencer, *An Autobiography*, 2 vols. (New York: D. Appleton and Co., 1904), 1:459.

10 Tillie Olsen, "Silences: When Writers Don't Write," in *Images of Women in Fiction*, ed. Susan Koppelman Cornillon (Ohio: Bowling Green University Popular Press, 1972), pp. 97–112.

11 George Eliot, "Woman in France: Madame de Sablé," in *Essays of George Eliot*, ed. Thomas Pinney (New York: Columbia University Press, 1963), p. 56.

12 Gordon Haight, *George Eliot* (Oxford: The Clarendon Press, 1968), p. 91.

13 George Eliot, *Middlemarch* (Boston: Houghton Mifflin, 1956), chap. 7. Subsequent chapter references will appear parenthetically in the text.

14 George Eliot, *Romola* (New York: Sm. L. Allison, n.d.), chap. 5. Subsequent chapter references will appear parenthetically in the text.

15 George Eliot, "The Legend of Jubal," *Poems*, 2:52–76. Subsequent references to poetical works will be placed in the text.

16 George Eliot, *Daniel Deronda* (Baltimore: Penguin Books, 1967), chap. 42. Subsequent chapter references will appear parenthetically in the text.

17 See Elaine Showalter's excellent essay on the importance of pseudonyms for many Victorian women novelists in "Women Writers and the Double Standard," *Woman in a Sexist Society*, ed. Vivian Gornick and Barbara K. Moran (New York: New American Library), pp. 452–79.

18 The failure of these visionary surrogates in Eliot's fiction helps explain Eliot's almost obsessive need to prove her success to herself through book sales, a mercenary impulse brilliantly traced and analyzed by Redinger, *George Eliot*, pp. 433–51.

19 Spencer, *Autobiography*, 458.

20 Eliot seems almost vindictive against the Princess when she causes her to regain her voice after marriage has ruled out the possibility of her ever using it again in public. This kind of plot is probably most obsessively evident in the short fiction of Mary Wilkins Freeman, as Judith Roman—a graduate student at

Indiana University—has pointed out to us.

21 "Life and Opinions of Milton," in *Essays of George Eliot*, p. 157.

22 Mary Shelley, "The Mortal Immortal," *Mary Shelley: Collected Tales and Stories*, ed. Charles E. Robinson (Baltimore and London: The Johns Hopkins University Press, 1976), pp. 219–30.

23 Mario Praz, *The Romantic Agony*, pp. 215–6.

24 George Eliot, *Felix Holt The Radical* (New York: Norton, 1970), chap. 5. Subsequent chapter references will appear parenthetically in the text.

25 Carlyle's conservative attitude toward women's proper sphere would only have complicated the tense relationship with Lewes and Eliot discussed by Redinger, *George Eliot*, pp. 269–70.

26 Curiously, there seems to be a full and wholly negative tradition associated with the name "Bertha." For instance, the self-assertive villainess of D. H. Lawrence's *Lady Chatterley's Lover* is certainly Mellor's sexually aggressive first wife, Bertha Coutts, whose name suggests at least an unconscious allusion to Bertha Mason Rochester. And of course certain World War I guns were called "Big Berthas."

27 The very difficulty of coming up with a word parallel to *misogyny* reveals the bias and basis of our linguistic inheritance.

28 Showalter, *A Literature of Their Own*, p. 126.

29 Woolf, "George Eliot," *The Common Reader*, p. 173.

30 See Mary Daly's discussion of female anti-feminism and the myth of feminine evil in *Beyond God the Father*, pp. 50–55.

31 Haight, *George Eliot*, p. 195.

32 Marghanita Laski discusses the possibility that Eliot discovered Lewes's infidelity after his death in *George Eliot and Her World* (London: Jarrold and Sons Ltd, 1973), pp. 111–12, but we are also indebted here to a conversation with U.C. Knoepflmacher. Regardless of her motives for the late marriage to Cross, Eliot's letters to him indicate her intense need to be looked after: she writes pathetically to him, "the sun it shines so cold, so cold, when there are no eyes to look love on me" (6:211–12).

33 Kenneth R. Johnston, "The Idiom of Vision," *New Perspectives on Coleridge and Wordsworth*, ed. Geoffrey H. Hartman (New York: Columbia University Press, 1971), pp. 1–39; Johnston, "'Home at Glasmere': Reclusive Song," *Studies in Romanticism* 14 (Winter 1975):1–28; Johnston, "Wordsworth's Last Beginning: *The Recluse* in 1808," *ELH* 43 (1976): 316–41. We are especially indebted to Kenneth Johnston's notes on the importance of the veil as a kind of "signature" of the visionary tradition that culminates in Yeats's *The Trembling of the Veil*. See also the discussion of Starobinski's and Poulet's image of the veil as a myth of transparency in Richard Macksey, "The Consciousness of the Critic: Georges Poulet and the Reader's Share," *Velocities of Change*, ed. Richard Macksey (Baltimore: The Johns Hopkins University Press, 1974), pp. 330–32.

34 "Christabel," lines 252–53. Also see Keat's "The Fall of Hyperion," lines 255–70, and Shelley's "The Witch of Atlas," which (interestingly) he dedicated to his wife, who, however, objected to the poem "upon the score of its containing no human interest."

35 Nathaniel Hawthorne, *The Blithedale Romance* (New York: Norton, 1958), pp. 127–28.

36 In "Methought I Saw My Late Espoused Saint," Milton describes the veiled face of his wife's spirit which visits him at night.

37 Christina Rossetti, "A Helpmeet for Him," *Poetical Works*, 2:214.

38 Mary Munro is currently writing on "Feminism and Spiritualism in Nineteenth-Century American Fiction" at Indiana University.

39 Harriet Beecher Stowe, "The Sullivan Looking-Glass," *Regional Sketches*, ed. John R. Adams (New Haven, Conn.: College & University Press, 1972), p. 114.

40 Doris Lessing's first allusion to the repetition of class and family structures of exploitation occurs in *A Proper Marriage* (New York: New American Library, 1952), p. 95.

41 Alexander Pope, *An Essay on Man*, 1. 193–94.

42 Elizabeth Barrett Browning, *Letters*, 2:445.

43 Emily Dickinson, *Letters*, 2:506.

44 Gordon Haight discusses several of Eliot's relationships with her "spiritual daughters," *George Eliot*, pp. 452–54.

45 See Lee Edwards, "Women, Energy and *Middlemarch*," *The Massachusetts Review* 13 (Winter/Spring 1972):223–83 and the response of Zelda Austen, "Why Feminist Critics Are Angry With George Eliot," *College English* 37 (1976): 549–61.

CHAPTER 14

Epigraphs: "A Description of One of the Pieces of Tapestry at Long-Leat," lines 1–13, *The Poems of Anne Countess of Winchilsea*, p. 47; "The Book of Urizen," chap. VIII, no. 7; *Daniel Deronda*, chap. 56.

1 W. H. Channing, J. F. Clarke and R. W. Emerson, *Memoirs of Margaret Fuller Ossoli*, 2 vols. (Boston: 1852), 1:248–49.

2 Ann Douglas, *The Feminization of American Culture*, p. 262.

3 Emily Dickinson, *Letters*, 2:551. In thanking Susan Gilbert Dickinson for a copy of *Daniel Deronda* Dickinson includes a poem of eulogy on Eliot's death: "Her Losses make our Gains ashamed—/She bore Life's empty Pack/As gallantly as if the East/Were swinging at her Back./Life's empty Pack is heaviest,/As every Porter knows—/In vain to punish Honey—/It only sweeter grows," *Letters*, 3:769–70.

4 Bell Gale Chevigny, ed. *The Woman and the Myth: Margaret Fuller's Life and Writing*, p. 57. This quote is taken from her journal and dated November 1835.

5 Ibid., p. 63. Quoted from the *Memoirs*, 1:297.

6 "Women in France: Madame de Sablé," *Essays of George Eliot*, p. 53.

7 Chevigny, ed., *The Woman and the Myth*, p. 216.

8 Margaret Fuller, *Woman in the Nineteenth Century* (New York: Norton, 1971), p. 115; Chevigny, ed., *The Woman and the Myth*, pp. 57–59.

9 *Woman in the Nineteenth Century*, p. 156.

10 Chevigny, ed., *The Woman and the Myth*, p. 203–05. Interestingly, in her essay "The Prose Works of Milton," Fuller explains that "if Milton be not absolutely

the greatest of human beings, it is hard to name one who combines so many features of God's own image, ideal grandeur, a life of spotless virtue, heroic endeavour and constancy, with such richness of gifts." See her *Papers on Literature and Art* (New York: Wiley and Putnam, 1846), p. 36.

11 Elizabeth Barrett Browning, *Letters to Mrs. David Ogilvy* ed. Peter N. Heydon and Philip Kelley (London: Murray, 1974), p. 31.

12 Elizabeth Barrett Browning to Mrs. Jameson, 12 April 1853, *Letters*, 2:110–11.

13 Emily Dickinson, *Letters*, 1:237.

14 "Silly Novels by Lady Novelists," in *Essays of George Eliot*, p. 319.

15 "Woman in France: Madame de Sablé," *Essays of George Eliot*, p. 53. Unfortunately Eliot never specifies about these distinctively female forms in art.

16 Elizabeth Ammons, "Heroines in *Uncle Tom's Cabin*," *American Literature* 49 (May 1977):172.

17 Harriet Beecher Stowe, *Uncle Tom's Cabin* (New York: Harper & Row, 1965), p. 447. Subsequent references will appear parenthetically in the text.

18 *Woman in the Nineteenth Century*, pp. 29–30.

19 Louisa May Alcott, *Little Women* (New York: Collier Books, 1962), p. 95.

20 To Tottie Fox, 24 December 1854; quoted by Winifred Gérin in *Elizabeth Gaskell: A Biography* (Oxford: Clarendon Press, 1976), p. 154.

21 Ibid., pp. 254–55.

22 George Eliot, *Scenes of Clerical Life* (Baltimore: Penguin, 1973), pp. 80–81. Subsequent citations appear parenthetically in the text. See Neil Roberts, *George Eliot: Her Belief and Her Art* (Pittsburgh: University of Pittsburgh Press, 1975), pp. 53–62, and Derek and Sybil Oldfield, "*Scenes of Clerical Life:* The Diagram and The Picture," *Critical Essays on George Eliot*, ed. Barbara Hardy (London: Routledge & Kegan Paul, 1970), pp. 1–18.

23 Alexander Welsh, *The City of Dickens*, pp. 182–84.

24 The title that seems to be an exception to this rule, *Romola*, is also a kind of camouflage since it takes the emphasis off the demonic, fallen double (Baldassarre) and his plot of revenge, and emphasizes the angelically exemplary heroine.

25 Carol Christ, "Aggression and Providential Death in George Eliot's Fiction," *Novel* (Winter 1976):130–40.

26 Nina Auerbach, "The Power of Hunger: Demonism and Maggie Tulliver," is probably the best essay on gothic elements in *The Mill on the Floss*, but Bernard Paris's discussion of Maggie's masochism is also very helpful. See *A Psychological Approach to Fiction* (Bloomington: Indiana University Press, 1974), pp. 165–89.

27 Ruby V. Redinger discusses Eliot's use of Antigone in Eliot's essay-review and in *The Mill on the Floss* in *George Eliot: The Emergent Self*, pp. 314–15, 325.

28 J. L. Borges, "The Library of Babel," *Ficciones* (New York: Grove Press, 1962), p. 85.

29 Gillian Beer discusses Eliot's knowledge of Mrs. Jameson's *Sacred and Legendary Art* and the legend of St. Dorothea in "*Middlemarch* and The Lifted Veil," *Essays on Middlemarch*, ed. Ian Adam, p. 108–09.

30 We are indebted to Rachel Blau DuPlessis's discussion of enthrallment in "The Transformation of Cultural Scripts in H.D.," at the Special Session on Women

Poets, convention of the Modern Language Association, December 1977.

31 Sylvia Plath, "Cut," in *Ariel*, pp. 13–14.

32 U. C. Knoepflmacher, "Fusing Fact and Myth: The New Reality of *Middlemarch*," *Essays on Middlemarch*, ed. Ian Adam, p. 54.

33 W. J. Harvey, "Introduction to *Middlemarch*," in *George Eliot's Middlemarch: A Casebook*, ed. Patrick Swinden (New York: Macmillan, 1972), p. 196.

34 See David Carroll's "*Middlemarch* and the Externality of Fact," in *Essays on Middlemarch*, ed. Ian Adam, pp. 73–90. Also Alan Mintz, *George Eliot and the Novel of Vocation* (Cambridge, Mass.: Harvard University Press, 1978), pp. 93–6, 115–21, 146–50.

35 Edward W. Said, *Beginnings: Intention and Method*, p. 76–77.

36 Gayatri Chakravorty Spivak, "Introduction," *Of Grammatology*, p. xi.

37 Margaret Atwood, "A Place: Fragments," anthologized in *Possibilities of Poetry*, ed. Richard Kostelanetz (New York: Delta Books, 1970), pp. 315–18.

38 Diane Wakoski, *Inside the Blood Factory* (New York: Doubleday, 1968), p. 67.

39 *The Diary of Alice James*, ed. Leon Edel (New York: Dodd, Mead & Co., 1964), p. 149.

40 *The Diary of Alice James*, pp. 40–41. In spite of her professed dislike for Eliot, Alice James's sense of paralysis and pent-in anger comes eerily close to Eliot's heroines' struggles. When the sister of illustrious William and Henry James came to the end of her invalid life of confinement, she dropped the tone of humor and spirit so valued by her family and dictated the final entry in her *Diary* to her nurse and companion, Katherine Loring: "All through Saturday, the 5th, and even in the night, Alice was making sentences. One of the last things she said to me was to make a correction in the sentence of March 4th 'moral discords and nervous horrors.' This dictation of March 4th was rushing about in her brain all day, and although she was very weak and it tired her much to dictate, she could not get her head quiet until she had had it written: then she was relieved . . ." (pp. 232–33).

41 Adrienne Rich, "Vesuvius at Home," in *Shakespeare's Sisters*, ed. Gilbert and Gubar, pp. 99–121.

42 Mary Ellmann, *Thinking About Women*, p. 194.

43 H. D., *Helen in Egypt* (New York: New Directions, 1961), p. 97.

44 "The Three Spinners," *The Complete Grimm's Fairy Tales*, ed. Joseph Campbell (New York: Pantheon, 1972), pp. 83–86.

45 Helen Diner, *Mothers and Amazons*, p. 16.

46 Reva Stump, *Movement and Vision in George Eliot's Novels* (Seattle: University of Washington Press, 1959), pp. 172–214; J. Hillis Miller, "Optic and Semiotic in *Middlemarch*," in *The Worlds of Victorian Fiction*, ed. Jerome Buckley (Cambridge, Mass.: Harvard University Press, 1976), pp. 125–45.

47 See J. Hillis Miller's "Optic and Semiotic in *Middlemarch*," p. 144; U. C. Knoepflmacher's "*Middlemarch*: An Avuncular View," *Nineteenth Century Fiction* 30 (June 1975): 53–81; and Kathleen Blake's "*Middlemarch* and the Woman Question," *Nineteenth-Century Fiction* 31 (December 1976): 285–312, which relies on the earlier essay "George Eliot in *Middlemarch*," by Quentin Anderson in

From Dickens to Hardy (Baltimore: Pelican, 1958), pp. 274–93. Although it is not concerned directly with gender, an extremely helpful analysis of the narrator's generalizing tendencies is Isobel Armstrong's *"Middlemarch*: A Note on George Eliot's Wisdom," *Critical Essays on George Eliot,* ed. Barbara Hardy, pp. 116–32.

48 Margaret Cavendish, *Poems and Fancies* (Scolar Press, 1972), pp. 2, 156.

49 U. C. Knoepflmacher mentions the importance of Ariadne and speculates on the possible meanings of the Minotaur in "Fusing Fact and Myth: The New Reality of *Middlemarch,*" in *This Particular Web,* ed. Ian Adams, pp. 43–72. J. Hillis Miller is also studying this myth, as his last essay on Middlemarch (with its concern with the web) and the title of his forthcoming book ("Ariadne's Thread") seem to indicate. With respect to women's literature, it is interesting that Elizabeth Barrett Browning chose to translate the myth of Bacchus finding Ariadne sleeping; her Bacchus calls Ariadne, "the true deed's true teller," in "How Bacchus Comforts Ariadne [Dionysiaca, Lib. XLVII]," *The Poetical Works,* pp. 514–15.

50 Barbara Hardy, *"Middlemarch* and the Passions," in *Essays on Middlemarch,* ed. Ian Adam, p. 16.

51 Adrienne Rich, "Natural Resources," *The Dream of a Common Language* (New York: Norton, 1978), p. 62.

52 The best discussion of Eliot's reputation with women writers appears in Showalter, *A Literature of Their Own,* pp. 107–10.

53 Chevigny, ed., *The Woman and the Myth,* p. 216.

CHAPTER 15

Epigraphs: "To George Sand: A Recognition," *Poetical Works of Elizabeth Barrett Browning,* p. 363; *A Room of One's Own,* p. 51; *The Letters of Elizabeth Barrett Browning,* 1:230–32; *After Great Pain: The Inner Life of Emily Dickinson* (Cambridge, Mass.: The Belknap Press of Harvard University Press, 1971), p. 495.

1 Compare Virginia Woolf's "For we think back through our mothers if we are women. It is useless to go to the great men writers for help, however much one may go to them for pleasure" (*A Room of One's Own,* p. 79).

2 Woolf, *A Room,* pp. 48–51.

3 Elizabeth Barrett Browning, *Letters,* 1:230–32.

4 Woolf, *A Room,* pp. 79–80.

5 Ibid., p. 98.

6 See "Aurora Leigh" and "I am Christina Rossetti" in *The Second Common Reader* (New York: Harcourt, Brace and Company, 1932), pp. 182–92 and 214–22.

7 Reprinted in Richard B. Sewall, ed., *Emily Dickinson: A Collection of Critical Essays* (Englewood Cliffs, N. J.: Prentice-Hall, 1963), p. 120. To do Reeves justice, we should note that he quotes this statement in order to dispute it.

8 Theodore Roethke, "The Poetry of Louise Bogan," *Selected Prose of Theodore Roethke,* ed. Ralph J. Mills, Jr. (Seattle: University of Washington Press, 1965), pp. 133–34.

9 "Emily Dickinson: A Poet Restored," in Sewall, ed., *Emily Dickinson,* p. 92.

10 Ibid., p. 89.

11 Quoted in Reeves, "Introduction to *Selected Poems*," p. 119.

12 Ransom, "Emily Dickinson: A Poet Restored," p. 97.

13 Gardner B. Taplin, *The Life of Elizabeth Barrett Browning* (New Haven: Yale University Press, 1957), p. 417.

14 *The Edinburgh Review* 189 (1899):420–39.

15 Samuel B. Holcombe, "Death of Mrs. Browning," *The Southern Literary Messenger* 33 (1861): 412–17.

16 *The Christian Examiner* 72 (1862):65–88.

17 "Poetic Aberrations," *Blackwood's* 87 (1860):490–94. The invidious comparison with Nightingale must have been particularly irritating to Barret Browning, who once commented that the famous nurse was still performing the age-old female function of handmaiden to men. (See *Letters*, 2:189.)

18 See Showalter, *A Literature of Their Own*, especially "The Double Critical Standard and the Feminine Novel," pp. 73–99. "We tend to forget how insistently Victorian reviewers made women the targets of *ad feminam* criticism," Showalter points out (p. 73).

19 *A Room*, p. 51. Woolf does also refer to lost novelists here, but it is plain from the succeeding paragraph that she really means to concentrate on poetry, which she defines as arising from the primary literary impulse.

20 Ibid., p. 65.

21 To Charlotte Brontë, March 1837.

22 "Conclusion" to *The Renaissance*.

23 See "An Essay on Criticism," part 1, lines 135–40.

24 "On Not Knowing Greek," *The Common Reader*, p. 24. In its context, this statement is curiously ambiguous: Woolf seems to mean that *all* modern readers are painfully ignorant of Greek. But her remark about "schoolboys," together with statements she makes elsewhere about female ignorance of classical languages, suggests that she really wants to speak primarily about women, and especially about herself (with her "we" being an editorial "we").

25 Ransom, "Emily Dickinson: A Poet Restored," p. 100.

26 *A Room*, p. 100.

27 See T. S. Eliot, "Tradition and the Individual Talent," and Emily Dickinson, letter to T. W. Higginson, July 1862, in *The Letters of Emily Dickinson*, ed. Johnson, 2:412.

28 Moers, *Literary Women*, p. 215.

29 See John Keats, letter to Benjamin Bailey, November 22, 1817.

30 *Maude: Prose and Verse*, edited and with an introduction by R. W. Crump (Hamden, Conn.: Archon Books, 1976), pp. 30–31.

31 Ibid, p. 37.

32 Ibid, pp. 35–36.

33 Ibid., p. 41.

34 Ibid, p. 53.

35 Ibid., p. 72.

36 Ibid., p. 32.

37 "Passing and Glassing," in *The Poetical Works of Christina G. Rossetti*, 2:115.

38 "Sleep and Poetry," lines 96–98.

39 See "To Homer," which begins "Standing aloof in giant ignorance, / Of thee I hear and of the Cyclades. . . ."

40 It is worth remembering here that twelve years after his sister wrote *Maude*, Dante Gabriel Rossetti—perhaps influenced by her story, perhaps by the Keats episode—buried his own poems in his wife's coffin. But the renunciation Christina imagines for her female poet did not prove viable for an ambitious male poet: within seven years Rossetti had his wife's body exhumed so that he could recover his poems for publication. For further details see Oswald Doughty, *A Victorian Romantic: Dante Gabriel Rossetti* (London: Frederick Muller Ltd., 1949), pp. 412–19.

41 *Maude*, p. 75. "On Keats," in *New Poems*, ed. W. M. Rossetti (1896), pp. 22–23.

42 To Charles Brown, 30 November 1820.

43 To Thomas Wentworth Higginson, 15 April 1862, *Letters*, 2:403.

44 Muriel Spark, *Child of Light*, pp. 48–49.

45 Richard Sewall, *The Life of Emily Dickinson*, in 2 volumes (New York: Farrar, Straus & Giroux, 1974), 2:541.

46 See Leslie Fiedler's introduction and notes to *Whitman: Selections from Leaves of Grass* (New York: Dell, 1959), especially pp. 7 and 183.

47 "Song of Myself," section 24.

48 Fiedler, introduction to *Selections from Leaves of Grass*, p. 8. See also Sewall, *The Life of Emily Dickinson*, 1:8.

49 Ransom, "Emily Dickinson: A Poet Restored," p. 98. For a further discussion of the striking Dickinson/Whitman polarities, see Terence Diggory, "Armoured Women, Naked Men," in *Shakespeare's Sisters*, ed. Gilbert and Gubar, pp. 135–52.

50 Albert Gelpi, "Emily Dickinson and the Deerslayer: The Dilemma of the Woman Poet in America," in *Shakespeare's Sisters*, ed. Gilbert and Gubar, pp. 122–34.

51 Rufus Griswold, ed., *The Female Poets of America* (Philadelphia: Carey & Hart, 1848). Caroline May, ed., *The American Female Poets* (New York: Leavitt & Allen Bros., 1869). The quotation is from "Preface," May, p. vi. For more about American "lady poets" in the nineteenth century, see Ann Douglas, *The Feminization of American Culture*. "Preface," to *American Female Poets*, p. vi.

52 May, loc. cit.

53 See Ruth Miller, *The Poetry of Emily Dickinson* (Middletown, Conn.: Wesleyan University Press, 1968), especially chapter 9, "The Practice of Poetry."

54 Jack L. Capps, *Emily Dickinson's Reading: 1836–1886* (Cambridge, Mass.: Harvard University Press, 1966), p. 86.

55 *Aurora Leigh*, in *The Poetical Works of Elizabeth Barrett Browning*, p. 8.

56 *Maude*, pp. 48–49.

57 D. H. Lawrence, Preface to *Collected Poems, 1928*, in *The Complete Poems of D. H. Lawrence*, ed. Vivian de Sola Pinto and Warren Roberts (New York: Viking, 1964), pp. 27—28.

58 To John Wheelock, 1 July 1935, in *What the Woman Lived: Selected Letters of*

Louise Bogan, 1920–1970, ed. Ruth Limmer (New York: Harcourt Brace Jovanovich, 1973), p. 86.

59 Sewall, *The Life of Emily Dickinson*, 2:580.
60 Miller, *The Poetry of Emily Dickinson*, pp. 24–25.
61 See Richard Wilbur, "Sumptuous Destitution," in Sewall, ed., *Emily Dickinson*, pp. 127–36.
62 "Goblin Market," *The Poetical Works of Christina G. Rossetti*, 1:3–22.
63 *Paradise Lost*, 9. 599–600, and 679.
64 Ibid., 9. 790–800.
65 See Ralph Wardle, *Mary Wollstonecraft*, p. 322.
66 Richard Polwhele, *The Unsex'd Females: A Poem* (New York: Garland, 1974; first published 1798), pp. 6–9. Polwhele complained in a footnote that "Botany has lately become a fashionable amusement with the ladies. But how the study of the sexual system of plants can accord with female modesty, I am not able to comprehend." And in his diatribe against Wollstonecraft he wrote that "I shudder at the new unpictur'd scene, / Where unsex'd woman vaunts the imperious mien; Where girls . . . With bliss botanic as their bosoms heave, / Still pluck forbidden fruit, with mother Eve, / For puberty in sighing florets pant, / Or point the prostitution of a plant; / Dissect its organ of unhallow'd lust, / And fondly gaze the titillating dust." He felt, in other words, that botanizing literally accompanied sexual and political self-assertion, as a sign of female depravity.
67 The dynamics of Jeanie's (and Laura's) disease are further illuminated by Rossetti's sonnet "The World." Here the speaker describes "The World" as a woman who is beautiful by day, offering "Ripe fruits, sweet flowers, and full satiety," but who becomes "a very monster void of love and prayer" by night. Thus "By day she stands a lie: by night she stands, / In all the naked horror of the truth, / With pushing horns and clawed and clutching hands." Clearly Rossetti has converted the traditional allegorical threesome of "the world, the flesh, and the devil" into a single terrifying figure who incarnates, among other things, her deep anxieties about female ambition, inspiration, and self-assertion. (See *Poetical Works*, 1:96.)
68 "From House to Home," Ibid., pp. 103–12.
69 See Woolf, "Aurora Leigh," in *The Second Common Reader*.
70 The hint of incest in the courtship of the lovers, together with the striking parallelism of Aurora Leigh's name with the name of Byron's half-sister Augusta Leigh, suggests that Barrett Browning may be simultaneously retelling and "purifying" the legendary story of Byron's shocking romance with Augusta. It has also been suggested that Mrs. Gaskell's *Ruth* was the source for the Marian Erle story.
71 *Aurora Leigh*, pp. 22–27.
72 Ibid., p. 173.
73 Ibid., p. 177.
74 Ibid., p. 178.
75 See J. 593, "I think I was enchanted / When first a sombre Girl— / I read that Foreign Lady— / The Dark—felt beautiful—"

CHAPTER 16

Epigraphs: Woman in the Nineteenth Century, p. 101; Higginson, quoted in Thomas Johnson, ed., *The Letters of Emily Dickinson,* 2:473; *Poems,* J. 669.

1 To T. W. Higginson, July 1862, *Letters* 2:412.

2 Richard B. Sewall, *The Life of Emily Dickinson,* 1:240.

3 Ibid.

4 See Suzanne Juhasz, *Naked and Fiery Forms, Modern American Poetry by Women: A New Tradition* (New York: Harper Colophon Books, 1976), chap. 1, "The Double Bind of the Woman Poet," pp. 1–6.

5 For a discussion of Dickinson's use of *Aurora Leigh,* see Ellen Moers, *Literary Women,* pp. 55–62. For other analyses of Dickinson's reading, see Jack L. Capps, *Emily Dickinson's Reading,* and Ruth Miller, *The Poetry of Emily Dickinson,* Appendix III, "Emily Dickinson's Reading," pp. 385–430.

6 Dickinson almost always referred to her home as "my Father's House." Her use of the phrase suggests her sense that she was an "Empress of Calvary" not unlike Christ, who did his "Father's business," but it also indicates her clear consciousness of the nature and power of the patriarchal culture in which she reached artistic maturity. That this father-dominated culture was one in which she had to read *furtively* is, moreover, one of the first points she made to Higginson: "Father . . . buys me many Books—but begs me not to read them—because he fears they joggle the Mind" (*Letters,* 2:404).

7 Ibid., p. 554.

8 See J. 271 ("A Solemn thing—it was—I said—/A woman—white—to be—"), J. 605 ("The Spider holds a Silver Ball/In unperceived Hands—/And dancing softly to Himself/His Yarn of Pearl unwinds—"), and J. 732 ("She rose to his Requirement . . . If ought she missed in Her new Day,/Of Amplitude, or Awe—/ . . . It lay unmentioned . . .").

9 See Blake, "To Nobodaddy" ("Why art thou silent & invisible,/Father of Jealousy?") and "When Klopstock England defied,/Uprose William Blake in his pride;/For old Nobodaddy aloft/Farted & Belched & cough'd."

10 See J. 528, "Mine—by the Right of the White Election!/Mine—by the Royal Seal!"

11 See J. 401, "What Soft—Cherubic Creatures—/These Gentlewomen are—/One would as soon assault a Plush—Or violate a Star—."

12 See Catherine Linton's speech to Nelly Dean in chapter 12 of *Wuthering Heights:* "I wish I were a girl again, half savage, and hardy, and free; and laughing at injuries, not maddening under them! Why am I so changed? why does my blood rush into a hell of tumult at a few words?"

13 *Letters,* 2:518–19.

14 See J. 510, "It was not Death, for I stood up,/And all the Dead, lie down/ . . . [and yet it was] As if my life were shaven/And fitted to a frame,/And could not breathe without a key," and J. 486, "I was the slightest in the House—/I took the smallest Room—."

15 See J. 1072, "Title divine—is mine!/The Wife—without the Sign!"

16 See Barbara Clarke Mossberg, "The Daughter Construct in Emily Dickinson's Poetry" (Ph.D. diss., Indiana University, 1977).

17 Higginson once described Dickinson in a letter as "my partially cracked poetess at Amherst." See Jay Leyda, ed., *The Years and Hours of Emily Dickinson* (New Haven: Yale University Press, 1960), 2:263.

18 *Letters*, 1:104.

19 Ibid., p. 99.

20 See J. 908, " 'Tis Sunrise—Little Maid—Hast Thou / No Station in the Day?"

21 *Letters*, 2:460.

22 Ibid., p. 439.

23 See, for instance, her high-spirited early letters to William Cowper Dickinson (14 February 1849), to George H. Gould [?] (February 1850), and to Elbridge G. Bowdoin (February 1851), *Letters*, 1:75–77, 91–93, 110.

24 Ransom, "Emily Dickinson: A Poet Restored," p. 97.

25 *Letters*, 3:777.

26 John Cody makes this suggestion in *After Great Pain*, pp. 416–22.

27 *Letters*, 1:209–10.

28 Quoted in Millicent Todd Bingham, *Emily Dickinson's Home: Letters of Edward Dickinson and His Family* (New York: Harper & Row, 1955), p. 407.

29 The quotation from Catherine Dickinson Sweetser appears in Bingham, *Home*, p. 17, and the quotation from Edward Dickinson in Sewall, *The Life of Emily Dickinson*, p. 47.

30 Leyda, *Years and Hours*, 1:30.

31 He "read lonely and rigorous books," *Letters*, 2:473; he "never played," ibid., p. 486; his "Heart was pure and terrible," ibid., p. 528.

32 He attacked "the Women's Suffrage People," Leyda, *Years and Hours*, 2:218; he was "thin, dry and speechless," *Letters*, 2:245.

33 *Letters*, 2:559 (to Louise and Frances Norcross).

34 *Jane Eyre*, chapter 34. The book itself is in the Houghton Library at Harvard University. Although Sewall does not include it in his list of volumes having marginal markings by Dickinson, the two thin lines which appear on these pages correspond exactly to the markings Sewall (and others) consider characteristic ED markings. See Sewall, 2:678–79, note 8.

35 Clark Griffith, *The Long Shadow: Emily Dickinson's Tragic Poetry* (Princeton: Princeton University Press, 1964), p. 155.

36 *Letters*, 2:391.

37 See J. 665, "Dropped into the Ether Acre—/ Wearing the Sod Gown . . . Journey of Down—and Whip of Diamond—/ Riding to meet the Earl—." In many ways this is Dickinson's most mordant (and morbid) comment on the genre of romance. By comparison, the much more famous "Because I could not stop for Death" (J. 712) is gently sentimental.

38 For the text of this letter and a discussion of it, see Winifred Gérin, *Charlotte Brontë*, pp. 290–93.

39 Charlotte Brontë, *Shirley*, chapter 1, "Levitical."

40 *Letters*, 2:391.

41 Gérin, *Charlotte Brontë*, p. 291.

42 Quoted in Bell Gale Chevigny, *The Woman and the Myth*, p. 278.

43 Quoted in Chevigny, p. 61.

44 See Cody, *After Great Pain*, p. 52.

45 *Letters*, 2:375.

46 We are indebted to Celeste Turner Wright for calling this poem to our attention.

47 George Eliot, *Armgart, Poems*, p. 92; Simone de Beauvoir, *The Second Sex*, p. 58.

48 Albert Gelpi, "Emily Dickinson and the Deerslayer."

49 See Northrop Frye, *Fearful Symmetry: A Study of William Blake* (Princeton: Princeton University Press, 1947), pp. 206–29, et passim.

50 William R. Sherwood, *Circumference and Circumstance: Stages in the Mind and Art of Emily Dickinson* (New York: Columbia University Press, 1968), pp. 152 and 231.

51 Herman Melville, *Moby Dick*, chapter 42, "The Whiteness of the Whale."

52 See J. 985, "The Missing All—prevented Me / From missing minor Things" and J. 532, "I tried to think a lonelier Thing / Than any I had seen— / Some Polar Expiation—An Omen in the Bone / Of Death's tremendous nearness—."

53 See Leslie Fiedler, *Love and Death in the American Novel* (New York: Dell, 1966), and Wendy Martin, "Seduced and Abandoned in the New World: The Image of Woman in American Fiction," in Vivian Gornick and Barbara K. Moran, ed., *Woman in Sexist Society: Studies in Power and Powerlessness* (New York: Basic Books, 1971).

54 See Alexander Welsh, *The City of Dickens*, chapter 11, "Two Angels of Death," pp. 180–95.

55 Elizabeth Barrett Browning, *Aurora Leigh, Poetical Works*, pp. 21, 28, 149.

56 Alfred, Lord Tennyson, "The Lady of Shalott," part 1, lines 24–27; part 2, lines 39, 72; part 3, line 116; part 4, lines 136, 146.

57 Nathaniel Hawthorne, "The Snow Image," *The Complete Novels and Selected Tales of Nathaniel Hawthorne*, ed. Norman Holmes Pearson (New York: Modern Library, 1937), p. 1167. Since Dickinson had certainly read Hawthorne, we might also speculate that her use of "Pearl" imagery was influenced by his characterization of little Pearl in *The Scarlet Letter*, a metaphorical child who is herself in part the fictional creation of her outcast mother. In addition, the lime-kiln into which Hawthorne's Ethan Brand plunges at the end of "Ethan Brand: An Abortive Romance," may well have helped suggest the forge Dickinson describes in "Dare you see a Soul *at the White Heat?*"

58 Harriet Beecher Stowe, *Uncle Tom's Cabin; or, Life Among the Lowly*, chapter 42, "An Authentic Ghost Story." Elizabeth Barrett Browning, *Poetical Works*, p. 21.

59 Christina Rossetti, "A Soul," in *New Poems by Christina Rossetti*, ed. William Michael Rossetti (New York: Macmillan & Co., 1896), p. 77.

60 Stowe, *Uncle Tom's Cabin*, chapter 42.

61 See *Letters*, 2:412: "Men do not call the surgeon, to commend—the Bone," Dickinson told Higginson in July 1862, "but to set it, Sir, and fracture within, is more critical."

62 Compare, for instance, Emily Brontë's "Julian M. and A. G. Rochelle" ("Silent

is the House—all are laid asleep") or her "Hope" ("Hope was but a timid friend; / She sat without my grated den"), in *The Complete Poems of Emily Jane Brontë*, ed. C. W. Hatfield (New York: Columbia University Press, 1941), pp. 192, 236.

63 See J. 1445, "Death is the supple Suitor / That wins at last— / It is a stealthy Wooing / Conducted first / By pallid innuendoes / And dim approach."

64 The parallels between this speaker and Sin, in *Paradise Lost*, are very striking. Sin is, after all, the Favorite of both metaphorical Doom (Satan) and literal Doom (Death), both of whom afflict her with turbulent children. In a more specifically personal sense, however, for Dickinson the burden with which this poem is pregnant is also the burden of the *body* of her poetry, which is a bandaged secret she must carry about with her. Similarly, the untimely burial she discusses also represents the untimely burial of her poetry, written in secret and hidden away (before her death) in a coffinlike bureau drawer. For a different treatment of this theme, see J. 1737, "Rearrange a 'Wife's' affection!... Big my Secret but it's bandaged— / It will never get away."

65 See *Jane Eyre*, chapter 25.

66 See J. 997 ("Crumbling is not an instant's Act"), J. 1356 ("The Rat is the concisest Tenant"), J. 793 ("Grief is a Mouse"), J. 1670 ("In Winter in my Room / I came upon a Worm— / Pink, lank and warm—"), J. 1275 ("The Spider as an Artist / Has never been employed— / ... Neglected Son of Genius / I take thee by the Hand—").

67 De Beauvoir, *The Second Sex*, p. 144. For poems about women as spiderlike weavers, see (among many others) Lucy Larcom, "Weaving," and Kathleen Raine, "The Clue," in Louise Bernikow, ed., *The World Split Open*: pp. 180, 200.

68 Compare H. D.'s "self-out-of-self, / /selfless, / that pearl-of-great-price," in *Trilogy* (New York: New Directions, 1973), p. 9.

69 Albert Gelpi, *Emily Dickinson: The Mind of the Poet*, p. 151. It is useful to compare Dickinson's vision of the spider spinning beauty—"Continents of Light"—from within him/herself, with Swift's disgust at the spider's art, which he defines as dirty because spun from the insect's bowels. There is a sense in which Dickinson is revising Swift, or at least Swift's tradition. (See Jonathan Swift, "The Spider and the Bee," in *The Battle of the Books*.)

70 *Letters*, 2:424.

71 Gelpi, *Emily Dickinson*, p. 152.

72 Ibid.

73 Webster's *New World Dictionary, College Edition* (Cleveland and New York: World Publishing Co., 1966).

74 Interestingly, in a memoir of Elizabeth Barrett Browning, her friend Mrs. Ogilvy wrote that "her letters were written in minute scratches no thicker than the hairs on a daisy stalk, on tiny note sheets, folded sometimes into tiny envelopes, the whole forming apparently a doll's epistle." A number of the E.B.B. MS poems in the Berg Collection are written in tiny notebooks, moreover. It seems as if many women artists may have half-consciously tried to make their work look like play. ("Recollections of Mrs. Browning, by Mrs. David Ogilvy,"

in *Elizabeth Barrett Browning's Letters to Mrs. David Ogilvy, 1849–1861* [New York: Quadrangle Books, 1973], p. xxxiii.)

75 See Thomas Johnson, Introduction to *The Poems of Emily Dickinson.*

76 Miller, *The Poetry of Emily Dickinson*, chapter 10, "The Fascicles."

77 *Letters*, 2:408, 409, 415.

78 Adrienne Rich, "When We Dead Awaken," in *Diving into the Wreck* (New York: Norton, 1973), p. 5.

79 *The Poetical Works of Elizabeth Barrett Browning*, p. 10; *The Poetical Works of Christina G. Rossetti*, 1:104–05.

80 See Christina Rossetti, "Mother Country," *Poetical Works*, 1:116, and Sylvia Plath, "Fever 103," *Ariel*, p. 55. Terence Diggory's "Armored Women, Naked Men" is particularly helpful in exploring the distinction between, on the one hand, male openness (or "nakedness") and assertiveness in American poetry, and, on the other hand, female evasiveness, reticence, and disguise.

81 *Letters*, 2:546.

Index

Abrams, M. H., 46
Adam, 195–99 passim, 225, 227, 254, 264, 283; in Austen and S. Richardson, 168; in Milton, 188, 194; in *Frankenstein*, 229–39 passim; and St. Paul, 385; in "A Drama of Exile," 391; in *Shirley*, 394; and "The Lifted Veil," 457; and Eliot, 496
Addison, Joseph, 131; and Richard Steele, *The Spectator*, 117
Aeschylus: *Prometheus Bound*, 195, 229; translations of, 546–47
Agoraphobia, xi, 101–02; in women, 53–59 passim; and escape, 84–85; of Dickinson, 555, 557, 583, 593, 595, 604, 606; in *Great Expectations*, 619
Alcott, Louisa May, 558; *Little Women*, 25, 64, 70, 350, 483–84; "Behind A Mask," 473
Alvarez, A., 284
Amnesia: in women's writing, 58–59; and female memory, 97–101; in *Romola*, 495
Ancestral mansion. *See* Architecture, ancestral mansion
Anderson, Quentin, 523
Androgyny, 65, 69; Woolf on, 192; in *Wuthering Heights*, 264–67, 276, 287, 295–98 passim, 306; in Eliot and E. Brontë, 307; in *The Professor*, 319, 325, 326, 327, 332; in *Villette*, 423, 432; in *The Mill on The Floss*, 492; and Fuller, 532; and female power, 616–17
Angel, woman as. *See* Woman as angel
Angel in the House, The. See Patmore, Coventry
"Anger, Jane": on women, 219
Anger. *See* Madness and anger
Animal symbolism: in Blake, 95; in Dickinson, 100, 595, 598–99, 602–03, 611, 631–33; in *Wuthering Heights*, 282, 303–05, 308; in *The Professor*, 323, 328; in *Jane Eyre*, 340, 351; in *Shirley*, 389, 397; in C. Brontë's letters, 399; in *Villette*, 412, 415, 428, 429; in Eliot, 467, 486, 492, 493, 497; in "Goblin Market," 567, 570. *See also* Birds; Dogs; Horses and riding; Insects; Serpents
Anonymity. *See* Names
Anorexia, xi, 25; in women, 53–59 passim; as escape, 85–86; in Austen, 142; in *Castle Rackrent*, 149, 150; in *Wuthering Heights*, 275, 282, 284–87, 292, 298, 301–02; in *Shirley*, 314, 390–91. *See also* Cooking; Food; Fruit; Starvation

Aphasia, 58. *See also* Amnesia; Language
Aquinas, Thomas, 501
Architecture, xi, 107, 120, 198, 209, 216–17, 375; in female fiction, 83–92, 312–13; in Austen, 121–22, 129, 154; in *Wuthering Heights*, 261, 271–74, 275, 280; in *Jane Eyre*, 336–71 passim, 612; in *Shirley*, 381, 384, 393; in *Villette*, 403–17 passim, 420–38 passim; in Eliot, 462–63, 470, 485, 487, 501–07; in Anne Finch, 478; in *Aurora Leigh*, 578–80; in Dickinson, 604, 607, 611–13, 631–33
—windows: in "Snow White," 37; in Dickinson, 146; in Milton, 202; in *Wuthering Heights*, 261, 271–74, 275, 280; in *Jane Eyre*, 336–71 passim, 612; in *Shirley*, 381, 517–19, 520; in *The Mill on the Floss*, 512; in *Uncle Tom's Cabin*, 534
—ancestral mansion: in "The Yellow Wallpaper," 89–91; in *Castle Rackrent*, 149–51; in Austen, 154, 177; in C. Brontë, 381, 438; in Stowe, 473, 533, 534; in Eliot, 485
—attic: in "The Yellow Wallpaper," 89–90; in Austen, 122, 348, 354, 360; in *Frankenstein*, 235; in *Jane Eyre*, 347–49; in *Villette*, 409, 425–26, 431, 438; in *The Mill on the Floss*, 491, 492; in *Uncle Tom's Cabin*, 533–34
—parlor/sitting room/drawing room: and Austen, 109–10, 112, 113, 122, 144, 153, 177, 179; and Edgeworth, 151–53; Woolf on, 153, 188; in *Shirley*, 378; in Eliot, 450, 454; in "The Snow Image," 618
—library: and Austen, 137; and Woolf, 192; in "The Lifted Veil," 464; in *Middlemarch*, 511, 530; and Alice James, 512. *See also* Christianity; Claustrophobia; Landscape; Prisons
Aristotle, 5, 7, 212; on femaleness, 53
Arnold, Matthew, 229, 257; "Philomela," 43; on *Villette*, 337, 338; "The Buried Life," 401–02; "Haworth Churchyard," 439
Arthritis, rheumatoid, 53
Attic. *See* Architecture, attic
Atwood, Margaret, 510; *Lady Oracle*, 57, 473
Auden, W. H., 174, 277; on Austen, 112
Auerbach, Erich, 46
Auerbach, Nina, 122, 415
Augustine, Saint, 30

Austen, Jane, xi, 9, 57, 72, 78, 80, 82, 101, 331, 373, 374, 395, 444, 491, 540, 562, 585; *Persuasion*, 7–8, 11–12, 13, 16, 27, 43, 44, 60, 112, 117, 119, 136, *174–83*, 405, 522, 627; *Northanger Abbey*, 58, 113, *128– 45*, 146, 149, 150, 152, 154, 160, 176, 177, 179, 238, 259, 275, 410, 585, 620, 643; *Emma*, 58, 136, *157–60*, 163, 173–74, 181, 183; "Bit of Ivory," 63, 83, 107–08; spatial metaphors about, 108–13; *Love and Freindship, 113–19*, 121, 122, 162, 171; and the picaresque, 114–15, 116; *The Watsons,* 115, 126; on romance, 116–21 passim, 132, 136, 142, 179; female characters in, 116–27 passim; *Pride and Prejudice,* 117, 120, 136, 157–58, 161, 172–73; *Sense and Sensibility,* 117, 120, 125, 136, 156–57, 172, 183; *Lady Susan,* 119, 155–56, 317; *Sanditon,* 119, 183; *Mansfield Park,* 120, *163–68,* 170–72; "Catharine," 122; "Frederic and Elfrida," 126, 127; "Jack and Alice," 126, 127; "Lesley Castle," 127; on history, 132–36; on education of women, 133–36 passim; and disease, 141, 162, 174, 177, 182–83, 335; and silence, 143–44, 160–62, 165, 169, 178; shrews in, 155, 169–74, 181, 183; Satanic heroes in, 206; as narrative "presence," 548
Authority: definition of, 4, 28, 45–46; and death, 14, 18, 36, 40; male anxiety about, 32, 110; monstrous female, 34–36, 66–67, 155, 159, 208, 209–10; of male genres, 67–71 passim; female anxiety about, 233, 316, 550–58. *See also* Madness and anger; Woman as monster
—male literary, 6–7, 11–16, 16–20 passim, 48, 59, 179, 188, 208–12 passim, 450, 556–57, 574; in Austen, 175; in Eliot, 499, 500–03, 505, 531; in Keats, 552–54; in "The Snow Image," 618–19
—patriarchal, 38–39, 138–40, 143–44, 198, 439; in *Middlemarch,* 214–18, 507–10; in *Wuthering Heights,* 280–82; in *The Professor,* 324; in *Jane Eyre,* 340, 357; in *Villette,* 430; in "The Lifted Veil,"464
—female struggle for, 71–75, 82, 99, 158, 227, 311, 317, 434–35, 437, 439, 446, 448–49; in *The Professor,* 329–31; in "Armgart," 454–55; and clairvoyance, 474; in Eliot, 485, 523–24, 531, 533; in Dickinson, 608, 616, 649
—female relinquishing of, 444; in Austen, 160–69; in Shirley, 394–95, 397; in Eliot, 450–51, 467; and C. Rossetti, 564–75; in Barrett Browning and C. Rossetti, 645

Bachelard, Gaston, xiii; *The Poetics of Space,* 87–88, 108
Balzac, Honoré de, 13, 540
Barnes, Djuna, *The Book of Repulsive Women,* 247
Barrett Browning, Elizabeth, 57, 124, 393, 444, 473, 474, 559, 562, 589; *Aurora Leigh,* 18–19, 23, 25–26, 35, 36, 37, 41, 44, 58, 99–100, 453, 506, 541, 559–61, 570, *575–80,* 582, 583, 587, 617, 621, 640, 643–44, 645, 648; on women writers, 66–67, 69, 71, 109, 481, 539–40; "An Essay On Mind," 70; "A Vision of Poets," 70; "An Island," 102–04; "A Drama of Exile," 189, 375, 391, 481; "Bertha in the Lane," 463; male critics on, 543–44; *Poems Before Congress,* 544; translation of *Prometheus Bound,* 547; and renunciation, 564; Dickinson on, 647–48
Bart, Pauline, 53
Barth, John, 374
Barthes, Roland, 10
Beddoes, Thomas Lovell, 242–43
Beethoven, Ludwig von, 453, 606
Behn, Aphra, 540; on female authorship, 63, 65, 66
Bell: Currer, Ellis, and Acton, 65
Bergman, Ingrid, 143
Bernard, Jessie, 53
Bersani, Leo, 11–12, 20, 165, 253, 258, 264, 268, 283, 291, 299
Bettelheim, Bruno, 37–41 passim, 303
Bewick, Thomas: *History of British Birds,* 339, 404
Bianchi, Martha Dickinson, 559, 563
Bible: *Genesis* and *Shirley,* 287, 395; Samson, 356, 368; John the Baptist, 365; Salome, 365; Saint John, 365; feminist revision of, 374, 385–86; Sisera and Jael, 412, 433, 455, 492; Vashti and *Villette,* 451, 456; *Exodus,* 469; and Biblical criticism, 502; "Female Scripture Characters" in *Middlemarch,* 520; *Ecclesiastes,* 524. *See also* Adam; Christ; Christianity; Eve; Fall, the; Satan; Sin; Virgin Mary
Bildungsroman: in Austen, 128; and *Frankenstein,* 238; *Wuthering Heights* as, 253–54, 259, 276; *The Professor* as, 315, 335; *Jane Eyre* as, 339–71 passim; and women, 426
Bingham, Millicent Todd, 563
Birds, symbolism of: in *Wuthering Heights,* 284; in *Shirley,* 377–78, 382–84; in *Villette,* 431; in Dickinson, 637–38
Blackmur, R. P., 541, 543, 545

Blackstone, Sir William, 155

Black subculture and women: 73–74, 120–21, 482

Blackwood, John, 488, 491

Blackwood's, 445

Blake, William, 205, 232, 233, 234, 242, 273, 276–83 passim, 295, 452, 469, 478, 530, 638, 645; on women, 12, 28, 200, 443; on "generation," 37; *For the Sexes,* 95; *The Marriage of Heaven and Hell,* 189, 308; *Milton,* 195, 200–01, 204; *The Book of Urizen,* 200–01, 268, 294, 297, 299, 300, 604; on imagination, 203, 612–13; on "Female Space," 213; on Milton and women, 218; on the Fall, 248; *Songs of Innocence,* 254; and E. Brontë, 254–55; on "Energy," 265–66; *The Book of Thel,* 567; on "Nobodaddy," 587, 594, 603; "The Mental Traveler," 611

Blindness. *See* Eye troubles and blindness

Bloom, Harold, xiii, 6, 145, 201, 221; *The Anxiety of Influence,* 46–53, 59, 188, 192, 193; on Milton, 191

Bogan, Louise, 477; and women's poetry, 541–42, 562

Bonheur, Rosa: on transvestism, 65–66

Borges, Jorge, 502

Borgia, Lucrezia, 459, 460

Boskind-Lodahl, Marlene, 86

Bowles, Samuel, 558, 559

Braddon, Mary Elizabeth, *Lady Audley's Secret,* 473

Bradstreet, Anne, 72, 258; on female authorship, 62, 65, 66

Branch, Anna Hempstead, 187

Brawne, Fanny, 553

Brillat-Savarin, Anthelme, 295

Brontë, Anne, 315, 375; *The Tenant of Wildfell Hall,* 80–83, 251, 317, 357; *Agnes Grey,* 250. *See also* Brontë, Emily, and Anne Brontë: Gondal writings; Brontë family, the

Brontë, Branwell, 315, 375; and Charlotte Brontë: Angrian writings, 251, 256, 312–18 passim, 332, 335, 336, 347, 640

Brontë, Charlotte, xi, 8, 58, 59, 73, 124, 213, 256, 444–45, 453, 533, 545; *Jane Eyre,* xii, 78, 80, 86, 99, 142, 205–06, 215, 250, 251, 314–28 passim, *336–71,* 372–96 passim, 399–404 passim, 417, 426, 431, 432, 433, 472, 473, 500, 570, 582, 583, 597, 604, 612, 622–30 passim; *Villette,* 59, 91, 314–28 passim, 369, 381, *399–440,* 443–44, 454, 467, 472, 492, 508, 620, 627, 643; to Southey, 63–64; *The Professor,* 70–71,

315–35, 336, 337, 339, 369, 372, 378, 381, 393, 394, 399, 400, 412, 447, 506, 620; on "the woman question," 77, 206; and women artists, 82; and spatial imagery, 84; on *Pride and Prejudice,* 109, 112; *Shirley,* 133, 189–208 passim, 251, 256, 287, 291, 305, 314, 317, 319, 369, *372–98,* 399, 400, 404, 426, 432, 438, 605; and Branwell Brontë: Angrian writings, 251, 256, 312–18 passim, 332, 335, 336, 347, 640; on *Wuthering Heights,* 253, 289, 305–06; Roe Head Journal, 311–13, 325, 334; life of, 319–24 passim, 329, 604–06; "Jane," 329–31; "Frances," 440–41; and Eliot, 463–66 passim, 486, 490, 498–99, 530; and Stowe, 444, 535; and *Aurora Leigh,* 575–78 passim; and Dickinson, 599–600. *See also* Brontë family, the

Brontë, Emily, 44, 58, 59, 78, 80, 82, 101, 315, 330, 374, 375, 381, 444, 463, 530; *Wuthering Heights,* 59, 142, 150, 189, 220, *248–308,* 378, 391, 393, 394, 423, 454, 472, 570, 583, 588, 595, 628, 630; and Anne Brontë: Gondal writings, 83, 99, 251, 256–58 passim, 265, 274–75, 279, 314, 640; and spatial imagery, 84; "No Coward Soul Is Mine," 254; and Anne Brontë: Diary Papers, 257–58, 259; "Often Rebuked Yet Always Back Returning," 258, 260; "Enough of Thought, Philosopher," 306; and *The Professor,* 306; in *Shirley,* 384; and Eliot, 586, 492–93; poetry of, 564, 627; landscapes in, 643; and Dickinson, 595, 628, 630, 646. *See also* Brontë, Charlotte; Brontë family, the

Brontë, Maria Branwell, 250

Brontë, Rev. Patrick, 250; and Milton, 252

Brontë family, the, 101, 150, 444, 455, 541, 559, 585; and pseudonyms, 65; juvenilia, 250–51; and sewing, 639–40

Broughton, Rhoda, 109

Brown, Norman O., 6, 13, 20, 68

Browne, Sir Thomas, 531

Browning, Elizabeth Barrett. *See* Barrett Browning, Elizabeth

Browning, Robert, "By the Fireside," 469

Brunton, Mary, 108, 121

Brydges, Sir Samuel Egerton, 107, 120

Bulimia. *See* Anorexia

Bunyan, John: *Pilgrim's Progress,* 314, 336–71 passim

Burgan, Mary, 137

Burgess, Anthony, 9

Burkhart, Charles, 425

Burlin, Katrin Ristkok, 139

Burney, Fanny, 120, 121, 133–34, 540; *Camilla,* 119, 131
Burton, Sir Thomas: *The Anatomy of Melancholy,* 501
Butler, Marilyn, 120, 147, 152
Byron, George Gordon, Lord, 23, 147, 191, 220, 227, 237, 242, 294, 312–15 passim, 365, 401, 452, 462, 529, 545, 553; *The Prisoner of Chillon,* 87, 279, 399, 631; *The Corsair,* 119; on Prometheus, 195; *Childe Harold,* 201, 347, 461; *Cain,* 202, 203, 204; *Manfred,* 202–09 passim, 221, 229, 258–59, 265, 347; *Lara,* 203; life of, 206, 207–09; on Rome, 247; Eliot on, 461–62. *See also* Byronic hero, the; Romanticism and Romantic poets; Satan
Byronic hero, the, 201–09 passim, 288; in *The Tenant of Wildfell Hall,* 81–82; Austen on, 119; in C. Brontë, 318, 332, 337, 338, 347, 354; Edward Dickinson as, 597–98

Cages. *See* Claustrophobia; Prisons
Capps, Jack, 559, 584
Carlyle, Thomas, 257, 560; on Byron and Goethe, 23, 314; on work, 365; *Sartor Resartus,* 462
Carroll, Lewis, *Through The Looking Glass,* 13, 552
Cather, Willa, *My Antonia,* 102
Cavendish, Margaret, Duchess of Newcastle, 189, 541, 544; on female authorship, 62–63, 65; on women, 219; and spinning, 525
Chapman, John, 450–51; as "Byron," 461–62
Chapone, Mrs. Hester, 116
Chartism, 205, 337
Chase, Richard, 9, 338, 351, 361, 368
Chaucer, Geoffrey: "The Wife of Bath's Tale," 11–12, 16, 78–79
Chesler, Phyllis, 53, 143
Chicago, Judy, 74
Childhood: in "Snow White," 38–41; male vs. female, 42–43; in Austen, 124, 125, 128; in *Frankenstein,* 230–31, 236; in *Wuthering Heights,* 264–67, 268, 283–84, 299; in *The Professor,* 331; in *Jane Eyre,* 339, 357–59, 361–62, 368; in *Villette,* 403, 416; in *The Mill on the Floss,* 491–92; in *Middlemarch,* 518; Dickinson's impersonation of, 583, 587–94, 602, 607–08, 616, 630–31, 640. *See also* Female Sexuality, initiation into; Games/charades/riddles; Infanticide; Maternity; Mothers
Chopin, Kate, *The Awakening,* 408
Christ, Carol, 491

Christ (Jesus), 194, 199, 476, 545, 566, 572–73. *See also* Christianity; Fall, the; God the father; Heaven/Eden/paradise; Hell
Christianity: in Austen, 163; and Milton, 198–201 passim, 209, 216–18, 255; in *Wuthering Heights,* 299; in *Jane Eyre,* 337, 338, 347, 365–66; in *Shirley,* 383–84, 389, 391, 397; in *Villette,* 417–18; and Eliot, 468, 473, 484, 488–89, 514; and Stowe, 482; in C. Rossetti, 566, 572–73; in Dickinson, 512–13, 614–15, 645–46. *See also* Adam; Bible; Christ (Jesus); Eve; God the father; Male sexuality, and celibacy; Satan, Virgin Mary; Woman as angel; Woman as nun
—Saints: in Eliot, 152, 468, 476, 503, 511; in *Jane Eyre,* 365; in *Shirley,* 385–86; in *Villette,* 411, 414
—clergy: in *Jane Eyre,* 365; in *Shirley,* 373–76 passim, 382, 390; in *Villette,* 410–11; in Eliot, 475, 484, 485, 488, 501, 503, 528
—Catholicism/anti-Catholicism: in *The Professor,* 322–25; in *Shirley,* 374; in *Villette,* 414–16, 420–21, 435
Christian Remembrancer, The, 337
Cicero, 501
Clairmont, Claire, 242, 288; and Byron, 207–08
Clairvoyance: of Sibyl, 96–97; and prophecy, 203; and Milton, 211; in *Jane Eyre,* 358–60, 362, 363, 367–68; and Stowe, 444–45, 535; in "The Lifted Veil," 446, 448–51, 464, 465; and Eliot, 458; and veil, 470; and women, 472–74, 476
Claustrophobia, xi, 65; in "In Duty Bound," 84; and escape, 85; in "The Yellow Wallpaper," 89–92 passim; in Austen, 114, 122, 124, 135, 141; in *Castle Rackrent,* 149–50; in *Wuthering Heights,* 278–79, 284, 288, 297; in *The Professor,* 320, 334; in *Jane Eyre,* 339–41, 348–49, 366; in *Shirley,* 376, 380, 389; in *Villette,* 405–06, 414–15, 427, 431; in Eliot, 462, 504–07, 512, 516; in Dickinson, 590–91, 606–07. *See also* Agoraphobia; Architecture; Death, and living burial; Prisons
Clergy. *See* Christianity
Clothing: veils and masks, 21, 274, 359, 360, 362, 443–44, 454, 463; 469–77, 590; in "Snow White," 40, 42, 54, 424; women's, 44, 85; "The Red Shoes," 45, 56–57; transvestism as metaphor, 65–67, 353, 355; Dickinson's white dress, 86, 549, 613–22, 636, 649; in Austen, 129; in *Wuthering Heights,* 273–74, 298; in *The*

Professor, 325; in *Jane Eyre,* 353, 355, 359;
in *Villette,* 404, 409, 413, 429, 432, 437; in
Eliot, 488, 496, 505, 520, 527; in Stowe,
534–35, 620; in C. Rossetti, 550, 553; "sod
gown" in Dickinson, 604, 610, 619; in
"The Snow Image," 617, 618–19; in *Great
Expectations,* 617, 619, 620; in *Aurora
Leigh,* 617, 621; in "The Lady of Shalott,"
617–18, 620; in *The Woman in White,*
619–20; and nakedness in Dickinson, 642,
645, 649. *See also* Ladyhood; Woman as
angel; Woman as male creation/creature/
art object; Woman as nun
Cody, John, 539, 543, 557, 558, 606, 625
Coleman, George, 116
Coleridge, Mary Elizabeth, 206; "The Other
Side of the Mirror," 15–16, 17, 37, 43, 76,
77, 141; "Blindness," 58; "The Witch,"
307
Coleridge, Samuel Taylor, 222, 265, 312,
351, 452, 469; on imagination, 5, 17;
"Christabel," 35, 235, 245, 307, 471;
"Kubla Khan," 87, 570; "The Ancient
Mariner," 235, 460–61. *See also* Romanti-
cism and Romantic poets
Collins, Wilkie: *The Woman in White,* 617,
619–20
Conduct books. *See* Education
Confinement. *See* Architecture; Claustro-
phobia; Maternity; Prisons
Cooking: in "Snow White," 40; in the cave,
94; in *Paradise Lost,* 193–94, 197, 209; and
Wuthering Heights, 291–92, 294–95; and
The Mill on the Floss, 492. *See also* Food;
Fruit; Housekeeping
Cowper, William, 156, 190, 382, 387
Craik, Mrs. Dinah, 169
Cross, John, 467
Curtius, Ernst Robert, 6

Dance: in "Snow White," 42–44, 53–57, 71,
424, 634; in Austen, 126, 129, 130, 138,
165; in Milton, 209; in Dickinson, 633–34,
643, 645
Dante Alighieri, 20–21, 260, 457, 467
Davis, Rebecca Harding: *Life in the Iron
Mills,* 102
Day, Thomas, 147–48
Death: and women, 14–15, 21, 24–27, 31,
443; in "Snow White," 37, 39–41, 618;
and "Lady of Shalott," 43, 617; of
Richard Edgeworth, 152; in Austen, 174,
180; in *Paradise Lost,* 197–98, 208–10; in
Middlemarch, 218, 464, 500, 505, 509,
512–14 passim; in *Frankenstein,* 232–35,
242, 244–45; in *Wuthering Heights,* 254,

270–71, 280, 284, 301–02, 306; in *The
Mill on the Floss,* 307, 494; as metaphor in
C. Brontë, 313, 325, 389, 401, 410, 427–
28, 429; and Eliot, 453, 467, 489, 491,
494–97 passim; in *Scenes of Clerical Life,*
485–88, 489–90; in *Daniel Deronda,* 495–
96; in *Adam Bede* and *Felix Holt,* 406; in
Dickinson, 622–33 passim. *See also* Christianity; Fall, the; Heaven/Eden/paradise;
Hell; Infanticide; Maternity
De Beauvoir, Simone, xiii, 161, 163, 521; on
female immanence, 14, 34, 88, 94–95,
102; on female aspirations, 76; on female
childhood, 107; on romance, 117–18; on
killing and transcendence, 610; on virginity, 632–33, 643
Deciphering: of Sibyl's leaves, 95–100; in
Austen, 140, 158, 449, 177–78; in M. Shelley, 223–24. *See also* Amnesia; Detective
fiction; Language
De Genlis, Mme. *See* Genlis, Stéphanie Félicité Ducrest de St. Aubin, Comtesse de
De Sable, Mme. *See* Sable, Mme. de
Descartes, René, 201
Detective fiction, 26, 67; in Austen, 135,
141–42; *Frankenstein* as, 224–25, 228,
249; and *Jane Eyre,* 349–51, 354–62
passim; and *Villette,* 426
Dickens, Charles, 86, 87, 540, 585; *Dombey
and Son,* 24–25; *The Old Curiosity Shop,* 25;
David Copperfield, 26; *Great Expectations,*
405, 617, 619, 620; "The Black Veil,"
469–70
Dickinson, Austen, 558, 563, 597
Dickinson, Edward: and family name, 555–
56; influence on Emily, 597–600
Dickinson, Emily, xi, 44, 57, 72, 78, 83, 88,
101, 146, 248, 256, 258, 274, 276, 289,
311, 336, 444, 455; on disease, 45, 51–53,
55, 59, 76, 92; on hunger, 58, 374, 564,
568, 573, 596; on language, 58–59, 392,
592–93, 641; and literary ambition, 64,
554–61, 563; literary theories, 73, 75,
107, 399, 403, 548, 581–650 passim;
claustrophobia/agoraphobia, 84–87, 102,
169, 555, 557, 583, 593, 595, 604, 606–50
passim; on memory, 100, 626–526; landscapes in, 100, 328, 570, 642–50; and sewing, 100, 633–42; on sun and noon, 102,
412, 581–650 passim; personality of, 176,
189, 213, 432, 475–76, 516, 581–650
passim; and *Jane Eyre,* 362, 582, 583, 597,
599–600, 604, 612, 622–30 passim; on
marriage, 370–71, 504, 587, 588–89,
595–96; on the Bible, 385; on Eve, 394,
648–50; and Eliot, 476, 480, 516; and

Dickinson, Emily (*continued*)
Stowe, 481; as spider, 525, 631–42
passim, 648; male critics on, 541, 542–43;
white dress, 86, 549, 613–22, 636, 649;
and Barrett Browning, 559–61, 575, 580,
647–48; estate of, 563–64, 641; poetry of,
581–650
—works discussed: "A word dropped careless on a page," 45, 51–53; "A word made
flesh," 568; "No romance sold unto," 581;
"Drama's vitallest expression is the common day," 586; "She rose to his
requirement—dropt," 588–91, 634; "I'm
'wife'—I've finished that—," 589;
" 'Arcturus' is his other name—," 592–93;
"Will there really be a 'morning?' " 593–
94; "Burglar! Banker—father," 594;
"Good morning—midnight," 594; "Before I got my eye put out," 595; "Where
bells no more affright the morn," 598;
"Papa above!" 598–99; "The daisy follows
soft the sun," 600–01; "The sun *just
touched* the morning," 601–02; "Master
letters," 602–06 passim, 607, 618, 626;
"Why make it doubt—it hurts it so," 603;
"Doom is the house without the door,"
604, 612; "A solemn thing it was—I said,"
608, 613–14; "My life had stood—a
loaded gun," 608–10, 611, 612; "A
wounded deer leaps highest," 611; "A
still—volcano—life," 611; "Dare you see a
soul at the white heat," 611–13, 621; "One
need not be a chamber—to be haunted,"
622, 624–25, 627; "The Soul has bandaged moments," 622–23; " 'Tis sunrise—little maid—hast thou," 623, 628,
629; "The First day's night had come,"
625–26; "I felt a cleaving in my mind,"
627–28, 639; "I felt a funeral in my
brain," 626–27, 639; "This chasm, sweet,"
629–31, 632, 639; "Alone and in a circumstance," 631–33; "The spider holds a
silver ball," 633; "I cannot dance upon my
toes," 634; "A spider sewed at night,"
635–38, 640–41; "Sang from the heart,
sir," 637–38; "Don't put up my thread and
needle," 640–41; "There is a morn by
men unseen," 643–50 passim; "Through
the dark sod—as education," 645–46;
"Sweet mountains—ye tell me no lie,"
646–50 passim; "Her face was in a bed of
hair," 647–50 passim; "I think I was enchanted," 647–50 passim; "Let me not
mar that perfect dream," 649–50
Dickinson, Lavinia, 563

Dickinson, Susan Gilbert, 563, 596, 602; as
schoolteacher, 558
Didion, Jean, 20
Dillon, Lord, 242–43
Diner, Helen, 95, 99, 521
Dinesen, Isak: on *Genesis,* 187
Dinnerstein, Dorothy, 14, 28, 34, 387
Disease/dis-ease/healing, 51–64 passim, 69,
71, 72, 74, 76, 91; in Austen, 107, 114,
118, 141–42, 146, 156–57, 160, 162, 165,
173–77 passim, 181–83 passim; and
Romanticism, 204; in *The Last Man,* 246–
47; in *Wuthering Heights,* 268, 280, 286; of
E. Brontë, 278; in *The Professor,* 330,
334–35; in *Jane Eyre,* 346, 370; in *Shirley,*
378, 388–92, 395; in *Villette,* 405, 415–22
passim, 425, 432–33; in Eliot, 445, 447,
448–53 passim, 462, 466, 485–90 passim,
493, 501–15 passim; in "Goblin Market,"
565; female genius as, 569–70; in Dickinson, 602–03, 633–42. *See also*
Agoraphobia; Anorexia; Arthritis; Claustrophobia; Fragmentation of personality;
Headaches; Madness and anger
Disney, Walt: *Snow White and the Seven
Dwarfs,* 36
Disobedience: in "Snow White," 40–41;
female, 50, 61, 73–75, 77–80, 82, 194–95,
196, 198–99, 201–06; male, 74; in Austen, 114–16, 118, 120–21, 145, 154, 157,
166–69 passim, 169–74; in *Wuthering
Heights,* 265–66, 299; in *The Professor,* 331,
333–34; in *Jane Eyre,* 337, 340, 343, 346–
47; in *Shirley,* 373; in *Villette,* 403, 409–11,
415, 417, 423–35; and the Romantics,
452; in Eliot, 454, 455, 465, 490, 511–14,
516; in "Goblin Market," 565; in *Aurora
Leigh,* 575–79 passim. *See also* Doubles;
Duplicity, female; Escape; Eve; Fall, the;
Madness and anger
Dixon, R. W., 3, 8, 10
Dogs, symbolism of, 198, 381, 383, 393; in
Wuthering Heights, 259–62 passim, 271–74
passim, 274, 287–89 passim, 296; in *The
Professor,* 332, 334; in *Shirley,* 393. *See also*
Animal symbolism
Donne, John, 86, 499, 549, 600; "Loves Al-
chymie," 245; on women, 295
Doolittle, Hilda. *See* H. D.
Dostoevsky, Fyodor, 51
Doubles, xi, 57, 69, 78, 85, 213; in "Snow
White," 36, 39–42; in Austen, 142, 159,
162, 167, 170–74; in *Frankenstein,* 231,
235; in *Wuthering Heights,* 265, 275–76,
280, 292, 293–97 passim; in *Shirley,* 374,

379, 382–84, 389; in *Villette*, 403–04, 412, 428–29; in female novel, 443, 545; in Eliot, 465, 495; in C. Rossetti, 551–52, 565–66; in *Aurora Leigh*, 577; in Dickinson, 591, 622–25 passim, 626, 631–33 —madwoman as; 77–80, 90–92, 162; in *Jane Eyre*, 339, 347, 359–62, 368; in *Villette*, 425–26, 431; in Eliot, 463–65, 472, 490, 496, 498; in Lessing, 474; in Stowe, 534. *See also* Disobedience; Duplicity, female; Escape; Fragmentation of personality; Madness and anger

Douglas, Ann, xii, 24–26, 111, 480

Dreams: of Annie Gottlieb, 52; in *Paradise Lost*, 202–03; and *Frankenstein*, 222, 232; in *Wuthering Heights*, 306–07; of C. Brontë, 312–13; in *Jane Eyre*, 357–59, 361–62, 363, 368; in *Villette*, 417; and Margaret Fuller, 480; in "Goblin Market," 569; and Dickinson, 598, 636, 649. *See also* Clairvoyance; Techniques of composition

Dryden, John: "Ode for St. Cecelia's Day," 457

Du Maurier, Daphne: *Rebecca*, 337

Duplicity, female, 32, 34, 69–77, 80–83, 87, 101, 111, 155, 197, 220, 331, 408–09, 641–42; in *The Angel in the House*, 25–27; in "Snow White," 39–42; in Austen, 118, 127, 128–31, 134, 137, 155, 157–58, 161–63, 165, 168–69, 173–74, 182–83; in Edgeworth, 150–51, 152; in Woolf, 205; in *Middlemarch*, 216–17, 511, 513–16 passim, 532; in *Frankenstein*, 232, 239, 243, 249; in *Wuthering Heights*, 249, 274; in C. Brontë's fiction, 314–15, 372; in *The Professor*, 322–24, 327; and male in *Jane Eyre*, 353, 354–56; in *Shirley*, 388; in *Villette*, 413, 414, 416, 418, 429; and Eliot, 454, 457, 484, 491, 498, 532; and veils, 473; and anger, 483–84; and *Little Women*, 483–84; in Mrs. Gaskell, 484; and sewing, 521; in *Uncle Tom's Cabin*, 534; in *Aurora Leigh*, 579–80; in Barrett Browning and C. Rossetti, 582–83; in Dickinson, 587, 590, 597–608, 620–21. *See also* Doubles; Parody

Eagleton, Terence, 256

Economics and women, 112–13, 115, 120, 122–26 passim, 134–37 passim, 142–43, 164, 171–80 passim; and "beggary" in *Frankenstein*, 227–28; in the Brontës, 251; in *The Professor*, 319, 326; in *Jane Eyre*, 364, 367; in *Shirley*, 374, 375, 377, 379,

381, 383, 387–90, 398; in *Villette*, 400, 402, 421, 438; and Eliot, 454, 486, 495; in Fuller and Eliot, 479; in *Middlemarch*, 506, 507–08, 511, 513, 515, 519, 529–30; and female novelists, 545; and "commercial" poetry, 558–59; and poverty as metaphor, 564. *See also* Governess, the; Housekeeping; Ladyhood; Prostitution; Women and work

Eden. *See* Heaven/Eden/paradise

Edgeworth, Maria, 101, 121, 146–53, 540; *Belinda*, 131, 151; *Letters for Literary Ladies*, 147–48; *Castle Rackrent*, 149–51, 152, 391, 583, 620; and Richard Lovell Edgeworth: *Professional Education*, 151

Edgeworth, Richard Lovell, 151–54 passim

Education: in *Love and Freindship*, 117; and Mary Shelley, 223–24; in *Frankenstein*, 237–40; male in *Wuthering Heights*, 295–96, 300, 303; male in *The Professor*, 320; male in *Jane Eyre*, 369; in *Villette*, 429–30, male in Keats, 553. *See also* Authority; Ladyhood; Woman as angel

—of women, 7, 30–31, 49, 53–54, 60, 71, 116–17, 131–34, 237–38, 546–47, 559–61; in Austen, 122, 138, 141, 144; in *Wuthering Heights*, 274–77, 279, 281, 287, 291; in *The Professor*, 320–31 passim; in *Jane Eyre*, 344–47, 361, 364; in Eliot, 447; in *Aurora Leigh*, 575–77

—in classics, 70, 133–34, 191, 192, 211, 214–18 passim, 220, 385; in *Wuthering Heights*, 281; in *Villette*, 429; and Eliot, 451, 467, 494, 501, 514, 531; and male poets, 546–47.

Eichner, Hans, 21–22, 55

Electra complex, 48, 50

Elements, the. *See also* Landscape, symbolic; Madness and anger; Nature/culture polarity

—snow and ice: in *Paradise Lost* and *Frankenstein*, 226, 246; in *Wuthering Heights*, 262; in *Jane Eyre*, 339, 366; in *Shirley*, 378; in *Villette*, 400, 404, 406, 427; in *Middlemarch*, 529; in Dickinson, 614, 616–19 passim

—stone: in *Shirley*, 372, 377–78, 379, 380, 384, 386, 390, 397–98; in *Villette*, 408, 410, 414, 438

—water and storms: in Austen, 79–80; in Woolf, 193; in *Shirley*, 387; in *Villette*, 406, 411, 415, 416–19, 427, 430–31, 434, 438, 449; in *Daniel Deronda*, 455; in Eliot, 456–57, 489, 490, 495, 497, 527; in *The Mill on the Floss*, 492–94; in *Adam Bede*,

Elements, (*continued*)
  496; in *Middlemarch*, 501, 504, 519; in *Romola*, 505; in *Felix Holt*, 517
—fire: in *Jane Eyre*, 339, 341, 343, 346–47, 353, 362, 368; in *Villette*, 408, 425, 426–27; in Eliot, 453, 463; in *Daniel Deronda*, 454; in *The Mill on the Floss*, 492; in Dickinson, 607, 611–13, 619
Eliade, Mircea, 259, 263
Eliot, George, 71, 78, 80, 82, 101, 148, 151, 546, 559, 564; on eye troubles, 58; headaches of, 64; male impersonation, 65; "Silly Novels by Lady Novelists," 72, 466; on woman question, 77; *Middlemarch*, 133, 142, 152, 189, 385, 450, 451, 456, 458, 460, 465, 468, 475–77 passim, 485, *499–532*, 502, 534, 578–79, 583, 585; *Daniel Deronda*, 134, 449, 450, 452, 454–55, 460, 477, 487, 495–99, 516–17, 528; on Milton, 214–18, 219, 220, 457–58; on marriage, 217, 446, 451–55, 459–60, 464, 467, 479, 485–90 passim, 494–95, 503–06, 511, 515, 518, 527, 530; *Adam Bede*, 232, 445, 468, 491, 496, 497–99 passim, 521, 523, 528, 570; *The Mill on the Floss*, 307, 445, 458, 460, 465, 468, 477, 485, 491–94, 496, 497–99 passim, 512, 516–18 passim, 520, 522, 526, 532, 570; and C. Brontë, 408, 463–65, 472, 490, 498–99, 530; and female subculture, 444–45, 466, 472–77 passim, 479–84, 486, 522, 526, 532–33; "The Lifted Veil," *445–77*, 479, 488, 497, 500, 502, 516, 518, 528; life of, 447–52 passim, 461–62, 466–68, 476, 484, 489, 502; *Letters*, 447, 448, 451, 461–67 passim, 471–79 passim, 489, 532, 533; "Women in France," 450; "Jubal," 451–52; *Romola*, 451–52, 472, 494–99 passim, 517, 522, 526–27; "Self and Life," 452; "Armgart," 453–54, 455, 522–23, 610; and M. Shelley, 455–58, 462, 490; *Felix Holt the Radical*, 461, 476, 485, 487, 491, 496–99 passim, 517–21; "Margaret Fuller and Mary Wollstonecraft," 466; on the veil, 468–77 passim; *Scenes of Clerical Life*, *484–91*, 495, 497, 499, 500, 516, 523; on sisterhood, 514–19 passim; female weaving in, 520–28 passim, 632. For "Amos Barton," "Mr. Gilfil's Love Story," and "Janet's Repentance," see *Scenes of Clerical Life* (above)
Eliot, T. S., 46, 201, 548; on Milton, 206
Ellis, Mrs. Sarah: precepts of, 24; *The Family Monitor*, 318; on women's work, 344–45

Ellmann, Mary, 120–21, 520
Emerson, Ralph Waldo, 113, 469, 584, 585; on Austen, 109
English, Deirdre, 54
Epic, 201; as male genre, 67; in Austen, 133; and Milton, 210–12; in *Frankenstein*, 237–38; in *Middlemarch*, 531; and Dickinson, 582
Equality, male-female: in *Persuasion*, 179–81; in *Jane Eyre*, 352–57, 369–71; in *Villette*, 428–29; in *Middlemarch*, 529–30. *See also* Feminism, rise of
Erikson, Erik, 88
Escape, xi, 16, 83, 85–86, 101; in "Snow White," 42, 44; in *The Tenant of Wildfell Hall*, 80–82; in Austen's juvenilia, 114; travel as, 122–24, 157, 380; in *Castle Rackrent*, 150; in Milton, 202, 203; in *Wuthering Heights*, 288; female fantasies of, 313–15, 317; in *Jane Eyre*, 362, 364, 366–67, 368; in Eliot, 489–90; in *Uncle Tom's Cabin*, 533–35; in "Goblin Market," 565, 571–74; in Dickinson, 606, 610, 621–22, 648–49
Eve: in Austen, 166; and S. Richardson, 168; in *Paradise Lost*, 188–212 passim; in *Shirley*, 193–95, 305, 375, 385; in *Frankenstein*, 225–47 passim; and *Wuthering Heights*, 254, 264–65, 269, 277, 283, 289, 300, 306; in "A Drama of Exile," 375, 391, 393; and Dickinson, 394, 648–50; in *Villette*, 423; in Eliot, 445, 452–54, 457, 460, 465, 496; as "Eva" in *Uncle Tom's Cabin*, 482; and "Goblin Market," 566, 567, 568. *See also* Adam; Bible; Christianity; Fall, the
Eye troubles and blindness, 58, 70–71, 360; and Milton, 211; in *Middlemarch*, 215, 501; in *The Professor*, 334; in *Jane Eyre*, 367, 368–69, 370; in *Aurora Leigh*, 577–80, 617; of Dickinson, 595–96, 640, 641. *See also* Disease/dis-ease/healing; Headaches

Fairytales: "Sleeping Beauty," 22; "Snow White," 23, 36–44, 68, 78, 89, 273, 616, 634; Bruno Bettelheim on, 37–41 passim; "The Juniper Tree," 42–43; and *Wuthering Heights*, 259, 263–64, 268, 290, 296–97, 298, 303; "Jack and the Beanstalk," 261; "Beauty and the Beast," 303; "The Frog Prince," 303; "Cinderella," 326, 342, 343, 347, 351, 354, 358, 363, 368; "The Ugly Duckling," 342; "Little Red Riding Hood," 344; elements in *Jane Eyre*, 351;

and C. Brontë, 399; in *Villette*, 430; Banshees, 431; and spinning, 520; "The Three Spinners," 521. *See also* Bible; Mythology, female figures in; Mythology, male figures in

Fall, the, 9, 80, 87, 101; and S. Richardson, 168; in *Persuasion*, 177; in *Paradise Lost*, and women writers, 187–212 passim; in *Frankenstein*, 226–27, 233–47; in *Wuthering Heights*, 248–308 passim; in C. Brontë, 330, 384–91 passim, 423, in Eliot, 447, 455, 466, 496; and "Goblin Market," 567–68; in *Aurora Leigh*, 577–78. *See also* Adam; Bible; Eve; God the father; Sin

Fanon, Franz, 73

Female artistry: in *The Tenant of Wildfell Hall*, 80–82; in *The Professor*, 326–31, 335; in *Jane Eyre*, 352, 357; in *Villette*, 421–25; in *Middlemarch*, 499–500; Woolf on, 540–41; in "Armgart," 453–55; and deprivation, 543; in *Aurora Leigh*, 575–80; and alienation, 617–18; in Dickinson, 636–40. *See also* Authority, female struggle for; Feminist poetics; Paintings and drawings

Female beauty: in "Snow White," 38, 40; in Milton, 197–99 passim, 209; in C. Brontë, 380, 437; and Eliot, 447, 452, 460–61, 509, 514, 520. *See also* Woman as male creation/creature/art object

Female impersonation: in *Jane Eyre*, 353, 355

Female sexuality: and powerlessness, 8–11, 13, 52, 60; male dread of, 12, 14–15, 29–36 passim; in "Snow White," 37, 38, 42; as wound, 44; J. Mitchell on, 49; and space, 88, 93–94; power of, 95–99 passim; in Austen, 155–58, 161, 172; in Milton, 240; in *Frankenstein*, 241–42, 244–46; in *Wuthering Heights*, 270–71, 286; in *The Professor*, 321, 330; in *Jane Eyre*, 338; in *Shirley*, 381, 391, 412; in *Villette*, 406, 411, 421, 424; in Eliot, 450, 463–65, 468, 485, 505, 514, 518; and literary career, 540; "fulfillment of," 543–44; in "Goblin Market," 566–67; and female genius, 569–75; in *Aurora Leigh*, 577; in Dickinson, 595–97; and virginity, 615, 632–33. *See also* Eve; Fall, the; Marriage; Maternity; Misogyny;

—initiation into, 37, 42, 504; in *The Voyage Out*, 193; in *Paradise Lost*, 197; and M. Shelley, 221–24, 227; in *Frankenstein*, 232–34; in *Wuthering Heights*, 259, 265,

269–78, 282; in *Jane Eyre*, 355; in *Maude*, 550–52; in Dickinson, 601–03

Female subculture, 444; and Eliot, 482, 498; in *Middlemarch*, 526. *See also* Feminism, rise of; History, female

Feminism, rise of, 23, 77, 92, 192, 200, 203–06, 219–21; and E. Brontë, 255–56; in *Wuthering Heights*, 265–66; and hunger strikes, 284; in C. Brontë, 313–15, 374; in *Shirley*, 305; in *Jane Eyre*, 338, 349, 353–54, 355, 369–71; and *Villette*, 399; and spiritualism, 472–73; and Fuller, 480; and Eliot, 528; and "Goblin Market," 566–67; in *Aurora Leigh*, 575–77; Edward Dickinson on, 597–98. *See also* Authority; Disobedience; Female sexuality; History, female

Feminist criticism. *See* Feminist poetics

Feminist poetics, xiii; search for self-definition, 17–20, 45–53, 71, 87, 96, 101, 220–21, 223–24; in *Villette*, 403, 424–25, 440; in Dickinson, 633–50 passim. *See also* Authority, female struggle for; Female subculture; Feminism, rise of; History, female literary

"Fern, Fanny," 213, 559, 560

Fiedler, Leslie, 557

Fielding, Henry, 31, 374; *Joseph Andrews*, 127

Finch, Anne, Countess of Winchilsea, 3, 7, 28, 31, 44, 73, 189, 211, 478, 541; on female authorship, 7–14 passim, 17, 32, 36, 43, 60, 65, 66; "The Spleen," 60–63; on spatial imagery, 84–85; on housekeeping, 210; on women, 219; on the fall, 225, 251, 283, 330; on spinning, 525; as woman poet, 564

Fish, Stanley, 196

Fitzgerald, Edward: on Austen, 109

Flowers: in Rossetti, 569–71; daisy in Dickinson, 596–97, 600–01, 602, 605, 615; lily in Dickinson, 615, 645–46. *See also* Fruit; Landscape, symbolic

"Folio, Fred": *Lucy Boston; or Women's Rights and Spiritualism*, 473

Food: in Austen, 135, 137; in *Castle Rackrent*, 149; in *Wuthering Heights*, 273, 274, 288, 292; in *Jane Eyre*, 345; in *Shirley*, 372–78 passim, 379–83 passim, 390–91, 396; in *Villette*, 404, 415, 417, 422, 425, 427, 429, 438; in Eliot, 528; in Stowe, 485; in C. Rossetti, 565–75 passim; in "La Belle Dame Sans Merci," 574. *See also* Anorexia; Cooking; Fruit; Housekeeping; Starvation

Fourier, François, 462
Fox: Ann Leah, Margaret, and Catherine, 473
Fragmentation of personality: in Edgeworth, 152; in Austen, 162, 163; in *Wuthering Heights*, 274, 278, 280, 284–87, 300, 303; in *The Professor*, 331; in *Jane Eyre*, 359–60; in *Villette*, 412; in Eliot, 476; and Dickinson, 590, 608, 620–33, 635, 639–41; and of Dickinson's fascicles, 640–42
French Revolution, 205
Freud, Sigmund, 14, 36, 93, 280, 281, 344, 444, 619; and M. Bloom, 46–51; on female hysteria, 53; on dream symbolism, 88; on penis envy, 234, 272–73; on "The Uncanny," 252; on childhood, 264; on female sexuality, 272–73, 330
Froude, James Anthony, 467
Fruit: in *The Bell Jar*, 311; in *Paradise Lost*, 196–99 passim, 234, 568; in *Villette*, 430; in *Adam Bede*, 496; in "Goblin Market," 565–75 passim; in "La Belle Dame Sans Merci," 574. *See also* Anorexia; Cooking; Food; Starvation
Frye, Northrop, 98–99, 103, 611
Fuller, Margaret, 426, 473, 532, 581; on womanhood, 71; *Woman in the Nineteenth Century*, 466; career of, 479–84 passim; "Master" letter, 604–06
Furniture, 85; wallpaper as text, 90–91; in Austen, 135, 139–40; in *Villette*, 408, 413, 425, 427, 437; in *Scenes of Clerical Life*, 486, 487; and keys in Eliot, 495, 507–13 passim; in *Middlemarch*, 503, 506, 507, 510, 530; in *Romola*, 526–27. *See also* Architecture; Housekeeping
Fuseli, Henry, 351

Games/charades/riddles, 549–50, 553; in *Emma*, 158–60; in *Jane Eyre*, 350, 356; and women's writing, 607–08, 640
Gaskell, Elizabeth, 151, 206, 484; on the Brontës, 70–71; *Mary Barton*, 205
Gass, William, 9
Gay, John: *Three Hours After Marriage*, 31–33
Gelpi, Albert, 14, 189, 558, 559, 562, 610, 635, 637
Genlis, Stéphanie Félicité Ducrest de St Aubin, Comtesse de, 116
Gerin, Winifred, 252, 312, 313, 315, 639
Gilbert, Susan. *See* Dickinson, Susan Gilbert
Gilman, Charlotte Perkins, 143, 443–44, 472; on female madness, 45; "In Duty Bound," 84; "The Yellow Wallpaper," 89–92, 508
Giorgione, 459
Girl's Book of Diversions, The, 146
Gluck, Christoph Wilibald, 453
God the father, 5–7, 15, 21; in Milton, 188–89, 192, 199, 201–02, 210–11; and *Frankenstein*, 236; and *Wuthering Heights*, 254, 262, 277–78; and *The Professor*, 330; and *Jane Eyre*, 343, 346, 365; and *Shirley*, 376, 384–85, 389, 391–92; and *Villette*, 406, 417, 429; and Eliot, 447, 455, 468, 486, 497, 509, 524; and Dickinson, 592, 594–600 passim, 598–99, 600. *See also* Bible; Christ (Jesus); Christianity; Fall, the
Godwin, Mrs., 223, 238
Godwin, William, 202, 221–24 passim, 227, 233, 250, 462, 555
Goethe, J. W., 220, 314, 452, 462, 479; *Das Ewig-Weibliche*, 21, 34, 55; on Makarie, 22–27 passim, 55, 56, 64, 75–76, 86, 314, 345–46, 418–19, 466, 480; *Faust*, 67, 460; on Prometheus, 195; *The Sorrows of Young Werther*, 237–38.
Goldsmith, Oliver, 131, 530; *History of England*, 133
Gose, Elliot, 258
Gothic fiction, 83, 101, 223, 234, 582; in *Northanger Abbey*, 129–43 passim; *Frankenstein* as, 229; by C. Brontë, 314; *Jane Eyre* as, 337; and women, 445, 458; and Eliot, 465, 477; and veil, 469–70; and Dickinson, 584–85, 591, 622–25 passim, 627–28
Gottlieb, Annie, 52, 59, 101
Governess, the, 558; in Austen, 136, 157–58; in *The Professor*, 319; in *Jane Eyre*, 338, 349, 388–89; in *Shirley*, 388–89, 394; in *Villette*, 403, 407; in Eliot, 487. *See also* Economics and women; Education; Women and work
Graves, Robert, *The White Goddess*, 199–200, 262
Gray, Thomas, 139
Greer, Germaine, 9
Gregory, Dr., 116
Griffith, Clark, 600
Grimm, Brothers, 36, 37; "Snow White," 408
Griswold, Rufus: *The Female Poets of America*, 9–10, 558; on women's writing, 60

Haight, Gordon, 450–51, 467
Harding, D. W., 158
Hardy, Thomas: *Tess of the D'Urbervilles*, 232

Harper, Frances: "Vashti," 422
Hartman, Geoffrey, 43
Hawthorne, Nathaniel, 51, 213; "The Minister's Black Veil," 469–70; *The Blithedale Romance,* 471, 473; "The Snow Image," 617, 618–19
Haydon, Benjamin, 215
Hazlitt, William, 198
H. D., 99, 189; *Palimpsest,* 73; and spatial imagery, 84; "Demeter," 504; *Helen in Egypt,* 521
Headaches, 71; of Goethe's Makarie, 55, 64, 75, 314; and Woolf, 64; and Eliot, 64, 446, 448; and women writers, 151; in Austen, 174; and Margaret Fuller, 480; in *Aurora Leigh,* 617. *See also* Disease/dis-ease/healing; Madness
Heaven/Eden/paradise: female, 99–104; in Blake and *Wuthering Heights,* 189, 308; in Milton, 191–212 passim, 221; in *Frankenstein,* 225, 226; in *Wuthering Heights,* 248–308 passim; in *Shirley,* 385, 386; in *Villette,* 423; in Blake, 443; in Eliot, 446, 454; in Dickinson, 592, 598, 642–50; in C. Rossetti, 644–45; male aesthetic, 646. *See also* Christianity; Fall, the; Myth of origin; Utopian visions
Hegel, Frederick, 252
Héger, Constantin, 604, 605
Héger, M. and Mme., 275
Heilbrun, Carolyn, 75
Heilman, Robert, 425
Hell: in Milton, 198, 202; in Blake, 200; and *Frankenstein,* 221, 226–27; and *Wuthering Heights,* 248–308 passim; in *Villette,* 423; in Eliot, 457. *See also* Christianity; Fall, the; Satan; Sin
Higginson, Thomas Wentworth, 554, 556, 585, 586, 589, 636, 641, 647, 650; on Dickinson, 581, 598; and Dickinson, 582, 583
History: female, xii; literary, 46–53 passim; female literary, 59–88 passim, 98–104, 187–89 passim, 540–41, 544–45, 559, 564, 635, 641–42; and Austen, 110–12, 132–34, 175, 182–83; in Woolf, 192; male literary, 211–12, 218, 327, 540, 546–47; of M. Shelley's family, 223–24, 227–28; in *Frankenstein,* 224, 235, 237–38; in *The Last Man,* 246–47; of Brontë family, 251–52; E. Brontë on, 260; and *Wuthering Heights,* 302; in *Shirley,* 314, 373, 375, 384, 395, 396–98; and Angrian tales, 318; and Fuller, 480; and Stowe, 482; in *Middlemarch,* 503, 522; in *Aurora Leigh,* 579–80; of Dickinson family, 597, 599. *See also* Bloom,

Harold; Milton, John; Romanticism and Romantic poets
Hobbs, John, 529
Hoffman, E. T. A., 350
Holland, Josiah, 559
Homer, 6, 211, 457, 514; studies of, 546, 547
Hopkins, Anne, 55
Hopkins, Gerard Manley: theory of poetry, 3–5, 7, 8, 10–11, 12; "On a Poetess," 43; "Spelt from Sibyl's Leaves," 96
Hopkins, Robert, 135
Horney, Karen, 14, 118; on male dread of women, 34
Horses and riding, symbolism of: in Austen, 123–24; in *Wuthering Heights,* 264; in Eliot, 497
Housekeeping, 85; and Finch, 8; and "Snow White," 40; in *Castle Rackrent,* 150; and Milton, 193, 196, 209–10; and E. Brontë, 257–58; in *Wuthering Heights,* 289–91, 299; in *Shirley,* 381–82; in "Goblin Market," 570; Dickinson on, 592–93. *See also* Cooking; Food; Women and work
Howells, William Dean, 109; *The Undiscovered Country,* 473
Hunt, Helen Fiske. *See* Jackson, Helen Hunt
Hunt, Leigh, 462, 553
Hunt, Thornton, 462

Imlay, Fanny, 241–42; and namelessness, 555
Incest: in Milton and Romantics, 207–09; in *Frankenstein,* 228–29, 234; in *Manfred* and *Wuthering Heights,* 258–59, 265; in *Wuthering Heights,* 290; and *Middlemarch,* 529–30
Infanticide: and Lilith, 35; in *Wuthering Heights,* 296–97; in Eliot, 496; in *Uncle Tom's Cabin,* 533–34. *See also* Childhood; Death; Motherhood, and mortality; Mothers, terrible
Insects, symbolism of: in *Shirley,* 377–78, 380, 393; in *Villette,* 412, 438; in Eliot, 460, 469, 474, 525; spiders in Dickinson, 615, 631–42 passim, 648; in *Great Expectations,* 619
Irwin, John, 6, 443

Jackson, Helen Hunt, 558, 559; and Dickinson, 563
Jackson, Laura Riding. *See* Riding, Laura
Jacobi, Dr. Mary Putnam, 54–55
Jacobins, 206
James, Alice: on female rage, 512–13
James, Henry, 113, 256, 528; on Austen, 110

Janeway, Elizabeth, 272
Jewsbury, Geraldine, 151
Johnson, E. D. H., 425
Johnson, Samuel, 5, 117, 118; on women, 31; _Rasselas_, 346
Johnson, Thomas, 586, 593, 640
Johnston, Kenneth, 469
Jong, Erica, 399
Jonson, Ben, 6
Joyce, James, 112, 256; _Ulysses_, 5
Juhasz, Suzanne, 584
Jung, Carl, 36

Kafka, Franz: _The Penal Colony_, 275; "A Hunger Artist," 287
Kant, Immanuel, 28
Keats, John, 209, 222, 284, 452, 546, 555, 557, 573, 584; on poetry, 5, 69, 549; "Ode On a Grecian Urn," 14, 610, 646; "Lamia," 35; on spatial metaphors, 87; on Milton, 191, 192, 211; "The Fall of Hyperion," 204, 471; and Milton, 215; "Negative Capability," 439; "La Belle Dame Sans Merci," 460, 574–75; and poetic ambition, 552–54; "This Living Hand," 575; "The Eve of St. Agnes," 582. _See also_ Romanticism and Romantic poets
Keepsake, The, 458, 477, 531
Kermode, Frank, 46
Kettle, Arnold, 258
Kiely, Robert, 258
Killigow, Anne, 62
Kinkead-Weekes, Mark, 277
Kipling, Rudyard: _The Janeites_, 110–13, 119
Kizer, Carolyn, 76, 83, 146
Knoepflmacher, U. C., 447, 505, 523
Künstlerroman, _Aurora Leigh_ as, 575

Ladyhood, 22; education in, 23–24; in "Snow White," 41; and invalidism, 54–55; in Austen, 108–10, 124, 128, 134, 136, 140, 161, 169, 174, 180, 181; and women writers, 146, 148, 153, 562–63; and M. Shelley, 242–43; in _Wuthering Heights_, 267–70, 280, 283, 285, 286, 289, 292, 303; C. Brontë on, 318; in _Jane Eyre_, 344–45; in C. Brontë, 378; in _Shirley_, 388, 390, 393, 394, 396; in _Middlemarch_, 403, 514, 522; in _Villette_, 420, 428; in _Scenes of Clerical Life_, 484; Dickinson on, 588, 590
Lakoff, Robin, 161
Landscape, symbolic: Austen as, 108; in Austen, 178; in _Frankenstein_, 226, 235, 246; in _Wuthering Heights_, 262; "male," 313–14; in _The Professor_, 328–29; in _Jane_

Eyre, 339, 366, 369–70; in _Villette_, 434–36; in _The Mill on the Floss_, 493; in "Goblin Market," 565, 567, 570, 573; in "From House to Home," 571–73; "La Belle Dame Sans Merci," 574; in Dickinson, 589, 591, 596, 607, 611–12, 627–29, 646–47; in women writers, 643–45. _See also_ Heaven/Eden/paradise; Hell
—gardens, 100, 144, 202; in _Wuthering Heights_, 299–308; in _The Professor_, 321; in _Shirley_, 374, 375, 381, 382; in _Villette_, 409–11, 412, 413, 418, 419, 429, 438; in _Scenes of Clerical Life_, 486, 490; in _Adam Bede_, 496
—moors, 195; in _Wuthering Heights_, 284, 300, 305–06, 492; in _Jane Eyre_, 342, 363–64
—caves, 247, 376; as female space, 93–104; leaves in Sibyl's, 95–97, 100–01.
Language: and women, 31, 43, 74, 127–28, 191; and female deciphering, 96–99; in Austen, 133, 138, 140, 156, 158, 169; and Milton, 211; in _Frankenstein_, 236; in _Wuthering Heights_, 294; in _The Professor_, 327; in _Shirley_, 388, 392–93; in _Villette_, 407, 415; female, and power, 568–69, 673; of Dickinson family, 583; of Dickinson, 591, 593, 599, 601, 602–03, 605, 609, 623, 626. _See also_ Aphasia; Deciphering; Education; Lyric poetry; Parody; Prosody
Lascelles, Mary, 120
Lawrence, D. H., 204, 356; _The Plumed Serpent_, 14; on Austen, 109–10; _The Rainbow_, 295; on "lady poets," 562
Lead, Jane: on female wisdom, 93; Sophia, 99; and E. Brontë, 255; on Eve, 306
Leavis, Q. D., 253, 258, 264, 289, 291, 292
Lederer, Wolfgang, 25; _The Fear of Women_, 14–15
Lee, Home, 169
Le Guin, Ursula: "The New Atlantis," 102
Leigh, Augusta, 208
Lennox, Charlotte, 121
Lerner, Gerda, xii–xiii
Lessing, Doris, 59; _Four-Gated City_, 78, 474; _Summer Before the Dark_, 144
Levertov, Denise, 241, 443–44, 472
Levine, George, 141–42
Lévi-Strauss, Claude: on myth, 257; _The Raw and the Cooked_, 273–74, 287, 294, 360; "The Jaguar's Wife," 303–05, 308
Lewes, George Henry, 373, 403, 448, 458, 462, 466, 467, 476
Lewis, "Monk," 227, 411
Library. _See_ Architecture, library

Lilith, 42; George MacDonald on, 35; Biblical story of, 35–36; in *Adam Bede*, 496; in *Middlemarch*, 514
Linton, Eliza Lynn, 531
"Little Snow White." *See* "Snow White"
Litz, A. Walton, 135
Locke, John, 501
Lovers' Vows, 167
Lucifer. *See* Satan
Lucifer the Light-Bearer, 205
Lyric poetry: as male genre, 68; and women, 83, 209, 539–650 passim; theories of, 541–49; "lady poets," 559–63, 627; as genre, 563; as mimesis, 586; vs. "prose" in Dickinson, 591; the aubade in Dickinson, 601; as literary criticism, 624–25

MacDonald, George; *Lilith*, vii, 35
Madness and anger, 85–89, 101, 111, 203, 220, 431, 477, 483–84, 486; as hysteria and spleen, 33, 53, 94, 448; in "Snow White," 38–42; in female artists, 43, 56, 544–45, 583; in "The Yellow Wallpaper," 89–92; in Woolf, 193; in *Frankenstein*, 236; in *Wuthering Heights*, 262–63, 269, 277–87, 302–08; in *The Professor*, 324, 332–34; in *Jane Eyre*, 338–71 passim; in *Villette*, 403, 414–15, 416, 423; in Eliot, 449, 462, 475, 484, 490–97 passim, 498, 518; in *Middlemarch*, 511, 512, 513, 516; in Dickinson, 608–12, 621–33, 648–49; and the color white, 617–18, 619–21. *See also* Disease/dis-ease/healing; Doubles; Fragmentation of personality
Madwomen. *See* Doubles
Male approval, female need for, 147–48, 151–54, 382; in "Snow White," 38; in Austen, 118, 165, 172; in Eliot, 403–04, 427–28, 449–50, 466–67, 492, 494, 506, 530, 532
Male as master; in *The Professor*, 317, 320, 325–27; in *The Professor* and "Jane," 329–31; in *Jane Eyre*, 351–57, 360; in *Shirley*, 394, 395; in *Villette*, 429–30; in Eliot, 486, 500, 506, 530; in *Uncle Tom's Cabin*, 533–34; in *Aurora Leigh*, 578–79; in Dickinson, 584, 594–606, 607, 608–10, 629, 646. *See also* Authority; Education
Male as muse, 208; in *Shirley*, 394; in *Villette*, 429–30; in Rossetti, 571; in Dickinson, 607–11, 636
Male impersonation: inauthenticity of, 72; in The *Professor*, 315–17; in C. Brontë, 372, 374, 381–82, 398, 399; in *Shirley*, 388; in *Villette*, 413, 432; and writing, 480;

and Eliot, 532. *See also* Duplicity, female; Names
Male sexuality: and literary power, 4, 6–7, 8–10; and killing, 14; definitions of masculinity, 130; and celibacy, 200; and power in *Wuthering Heights*, 277; and *Jane Eyre*, 338, 351, 354, 355, 368; female dread of, 392; in *Middlemarch*, 505; and evil in "Goblin Market," 566–67, 570; in Dickinson, 600–02; 609–10
Marchand, Leslie, 207
Marlowe, Christopher, 231
Marriage: and killing, 14; in "Snow White," 41–42; in *The Tenant of Wildfell Hall*, 80–82; in Austen, 109, 126–27, 128, 130, 132, 136, 144, 160–61, 163, 178–81, 181–83; in *Castle Rackrent*, 149–50; and law, 154–55; and Milton, 190, 458; in *Middlemarch*, 217, 503–06, 511, 514–16, 518, 530; in *Frankenstein*, 228–29; in *Wuthering Heights*, 269–70, 275–78, 290; in *The Professor*, 318, 324, 331; in *Jane Eyre*, 350–62 passim, 364, 367, 368–71 passim; and money in C. Brontë, 375, 376, 377; in *Shirley*, 388, 392, 395–97; in *Villette*, 407; in "The Lifted Veil," 446, 459–60, 464, 479; and "Armgart," 453–54; of Eliot, 467; in *Scenes of Clerical Life*, 485–90 passim; in *Romola*, 494–95, 505; in *Daniel Deronda*, 495, 505; and myth, 527; in *Aurora Leigh*, 578–80, 582; as metaphor in Dickinson, 587; Dickinson on, 588–89, 595–96; Edward Dickinson on, 597. *See also* Economics and women; Female sexuality; Housekeeping; Male sexuality; Women and work
Martin, Wendy, 55
Mary, Queen of Scots, 215
Masochism: female, in Austen, 118; in *Wuthering Heights*, 284–85; and Eliot, 466; in Rossetti, 553, 571–74; in Dickinson, 595–96, 602
Maternity and childbirth: and mortality, 26, 88, 94–95, 222–23; in *Aurora Leigh*, 59; anxiety about, 88–89, 125–26, 156, 181, 198, 455; in the cave, 94; and motherland, 99–104; in Austen, 114–16, 172, 174; in *Paradise Lost*, 197–98, 211, 222–24; and nursing, 198, 224; in *Frankenstein*, 232–34, 238; and pregnancy in *Frankenstein*, 241; in *Maria*, 246–47; mock, in *Wuthering Heights*, 266; in *Wuthering Heights*, 270–71; and pregnancy in *Wuthering Heights*, 285–87; and mortality in *Wuthering Heights*, 286–87; in *Scenes of Clerical Life*,

Maternity (*continued*)
485–87 passim; and motherland in Eliot, 495; and Eliot, 499; in *Middlemarch*, 514; and matriarchy, 528; and pregnancy, symbolic in Dickinson, 630–31. *See also* Female sexuality; Mothers

Matrilineality, 45, 59; literary, 49–53 passim, 98–104 passim. *See also* Maternity; Mothers

May, Caroline: *American Female Poets*, 558–59

Mazzini, Giuseppe, 467, 479

Melville, Herman: *Moby Dick*, 614–15, 621

Memory. *See* Amnesia

Mill, John, 349, 370

Millay, Edna St. Vincent: on female writing, 56–57

Miller, J. Hillis, xiii, 46, 52, 264, 523

Miller, Ruth, 559, 563, 584, 641

Millett, Kate, 420

Milton, John, 12, 46, 131, 529, 533, 562; "Methought I Saw My Late Espoused Saint," 20–21, 472, 615; Sin and Eve, 30–33; misogyny of, 80; *Paradise Lost* (and women), 187–308 passim, 357, 457, 582, 615, 646, 648; *Lycidas*, 192, 224; *Comus*, 193, 224; and his daughters, 210, 214–15, 219–21, 265, 578–79; blindness of, 211; in *Middlemarch*, 217–18, 385, 451, 500, 511, 529; *Areopagitica*, 224; *Paradise Regained*, 224; and C. Brontë, 314, 328, 374, 378, 384, 429; on marriage, 458; and Fuller, 481; and "Goblin Market," 567–68. *See also* Christianity; Eve; Fall, the; God the father; Reading; Revision

Mirrors, 44, 54, 57, 85; Riding on, 3; M. E. Coleridge on, 15–16, 17, 77; and female self-loathing, 34, 36; in "Snow White," 36–38, 42, 43, 46; texts as, 53, 71, 76–77, 82; and narcissism, 118; in *Persuasion*, 122, 175, 176, 177, 180; in *Northanger Abbey*, 144; in *Paradise Lost*, 203; in *Frankenstein*, 240; in *Wuthering Heights*, 282–85 passim; in *Jane Eyre*, 340–41, 359, 360, 362; in *Shirley*, 386; in *Villette*, 434, 436, 437; and M. Atwood, 473; and H. B. Stowe, 473; in *Scenes of Clerical Life*, 486; in *Middlemarch*, 515–16, 526; in Eliot, 517; and C. Rossetti, 552

Misogyny, 214, 266; underlying patriarchy, 13–15, 30–31; in Milton, 21, 80, 188–212 passim, 252, 307; in Finch and Pope, 60–61; female, 62–63, 70; in *The Tenant of Wildfell Hall*, 82; in Austen, 139–40; in *Letters for Literary Ladies*, 148; patristic, 240; in *Frankenstein*, 243; in Donne, 245;

and the Bible, 385, 391; and authorship in *Shirley*, 396; in "The Lifted Veil," 459–60, 461; and Eliot, 462, 465–66, 494–95; in *Scenes of Clerical Life*, 489; in *Middlemarch*, 501, 507

Mitchell, Juliet, 272; on Freud, 47, 49–50

Mitchell, S. Weir, 89, 91–92; on female madness, 45

Moers, Ellen, xii, 39, 116, 136, 142, 205, 222, 228–29, 232, 548, 584; on female Gothic, 83

Moglen, Helene, 208

Monsters. *See* Woman as monster

Moon, symbolism of: in "The Yellow Wallpaper," 90; Robert Graves on, 199; in *Jane Eyre*, 342, 363, 365, 367; in *Villette*, 405, 411, 422–23, 434, 436, 438; in *Middlemarch*, 501; in Margaret Fuller, 606; in Dickinson, 647. *See also* Elements; Times of Day

More, Mrs. Hannah, 116, 467

Moschus: "Lament for Bion," 68

Mossberg, Barbara Clarke, 591

Mother Goose, 547, 582

Mothers: Dickinson on, 53; in Austen, 124–26, 171; educating, 138, 392; in *Jane Eyre*, 342, 345; and Eliot, 476; and myth of Demeter, 504; and Stowe, 532–33, 535; in Dickinson, 589, 647. *See also* Female sexuality; Maternity; Matrilineality

—dead, 18–19, 97, 222–24, 263, 267, 447; in *Frankenstein*, 242–46; in *Middlemarch*, 510

—goddesses, 19, 20–21, 95, 99, 384, 398, 521; in *Wuthering Heights*, 303; in *Jane Eyre*, 357, 363; in Dickinson, 646–49

—terrible, 19, 28, 33–44 passim, 52, 79, 298; in *Villette*, 431

—good, 39, 88, 91, 383, 474; in *Jane Eyre*, 346; in *Villette*, 403, 417, 420; in Stowe, 482–83

—stepmother, 181, 315; in *Wuthering Heights*, 269–70; in *Jane Eyre*, 342–43; in *Villette*, 414

—absent, 376, 378, 529; in Austen, 176, 178; in *Middlemarch*, 506

Mozart, Wolfgang Amadeus, *The Magic Flute*, 172

Mozley, Anne: on *Jane Eyre*, 337, 338

Mudrick, Marvin, 120

Murder: in *Frankenstein*, 228, 231, 236, 241, 242–44; in *Maria*, 246–67; in *Wuthering Heights*, 296–97

Muse, female: in Keats, 574; in Dickinson, 647–49

Muse, male. *See* Male as muse

"Myrtle, Minny," 559

Myth of origin: *Paradise Lost* as, 188–212 passim; *Frankenstein* as, 224–27 passim; *Wuthering Heights* as, 248–308; American Indian, 303–04; in *Shirley*, 391

Mythology, female figures in, 198; Galatea, 12, 41; Sophia, 12, 93, 103–04, 198; Minerva, 12, 472, 481, 529; Medusa, 17, 18, 34, 80, 198, 380, 387, 471–72, 477, 491–92, 529; Muse, 18, 47, 49, 62, 182, 210, 450, 458, 471–72, 529; Lamia, 18, 79, 455, 464; Psyche, 18, 234, 508; Sirens, 29, 166, 460; Circe, 30, 34, 80, 632; Medea, 30, 42, 68; Scylla, 30, 79; Delila, 34; Kali, 34; Sphinx, 34, 79; Salome, 34, 476; Procne, 43; Philomel, 43, 521, 642; Gorgons, 79; Helen, 80; Leda, 80; Persephone, 80, 273, 504, 506, 527, 532; Cassandra, 80, 450; Demeter, 95; Gaea, 95; Fates, the, 95, 521, 524; Norns, 95, 521, 532; Sibyl, 95–99; Eurydice, 99; Isis, 99, 471; Urania, 197; Pandora, 234; Diana, 364–65, 616, 647; Lady Bountiful, 382, 388; mermaid, 386–87, 515; Cleopatra, 420–21, 460, 527; Maenad, 453; Melusina, 455; Arachne, 478; Pallas, 478; Pollian, 479; Penelope, 481, 521, 523, 642; Nemesis, 490, 495, 498, 524; Bacchante, 494; Antigone, 494, 504, 532; Fortune, 524; Erinna, 525; Ariadne, 526–28, 532, 629, 642; Aurora, 578. *See also* Eve; Lilith; Sin; Virgin Mary

Mythology, male figures in: Titans, 194–96; Prometheus, 194–96, 201, 203, 204, 206, 207, 224, 225, 234, 237, 247, 347, 542; Albion, 195; Jove, 198, 231, 237; Cain, 204, 207; Tiresias, 211; Samson, 215; Achilles, 272; Fisher King, the, 272; Oedipus, 272; Hercules, 356, 368; Charon, 406; Apollyon, 409; Apollo, 412, 578, 595; Cupid, 508; Minotaur, 527; Theseus, 527; Bacchus, 527, 529; Pegasus, 529. *See also* Adam; Satan

Names: and pseudonyms, 64–71 passim, 446; and male impersonation, 65, 380, 381; and Maria Edgeworth, 146–47; and Austen, 175; and namelessness in *Frankenstein*, 239, 241–42; in *Wuthering Heights*, 259, 276, 300, 302–03; in *Jane Eyre*, 342, 358; and namelessness in *Jane Eyre*, 364–65; of C. Brontë, 374; and Eliot, 450–52, 466, 491, 502, 531; and legitimacy, 462; of Bertha, 463; and Barrett Browning, 474; and sewing, 478; and female namelessness, 555; of women

writers, 562–63; in Dickinson, 583; and namelessness in women's writing, 627

Narcissism: Bettelheim on, 37; in "Snow White," 38, 41; in Austen's juvenilia, 117–18; in *Paradise Lost*, 203; female, 240; in *Villette*, 410; and "The Lifted Veil," 457; in *Middlemarch*, 514, 516

Narrative technique: in Austen, 153–55, 179; in *Frankenstein*, 224–27 passim, 249–50; in *Wuthering Heights*, 249–50, 267, 288, 290; in C. Brontë, 314; in *The Professor*, 315–18, 333; epistolary novel, 317–18; in novel as compared to poetry, 538; dramatic monologue in Dickinson, 583, 623, 628–30

Nature/culture polarity: woman as cultural outsider, 19, 28, 48–49, 205, 384, 387, 398, 456–57, 492–94, 525–26; and Austen, 134, 179–80; and *Wuthering Heights*, 257, 264, 268, 273–74, 287, 288; in *Lear* and *Wuthering Heights*, 259; nature as female, 262, 646–47, 648; nature as female in *Wuthering Heights*, 293–308 passim; and nineteenth century, 301–02, 621; in *Shirley*, 394; nature as female in Eliot, 492–94, 497–98, 526

Newcastle, Duchess of. *See* Cavendish, Margaret

Nietzsche, Friedrich, 206

Nightingale, Florence, 544

Niles, Thomas, 559

Nin, Anaïs, 3, 7

Norcross, Louise, 593

Novel as genre: and women, 67–72, 138–39, 140; 563; Austen on, 131–33, 138–39, 168; in *Frankenstein*, 237; and *Wuthering Heights*, 252, 258–59; and myth, 256–57; and C. Brontë, 315; and women in *Shirley*, 395–98; and women writers, 540–41, 545–49; and Dickinson, 582, 583–86. *See also* Parody; Reading; Revision; Romance

Oates, Joyce Carol, 548; on author and characters, 68–69

Oliphant, Mrs. Margaret, 531; on *Jane Eyre*, 337, 338

Olsen, Tillie, 449

Orphanhood: in *Mansfield Park*, 164; in *Frankenstein*, 227–28, 232, 239, 244; and the Brontës, 251, 312, 315, 319, 583; and *Wuthering Heights*, 255; in *The Professor*, 325; in *Jane Eyre*, 336–71 passim; in *Shirley*, 394; in *Villette*, 400, 415; in *Adam Bede*, 446; in "The Lifted Veil," 457, 463; in "The Mortal Immortal," 458; in *Scenes of Clerical Life*, 486. *See also* Childhood;

Orphanhood, (*continued*)
  Economics and women, and "beggary";
  Infanticide; Mothers
Ortner, Sherry, 295, 300; "Is Female to Male
  As Nature Is To Culture," 18–19, 28
Otherness of female. *See* Nature/culture po-
  larity
Ovid: *Metamorphoses,* 527

Paintings and drawings, 85, 123, 129; in *Aurora Leigh,* 18–19; Judy Chicago on
  female, 74; in *The Tenant of Wildfell Hall,*
  81–82; by Raphael, 98; on ivory, 107–08;
  in Austen, 138, 140, 141; of Milton, 215;
  in *The Professor,* 327, 333–34; in *Jane Eyre,*
  352, 357, 433; in *Villette,* 420–21, 432; in
  "The Lifted Veil," 459, in *Middlemarch,*
  500, 506, 529; of Eliot, 533; daguerrotype
  of Whitman, 556. *See also* Female artistry
Palimpsest. *See* Duplicity, female
Paradise Lost. See Milton, John
Parlor. *See* Architecture, parlor/sitting
  room/drawing room
Parody, 58; in "Snow White," 39–42; as
  female revision, 80; in Kipling, 111; in
  Austen, 112, 113–27 passim, 130, 132,
  133, 139, 141, 145, 153, 164, 170; in
  Frankenstein, 236, 241; in *Wuthering
  Heights,* 261, 262, 266, 277, 288, 296–98,
  302; in *Jane Eyre,* 370; in *Shirley,* 387, 388,
  394–95; in *Villette,* 402, 409, 413, 418,
  420; and women, 457, 461; in
  Middlemarch, 507; in Dickinson, 623,
  628–30. *See also* Duplicity, female; Narrative technique; Novel as genre
Pater, Sir Walter, 545–46
Paternity: as metaphor, 3–16, 46–47, 60, 74,
  188, 220–21, 456; and patricide, 114; and
  patricide in Austen, 116; in Austen, 128,
  137, 139, 166–67; and Edgeworth, 147–
  48, 151–52; and death, 198, 357; in
  Wuthering Heights, 253, 266, 281, 296–98,
  299, 301; in *Jane Eyre,* 346; in *Villette,* 415;
  in Dickinson, 587; Dickinson and her
  father, 597–600. *See also* Authority; Male
  sexuality; Patrilineality
Patmore, Coventry, 344; *The Angel In the
  House,* 22–29 passim, 32, 86
Patrilineality, 202; exclusion of female artist, 48–49, 51; in Austen, 120; in *Frankenstein,* 243; and legitimacy in *Wuthering
  Heights,* 301–03, 305. *See also* Architecture; Authority; Paternity
Peterson, M. Jeanne, 349
Petrarch, 23, 68

Physiognomy: as symbol in Dickinson,
  637–38
Piercy, Marge: "Unlearning To Not Speak,"
  83
Plath, Sylvia, xi, 143, 189, 209, 286, 311,
  425, 477, 505; "Lady Lazarus," 17–18,
  283, 424–25, 623, 639; "Elm," 76; "In
  Plaster," 78, 241; and spatial imagery, 84;
  "Stings," 92; "Nick and the Candlestick,"
  102; "Daddy," 206–07; "Ariel," 220, 648;
  on the fall, 225; "Confusion," 284;
  "Tulips," 335; "Two Sisters of Persephone," 504; *The Bell Jar,* 508; suicide of, 549
Plato, 87, 103, 546; the parable of the cave,
  93–96
Plutarch: *Lives,* 237–38; *Stories of Great Men,*
  531
Poe, Edgar Allan, 109, 620, 631; on women,
  25; and architecture, 86, 87; "Ligeia," 87;
  and spatial metaphor, 93–94; "The Case
  of M. Valdemar," 469–70
Poison, 57–58, 126, 198; in "Snow White,"
  40–41; in *Wuthering Heights,* 303; in "The
  Lifted Veil," 464–65; in *Middlemarch,* 509
Politics: and Austen, 135–36; and oppres-
  sion in *The Professor,* 333, 334; male in
  Aurora Leigh, 575–76, 579–80. *See also*
  History
Polwhele, Richard, 569
Pope, Alexander, 61, 116–17, 131, 139, 141,
  192; *Three Hours After Marriage,* 31–33;
  on women, 32, 60–61; "The Dunciad,"
  32–35 passim; *The Rape of the Lock,* 33;
  "An Essay On Man," 70, 474; "An Essay
  on Criticism," 546
Praz, Mario, 460
Pre-Raphaelite Brotherhood, The, 573
"Pre-Romantics," the, 205
Prior, Matthew, 131
Prisons, 86–87, 313, 399; and prisoners in
  Northanger Abbey, 140–41; and prisoners
  in *Castle Rackrent,* 149–50; in E. Brontë,
  273–76 passim, 279–84 passim, 297; in C.
  Brontë, 276–77, 399; and cages, 384, 399;
  in *Villette,* 407; in *Middlemarch,* 516. *See
  also* Claustrophobia
Prophecy. *See* Clairvoyance
Prosody: English, 547; female, 582; unor-
  thodox in Dickinson, 602–03, 641
Prostitution: in *Jane Eyre,* 350; in *Aurora
  Leigh,* 577. *See also* Economics and women;
  Women and work

Quarles, Francis, 584
Quarterly Review, The, 337

Rachel, 423

Racine: *Phaedre*, 423

Radcliffe, Ann, 83, 115, 121, 129, 135, 143, 540, 585; *The Mysteries of Udolpho*, 340, 347, 620

Ransom, John Crowe: on Dickinson, 541, 542–43, 583, 594; on Whitman, 557

Raphael, 98

Ratchford, Fanny, 256, 258

Reading, 78; as male activity, 8, 49; as invasion of privacy, 20, 52; and anxiety, 30–31, 32, 55–56, 64, 187–212 passim, 221–24; and misreading, 79, 201, 402; and revision, 205; and sex, 224; in *Frankenstein*, 225, 230, 237, 240, 244–46; male, of women writers, 541–44; and Dickinson, 559–61, 582–650 passim. *See also* Authority; Duplicity, female; Parody; Revision

—female; 117–21 passim, 215–308 passim, 314; in Austen, 113–14, 115, 123, 127–45 passim; in *Wuthering Heights*, 248–308 passim; in *Jane Eyre*, 356; in *Shirley*, 382; in *Villette*, 404–05, 439; and Eliot, 451, 484, 493, 531

Redinger, Ruby, 447

Reeves, James, 541

Renoir, Auguste, 6

Renunciation. *See* Authority, female relinquishing of

Revision: literary, xii; A. Rich on, 49; H. Bloom on, 73–74; female literary, 73–75, 76–77, 80, 103, 220–21; by Austen, 119–21, 135–43; by M. Shelley, 221–46 passim; by E. Brontë, 248–60 passim; by C. Brontë, 336–71 passim, 374, 402, 405–06; by Eliot, 465, 492, 496, 519, 527. *See also* Parody; Reading

Rhys, Jean, 336

Rich, Adrienne, 346, 530; "Planetarium," 29, 89, 240–41; on revision, 49; on Dickinson, 83; "Re-forming the Crystal," 99, 101; "Living in the Cave," 102; on *Jane Eyre*, 361–65 passim; "When We Dead Awaken," 408; on sewing, 642

Richardson, Dorothy, 531

Richardson, Samuel, 290, 577; *Pamela*, 67, 68, 119, 337, 352, 354; *Clarissa*, 119, 129, 620; *Sir Charles Grandison*, 168; and women, 317–18, 321

Riding, Laura: "Eve's Side Of It," vii, 35; "In the End," 3

Rieger, James, 238

Rigby, Elizabeth, 354, 369, 370, 389; on *Jane Eyre*, 205–06, 337, 338

Riley, Bridget, 6

Robbins, Elizabeth, 531

Rochester, John Wilmot, Earl of, 6, 354

Roethke, Theodore, 562; on women poets, 541–42

Romance: and women, 68, 605–06; in Austen, 115–18, 123, 126, 130–32, 158, 179, 275; *Wuthering Heights* as, 249, 255, 288, 291; in *Shirley*, 396–98; in *Villette*, 420, 427–28, 434, 436; images of women in, 323; in Eliot, 493, 529; and women poets, 543; and Dickinson, 582, 594, 600–02; and *Great Expectations*, 619. *See also* Novel as genre; Parody; Reading; Revision

Romanticism and Romantic poets: on imagination, 55, 312; and revolutionary politics, 82, 201–06 passim, 211, 315, 327, 580; and women, 98–99, 103, 156, 219, 220, 401–03, 438, 445, 460–62; and Milton, 211–12, 221; on *Frankenstein*, 221–46 passim; on maternity, 245; and Jane Eyre, 351; and Eliot, 460–62, 469–72; and theology, 546, 612; and self-assertion, 587; and Dickinson, 597, 648–50; and whiteness, 615. *See also* History, literary; Lyric poetry; Parody; Reading; Revision

Root, Abiah, 592, 593

Rosenfeld, Claire, 360

Ross, Anne, 431–32

Rossetti, Christina, 191, 414, 444, 541, 589; "In an Artist's Studio," 18; on hunger, 58; "The Keynote," 59, 93, 98; religion in, 83; "Mother Country," 100–01; "Goblin Market," 189, 220, 582, 583, *564–75;* and veils, 472; *Maude, 549–54*, 561–62, 564–65, 570–71, 573, 617; "Some Ladies Dress in Muslin," 550; "She Sat and Sang," 551; "All Things That Pass," 552; "Speaking Likenesses," 552; "On Keats," 553–54; and literary ambition, 558; "From House to Home," 571–75 passim, 578, 582, 645; and renunciation, 587; "A Soul," 621

Rossetti, Dante Gabriel: "The Blessed Damozel," 27; and Elizabeth Siddal, 27

Rossetti, Elizabeth Siddal, 27, 427

Rossi, Alice, xii

Rousseau, Jean Jacques, 147, 382, 456

Rubenstein, Marc, 232

Rukeyser, Muriel: "Myth," 79; "In the Underworld," 504

Rush, Florence, 143

Ruskin, John: "On Imagination," 5; on woman's place, 24

Russ, Joanna, 69

Sade, Donatien Alphonse François, Marquis de, 10, 424

Said, Edward, 4–5, 6, 510
Saint Pierre, Bernardin de: *Paul et Virginie*, 438, 439
Sand, George, 65–67, 463, 479, 559
Sappho, 70, 146
Sarton, May: "Birthday on the Acropolis," 76; "The Muse as Medusa," 477
Sartre, Jean Paul, 12, 295
Satan, 35, 82, 101, 214, 216, 218, 219, 225, 227, 242, 293, 296, 298, 300, 301, 303, 314, 316, 328, 332, 445, 597, 615; in Austen, 167; in *Paradise Lost*, 188–212 passim; and *Frankenstein*, 226, 229–40 passim; and *Wuthering Heights*, 253, 254, 255, 261, 266, 271, 280, 288, 306; and *Villette*, 430, 434, 437; and Eliot, 452, 453, 455, 456, 457; and "Goblin Market," 566, 567; and Dickinson, 600, 609, 649. *See also* Christianity; Fall, the; Hell; Milton
Satire, 68; and misogyny, 30–34
Schiller, Johann Friedrich, 439; "Das Mädchens Klage," 428; "The Veiled Image of Saia," 471
Schorer, Mark, 249, 253, 258, 292
Schreiner, Olive, 151
Scott, Sir Walter, 112, 312, 531, 545; on Austen, 108–09
Serpents and snakes, symbolism of, 196, 197, 203, 455, 457, 472, 514, 567–68; in "The Lifted Veil," 460; in *Scenes of Clerical Life*, 489–90; in *The Mill on the Floss*, 491
Sewing and weaving: in "Snow White," 37, 42, 517; and C. Brontë, 323, 325, 377, 378, 428, 434; in the cave, 94–95, 97, 102; in Dickinson, 100, 532–42; and Austen, 110, 171, 182; in Blake, 443, 478; threads, 454; in Eliot, 459, 485, 500, 520–26, 535; and witchcraft, 471; in Anne Finch, 478; and fairy tales, 520; and myth, 521, 527–28; as female activity, 638–42; in *Aurora Leigh*, 640. *See also* Clothing; Housekeeping
Sexton, Anne, 549; on mothers, 45; "The Red Shoes," 56–57
Shakespeare, William, 5, 87, 530, 540, 548, 557, 560, 584; *King Lear*, 30, 34, 68, 120, 241, 248, 268, 285; *Macbeth*, 30, 35, 66, 68; *Hamlet*, 68, 285, 618; *King Lear*, 259, 262, 263, 266, 296–98 passim; *Coriolanus*, 377, 383, 404
"Shakespeare's sister." *See* Woolf, Virginia
Shelley, Mary, 57, 58, 73, 80, 82, 142, 201, 207, 209, 270, 330, 374, 444, 445, 453, 455, 462, 463, 530; *Frankenstein*, 59, 68, 78, 79, 189, 220, *221–47*, 269, 283, 293,

296, 298, 307, 328, 331, 357, 423, 508, 615; *The Last Man*, 95–104, 246–47, 456, 642; as literary heiress, 221–24; journal of, 223–24; *Frankenstein* compared to *Wuthering Heights*, 249–52, 262; *Frankenstein* and "The Lifted Veil," 455–57; "The Mortal Immortal" and Eliot, 458; *Frankenstein* and revenge, 490; on Proserpine, 504
Shelley, Percy Bysshe, 95, 202, 203, 205, 242, 401, 452, 461, 462, 529, 553; "On Poetry," 5; on women, 12; *Prometheus Unbound*, 195, 201, 204, 221; literary theory of, 211–12; and reading, 223; preface to *Frankenstein*, 239; on Rome, 247; "Medusa," 460; *Adonais*, 469; "Lift Not the Painted Veil," 469–70; *The Witch of Atlas*, 471; studies of the classics, 546, 547; "Mont Blanc," 615. *See also* Romanticism and Romantic poets
Sheridan, Richard Brinsley, 30, 116; *The Rivals*, 127
Sherwood, William, R., 614, 620
Showalter, Elaine, xii, 50, 61, 75, 294, 465, 544
Siddal, Elizabeth. *See* Rossetti, Dante Gabriel
Sidney, Sir Phillip, 5; "Arcadia," 30
Sigourney, Lydia, 558, 559
Sin (in *Paradise Lost*), 30, 33; and Eve, 197–99; and *Frankenstein*, 229, 233, 235, 239, 242, 243, 244; and *Wuthering Heights*, 270, 297, 300; and *Shirley*, 387; and Eliot, 455. *See also* Fall, the; Woman as monster
Sisterhood: in Austen, 29–30, 126, 156–62, 165, 170, 183; difficulty of bonding, 38; literary, 50–51, 132, 135; in *Jane Eyre*, 342, 350, 364–65; in *Shirley*, 392; in *Villette*, 410; nuns as, 462; in Eliot, 503, 517–19; and Dickinson estate, 563–64; in "Goblin Market," 565–67. *See also* Female subculture; Feminism, rise of
Slavery and anti-slavery movement, 205
Smith, Catherine, 255
Smith, Charlotte, 129
Smollett, Tobias, 31; *Humphrey Clinker*, 127
Snodgrass, DeWitt, 56
"Snow White," 46, 49, 54–57, 144, 165, 424, 517; and the Queen, 156, 166, 172
Sophocles: *Oedipus Rex*, 67, 68; *Electra*, 291; *Antigone*, 494
Southey, Robert, 63–64; on female authorship, 8, 545
Spacks, Patricia Meyer, 75
Spark, Muriel, 223, 229, 246, 555
Spencer, Herbert, 448, 467

Spenser, Edmund: *The Faerie Queene*, 30, 33, 34, 42, 63, 73, 197, 471
Spinsterhood, 109; dread of, 88; Gertrude Stein on, 107; in *Emma*, 111; and Austen, 112, 136; and C. Brontë, 380, 426; in *Shirley*, 389; in *Villette*, 406–07, 428; in *Middlemarch*, 528; and Dickinson, 542–43, 632–33, 635; in C. Rossetti, 552
Spivak, Gayatri Chakravorty, 510
Springfield Republican, The, 558
Stanton, Elizabeth Cady, 473; *Woman's Bible*, 385
Starvation: in *Castle Rackrent*, 149–51; in *Wuthering Heights*, 278–79; in *Jane Eyre*, 336, 339, 341, 364; in *Shirley*, 372, 373, 374, 377–78; in *Villette*, 404, 415, 422, 427; and poetry, 573–74. *See also* Anorexia; Food
Steele, Richard, 131; *Tender Husband*, 116. *See also* Addison, Joseph
Stein, Gertrude: on patriarchal poetry, xi, xiii, 101, 187–88, 189; on spinsterhood, 107; on telepathy, 473
Stephen, Sir Leslie, 531; Woolf on, 191–92
Sterne, Lawrence, 131; *A Sentimental Journey*, 120
Stewart, Dugald, 443
Stimpson, Catherine, 75
Stone, Lucy, 473
Stone, Ruth, 372
Stowe, Harriet Beecher, 444–45, 473; *Uncle Tom's Cabin*, 25, 205, 481–83, 533–35, 620–21, 624; *My Wife and I*, 69–70; "The True Story of Lord Byron's Life," 461; "The Sullivan Looking-Glass," 473; and Eliot, 479, 481–84, 532–33
Strauss, David Friedrich, 468; *The Life of Jesus*, 450, 502
Suicide: in *Wuthering Heights*, 284, 298; in *Shirley*, 390; in *Little Women*, 483; of Judith Shakespeare, 540, 549; fantasies in Dickinson, 623, 629–31; and sewing, 638–39. *See also* Death; Masochism
Sun, symbolism of: in *Villette*, 422–23; in *Middlemarch*, 504, 530; in *Aurora Leigh*, 577–78; in Dickinson, 595–97; in Fuller and Dickinson, 606. *See also* Moon, symbolism of; Times of day
Supernatural and ghosts: and Austen, 175; in *Wuthering Heights*, 260, 263, 279, 292, 300; in C. Brontë, 378; in *Villette*, 404, 407, 422, 425–26, 432; goblins in "Goblin Market," 565, 567, 569–70; in Keats and Rossetti, 574; goblins in Dickinson, 622–23; in *Uncle Tom's Cabin*, 624; in Dickin-

son, 624–25; Dickinson as "gnome," 636. *See also* Clairvoyance; Death; Gothic fiction
Swift, Jonathan, 12, 456, 459, 522, 529; on women, 31–34; *The Battle of the Books*, 33; *Gulliver's Travels*, 241
Swinburne, Algernon, 460, 469

Tales from Blackwood, 446
Tave, Stuart, 178
Taylor, Bayard, *Hannah Thurston*, 473
Techniques of composition: "trance-writing," 58, 150, 311–15, 316–17, 327, 335, 473; "common sittingroom," 151–55; and women poets, 548–49; Dickinson's fascicles, 607–08, 640–42
Tennyson, Alfred, Lord, 456, 573; "The Palace of Art," xi, 73, 87; "The Lady of Shalott," 617–20 passim
Tertullian, 30, 240
Thackeray, William Makepeace, 373, 540, 546; *Vanity Fair*, 29
Theatre and acting: in *Mansfield Park*, 164, 166–68; in *Villette*, 413, 418, 421–25, 426, 435, 437; in "Armgart," 464; in *Daniel Deronda*, 455; in "The Lifted Veil," 464; in *Middlemarch*, 499–500, 520; and Eliot, 532; in *Uncle Tom's Cabin*, 533–35, 620; women in Elizabethan theatre, 540; in Dickinson, 582–650 passim. *See also* Clothing; Duplicity, female; Parody; Romance
Times of day: dawn, 58–59; night, 99, 101; noon, 102; night in *Paradise Lost*, 202–03; night in *Wuthering Heights*, 300; night in "Goblin Market," 569; symbolic in *Aurora Leigh*, 576, 578, 580; symbolic in Dickinson, 593–94; noon in Dickinson, 595–97, 598, 606, 607, 617; dawn/morning in Dickinson, 600–04, 623, 642–43; night in Dickinson, 625–26, 635–36. *See also* Moon, symbolism of; Sun, symbolism of
Todd, Mabel Loomis, 563
Transvestism. *See* Clothing; Female impersonation; Male impersonation; Theatre and acting
Twain, Mark, 109, 558

Utopian visions: female, 102–04; female in *Wuthering Heights*, 265; female in *The Professor*, 235; female in *Aurora Leigh*, 578–80; female in Dickinson, 642–50; male aesthetic, 646. *See also* Feminism, rise of; Heaven/Eden/paradise

Van Ghent, Dorothy, 278
Venus in the Cloister, or the Nun in Her Smock, 411
Vicinus, Martha, xii
Victorian culture: male sexuality in, 4; woman's place in, 20, 54–55, 194, 381, 462, 482, 505; death in, 24–27; and morality, 63, 444–45; female sexuality in, 94. *See also* History
Virgin Mary, 18, 20–21, 365; in *Shirley,* 397; in *Villette,* 415; in Eliot, 468, 485, 490, 492–98 passim, 501. *See also* Christianity; Mothers, goddesses

Wagner, Richard, 284
Wakoski, Diane: "Sun," 510
Walpole, Horace; on Mary Wollstonecraft, 31; *The Castle of Otranto,* 347
Weininger, Otto, 8
Weisstein, Naomi, 53
Welsh, Alexander, 24–26 passim, 490, 616
West, Rebecca, 372
Westminster Review, 450, 482, 530
Wheelock, John Hall, 562
Whiteness: symbolism of, 21, 613–22; in "Snow White," 37–39 passim; and Dickinson, 86, 613–22, 636, 640, 645, 556; and *Villette,* 437; and Milton, 472; in *Uncle Tom's Cabin,* 534–35, 620; in *Moby Dick,* 614–15, 621. *See also* Clothing
Whitman, Walt, 554, 560–61; and literary ambition, 556–57; *Leaves of Grass,* 556–57; "A Noiseless, Patient Spider," 639
Widowhood: Hopkins on, 10–11; in Austen, 136, 170, 172, 181–82; in *Villette,* 420; in Eliot, 522. *See also* Female sexuality; Marriage
Wilbur, Richard, 564
Wilde, Oscar: *Salome,* 365
Winchilsea, Anne, Countess of. *See* Finch, Anne
Winthrop, John, 55
Witch, the. *See* Woman as witch
Wittreich, Joseph, 212
Wollstonecraft, Mary, 31, 97, 211, 250, 349, 370, 444, 449, 453, 455; on female education, 116; *A Vindication of the Rights of Women,* 124–25, 205, 222, 466, 569; on "the sublime," 204; on Milton, 213; *Mary,* 222; *Posthumous Works,* 222; and M. Shelley, 222–24, 242; *Maria,* 232, 245–46, 620
Woman as angel, 64, 86, 101, 197, 444; history of, 17–27 passim; in Barrett Browning, 18, 26, 463; and death, 24–27, 490–91, 535; linked with monster, 28–31, 34,

44, 46, 48, 68, 76, 78–79, 194, 196, 203, 219, 240, 244, 314, 321–23, 345–46; in "Snow White," 39–42 passim; and disease, 55; and silence, 71; in Goethe, 75; in Austen, 119, 165, 166; in *Frankenstein,* 229, 232; in *Wuthering Heights,* 261, 267, 289, 299–300; in Eliot, 307, 455, 479, 485, 491–92, 514; in C. Brontë, 318, 344–46, 376, 386, 421; and veils, 471; and Fuller, 480; in "Goblin Market," 567; in C. Rossetti and Eliot, 583; whiteness of, 615–16. *See also* Christianity; Ladyhead; Woman as monster
Woman as male agent: in *The Professor,* 326; in *Jane Eyre,* 348, 350–51; in *Villette,* 432–33
Woman as male creation/creature/art object, 54–55, 187, 197–98, 208–09, 224, 235, 239, 243–44, 429, 616; theories about, 13–19 passim; in "Snow White," 41–42; and Austen, 111; and Edgeworth, 148; and Eliot, 450, 457, 461, 486. *See also* Authority; Paternity
Woman as monster, 89, 99, 101, 222, 345, 444, 545–46; autonomy of, 16, 27, 28, 34, 60, 79; images of, 16–20 passim; history of, 27–36; and escape, 86; in *Paradise Lost,* 30, 33, 197; in Austen, 129, 141, 155, 159–74, 181, 183; in Edgeworth, 148; in *Frankenstein,* 225, 232–47 passim; in *The Professor,* 322; in *Jane Eyre,* 361–62; and Eliot, 455, 477, 489, 491–92; and Hannah More, 467; and veil, 471–72. *See also* Authority, monstrous female; Doubles; Fragmentation of personality; Madness; Supernatural and ghosts; Woman as witch
Woman as nun: in Austen, 135; in *Shirley,* 386, 389; in *Villette,* 406, 410–15 passim, 419; 425–33 passim, 434–36, 438, 472, 476; in Dickinson, 621, 647. *See also* Christianity
Woman as witch, 25, 27, 37, 38, 42, 79; and Lilith, 35; in *Wuthering Heights,* 207, 262, 292–96, 306–07; in *Villette,* 406, 430–33 passim; in "The Lifted Veil," 459; in *The Witch of Atlas,* 471; in *The Mill on the Floss,* 493; and Eliot, 447–517; in "Goblin Market," 569–70; in Dickinson, 647–49. *See also* Woman as monster; Supernatural and ghosts
"Woman's Poem, A," 18
Women and work: nurse in *Persuasion,* 182–83; teacher in *The Professor,* 323, 325, 331; need for, in *Jane Eyre,* 347–49; teacher in *Jane Eyre,* 364; singing teacher

in *Daniel Deronda,* 450; maid in "The Lifted Veil," 447, 460; need for, according to Eliot, 468, 532; "commercial writing," 545, 558–59; schoolteacher, 558; Barrett Browning on, 559–61; social service in *Aurora Leigh,* 575–76; Dickinson on, 588–91, 634. *See also* Economics and women; Governess, the; Housekeeping; Marriage; Prostitution; Theatre and acting

Woodhull, Victoria, 473

Woolf, Virginia, xi, 202, 203, 211, 256, 336; on "the angel in the house," 17, 20, 23; on Cavendish, 63; on female authorship, 64, 546–49 passim, 559 (*see also* on "Judith Shakespeare," below); *Mrs. Dalloway,* 78, 642; on "Judith Shakespeare," 99, 187–88, 195, 539–41, 544–45, 548–49, 558, 563–64, 583; *The Years,* 133, *Three Guineas,* 134, 205; on Austen, 147, 153–55; on Milton, 187–95 passim, 212, 213, 307; *A Writer's Diary,* 189–90; *Orlando,* 192, 220; *Between the Acts,* 192; *A Room of One's Own,* 192, 243, 292 (*see also* on "Judith Shakespeare," above); *The Voyage Out,* 192–93; on misogyny, 218; on Eliot, 466; *To the Lighthouse,* 514, 642; on *Aurora Leigh,* 575

Wordsworth, William, 312, 327, 330, 401, 411, 415–16, 439, 445, 461, 469, 474, 588; "Intimations" ode, 87; literary theory, 211–12; "Lucy Gray," 307, 342, 404, 405, 618; "Strange Fits of Passion," 405; *Lyrical Ballads,* 496; "The Thorn," 496; *The Prelude,* 582. *See also* Romanticism and Romantic poets

Wounds as female metaphor, 311, 317; in *Wuthering Heights,* 272–73, 279, 284, 595; in "Jane" and *The Professor,* 329–31, 335; in *Shirley,* 393; in Dickinson, 595, 603–04, 606–07, 611. *See also* Disease/dis-ease/healing; Female sexuality

Wyatt, Sir Thomas, "The Lover Compareth His Heart to the Overcharged Gun," 609–10

Wylie, Elinor, 187, 372

Yeats, William Butler, 12, 204, 206, 548; "Sailing to Byzantium," 646

Yonge, Charlotte Mary, 169

Zietlow, Paul, 181